THE CHAPTER VII POWERS OF THE UNITED NATIONS SECURITY COUNCIL

This study provides a comprehensive analysis of the questions pertaining to the powers of the Security Council under Chapter VII of the Charter. It departs from the premise that an analysis of the limitations to the powers of the Security Council and an analysis of judicial review of such limitations by the ICJ, respectively, are inter-dependent. On the one hand, judicial review would only become relevant if and to the extent that the powers granted to the Security Council under Chapter VII of the Charter are subject to justiciable limitations. On the other hand, the relevance of any limitation to the powers of the Security Council would remain limited if it could not be enforced by judicial review.

This inter-dependence is reflected by the fact that chapters 2 and 3 focus on judicial review in advisory and contentious proceedings, respectively, whereas chapters 4 to 9 examine the limits to the powers of the Security Council. The concluding chapter subsequently illuminates how the respective limits to the Security Council's enforcement powers could be enforced by judicial review. It also explores an alternative mode of review of binding Security Council decisions that could complement judicial review by the ICJ, notably the right of states to reject illegal Security Council decisions as a 'right of last resort'.

The space and attention devoted to the limits to the Security Council's enforcement powers reflects the second aim of this study, namely to provide new direction to this aspect of the debate on the Security Council's powers under Chapter VII of the Charter. It does so by paying particular attention to the role of human rights norms in limiting the type of enforcement measures that the Security Council can resort to in order to maintain or restore international peace and security.

Volume 3 in the series, Studies in International Law

Studies in International Law

Volume 1: Between Light and Shadow: The World Bank, the International Monetary Fund and International Human Rights Law *Mac Darrow*

Volume 2: Toxics and Transnational Law: International and European Regulation of Toxic Substances as Legal Symbolism *Marc Pallemaerts*

Volume 3: The Chapter VII Powers of the United Nations Security Council *Erika de Wet*

The Chapter VII Powers of the United Nations Security Council

ERIKA DE WET

B Iur, LL B, LL D (University of the Free State);
LL M (Harvard); Habil (University of Zurich)

·HART·
PUBLISHING

OXFORD AND PORTLAND OREGON
2004

Published in North America (US and Canada) by
Hart Publishing
c/o International Specialized Book Services
5804 NE Hassalo Street
Portland, Oregon
97213-3644
USA

Hart Publishing is a specialist legal publisher based in Oxford, England.
To order further copies of this book or to request a list of other
publications please write to:

Hart Publishing, Salters Boatyard, Folly Bridge, Abingdon Rd, Oxford,
OX1 4LB Telephone: +44 (0)1865 245533 Fax: +44 (0) 1865 794882
email: mail@hartpub.co.uk
WEBSITE: http//:www.hartpub.co.uk

British Library Cataloguing in Publication Data
Data Available

ISBN 1-84113-422-8 (hardback)

Typeset by Olympus Infotech Pvt. Ltd., India, in Palatino 10/12 pt
Printed and bound in Great Britain by
MPG Books Ltd, Bodmin, Cornwall

Acknowledgements

This publication is a revised version of my *Habilitationsschrift* which was commenced under the supervision of *Justice Luzius Wilhaber* at the Faculty of Law of the University of Basel in 1997. After *Justice Wilhaber* joined the European Court of Justice on a full-time basis in 1998, the supervision was continued by *Professor Dr Daniel Thürer* from the Faculty of Law of the University of Zurich, where the *Habilitationsschrift* was accepted in 2002. I am deeply indebted to both *Justice Wildhaber* and *Professor Dr Thürer* for their generous support during this period, without which a successful completion of this manuscript would not have been possible. I would also like to extend my sincere gratitude to *Professor Dr Heinrich Koller* for encouraging me to pursue the *Habilitationsschrift* and for putting me in touch with *Justice Wildhaber*.

Indispensable for the completion of this manuscript was also the generous financial support of the *Swiss National Science Foundation* that facilitated an LL M at *Harvard Law School* and a research sabbatical at the *T M C Asser Institute* in The Hague. I am also indebted to the Direction of the *Swiss Institute of Comparative Law (ISDC)* for granting me a sabbatical in order to pursue these endeavours. In addition, I would like to thank the library personnel of the *ISDC, Harvard Law School*, the *Peace Palace, Leiden University* and the *University of Amsterdam* for allowing me to use their research facilities, as well assisting me in finding the necessary research material.

During the past five years I have also had the privilege of relying on the personal and academic support of a variety of friends and colleagues. In this context I would like to single out *Professor Dr Gudmundur Alfredsson* for his assistance in selecting the topic of the *Habilitationsschrift*, as well as for the many conversations of encouragement over the years. Similarly, I would like to single out *Professor Dr Christof Heyns* and *Dr Natascha Schulze* for their sustained interest and support of my research. I also think back frequently to the many inspiring conversations with the late *Professor Abram Chayes* during my LL M year in *Harvard Law School*; as well as exchanges with colleagues in The Netherlands, where the manuscript was completed. These include *Professor Dr Niels Blokker, Professor Dr John Dugard, Professor Dr Terry Gill* and *Mr Gabriel Oosthuizen*, LL M. In this context I would particularly like to thank *Dr Elsbeth de Vos* and *Professor Dr André Nollkaemper* for the time they invested in reviewing the final draft(s) of the manuscript, as well as *Professor Dr Friedl Weiss* for the role he played as *Zweitgutachter*. Last but not least I would like to thank my family in South Africa, for their unconditional support during all my years abroad.

Erika de Wet
Amsterdam, November 2003

Contents

Table of Cases

ARBITRATION

TREATY BODIES

NATIONAL JURISDICTIONS

Bosnia-Herzegovina

Canada

1

Introduction

1. BACKGROUND

THE FALL OF the Berlin wall in October 1989 symbolised the end of the Cold War which had polarised and lamed international relations since the end of World War II. In the post Cold War era, the reduction in the tension between the major powers in the East and West created new possibilities for cooperation which also had significant consequences for the Security Council of the United Nations. As the organ which is endowed with the primary responsibility for the maintenance of international peace in security,[1] Chapter VII of the Charter of the United Nations (hereinafter the Charter) allows the Security Council to take far-reaching decisions which are binding on member states.[2] During the Cold War the Security Council was unable to exercise this exclusive power, as it was almost impossible to obtain a consensus amongst its five permanent members which is a prerequisite for triggering the Security Council's binding authority.[3] Between 1945 and 1990, the recommendation to use force against North Korea, as well as the economic and military sanctions adopted against Southern Rhodesia and South Africa, respectively, formed the only occasions during which the Security Council endorsed enforcement measures under Chapter VII of the Charter in response to a breach of or a threat to international peace.[4]

The new era of cooperation within the Security Council was introduced by its reaction following the Iraqi invasion of Kuwait on 1 August 1990. Within 24 hours of the invasion, the Security Council adopted Resolution 660 of 2 August 1990, determining that this invasion constituted a breach of the peace. Subsequently, the Security Council also adopted far-reaching coercive measures against Iraq, including the armed liberation

---

[1] Art 24(1) of the Charter.
[2] Art 25 of the Charter.
[3] Art 27(3) of the Charter.
[4] See also Bernd Martenczuk, *Rechtsbindung und Rechtskontrolle des Weltsicherheitsrats. Die Überprüfung nichtmilitärischer Zwangsmassnahmen durch den internationalen Gerichtshof* 19 (Berlin, Duncker & Humblot, 1996).

of Kuwait.[5] In the years since the Gulf War, the Security Council resorted to Chapter VII on a regular basis and adopted a wide variety of enforcement measures in the process. These ranged from extensive economic embargoes to the authorisation of member states and regional organisations to use force; the creation of quasi-judicial organs; as well as the authorisation of the civil administration of territories by the United Nations.

This sustained increase in the activity of the Security Council since the end of the Cold War has rekindled interest amongst international lawyers regarding the limitations to the powers of the Security Council under Chapter VII of the Charter. On the one hand, the question arose whether there were limits to the Security Council's discretion in determining that a threat to peace, breach of the peace or an act of aggression existed, as such a determination is a prerequisite for triggering the Chapter VII enforcement mechanism.[6] On the other hand, it also became pertinent to determine whether there were limits to the type of enforcement measures that the Security Council could resort to in order to restore or maintain international peace and security.[7] In addition, the question arose whether the International Court of Justice (ICJ) as the principal legal organ of the United Nations had a role to play in determining if and to what extent limitations to the powers of the Security Council existed.

The relevance of these questions came to the for in a rather dramatic fashion during the so-called *Lockerbie* case which—at the time of writing —had already been on the role of the ICJ for more than 10 years. It also arose briefly in the proceedings between *Bosnia-Herzegovina v Serbia and Montenegro* between 1993 and 1994. The following passages will give an overview of both cases in order to introduce the reader to the current status of the debate, as well as give an indication of those issues which are hotly disputed and in need of in-depth analysis. It also provides the reader with background information which is necessary for a clear understanding of the analyses that follow in subsequent chapters.

2.   THE *LOCKERBIE* CASE

2.1.   The Provisional Measures Phase

On 27 November 1991, the British and United States Governments jointly demanded the extradition of two Libyan nationals for their alleged

---

[5] SC Res 661 of 6 August 1990, SC Res 678 of 29 November 1990, and SC Res 687 of 3 April 1991.
[6] See Art 39 of the Charter.
[7] See Art 40 to Art 42 of the Charter.

involvement in the explosion of Pan Am flight 103 over *Lockerbie*, Scotland, on 21 September 1988.[8] This request was subsequently complemented by a non-binding Security Council resolution,[9] requesting Libya to comply with the request made by the British and American governments, including their call for the extradition of the two suspects and to pay appropriate compensation.[10] Libya, for its part, regarded the question of extradition as falling within the scope of application of the Montreal Convention for the Suppression of Unlawful Acts against the Safety of Civil Aviation of 23 September 1971[11] (hereinafter the Montreal Convention), to which all three states were parties.[12]

---

[8] The Joint Declaration by the United States and the United Kingdom to this effect was included in the Statement issued by the Government of the United States on 27 November 1991 (S/23309) regarding the bombing of Pan Am 103, reprinted in 31 *International Legal Materials* 723 (1992):
"The British and American Governments today declare that the Government of Libya must:

— surrender for trial all those charged with the crime; and accept responsibility for the actions of Libyan officials;
— disclose all it knows of the crime, including the names of all those responsible, and allow full access to all witnesses, documents and other material evidence, including all the remaining timers;
— pay appropriate compensation.

We expect Libya to comply promptly and in full."
[9] SC Res 731 of 22 January 1992:
"*The Security Council,*
....

Deeply concerned over the results of investigations, which implicate officials of the Libyan Government and which are contained in Security Council documents that include the requests addressed to the Libyan authorities by France, the United Kingdom of Great Britain and Northern Ireland and the United States of America, in connection with the legal procedures related to the attacks carried out against Pan American flight 103 and Union de transports areans flight 772;
Determined to eliminate international terrorism,
....

3. *Urges* the Libyan Government immediately to provide a full and effective response to those requests so as to contribute to the elimination of international terrorism;

...."
[10] For an extensive discussion of the *Lockerbie* incident, see Marcella David, "Passport to Justice: Internationalising the Political Question Doctrine for Application in the World Court, 40 *Harvard International Law Journal* 81 ff (1999). Cf Michael Plachta, "The Lockerbie Case: The Role of the Security Council in Enforcing the Principle *Aut Dedere Aut Judicare*", 12 *European Journal of International Law* 127 ff (2001); Martenczuk (Rechtskontrolle), above n 4, at 92.
[11] Reprinted in 10 *International Legal Materials* 1151 ff (1971).
[12] See also Peter Malanczuk, "Reconsidering the Relationship between the ICJ and the Security Council", in Wybo P Heere (ed), *International Law and the Hague's 750th Anniversary* 6 (The Hague, TMC Asser, 1999).

On the basis of the compromisary clause contained in the Montreal Convention,[13] Libya filed a claim with the ICJ on 3 March 1992.[14] Relying on the principle *aut dedere aut iudicare*,[15] Libya requested the ICJ to find that it had complied with all of its obligations under the Montreal Convention, that the United Kingdom and the United States were in violation of their obligations under that Convention and that they were obliged to desist from the use of any force or threats against Libya.[16] In addition, Libya submitted a request for provisional measures on the basis that the ICJ statute provides for such an order in circumstances where it is necessary to preserve the respective rights of the parties.[17] These included a request to enjoin the United States and the United Kingdom from taking any action against Libya, calculated to coerce or compel it to surrender the accused individuals to any jurisdiction outside of Libya. It also had to be ensured that no steps were taken that would prejudice in any way the rights of Libya with respect to the legal proceedings that were the subject of Libya's application.[18]

On 31 March 1992, three days after the closing of the hearings on the request for provisional measures and whilst the ICJ was still in deliberation, the Security Council adopted Resolution 748 under Chapter VII of the Charter.[19] It determined that the failure by the Libyan Government to

---

[13] Art 14(1).

[14] See *Case Concerning Questions of Interpretation and Application of the 1971 Montreal Convention Arising from the Aerial Incident at Lockerbie (Libyan Arab Jamahiriya v United Kingdom)*, Provisional Measures, ICJ Rep 1992, at 3 ff; *Case Concerning Questions of Interpretation and Application of the 1971 Montreal Convention Arising from the Aerial Incident at Lockerbie (Libyan Arab Jamahiriya v United States of America)*, Provisional Measures, ICJ Rep 1992, at 114 ff. These two orders will hereinafter be referred to as *Libya v United Kingdom*, provisional measures and *Libya v United States*, provisional measures, respectively. However, since the two orders are essentially the same, both will hereinafter be referred to as *Libya v United States*, provisional measures. Separate reference to *Libya v United Kingdom*, provisional measures, is only made where it contains additional information.

[15] The principle, which is also contained in Art 7 of the Montreal Convention, determines that if the custodial state does not extradite the suspects, it is obliged without exception whatsoever to prosecute under its domestic jurisdiction. See also Jochen A Frowein, "Die Verpflichtungen *erga omnes* im Völkerrecht und ihre Durchsetzung", in Rudolf Bernhardt *et al* (eds), *Völkerrecht als Rechtsordnung. Internationale Gerichtsbarkeit. Menschenrechte: Festschrift für Hermann Mosler* 252 (Berlin, Springer, 1983). See also Wladsylaw Czaplinksi, "The Lockerbie *Case*—some Comments", 20 *Polish Yearbook of International Law* 39 (1993).

[16] Bernd Martenczuk, "The Security Council, the International Court and Judicial Review: What Lessons from Lockerbie?", 10 *European Journal of International Law* 520 (1999).

[17] Art 41 of the ICJ statute.

[18] *Libya v United States*, provisional measures, above n 14, at 119; Martenczuk, above n 16, at 520, see also David above n 10, at 103.

[19] SC Res 748 of 31 March 1992:

"*The Security Council,*

....

Determining, in this context that the failure by the Libyan Government to demonstrate by concrete actions its renunciation of terrorism and in particular its continued failure to

demonstrate by concrete actions its renunciation of terrorism and in particular its continued failure to respond fully and effectively to the requests in Resolution 731 (1992), constituted a threat to international peace and security. It also decided that Libya had to comply with the extradition requests expressed in the joint declaration of the British and American governments. In the case of non-compliance, the Security Council would impose an arms embargo against Libya, as well as an embargo on air travel to and from that country.[20]

Confronted with this new situation directly affecting the legal question of extradition before it, the ICJ held that under the circumstances of the case it was not necessary to indicate provisional measures. When issuing this order on 14 April 1992, the majority of 10 judges stated that it did not make definite findings either of fact or law on the issues relating to the merits. It stressed that the right of the parties to contest such issues at the stage of the merits must remain unaffected by the order.[21] However, at the stage of provisional measures the member states had a *prima facie* obligation to give effect to Resolution 748 (1992). This followed from Articles 25 and 103 of the Charter, according to which member states are obliged to carry out binding decisions of the Security Council, and according to

respond fully and effectively to the requests in resolution 731 (1992) constitute a threat to international peace and security,

(...),

Acting under Chapter VII of the Charter,

1. *Decides* that the Libyan Government must now comply without any further delay with para 3 of resolution 731 (1992) regarding the requests contained in documents S/23306, S/23308, S/23309;
2. *Decides also* that the Libyan Government must commit itself definitely to cease all forms of terrorist action and all assistance to terrorist groups and that it must promptly, by concrete actions, demonstrate its renunciation of terrorism;
3. *Decides* that, on 15 April 1992, all States shall adopt the measures set out below, which shall apply until the Security Council decides that the Libyan Government has complied with paras 1 and 2 above;

...."

[20] In the Security Council debates leading up to the SC Res 748 of 31 March 1992, several delegates indicated that the Security Council should wait until the Court had made a determination. The Zimbabwean delegate warned that the action of the Security Council could lead to a major institutional crisis. See the statements of the representatives of Cape Verde, Zimbabwe and India in S/PV 3063 46 ff (1992). The states that voted for SC Res 748 of 31 March 1992 were the United States, the United Kingdom, France, Russia, Austria, Belgium, Ecuador, Hungary, Japan, and Venezuela. Abstaining were China, Cape Verde, India, Morocco and Zimbabwe. See also Fiona Beveridge, "The Lockerbie Affair", 41 *International and Comparative Law Quarterly* 911 (1992); Gerald P McGinley, "The ICJ's decision in the Lockerbie cases" 22 *Georgia Journal of International and Comparative Law* 589 (1992); Martenczuk, above n 16, at 521; Malanczuk, above n 12, at 93.

[21] *Libya v United States*, provisional measures, above n 14, at 126–27. In *Libya v United Kingdom*, provisional measures, above n 14, it was rejected by 11 of 16 judges. See also Martenczuk, above n 16, at 521; Nigel White, "To Review or Not to Review? The Lockerbie Cases Before the World Court", 12 *Leiden Journal of International Law* 405 (1999).

which obligations under the Charter prevailed over their obligations under international agreements, including the Montreal Convention.[22]

Whilst the majority avoided any direct reference to the complex questions raised by the proceedings, some of them were articulated in the dissenting opinions. Judge Bedjaoui, for example, expressed discomfort with the fact that the *Lockerbie* bombing should be seen as an urgent threat to the peace three years after its occurrence, but was not sure whether the ICJ could concern itself with this question.[23] Judge Weeramantry was more outspoken on this point and concluded that a determination under Article 39 of the Charter is one entirely within the discretion of the Security Council. Consequently it does not appear, *prima facie*, to be one with which the ICJ can properly deal.[24] Judge *ad hoc* El-Kosheri, for his part, argued that Resolution 748 (1992) was in violation of Article 92 of the Charter, by virtue of having interfered with pending proceedings before the ICJ.[25] He also suggested *proprio motu* provisional measures[26] to the extent that the suspects be placed in the custody of another state that could provide a mutually agreeable and appropriate forum for trial.[27]

2.2. The Preliminary Objections Phase

On 27 February 1998, almost 6 years after the filing of the applications, the ICJ reached a decision on the preliminary objections raised by the respondents.[28] The United Kingdom and the United States had raised objections to the jurisdiction of the ICJ and to the admissibility of

---

[22] *Ibid*; see also Martenczuk, above n 16, at 521; Malanczuk, above n 12, at 93.

[23] Dissenting opinion of Judge Bedjaoui, *Libya v United States*, provisional measures, above n 14, at 153; Martenczuk, above n 16, at 522.

[24] Dissenting opinion of Judge Weeramantry, *Libya v United States*, provisional measures, above n 14, at 176.

[25] Dissenting opinion of Judge *ad hoc* El-Kosheri, *Libya v United States*, provisional measures, above n 14, at 210.

[26] As is provided for in Art 41 of the ICJ statute, as well as Rule 75 of the ICJ's Rules of Procedure.

[27] Judge *ad hoc* El-Kosheri, *Libya v United States*, provisional measures, above n 14, at 217. But see the dissenting opinion of Judge Bedjaoui, *ibid* at 157–58. He concluded that the request for provisional measures was in itself justified, but that its effects had ceased to exist due to the prima facie binding effect of SC Res 748 of 31 March 1992. The ICJ did, however, also have the option of indicating provisional measures *proprio motu*, which it might have considered more appropriate than those requested by Libya. See also the dissenting opinions of Judge Ajibola, *ibid*, at 194–95; Judge Ranjeva, *ibid*, at 182 and Judge Weeramantry, *ibid*, at 180. Cf Martenczuk, above n 16, at 521; Angus M Gunn, "Council and Court: Prospects in Lockerbie for an International Rule of Law", 52 *University of Toronto Faculty of Law Review* 218–19 (1993).

[28] *Case Concerning Questions of Interpretation and Application of the 1971 Montreal Convention Arising from The Aerial Incident at Lockerbie (Libyan Arab Jamahiriya v United Kingdom)*, Preliminary Objections, *and Case Concerning Questions of Interpretation and Application*

the application. They also regarded these objections to be of an essentially preliminary character which had to be decided prior to a determination on the merits of the case. In the meantime, the Security Council had repeated its finding that Libya's refusal to extradite the suspects constituted a threat to international peace and further tightened sanctions with Resolution 883 of 11 November 1993.[29]

2.2.1. Objections Relating to Jurisdiction

As Libya never accepted the ICJ's compulsory jurisdiction in terms of Article 36(2) of the ICJ statute, it could only refer the dispute to the ICJ by relying on the compromisary clause contained in Article 14(1) of the Montreal Convention.[30] However, the United Kingdom and the United States (the respondents) argued that the jurisdiction of the ICJ could not be based on Article 14(1) of the Montreal Convention, since there was no dispute concerning the interpretation or application of this Convention.

of the 1971 Montreal Convention Arising from The Aerial Incident at Lockerbie (Libyan Arab Jamahiriya v United States), Preliminary Objections. Both decisions are available at www.icj-cij.org/. See also 37 *International Legal Materials* 587 ff (1998). These two decisions will hereinafter be referred to as *Libya v United Kingdom*, preliminary objections and *Libya v United States*, preliminary objections, respectively. However, since the two orders are essentially the same, both will hereinafter be referred to as *Libya v United States*, preliminary objections. Separate reference to *Libya v United Kingdom*, preliminary objections, is only made where it contains additional information.

[29] SC Res 883 of 11 November 1993:
  "*The Security Council,*
  ....
  Determined to eliminate international terrorism,
  ....
  Convinced also that the suppression of acts of international terrorism, including those in which states are directly or indirectly involved, is essential for the maintenance of international peace and security,
  Determining, in this context, that the continued failure by the Libyan Government to demonstrate by concrete actions its renunciation of terrorism, and in particular its continued failure to respond fully and effectively to the requests and decisions in resolution 731 (1992) and resolution 748 (1992), constitute a threat to international peace and security,
  ....
  Acting under Chapter VII of the Charter,
  1. *Demands* once again that the Libyan Government comply without any further delay with resolutions 731 (1992) and 748 (1992); ....." See also Malanczuk, above n 12, at 94; Martenczuk, above n 16, at 522.

[30] Art 14(1) of the Montreal Convention reads as follows:
  "Any dispute between two or more Contracting States concerning the interpretation or application of this Convention which cannot be settled through negotiation, shall, at the request of one of them, be submitted to arbitration. If within six months from the date of the request for arbitration the Parties are unable to agree on the organisation of the arbitration, any one of those parties may refer the dispute to the International Court of Justice by request in conformity with the Statute of the Court."

According to the respondents, neither of them relied upon the Montreal Convention as the basis for their extradition demands, as a result of which Libya's claims could not concern the interpretation or application of that convention.[31] They did not deny that the facts of the case could fall within the terms of the Montreal Convention, but regarded it as irrelevant in the light of the subsequent binding Security Council resolution 748 (1992).[32] Their failure to rely on the Montreal Convention would preclude Libya from invoking it defensively and arguing the illegality of the extradition demands against the convention's provisions. The ICJ would therefore not have jurisdiction under Article 14(1) of the Montreal Convention and since this convention was the sole jurisdictional basis advanced by Libya, the jurisdiction of the ICJ would be precluded.[33]

In addition, the respondents claimed that even if Libya enjoyed the rights it claimed under the Montreal Convention, they were suspended by Resolution 748 (1992) and Resolution 883 (1993). Under Articles 25 and 103 of the Charter they would have priority over all rights and obligations arising from the Montreal Convention. Due to these resolutions the only dispute that still existed was between Libya and the Security Council, which was a dispute that the ICJ could not entertain.[34]

The ICJ rejected both objections. First, it ruled that the difference between the parties as to whether the destruction of the Pan Am Aircraft over *Lockerbie* is governed by the Montreal Convention constitutes a dispute between them regarding the legal regime applicable to this event. According to the majority, this did concern the interpretation and application of the Montreal Convention which falls to be decided by the ICJ.[35] The ICJ rejected the second objection on the basis that the Chapter VII resolutions were adopted later than Libya's filing of the application on 3 March 1992.[36] Referring to its earlier jurisprudence in the *Nottebohm case (Liechtenstein v Guatemala)*[37] and the case concerning *Right of Passage over Indian Territory (Portugal v India)*,[38] the ICJ determined that if it had jurisdiction on the filing date it continued to do so. The subsequent coming into existence of the above-mentioned resolutions cannot affect its jurisdiction once established.[39]

---

[31] *Libya v United States*, preliminary objections, above n 28, at 599.
[32] *Ibid.*
[33] See David, above n 10, at 107; Martenczuk above n 16, at 523; White, above n 21, at 407.
[34] *Libya v United States*, preliminary objections, above n 28, at 603–04; see also Martenczuk, above n 16, at 523; Malanczuk, above n 12, at 94.
[35] *Libya v United States*, preliminary objections, above n 28, at 599; Martenczuk above n 16, at 523; White, above n 21, at 407.
[36] *Libya v United States*, preliminary objections, above n 28, at 604.
[37] Preliminary Objections, ICJ Rep 1952, at 122.
[38] Preliminary Objections, ICJ Rep 1957, at 142.
[39] *Libya v United States*, preliminary objections, above n 28, at 604; Malanczuk, above n 12, at 95.

This rather cryptic finding of the majority was criticised in the dissenting opinions of Judges Schwebel, Oda and Judge *ad hoc* Jennings, who saw the only dispute as one relating to the meaning, legality and effectiveness of the pertinent Security Council resolutions. This amounted to a dispute between Libya and the Security Council, which is something different from a dispute between the parties with respect to the interpretation or application of the Montreal Convention.[40]

The second majority conclusion pertaining to jurisdiction was also questioned by the dissenting judges, who regarded the present situation as completely different from that which was present in the *Nottebohm* and *Right of Passage* cases.[41] In those instances the respondent states attempted to divest the ICJ of jurisdiction validly seized by subsequent unilateral action, such as terminating their declaration of acceptance of the ICJ's jurisdiction. In the current case, the jurisdiction was terminated by the multi-lateral action by the Security Council in terms of Chapter VII of the Charter.[42]

2.2.2.   *Objections Relating to Admissibility*

The respondents' objection to admissibility also centred around the argument that the dispute was now regulated by binding decisions of the Security Council in terms of Chapter VII of the Charter. In case of any conflict with other rights or obligations under international law, these resolution have overriding effect under Article 103 of the Charter.[43] In a second, closely related argument they submitted that the events subsequent to the filing of the application, ie the adoption of the Security Council resolutions, had rendered the application without object (moot).[44] This means that if the case were admissible, it would determine the legal position as it existed prior to the subsequent adoption of the Chapter VII resolutions. However, as the Security Council had taken jurisdiction over the dispute under Chapter VII and Libya was required to comply with the measures set forth in those resolutions, this would be a futile exercise.[45]

The ICJ majority rejected the first argument on temporal grounds. It stated that Libya's application pre-dated the adoption of the resolutions

---

[40] Dissenting opinion of President Schwebel in *Libya v United States*, preliminary objections, above n 28, at 621, dissenting opinion of Judge Oda, *ibid*, at 636–37; dissenting opinion of Judge *ad hoc* Jennings, *Libya v United Kingdom*, preliminary objections, above n 28; Martenczuk, above n 16, at 525.

[41] Notably the dissenting opinion of President Schwebel in *Libya v United States*, preliminary objections, above n 28, at 620–21.

[42] *Ibid.*

[43] *Libya v United States*, preliminary objections, above n 28, at para 41; White, above n 21, at 408.

[44] *Libya v United States*, preliminary objections, above n 28, at para 46.

[45] See David, above n 10, at 112; White, above n 21, at 409; Martenczuk, above n 16, at 524.

and that the date of application was the only relevant date for determining admissibility.[46] With respect to the second argument, the majority determined that the matter required the discussion of many complicated issues which were inextricably linked with the merits. If the objection had to be sustained at the preliminary phase of the case, it would not only affect Libya's rights on the merits, but would constitute in many respects the very subject-matter of that decision.[47] The objection did not have an exclusively preliminary character within the meaning of Article 79 of the Rules of Prodecure,[48] in which case the ICJ would have to decide it at the preliminary stage.

This reasoning was criticised by a minority of five dissenting judges.[49] First, some of them regarded the decisive effect of the date of filing of the application for the purposes of admissibility as too rigid and formalistic.[50] Although this date is normally regarded as decisive, the relevant case law acknowledges that subsequent events may also have an impact on admissibility.[51] In the current case, such events in the form of the adoption of binding Security Council resolutions have rendered Libya's application without object.[52] These resolutions did not take position on whether the

---

[46] *Libya v United States*, preliminary objections, above n 28, at 650. It also indicated that although SC Res 731 of 22 January 1992 was adopted prior to the date of filing, it had no effect on the admissibility as it was a non-binding recommendation. See also David, above n 10, at 110; Malanczuk, above n 12, at 95; White, above n 21, at 409.

[47] *Libya v United States*, preliminary objections, above n 28, at 608. The reluctance of the ICJ to determine the issue of mootness of Libya's claim at the preliminary objections stage seems to flow from an element of contingency inherent to it. The question of whether Libya's claim was without object was dependent on the effect of the Security Council resolutions on that claim. They would only be deprived of their legal foundation if it were clear that the Security Council superseded them, as a result of which Libya had to hand over the suspects. Libya questioned both the legality of SC Res 748 of 31 March 1992 and SC Res 883 of 11 November 1993 and their effects on the Montreal Convention. As a result of these unresolved issues the majority distinguished Libya's claims from previous occasions where the ICJ determined that factual developments after the filing of the application rendered the measures requested by the applicant without object. See Martenczuk, above n 16, at 532–33; White, above n 21, at 409–10.

[48] Art 79(7) of the Rules of Procedure determines that: "After hearing the parties, the Court shall give its decision in the form of a judgment, by which it shall either uphold the objection, reject it, or declare that the objection does not possess, in the circumstances of the case, an exclusively preliminary character. If the Court rejects the objection or declares that it does not possess an exclusively preliminary character, it shall fix time-limits for the further proceedings."

[49] These included President Schwebel and Judges Oda, Guillaume, Herczegh and Fleischhauer. In the case of *Libya v the United Kingdom* there were six dissenting judges, including Judge *ad hoc* Jennings.

[50] See dissenting opinion of President Schwebel in *Libya v United States*, preliminary objections, above n 28, at 622–24.

[51] For example the *South West Africa cases*, Preliminary Objections, ICJ Rep 1962, at 344; *Border and Transborder Armed Actions (Nicaragua v Honduras)*, Jurisdiction and Admissibility, ICJ Rep 1988, at 95.

[52] See dissenting opinion of President Schwebel in *Libya v United States*, preliminary objections, above n 28, at 624; see also declaration of Judge Herczegh, *ibid* and the dissenting opinion of Judge *ad hoc* Jennings, *Libya v United Kingdom*, preliminary objections, above n 28.

Montreal Convention is applicable to the *Lockerbie* incident, but imposed obligations on Libya which where necessary for the maintenance of international peace and security.[53] In accordance with Article 103 of the Charter, those obligations override all other obligations of the parties, irrespective of whether the latter obligations were contested between the parties or whether they were complied with or not.[54]

This lack of connection between the Security Council resolutions and the position of the parties under the Montreal Convention necessitated an acceptance of the objection of mootness as an exclusively preliminary issue, which would have brought the case to an end at that stage.[55]

2.3. The Current State of Affairs

By 1998 the idea of a trial in a neutral form was raised again, as the parties were no closer to a solution, even though 10 years had passed since the explosion. In addition, support for the sanctions had begun to erode by 1997. First, the Arab League threatened to stop abiding by the sanctions. This was followed by a threat of the entire membership of the Organisation of African Unity (OAU) not to continue the sanctions after December 1998, unless the impasse over the *Lockerbie* incident were resolved by negotiation.[56] Consequently the United Kingdom and the United States proposed a trial in the Netherlands before a panel of Scottish jurists who would apply Scottish law.[57] Thereafter the Security Council adopted Resolution 1192 of 27 August 1998,[58] which proposed the automatic suspension of the sanctions upon the delivery of the

---

[53] Joint declaration of Judges Guillaume and Fleischhauer in *Libya v United States*, preliminary objections, above n 28, at 611.

[54] *Ibid*, at 611–12

[55] *Ibid*, at 612. See also the dissenting opinion of President Schwebel in *Libya v United States*, preliminary objections, above n 28, at 624–25; dissenting opinion of Judge Oda, *ibid*, at 637; declaration of Judge Herczegh in *Libya v United Kingdom*, preliminary objections, above n 28; dissenting opinion of Judge *ad hoc* Jennings, *ibid*. But see the joint declaration of Judges Bedjaoui, Ranjeva and Koroma, *ibid*. According to them it is not sufficient to invoke Chapter VII provisions of the Charter so as to bring to and end, ipso facto and with immediate effect, all argument on the decisions of the Security Council. See also Martenczuk, above n 16, at 425; David, above n 10, at 116–17.

[56] The OAU decision was announced at the conclusion of the OAU Summit in Ouagadougu on 10 June 1998 (see AHG/Dec XXXIV (1998)). See Princeton L Nyman, "Saving the UN Security Council—A Challenge for the United Nations", 4 *Max Planck Yearbook of United Nations Law* 132 (2000); Tshibangu Kalulu, "La Décision de l'OAU de ne plus Respecter Les Sanctions Décrétées par l'ONU contre la Libye: Désobéissance Civile des États Africains à l'Égard de L'ONU", 32 *Revue belge de droit international* 545 ff (1999).

[57] S/1997/991, Annex; David, above n 10, at 86; Plachta, above n 10, at 132.

[58] SC Res 1992 of 27 August 1998:

"*The Security Council,*

...

Acting under Chapter VII of the Charter of the United Nations,

suspects to the Netherlands.[59] On 5 April 1999 the two Libyan nationals in question arrived in the Netherlands and the sanctions under Resolution 748 (1992) and Resolution 883 (1993) were suspended.[60] This allowed international air travel and the sale of vital industrial equipment to resume and facilitated the release of Libyan assets that had been frozen in a number of countries.[61]

In the subsequent trial held at Camp Zeist in The Netherlands, Abdelbaset Ali Mohamed Al Megrahi was found guilty of introducing the explosive device in the Pan Am aircraft, whereas Al Amin Khalifa Fhima was acquitted of the same charge.[62] The Court left the question whether the Libyan government was involved in the terrorist attack unanswered. After the affirmation of the one conviction during the appeals procedure, and Libya's subsequent acceptance of "responsibility for the actions of its officials", the case was removed from the ICJ's role at the joint request of the parties on 10 September 2003.[63] This means that any pronouncement of the ICJ on its (in)ability to review the legality of Security Council decisions in contentious proceedings will remain unlikely in the immediate future.

3.   THE CASE OF BOSNIA AND HERZEGOVINA v SERBIA AND MONTENEGRO

In the *Case Concerning Application of the Convention on the Prevention and Punishment of the Crime of Genocide (Bosnia and Herzegovina v Yugoslavia (Serbia and Montenegro)*,[64] Bosnia-Herzegovina sued the Federal Republic

8.   *Reaffirms* that the measures set forth in its resolutions 748 (1992) and 883 (1993) remain in effect and binding on all Member States, ... and *decides* that the aforementioned measures shall be suspended immediately if the Secretary-General reports to the Council that the two accused have arrived in the Netherlands for the purpose of trial before the court described in para 2 or have appeared for trial before an appropriate court in the United Kingdom or the United States, and that the Libyan Government has satisfied the French judicial authorities with regard to the bombing of UTA 772 ....". See also David, above n 10, at 87; Martenczuk, above n 16, at 518; Nyman, above n 88, at 133.

[59] The sanctions were finally lifted completely in SC Res 1506 of 12 September 2003, at para 1. See also below n 63.
[60] See statement of the President of the Security Council in S/PRST/1999/10 of 8 April 1999.
[61] Plachta, above n 10, at 135.
[62] Decision of the High Court of Justiciary at Camp Zeist, Case No 1475/1999, *Her Majesty's Advocate v Abdelbaset ali Mohamed al Megrahi and Al Amin Khalifa Fhimah*, at para 84 ff, in 40 *International Legal Materials* 611 ff (2001).
[63] The conviction of Abdelbaset Ali Mohamed Al Megrahi was affirmed unanimously on appeal on 14 March 2002. It is noteworthy that Libya's acceptance of responsibility was broadly formulated. One should therefore be careful to interpret it as an acknowledgement of guilt, as such acceptance and the subsequent payment of compensation could also be seen as ex gratia actions. See S/2003/818; ICJ Press Release 2003/39 of 10 September 2003.
[64] Provisional Measures, ICJ Rep 1993, at 3 ff. Hereinafter referred to as *Bosnia-Herzegovina v Serbia and Montenegro*, provisional measures I.

of Yugoslavia (FRY) for acts of genocide of the FRY forces in Bosnia and for the FRY's support of genocide carried out by Bosnian Serb forces, which arguably engaged the FRY's state responsibility under the Convention on the Prevention and Punishment of the Crime of Genocide of 1948 (hereinafter the Genocide Convention).[65] The proceedings were initiated on the basis of the contentious jurisdiction of the ICJ by virtue of the compromisary clause in Article IX on the Genocide Convention.[66] Due to the urgency of the matter, Bosnia-Herzegovina also requested provisional measures. The ICJ first gave effect to this request in April 1993 by ordering the FRY to cease and desist from all genocidal actions.[67] In September of that year the ICJ reaffirmed its position in a second order for provisional measures, after Bosnia-Herzegovina had claimed that the FRY was not complying with the first order.[68]

While Bosnia-Herzegovina's central claim at each stage of the case concerned the FRY's legal responsibility for acts of genocide, it also wanted the ICJ to consider the legal status and effects of the mandatory arms embargo that was imposed by Security Council Resolution 713 of 25 September 1991 against (all the territories of) the former Socialist Federal Republic of Yugoslavia.[69] In particular, Bosnia-Herzegovina wished to know whether Article 51 of the Charter granted it the right of access to the means (including arms) to defend itself against the genocide of its own people, and whether other states parties to the Genocide Convention had the right to provide military equipment to Bosnia-Herzegovina for this purpose. In addition, it wanted clarification as

---

[65] *Bosnia-Herzegovina v Serbia and Montenegro*, provisional measures I, above n 54, at 5 ff; Craig Scott *et al*, "Memorial for Bosnia: Framework of Legal Arguments Concerning the Lawfulness of the Maintenance of the United Nations Security Council's Arms Embargo on Bosnia and Herzegovina", 16 *Michigan Journal of International Law* 8 (1994).

[66] Art 1 of the Genocide Convention confirms that genocide, whether committed in time of peace or in time of war, is a crime under international law which parties undertake to prevent and to punish. The Genocide Convention thus does not only prohibit acts of genocide, but also obliges states to undertake positive obligations to prevent and punish genocide. See the separate opinion of Judge *ad hoc* Lauterpacht, *Case Concerning Application of the Convention on the Prevention and Punishment of the Crime of Genocide (Bosnia and Herzegovina v Yugoslavia (Serbia and Montenegro))*, Further Requests for the Indication of Provisional Measures, ICJ Rep 1993, at 436. Hereinafter referred to as *Bosnia-Herzegovina v Serbia and Montenegro*, provisional measures II. See also Scott *et al*, above n 55, at 36.

[67] *Bosnia-Herzegovina v Serbia and Montenegro*, provisional measures I, above n 129, at 24 ff; Scott *et al*, above n 55, at 9.

[68] *Bosnia-Herzegovina v Serbia and Montenegro*, provisional measures II, above n 56 at 325 ff.

[69] Within one month of the adoption of SC Res 713 of 25 September 1991, the borders of the country became a matter of doubt and by 22 May 1992 Bosnia-Herzegovina was admitted as a new member to the United Nations. The Security Council nonetheless reaffirmed the embargo on a number of occasions and intended for it to apply to Bosnia-Herzegovina as well. See the preambles of SC Res 752 of 15 May 1992, and SC Res 757 of 30 May 1992. See also separate opinion of Judge *ad hoc* Lauterpacht in *Bosnia-Herzegovina v Serbia and Montenegro*, provisional measures II, above n 56, at 438.

to whether these rights prevailed over the obligations flowing from Resolution 713 (1991).[70]

From a procedural point of view, this request was problematic to the extent that the obligations stemming from Resolution 713 (1991) primarily affected the relationship between third parties to the Genocide Convention and Bosnia-Herzegovina. It was not, however, a necessary issue in deciding whether or not the FRY had breached the Genocide Convention in the manner alleged by Bosnia-Herzegovina. Given that Bosnia-Herzegovina and the FRY were the only parties to the case, the question arose whether the ICJ could deal with the implications of Resolution 713 (1991) in the context of a request for provisional measures directed at the FRY.[71]

In both requests for provisional measures the ICJ answered this question in the negative, as it saw its power to issue provisional measures in terms of Article 41 of its Statute as limited to the preservation of rights which could be the subject of a binding legal judgment at the eventual merits stage of the case.[72] Since the eventual judgment on the merits is only binding on the states that are party to the proceedings, the provisional measures also could only apply to those states (or to one of them) and not to third states that would not be bound by the judgment on the merits.[73] Judge Ajibola went one step further in his separate opinion by stating that complaints concerning the consequences of Resolution 713 (1991) had to be presented to the Security Council as opposed to the ICJ.[74] Even Judge *ad hoc* Lauterpacht, who questioned the legality of the arms embargo during the second request for provisional measures,[75] was concerned that the bilateral relationship of the case made it difficult for the

---

[70] *Bosnia-Herzegovina v Serbia and Montenegro*, provisional measures I, above n 54, at 6; *Bosnia-Herzegovina v Serbia and Montenegro*, provisional measures II, above n 56, at 328.; Scott *et al*, above n 55, at 10.

[71] See especially separate opinion of Judge *ad hoc* Lauterpacht, in *Bosnia-Herzegovina v Serbia and Montenegro*, provisional measures II, above n 56, at 442; Scott *et al*, above n 55, at 10; Martenczuk (Rechtskontrolle), above n 4, at 26.

[72] Art 41(1) of the ICJ statute determines that: "The Court shall have the power to indicate, if it considers that circumstances so require, any provisional measures which ought to be taken to preserve the respective rights of either party."

[73] *Bosnia-Herzegovina v Serbia and Montenegro*, provisional measures I, above n 54, at 20; *Bosnia-Herzegovina v Serbia and Montenegro*, provisional measures II, above n 56, at 344–55. See also Lucius Caflish, "Is the International Court Entitled to Review Security Council Resolution Adopted under Chapter VII of the United Nations Charter?", in Najeeb Al-Naumi & Richard Meese, *International Legal Issues Arising under the United Nations Decade of International Law* 649 (Martinus Nijhoff, The Hague, 1995); Scott *et al*, above n 55, at 10.

[74] Separate opinion of Judge Ajibola in *Bosnia-Herzegovina v Serbia and Montenegro*, provisional measures II, above n 56, at 405.

[75] Separate opinion of Judge *ad hoc* Lauterpacht in *Bosnia-Herzegovina v Serbia and Montenegro*, provisional measures II, above n 56, at 339 ff.

ICJ to assess directly the legal status of the arms embargo imposed by Resolution 713 (1991).[76]

In the light of this cool reception at the provisional measures stage, Bosnia-Herzegovina retracted the issue of the legality of the arms embargo from the dispute in 1994. It had apparently decided that its chances for securing an ICJ decision would be better served by focussing on the FRY's violation of the Genocide Convention, than by attempting to force the ICJ into taking a position on the legality of Resolution 713 (1991).[77] As a result, the question of judicial review of Security Council resolutions by the ICJ in contentious proceedings will not be at issue at the merits stage of this case.

4.   ISSUES IDENTIFIED FOR ANALYSIS

From the above overview one can conclude that the ICJ's competence to review the legality of Security Council decisions during the merits stage of contentious proceedings still constitutes a major point of controversy amongst international lawyers. In addition to the controversy surrounding the ICJ's role in determining the limitations to the powers of the Security Council, the *Lockerbie* case revealed disagreement as to whether the Security Council's powers are subject to limitations at all. In this regard the question whether a determination in terms of Article 39 of the Charter is of a non-justiciable (political) nature, formed a particular bone of contention.

Finally, the *Bosnia-Herzegovina v Serbia and Montenegro* proceedings illustrated that a determination that a particular situation constitutes a threat to peace is not the only situation in which the discretion of a Security Council decision might be at issue. It also needs to be clarified whether the Security Council's discretion in choosing the type of enforcement measures for restoring or maintaining international peace and security, is subject to limitation. In essence therefore, questions concerning the limitations to the powers of the Security Council pertain both to the "when" and "how" of Security Council action.

---

[76] Separate opinion of Judge *ad hoc* Lauterpacht in *Bosnia-Herzegovina v Serbia and Montenegro*, provisional measures II, above n 56, at 442. He was prepared to indicate provisional measures in the following terms: "between the Applicant and the Respondent the continuing validity of the embargo in its bearing on the applicant has become a matter of doubt requiring further consideration by the Security Council." See also Scott *et al*, above n 55, at 11.

[77] Bosnia-Herzegovina had considered also initiating proceedings on the basis of Art IX of the Genocide Convention against the United Kingdom. By commencing proceedings against a third party to the Genocide Convention, it would have placed the legality of Resolution 713 (1991) directly at issue. However, due to political considerations Bosnia-Herzegovina did not pursue the matter. See Scott *et al*, above n 55, at 12–13; see also Martenczuk, above n 16, at 26.

The following chapters will attempt to provide some answers to the above questions on the basis of primary and secondary sources available before 30 June 2003. At first sight, one might wonder why the author would undertake such a project, given the already existing wealth of literature on the subject matter. For example, the *Lockerbie* incident has sparked several publications on the possibility of judicial review of binding Security Council decisions in contentious proceedings.[78] As far as the limits to the powers of the Security Council is concerned, several studies have been undertaken in relation to the justiciability of Article 39 of the Charter.[79] The frequency with which the Security Council has since 1991 authorised the use of force for the purpose of restoring or maintaining international peace and security, has also resulted in studies on the Security Council's ability to delegate its powers to member states and regional organisations.[80] Other authors have devoted attention to the question whether the Security Council's powers to impose economic sanctions would be limited by basic human rights norms and basic norms of humanitarian law.[81]

However, whilst these and other studies have made a valuable contribution to the debate on the powers of the Security Council, the scope of their analysis remains limited in that they only deal with one or some of the vexing questions raised above. The first aim of this study therefore is

[78] See for example Gunn, above n 27, at 228 ff; Martenczuk, above n 16, at 538 ff; Czaplinksi, above n 15; David, above n 10; Plachta, above n 10.

[79] See for example Martenczuk (Rechtskontrolle), above n 4; Jochen A Frowein, "Art 39", in Bruno Simma (ed), *Charter of the United Nations. A Commentary* 618 (Oxford, Oxford University Press, 1994); TD Gill, "Legal and Some Political Limitations on the Power of the UN Security Council to Exercise its Enforcement Powers under Chapter VII of the Charter", 26 *Netherlands Yearbook of International Law* 60 (1995); Ruth Gordon, "United Nations Intervention in Internal Conflicts: Iraq, Somalia, and Beyond", 15 *Michigan Journal of International Law* 563 (1993); Vera Gowlland-Debbas, "Security Council Enforcement Action and Issues of State Responsibility", 43 *International and Comparative Law Quarterly* 60 ff (1994); Matthias Herdegen, *Die Befugnisse des UN-Sicherheitsrates: aufgeklärter Absolitismus im Völkerrecht?* (Heidelberg, Müller, 1998).

[80] See for example Danesh Sarooshi, *The United Nations and the Development of Collective Security* (Oxford, Oxford University Press, 1999); Christian Walter, *Vereinte Nationen und Regionalorganisationen* (Berlin, Springer, 1996); Nigel D White & Özlem Ülgen, "The Security Council and the Decentralized Military Option: Constitutionality and Function", 44 *Netherlands International Law Review* 385 ff (1997).

[81] See, for example, Dorothee Starck, *Die Rechtsmässigkeit von UNO-Wirtschaftssanktionen in Anbetracht ihrer Auswirkungen auf die Zivilbevölkerung* (Berlin, Duncker & Humblot, 2000); Roger Normand, "A Human Rights Assessment of Sanctions: The Case of Iraq, 1990–997", in Willem JM van Genugten & Gerard A de Groot (eds), *United Nations Sanctions. Effectiveness and Effects, Especially in the Field of Human Rights. A Multi-disciplinary Approach* 23 ff (Antwerp, Intersentia, 1999); Hans-Peter Gasser, "Collective Economic Sanctions and International Humanitarian Law", 56 *Zeitschrift für ausländisches öffentliches Recht und Völkerrecht* 880 ff (1996); Andrew K Fishman, "Between Iraq and a Hard Place: The Use of Economic Sanctions and Threat to International Peace and Security", 13 *Emory International Law Review* 702 ff (1999).

to provide a coherent and comprehensive analysis of the questions pertaining to the powers of the Security Council under Chapter VII of the Charter. It departs from the premise that an analysis of the limitations to the powers of the Security Council and an analysis of judicial review of such limitations, respectively, are inter-dependent. On the one hand, judicial review would only become relevant if and to the extent that the powers granted to the Security Council under Chapter VII of the Charter are subject to justiciable limitations. On the other hand, the relevance of any limitation to the powers of the Security Council would remain limited if it could not be enforced by judicial review.

This inter-dependence is reflected by the fact that the next two chapters (chapters 2 and 3) are devoted to questions pertaining to judicial review, whereafter chapters 4 to 9 examine the limits to the powers of the Security Council. The concluding chapter (chapter 10) subsequently illuminates how the respective limits to the Security Council's enforcement powers could be enforced by judicial review. It also explores an alternative mode of review of binding Security Council decisions that could complement judicial review by the ICJ, namely the right of states to reject illegal Security Council decisions as a "right of last resort".

The space and attention devoted to the limits to the Security Council's enforcement powers reflect the second aim of this study, namely to provide new direction to this aspect of the debate on the Security Council's powers under Chapter VII of the Charter. It does so by paying particular attention to the role of human rights norms in limiting the type of enforcement measures that the Security Council can resort to in order to maintain or restore international peace and security. Although some studies have, for example, drawn attention to the impact of Security Council sanctions on socio-economic rights, there still is considerable scope for the development of the human rights angle of the debate. There is, in particular, a need for a systematic analysis of the implications of international human rights norms for all enforcement measures undertaken by the Security Council, including quasi-judicial measures and authorisations relating to the administration of territories.

4.1.   Chapter Overview

The analysis commences with an inquiry into the potential role of the ICJ in determining the legality of decisions of the Security Council. Chapter 2 focuses on the advisory opinion procedure provided for in Article 96(1) of the Charter as a mechanism for judicial review. As the question of judicial review featured before the ICJ during the advisory opinions procedure well before it did so during contentious proceedings, it seems fitting to examine the implications of these opinions at this early stage of the analysis.

It also highlights the fact that there may exist other avenues for judicial review of Security Council decisions than contentious proceedings. This fact has often been neglected, due to the preoccupation with judicial review in contentious proceedings since the *Lockerbie* affair.

Chapter 2 first examines the extent to which the ICJ has already reviewed Security Council resolutions by means of advisory opinions. Thereafter it analyses several general questions which are central to this type of judicial review. They evolve around the propriety of judicial review *versus* the development of a political question doctrine; the consequences of an illegal Security Council resolution, and the (overcoming of the) reluctance of United Nations organs to make frequent use of the advisory opinion procedure.

Chapter 3 deals with judicial review by the ICJ in contentious proceedings. It first illuminates that both the defenders and critics of such review rely on the same arguments (ie the principle of efficiency, the need for cooperation between the principle organs of the United Nations, and the drafting history of the Charter), in order to reach very different conclusions. As the arguments on both sides carry considerable weight, the discussion currently seems to find itself in an impasse. Consequently, the chapter then attempts to steer the debate in a new direction by examining whether judicial review can be regarded as a general principle within municipal orders. If a survey of municipal orders were to indicate that judicial review of the decisions of political organs within States was (or was not) emerging as a general principle of law, this could tip the scale of the debate one way or the other. For example, if the rationale for accepting such control would seem to have become generally accepted, the ICJ could transpose it to the international order through Article 38(1)(c) of its Statute. As this line of argument presupposes that a comparison with judicial review in municipal law is tenable, chapter 3 also examines whether the structural differences between the municipal legal orders on the one hand and the international legal order on the other, would necessarily exclude such a comparison.

In chapter 4 and subsequent chapters the attention shifts from the mechanisms for facilitating judicial review within the United Nations system to the criteria to be applied during judicial review. These chapters examine if and to what extent the broad discretion of the Security Council under Chapter VII of the Charter can be limited. Before the Security Council may impose coercive measures of a non-military or military nature under Articles 40, 41 and 42 of the Charter, it must determine the existence of "a threat to the peace, breach of the peace, or an act of aggression" within the meaning of Article 39 of the Charter. This means that the Security Council has a discretion both in deciding when to act (Article 39) and how to act (Articles 40, 41 and 42).

Chapter 4 examines whether an Article 39 determination lies purely within the Security Council's discretion, or whether it can be measured by judicial criteria. It commences with an abstract analysis of the nature of the Security Council's determination under Article 39. This includes an attempt to define the concepts "threat to peace", "breach of the peace" and an "act of aggression" in legal terms by interpreting them according to their ordinary meaning, in context and with due consideration to the object and purpose of the Charter. Due to its dominant role in practice the term "threat to peace" will form the centre of the analysis, followed by a concise discussion of the concepts "breach of the peace" and "act of aggression". Thereafter chapter 4 concentrates on the practice of the Security Council in order to determine if and to what extent it corresponds to any of the preliminary conclusions flowing from the abstract analysis of Article 39.

As of chapter 5, the extent of the Security Council's discretion in terms of Articles 40, 41 and 42 of the Charter becomes the focal point of the analysis. Chapter 5 gives an overview of the nature of the Security Council's discretion when resorting to enforcement measures, as well as the substantive limits to its discretion in this regard. These "substantive" limits can be distinguished from the "structural" limits inherent in the Charter and which affect, in particular, the power of the Security Council to delegate certain powers to sub-organs or other entities. The implications of these structural limits for the Security Council are first examined in chapter 7.

Chapter 5 first inquires whether the Charter intended the Security Council's broad discretion to be limited by substantive norms at all. After answering this question in the affirmative, the chapter examines where these limitations can be found. It subsequently identifies the norms of *ius cogens* and the purposes and principles of the United Nations as the main substantive limitations to the Security Council's discretion during enforcement action. In accordance with these limitations, the Security Council is prevented from adopting measures that violate core elements of human rights and international humanitarian law; that violate the right to self-defence; that impose a settlement on parties; or that completely undermine state sovereignty.

Chapter 5 further pays particular attention to the limits flowing from the Charter principle of good faith, in accordance with which the organs of the United Nations have to fulfil legal expectations previously created by their own actions. It examines the interaction of this principle with the Charter purpose of promoting human rights and humanitarian norms. The analysis remains general in that it does not engage in an application of any of the substantive limits identified to Security Council practice. Such an application is undertaken in chapters 6, 8 and 9. Chapter 5 thus constitutes the principled foundation on which the subsequent evaluation of the conformity of Security Council practice with substantive (human rights) limitations is based.

Chapter 6 identifies in a more concrete fashion the extent to which human rights would limit the Security Council's ability to adopt non-military enforcement measures in the form of economic sanctions. The chapter commences by elaborating on the nature of the particular human rights which pose a limitation on economic embargoes. In doing so, it concentrates on the right to life and the right to health, as practice has shown that these rights are the most likely to be affected by broad economic embargoes. Thereafter it applies the yardsticks identified during this inquiry to the most controversial economic sanctions regimes which the Security Council has adopted during the existence of the United Nations.

Chapter 6 also explores the limitations implied by the right to self-defence for economic sanctions in situations of armed conflict. The final section of the chapter illustrates that this right becomes particularly relevant in situations where the Security Council imposes an arms embargo upon states involved in an inter-state conflict that involves an armed attack.

In Chapter 7 the focus (temporarily) shifts from the Security Council's non-military enforcement powers to its competence to resort to military measures under Chapter VII of the Charter. As the Security Council has developed the practice of authorising member states or regional (defence) organisations to use force on its behalf, Chapter 7 examines whether these authorisations are permissible. Since an authorisation to use force amounts to the delegation of a power which is centralised with the Security Council, it has to be determined if and to what extent the Charter facilitates such a delegation. Chapter 7 does so by drawing a distinction between the authorisation of states, on the one hand, and regional (defence) organisations, on the other, to engage in military action. In both instances it follows the same methodology. It first identifies the Charter requirements for such an authorisation and then applies them to the Security Council practice.

The issue of the delegation of powers centralised in the Security Council also forms a focal point in chapter 8, which examines the extent to which the Security Council is empowered to authorise the civil administration of territories under Chapter VII of the Charter. As these mandates for civil administration imply a delegation of the Security Council's power to take binding decisions to a Special Representative of the Secretary-General, the chapter first examines the nature of these mandates. In doing so, it builds on the delegation model that was developed in chapter 7. This means that it extends the delegation model developed in the context of military authorisations to mandates involving the delegation of binding Security Council powers of a non-military nature. Thereafter chapter 8 once again draws attention to the Security Council's obligation to respect human rights norms. In doing so, it places particular emphasis on the right to self-determination, as this right may arguably turn out to be one of the rights most severely affected by the long term civil administrations in the respective territories.

Chapter 9 examines the competence of the Security Council to adopt quasi-judicial measures in one form or another, as a mechanism to restore or maintain international peace and security. It first focuses on the establishment of the International Criminal Tribunal for the former Yugoslavia (ICTY) and the International Criminal Tribunal for Rwanda (ICTR), as the jurisprudence relating to these tribunals form an important point of reference for determining the legality of other Security Council decisions that affected the criminal prosecution of individuals. This concerns, in particular, the Security Council resolutions demanding the extradition of suspected international terrorists, as well as those requiring the freezing of assets of individuals associated with international terrorism. Thereafter the analysis concentrates on the legality of quasi-judicial bodies whose decisions were directed against states rather than individuals, namely the United Nations Compensation Commission for Iraq and the Iraq-Kuwait Boundary Demarcation Commission.

The final, concluding chapter recaptures the limitations to the Chapter VII power of the Security Council, as well as the role of the ICJ in enforcing these limitations. Thereafter it explores an alternative (or complementary) mode of enforcement in the decentralised international order, namely the right of member states to reject illegal Security Council decisions as a "right of last resort".

Part I

Judicial Review

2

Advisory Opinions of the International Court of Justice (ICJ) as a Mechanism for Judicial Review

1. INTRODUCTION

AS THE QUESTION of legal constraints upon the Security Council and the role of the ICJ in enforcing these constraints first featured in an ICJ advisory opinion, it seems fitting to examine the implications of advisory opinions at this early stage of the analysis. A clear understanding of these opinions introduces the reader to a variety of questions surrounding the (limitations to the) powers of the Security Council and thus provides a comprehensive background against which subsequent chapters can unfold. In addition, a certain fixation on judicial review in contentious procedures following the *Lockerbie* incident,[1] has led to a neglect of the potential of advisory opinions as an avenue for judicial review. It is therefore important to highlight that if the real issue is legality, the pronouncements of the ICJ in advisory opinions on the legality of the actions of a United Nations organ deserve more attention.[2]

The value of advisory opinions in this regard becomes apparent if one considers that a variety of domestic legal systems and international institutions recognise advisory opinions as an avenue for obtaining authoritative interpretations of the law, which can place constraints on the actions of political organs. Article 143 of the Constitution of India, for example, calls upon the Supreme Court to counsel the President of India on matters of public importance. As a consequence, the President has referred questions to the Supreme Court on issues varying from the constitutionality of an existing law to the implementation of an international agreement.[3] Equally, in Canadian constitutional matters, the advisory opinion or

---

[1] See extensively ch 1, at s 2.
[2] See Jose E Alvarez, "Judging the Security Council", 90 *American Journal of International Law*, 8 (1996).
[3] India Const pt V; See Ashok K Johari, *The Supreme Court's Advisory Function* 1 (Aligarh, Naraina Publishers, 1984).

constitutional reference (as it is also known) plays an important role at both the federal and provincial levels of government.[4] Pursuant to its reference jurisdiction, the Supreme Court of Canada issues advisory opinions on a wide range of legal questions at the request of the Governor.[5] Also in the United States several state courts[6] render advisory opinions to governors and state legislatures.[7] In the United Kingdom the Law Commission of England and Wales has drawn attention to the practical value of public law cases.[8] The Commission reported that in its extensive consultations there was widespread support for the High Court having the power to grant advisory declarations, provided that the jurisdiction was carefully exercised. Individuals and public authorities faced with the interpretation of complex statutes drafted in very general terms could benefit from such advice. As it was unclear whether the High Court (implicitly) possessed such a power, the Commission recommended that it be granted explicit power to make advisory declarations on points of general public importance.[9]

On the international level the Inter-American Court of Human Rights has a far-reaching advisory power. Article 64(1) of the Inter-American Convention of Human Rights provides that member states may consult

[4] Joseph Jaconelli, "Hypothetical Disputes, Moot Points of Law, and Advisory Opinions", 101 *Law Quarterly Review* 600 (1985).

[5] See Supreme Court Act, Can Rev Stat ch S–26, § 53 (1985); see also James L Huffman & Mardilyn Saathoff, "Advisory Opinions and Canadian Constitutional Development: The Supreme Court's Reference Jurisdiction", 74 *Minnesota Law Review* 1251 (1990). See also Luzius Wildhaber, *Advisory opinions. Rechtsgutachten höchster Gerichte* 103 ff (1962).

[6] For a state's authority to issue advisory opinions, see Colo Const, Art VI, § 3; Fla Const Art IV, § 1(c); Me Const Art VI, § 3; Mass Const pt 2, ch 3, Art III; Mich Const, Art III, § 8; NH Const pt 2, Art 74; RI Const Art 10, § 3; SD Const Art V, § 5; Ala Code § 12–2–10 (1975); Del Code Ann tit 10, § 141 (1975); Okla Stat Ann tit 22 §§ 1002, 1003. See Robert H Kennedy, "Advisory Opinions: Cautions About Non-Judicial Undertakings", 23 *University of Richmond Law Review* 174 (1989). For a discussion of advisory opinions in the different states, see Wildhaber, above n 5, at 41 ff.

[7] However, federal courts in the United States have not rendered advisory opinions since the Supreme Court refused to do so in the late 1700s. In 1792 it refused to advise Congress and the Secretary of War on certain pension applications. In 1793 it also refused to advise President Washington on questions relating to United States neutrality in the European War of 1793. The most important reason seemed to be that judicial rendering of advisory opinions would offend the separation of powers as enshrined in the United States Constitution, and the constitutional limitation of federal court jurisdiction to cases or controversies. See US Const, Art III, § 2, cl 1; *Hayburn's Case*, 2 US (2 Dall) 409 (1792); see also *Alabama State Fed'n of Labor v McAdory*, 325 US 450, 461 (1945); see Huffman & Saathoff, above n 5, at 1251 ff.

[8] Law Commission, *Administrative Law—Judicial Review and Statutory Appeals* (Law Comm 226, 1994), para 8.9 ff. See Kenneth Keith,' The Advisory Jurisdiction of the International Court of Justice: Some Comparative Reflections', 17 *Australian Yearbook of International Law* 40 (1996).

[9] Law Commission, above n 8; Keith, above n 8, at 40. For an overview of the history of advisory opinions as requested by the House of Lords and the Crown, respectively, see Luzius Wildhaber, above n 5, at 9 ff. In the case of the House of Lords, requests for advisory opinions fell into disuse by the early twentieth century. With respect to the Crown it fell into disuse more than two centuries ago.

the court as regards the interpretation, not only of the Convention itself, but also of other treaties concerning the protection of human rights in the American states.[10] The second paragraph of the same Article also provides that any member state may request the Inter-American Court's opinion regarding the compatibility of any of its domestic laws with the aforesaid international instruments.[11] In Africa, both the African Commission of Human Rights[12] and the future African Court of Human and Peoples' Rights[13] will be able to provide advisory opinions on the interpretation and application of the African Charter of Human and Peoples' Rights, when requested to do so by the African Union (formerly the Organisation of African States) or any of its organs, member states, or organisations recognised by the African Union.

The European Convention of Human Rights and Freedoms itself does not grant the European Court of Human Rights the right to render advisory opinions. However, the second protocol to the Convention grants the European Court the right to respond to certain types of questions filed by the Committee of Ministers (which may not relate to the content or scope of the rights or freedoms defined in the European Convention or its protocols).[14] Finally, the European Court of Justice enjoys no general power to render advisory opinions, but the constituent documents specify a limited advisory jurisdiction of which Article 300(6) of the Treaty establishing the European Community is worth mentioning. It concerns the right of certain organs of the European Community and its member states to request an advisory opinion from the European Court of Justice on the legality of the entry into proposed treaties by the European Community.[15] In practice this has proved to be a useful method for deciding whether the competence for entering the treaty lies with the European Community or the member states.[16]

---

[10] Available at www.oas.org. See also Scott Davidson, *The Inter-American Court of Human Rights* 233 (1992); Jo M Pasqualucci, "Advisory Practice of the Inter-American Court of Human Rights: Contributing to the Evolution of International Human Rights Law", 38 *Stanford Journal of International Law* 241 ff (2002).

[11] Jaconelli, above n 4, at 605.

[12] Art 45(3) of the African Charter of Human and Peoples' Rights, available at www.up.ac.za/chr/. See also CH Heyns (ed), *Human Rights in Africa Series Vol I* (Kluwer, The Hague, 1996).

[13] Art 4 of the Protocol to the African Charter of Human and Peoples' Rights (OAU/LEG/ EXP/AFCHPR/PROT(III)), available at www.up.ac.za/chr/.

[14] Available at www.ceo.fr.

[15] The text of the TEC is available at www.europa.eu.int/.

[16] See also Hans van der Groeben *et al*, *Kommentar zum EU-/EG-Vertrag* 5/515–16 (Baden-Baden, Nomos 1997). If the European Court of Justice (ECJ) finds that it would be illegal in terms of the Treaty establishing the European Community (TEC) to enter the international agreement, the latter could only be entered into after amending the TEC. If the ECJ does not object to the legality of entering the international agreement, the way is free for ratification. However, this would not preclude objections against the international agreement on the basis of other articles of the TEC at a later stage, for example, during its implementation.

The utility and propriety has been debated in all the above mentioned forums.[17] Critics raise objections to the nature of advisory opinions, arguing that they are merely advisory in nature and bind neither those who requested the advice nor the judges.[18] Second, the advisory opinions are criticised on the ground that they are speculative and based on hypothetical, abstract and academic considerations. Some argue that it might turn out to be practically impossible to define a principle adequately and safely without previous ascertainment of the exact facts to which it was to be applied.[19] American Supreme Court Justice Frankfurter submitted that an advisory opinion was void of any intrinsic value, because of the psychologically unreal atmosphere in which the opinion moves on account of the questions being sterilised and mutilated for want of the impact of actuality and intensities of immediacy.[20] Courts would require the specific facts of an actual controversy to illuminate the complexities of legal issues and therefore should not and cannot resolve abstract legal questions.[21] Third, the critics are afraid that the executive would abuse advisory opinion for political purposes by referring to the courts questions involving political issues. Consequently, the judiciary would be drawn into political controversies with the danger of loss of popular respect, impartial image and abandonment of truly judicial standards.[22]

Those in favour of advisory opinions counter these arguments by underlining that the so-called non-binding nature of the opinions is merely a technical point. In practice advisory opinions are treated as having the same efficacy, authority and precedential value as a judgment in contentious proceedings and the referring authority has almost always honoured the opinions given.[23] Also, although there is a risk that advisory

---

[17] See Manley O Hudson, "Advisory Opinions of National and International Courts", 37 *Harvard Law Review* 970 (1923–24); Felix Frankfurter, "A Note on Advisory Opinions", *ibid*, at 1002; Christine Bray, "Advisory Opinions and the European Court of Justice", 8 *European Law Review* 36 (1985).

[18] Johari above n 3, at 11; see also Bray, above n 17, at 36.

[19] Johari above n 3, at 12.

[20] Frankfurter, above, n 17, at 1006; See Kennedy, above n 6, at 175.

[21] Frankfurter, above n 17, at 1006. See Huffman & Saathoff, above n 5, at 1267, 1270 for submissions that the arguments in advisory proceedings move in an unreal atmosphere and possible situations which would arise are imagined. See also Johari above n 3, at 14. Kennedy, above n 6, at 193.

[22] Johari above n 3, at 13–14. See also Kennedy above n 6, at 179, who argued that the characteristic agenda of an advisory opinion is political rather than judicial. This argument is closely linked to the objection that the advising of the executive by the judiciary violates the principles of separation of powers, since advising the executive or legislature is an executive function as opposed to a legal one. See Huffman and Saathoff, above n 5, at 1268.

[23] Johari, above n 3, at 14–15; Bray above n 17, at 24; Davidson, above n 10, at 232. See also Huffman and Saathoff above n 5, at 1284, who illustrated that the Supreme Court of Canada itself has often relied on earlier reference opinions as precedent, and rarely rejects them as relevant precedent. See also Paul M Bator *et al*; *Hart and Wechsler's The Federal Courts and the Federal System* 69 (Westbury, Foundation, 1988). In the United States, the advisory opinion in

opinions may relate to speculative, abstract and academic considerations the experience with the institution so far does not seem to present a serious threat in this regard. This is partly due to the fact that the advisory procedure usually provides the courts with discretion to decline to give opinions in such circumstances.[24] The fear of the improper involvement of the judiciary in political disputes can also be diluted if both the referring and answering authorities act with self-restraint.[25]

It will become apparent that almost identical arguments make up the debate about the advisory procedure of the ICJ. The merits of these arguments will be addressed at a later stage of the chapter. At the moment the important point is that the advisory procedure, whilst not universally accepted, cannot be regarded as an outlier either. It is an internationally acknowledged avenue for obtaining authoritative legal advice. Even many of those opposed to it agree that advisory opinions, once rendered, have power not unlike ordinary judicial opinions.[26] An enquiry into the advisory opinions of the ICJ as a mechanism to guide or constrain actions of United Nations organs (notably the Security Council) would therefore be appropriate. This becomes all the more apparent if one considers that the possibility for judicial review by the ICJ is otherwise very limited, since it cannot assert jurisdiction over states without their consent.[27] The advisory opinion would thus provide a compensation for such limited jurisdiction.[28]

This chapter is an attempt to evaluate the advisory opinions of the ICJ as a mode for judicial review of actions of the Security Council. At the outset it will examine the extent to which the ICJ has already exercised review in the *Certain Expenses of the United Nations* advisory opinion[29] and the *Legal Consequences for States of the Continued Presence of South Africa and Namibia (South West Africa) Notwithstanding Security Council Resolution 276 (1970)* advisory opinion.[30] Whilst the ICJ effectively reviewed the legality of a binding Chapter VII resolution in the *Namibia* opinion,[31] the *Certain Expenses* opinion reviewed the scope of the powers of the General

---

Massachusetts seems to have the longest and most frequent use. Although non-binding, they have usually been followed when the same issues also featured in litigation.

[24] Johari, above n 3, at 15.
[25] *Ibid.*
[26] See Kennedy, above n 6, at 198; Wildhaber, above n 5, at 7.
[27] Art 35 of the ICJ Statute. See Jaconelli, above n 4, at 603. Cf W Michael Reisman, "The Constitutional Crisis in the United Nations", 87 *American Journal of International Law* 92–93 (1993). See also ch 3 at s 1.
[28] See Michael Fraas, *Sicherheitsrat der Vereinten Nationen und Internationaler Gerichtshof* 29 (Peter Lang, Frankfurt a/M, 1998).
[29] ICJ Rep 1962, at 151 ff. Hereinafter referred to as the *Certain Expenses* opinion.
[30] ICJ Rep 1971, at 12 ff. Hereinafter referred to as the *Namibia* opinion.
[31] See below in s 2.2.1.

Assembly and the Secretary-General.[32] However, since this advisory opinion also sheds light on the relationship ("division of labour") between the Security Council and the General Assembly, it is of significant importance for understanding the role of the Security Council in the Charter system. In addition, the *Certain Expenses* opinion is illustrative of certain general techniques and principles which the ICJ utilises when reviewing the powers of political organs of the United Nations—whether the Security Council or otherwise.[33]

After concentrating on the *Certain Expenses* and *Namibia* opinions, the chapter analyses several general questions which are central to judicial review of the Security Council by means of advisory opinions. They evolve around the propriety of judicial review *versus* the development of a political question doctrine; the consequences of an illegal Security Council resolution, and the reluctance of United Nations organs to make frequent use of the advisory opinion procedure. Finally, the chapter draws some conclusions for the future of advisory opinions as a mode for judicial review and the potential role of the Secretary-General in this context.

2.   EXERCISING REVIEW THROUGH ADVISORY OPINIONS

2.1.   Legitimating the Concept of Peace-Keeping (*Certain Expenses* Opinion)

The *Certain Expenses* opinion[34] had a significant impact on the scope of the General Assembly's powers *vis a vis* the Security Council. It limited the action with respect to which the Security Council has the exclusive competence to that of enforcement action and allowed the General Assembly to initiate peace-keeping action. It also gave legitimacy to the concept of peace-keeping, which was not explicitly provided for in the Charter.[35]

The concept of peace-keeping was invented in the wake of the Suez-crisis in 1956,[36] when the laming of the Security Council in the wake of the Cold War prompted the General Assembly to invoke the Uniting for

---

[32] See below in s 2.1.

[33] For the same reason, reference will occasionally also be made to other advisory opinions in which the ICJ reviewed the competencies of the General Assembly, or of political organs of other international organisations.

[34] See above n 29.

[35] Malcom Shaw, *International Law* 250 (Cambridge, Cambridge University Press, 1997); Alvarez, above n 2 at 8 fn 46; cf Halderman, "Some Legal Aspects of Sanctions in the Rhodesian Case", 17 *International & Comparative Law Quarterly* 682 (1968).

[36] See Abram Chayes *et al* (eds), *International Legal Process* 36 (Boston, Little & Brown, 1968). See also John W Halderman, above n 35, at 676.

Peace Resolution.[37] In the resulting General Assembly session it adopted a resolution that inter alia authorised the Secretary-General to create a United Nations emergency Force (hereinafter UNEF), which would supervise and secure a cease-fire agreed to by the parties.[38]

The United Nations Operations in the Congo (hereinafter ONUC) was created by the Security Council in the face of the violence which erupted in the Congo after independence on 30 June 1960. The Security Council subsequently passed Resolution 143 of 14 July 1960, authorising the Secretary-General to organise a peacekeeping force modelled after UNEF.[39] By September of 1960 the Congolese government had disintegrated and consensus within the Security Council had collapsed.[40] The General Assembly was then called into emergency session under the Uniting for Peace procedure[41] and passed a resolution approving the Secretary General's conduct of ONUC.[42]

With respect to both UNEF and ONUC disagreements arose as to whether the operations should be financed by the participating states or by the United Nations as a whole.[43] By December 1961 the United Nations

[37] GA Res 377(V) of 3 November 1950. Its essential feature is an assertion of a right on the part of the General Assembly to act to maintain international peace and security when the Security Council, because of the veto, is unable to do so. The General Assembly can then recommend the members to take collective action. It may meet in an emergency special session within 24 hours of a request by the Security Council on the vote of any seven (now nine) members or by a majority of the members of the United Nations. See also Finn Seyersted, *United Nations Forces in the Law of Peace and War* 42 (AW Seythoff, Leyden, 1966); also Blaine Sloan, *United Nations General Assembly Resolutions in Our Changing World* 25 (Ardsley-on-Hudson NY, Transnational Publications, 1991).

[38] GA Res 1000 (ES–I) of 5 November 1956, at para 1. The Force was equipped with normal regimental weapons, but not with heavy arms and its troops had a right to fire in self-defence. However, they were never to take the initiative in the use of arms, but may have responded with force to an armed attack upon them. This included attempts to use force to make them withdraw from positions which they occupied under orders from the Commander. See A/3302 (1956); Chayes, above n 36, at 38–39. Michael Bothe, "Peace-Keeping", in Bruno Simma (eds), *The Charter of the United Nations. A Commentary* (Oxford, Oxford University Press, 1994) at 589 fn 144; Seyersted, above n 37, at 45–46.

[39] At para 2. See also SC Res 145 of 22 July 1960 and SC Res 146 of 9 August 1960.

[40] The Secretary General's representative in charge of ONUC took steps seeking to head off or at least contain the civil war. A Soviet resolution opposing these activities was defeated and a resolution praising them was vetoed. See Chayes, above n 36, at 40.

[41] See SC Res 157 of 17 September 1960.

[42] GA Res 1474 (ES–IV) of 20 September 1960; See also GA Res 1600 (XV) of 15 April 1961. By 1961 some measure of consent had been re-established within the Security Council. For example, in SC Res 169 of 24 November 1961, it authorised the Secretary-General to take "vigorous action" including the requisite measure of force, if necessary, for the immediate apprehension of foreign military personnel. See also SC Res 161 of 21 February 1961; Seyersted, above n 37, at 69.

[43] The United States favoured characterising the costs as "expenses of the organisation", and financing them on the usual scale of assessments. The Soviet Union insisted that UNEF costs be borne by Britain, France and Israel. The General Assembly finally provided that assessments should be made on all members, but on a sliding scale with low-income members paying less than their usual share and the difference being made up by voluntary contributions. See GA Res 1583 of 20 December 1960; Chayes, above n 36, at 40 ff.

financial statement reflected the failure of many nations to pay their assessments for ONUC and UNEF. In an effort to solve the financial crisis, the General Assembly submitted a request to the ICJ on whether certain expenditures which were authorised by the General Assembly to cover the costs of ONUC and UNEF constituted expenses of the organisation within the meaning of paragraph 2 of Article 17 of the Charter. The ICJ concluded that in both instances the financial obligations incurred fell within the purposes of the Charter and were incurred by organs which were authorised under the Charter to do so.[44]

The ICJ conceded that in accordance with Article 24 of the Charter the Security Council had the primary responsibility for the maintenance of peace and security. It also stated, however, that this primary responsibility was not an exclusive one. The Charter made it abundantly clear that the General Assembly was also to be concerned with international peace and security. Article 14 authorises the General Assembly to recommend measures for the peaceful adjustment of any situation, including those resulting from a violation of the provisions of the Charter. The only limitation which Article 14 imposes on the General Assembly is the restriction found in Article 12, namely that the Assembly should not recommend measures while the Security Council is dealing with the same matter, unless the Security Council requests it to do so.[45]

A further restriction on the powers of the General Assembly is found in paragraph 2 of Article 11, according to which it has to refer questions on which "action" is necessary to the Security Council. The ICJ limited the kind of action falling exclusively in the jurisdiction of the Security Council to enforcement action, by stating that it is only the Security Council that can require enforcement by coercive action against an aggressor in terms of Chapter VII of the Charter.[46] Such action was to be distinguished from peace-keeping operations, which were performed at the request or with the consent of the states concerned, and which could therefore be initiated by the General Assembly.[47] This distinction between peace-keeping

---

[44]*Certain Expenses* opinion, above n 29, at 185, 188; See also Hans W Baade, "Nullity and Avoidance in Public International Law: A Preliminary Survey and a Theoretical Orientation", 39 *Indiana Law Journal* 520 (1963–64); Elihu Lauterpacht, "The Legal Effect of Illegal Acts of International Organisations", in *Cambridge Essays in International Law. Essays in Honour of Lord McNair* 107 (London, Stevens & Sons, 1965); Dapo Akande, "The International Court of Justice and the Security Council: Is there Room for Judicial Control of Decisions of Political Organs of the United Nations?", 46 *International & Comparative Law Quarterly* 328 (1997).
[45]*Ibid*, at 163. For the implications of this limitation contained in Art 12, see below, at s 5.1.
[46]*Certain Expenses* opinion, above n 29, at 178. See Robert Y Jennings, "Advisory Opinion of July 20 1962", 11 *International and Comparative Law Quarterly* 1173 (1962).
[47]*Ibid*. But see dissenting opinion of Judge Koretsky, *ibid*, at 204–05. Only the Security Council may take action with regard to a question relating to the maintenance of international peace and security. He criticised the definition of enforcement action as action directed against a state. He was unable to find any direct reference in Art 39 of the Charter to the fact

and "action" in terms of paragraph 2 of Article 11 of the Charter will be discussed again in the context of the *Namibia* opinion.[48]

The essence of this reasoning is that the General Assembly could initiate a peace-keeping operation such as UNEF if it had the *consent* of the parties involved. Had this consent been absent or had the operation involved enforcement action, the General Assembly would have lacked the authority to undertake the military operation.[49] In this context it is worth noting that the nature of ONUC was slightly different, as it was initially authorised by the Security Council and then continued by the General Assembly and the Secretary-General when consensus within the Security Council disintegrated. The operation was nonetheless similar to UNEF in that it enjoyed the consent of the Congolese government.[50] According to the ICJ the operations of ONUC did not include a use of armed force against a state which the Security Council, under Article 39, determined to have committed an act of aggression or to have breached the peace. The operation did not involve preventative or enforcement measures against any state under Chapter VII and therefore did not constitute "action" as that term is used in Article 11.[51]

In summary therefore, the ICJ in the *Certain Expenses* opinion upheld the General Assembly and Security Council resolutions which created the concept of peace-keeping. In addition it legitimised the criteria which have by now become classic for traditional peace-keeping operations.[52] These include the consent of the states on whose territory the operations take place, impartiality and the use of force in self-defence. In the case of UNOC the ICJ downplayed the fact that the use of force extended beyond self-defence, by emphasising the consent of the Congolese government to the United Nations action.[53]

---

that measures to be taken by the Security Council for the maintenance of international peace and security should be directed against a state. See dissenting opinion of Judge Winiarski, *ibid*, at 230.

[48] See below, at s 2.2.1.
[49] See *Certain Expenses* opinion, above n 29, at 184.
[50] *Ibid*, at 186.
[51] *Ibid*. The ICJ thus did not regard the expanded use of force which was authorised in SC Res 169 of 24 November 1961 as "enforcement action", as it was directed at groups such as mercenaries and foreign military personnel, but not against the Congolese government itself.
[52] See Secretary-General's Supplement to an Agenda for Peace, A/50/60 – S/1995/1 para 33 (1995); Report of the Panel on United Nations Peace Operations (Brahimi Report), A/55/305–S/2000/809 para 48 (2000).
[53] See Elina Kalkku, "The United Nations Authorisation to Peace Enforcement with the Use of Armed Forces in the Light of the Practice of the UN Security Council", 9 *Finnish Yearbook of International Law* 359 (1998). She stated that SC Res 169 of 24 November 1961, clearly authorised the use of armed force beyond what can be considered necessary for mere self-defence. See also Seyersted, above n 37, at 69. But see Bothe (in Simma), above n 38, at 589, who referred to this type of action as active self-defence, which could become necessary

These criteria also implicitly place a limit on the residual roles of the General Assembly and Secretary-General in initiating and executing peace-keeping operations when the Security Council is unable to fulfil its primary responsibility in this regard. For example, it would be illegal for them to extend their authority to enforcement action under Chapter VII of the Charter.[54] One could illustrate this point by drawing an analogy with the inability of the Security Council to intervene militarily in Kosovo in 1999, due to Russian and Chinese opposition. Initiating the Uniting for Peace procedure to overcome this deadlock[55] would only have been legal to the extent that an intervention had the consent of the authorities of the Federal Republic of Yugoslavia. In the absence of such consent a full military intervention by NATO would have remained illegal under the Charter, even though broad support by the General Assembly would have provided political legitimisation. This point is taken up again in chapter 7 at section 3.1.2., when examining the Security Council and General Assembly resolutions that authorised the use of force against North Korea in 1950.

2.2.   Termination of Mandates (*Namibia* Opinion)

The *Namibia* opinion confirmed that a mandate can be regarded as terminated where the mandatory power deliberately and persistently violated obligations and therefore destroyed the very object and purpose of

---

where the peace-keeping forces are not merely of an inter-positionary nature. The force would assert its right of freedom of movement and any attempt to hinder the exercise of this right could be countered by force in the name of self-defence. However, this interpretation remains controversial as it blurs the distinction with enforcement action, as is indicated by Kalkku, above n 53, at 358.

[54] This would, to some extent, counter the argument forwarded by Kay Hailbronner & Eckart Klein, "Article 12" in Bruno Simma (ed), *The Charter of the United Nations. A Commentary* 257 (Oxford, Oxford University Press, 1994). They regarded the Uniting for Peace resolution as problematic, since the exercise of the veto is not necessarily aimed at paralysing the security mechanism of the United Nations. It may well be based on the conviction of a permanent member that there is no threat to the peace. To then accord a power of assessment of the situation to the General Assembly would amount to placing the Security Council under the supervision of the General Assembly. This is not in line with the Charter and the permanent members' explicit right to veto power in Art 27(3). However, as long as the action taken in terms of the Uniting for Peace resolution is based on the consent of the states concerned, there would not be any control of the Security Council by the General Assembly. The Security Council is not forced to adopt any decision and it remains the only organ that can adopt binding decisions for member states. See Danesh Sarooshi, *The United Nations and the Development of Collective Security* 136 (Oxford, Oxford University, 1999).

[55] As suggested by Walter Kälin, "Humanitäre Intervention: Legitimation durch Verfahren? Zehn Thesen zur Kosovo-Krise", 10 *Schweizerische Zeitschrift für Internationales und Europäisches Recht* 171 (2000); cf Daniel Thürer, Der Wefall effektiver Staatsgewalt: "The Failed State", 34 *Berichte der Deutschen Gesellschaft für Völkerrecht* 38 (1995).

that relationship. The ICJ also found that whereas the General Assembly had the power to terminate the mandate, the withdrawal of the illegal administration could only be enforced by the Security Council.

It can thus be argued that the ICJ created a two-step procedure for the termination of mandates. This first step is the termination of the mandate by the General Assembly due to a violation of core obligations by the mandatory power.[56] The second step consists of the enforcement of the termination by the Security Council by means of a binding resolution demanding South Africa's withdrawal.[57] Most importantly, this enforcement action by the Security Council implied that the breach of a mandate by the mandatory power can—and in this particular case has—resulted in a threat to international peace and security under Article 39 of Chapter VII of the Charter.[58]

The *Namibia* opinion resulted from the Security Council's only request to date for an advisory opinion. The request was aimed at clarifying the legal consequences for states of the continued presence of South Africa in Namibia, notwithstanding Security Council resolution 276 of 30 January 1970. The opinion had a long history which began with the General Assembly's adoption of Resolution 2145 (XXI) of 27 October 1966. By this resolution it decided that the mandate for South-West Africa was terminated and that South Africa had no other right to administer the territory. Subsequently the Security Council adopted various resolutions including resolution 276 (1970), declaring the continued presence of South Africa in Namibia illegal.

In response to South Africa's objections against the validity of these resolutions, the ICJ stated that it did not possess powers of judicial review or appeal in relation to the United Nations organs in question. Nor did the validity of the resolutions form the subject of the request for an advisory opinion. The ICJ nevertheless, in the exercise of its judicial function, considered their validity before elaborating on the legal consequences arising from those resolutions.[59] The ICJ's obligation to do so was especially

---

[56] See Alvarez, above n 2, at 8 fn 46.
[57] See Rosalyn Higgins, "The Advisory Opinion on Namibia: Which UN Resolutions are Binding under Art 25 of the Charter?", 21 *International & Comparative Law Quarterly* 273 (1972).
[58] See Akande, above n 44, at 331.
[59] *Namibia* opinion, above n 30, at 45. See also Akande, above n 44, at 331; Shaw, above n 35, at 251. See James Crawford, "The General Assembly, the International Court and Self-determination", in Vaughan Lowe & Malgosia Fitzmaurice (eds), *Fifty Years of the International Court of Justice. Essays in Honour of Sir Robert Jennings* 590 (Cambridge, Cambridge University Press, 1996). The ICJ declined to treat at face value the Security Council's request for an advisory opinion. The request focused on the legal effects of the relevant resolutions rather than on the validity of the termination of the mandate as such. But the ICJ pointed out that the one presupposed the other and went on to deal with the underlying issues.

strongly worded in some of the dissenting opinions. Judge Fitzmaurice, for example, did not conceive it as compatible with the judicial function of the ICJ to state the consequences of acts whose validity is assumed, without itself testing the lawfulness of those acts. Therefore he was of the view that the ICJ had a duty to examine the legality of General Assembly resolution 2145 (XXI) (1966). It also had an equal duty to examine all relevant resolutions of the Security Council for the same purpose.[60]

In reviewing these resolutions the ICJ concluded that Resolution 2145 (XXI) (1966) determined that there had been a material breach of the mandate. South Africa had failed to fulfil its obligations in respect of the administration of the mandated territory and to ensure the moral and material well-being and security of the indigenous inhabitants of South-West Africa and has disavowed the mandate.[61] The resolution in question was therefore to be viewed as the exercise of the right to terminate a relationship in case of a deliberate and persistent violation of obligations which destroys the very object and purpose of that relationship.[62]

It would not be correct to assume that because of its recommendatory powers, the General Assembly is debarred from adopting, in special cases within the framework of its competence, resolutions which make determinations or have operative effect. However, the General Assembly lacked the necessary powers to ensure the withdrawal of South Africa from the territory and therefore, acting in accordance with paragraph 2 of Article 11 of the Charter, enlisted the cooperation of the Security Council.[63] According to the ICJ, having considered the terms of the Security Council resolutions leading up to resolution 276 (1970), the discussions preceding it and the Charter provisions invoked, these resolutions were adopted in conformity with the purposes and principles of the Charter and in accordance with the Security Council's primary responsibility for the maintenance of international peace and security in Articles 24 and 25.[64] Consequently the decisions were binding on all member states.[65] The implications thereof were, *inter alia*, that South Africa was under an obligation to withdraw its administration from Namibia immediately and thus put an end to its occupation of the territory.

---

[60] Dissenting opinion of Judge Fitzmaurice in *Namibia* opinion, above n 30, at 294. See the separate opinion of Judge Onyeama *ibid*, at 143–44. He submitted that the ICJ's powers are clearly defined by its Statute and do not include powers to review decisions of other organs of the United Nations. But when, as in the present proceedings, such decisions bear upon a case properly instituted before the ICJ and a correct judgment or opinion could not be rendered without determining the validity of such decisions, the ICJ could not possibly avoid such a determination without abdicating its role of a judicial organ.
[61] *Namibia* opinion, above n 30, at 46.
[62] *Ibid*, at 47.
[63] *Ibid*, at 51.
[64] See *Namibia* opinion, above n 30, at 51.
[65] *Ibid*, at 53.

2.2.1. Did the Security Council Enforce Termination under Chapter VII?

It is important to point out that none of the Security Council resolutions stated that South Africa's behaviour constituted a threat to or breach of the peace in terms of Article 39 of the Charter. Neither was the chapter under which the relevant Security Council resolutions fell, clearly designated.[66] The ICJ also went to great lengths in explaining that it did not find in the Charter any support for the view that Article 25 applies only to enforcement measures adopted under Chapter VII of the Charter. The ICJ submitted instead that it applied to all decisions of the Security Council adopted in accordance with the Charter.[67] Article 25 is placed not in Chapter VII, but immediately after Article 24 in that part of the Charter which deals with the functions and powers of the Security Council. If Article 25 had reference solely to decisions of the Security Council concerning enforcement action under Articles 41 and 42 of the Charter, that is to say, if it were only such decisions which had binding effect, then Article 25 would be superfluous, since this effect is secured by Articles 48 and 49 of the Charter.[68]

The implication thus is that any resolution adopted by the Security Council pursuant to the exercise of its primary responsibility for international peace and security—including those resolutions adopted under Chapter VI—could constitute a binding decision, since Article 25 would also apply to that chapter.[69] Moreover, by elaborating on the possibility of adopting binding resolutions under Chapter VI, the ICJ implied that in the present case the Security Council acted under Chapter VI rather than Chapter VII.

---

[66] Higgins, above n 57, at 275.

[67] *Namibia* opinion, above n 30, at 53. Some support for this interpretation can be drawn from the *travaux préparatoires* of Art 25. The Dumbarto Oaks version of Art 25 determined that "all members of the Organisation should obligate themselves to accept the decisions of the Security Council and to carry them out in accordance with the provisions of the Charter." At San Francisco Belgium suggested that the words "taken under Chapter VIII" (which later become Chapter VII), be added after the words "Security Council". In this way Belgium wanted to clarify that the obligation to accept the decisions of the Security Council referred solely to its powers under Chapter VII. However, this proposal was rejected since states such as the United Kingdom and the Soviet Union found such a qualification too restrictive. Instead, they preferred a text that obliged members to carry out all decisions of the Security Council. See XI *United Nations Conference on International Organisation* 392–95 (1945); see also Wilhelm A Kewenig, "Die Problematik der Bindungswirkung von Entscheidungen des Sicherheitsrates", in Horst Emhke *et al* (eds), *Festschrift für Ulrich Scheuner zum 70. Geburtstag* 275–76 (Berlin, Duncker & Humblot, 1973).

[68] *Ibid*; See Jost Delbrück, "Article 25", in Bruno Simma (ed), *The Charter of the United Nations. A Commentary* 410 (Oxford, Oxford University Press, 1994).

[69] Higgins, above n 57, at 272, 278. She also noted that if Art 25 applied only to Chapter VII, one might perhaps have expected to see it located in that chapter. See also Kewenig, above n 67, at 282–83; Olivier J Lissitzyn, "International Law and the Advisory opinion on Namibia", 11 *Columbia Journal of International Law* 63 (1972).

However, this assumption can be countered by several arguments. First, the conclusion that the binding effect of Security Council resolutions under Chapter VII is secured by Articles 48 and 49 of the Charter, as opposed to Article 25, is flawed. Articles 48 and 49 relate only to the choosing of the states who would enforce the binding measures. It does not deal with when and how such binding measure can be adopted.[70] Furthermore, the ICJ also stated that the General Assembly enlisted the cooperation of the Security Council in accordance with *paragraph 2 of Article 11* (emphasis added), since it lacked the necessary powers to ensure the withdrawal of South Africa from the territory. As has been indicated in the *Certain Expenses* opinion,[71] the action in paragraph 2 of Article 11 that the General Assembly cannot exercise is enforcement action under Chapter VII. The referral to paragraph 2 of Article 11 thus necessarily implies enforcement action under Chapter VII.

One should also keep in mind that the opportunities for the Security Council to take binding decisions under Chapter VI are extremely small, since the wording of the paragraphs mainly refers to recommendations as opposed to decisions by the Security Council.[72] The only exception contained in Chapter VI is Article 34, according to which the Security Council may investigate any dispute, or any situation which might lead to international friction or give rise to a dispute, in order to determine whether the continuance of the dispute or situation is likely to endanger the maintenance of international peace and security.[73] According to several authors this wording suggests the binding nature of a decision to carry out an investigation, since it does not contain any proviso that an investigation decided by the Security Council need the consent of the

---

[70] See Fraas, above n 28, at 55 fn 63; Kewenig, above n 67, at 274.

[71] Above n 29.

[72] See Higgins, above n 57, at 282, who acknowledged this limitation; Delbrück (in Simma), above n 68, at 411. The mere fact that the Charter distinguishes between decisions and recommendations indicates that the Security Council may make either binding decisions or non-binding recommendations. See also Jochen A Frowein, "Collective Enforcement of International Obligations", 47 *Zeitschrift für ausländisches öffentliches Recht und Völkerrecht* 69–70 (1987). He stated that it was very doubtful whether Art 25 gave special powers to the Security Council outside of Chapter VII. If under the relevant Chapter or Article of the Charter a decision is not binding, Art 25 cannot make it so.

[73] The only exception outside of Chapter VI is Art 94(2) of the Charter. It provides that if any party to a case before the ICJ fails to execute a judgment rendered by that court, the other party may have recourse to the Security Council. The latter may, if it deems necessary, make recommendations or decide upon measures to be taken to give effect to the judgment. This clause thus gives the Security Council the power to enforce decisions of the ICJ. It stands apart from the collective security system in that it is not dependent on whether the non-compliance with an ICJ judgment constitutes a threat to peace. It has, however, fallen into complete disuse with the Charter system. See Gaetano Arangio-Ruiz, "On the Security Council's "Law-Making", 83 *Rivista di Diritto Internazionale* 622 (2000); Kewenig, above n 67, at 279–80.

state concerned.[74] They submit that only such a provision could be seen as indicating the non-binding character of the recommendations concerning investments. Stated differently, they do not regard Article 34's systematic placement within Chapter VI as enough to rob it of binding character.[75]

However, the importance of Article's 34 placement in Chapter VI is not to be under-estimated. Allowing the Security Council to adopt binding measures under Chapter VI would undermine the structural division of competencies foreseen by Chapters VI and VII, respectively. The whole aim of separating these chapters is to distinguish between voluntary and binding measures. Whereas the pacific settlement of disputes provided by the former is underpinned by the consent of the parties, binding measures in terms of Chapter VII are characterised by the absence of such consent.[76] A further indication of the non-binding nature of measures taken in terms of Chapter VI is the obligation on members of the Security Council who are parties to a dispute, to refrain from voting when resolutions under Chapter VI are adopted.[77] No similar obligation exists with respect to binding resolutions adopted under Chapter VII.[78] Therefore one can argue that if resolutions under Article 34 were binding, this Article would have been exempted from the voting qualification, just like the other binding measures in Chapter VII. Since this is not the case, the conclusion has to be that Security Council resolutions in terms of Article 34 are non-binding.

The proponents of the binding nature of Article 34 resolutions also argue that such binding force is necessary to give effective execution to Security Council measures. If it were impossible for the Security Council to effect an investigation of a disputed matter by issuing a binding decision, a core element of the system for maintaining world peace would be jeopardised.[79] This argument would have carried significant weight if the Security Council were indeed obliged to resort to investigation before determining that an Article 39 threat to the peace exists. However, as it

---

[74] Delbrück (in Simma), above n 68, at 412; Kewenig, above n 67, at 283; Theodor Schweisfurth, "Article 34", in Bruno Simma (ed), *The Charter of the United Nations. A Commentary* 525 (Oxford, Oxford University Press, 1994). Cf Ernest L Kerley, "The Powers of Investigation of the United Nations Security Council", in 55 *American Journal of International Law* (1961), at 892 ff.

[75] Delbrück (in Simma), above n 68, at 412.

[76] Fraas, above n 28, at 55–56. However, he did not seem to regard the termination of the mandate as action in terms of Chapter VII. He rather saw the termination of mandates as a special case, but failed to indicate interms of which Articles of the Charter such special resolutions would be justified. See also the separate opinion of Judge Dillard in the *Namibia* opinion, above n 30, at 150.

[77] As stipulated by Art 27(3) of the Charter.

[78] As is conceded by Delbrück (in Simma), above n 68, at 412.

[79] Delbrück (in Simma), above n 68, at 412; Kewenig, above n 67, at 266–67; Schweisfurth (in Simma), above n 74, at 525.

stands, the Security Council is by no means obliged to do so and has resorted to Article 34 only twice in the past.[80] In the light of the practical unimportance of Article 34 resolutions, attempts to discover their binding character from the principle of effectiveness would thus not seem to be convincing.

Finally, even if one were to accept that recommendations to investigate under Article 34 were of a binding nature, this would not enhance the Security Council's power outside of Chapter VII in any material way. The reason is that states would only have to permit the Security Council to gather comprehensive information about a dispute or situation and to support the Security Council to this effect.[81] The Article does not allow for imposing any procedure, method, or substantial settlement of a dispute on the parties. In that respect Article 34 reflects the general tenor of Chapter VI, namely to leave the free choice of the method of dispute settlement to the parties.[82]

If one applies this reasoning to the *Namibia* opinion, the decisive point is that none of the Articles under Chapter VI facilitate the adoption of the type of binding measures that were adopted by the Security Council in Resolution 276 (1970). Thus, the argument that the *Namibia* opinion would be a case where the ICJ merely reviewed whether the Security Council had the competence in the specific instance to adopt a binding resolution outside of Chapter VII, as opposed to a situation where the legality of a Chapter VII resolution is being reviewed,[83] is not convincing. Resolution 276 (1970) was indeed adopted in terms of Chapter VII, even though the ICJ went to some length to give the opposite impression.

In order to take action under Chapter VII, the Security Council must find (even if only implicitly) a threat to peace, breach of the peace, or an act of aggression.[84] The majority in the *Namibia* opinion found that South Africa's behaviour amounted to such, albeit implicitly. This is reflected by their regarding the relevant Security Council resolutions as being adopted in

---

[80] These were the Greek Frontier Incidents Question (SC Res 15 of 19 December 1946), and the India-Pakistan Question (SC Res 39 of 20 January 1948). Cf Kewenig, above n 67, at 266.

[81] Schweisfurth (in Simma), above n 74, at 525.

[82] *Ibid.* The same can be said of a resolution of the Security Council in terms of Art 33, calling on states to have recourse to pacific measures of dispute resolution. Moreover, the duty of the members to have recourse to such measures is not created by such a resolution of the Security Council—the resolution would be a mere declaration emphasising a duty of the members which flows directly from the Charter itself. See Delbrück (in Simma), above n 68, at 411.

[83] As was argued by Barbara Lorinser, *Bindende Resolutionen des Sicherheitsrates* 65 (Baden-Baden, Nomos, 1996). Due to the fact that she regarded the *Namibia* opinion as not relating to binding Chapter VII resolutions, she came to the conclusion that it had very limited precedential value for the question whether the ICJ could actually review the validity of binding resolutions adopted under that Chapter.

[84] Art 39 of the Charter.

accordance with that organ's primary responsibility for peace and security, and as being binding on all member states. However, differences of opinion in this regard featured in several of the dissenting opinions. For example, Judge Fitzmaurice stated that in the situation before the ICJ there was no threat to peace and security other than such as might have been artificially created as a pretext for the realisation of ulterior purposes.[85] These differences of opinion are closely related to the question whether the discretion of the Security Council in determining a threat to peace is unlimited, or whether it is subjected to legal criteria—a matter which is discussed extensively in chapter 4.

The question that remains is how to understand the ICJ's own acknowledgement that it has no power of judicial review. The only conclusion would seem to be that it has no right to judicial review in the sense where this is a separate or special institution as known in national law.[86] But the ICJ's statement provides no ground for thinking that the legal basis of resolutions of the Security Council or the General Assembly is somehow privileged and immune from scrutiny.[87] This becomes all the more apparent if one takes note of the fact that several judges in the *Namibia* opinion were prepared to regard the Security Council's resolutions as invalid. As has been mentioned, Judge Fitzmaurice was not convinced by the fact that the Union of South Africa's administration of the mandate resulted in a threat to the peace.[88] Although one may disagree with him with respect to his conclusion on the facts, there is a lot to say for his warning that limitations on the powers of the Security Council are necessary because of the all too great ease with which any acutely controversial international situation can be represented as involving a latent threat to peace and security, even where it is really too remote to genuinely constitute one.[89]

---

[85] See the dissenting opinion of Judge Fitzmaurice in the *Namibia* opinion, above n 30, at 293; see also the dissenting opinion of Judge Gros, *ibid*, at 340; cf Akande, above n 44, at 337.

[86] See Akande, above n 44, at 333. The ICJ seemed to be saying that it lacked powers of judicial review in the sense of being able to quash definitively the decisions of the political organs of the United Nations. See also Lorinser, above n 83, at 65, 74; Bernd Martenczuk, "The Security Council, the International Court and Judicial Review: What Lessons from Lockerbie?", 10 *European Journal of International Law* 526–27 (1999).

[87] Crawford, above n 59, at 590, Shaw, above n 35, at 252. See Vera Gowlland-Debbas, "The Relationship between the International Court of Justice and the Security Council in the Light of the Lockerbie Case", 88 *American Journal of International Law* 663 (1994); see also Blaine Sloan, "The United Nations Charter as a Constitution", 1 *Pace Yearbook of International Law* 77 (1989).

[88] Dissenting opinion of Judge Fitzmaurice in the *Namibia* opinion, above n 30, at 340.

[88] *Ibid*, at 294.

[89] *Ibid*. He also warned that: "it was to keep the peace, not to change the world order, that the Security Council was set up".

3.   QUESTIONS RELATING TO JUDICIAL REVIEW THROUGH ADVISORY OPINIONS

From the above presentation it emerges that questions of review of the legality of resolutions of political organs of the United Nations may arise in advisory opinions even without an express request to this extent from the organ that requests the opinion. It occurs where the ICJ is asked to decide upon the legal obligations arising from, or the legal consequences that flow from a particular resolution or decision.[90] Where this is the case the ICJ has an obligation to take into account all legal aspects relevant to the situation. It cannot pronounce upon such obligations or consequences without determining the legal basis of the origins of such obligations or consequences.[91]

In reviewing the resolutions of political organs of the United Nations the ICJ does so with care and with the respect due to other principal organs of the organisation, reflecting a spirit of cooperation.[92] This is due to the fact that the ICJ was established as the principal judicial organ within the United Nations. This provided the basis for the judicial duty to cooperate, which entails the overcoming of difficulties in order to extend maximal assistance to fellow organs of the United Nations.[93] The duty to cooperate also gains support from the inherent right of each organ of the United Nations to interpret the Charter in relation to its authority.[94]

In the following paragraphs some of the central questions intrinsically linked to the doctrine of cooperation will be addressed. The first question is whether the ICJ should actually be engaging in judicial review at all, or whether the doctrine of cooperation would necessitate the development of a political question doctrine. For example, should the ICJ refrain from engaging in a review of the legality of binding resolutions of the Security Council under Chapter VII of the Charter? Questions also arise with respect to the consequences of an invalid Security Council resolution, and whether this would result in the nullity of the resolution. One can also ask why the advisory opinion procedure is not used more often, and whether this under-utilisation of the ICJ can be overcome by extending the authority to request advisory opinions to the Secretary-General.

---

[90] Shaw, above n 35, at 257. See also Sloan, above n 119, at 76.
[91] Akande, above n 44, at 330.
[92] Shaw, above n 35, at 257.
[93] Michla Pomerance, "Advisory Role of the International Court of Justice and its Judicial Character: Past and Future Prisms", in Alexander S Muller, *et al* (eds), *The International Court of Justice—Its Future Role after Fifty Years* 290 (The Hague, Martinus Nijhoff, 1997).
[94] Cf Akande, above n 44, at 341; separate opinion of Judge de Castro in the *Namibia* opinion, above n 30, at 185. See Matthias J Herdegen, "The 'Constitutionalisation' of the UN Security System", 27 *Vanderbilt Journal of Transnational Law* 110 (1994). He referred to the right of each organ to interpret the Charter with respect to its own functions as a limited *Kompetenz-Kompetenz*.

3.1.   The Political Question Doctrine

The political question doctrine relates to the propriety of the ICJ to render an advisory opinion, in the light of the political context in which the request was submitted. Should the ICJ refrain from dealing with a request for an advisory opinion, on the basis that it concerns a political rather than a legal matter? This question has to be distinguished from the scope of the General Assembly and the Security Council to ask for an advisory opinion. The latter is the preliminary question. Only when the competence of the General Assembly or the Security Council to submit a request to the ICJ has been determined, does the issue whether the ICJ has to exercise its discretion and render an opinion arise.

3.1.1.   *The Competence of the General Assembly and Security Council to Request Advisory Opinions*

According to Article 96(1) of the Charter, the General Assembly or the Security Council may request the ICJ to give an advisory opinion on any legal question. This clause is phrased in wide language and has been interpreted to mean both abstract and concrete questions. Also, the interpretation of the Charter by the ICJ was regarded as an interpretative function which falls within the normal judicial powers of the principal organ of the United Nations.[95]

This broad authorisation has to be distinguished from that defined in Article 96(2). According to the latter, the General Assembly can permit the other organs of the United Nations and specialised agencies to request advisory opinions on legal questions "arising within the scope of their activities". No such restriction is imposed upon the analogous competence of the General Assembly and of the Security Council in Article 96(1). Therefore some are of the opinion that the reference to "any legal question" would allow the General Assembly and the Security Council to ask questions falling outside their activities.[96] On the other hand, it has been contended that these organs too are competent to request advisory opinions on legal questions only if such questions arise within the scope of their activities.[97] After all, the interpretation of any organ's jurisdiction

---

[95] *Conditions of Admission to Membership in the United Nations*, Advisory Opinion, ICJ Rep 1947–48, at 61.
[96] Akande, above n 44, at 328; cf Rosalyn Higgins, "A Comment on the Current Health of Advisory Opinions", in Vaughan Lowe & Malgosia Fitzmaurice (eds), *Fifty Years of the International Court of Justice. Essays in Honour of Sir Robert Jennings* 577 (1996), who submitted that a question outside the jurisdiction would not entail a substantive enlargement of the scope of activity of the requesting organ, but merely the seeking of advice.
[97] Hans Kelsen, *Principles of International Law* 546 (New York, Holt, 1967).

implies the norm not to act beyond the scope of its activity as determined by the legal instrument instituting the organ.[98]

To a certain extent the debate is academic, since both the Security Council and the General Assembly have a wide mandate.[99] It is also unlikely that the one or the other organ would obtain the requisite majority for submitting a request for an advisory opinion that does not relate to its activities.[100] A more compelling question concerns the possible overlap of activities of the General Assembly and the Security Council in the field of international peace and security. Since the Security Council does not have the exclusive responsibility for the maintenance of international peace and security,[101] one may ask whether the General Assembly could request the ICJ to give an advisory opinion on the legality of resolutions of the Security Council in this field, where the latter is unwilling to submit such a request itself. It seems that the *Legality of the Threat or Use of*

---

[98] See Kelsen, above n 97, at 546; Stephen M Schwebel, "Justice in International Law" 79 (Cambridge, Grotius, 1994). See also *Legality of the Threat or Use of Nuclear Weapons*, Advisory Opinion, 35 *International Legal Materials* 817 (1996). Some states which opposed the giving of an opinion by the ICJ argued that the General Assembly and Security Council are not entitled to ask for opinions on matters totally unrelated to their work. They suggested that, as in the case of organs and agencies acting under Art 96(2) of the Charter, and notwithstanding the difference in wording between that provision and Art 96(1), the General Assembly and Security Council may ask for an advisory opinion on a legal question only when within the scope of their activities.

[99] The only instance in the history of the ICJ where it was found that the request for an advisory opinion fell outside the activities of the organisation concerned the World Health Organisation (hereinafter WHO), in the *Legality of the use by a State of Nuclear Weapons in Armed Conflict*, Advisory Opinion, ICJ Rep 1996, at 66. Hereinafter *Legality of Nuclear Weapons (WHO) opinion*.

[100] It does seem that the legal question to which Art 96(1) refers, must be a question that is being discussed in the United Nations. In November 1992 the General Assembly was presented with a request to seek an advisory opinion from the Court (A/47/249/Add.1/Corr.1 (1992)). This came from virtually all of the Latin American members, supplemented by Spain, Portugal, and later Iran. The demand arose out of the findings of the Supreme Court of the United States concerning the abduction of Mr Alvarez Machain. The latter was suspected of kidnapping, torturing and murdering of a United States drug enforcement agent, as a consequence of which he was kidnapped from Mexico and transferred to the United States to stand trial. The United States Supreme Court decided that this sequence of events did not violate the extradition treaty between Mexico and the United States and render the United States courts without jurisdiction. The draft resolution proposed for the Court was in abstract terms, carefully avoiding mention of Mr Alvarez-Machain and the ensuing dispute between Mexico and the United States. The sponsors hoped that the breadth of the General Assembly's competence under Art 96(1) would have been sufficient for the request to be submitted to the Court. However, the proposal was effectively rejected (A/48/619 (1993)). The clear implication was that the phrase "any legal question" must refer to a legal question under consideration within the United Nations. In spite of the abstract formulation, it was clear that the matter had only been brought to the United Nations for the purpose of seeking an advisory opinion. See Higgins (Comment), above n 96, at 580.

[101] See the *Certain Expenses* opinion, above n 29, at 163. See also the *Legality of the Threat or Use of Nuclear Weapons* opinion, above n 98, at 817. It underlined that Art 11 of the Charter has specifically provided the General Assembly with a competence to consider the general principle of the maintenance of international peace and security.

Nuclear Weapons[102] would support this line of argument. The ICJ concluded that the General Assembly has competence to request an opinion relating to *any* question within the scope of the Charter.[103] It is submitted that this would include questions relating to resolutions taken by the Security Council, whether taken in terms of Chapter VII or otherwise.

The wording of Article 10 in conjunction with Article 12 could also be read to support such a conclusion. Article 10 of the Charter provides the General Assembly with the power to discuss and make recommendations with respect to any issue within the scope of organisation. Even though Article 12(1) of the Charter prevents the General Assembly from making recommendations concerning issues being dealt with by the Security Council, it does not prevent the General Assembly from discussing those issues. The General Assembly would thus maintain some competence with respect to matters under discussion be the Security Council.[104] The question thus becomes whether the request for a legal opinion would amount to a recommendation, in which case the General Assembly would not be allowed to submit it to the ICJ, or whether it remains something different from a recommendation.[105]

One can argue that the request for an advisory opinion is not a recommendation directed towards member states, but an internal decision directed at another principal organ.[106] Moreover, by defining the request for an advisory opinion as a recommendation, one would end up with a circular argument. By submitting such a request the General Assembly seeks to clarify whether a Security Council resolution is legal. Only when this is indeed the case, can the General Assembly be barred from making recommendations under Article 12(1) of the Charter. Allowing the General Assembly to submit a request for an advisory opinion on the legality of Security Council resolutions would thus be pre-supposed by Article 12.[107]

---

[102] Above n 98, at 813.

[103] *Ibid*, at 817. The Charter cannot be read as limiting the ability of the General Assembly to request an opinion only in those circumstances in which it can take binding decisions. The fact that the General Assembly can only make recommendations has no bearing on the issue of whether it had the competence to put to the ICJ the question of which it is seized. See also Thomas M Franck, "The Political and the Judicial Empires: Must there be Conflict over Conflict-Resolution?", in Najeeb Al-Naumi & Richard Meese (eds), *International Legal Issues Arising under the United Nations Decade of International Law* 631 (The Hague, Martinus Nijhoff, 1995). He regarded Art 96(1) as providing the ICJ with an irrefutable basis of jurisdiction. It would also enhance political legitimisation of requests which were supported by a large majority of voting members. It would rebut a charge of judicial self-aggrandisement which might be levelled where the ICJ challenged the validity of a resolution in contentious proceeding, in response to the pleading of just one state.

[104] Fraas, above n 28, at 183.

[105] See Jochen Herbst, *Rechtskontrolle des UN-Sicherheitsrates* 404 (Frankfurt a/M, Peter Lang, 1999).

[106] *Ibid*, at 404–05.

[107] *Ibid*, at 405. See also Fraas, above n 28, at 183–84. Although the spirit of submission contained in Art 12 would prevent the General Assembly from judging the legality of Security

Finally, even if one were to conclude that a request of the General Assembly for an advisory opinion on the legality of Security Council action would amount to a recommendation, Article 12(1) would not necessarily prevent the General Assembly from submitting such a request. The reason is that in practice Article 12(1) has been constructed in a way that allows the General Assembly to make recommendations on issues with which the Security Council was itself dealing quite actively. Examples include General Assembly recommendations on the racial policies of South Africa, the situation in Angola, the territories under Portuguese administration and in Southern Rhodesia, as well as the Tunisian case and the question of Cyprus.[108] The member states, for their part, did not object to this practice.[109]

This means that Article 12(1) has in practice been reduced to merely preventing the General Assembly from making recommendations that directly and formally conflict with those of the Security Council.[110] Of particular importance is that such direct opposition would not be present where the General Assembly makes a recommendation on an issue on which the Security Council refrained from so doing, due to the exercise of the veto power by one of the permanent members. This follows from the General Assembly's Uniting for Peace resolution.[111] According to this resolution—which was condoned by the member states as well as the ICJ[112]—the General Assembly could recommend measures where the Security Council, because of the veto power of the permanent members, failed to exercise its primary responsibility for the maintenance of international peace and security. This in effect amounts to saying that if a veto cast by a permanent member prevents the Security Council from taking a decision, the latter will not be exercising its functions within the meaning

---

Council action by itself, this would not mean that the General Assembly is prevented from submitting a mere question on the matter to the ICJ. The same point is argued by Bernd Martenczuk, *Rechtsbindung und Rechtskontrolle des Weltsicherheitsrats. Die Überprüfung nicht-militärischer Zwangsmassnahmen durch den internationalen Gerichtshof* 76 fn 46 (Berlin, Duncker & Humblot, 1996). But see Gowlland-Debbas, above n 87, at 670 fn 149, who stated that the General Assembly may not question a Security Council interpretation of Charter provisions governing the functioning of the Security Council. Cf Mohammed Bedjaoui, *The New World Order and the Security Council* 79 (Dordrecht, Martinus Nijhoff, 1994).

[107] *Certain Expenses* opinion, above n 29, at 155; see also Higgins (Comment), above n 96, at 577.

[108] Hailbronner & Klein (in Simma), above n 54, at 256. Cf Philip Alston, "The Security Council and Human Rights: Lessons to be Learned from the Iraq-Kuwait Crisis and its Aftermath", 13 *Australian Yearbook of International law* 140 (1990/ 1991).

[109] As noted by the Legal Council of the Secretary General in *United Nations Juridical Yearbook* 237 (1964) and *United Nations Juridical Yearbook* 185 (1968); Hailbronner & Klein (in Simma), above n 54, at 256, 261.

[110] Hailbronner & Klein (in Simma), above n 54, at 261.

[111] See above fn 32.

[112] See the *Certain Expenses* opinion, above n 29.

of Article 12(1). As a result, the General Assembly will not be barred from making recommendations.[113]

Even though this resolution was adopted in the context of peace-keeping, it would only be consistent to demand that the same interpretation of Article 12(1) applies where the veto power of a permanent member prevents the Security Council from submitting a request for a legal opinion to the ICJ. The logical conclusion would be that this would not prevent the General Assembly from making a recommendation to this effect.

3.1.2. *The ICJ's Discretion to Refrain from Rendering Advisory Opinions*

The fact that the General Assembly (or the Security Council) has the right to submit a request to the ICJ in terms of Article 96(1) does not mean that the ICJ is obliged to give an opinion. The ICJ must then exercise its discretion whether, in the particular case, it would be appropriate to render one. This follows from Article 65 of the Statute of the ICJ, according to which it may give an advisory opinion on any legal question at the request of whatever body that may be authorised by or in accordance with the Charter to make such a request. The permissive character of Article 65 thus gives the ICJ the power to examine whether the circumstances of the case are such that it should decline to answer the request.[114]

The ICJ itself has always taken the attitude that its reply to a request should in principle not be refused, since the ICJ is an organ of the United Nations and its reply to a request represents its participation in the activities of the organisation. Only compelling reasons should lead it to refuse to give a requested advisory opinion.[115] The ICJ has consistently rejected the notion that the political context in which the request was submitted would amount to such a compelling reason.

Since its very beginning the ICJ made it clear that it could not attribute a political character to a request which invited it to undertake an essentially judicial task, namely the interpretation of a treaty provision and that it is not concerned with the motives which may have inspired this request.[116] The ICJ indicated that questions framed in terms of law and raising problems of international law are by their very nature susceptible

---

[113] Hailbronner & Klein (in Simma), above n 54, at 257.

[114] *Certain Expenses* opinion, above n 29, at 155; see also Higgins (Comment), above n 96, at 577.

[115] See, inter alia, *Certain Expenses* opinion, above n 29, at 155; *Namibia* opinion, above n 30, at 27; *Western Sahara*, Advisory Opinion, ICJ Rep 1975, at 21; *Legality of the Threat or Use of Nuclear Weapons* opinion, above n 98, at 818.

[116] *Conditions of Admissions* opinion, above n 95, at 61; *Competence of the General Assembly for the Admission of a State to the United Nations*, Advisory Opinion, ICJ Rep 1950, at 6. Cf Herdegen, above n 94, at 106.

of a reply based on law, and appear to be questions of a legal character.[117] Moreover, in situations in which political considerations are prominent it may be particularly necessary for an international organisation to obtain an advisory opinion from the ICJ as to the legal principles applicable with respect to the matter under debate.[118]

The ICJ showed itself to be aware that no matter what its conclusions in any opinion it might give, they would have relevance for the continuing debate and would present an additional element in the negotiations on the matter. Beyond that, the effect of the opinion (whether it would be advantageous or detrimental to negotiations) is a matter of appreciation which cannot be regarded by the ICJ as a compelling reason to decline to exercise its jurisdiction.[119] From the *Namibia* opinion[120] one can conclude that the ICJ also applies this approach to the Security Council and that it does not regard binding Security Council resolutions as falling in a distinct political category that would make the rendering of an advisory opinion inappropriate.

In the *Namibia* opinion the ICJ did not explicitly address the question of whether it should refrain from giving an advisory opinion when the request relates to judicial review of binding resolutions of the Security Council. However, *de facto* the ICJ did review these resolutions. It stated that the Security Council resolutions in question were adopted in conformity with the purposes and principles of the Charter and its Articles 24 and 25, and consequently were binding on all members states of the United Nations.[121] By effectively engaging in judicial review of a binding resolution—which, as was pointed out in 2.2.1, must be regarded as a Chapter VII resolution—the ICJ by implication confirmed that it did not regard their binding nature as a factor which should deter it from rendering an advisory opinion.

3.1.3. *The ICJ's Reluctance to Refrain from Rendering Advisory Opinions*

The ICJ's reluctance to decline to give an opinion has been criticised in dissenting opinions as well as in the literature. The ICJ has been accused

---

[117] *Legality of the Threat or Use of Nuclear Weapons* opinion, above n 98, at 817–18; *Western Sahara* opinion, above n 115, at 18; *Conditions of Admission* opinion, above n 95, at 61–62; *Competence of the General Assembly* opinion, above n 116, at 155. See also Gowlland-Debbas, above n 87, at 648.

[118] *Legality of the Threat or Use of Nuclear Weapons* opinion, above n 98, at 818. It is not for the ICJ to decide whether or not an advisory opinion is needed by the General Assembly for the performance of its functions. The General Assembly has the right to decide for itself on the usefulness of an opinion in the light of its own needs.

[119] *Conditions of Admission* opinion, above n 95; *Admissibility of Hearings of Petitioners by the Committee on South West Africa*, Advisory Opinion, ICJ Rep 1956 (hereinafter *South-West Africa (Petitioners) opinion*); *Legality of the Threat or Use of Nuclear Weapons* opinion, above n 98, at 819.

[120] Above, n 87.

[121] *Namibia* opinion, above n 30, at 53. See also Akande, above n 44, at 335.

of making political decisions and thus acting as a quasi-legislator, especially when confronted with legal opinions in abstract terms.[122] Some also felt that the powers of organs of the United Nations should be interpreted by the organs themselves rather than by the ICJ.[123]

Others believed that the political environment of the Cold War in which the organisation functioned for so many decades made codification and quasi-legislation by resolution preferable to adjudication and that it was naïve to believe that a strict legal interpretation of the disputed text would serve to relieve the tension.[124] When the ICJ's advisory jurisdiction was utilised, it was often turned to not for the purpose of genuine legal clarification and problem-solving, but for propaganda advantages and judicial legitimisation of options already firmly taken by the political organs.[125] The resolutions requesting the ICJ's opinions were frequently adopted with many states opposing or abstaining in the vote. They were also often pushed through in the face of the outright opposition of the states without whose cooperation implementation of the resultant opinion was virtually unthinkable.[126]

Consequently, some international lawyers submitted that the motive for invoking the ICJ's jurisdiction was not to bring about a settlement acceptable to all sides, but to exert political pressure on the recalcitrant minority.[127] This was regarded as an abuse of the advisory procedure in order to avoid restrictions on the ICJ's compulsory jurisdiction, and it was also considered that it jeopardised the ICJ's prestige and cast doubt on its own impartiality. As a result some authors believe that the ICJ should be more willing to refrain from giving an opinion.[128] They argue that where

---

[122] See, for example, the dissenting opinion of Judge Krylov in the *Conditions of Admission* opinion, above n 95, at 109. He regarded the opinion as relating to conditions of admission which cannot even be foreseen at the present time, as a consequence of which the political organs of the UN eventually may depart from it.

[123] *Ibid*, See also dissenting opinion of Judge Zoricic, *ibid*, at 94 ff.

[124] DW Greig, "The Advisory Jurisdiction of the International Court and the Settlement of Disputes between States", *International & Comparative Law Quarterly* 339 (1966); Paul C Szasz, "Enhancing the Advisory Competence of the World Court", in Leo Gross, (ed), *The Future of the International Court of Justice Vol II* 523 (Dobbs Ferry, Oceana Publications, 1976). The more entities the ICJ involves in reaching its decision and the more factors it weighs, the more it appears to be legislating and the greater the authority that will accrue to the resulting nonbinding opinion.

[125] Pomerance, above n 93, at 295.

[126] *Ibid*, at 295–96. She argued that action taken simultaneously with the requesting resolution sometimes revealed how insincere the professed desire for judicial clarification was, since the very measures still to be judicially determined were forcefully reasserted. The Security Council itself, for example, spelled out the legal consequences for states of the continued presence of South Africa in Namibia in SC Res 283 of 29 July 1970, notwithstanding its request for an advisory opinion. Also, the language of the requesting resolution sometimes appeared to state rather than query the legal premises upon which the ICJ was to proceed to answer the questions posed.

[127] Greig, above n 124, at 327.

[128] *Ibid*, at 325, 327; Pomerance, above n 93, at 321.

the political implications do not outweigh the legal characteristics of the situation, it is probable that the ICJ can play a useful interpretative role. But if the legal issues are clearly secondary to a fundamental political conflict, the ICJ's pronouncements may well be looked upon as an attempt to alter the meaning of the relevant text at the will of the majority in circumstances where formal amendment would be impossible.[129] If the ICJ is to serve as the principal judicial organ of organised international society and if it is to maintain the prestige which is essential to its functioning as such, it must not be pressed to assume political functions and it cannot be made a substitute for effective political agencies.[130]

It is submitted that these ongoing arguments as to whether a question is predominantly political or legal and therefore justiciable are misdirected.[131] It is unfortunate that in the effort to establish international tribunals so much effort was and still is devoted to the distinction between legal and political questions, at the expense of the important distinction between legal and political determination of a legal dispute.[132] What is relevant is the distinction between a political method and a legal method of solving disputes.[133] A dispute that cannot be reduced to specific issues of fact or law between the parties would be purely political, whereas a legal dispute implies both a legal answer and a political answer.[134] Since in the case of advisory opinions the ICJ has quite a wide discretion to re-formulate questions put to it, it could focus upon the sometimes obscured legal questions.[135]

---

[129] Greig, above n 124, at 365; Pomerance, above n 93, at 321; cf Takane Sugihara, "The Judicial Function of the International Court of Justice with Respect to Disputes Involving Highly Political Issues", in Alexander S Muller, *et al* (eds). *The International Court of Justice— Its Future Role after Fifty Years* 132 (The Hague, Martinus Nijhoff, 1997).

[130] Greig, above n 124, at 368; Pomerance, above n 93, at 321.

[131] The political question debate is also futile from a pragmatic point of view. From the very first advisory opinion the ICJ evidenced a willingness to consider questions involving treaty interpretation as *ipso facto* legal and to leave aside the circumstances leading up to the request or the probable aftermath of the opinions. This was even conceded by Pomerance, above n 93, at 309. See Fraas, above n 28, at 127–29, who noted the futility of theoretical attempts to distinguish between legal and political questions.

[132] Shaw, above n 35, at 240.

[133] *Ibid,* Rosalyn Higgins, "Policy Considerations and the International Judicial Process", 17 *International & Comparative Law Quarterly* 63 (1968). See Kelsen, above n 97, at 526; Gowlland-Debbas, above n 87, at 654.

[134] Shaw, above n 35, at 240. See also Dapo Akande, "The Role of the International Court of Justice in the Maintenance of International Peace", 8 *African Journal of International and Comparative Law* 602 (1996); He submitted that the political nature of the proceedings is inevitable, since it concerns political entities. Cf Martenczuk, above n 86, at 528–29

[135] Shaw, above n 35, at 241. See also Pomerance, above n 93, at 317, who remarked that this need was not always attributable to poor drafting. Often it was due to the desire to overcome major objections to compliance with the request. Also see TD Gill, "Legal and Some Political Limitations on the Power of the UN Security Council to Exercise its Enforcement Powers under Chapter VII of the Charter", 26 *Netherlands Yearbook of International Law* 123 (1995).

Moreover, in (re)formulating and answering the questions put before it, the ICJ has consistently given recognition to the political sensitivities involved by showing considerable deference to the political organs. This is illustrated by the fact that the ICJ has so far upheld the legality of the decisions of the political organs of the United Nations in all instances where it has had cause to examine their legality in advisory opinions.[136] Methodologically the ICJ achieved this by attributing a presumption of validity to the decisions of these organs. It concluded that when the organisation takes action which is appropriate for the fulfilment of one its purposes, the presumption is that such action is not *ultra vires* the organisation.[137] As a result, the onus rests on those claiming that the political organ has acted beyond its powers to prove that this indeed has been the case.[138]

In addition, the ICJ attached significant weight to the power of the organs of the United Nations to interpret their own competencies. It sometimes limited the criteria for establishing whether a resolution is *intra vires* to the specific organ's interpretation of its competencies and its subsequent actions. Since this issue will be discussed in more detail in chapter 3 at section 4.3, it will suffice to mention the ICJ's interpretation of Article 27(3) of the Charter in the *Namibia* opinion. The ICJ accepted the Security Council's interpretation whereby the withholding of a vote by a permanent member is regarded as a concurring vote. Such an interpretation does not strictly correspond to the wording of the Article.[139] The ICJ supported it, pointing out that it has consistently been followed by the Security Council and has been accepted by states in practice.[140] By adopting this approach the ICJ affirmed that judicial restraint can also be effected by the way in which the ICJ involves itself in an advisory opinion, and not merely by refusing to give the advisory opinion altogether.

One can furthermore question whether advisory opinions would lead to a misuse of the ICJ. To the contrary, the requirement that an advisory

---

[136] Akande, above n 44, at 336; Cf Louis B Sohn, "Important Improvements in the Functioning of the Principal Organs of the United Nations that can be Made without Charter Revision", 91 *American Journal of International Law* 659 (1997).

[137] Gowlland-Debbas, above n 87, at 665, 670. See also *Certain Expenses* opinion, above n 29, at 168; Jennings, above n 46, at 1178; Jochen A Frowein, "The Internal and External Effects of Resolutions by International Organisations", 49 *Zeitschrift für ausländisches öffentliches Recht und Völkerrecht* 781 (1989). See also Lorinser, above n 83, at 142; Martenczuk, above n 86, at 539.

[138] Akande, above n 44, at 342.

[139] Art 27(3) of the Charter reads as follows: "Decisions of the Security Council on all other matters shall be made by an affirmative vote of nine members including the concurring votes of the permanent members..." See also Fraas, above n 28 , at 19.

[140] *Namibia* opinion, above n 30, at 22; see Herdegen, above n 94, at 112. Lissitzyn, above n 69, at 55.

opinion must be requested by a qualified majority of states in either the General Assembly or Security Council, would ensure that the ICJ will not be engaged as a matter of partisan policy by a minority of states, but only in situations in which a significant number of states are convinced of the need for legal guidance and review.[141] It is also difficult to see why an advisory opinion given against the will of several members would necessarily impose the will of the majority on that of the minority. The *Legality of the Threat or Use of Nuclear Weapons* opinion illustrated that it will not necessarily give the majority the answer they want to hear. One may disagree with the way in which the ICJ opened the back-door for legitimating the use or threat to use nuclear weapons in certain circumstances, but the fact remains that the ICJ did not merely "capitulate" to the will of the majority be declaring the use of nuclear weapons illegal in all circumstances.[142]

Moreover, in those cases where the ICJ does confirm the view of the majority, it should not be seen as the imposition of one group's opinion on another or an amendment of the Charter against their will, but as the *clarification* of the law by the principal judicial organ of the United Nations.[143] There is, of course, always the risk that the advisory opinion would not be complied with in the face of opposition of states. But the ICJ has to build on the perception that the clearer the law, the greater the possibility for compliance. This point will be addressed again in section 4 below.

It is nevertheless conceded that one might question the value of a legal opinion relating to a completely abstract set of facts. In the history of the ICJ there has only been one such occurrence, namely the *Legality of the Threat or Use of Nuclear Weapons* opinion.[144] The question was unrelated either to a concrete dispute or to a concrete problem awaiting a practical solution.[145] One can ask whether the inability of the ICJ to come to a conclusive answer in the *Legality of the Threat or Use of Nuclear Weapons*

---

[141] Gill, above n 135, at 123.
[142] Above, n 98, at 813. The General Assembly requested the ICJ to render an opinion on whether the threat or use of nuclear weapons was in any circumstance permitted under international law. The ICJ concluded that in view of the unique characteristics of nuclear weapons, the use of such weapons seem scarcely reconcilable with the requirements of the law of armed conflict. Nevertheless, the ICJ considered that it did not have sufficient information to enable it to conclude with certainty that the use of nuclear weapons would necessarily be at variance with the principles and rules of the law of armed conflict in any circumstance.
[143] *Ibid*, at 122.
[144] Above, n 157.
[145] This was not the case with other abstractly formulated opinions, such as the *Conditions of Admission* opinion, above n 95. Despite the abstract formulation, it related to a difference of opinion as to how the criteria for the admission of new member states should be interpreted in a concrete situation. See also Keith, above n 8, at 42.

opinion was at least partly the result of the abstract situation in which it was given. It is only when a legal rule is applied in a particular set of circumstances that it is possible to determine its outcome. As it were, the rendering of an opinion in the absence of such a factual situation did not contribute to the credibility of the ICJ. It was contradictory to decide with near unanimity to comply with the General Assembly's request for an advisory opinion, and then to reply by a bare majority that the ICJ cannot answer the substance of the question conclusively.[146] It might have been better had the ICJ refused to give an opinion on the basis that the question was too abstract.

3.2. Abusing the Advisory Opinions Procedure to Address Disputes between States

The ICJ has also been criticised for rendering advisory opinions in instances where the requests related to disputes between states of which one objected to the request for an opinion. Those raising this objection have often referred to the Permanent Court of International Justice (PCIJ) which refused to give an opinion on the *Status of Eastern Carelia*.[147] They argued that the PCIJ declined to rule upon the question referred to it, because it was directly related to the main point of a dispute actually pending between two states.[148]

The ICJ has always found a way to reject the *Eastern Carelia* opinion as irrelevant for the facts of the case.[149] For example, in the *Namibia* opinion it remarked that in the *Eastern Carelia* opinion one of the states concerned was not at the time a member of the League of Nations and did not appear before the PCIJ. South Africa, as a member of the United Nations, was bound by Article 96 of the Charter which empowers the Security Council to request advisory opinions on any legal question. Furthermore, it appeared before the ICJ, participated in both the written and oral proceedings and, while raising specific objections against the competence of the ICJ, addressed itself to the merits of the question.[150] It was also not the

---

[146] See the dissenting opinions of Judges Oda and Shahabuddeen in *Legality of the Threat or Use of Nuclear Weapons* opinion, above n 98, at 860–61, respectively.

[147] PCIL Rep 1923 (ser B), No 5.

[148] *Namibia* opinion, above n 30, at 23.

[149] See Pomerance, above n 93, at 307. It appears that the reaffirmation of the *Status of Eastern Carelia* opinion, above n 147, notwithstanding, the prospects that the ICJ will refuse to give an opinion because of the absence of states' consent are remote. See also Higgins (Comment), above n 96, at 571.

[150] *Namibia* opinion, above n 30, at 23–24; South Africa submitted inter alia that the question related to a dispute between itself and other members of the United Nations and that South Africa should have been invited to participate in the discussions of the Security Council according to Art 32 of the Charter. Also, the provision in Art 27(2) of the Charter, requiring

purpose of the request to obtain the assistance of the ICJ in the exercise of the Security Council's functions relating to the pacific settlement of a dispute between two or more states. The request was put forward by a United Nations organ with reference to its own decisions and it sought legal advice from the ICJ on the consequences and implications of these decisions.[151]

It can thus be concluded that the ICJ would not easily regard the lack of consent of a state directly implicated in an advisory opinion as a compelling reason to refuse the requested opinion. Where the main objective of the opinion is to guide the United Nations concerning its own actions, and if the ICJ is in a position to obtain full information about the facts, it will render the opinion.[152] States that are members of the United Nations undertake to respect the principles and purposes of the organisation and thus accept that their actions can have consequences for the organisation as a whole. Therefore they have to take into account that a dispute between them may have implications for the action to be taken by the organisation. This also implies the risk that the organisation may need clarification from the ICJ as to the action it should take, regardless of whether this is consented to by (one of) the states involved in the dispute.[153] In the present history of the ICJ there has been no instance where the ICJ has, on the basis of its discretionary power, declined to give an opinion.[154]

---

members of the Security Council which are parties to a dispute to abstain from voting, should have been observed. The ICJ rejected this argument. The question of Namibia was placed on the agenda of the Council as a "situation" (as opposed to a "dispute") and the South African Government failed to draw the Council's attention to the necessity in its eyes of treating it as a dispute. The language of Art 32 is mandatory, but the question whether the Security Council must extend an invitation in accordance with that provision depends on whether it has made a determination that the matter under its consideration is in the nature of a dispute. In the absence of such a determination Art 32 does not apply. The same applies to the related objection based on the provision to Art 27(3) of the Charter. See also Pomerance, above n 93, at 302.

[151] *Namibia* opinion, above n 30, at 24. At a later stage the ICJ also submitted that in the *Status of Eastern Carelia* opinion, above n 147, the lack of consent of a state concerned and its non-participation in the opinion was only a secondary reason for the refusal to render and opinion. It was the actual lack of materials sufficient to enable it to arrive at any judicial conclusion upon the question of fact which, for reasons of judicial propriety, prevented it from giving an opinion. See the Western Sahara opinion, above n 115, at 28.

[152] Cf Higgins (Comment), above n 96, at 571. Since the early years the implication has been that a member of the United Nations must be prepared to bear the risk of the ICJ fulfilling its advisory function in these circumstances, and that this was a differentiating factor from *the Status of Eastern Carelia* opinion, above n 147.

[153] See Gill, above n 135, at 122, who stated that the advisory competence of the ICJ is first and foremost designed and intended to provide the organisation with the necessary legal advice and judicial assistance.

[154] As already mentioned, in the *Legality of Nuclear Weapons (WHO)* opinion, above n 99, the refusal to give the WHO the advisory opinion it requested, was based on the ICJ's lack of jurisdiction in that case. See Greig, above n 124, at 326, Keith, above n 8, at 47.

4.   LEGAL EFFECTS OF ADVISORY OPINIONS

4.1.   General

Both the ICJ and legal authorities have attached great weight to the legal effects of advisory opinions.[155] They have stressed that although the advisory opinions are not legally binding in that they do not impose legal obligations either upon the requesting body or upon states, such opinions are not devoid of effect as they remain the law recognised by the United Nations.[156] A legal opinion soundly based on law will assist in building up a climate of opinion in which law is respected. It will enhance the authority of the ICJ as it will be seen to be discharging its duty of clarifying and developing the law, regardless of political considerations.[157] The clarification of the law is an end in itself, and not merely a means to an end. When the law is clear, there is a greater chance of compliance than when it is shrouded in obscurity.[158] It should also be kept in mind that even in contentious cases the decision is only binding (in the strict sense) *inter partes*.[159] Therefore it would not be correct to give the impression that this is a deficit peculiar to advisory opinions.[160]

These submissions do not deny the fact that requests formulated by the General Assembly and the Security Council have sometimes been preceded by deep political divisions which survived even after the ICJ

---

[155] See A/17/962 para (1962), for the debate in the General Assembly's Fifth Committee following the *Certain Expenses* opinion. According to the representative of the United Kingdom the opinion had to be complied with. To do otherwise would be a blow to the authority and standing of the ICJ and the General Assembly in a matter vital to the future of the United Nations. It would also show scant respect for the rule of law and it would be absurd for the General Assembly merely to note the opinion of the ICJ when it had expressly asked for authoritative legal guidance. According to the representative of the United States (*ibid*, at para 20), such a step was unheard of in the practice of the Council of the League of Nations or of the United Nations General Assembly. Cf Greig, above n 124, at 363–64.

[156] Dissenting opinion of Judge Koroma in the *Legality of the Threat or Use of Nuclear Weapons* opinion, above n 98, at 930; see also Martenczuk, above n 86, at 528.

[157] Szasz, above n 124, at 508. See also Fraas, above n 28, at 33; Lauterpacht above n 44, at 113.

[158] Keith, above n 8, at 42.

[159] Karl Doehring, "Unlawful Resolutions of the Security Council and their Legal Consequences", 1 *Max Planck Yearbook of United Nations Law* 91 (1997); Derek Bowett, "The Impact of Security Council Decisions on Dispute Settlement Procedures", 5 *European Journal of International Law* 98 (1994).

[160] The same would apply to the criticism that the control function of the advisory opinion is limited, since it is always after the fact, as is argued by Bernhard Graefrath, "Die Vereinten Nationen im Übergang—Die Gratwanderung des Sicherheitsrates zwischen Rechtsanwendung und Rechtsanmassung", *Die Reform der Vereinten Nationen* 43 (Opladen, Leske & Budrich, 1994).

had rendered its opinion. One such example was the *Certain Expenses* opinion.[161] After its adoption by the General Assembly,[162] the United States insisted that Article 19 of the Charter had mandatory and automatic effect.[163] According to this Article, a member of the United Nations which is in arrears in the payment of its financial contributions to the organisation shall have no vote in the General Assembly if the amount of its arrears equals or exceeds the amount of the contributions due from it for the preceding two full years. Other countries such as Czechoslovakia argued that a suspension of voting rights in terms of Article 19 could only follow a vote in the General Assembly in which a two-thirds majority were in favour of such suspension.[164]

An acceptance of the position of the United States would have meant, *inter alia*, that the voting rights of the Soviet Union would have been suspended, since its arrearages were to exceed the two-year limitation by 1965, if peace-keeping assessments were counted as expenses of the organisation.[165] Thus, as a result of the United States' position the issue of arrearages was widely interpreted as a confrontation between major powers, rather than between the non-paying members and the law of the United Nations. Eventually the United States conceded that it did not have the support it needed for enforcing its interpretation of Article 19 of the Charter.[166] Although it maintained its position on the interpretation of Article 19, it concluded that the General Assembly at that point in time was not prepared to enforce that provision.[167]

Thereafter some authors argued that the General Assembly itself did not adhere to the *Certain Expenses* opinion, since it never gathered the courage to suspend the voting rights of certain member states.[168] It is submitted that this was a too undifferentiated view of the outcome of that opinion. First, no one thought that the advisory opinion would end all debate, but many nations had indicated that they would pay their assessments if the ICJ held them responsible. Several indeed also lived up to this promise after the ICJ rendered its opinion.[169] From this perspective

---

[161] Above n 29.
[162] GA Res 1854 A (XVII) of 19 December 1962; A/PV199 (1964); see Chayes, above n 36, at 216.
[163] Chayes, above n 36, at 219.
[164] *Ibid*, at 218.
[165] *Ibid*, at 245.
[166] The General Assembly initially attempted to avoid a confrontation prior to the recess of that session. It planned to set up machinery for negotiations during the recess which would review all the aspects of peace-keeping operations in order to come to an agreed solution. This effort was undermined, amongst others, by the Albanian delegate who questioned the legality of such a consensual arrangement on which no prior vote had been taken. See Chayes, above n 36, at 232, 235, 239.
[167] *Ibid*, at 241.
[168] Szasz, above n 124, at 508.
[169] See Chayes, above n 36, at 167, 217.

the opinion was at least partially complied with. The real problem related to the fact that the United States went a step further and justified their interpretation of Article 19 of the Charter on the basis of the *Certain Expenses* opinion—although the ICJ itself did not attempt to interpret Article 19 or its relationship with Article 17 in that opinion. It is thus not so much the *Certain Expenses* opinion that was not complied with, but an interpretation of the United States of an Article of the Charter that—although related to the issue in the *Certain Expenses* opinion—was not addressed by it.

At the same time one has to acknowledge that there are no guarantees that advisory opinions will be complied with, as South Africa's persistent disregard of the *Namibia* opinion illustrated.[170] But despite these instances of non-compliance, advisory opinions still provides authoritative statements of those points of international law to which they are addressed and consequently may in effect be dispositive of the issue submitted.[171] One should also remember that non-compliance is not a risk peculiar to advisory opinions, but also exists with respect to decisions in contentious proceedings.

Moreover, by elaborating on principles of international law in advisory opinions the ICJ reinforces their position in the general international legal discourse. Even those who do not approve of the advisory opinion cannot refrain from considering it when arguing the disputed issue, since it is rendered by a court of law which is also the principal judicial organ of the United Nations. They would therefore have to shape their argument in the shadow of the law.[172] The principles developed in the course of a legal opinion will also have precedential value for the ICJ itself. The ICJ will rely on them when related issues arise in future proceedings, whether of a contentious or advisory nature. This should not only enhance the chances of compliance by organs of the United Nations and member states with the advisory opinion, but should strengthen the value of the Charter as a legal document that defines the boundaries of United Nations action in the international legal order.

---

[170] In the *Conditions of Admission* opinion, above n 95, certain members on the Security Council also disregarded the ICJ's strictures against the admission of members of the basis of package deals. See also Szasz, above n 124, at 507–08; Michla Pomerance, "The ICJ and South West Africa (Namibia): A Retrospective Legal/ Political Assessment", 12 *Leiden Journal of International Law* 427–32 (1999).

[171] See Greig, above n 124, at 362: If the ICJ does make a pronouncement on what the law is in a particular field, such a pronouncement must surely be "binding" as an authoritative statement of international law. See also Alvarez, above n 2, at 8; Gowlland-Debbas, above n 87, at 671. But see Pomerance (Namibia), above n 170, at 434, who regarded advisory opinions as a vehicle for the legitimisation of a preconceived political stand, rather than the clarification of the law.

[172] Herbst, above n 105, at 107.

4.2.   The Consequences of a Determination of (Il)legality of a binding Security Council Resolution

The question now to be answered concerns the consequences of an advisory opinion specifically relating to the legality of a binding Chapter VII resolution of the Security Council. In particular, it has to be determined what would happen if the presumption of validity of such a resolution were successfully rebutted, as a result of which the ICJ were to determine its illegality. After all, the presumption of legality does not imply deference to the political organ at all times, as this would undermine the judicial function which requires the ICJ itself to decide on questions of law before it. The concept of a presumption of validity bears with it the seeds of a finding of illegality.[173]

It is often emphasised that the ICJ cannot strike down a resolution of the Security Council and declare it null and void, as would be the case with a court that has the "classic" power of judicial review. So, even if the ICJ were to give an opinion against a specific resolution, it would still remain valid.[174] This is a very narrow and formal view of judicial review that reduces its value to whether or not a court can annul the decision of the political organ in question.[175] It underestimates the fact that a determination of the ICJ to the effect that a binding Security Council resolution is illegal would undermine the legitimacy of that resolution and weaken its claim to compliance. A determination in an advisory opinion that a Security Council resolution is illegal would justify non-compliance by states and would strengthen disrespect for the resolution.[176] This raises the question of how far this rejection of resolutions by states could go and whether they should regard the resolution as null and void *ab initio*.

In his separate opinion in the *Certain Expenses* opinion Judge Morelli argued that illegal resolutions of United Nations organs were null and void *ab initio*, since voidability did not exist in international law. He drew

---

[173] Akande, above n 44, at 342. But see the separate opinion of Judge Morelli in the *Certain Expenses* opinion, above n 29, at 221–24. He favoured a very strong presumption of legality of actions of UN organs, in the interest of legal certainty and efficiency of the organisation. It is only in especially serious cases that an act of the organisation could be regarded as invalid. This would be the case, for example, where the organ had not obtained the required majority, or a resolution was vitiated by a manifest *excès de pouvoir*, such as a resolution which had nothing to do with the purposes of the organisation. For Judge Morelli an *ultra vires* act by an organ would not constitute an *excès de pouvoir*. It is questionable whether this restrictive interpretation of an *excès de pouvoir* is correct, since it would render the concept meaningless and make it virtually impossible to overcome the presumption of validity. See Lorinser, above n 83, at 66.

[174] Kaiyan H Kaikobad, "The Court, the Council and Interim Protection: A Commentary on the Lockerbie Order of 14 April 1992", 17 *Australian Yearbook of International Law* 128 (1996). See also Doehring, above n 159, at 100; Lorinser, above n 83, at 91, 119.

[175] See Kaikobad, above n 238, at 139. See also ch 3, at s 4.2, for a discussion of the effects of judicial review in municipal legal orders.

[176] Akande, above n 44, at 335; David, above n 49, at 117.

parallels with municipal law, illustrating that in the latter there are several cases in which the non-conformity of an act with the legal rule constitutes a mere irregularity, having no effect on the validity of the act. In more serious cases lack of conformity entails the invalidity of the act. Such invalidity may well constitute an absolute nullity, operating *ipso jure* so that the act which it affects produces no legal effects.[177]

In municipal law cases of absolute nullity are of a quite exceptional character. In general, the invalidity of acts in municipal law involves not the nullity but rather the voidability of the act. A voidable act is an act that produces all its effect in spite of the defects by which it is vitiated, as long as it is not annulled by the competent organ. It is only as a result of being annulled that the act loses, retroactively, its effectiveness. This concept of voidability in municipal law is closely linked with the means of recourse open in some domestic legal systems against the legality of administrative acts and which have to be used in a prescribed form and within a fixed time-limit.[178]

In the case of acts of international organisations and in particular the acts of the United Nations there is nothing comparable to the remedies existing in domestic law in connection with administrative acts.[179] The consequence of this is that there is no possibility of applying the concept of voidability to the acts of the United Nations. If an act of an organ of the United Nations had to be considered as an invalid act, such invalidity could constitute only the absolute nullity of the act. There are only two alternatives for the acts of the organisation. Either the act is fully valid or it is an absolute nullity, because absolute nullity is the only form in which invalidity of an act of the organisation can occur.[180]

Judge Morelli's argument is based on the premise that there is no tribunal equipped to exercise judicial review on the legality of a decision of a United Nations organ. This is rather ironic, in the light of the fact that in the *Certain Expenses* opinion the ICJ indeed engaged in such review, albeit by an advisory opinion. It is thus submitted that Judge Morelli's analysis is too restrictive. Not only does judicial review exist within the United Nations,[181] but one should distinguish between the nullity of a resolution as such, and that of the acts based on the resolution.

[177] Separate opinion of Judge Morelli in the *Certain Expenses* opinion, above n 29, at 221.
[178] *Ibid*, at 121–22.
[179] *Ibid*, at 222. One of the few international constitutive documents which provides for a system in which decisions of political organs can be annulled, is the Treaty of the European Community (TEC), available at www.europa.eu.int/. According to Art 230 and Art 231, resolutions which have binding force for the member states concerned, ie regulations, directives or decisions, can be attacked before and annulled by the European Court of Justice. Cf Frowein (Effects of Resolutions), above n 137, at 781.
[180] *Ibid*. See also dissenting opinion of Judge Winiarski in *Certain Expenses* opinion, above n 29, at 232.
[181] See Jochen A Frowein, "Nullity in International Law", 7 *Encyclopedia of Public International Law* 363 (1983). He relied on the *Namibia* opinion, above n 30, at 44–45, when arguing that

The practice of states concerning treaties later declared null and void can be illuminating and serve as a useful analogy in this regard. Practice shows that a distinction must be made between the treaty itself and acts performed on the basis of it. While the treaty itself will normally be considered void *ab initio (ex tunc)*, acts performed on the basis of the treaty are not affected.[182] This results from the need for legal certainty in a situation where nullity will be established at a time where several acts may have already been performed on the basis of the treaty.[183] A similar situation would exist in cases where the ICJ had to render an advisory opinion on the legality of a resolution of one of the organs of the United Nations. No suspensory effect arises out of the request for an advisory opinion[184] and it would take several weeks or months to render an opinion, especially if member states and the Secretary-General are invited to submit their views to the ICJ.[185] It is therefore very likely that by the time the ICJ opined on the legality of the resolution, several states would have acted on it.

Moreover, it might also be necessary for states to act speedily on resolutions in order to avoid seriously compromising the effectiveness of the organisation.[186] Collective security measures such as sanctions adopted by the Security Council may serve as a good example. They are often effective immediately upon adoption, in view of the urgency of the situations that trigger them and the initial need for certainty to assure their implementation.[187] However, as will be illuminated extensively in chapter 6, these sanctions may at some point become illegal. This may be the case, for example, where they were indeterminate without a clear cut-off date, as is often the case. With the passage of time the majority of states may feel that the impact of the sanctions are violating basic human rights. But the Security Council can be blocked from terminating the sanctions by the "reverse veto" of one of the permanent members.[188]

If in such a case, the ICJ were requested by the General Assembly to opine on the legality of continued sanctions, the ICJ may come to the conclusion that the resolution imposing sanctions had become illegal. As a result, member states would not be bound to the resolution with respect

---

the ICJ can always be used as a judicial organ to give an advisory opinion on whether an act of the United Nations is valid or not.

[182] Frowein (Nullity), above n 181, at 362.
[183] *Ibid.*
[184] See Bedjaoui, above n 106, at 57.
[185] Bowett, above n 159, at 99.
[186] See Lorinser, above n 83, at 129, where she stressed the importance of efficient implementation of Security Council resolutions.
[187] Gowlland-Debbas, above n 87, at 673.
[188] *Ibid.* See also Herbst, above n 105, at 359; Lorinser, above n 83, at 50.

to the future.[189] However, action taken up to the ICJ's advisory opinion would not be affected. In this way it can be avoided that states refrain from acting on a resolution altogether out of the resulting legal uncertainty. If they fear that the respective resolution and all state acts resulting from it may later be declared illegal, they would be reluctant to implement the resolution in the first place. As this would erode the efficiency of the Security Council, it is important to exercise judicial review in a way that takes due consideration of legal certainty.[190]

Finally, the advisory opinion would also provide a powerful incentive to the Security Council to rethink its decision and amend it in a way which would avoid violation of fundamental rules and principles of international law.[191] Even though the advisory opinion is non-binding it would inevitably influence the Security Council's deliberations and the positions of states with regard to its decision. Although one or more of the permanent members could use their veto power to block reversal or modification of such a decision, the advisory opinion may nonetheless serve to prevent similar illegal decisions from being taken in the future.[192]

5. THE RELUCTANCE OF THE UNITED NATIONS ORGANS TO REQUEST ADVISORY OPINIONS

From the above opinions it emerged that the use of advisory opinions to test the legality of actions of the Security Council or General Assembly emerged at times when there were uncertainties about the institutional arrangements within the United Nations, and particularly about the distribution of power between different organs or between the United Nations

---

[189] Herdegen, above n 94, at 119. See also Lorinser, above n 83, at 147. Due to the initial presumption of validity of the (illegal) Security Council resolution, state action on the basis of that resolution would be justified up to the point where the ICJ declared the resolution *ultra vires*.

[190] But see Martenczuk (Rechtskontrolle), above n 106, at 285–87, who regarded the Security Council resolutions reviewable only at the time of adoption. Once Security Council resolutions have been adopted, they have to be regarded as legal, even if the conditions change and a removal of the sanctions is blocked by one state. The discretion of the Security Council in deciding to remove the measures would not be reviewable by the ICJ, as this would undermine legal certainty. Similarly Christopher Greenwood, "The Impact of Decisions and Resolutions of the Security Council on the International Court of Justice", in Wybo P Heere (ed), *International Law and The Hague's 750th Anniversary* 86 (The Hague, TMC Asser, 1999). Cf Lauterpacht, above n 44, at 93.

[191] Gill, above n 135, at 124; Herdegen, above n 94, at 119. He concedes that the Security Council would be obliged to reconsider its resolution in such a case, in the light of the mutual doctrine of cooperation. See Doehring, above n 159, at 92; Gowlland-Debbas, above n 87, at 673.

[192] *Ibid.*

and its member states.[193] Typically, such uncertainties emerge during the first years in the life of an organisation, or during times of institutional turmoil.[194] Most of the legal opinions were given during the first 10 years of the ICJ's existence, with only a handful of comparable advices sought in subsequent years.

In recent years the ending of the Cold War has had profound implications for the United Nations. The Security Council has the possibility of operating in areas previously precluded by the veto. But it is often beyond the limits of a strict textual reading of the Charter and by means other than those explicitly envisaged under the Charter. The changes in the distribution of power among the permanent members also have implications for the relationship between the Security Council and the General Assembly.[195] Consequently one might think that the situation has returned to the underlying conditions of the first 10 years of the United Nations, in the sense that the legality of the distribution of competencies among United Nations organs or between the United Nations and its members would once again need to be tested through advisory opinions.[196]

Unfortunately requests for such opinions are not forthcoming. No request can be submitted to the ICJ for an advisory opinion unless a decision for such a request is obtained by the necessary majority in the organ concerned. These majorities are difficult to obtain, since the political organs have developed their own practices.[197] The longer they are in existence, the less they are likely to want advice on their practices from the ICJ. It is also unlikely that the Security Council in particular would ask for an advisory opinion if the risk of embarrassment were too great, or the possibility of an adverse opinion unacceptable.[198]

The question that comes to mind is how this problem might be overcome without amending the Charter. Any amendment would require unanimity of the five permanent members of the Security Council, which cannot be obtained as long as some of them are fundamentally opposed to any extension of the activities of the ICJ.[199] In this context one should bear in mind that most of the permanent members of the Security Council has a rather cool relationship with the ICJ.[200] Russia and China have never been

---

[193] Higgins (Comment), above n 96, at 575.
[194] *Ibid*, at 575, 581.
[195] Higgins (Comment), above n 96, at 575.
[196] *Ibid*, at 576.
[197] *Ibid*.
[198] *Ibid*. See also Alvarez, above n 2, at 8, Lorinser, above n 83, at 113 fn 38. See Herbst, above n 105, at 153, 181 who illustrated that attempts to convince the Security Council to request advisory opinions during the Indonesian conflict in 1947 and the Anglo Iranian Oil Company 1951, respectively, failed.
[199] Szasz, above n 124, at 509.
[200] Herbst, above n 105, at 403.

members, whereas France has, untily very recently, effectively avoided the ICJ since the nuclear test incidents of 1974.[201] The relationship of the United States with the ICJ has been ambivalent, to say the least, since the *Nicaragua* decision[202] and lately also in the *Lockerbie* case.[203]

One must therefore consider alternatives which would side-step the voting procedure required by the General Assembly and Security Council for requesting advisory opinions, but which remain within the Charter framework. One such possibility would be for the General Assembly to grant the Secretary-General the power to request advisory opinions in terms of Article 96(2) of the Charter.[204]

6.   THE SECRETARY-GENERAL AND ADVISORY OPINIONS

The suggestion that the Secretary-General be authorised to request advisory opinions is not new. As long ago as 1950 the Secretary-General prepared a report on the Human Rights Committee to be established under the International Covenant for Civil and Political Rights, and addressed the possibility that it might be authorised to request advisory opinions.[205] It concluded that as the Human Rights Committee would be a treaty body

---

[201] France recently appeared before the ICJ in the *Case Concerning Certain Criminal Proceedings in France (Republic of Congo v France)*, Provisional Measures, 17 June 2003, availabe at www.icj-cij.org. See also Herbst, above n 105, at 403 fn 12.

[202] *Military and Paramilitary Activities in and Against Nicaragua (Nicaragua v United States)*, Jurisdiction and Admissibility, ICJ Rep 1984, at 392.

[203] Herbst, above n 105, at 403.

[204] Cf Sohn, above n 136, at 660. He suggested an alternative, namely that the General Assembly establishes a special committee that would serve as a channel for sending questions for advisory opinions to the ICJ. This new committee should be composed of legal experts nominated by members of the General Committee of the Assembly. (In addition to the six or seven chairpersons of the main committees of the General Assembly, this committee always includes the five permanent members of the Security Council among the 17 vice-presidents who complement the composition of the General Committee.) This new committee would have discretion to decide which requests should be forwarded to the ICJ, taking into account the importance of the case and its urgency, as well as the need not to overburden the ICJ with too many requests, especially when the docket of the ICJ is already full. However, it is questionable whether such a new committee would be effective. Since it would reflect the composition of the General Assembly it would most probably find it equally difficult to obtain the necessary majority for submitting a request for an advisory opinion to the ICJ.

[205] E/1732 (1950). See Higgins (Comment), above n 96, at 567. Cf Kelsen, above n 97, at 547 questioned whether it is the Secretary-General or the Secretariat that may be authorised by the General Assembly to request advisory opinions. He submitted that Art 65 of the ICJ Statute is not quite in conformity with Art 96 of the Charter. Under Art 65 of the ICJ Statute, the Court is authorised to give advisory opinions only to a "body" (collegiate organ). This would imply that it could not give an opinion to a person such as the Secretary-General. But see Schwebel, above n 98, at 79–80. He rightly points out that the objection could be overcome by simply vesting the authority to request an advisory opinion in the Secretariat. Since the Secretariat is expressly nominated as a principal organ of the United Nations by Art 7(1) of the Charter, it is clear that the General Assembly may authorise the Secretariat to request

and not an organ of the United Nations or a specialised agency, it could not be so authorised by the General Assembly under paragraph 2 of Article 96 of the Charter. Since the Secretary-General could be so authorised it (unsuccessfully) suggested that it be entrusted by the General Assembly to consider suggestions of the Human Rights Committee in order to request advisory opinions arising out of that Committee's work.[206] Since the end of the Cold War the matter has again been receiving attention. One example is the Report of the Special Committee on the Charter of the United Nations and on the Strengthening of the Role of the Organisation, in which the Secretary General proposed that he be authorised to request advisory opinions from the ICJ.[207]

If the Secretary-General were to be authorised by the General Assembly to request advisory opinions, those opinions could by reason of paragraph 2 of Article 96 only be on questions arising within the scope of his activities. That raises the question as to how broad these activities are. Article 98 of the Charter provides that the Secretary-General shall act in that capacity in all meetings of the General Assembly, of the Security Council, of the Economic and Social Council, and of the Trusteeship Council and shall perform such other functions as are entrusted to him by these organs. This can be interpreted to mean that all the activities of these organs are *ipso facto* within the scope of the activities of the Secretary-General.[208] The Secretary-General's scope of activities would be so broad as to be coextensive with all the organisation's activities—including those of the Security Council.

On the other hand, there are those who argue that the activities of an organ may be more reasonably seen as its activities and not the services of the Secretariat that are incidental to them. In so far as those services (or delegated powers under Article 98) are at issue, a question would be within the scope of the Secretary-General's activities. But that does not mean that the activities of those organs would of themselves pose questions on which the Secretary-General would be entitled to request advisory opinions.[209]

---

advisory opinions from the Court. However, since the Secretariat's political functions are embodied in the Secretary-General, it would still be the latter who would submit the request. Cf Szasz above, n 124, at 513.

[206] Higgins (Comment), above, no 96, at 569. The issue had also arisen as to whether the United Nations Commission on Human Rights should become an authorised organ under Art 96(2). This body, unlike the Committee on Human Rights, is undoubtedly a subsidiary organ of the United Nations. Here too the Secretary-General suggested that he should be substituted, as a principal organ, to deal with all requests from that Commission.

[207] A/47/33 9 (1992); see also the Agenda for Peace, A/47/277 (1992); Higgins (Comment), above n 96, at 573.

[208] Schwebel, above n 98, at 78.

[209] *Ibid.* See also Lucius Caflish, *"Is the International Court Entitled to Review Security Council Resolutions adopted under Chapter VII of the United Nations Charter?"*, in Najeeb Al-Nauimi *et al*

The General Assembly fears that a broad interpretation of the scope of activities of the Secretary-General may cause an institutional imbalance.[210] It fears that the Secretary-General would be politically over-strengthened if he were able to obtain from the ICJ opinions that might encourage him to exercise greater autonomy in his action with respect to, inter alia, the Security Council. If his activities were to involve every sector of the organisation's work, he could submit to the ICJ a legal question with which the Security Council is confronted. This potential omnipresence of the Secretary-General would imply that it might be dangerous to endow him with the power of seizing the ICJ *proprio motu*, since he could force the hand of the principal organ facing the question concerned.[211]

To vest in a single person such as the Secretary-General the authority to request advisory opinions would also constitute a major departure from prevailing concepts and would undoubtedly encounter severe political resistance.[212] Many would fear that the Secretary-General's recourse to advisory proceedings would be less visible and vivid than those of the General Assembly and the Security Council as a consequence of which the Secretary-General would be able to submit questions to the ICJ that would raise delicate international questions.[213]

This is possible, and the question then comes down to whether the advantages of authorising the Secretary-General to request advisory opinions on questions concerning the legality of actions of United Nations organs outweigh the risks. There may be room for difference of view over the answer to that question, but it is submitted that the advantages outweigh the risks in an organisation committed to the rule of law. The controversy surrounding the constitutionality of the Security Council resolution creating the International Tribunal for the Prosecution of Persons Responsible for Serious Violations of International Humanitarian Law Committed in the Territory of Former Yugoslavia since 1991 (hereinafter ICTY) could serve as an example.

When the appeals chamber of the ICTY was confronted with the question whether the establishment of the ICTY was lawful, it found that it

---

(eds), *International Legal Issues Arising under the United Nations Decade of International Law* 658 (The Hague, Martinus Nijhoff, 1995).

[210] Bedjaoui above n 106, at 78.
[211] *Ibid*, at 78–79.
[212] See Higgins (Comment), above n 96, at 573–74 who regarded it as alarming that the Secretary-General could secure a reference to the Court for an advisory opinion when the Security Council or the General Assembly would not themselves agree to make the request.
[213] See Pomerance above n 93, at 322. The proliferation of organs with access to the Court's advisory function may amplify opportunities for inappropriate use of the advisory jurisdiction for matters outside the Court's area of expertise. It may also increase the temptation to utilise the Court for political purposes and to circumvent the fundamental principle that no state may be subjected to international justice without its consent.

had the jurisdiction to deal with this question itself.[214] The appeals Chamber concluded that it had the incidental or inherent jurisdiction to determine its own jurisdiction as a necessary component in the exercise of judicial function.[215] By doing so, the ICTY acted as judge in its own affair which added to the controversy surrounding its establishment. Strictly speaking, it should have referred the matter to the Security Council for the purpose of requesting an advisory opinion on the legality of the ICTY's establishment from the ICJ. However, the ICTY refrained from pursuing this option, since it knew that the Security Council would never have cooperated.[216] One may ask whether this deadlock could have been avoided if the Secretary-General had possessed an extensive power to submit requests for advisory opinions to the ICJ. In that case the ICTY could have requested the Secretary-General to submit the question to the ICJ for an authoritative legal opinion, which would have prevented the ICTY from acting as judge in its own affair, and therefore enhanced its credibility.

In conclusion it is submitted that in order to enhance the utilisation of the advisory procedure of the ICJ with respect to questions of legality of actions of United Nations organs such as the Security Council, the Secretary-General should be authorised to request advisory opinions from the ICJ. This authorisation should be interpreted broadly, in the sense that the Secretary-General's scope of activities should be interpreted so as to co-exist with the activities of the other organs of the United Nations. In this way the Secretary-General can approach the ICJ for authoritative advice that can guide the Security Council with respect to the legality of its own actions.[217]

---

[214] *Prosecutor v Dusco Tadic*, Decision on the Defence Motion for Interlocutory Appeal and Jurisdiction, case no IT–94–1–T, 2 October 1995, Appeals Chamber, available at www.itcy.org. See also ch 9 at s 2.1.

[215] *Ibid.*

[216] George Abi-Saab "Strengthening the Role of the Court as the Principal Judicial Organ of the UN", in Connie Peck *et al* (eds), *Increasing the Effectiveness of the International Court of Justice* 277 (The Hague, Martinus Nijhoff, 1997).

[217] This should be distinguished from an affirmative answer to the question whether the Secretary-General should be able to request an advisory opinion with respect to disputes between states. In that situation the advisory opinion would be directed at the disputing states and not at the actions of the organisation as a whole. The Secretary-General has suggested that he should have such competence, when exercising his good offices and with the consent of the parties to the dispute (A/47/33, 10 (1992)). This proposal was criticised for the fact that it would allow states to request advisory opinions from the Court by the back door, although they are not entitled to do so under the Charter. The practical use of such power of the Secretary-General was also questioned, since states that have consented to submit their disputes to international settlement are already offered a sufficient choice and range of procedures. See Higgins (Comment), above n 96, at 572–74. See Cf Vera Gowlland-Debbas "Strengthening the Role of the Court as the Principal Judicial Organ of the UN", in Connie Peck *et al* (eds), *Increasing the Effectiveness of the International Court of Justice* 261–62 (The Hague, Martinus Nijhoff, 1997). She does, however, support the notion that the

7. CONCLUSION

Advisory opinions are an acknowledged avenue for obtaining authoritative interpretations of the law in a variety of national and international forms. This is also the case within the United Nations system, where advisory opinions of the ICJ have proved to be a mode for judicial review of the organisation's political organs, including the Security Council. Although none of the relevant advisory opinions has lead to a finding of illegality, they nonetheless affirm that advisory opinions can serve to guide the actions of an organ such as the Security Council and strengthen its legitimacy.

In the process, the ICJ has shown itself capable of exercising judicial restraint by attaching a presumption of legality to United Nations resolutions, as well as deference to the political organs' own interpretation of the scope of their competencies. By doing so, the ICJ has paid due respect to the principle of cooperation underpinning its relationship with other principal organs of the organisation, as well as the doctrine of efficiency. It also implies that a determination of illegality of a Security Council resolution could only be expected in clear and extreme cases and that a fear of excessive judicial activism in this regard would be unfounded.

However, an essential prerequisite for (de)legitimisation of United Nations action by means of advisory opinions, is that sufficient use must be made of the advisory procedure as a mode for judicial review. The ICJ can only contribute in the developing of standards for the legality of United Nations action if it is given the opportunity to do so. The underutilisation of the advisory procedure has played a major rule in reinforcing the view that no procedure for reviewing the legality of Security Council resolutions exists within the United Nations system. It is therefore important to develop means by which this deficit can be overcome. Authorising the Secretary-General to request advisory opinions for the purpose of guiding the organisation with respect to (the legality of) its own actions, poses one such a possibility.

Finally, it is conceded that the mode for judicial review offered by the advisory opinion procedure is a limited one. It is limited in the sense that it would never be as comprehensive as a fully fledged national appeals system with mechanisms ensuring enforcement of its decisions. But it nonetheless introduces or reinforces the importance of certain legal

---

Secretary-General be authorised to request advisory opinions originating from subsidiary organs or human rights treaty bodies, where these represent the interests of non-state entities debarred from access to international fora. Such bodies as the United Nations High Commissioner for Refugees, the Committee on the Rights of the Child, or the Committee on the Convention on the Elimination of Discrimination Against Women, would then have an alternative channel to the Court than that offered by the General Assembly or the Economic and Social Council.

principles in the international legal discourse and in this way encourages the organs of the organisation as well as member states to adhere to the law. In the long term this should also strengthen the value of the Charter as a legal document, and the notion of the existence of and adherence to an international rule of law.

3

Judicial Review as an Emerging General Principle of Law and its Implications for Contentious Proceedings before the ICJ

1. INTRODUCTION

THE CURRENT CHAPTER will examine whether judicial review, meaning the reviewing of the legality of decisions of political organs by an independent court of law, can be regarded as a general principle of law of civilised nations in terms of Article 38(1)(c) of the Statute of the International Court of Justice (ICJ).[1] The purpose of this analysis is to provide new direction in the debate as to whether the ICJ can review the legality of resolutions of the Security Council during contentious proceedings between states. This is necessitated by the fact that this debate arguably finds itself at an impasse from where it is difficult to come to any convincing conclusions.

Section 2 of the current chapter will illustrate that supporters and critics of a review power for the ICJ in contentious proceedings rely on the same arguments in order to come to very different conclusions. Due to the silence of the Charter on this issue, both camps resort to arguments relating to the principle of efficiency, the need for cooperation between the principle organs of the United Nations, and the drafting history of the Charter. Section 2 will also reveal that the latter argument forms the

---

[1] Art 38(1) reads as follows: "The Court, whose function is to decide in accordance with international law such disputes as are submitted to it shall apply:

    (a)   international conventions, whether general or particular, establishing rules expressly recognized by the contesting states;
    (b)   international custom, as evidence of a general practice accepted as law;
    (c)   the general principles of law recognized by civilized nations,
    (d)   subject to the provisions of Art 59, judicial decisions and the teachings of the most highly qualified publicists of the various nations, as subsidiary means for the determination of rules of law."

weakest link on both sides, as the drafting history did not really address the matter at all.[2] As far as the principle of efficiency and the need for cooperation between the principle organs are concerned, the arguments on both sides carry considerable weight. As a result, the debate finds itself at an impasse and in search of new perspectives.

At this point it is worth mentioning that the opportunity for the ICJ to review the resolutions of the Security Council during contentious proceedings will remain few and far between. Since the political organs of the United Nations cannot be a party to contentious proceedings, the question of legality of Security Council resolutions will have to arise *incidentally* in proceedings between states. This means that for a state to initiate the examination of the legality of a Security Council decision by the ICJ, such an examination must be necessary for the decision of a dispute between parties. One should also keep in mind that the ICJ does not have a general competence to enforce the law between states. Instead, it is dependent on the consent of states for jurisdiction *ratio personae* as well as *ratio materiae*.[3] The fact that the incidental questioning of the legality of Security Council resolutions remains contingent on a dispute between states and their willingness to subject it to the ICJ's jurisdiction, makes this avenue for judicial review the exception rather than the rule.[4]

Even so, the controversy surrounding the *Lockerbie* incident[5] has illustrated that on the rare occasion that this avenue of revue is triggered, it can have considerable repercussions for the legitimacy of the Charter system. In addition, contentious proceedings remain the only avenue by means of which *individual states* can initiate judicial review, as the Charter does not grant them the (individual) right to request an advisory opinion from the ICJ. Article 96(1) of the Charter reserves the right to test the legality of Security Council resolutions by means of an advisory opinion for the General Assembly and the Security Council. It therefore remains important to attempt to resolve the question whether the ICJ has the power to review the legality of Security Council proceedings during contentious proceedings.

---

[2] Other problems affecting the value of the *travaux préparatoires* will be discussed below at s 5.3.1.

[3] See Art 36(1) and Art 36(2) of the ICJ statute.

[4] See Barbara Lorinser, *Bindende Resolutionen des Sicherheitsrates* 97 (Baden-Baden, Nomos, 1996); Christian Tomuschat, "Tyrannei der Minderheit?", 19 *German Yearbook of International Law* 278 (1976); Bardo Fassbender, "The United Nations Charter as Constitution of the International Community", 36 *Columbia Journal of Transnational Law* 575 (1998); Blaine Sloan, "The United Nations Charter as a Constitution", 1 *Pace Yearbook of International Law* 73 (1989); see also Konrad Ginther, "Die Verfassung der Völkerrechtsgemeinschaft im Lichte der Entscheidung des internationalen Gerichtshofes im sogenannten Südwestafrika-Streit", in René Marcic *et al* (eds), *International Festschrift für Verdross zum 80. Geburtstag* 100 (München, Wilhelm Fink, 1971).

[5] See also extensively ch 1, at s 2.

As of section 3, the current chapter attempts to provide new impulses to the debate by examining whether judicial review is emerging as a general principle of law within municipal orders. If a survey of municipal orders were to indicate that judicial review of the decisions of political organs within states was (or was not) emerging as a general principle of law, this could tip the scale of the debate one way or the other. For example, if the rationale for accepting such control would seem to have become generally accepted, the ICJ could transpose it to the international order through Article 38(1)(c) of its Statute. This presupposes that a comparison with judicial review in municipal law is justified in the light of the difference in structure between municipal orders and the international legal order. Until now several authors have rejected such a comparison out of hand, arguing that any comparison with municipal treatment of judicial review would be out of place.[6]

However, although it is correct to point out that comparative analogies have to be undertaken with care and that they should not serve to replace the autonomous stipulations of international law, this is no reason for a priori rejecting them. They can serve to *support* (emerging) international doctrine, especially in dynamic areas such as judicial review which has gained considerable momentum in all parts of the world since the early 1990s. It would therefore be just as premature to reject analogies with judicial review in municipal law—without first having done some analysis of the issue—as it would be to overtake national constitutional concepts blindly, without having examined whether the conditions in which they are applied domestically would correspond to those on the international plane.

The analysis of judicial review in municipal orders and its implications for the ICJ consists of three parts. The first concentrates on the meaning of general principles, ie the conditions to be met for a principle to qualify as a general principle of law. These would include the extent to which it is present in the different municipal systems. One also has to consider whether a mere theoretical presence in a majority of legal systems suffices, or whether effective enforcement is a pre-requisite as well. Furthermore, once it has been established that a particular principle is widely acknowledged, one has to determine whether it has a core content that is in conformity with the structure of the international legal order, as a result of which it could be transposed thereto.

---

[6] See for example Gaetano Arangio-Ruiz, "The 'Federal Analogy' and UN Character Interpretation: A Crucial Issue", 8 *European Journal of International Law* 20–21 (1997), who regarded, inter alia, the differences in the composition of international organisations and states as an insurmountable barrier for the purposes of constitutional analogy. See also Jochen Herbst, *Rechtsbindung des UN-Sicherheitsrates* 389–91 (Frankfurt a/M, Peter Lang, 1999) and Michael Fraas, *Sicherheitsrat der Vereinten Nationen und Internationaler Gerichtshof* 4 (Frankfurt a/M, Peter Lang, 1998).

From this abstract level the chapter moves to the more concrete issue of the use of constitutional analogies for international organisations. Their constitutive documents show similarities with constitutions and their functions similarities with municipal administrations. Of particular interest is whether these similarities between municipal constitutions and the Charter would justify a comparative analysis when analysing the question of judicial review by the ICJ, despite structural differences remaining between the systems. Stated differently, one has to determine whether such a comparison would result in an over-extension of the analogy. In order to answer this question it is first necessary to examine the constitutional character of the Charter. Only once it has been established that the Charter would possess the core elements usually associated with municipal constitutions, could one progress to drawing comparisons with municipal orders in relation to judicial review. The constitutional character of the Charter is explored in the second part of the chapter and the constitutional elements singled out as characteristic include the normative quality of a constitutional document, its superiority and inclusivity, its dynamic and evolutionary character, and the protection of the separation of powers.

After concluding that the Charter possesses these qualities—albeit only in a rudimentary form—the chapter concentrates on judicial review as an emerging general principle of law. It first outlines the growing significance of judicial review in municipal orders in recent years. It then examines whether these developments in the municipal orders are underpinned by a common rational or core value, and if so, whether it would find resonance on the international plane. Thereafter it questions whether, on the basis of such a common rational, judicial review could be recognised as a general principle of law in terms of Article 38(1)(c) of the ICJ statute, despite the different ways in which it manifests itself in the various municipal orders.

2.   LEGAL IMPLICATIONS OF THE *LOCKERBIE* CASE FOR JUDICIAL REVIEW IN CONTENTIOUS PROCEEDINGS

2.1.   Legal Implications of the Rejection of Provisional Measures

The statements made by judges at the provisional measure stage of the *Lockerbie* proceedings[7]—concurring or dissenting alike—reflect considerable differences in the motivations that underpinned the judges' reasoning.

---

[7] *Case Concerning Questions of Interpretation and Application of the 1971 Montreal Convention Arising from the Aerial Incident at Lockerbie (Libyan Arab Jamahiriya v United Kingdom)*, Provisional Measures, ICJ Rep 1992, at 3 ff; *Case Concerning Questions of Interpretation and Application of the 1971 Montreal Convention Arising from the Aerial Incident at Lockerbie (Libyan Arab Jamahiriya v United States of America)*, Provisional Measures, ICJ Rep 1992, at 114 ff.

In addition, they are notable for their cautious and sometimes ambiguous language that emphasises the prima facie validity of Security Council resolutions during preliminary proceedings. As this clearly reflects the unease and uncertainty within the ICJ regarding the question of judicial review of Security Council resolutions at the merits stage of the proceedings, one should be careful to draw any extensive conclusions from this decision. One could neither conclude from it that the ICJ would be prepared to review fully the legality of Chapter VII resolutions at the merits stage,[8] nor that it would be unwilling to do so. Even though there is a resemblance to the *Marbury v Madison*[9] decision, where the United States Supreme Court had to stake out its own role with respect to judicial review,[10] it would be premature to argue that the ICJ had or had not asserted a similar power unto itself in contentious proceedings.[11] The fact is that the ICJ had left the essence of the question of whether it was competent to review Security Council decisions in contentious proceedings unresolved.[12]

The most that one can conclude is that there exists an almost irrebuttable presumption of legality of Security Council resolutions at the provisional measures stage.[13] This implies that the ICJ would only adopt provisional measures if they do not conflict with the disputed Security Council resolution. This position is supported by the order for provisional measures relating to the *Armed Activities on the Territory of the Congo (Democratic Republic of the Congo v Uganda)*.[14] In July 2000 the ICJ granted the Congo's request for provisional measures and ordered the parties to refrain forthwith from any armed action. It also enjoined them to ensure

---

These two orders will hereinafter be referred to as *Libya v United Kingdom*, provisional measures and *Libya v United States*, provisional measures, respectively. However, since the two orders are essentially the same, both will hereinafter be referred to as *Libya v United States*, provisional measures. See also ch 1, at s 2.1.

[8] Nigel White, "To Review or Not to Review? The Lockerbie Cases Before the World Court", 12 *Leiden Journal of International Law* 405–06 (1999). He submitted that the ICJ strongly suggested that this presumption of the superseding character of the Security Council resolution will be reconsidered by the ICJ at the merits stage. However, it would be reading too much into the ICJ's order to teach such a conclusion.

[9] 5 US (1 Cranch) 137 (1803).

[10] Thomas M Franck, "The 'Powers of Appreciation': Who Is the Ultimate Guardian of UN Legality?", 86 *American Journal of International Law* 519 (1992).

[11] See Ken Roberts, "Second-Guessing the Security Council: the International Court of Justice and its Powers of Judicial Review", 7 *Pace International Law Review* 308 (1995).

[12] Robert F Kennedy, "Libya v United States: The International Court of Justice and the Power of Judicial Review", 33 *Virginia Journal of International Law* 909 (1993).

[13] White, above n 8, at 403; Bernd Martenczuk, "The Security Council, the International Court and Judicial Review: What Lessons from Lockerbie?", 10 *European Journal of International Law* 521 (1999), noted that it would have been inappropriate for the ICJ to question the Security Council's authority at the provisional stage of the procedure without sufficient investigation, briefing, argument and deliberation.

[14] Reprinted in 39 *International Legal Materials* 1100 ff (2000). Hereinafter referred to as *Congo v Uganda*, provisional measures.

full respect within the zone of conflict for fundamental human rights.[15] This order was preceded by Resolution 1304 of 16 June 2000, which was adopted under Chapter VII and called on all parties to cease hostilities throughout the Congo.[16] The ICJ nonetheless granted the provisional measures, as there was no prima facie conflict between the measures requested by the Congo and the obligations contained in Resolution 1304 (2000).[17]

2.2. Legal Implications of the Rejection of the Preliminary Objections

The majority decision at the preliminary objections phase of the *Lockerbie* proceedings[18] was equally cryptic and cautious. On the one hand, this stage of the proceedings confirmed that a binding Security Council resolution does not automatically trump the ICJ's ability to render a meaningful judgment at the merits stage. At the same time, the ICJ did not give an answer as to whether the ICJ would actually review in substance the legality of the Security Council's decisions. The real conflict had thus been postponed again.[19] This inevitably leads to the question why the ICJ is so hesitant to take a stand on the issue. The answer can be found in the deep divisions within the ICJ (and amongst international lawyers in general) with respect to whether it has the power to review the legality of Security Council decisions in contentious proceedings.

The opponents of judicial review base their argument on the Security Council's primary responsibility for international peace and security and the need for this organ to execute its function efficiently. These factors would oblige other principal organs of the United Nations, including the ICJ, to cooperate with the Security Council by giving effect to its decisions wherever necessary.[20] They fear that the eventual finding of illegality of a

---

[15] *Congo v Uganda*, provisional measures, above n 14, at 1113.
[16] SC Res 1204 of 16 June 2000, at paras 1–3.
[17] *Congo v Uganda*, provisional measures, above n 14, at 1111.
[18] *Case Concerning Questions of Interpretation and Application of the 1971 Montreal Convention Arising from The Aerial Incident at Lockerbie (Libyan Arab Jamahiriya v United Kingdom)*, Preliminary Objections, *and Case Concerning Questions of Interpretation and Application of the 1971 Montreal Convention Arising from The Aerial Incident at Lockerbie (Libyan Arab Jamahiriya v United States)*, Preliminary Objections. Both decisions are available at www.icj-cij.org/. See also 37 *International Legal Materials* 587 ff (1998). These two decisions will hereinafter be referred to as *Libya v United Kingdom*, preliminary objections and *Libya v United States*, preliminary objections, respectively. However, since the two orders are essentially the same, both will hereinafter be referred to as *Libya v United States*, preliminary objections. Separate reference to *Libya v United Kingdom*, preliminary objections, is only made where it contains additional information. See also ch 2, at 2.2.
[19] See Martenczuk, above n 13, at 525.
[20] Dissenting opinion of President Schwebel, *Libya v United States*, preliminary objections, above n 18, at 630; Scott S Evans, "The Lockerbie Incident Cases: Libyan-Sponsored Terrorism, Judicial Review and the Political Question Doctrine", 18 *Maryland Journal of International Law and Trade* (1994)

Security Council resolution would frustrate the latter's workings, and in that way aggravate the peaceful settlement of a situation instead of promoting it.[21] Consequently the ICJ had to foreclose immediately even the suggestion of judicial review, as anything else would contribute in challenging the integrity and authority of the Security Council. A decision by the ICJ to hear the claim may be interpreted as justification for continued defiance of the Security Council's binding resolutions.[22] In addition, it would set a precedent for recalcitrant states to use the alleged illegality of binding Security Council measures as a pretext to frustrate decisions of the Security Council.[23]

They underline that these fears were already expressed during the drafting of the Charter at the United Nations Conference on International Organization at San Francisco in 1945.[24] When deliberating the chapter on the peaceful settlement of disputes, Belgium submitted two proposals that would have granted individual states the possibility of requesting advisory opinions from the ICJ for the purpose of reviewing the legality of proposed Security Council resolutions. However, both proposals were rejected.[25] Seen against this background, the absence of any provision in the Charter that would provide for judicial review in

---

[21] Evans, above n 20, at 64; W Michael Reisman, "The Constitutional Crisis in the United Nations", 87 *American Journal of International Law* 88 (1993).

[22] Dissenting opinion of President Schwebel, *Libya v United States*, preliminary objections, above n 18, at 630. Cf Evans, above n 20, at 64.

[23] See the dissenting opinion of President Schwebel, *Libya v United States*, preliminary objections, above n 18, at 630; separate opinion of Judge *ad hoc* Jennings, *Libya v United Kingdom*, preliminary objections, above n 18. Cf Marcella David, "Passport to Justice: Internationalizing the Political Question Doctrine for Application in the World Court, 40 *Harvard International Law Journal* 121 (1999); White, above n 8, at 421.

[24] See, for example, the statements of the USSR in 12 *United Nation Conference on International Organization* 49 (1945); the United Kingdom, *ibid*, at 65, the United States, *ibid*, at 49; and France, *ibid*, at 50. The Soviet Union was concerned that the Belgian amendment would weaken the Security Council; the United Kingdom delegate feared that the amendment could cause unacceptable delays to the advantage of an aggressor state; the American delegate regarded the requirement that the Security Council work in accordance with the principles of the organisation and with due regard for the principles of justice and international law as sufficient control over the Security Council; the French delegate was opposed to a dispersal of responsibilities in the organisation. See Roberts, above n 11, at 290; see also Craig Scott *et al*, "Memorial for Bosnia: Framework of Legal Arguments Concerning the Lawfulness of the Maintenance of the United Nations Security Council's Arms Embargo on Bosnia and Herzegovina", 16 *Michigan Journal of International Law* 82 ff (1994).

[25] The Belgian proposal read as follows: "Any state, party to a dispute brought before the Security Council, shall have the right to ask the Permanent Court of International Justice whether a recommendation or a decision made by the Council or proposed if it infringes on its essential rights. If the Court considers that such rights have been disregarded or are threatened, it is for the Council either to reconsider the question or to refer the dispute to the Assembly for decision." See 3 *United Nation Conference on International Organization* 336 (1945); see also 13 *United Nation Conference on International Organization* 653–54 (1945); Roberts, above n 11, at 292; Scott *et al*, above n 24, at 84.

contentious proceedings could only mean that the ICJ would not possess such a power.[26]

The supporters of judicial review of Security Council decisions, on the other hand, note that the obligation to cooperate with other principal organs applies equally to the ICJ and the Security Council. Consequently the Security Council may not frustrate the working of the ICJ by attempting to prevent it from giving a decision over which the ICJ has established jurisdiction, as the Security Council attempted to do by adopting Resolution 748 (1992).[27] By the time the Security Council adopted this resolution, Libya had already initiated proceedings before the ICJ under Article 14(1) of the Montreal Convention. Not only had the claim been filed, but the parties had already presented their oral arguments and the ICJ was in deliberation. By taking binding action without awaiting the outcome of the ICJ's decision, the Security Council undermined its jurisdiction.[28]

The supporters of judicial review reject claims that this intervention was not aimed at undermining the ICJ, but rather at preventing Libya from abusing the dispute settlement procedures. There would be no reason why the ICJ could not prevent such abuse itself, as concerns about abuse of process could be presented as a legal argument.[29] For example, the respondents could argue that the Montreal Convention was not intended to enable states with a long record of terrorist activities to protect their terrorist agents from prosecution.[30] This would amount to the Montreal Convention containing an implied condition that prohibits such states from exercising jurisdiction over terrorist suspects. As a result, they would have to extradite the suspects to one of the other states that could claim jurisdiction in terms of the Montreal Convention.[31]

---

[26] Dissenting opinion of President Schwebel, *Libya v United States*, preliminary objections, above n 18, at 630. See Reisman, above n 21, at 95. The United Nations Charter did not incorporate judicial review as a form of checks and balances, but limited control over the Security Council to the veto power assigned to its permanent members.

[27] Evans, above n 20, at 60–61; Martenczuk, above n 13, at 533; Malanczuk, "Reconsidering the Relationship between the ICJ and the Security Council", in Wybo P Heere (ed), *International Law and the Hague's 750th* Anniversary 90 (The Hague, TMC Asser, 1999); Edward McWhinney, "Judicial Wisdom, and the World Court as Special Constitutional Court", in Beyerlein, Ulrich *et al* (eds), *Recht zwischen Umbruch und Bewahrung; Völkerrecht, Europarecht, Staatsrecht: Festschrift für Rudolf Berhnardt* 709 (Berlin, Springer, 1995).

[28] David, above n 23, at 119; GA Sarpong, "The Lockerbie Incident and the International Court of Justice: Reality in the New World Order", *African Society of International and Comparative Law. Proceedings of the fifth Annual Conference* 70–71 (1993).

[29] David, above n 23, at 118.

[30] *Ibid.*

[31] *Ibid.* The objections of the respondents (and dissenting judges) against the jurisdiction of the ICJ in the *Lockerbie* case assumed that the Montreal Convention was necessarily in contradiction with and therefore trumped by SC Res 748 of 31 March 1992 and SC Res 883 of 11 November 1993. It overlooked the fact that the Montreal Convention may not have been intended to apply to instances of state-sponsored terrorism. Whether this was indeed the case, depends on the interpretation of Art 7 of the Montreal Convention and the extent of its application. The ICJ would first have to determine whether the choice of the custodial

If Resolution 748 (1992) were to prevent the ICJ from considering these (and other) legal arguments, it would open the way for one party to a dispute to abuse a political organ for the purposes of avoiding its legal obligations.[32] It would set a precedent for powerful states that exert substantial influence in the Security Council to suspend settlement procedures under an international convention which it had previously accepted, by instrumentalising the Security Council in their own interest. In the process the independence of the ICJ and ultimately the legitimacy and efficiency of the United Nations would be severely compromised.[33]

In addition, the supporters of judicial review do not regard the absence in the Charter of an explicit provision for judicial review in contentious proceedings as an insurmountable obstacle. This power would be implicitly provided for in Article 92, which describes the ICJ as the principal judicial organ of the United Nations.[34] Moreover, it is incorrect to conclude from the Charter's drafting history that Belgium withdrew its first proposal because the framers had reached a consensus that judicial review of binding Chapter VII Security Council decisions was undesirable.[35] It was withdrawn, for when acting within the chapter on the peaceful settlement of disputes (that later became Chapter VI), the Security Council's power to recommend a solution would be merely advisory and not possess any obligatory effect.[36]

Furthermore, even though the second Belgian proposal was defeated as well, the Statement on Interpretation of the Charter, which was ultimately

state between prosecuting the suspects itself or extraditing them was intended to enable states with a long record of terrorist activities to protect their terrorist agents from prosecution. If it concluded that Art 7 of the Montreal Convention was not intended to apply under such circumstances and therefore was not applicable in the current case, the ICJ would interpret the Montreal Convention in a way that avoided conflict with these resolutions. It is only when the ICJ were to decide that Art 7 of the Montreal Convention granted Libya the right not to extradite the suspects, that it would have to rule on the legality of the resolutions. The ICJ would then be confronted with a direct conflict of obligations, which would make an examination of the validity of the resolutions inevitable. See also Stefan Sohm, "Zur Bekämpfung des internationalen Terrorismus", *Humanitäres Völkerrecht* 173 (1994); Peter HF Bekker, "International Decisions: Questions of Interpretation and Application of the 1971 Montreal Convention Arising from the Aerial Incident at Lockerbie", 92 *American Journal of International Law* 504 (1998); Martenczuk, above n 13, at 529–30; White, above n 8, at 407.

[32] Bernhard Graefrath, "Leave to the Court what Belongs to the Court": The Libyan Case', 4 *European Journal of International Law* 204 (1993); David, above n 23, at 119; Sarpong, above n 28, at 71.
[33] Graefrath, above n 32, at 204; David, above n 23, at 119.
[34] Scott *et al*, above n 24, at 96. See also John Dugard, "Judicial Review of Sanctions", in Vera Gowlland-Debbas (ed), *United Nations Sanctions and International Law* 85 (The Hague, Kluwer, 2001); But see Roberts, above n 11, at 286, who is more sceptical.
[35] Scott *et al*, above n 24, at 84.
[36] 12 *United Nation Conference on International Organization* 65–66 (1945); Roberts, above n 11, at 291–92; Scott *et al*, above n 24, at 84.

adopted by the Committee on Legal Problems, did favour judicial review.[37] It provided that each United Nations organ would in the first instance interpret the parts of the Charter applicable to its functions itself. In the event that two organs expressed or acted upon different interpretations of the Charter, they could ask for an advisory opinion of the Court, or set up an *ad hoc* committee of jurists to examine the question.[38]

A significant factor of the above mentioned arguments is that the opponents and supporters of judicial review in contentious proceedings use similar arguments to reach different conclusions. Both groups refer to the importance of the efficient functioning of the organisation and the principle of cooperation between principal organs, when arguing that judicial review is not only (not) desirable, but also (not) provided for in the Charter. In addition, both groups attempt to support their conclusions with the drafting history of the Charter.[39] This latter argument poses the weakest link in the argument on both sides, as it is doubtful whether any significant conclusions can be drawn from the drafting history. Apart from being rather ambiguous in nature, the debate did not address the core of the current debate, namely whether binding Security Council decisions can be subjected to judicial review by the ICJ in contentious proceedings.[40]

The debate at San Francisco concentrated exclusively on the possible testing of non-binding Security Council resolutions under Chapter VI of the Charter.[41] It did not give any indication of the intentions of the drafters with respect to the reviewing of binding Security Council resolutions under Chapter VII. Second, the debate was limited to whether an *advisory opinion* procedure for *individual states* should be introduced. It did not include any discussion on the testing of binding Security Council decisions during contentious proceedings.

As far as the principle of efficiency and the need for cooperation between the principle organs are concerned, the arguments on both sides carry considerable weight. This is reflected in the strong divisions within the ICJ, as well as the fact that both sides of the argument enjoy strong support amongst authors. As a result, the discussion on whether the ICJ has the competence to review the legality of a Security Council resolution during contentious proceedings arguably finds itself at an impasse and in

---

[37] Scott *et al*, above n 24, at 84.
[38] 13 *United Nations Conference on International Organization* 710 (1945); Scott *et al*, above n 24, at 84. See also Andreas Stein, *Der Sicherheitsrat der Vereinten Nationen und die Rule of Law* 350 (Baden-Baden, Nomos, 1999).
[39] Herbst, above n 6, at 98, Lorinser, above n 4, at 62; José E Alvarez "Judging the Security Council", 90 *American Journal of International Law* 3–4 (1996).
[40] Herbst, above n 6, at 62. Cf Blaine Sloan, above n 4, at 72, 74–75.
[41] Lorinser, above n 4, at 62; Herbst, above n 6, at 98.

need of a new perspective. In an attempt to respond to this situation, the subsequent passages will examine whether judicial review is emerging as a general principle of law within municipal orders and, if so, what it would imply for judicial review of Security Council decisions during contentious proceedings before the ICJ.

3. THE MEANING OF "GENERAL PRINCIPLES OF THE LAW RECOGNISED BY CIVILISED NATIONS"

The concept of general principles of law in terms of Article 38(1)(c) of the ICJ statute was first inserted in Article 38 of the Statute of the Permanent Court of International Justice (PCIJ), the forerunner of the ICJ.[42] It was intended to provide a solution in cases where treaties and custom provided no (clear) answers to the case at hand. In this way situations in which the ICJ would be unable to decide cases because of gaps in treaty and customary law were to be avoided.[43]

Article 38 not only determines the law to be applied by the ICJ, but also the order in which it has to examine the groups of law listed in its first paragraph.[44] It indicates that judges will first resort to treaty or

---

[42] Peter Malanczuk, *Akehurst's Modern Introduction to International Law* 48 (London, Routledge, 1997); Hermann Mosler, 2 *Encyclopedia of Public International Law* 515 (1995). The first attempt at codifying the consideration that domestic legal orders influence the application and development of international law by international courts occurred during the second Hague Peace Conference in 1907. During this time it was attempted to create a permanent international court of arbitral justice. Attached to the draft statute worked out for this court, the following explanation was found: "Different systems of law exist in different states, but an international court must embrace the various systems of the world. If the Court is to judge according to equity and international law, it must not be the equity of any one system, but the equity which is the resultant of the various systems of law. For the purpose of the Court municipal law must be internationalised". The draft project did not succeed at the time, because it was impossible to reach agreement at the conference on the composition of the court. However, even without such codification arbitration tribunals have frequently resorted to municipal analogies since the nineteenth century. See, for example, Alfred Verdross, "Les principes généraux du droit dans la jurisprudence international", 52 *Recueil des Cours de l'académie de droit international de la Haye* 196 ff (1935 II); Ian Brownlie, *Principles of Public International Law* 17 (Oxford, Clarendon Press, 1998); Robert Jennings & Arthur Watts, *Oppenheim's International Law* 39 (London, Longman, 1992).

[43] Malanczuk, above n 42, at 48. For an indication of the intention of the drafters of Art 38(1)(c) to this effect, see Advisory Committee of Jurists, *Procés-Verbaux of the Proceedings of the Committee* 294 ff (The Hague, 1920). These *travaux préparatoires* concerned the Statute of the PCIJ. Since Art 38 was in essence over-taken in the statute of the ICJ without any lengthy debate, the *travaux préparatoires* are still deemed relevant. See Vladimir-Djuro Degan, "General Principles of Law", 3 *Finnish Yearbook of International Law* 33–41 (1992); GJH van Hoof, *Rethinking the Sources of International Law* 136–39 (The Hague, Kluwer, 1983).

[44] Mosler (Encyclopedia), above n 42, at 516.

customary law, but in situations where these sources do not provide any answers they will have to resort to municipal law.[45] Also, where the answers provided by treaties or custom are uncertain or ambiguous they may be interpreted in the light of general principles of municipal law.[46] The municipal law would thus be a supplementary argument in case the contentions based on customary law or treaties fail to convince.[47]

This means that the application of general principles usually does not follow when the relevant rights and obligations, whether regulated by treaty or customary international law, have already developed a clear content.[48] Even though the wording of Article 38 would not constitute a hierarchy, this would follow from the *principle lex specialis derogat lege generali* (which in itself is a general principle).[49] Gaps in the law or ambiguities would be particularly prevalent when international courts are confronted with new problems which are not yet regulated by customary or treaty law. In these situations the judges have no choice but to create a fitting solution themselves.[50] They can do so by considering whether the main legal systems of the world reflect a similar principle that would be applicable to the case at hand.[51]

---

[45] Hermann Mosler, "Rechtsvergleichung vor völkerrechtlichen Gerichten", in René Marcic *et al* (eds), *Festschrift für Verdross zum 80. Geburtstag* 382 (München, Fink, 1971). Virtually immediately following its foundation the ICJ had to resort to municipal law for the purposes of drafting its rules of procedure. See also Michael Bothe & Georg Ress, "The Comparative Method and Public International Law", in William E Butler, *International Law in a Comparative Perspective* 61 (Alphen aan den Rijn, Sijthoff & Noordhoff, 1980).

[46] Johan G Lammers, "General Principles of Law Recognized by Civilized Nations", in Frits Kalshoven *et al* (eds), *Essays on the Development of the International Legal Order in Memory of Haro F Van Panhuys* 64–65 (Alphen aan den Rijn, Sijthoff & Noordhoff, 1980).

[47] HWA Thirlway "The Law and Procedure of the International Court of Justice: Part Two", 61 *British Yearbook of International Law* 112 (1990).

[48] Paul Guggenheim, "Landesrechtliche Begriffe im Völkerrecht, vor allem im Bereich der internationalen Organisationen", in Walter Schaetzel & Hans-Juergen Schlochauer (eds), *Rechtsfragen der internationalen Organisationen. Festschrift für Hans Wehberg zu seinem 70 Geburtstag* 142 (Frankfurt am Main, Vittorio Klostermann, 1956); Degan above n 43, at 53.

[49] Degan, above n 43, at 3; Lammers, above n 46, at 66. See also Cherif Bassiouni, "A Functional approach to 'General Principles of International Law'", 11 *Michigan Journal of International Law* 783–85, 800 (1989). Although he argued that Art 38(1) did not foresee a hierarchy between the different sources of law mentioned by it, he conceded that in practice the general principles of law do not come into play where clear answers are provided by treaties or custom.

[50] Michael Bothe, "Die Bedeutung der Rechtsvergleichung in der Praxis internationaler Gerichte", 36 *Zeitschrift für ausländisches öffentliches Recht und Völkerrecht* 291 (1976); Guggenheim (Festschrift für Wehberg), above n 48, at 143. See also Bothe & Ress, above n 45, at 49; Malanczuk, above n 42, at 49.

[51] Guggenheim (Festschrift für Wehberg), above n 48, at 133, 140. See also Mosler (Encyclopedia), above n 42, at 518. It may well be possible that general principles are not the only basis for reaching a decision but that they are used jointly either with treaty law or customary law. This could make the boundary between a customary rule and a general principle difficult to distinguish.

There are different opinions concerning the nature of the general principles to be applied by the ICJ in such situations.[52] Many authors still argue that the majority of the drafters of Article 38(1)(c) intended to restrict the general principles to those applied in *foro domestico*, ie to maxims of law. Therefore it would not be enough that the general principles are common to most legal systems, but they should also form the basis of those systems.[53] In addition to being widely accepted in municipal systems, the relevant principle must possess such a degree of reasonableness and appropriateness for application on the international plane, that a state which acts in a contrary manner must at least have been conscious of a possibility that a rule of law might point in the opposite direction.[54] Examples would be the principles of good faith or *res judicata*.[55]

---

[52] It is also disputed among writers whether general principles of law refer to those observed only in national jurisdictions, or whether in addition general principles can be deducted from international law through analogy as well. For present purposes, the focus will merely be on the general principles derived from municipal law. For a discussion see Mosler (Encyclopedia), above n 42, at 513 ff; Van Hoof, above n 43, at 143–44; Lammers, above n 46, at 56–57; cf Olufemi Elias & Chin Lim, "'General Principles of Law', 'Soft' Law and the Identification of International Law", 28 *Netherlands Yearbook of International Law* 28–35 (1997).

[53] For discussion of the theoretical opinions see Degan, above n 43, at 1–6; Lammers, above n 46, at 56–59; B Vitanyi, "Les positions doctrinales concernant le sens de la notion de 'principe généraux de droit reconnus par les nations civilisées'", 86 *Revue générale de droit international public* 48 (1982).

[54] Thirlway, above n 47, at 113. A minority of scholars (Soviet lawyers in particular), did not accept general principles as a source of international law at all. They rejected the notion that socialist and capitalist systems can have normative principles in common. Furthermore, according to the Soviet interpretation of Art 38(1)(c), the general principles are merely the ones that can be deducted from the relations between states and customary international law and which are contained in court decisions. See G Tunkin, *Theory of International Law*, translation by W Butler 199–203 (London, Allen Unwin, 1974). For a similar sceptical view of a "bourgeois" writer, see Hans Kelsen, *Principles of International Law* 540 (New York, Holt, Rhinehart and Winston, 1966). Against Ignaz Seidl-Hohenveldern, `Die Rolle der Rechtsvergleichung im Völkerrecht', in FA von der Heydte, *Völkerrecht und rechtliches Weltbild : Festschrift für Alfred Verdross* 255–56 (Vienna, Springer, 1960). He refuted this by pointing out that such interpretation would render Art 38(1)(c) a meaningless pleonasm. After all, general principles of *international law* (as opposed to those of states) are already acknowledged as a source of international law in Art 38(1)(b), by means of the reference to customary international law. This is, of course, in so far as these principles are not already concretised in international treaties. To this criticism of Seidl-Hohenveldern one can add that the Soviet interpretation probably does not hold much weight since the demise of the socialist ideology. See also Elias & Lim, above n 52, at 21; Van Hoof, above n 43, at 132–33.

[55] See Alfred Verdross & Bruno Simma, *Universelles Völkerrecht* 384 (Berlin, Duncker & Humblot, 1984). Their view would be comparable with statements of Baron Decampes of Belgium in the *Procés Verbaux*, above n 43, at 310–31. He referred to the fundamental law of justice and injustice deeply engraved on the heart of every human being and which is given its highest and most authoritative expression in the legal conscience of civilised nations. See also HC Gutteridge, "The Meaning of the Scope of Art 38(1)(c) of the Statute of the International Court of Justice", 38 *Transactions of the Grotius Society* 127 (1952) who described the general principles as extremely rare.

Others points out—it is submitted, correctly—that it is not necessary to restrict the notion of general principles in such a way.[56] For the drafters of the ICJ statute the decisive point was that such principles were not to be derived from mere speculation. They had to be made objective through some sort of general acceptance or recognition by states.[57] Furthermore, even if a narrow interpretation were intended by the drafters, the concept of general principles has been extended in international decisions through creative interpretation.[58] This recognises a dynamic function inherent in Article 38(1)(c) that it anticipates the prospective need for evolution and change in the development of international law.[59] It would be stifling not to inject into the sources of international law the capability of growth and development. Every national legal system includes such a process, either through the jurisprudence of its courts or through doctrine as developed by scholars. Thus, it can be said that national legal principles evolve and that a legal mechanism or process for recognition of this evolutionary aspect of law must exist in international law.[60]

In spite of these ongoing doctrinal debates, it is generally accepted that the term "civilised nations" today refers to all members of the international community.[61] No state or group of states may be excluded on the basis of not being a civilised nation. [62] There is also agreement that a principle originating in national law need not be observed by all states in the world, so long as there is evidence that it is applied by a representative majority which includes the principal legal systems of the world.[63] In this

---

[56] Bruno Simma & Philip Alston, "The Sources of Human Rights Law: Custom, Ius Cogens, and General Principles", 12 *Australian Yearbook of International Law* 102 (1992).

[57] *Ibid*, at 102.

[58] Mosler (Encyclopedia), above n 42, at 517.

[59] Bassiouni, above n 49, at 777.

[60] *Ibid*. See also Henry Schermers & Niels M Blokker, *International Institutional Law* 824 (The Hague, Martinus Nijhoff, 1994). See Van Hoof, above n 43, at 138–39. In order to understand the line of reasoning of the drafting Committee, one should keep in mind the time-frame of its work. At the time that this clause was drafted in 1920, the international society was still relatively homogenous (ie Western) as far as conceptions of international law were concerned. The drafters were convinced that the rules which they had in mind and which were strongly influenced by natural law, were indeed accepted by the national legal systems of states. Even though this may have been correct at the time for the group of states they had in mind, the picture has changed as a result of the developments in the composition of the international society. This statement can be interpreted as acknowledging the evolutionary nature of international society and as a result also of its sources of law such as general principles.

[61] Mosler (Encyclopedia), above n 42, at 517; Kay Hailbronner, "Ziele und Methoden völkerrechtlich relevanter Rechtsvergleichung", 36 *Zeitschrift für ausländisches öffentliches Recht und Völkerrecht* 207 (1976). See also Mosler (Festschrift für Verdross), above n 45, at 382 where he stated that the concept of civilised nations is outdated.

[62] Hailbronner, above n 61, at 208. Degan, above n 43, at 54 indicated that Art 38(1)(c) may be repugnant to many modern scholars, simply because of the term "civilised nations".

[63] Gutteridge, above n 55, at 127. See also Bernd Martenczuk, *Rechtsbindung und Rechtskontrolle des Weltsicherheitsrates. Die Überprüfung nichtmilitärischer Zwangsmassnahme durch den Internationalen Gerichtshof* 64 (Berlin, Duncker & Humblot, 1996), who favoured a

way one or more countries can be prevented from dressing-up specific interests of their own as rules of international law.[64]

This would mean that the mere absence of a legal principle in a particular system would not necessarily prevent it from being recognised as a general principle, since the finding of a general principle is not a mathematical process in which the (smallest) common denominator is to be found.[65] Legal principles could be described as general when they are to be found only in some legal systems, but can nonetheless be reconciled with the other legal systems. Most acknowledged general principles seem to be of this kind.[66] The test to be applied is a negative one, according to which the solution found by the international court may not violate any principles of law in member states.[67] Where some states show a contradictory rule to the so-called general principle, this cannot be ignored.[68]

Once it has been established that a particular principle is present in most major legal systems, the question becomes whether it also has to be enforced effectively in order to be recognised as a general principle. Some authors question whether the mere existence of a principle in the constitution or other municipal statutes would suffice.[69] They argue that these principles often do not correspond to the actual state practice and that

large majority of states recognising the general principle. Bassiouni, above n 49, at 812 described the main families as the (a) Romanist-civilist-Germanic systems; (b) common law systems; (c) Marxist-socialist systems; (d) Islamic systems and (e) Asian systems. He omitted the African systems from this listing. See Hailbronner, above n 61, at 208. He pointed to the difficulty of obtaining information about African and Asian customary law. At the same time, he submitted that these states have to a large extent taken over the legal systems of other countries. Therefore the relevance of the customary systems for the determination of general principles is reduced.

[64] See also Helmut Steinberger, "Comparative Jurisprudence and Judicial Protection of the Individual against the Executive: A Method for Ascertaining International Law?", in Herman Mosler *Judicial Protection against the Executive, vol III* 275 (Cologne, Carl Heymanns, 1971); Seidl-Hohenveldern, above n 54, at 255–56.

[65] Karl Zemanek, "Was kann die Vergleichung staatlichen öffentlichen Rechts für das Recht der internationalen Organisation leisten?", in 24 *Zeitschrift für ausländisches öffentliches Recht und Völkerrecht* 464 (1964).

[66] *Ibid*, at 465; see Steinberger, above n 64, at 269.

[67] Georg Ress, "Die Bedeutung der Rechtsvergleichung für das Recht internationaler Organisationen", in 36 *Zeitschrift für ausländisches öffentliches Recht und Völkerrecht* 236 fn 20 (1976). This can be a difficult test to pass. It is often easier to find commonalities, since for the negative test one has to operate more or less exhaustively.

[68] Hailbronner, above n 61, at 208–09. This would not include states that are deviating from a general rule due to special circumstances such as civil war. The international legal order builds on a normal situation and does not have to consider a state of emergency for the purposes of the recognition of a general principle. The same applies where the legal order has reached a certain level of development, but a certain group of people are excluded from legal protection due to racial, political or religious discrimination. The existence of the general principle of equality before the law, for example, would not be thwarted by an apartheid system. Cf Thirlway, above n 47, at 119.

[69] Bothe & Ress, above n 45, at 51.

states merely exercise constitutional or statutory lip-service to particular principles.[70] However, although a legal principle cannot be interpreted completely separately from its application, one should refrain from over-emphasising intra-state practice.

First, many aspects of international law are based on principles which are interpreted very differently by different states.[71] A typical example would be human rights, which are enforced and protected in different ways in the different countries that recognise them. Therefore the fact that a particular right is acknowledged in most legal orders is to be taken account of, and not that many countries do not effectively guarantee its exercise.[72] Similarly, general principles can develop which are broad enough to cover big differences in implementation in the national legal orders. Moreover, determining whether the principle is effectively enforced in all countries would be a virtually impossible task, which would render the whole comparative exercise meaningless.

Consequently the mere recognition of the principle is to be used as the starting point. Thereafter it has to be determined whether a core content can be deducted from the principle, despite its different manifestations in the different municipal orders. Ultimately this core content will be considered for transferral to the international order.[73]

3.1. Identifying the Transferable Elements of General Principles in Municipal Law

The identification of the core elements of a general principle is a difficult issue which requires caution. Comparatists and international judges have to be careful not to restrict themselves to notions peculiar to their own municipal law.[74] Moreover, they have to keep in mind that not every relation between states has its counterpart in municipal law. Mere parallelism of specific rules or principles in the municipal legal systems is not sufficient to establish their validity in international law. The municipal rules or principles must in addition be in conformity with the fundamental

---

[70] *Ibid.*

[71] Hailbronner, above n 61, at 210.

[72] *Ibid*, at 199. See also Rudolf Bernhardt, "Eigenheiten und Ziele der Rechtsvergleichung im öffentlichen Recht", 24 *Zeitschrift für ausländisches öffentliches Recht und Völkerrecht* 447 (1964). He took the principled approach according to which the formal recognition of the norm has to weigh more than actual incidents of non-compliance with it. Cf Elias & Lim, above n 52, at 37.

[73] See Hailbronner, above n 61, at 210.

[74] M Shahabuddeen, "Municipal law reasoning in international law", in Vaughan Lowe & Malgosia Fitzmaurice (eds), *Fifty years of the International Court of Justice. Essays in honor of Sir Robert Jennings* 92 (Cambridge, Cambridge University Press, 1996); Gutteridge, above n 55, at 127.

structure of international law as a system of legal coordination between states, other subjects such as international organisations, and (in limited instances) individuals.[75] There thus cannot be an unreserved transferral of municipal law into international law and the procedures of international courts, since the character of the rights and obligations are of another kind.[76]

Nevertheless, it is one thing to caution against the dangers of unbridled comparative analysis. It is something else to attempt, almost as a matter of ideological faith, to come to grips with international law notions rigidly divorced from a municipal conceptual framework, which in many instances influenced their formation.[77] The eventual structural differences in seemingly similar concepts in municipal and international law do not have to mean that the municipal idea is to be abandoned and the international concept left to be ascertained independently.[78] At the very least, the differences between the municipal law and international law concept can help to clarify the latter.[79]

Furthermore, the municipal law concept can still be transferred to the international level if correctly handled and rightly understood. The differences may call for adaptation, not necessarily for outright rejection.[80] The particular need or problem that exists in the international order is to be the starting point and the comparable legal institutions in domestic legal systems should be adapted to provide a functional solution, corresponding to the purpose and structure of the international order.[81] The international judges could thus use the substance of the municipal idea, whilst construing it with the modifications and exceptions required by the different international context. In this way they can benefit from the general guidance of the idea when searching for the appropriate rule governing the particular problem before them.[82]

---

[75] Bothe & Ress, above n 45, at 50. See also Thirlway, above n 47, at 113.

[76] Shahabuddeen, above n 74, at 93, 100; Jennings & Watts above n 42, at 37.

[77] Shahabuddeen, above n 74, at 102–03. See also Zemanek, above n 65, at 454. Many of the terms of international law are not autonomous but stem from other legal systems or disciplines. It is therefore inherent in international law that it would constantly be complemented by institutions and principles stemming from municipal law.

[78] Shahabuddeen, above n 74, at 101.

[79] *Ibid*, at 93.

[80] *Ibid*, at 99–100.

[81] Bothe & Ress, above n 45, at 57; Bernhardt (Eigenheiten und Ziele), above n 72, at 450 Cf Ress (Die Bedeutung der Rechtsvergleichung), above n 69, at 234 fn 13. Where an international organ can refer to a comparable regulation or concept in some of the member states, it adds to the weight of the decision of the international organ, even if the issue at hand would not yet qualify as a general principle of law. On the other hand, where a (foreseen) decision of the international organ does not have any parallel in the member states, this may discourage the organ from adopting the decision, since it is unclear how it will be received by the member states.

[82] Shahabuddeen, above n 74, at 102. Mosler (Encyclopedia), above n 42, at 517.

The common ground provided by a given legal principle can give only a very basic or general orientation.[83] In each national system the principle has become concrete by legislation or well-settled custom. Within certain legal families these details may more or less correspond. They hardly coincide, however, in all representative legal systems. The more one delves into detail, the more differences in the systems one will encounter. Therefore the principles can only be overtaken in a very general way and the specific concretisation that they underwent in the municipal orders is not necessarily transferable.[84] Stated differently, the values underpinned by the legal concept must be present in the legal systems of most member states, but the procedure which is used to realise this value may come from one or some of the systems.[85]

The question arises whether one can criticise this mere touching of the different legal systems for lack of thoroughness. Although this is a legitimate concern, one should beware of a too scientific or academic approach to comparative analysis. By becoming too detailed, there is a danger that the use of comparative analogies to develop international law would be severely limited, since the task would become unmanageable.[86] Also, one should keep in mind that international courts and tribunals are usually composed of judges representing the major legal systems. If they were to transfer a municipal principle into international law, their representative composition can give some assurance that such a principle is reconcilable with the major legal systems of the world.[87] The more agreement there is amongst judges concerning the existence of a general principle, the more weight it will carry.[88] On the other hand, the mere fact that there is a minority of judges in disagreement, would not be enough to deny

---

[83] Bothe, above n 50, at 287; Mosler (Encyclopedia), above n 42, at 517–18.

[84] Mosler (Festschrift für Verdross), above n 45, at 404; Bothe, above n 50, at 298.

[85] Zemanek, above n 65, at 463.

[86] Ress (Die Bedeutung der Rechtsvergleichung), above n 69, at 236. For a more cautious approach see Bothe & Ress, above n 45, at 53. Using the European Union as a starting point, they claimed that the different legal systems of the member states had much in common with respect to, inter alia, fundamental rights as far as the mere principles are concerned. There nonetheless remain considerable differences with respect to details. This would make it impossible to dispense with a more detailed examination of lawful restriction on these fundamental rights. If this proved to be true for the member states of the European Union, it would be surely true for any other group of states. A comparative study has to penetrate deeper in order to extract all relevant elements of the principle or right involved.

[87] Bothe, above n 50, at 287; Ress (Die Bedeutung der Rechtsvergleichung), above n 69, at 236–37 fn 23. In regional courts where all the countries are represented on the bench, one can assume that knowledge from all the legal systems flow into the decision. See also Michel Virally, "The Sources of International Law", in Mark Soerensen (ed), *Manual of Public International Law* 146 (London, Macmillan, 1968).

[88] At the ICJ a quorum of 9 judges is required to constitute the court. In theory a decision that a general principle exists could be taken by only 5 judges. However, it is unlikely that a decision carried by only a third of the judges would carry significant weight. See Van Hoof, above n 43, at 142 fn 580.

the existence of a general principle. They would have to offer convincing arguments as to why an alleged principle violates the fundamental concepts of a particular system of law. Only then could one conclude that the majority was wrong and that such a principle of law does not exist at all.[89]

International judges thus have the creative task of maintaining the essential features of the general principle while at the same time finding the appropriate solution for the international legal relation upon which they have to pass judgment.[90] They are not merely replacing the individual subjects of law between whom the municipal principle operates with the subjects of international law.[91] Through transfer of the norm they change the area of its application, and possibly also its content. The general principle is loosened from its municipal roots in order to be of use for the interpretation of a treaty or general international law. In the process it becomes an autonomous term of international law.[92] Moreover, it acquires a different meaning on the international plane than in a particular municipal context, even though its form may still resemble that of (a) certain legal system(s).[93]

3.2. The ICJ's Approach to General Principles of Law

The ICJ has resorted to general principles only sparingly, and has attempted to resolve the issue at hand by relying only on treaty or custom.[94] For example, in the *Right of Passage* case, it applied a custom which had

---

[89] Degan, above n 43, at 57. The scarcity of reference to general principles of law by the ICJ reflects a reluctance by judges to deal openly with possible disagreement on whether a general principle of law exists or not. The majority would rather abolish the line of reasoning and choose another motive to substantiate their arguments than force the issue.

[90] Brownlie, above n 42, at 16. Mosler (Encyclopedia), above n 45, at 518. It is only on rare occasions that a general principle exists which can be transferred to international law with the same characteristics and limitations as it possesses in national law. Also see the separate opinion of Judge McNair, *International Status of South West Africa*, Advisory Opinion, ICJ Rep 1950, at 148, who submitted that international law did not import the institutions of municipal law in a lock, stock and barrel, ready-made fashion. Rather, international tribunals should regard any features or terminology which are reminiscent of the rules and institutions of municipal law as an indication of policy and principles rather than as directly importing these rules and institutions. (He referred more pertinently to private municipal law, but one could make the argument applicable to municipal law in the broad sense). See also Shahabuddeen, above n 74, at 99; Mosler (Festschrift für Verdross), above n 45, at 411.

[91] As is suggested by Thirlway, above n 47, at 118.

[92] Mosler, (Festschrift für Verdross), above n 45, at 404–05, 411. See also Bothe, above n 50, at 298. The purpose of comparative law is not to take away the international court's responsibility of finding a suitable solution in a particular case, by providing it with ready made solutions. It can, however, assist the court by expanding the alternative solutions at hand.

[93] Zemanek, above n 65, at 463–64; Hailbronner, above n 61, at 199; Bothe & Ress, above n 45, at 56.

[94] For an overview of general principles as applied by the Permanent Court of International Justice (PCIJ), see Degan, above n 43, at 41–46.

only been developed between India and Portugal.[95] In that case the ICJ was asked to determine whether Portugal had a right of passage between its enclaves over Indian territory. Since it found that the Indian and Portuguese authorities had an established practice according to which consent for passage was required, it was not necessary to resort to general principles of law (as was requested by Portugal).[96]

In the cases in which the ICJ did resort to municipal law, it did not elaborate or give any detailed reasons. Instead it regarded the principles as self-evident and as directly relevant to the issue at hand.[97] For example, in the *Corfu Channel* case the majority decision simply stated that circumstantial evidence was admissible since it was allowed in all legal systems and its use was sanctioned by international courts.[98] In the *Effect of Awards* case it supported its conclusion that the General Assembly is capable of creating a tribunal competent to make decisions binding on itself by a matter-of-fact reference to municipal law.[99] The ICJ concluded that it is common practice in national legislatures to create courts with the capacity to render decisions legally binding on the legislatures which brought them into being.[100]

In the *Barcelona Traction* case the ICJ relied upon the municipal law concept of the limited liability company.[101] It stated that to do otherwise would invite serious legal difficulties, for there are no corresponding institutions of international law to which the ICJ could resort. The ICJ did not elaborate on the municipal law of a particular state, but referred generally to the rules accepted by municipal legal systems which recognise the idea of the limited company.[102] Also, in the *North Sea Continental Shelf* case the ICJ determined that the equity of its decision was inherent in the function of a court of law.[103] In order for it to come to this conclusion, the

[95] *Right of Passage Over Indian Territory (Port v India)*, Merits, ICJ Rep 1960, at 43. Bassiouni, above n 49, at 797.

[96] See also, Bassiouni, above n 49, at 798–99.

[97] Mosler (Festschrift für Verdross), above n 45, at 401; Bernhardt (Eigenheiten und Ziele), above n 72, at 447; Degan, above n 43, at 46. Bassiouni, above n 49, at 778 remarks that the PCIJ or ICJ did not apply the general principles in a way that significantly influenced the growth of new rules.

[98] *Corfu Channel (United Kingdom v Albania)*, Merits, ICJ Rep 1949, at 18; Mosler (Festschrift für Verdross), above n 45, at 401.

[99] *Effect of Awards of Compensation Made by the United Nations Administrative Tribunal*, Advisory Opinion, ICJ Rep 1954, at 61.

[100] *Ibid*, see also Shahabuddeen, above n 74, at 101.

[101] *Barcelona Traction, Light and Power Company, Limited (Belgium v Spain)*, second phase, ICJ Rep 1970, at 3.

[102] See also Malcom Shaw, *International Law* 87 (Cambridge, Cambridge University Press, 1997); Brownlie, above n 42, at 18. Thirlway, above n 47, at 126–27 criticised the transferral of the municipal concept of limited liability to the international level. The rights of shareholders would only exist in municipal law, and would not fit the pattern of relationships of the subjects of international law.

[103] ICJ Rep 1969, at para 88; Mosler (Festschrift für Verdross), above n 45, at 390.

ICJ must have been influenced, whether knowingly or unknowingly, by general notions in municipal law of the function of a court of law. It was a kind of unreflective comparative analysis which applied a principle that was generally accepted in the "collective legal sub-conscience".[104]

The ICJ also sometimes invoked the general principles in a negative sense, when it intended to prove the lack of an applicable general principle of law.[105] In the advisory opinion on the *Application of Judgement No 158 of the United Nations Administrative Tribunal*, for example, the ICJ stated that there was no general principle of law which requires that in review proceedings the interested parties should have an opportunity to submit oral statements to the review tribunal.[106] Although the general principles of law and the judicial character of the court would require that all parties have an equal chance to state the relevant elements to the review tribunal, this could also be done in written form.[107]

There are several reasons for the ICJ's reluctance to rely on general principles of international law. One may simply be that international judges are uncomfortable when dealing with fields of law which they are not familiar with—especially if they might be accused of dealing inaccurately with complicated matters of municipal law.[108] The cases in which the ICJ has to resort to general principles of law are also relatively few. Not only do international custom and treaty usually provide the answers, but the peculiarities of international law may make analogies with municipal law difficult.[109] Moreover, the fact that the international community is made up of more than 190 states also makes it quite cumbersome from a practical point of view to establish the existence of a general principle of law.[110]

---

[104] See Mosler (Festschrift für Verdross), above n 45, at 391.

[105] Degan, above n 43, at 41. However, in his separate opinion in the *North Sea Continental Shelf* case, above n 103, at 135 Judge Ammoun based his argument concerning the equitable delimitation of the continental shelf on the principle of equity found in the common law, Muslim law, Chinese law, Soviet law, Hindu law and the law of other African and Asian countries. See also Thirlway, above n 47, at 123.

[106] Advisory Opinion, ICJ Rep 1973, at 181.

[107] An unfortunate negative application of general principles of law occurred in *South West Africa* Judgment, Second Phase, ICJ Rep 1966, at 47, when it determined that the *actio popularis* was not a general principle of law. By concentrating on the non-existence of the general principle in municipal law the ICJ disregarded the clear language of Art 7 of the mandate relating to South-West Africa. The latter should have been determinative in deciding whether the claimants had a legal interest in the matter and this was indeed the view of the ICJ in the *South West Africa* Judgment, Preliminary Objections, ICJ Rep 1962, at 343. Discussed in Degan, above n 43, at 49–51.

[108] Mosler (Festschrift für Verdross), above n 45, at 409. Zemanek, above n 65, at 457.

[109] Mosler (Festschrift für Verdross), above n 45, at 410; Bernhardt (Eigenheiten und Ziele), above n 72, at 447; Lammers, above n 46, at 71.

[110] Van Hoof, above n 43, at 146.

Another factor relates to the voluntary jurisdiction of the ICJ and the fear that a too activist approach may lead states to withhold or withdraw acceptance of its jurisdiction with respect to future cases.[111] This concern would be closely connected to a deep-rooted fear that any explicit references to municipal law may come across as overtly political. After all, by illustrating the different alternatives to a particular problem through a comparative analysis of municipal law, the different underpinning policy issues are exposed as well. The task of the judge would thus have strong (or rather more overt) political undertones in such a case.[112] In order not to be accused of being overtly political or activist, international judges may prefer to make more discrete use of municipal law.

One could argue that such discreteness results in a lack of transparency that is counter-productive. It further undermines faith in an international judicial settlement procedure that already leaves much to be desired. A careful, informative and more open use of comparative analysis would render international judgments more plausible and convincing. It could illustrate that the court indeed attempted to take into consideration countries that are representative of all the major legal orders when deciding to transpose a particular municipal concept into international law.[113] The comparative law method has the merit of scientific verifiability and constitutes a proper defence against complaints of subjectivism in the determination of general principles of law.[114]

3.3.   The Significance of Municipal Analogies for International Organisations

The great majority of general principles of law which have been incorporated into international law are derived from private law and the law of civil procedure, such as the principle of good faith, *pacta sunt servanda, res judicata*, estoppel and unjustified enrichment.[115] This is mainly due to the fact that international law was initially limited to regulating relations between equal sovereign states, for which private law concepts (especially Roman law) proved to be the appropriate analogy.[116] Another reason would be that public law and administrative law in particular developed much later than private law. It also manifested itself very differently in the different legal systems. This lack of international homogeneity could

---

[111] *Ibid.*

[112] Bothe, above n 50, at 291; Cf Bernhardt (Eigenheiten und Ziele), above n 72, at 449.

[113] Bothe & Ress, above n 45, at 61

[114] Lammers, above n 46, at 62.

[115] Bothe & Ress, above n 45, at 51. See generally on this topic Hersch Lauterpacht, *Private Law Sources and Analogies of International Law* (Hambden, Conn, Archon, 1971).

[116] Zemanek, above n 65, at 454.

also explain why public law principles did not serve as a traditional source for public international law.[117]

However, in the last century the character of international law changed due to the development of international organisations. Especially since the end of World War II, most international organisations have developed a structure which is comparable to public law institutions in municipal law. Their constitutive documents show similarities with constitutions and their functions similarities with municipal administrations.[118] This is due to the fact that the normative content of a constitutive treaty of an international organisation and the secondary law produced by the organisation are characterised by a hierarchy of norms, comparable to that which exists between the state and individuals in municipal law.[119] This remains so despite the structural differences between an international organisation composed of states, and that of states which are made up of individuals.[120] Structural differences nonetheless are important for the extent to which comparisons can be drawn between the constitutive documents of an organisation and the constitutions of states. The more similar the structure of the legal concept or institution of the state(s) to that of the organisation, the more fruitful the comparison with national solutions can be.[121]

For example, the internal law of an international organisation is regarded as structurally closer to administrative municipal law than the "constitutional law" of an international organisation to that of municipal jurisdictions.[122] The administrative courts of international organisations can illustrate the point. Their main purpose is to interpret statutes relating to the relationship between the organisations and its civil servants. Since the questions that arose at the time had not been dealt with yet in international law, the tribunals have relied heavily on municipal law for exercising their functions.[123] Amongst others, the legal nature of the relationship

---

[117] *Ibid.*

[118] *Ibid*; Bothe & Ress, above n 45, at 55.

[119] Ress (Die Bedeutung der Rechtsvergleichung), above n 69, at 247, 249–50; Zemanek, above n 65, at 461.

[120] Shahabuddeen, above n 74, at 101; Bothe & Ress, above n 45, at 56; Guggenheim (Festschrift für Wehberg), above n 48, at 146–47. See Malanczuk, above n 42, at 49–50. But see Arangio-Ruiz, above n 6, at 20–21, who regarded the differences in the composition of international organisations and states, respectively, as an insurmountable barrier for the purposes of constitutional analogy.

[121] Bothe & Ress, above n 45, at 53. See also Ress (Die Bedeutung der Rechtsvergleichung), above n 69, at 278. He submitted that it was necessary to differentiate between those parts of the constitutive document which are consensual and those which are normative. Analogies with institutions of municipal public law would only be appropriate with respect to the normative elements.

[122] Hailbronner, above n 61, at 224. See Mosler (Encyclopedia), above n 45, at 521–22, who mentioned that the general principles developed in municipal administrative law have become increasingly important for the internal law of international organisations.

[123] Guggenheim (Festschrift für Wehberg), above n 48, at 143; Bernhardt (Eigenheiten und Ziele), above n 72, at 448.

between the civil servant and the organisation had to be determined. It was unclear whether it was a mere private law contract, or rights and obligations resulting from a one-sided administrative act of a statutory nature.[124] The solution of the Administrative Tribunal of the United Nations (UNAT) reflected the approach of French administrative law, according to which the relationship was partly a private law contract and partly a one-sided act of a statutory nature.[125]

Regional organisations which can restrict themselves to a comparison of the (relatively similar) legal systems of the members states may also come up with more similarities than organisations such as the United Nations, which are aimed at universal membership and have to take into account more diverse legal systems.[126] The reliance on municipal analogies in a regional organisation such as the European Union is also enhanced by its intention of integrating the member states by assuming more and more of their authority and by unifying their respective municipal law. This is not the aim of a more loose community such as the United Nations.[127] The intensity of the collaboration of the member states of an organisation can therefore have important implications for the extent to which principles of national constitutional and administrative law could be used to interpret and develop the law of an international organisation.[128]

The question which is of particular interest in the context of this chapter is whether these structural differences between municipal constitutions and the Charter as a constitutive document of an international organisation would prevent a comparative analysis in relation to judicial review by the ICJ on the one hand, and municipal courts on the other. In order to answer this question a closer look will now be taken at the constitutional character of the Charter.

4.   THE CONSTITUTIONAL CHARACTER OF THE CHARTER

The municipal constitution as we know it today is a concept invented by eighteenth and nineteenth century legal philosophy, in order to facilitate the

---

[124] Guggenheim (Festschrift für Wehberg), above n 48, at 143.

[125] *Ibid*, at 145. At the same time this analogy with the French system was never explicitly stated and the jurisprudence of the UNAT is not completely tailored to the administrative system of just one country. From this one can draw the conclusion that the UNAT does attempt to draw from principles that would be representative of the different legal systems of its members. See also Bothe & Ress, above n 45, at 56–57; Ress (Die Bedeutung der Rechtsvergleichung), above n 69, at 261. See generally Chittharanjan F Amerasinghe, *Principles of the institutional law of international organizations* (Cambridge, Cambridge University Press, 1996).

[126] Ress (Die Bedeutung der Rechtsvergleichung), above n 69, at 230.

[127] Zemanek, above n 65, at 459. Bothe & Ress, above n 45, at 53.

[128] Ress (Die Bedeutung der Rechtsvergleichung), above n 69, at 230.

transition from feudalism to liberalism. Written constitutions were favoured as a means of limiting state intrusion on private rights and liberties and of ensuring political participation of citizens.[129] Although this concept of constitutionalism initially stems from Western legal and political thought, it can no longer be said to be confined to those cultures. This is reflected by, inter alia, the universal recognition of fundamental human rights as well as the increasingly widespread recognition of the importance of democracy in non-western cultures.[130] For their part, non-western cultures have contributed to modern constitutionalism by promoting the constitutional protection of economic, social and cultural rights and the fight against colonialism and racism.

All this points to a growing stock of common constitutional values that is more substantial than sometimes believed—notwithstanding special features responding to particular historical or political conditions.[131] Most municipal constitutions today provide a legal framework for the political life of a community for an indefinite time.[132] They present a complex of fundamental norms governing the organisation and performance of governmental functions in a given state and the relationship between state authorities and citizens.[133]

As far as international law is concerned, the notion of a constitution has been introduced to distinguish treaties establishing an institution from other international agreements. The Charter in this sense is synonymous for what Article 5 of the Vienna Convention on the Law of Treaties of 1969[134] calls a constituent document.[135] On the one hand, this terminology does not change the generally accepted notion that the Charter is an international treaty and that one is not dealing with a super-state or world government.[136] On the other hand, it does illustrate that the Charter is a very special treaty that has normative character as a result of which it has

---

[129] Fassbender, above n 4, at 553.

[130] *Ibid*, at 553–54; Christian Tomuschat, "Obligations Arising for States without or against their Will", *Recueil des Cours de l'académie de droit international de la Haye* 235 (1993 IV); Thomas M Franck, "The Emerging Right to Democratic Governance", 86 *American Journal of International Law* 46 ff (1992).

[131] Fassbender, above n 4, at 553–54. The new constitution in post-apartheid South Africa, for example, demonstrates a profound belief in a constitution as an instrument of organising government and which secures freedom for individuals and communities. President Thabo Mbeki (quoted in Fassbender) emphasised the African character of this constitution and described it as a creation of African hands and African minds.

[132] Fassbender, above n 4, at 536.

[133] *Ibid*, at 534.

[134] Reprinted in 8 *International Legal Materials* 679 ff (1969). Hereinafter referred to as the Vienna Convention.

[135] *Ibid*, at 538.

[136] Lorinser, above n 4, at 85; Sloan, above n 4, at 81. See the *Certain Expenses of the United Nations*, Advisory Opinion, ICJ Rep 1962, at 157. Hereinafter referred to as *Certain Expenses* opinion.

evolved beyond a mere treaty.[137] The question that now has to be answered is to what extent this normative character would correspond to the core elements of municipal constitutions. In the following passages the characteristics which are arguably the most typical of municipal constitutions will be illuminated. These include their normative character, their supremacy and inclusivity, their dynamic nature and their protection of the separation of powers.

4.1. The Charter as a Normative Framework

It is fair to say that states, as the main actors in the field of international politics, have never come consciously together to establish a constitution regulating the international public order and setting forth the guiding principles for the main functions of international governance.[138] However, over time the idea of a legal framework determining certain common values and principles for the international community developed. The Charter constitutes a definitive moment in this process in that it created the United Nations that represents the international community.[139] The Charter defines the structure of the organisation (and in that sense of the community), sets forth the powers and function of its organs and the rights and duties of its members. It provides states with binding values and aims, as well as procedures for interaction.[140]

These are mainly to be found in Articles 1 and 2 of the Charter. They concern the maintenance of peace and security along with the prohibition of the use of force;[141] the peaceful settlement of disputes;[142] equal rights and self-determination of peoples;[143] the principle of cooperation

---

[137] Lorinser, above n 4, at 85; Verdross & Simma, above n 55, at 77–78. See also Shabtai Rosenne, *Developments in the law of treaties 1945–1986* 194 (Cambridge, Cambridge University Press, 1989).

[138] Tomuschat (Obligations), above n 130, at 219.

[139] *Ibid*, at 236; Fassbender, above n 4, at 573.

[140] Daniel Thürer, "Internationales 'Rule of Law'—innerstaatliche Demokratie", *Schweizerische Zeitschrift für Internationales and Europäisches Recht* 457(1995); Sloan, above n 4, at 62, 116. See also Lorinser, above n 4, at 87 who stated that the Charter, like a national constitution, expresses a political compromise that reflects a basic consensus between the different groups of power. Cf Pierre-Marie Dupuy, "The Constitutional Dimension of the Charter of the United Nations Revisited", 1 *Max Planck Yearbook of International Law* 3 (1997). He distinguished between substantial and institutional aspects of the constitutions. The former relates to the rules and values to be promoted, whereas the latter points to the designation of public organs, the separation of powers and the different institutions which are endowed with competencies. He acknowledged that the substantial and institutional aspects are intertwined, since the institutional instrument is necessary for the promotion of the first.

[141] Art 1(1) and Art 2(4).

[142] Art 1(1), Art 2(3) and Art 33.

[143] Art 1(2).

(which extends to every field of international problems, in particular those concerned with an economic, social, cultural or humanitarian character);[144] the promotion of respect for human rights and for fundamental freedoms without any form of discrimination;[145] and the respect for the sovereign equality of all states.[146] These norms, which are formulated in the broad manner which is typical of a constitution, have derived their content from the activities of the principal organs of the organisation. One example is the Declaration on Principles of International Law concerning Friendly Relations and Cooperation among States (Friendly Relations Declaration).[147]

Although the Charter is the major point of reference for the rights and obligations of the international community, it does not contain all normative elements that form part of the constitutional order.[148] It is supplemented by *ius cogens*, ie peremptory norms of general international law which are accepted by the international community of states as a whole from which no derogation is permitted, and which can be modified only by a subsequent norm of general international law having the same character.[149] At the same time there is a partial overlap between *ius cogens* and certain Charter norms.[150] In some cases a principle may have developed to a peremptory norm due to its inclusion in the Charter, such as the prohibition of the use of force.[151] In other cases a norm affirmed by the Charter may have already existed as a peremptory norm of international law before its enunciation in the Charter. This would be the case with the right to self-defence, or the sovereign equality of states.[152]

This observation does not undermine the potential constitutional character of the Charter. It demonstrates that its founders had intended to reiterate and summarise in one fundamental text the basic principles which had already served as the cornerstone of interstate relations. At the same time they wanted to add to these principles some new ones,

---

[144] Art 1(3).

[145] *Ibid*. This reference to human rights is complemented by Art 55 and Art 56 of the Charter which affirm the universal respect for and observance of human rights and fundamental freedoms for all without distinction as to race, sex, language or religion.

[146] Art 2(1); see Dupuy, above n 140, at 6.

[147] GA Res 2625 (XXV) of 24 October 1970; see also Dupuy, above n 140, at 31; Fassbender, above n 4, at 573. Cf Ronald St J Macdonald, "The Charter of the United Nations in Constitutional Perspective", in 20 *Australian Yearbook of International Law* 214–15 (1999).

[148] Dupuy, above n 140, at 31.

[149] Art 53 of the Vienna Convention, above n 134; see also Jochen A Frowein, "Ius Cogens", III *Encyclopedia of Public International Law* 66 (1995); Fassbender, above n 4, at 589.

[150] Dupuy, above n 140, at 7; Fassbender, above n 4, at 589.

[151] See Frowein (*Ius Cogens*), above n 149, at 67, who stated that it is generally recognised that the prohibition of the use of force has the character of *ius cogens*.

[152] Dupuy, above n 140, at 7. *Military and Paramilitary Activities in and Against Nicaragua (Nicaragua v United States of America)*, Merits, ICJ Rep 1986, at 95, 102. Hereinafter referred to as *Nicaragua v United States*, merits.

aimed at reinforcing and enhancing the former.[153] A similar development can occur in municipal constitutional law, where some rights and duties have been recognised in a particular legal system long before they are actually concretised in the constitution.

Similarly, the fact that a customary rule can become peremptory without being explicitly enunciated in the Charter, would not undermine the constitutional character of the Charter either. In municipal law the content of the constitutional order is not necessarily limited to a written document.[154] Even though most countries attempt to arrange their constitution in a single written document, a constitution can grow contingently, as it is moulded by the manifold political and historical forces at work within the community whose fundamental order it determines.[155] In the process new, unwritten norms appear which are inter-linked with those already codified in the written text.

In the international constitutional order the rule of non-intervention in the internal affairs of a sovereign state seemed to have developed to such an "uncodified" peremptory norm. In the case concerning the *Military and Paramilitary Activities in and against Nicaragua*,[156] the ICJ did not explicitly qualify the rule as a peremptory norm. Nevertheless, it insisted on its "paramount importance" for the promotion of peaceful international relations which reflects its peremptory nature. Even though the rule of non-intervention is not spelt out in the Charter, it is linked to it, in that it is directly derived from the principle of the sovereign equality of states.[157] The same conclusion could be drawn with regard to other norms which are usually categorised as *ius cogens*, without being explicitly mentioned in the Charter. Examples in the field of human rights would include the prohibition of slavery and genocide. These norms can be derived from the logical implications of the generic rules established in the Charter, which provide the ethical and legal matrix for all peremptory norms.[158]

---

[153] Dupuy, above n 140, at 8.
[154] Tomuschat (Obligations), above n 130, at 217–18.
[155] *Ibid.* The rules on government in the United Kingdom constitute the prime example of a constitution whose relevant components cannot be found in a single document.
[156] Above n 118, at 100; Dupuy, above n 140, at 8–9.
[157] Dupuy, above n 140, at 9–10. The ICJ proceeded in a similar way in *United States Diplomatic and Consular Staff in Tehran (United States of America v Iran)*, Judgment, ICJ Rep 1980, at 3. Hereinafter referred to as *United States v Iran*. The emphatic way in which it stressed the importance of the obligation of states to respect the diplomatic and consular immunities attached to the representatives of foreign countries, suggest peremptory character. Although the respect for diplomatic immunity is not mentioned in the Charter, it can also be linked with the principle of equality of sovereign states. Cf Vera Gowlland-Debbas, "Security Council Enforcement Actions and Issues of State Responsibility", 43 *International and Comparative Law Quarterly* 69 (1994).
[158] Dupuy, above n 140, at 10–11, 31.

Such a constitutional outlook on the Charter and other peremptory norms offers a coherent explanation of current developments in international law by emphasising the growing interests of the international community as a whole over those of individual states.[159] This opens up the international community to a new collective sub-conscience which mobilises the potential of collective action and development.[160]

4.2.   Supremacy and Inclusivity of a Constitution

In municipal law a constitution is of paramount importance for every member of the social community ruled by it.[161] It binds all state organs and members of the society and implies a hierarchy of norms, at the top of which are the legal principles belonging to the constitution.[162] Due to the almost universal membership of the United Nations and the fact that its basic principles have also been accepted by the few non-members,[163] the normative framework enshrined in the Charter constitutes the constitution of the international legal order.[164]

Whether this constitutional character would extend beyond the Charter's fundamental *normative* principles to include the *enforcement* system under Chapter VII of the Charter, is debatable. On the one hand, the Security Council has been addressing its resolutions under Chapter VII to "all states" for more than 20 years. As this practice has silently been accepted by states, it could be interpreted as evidence of the customary nature of Chapter VII.[165] One could also argue that non-members would enjoy an unfair advantage over member-states if they were not subjected

---

[159] Fassbender, above n 4, at 553.

[160] See Thürer, above n 140, at 457–58. Within this new perspective of the international constitutional community new fields of activity arise whilst traditional state communities lose (some of their) significance. Also, classic concepts such as state sovereignty and state develop a new meaning and may even become obsolete in the long run. This fact seems to be over-looked by Arangio-Ruiz, above n 6, at 4, when stating that state sovereignty and domestic jurisdiction are expressly reserved by Art 2(7) of the Charter. As a result, he did not recognise the constitutional character of the Charter.

[161] Thomas M Franck, "The Political and the Judicial Empires: Must there be a Conflict over Conflict-Resolution?", in Najeeb Al-Naumi & Richard Meese, *International Legal Issues Arising under the United Nations Decade of International Law* 627 (1995); Dupuy, above n 140, at 28; Sloan, above n 4, at 117.

[162] Dupuy, above n 140, at 3; Fassbender, above n 4, at 581.

[163] The only countries that are not members of the UN are the Holy See (Vatican City State) and Taiwan. See www.un.org; Fassbender, above n 4, at 567.

[164] For example, after the invasion of Kuwait by Iraq, the Swiss Federal Council explicitly stated that Art 2(4) of the Charter is a norm of customary international law. See 1 *Schweizerische Zeitschrift für Internationales und Europäisches Recht* 561 (1991). See also Verdross & Simma, above n 55, at 72; Fassbender, above n 4, at 542.

[165] Bardo Fassbender, *UN Security Council Reform and the Right of Veto. A Constitutional Perspective* 130 (The Hague, Kluwer, 1998). At 109 he also submits that it is not possible to separate the basic principles (ie normative element) of the Charter from the machinery

to Chapter VII, as they would profit from the security system provided by the Charter, without having to fulfil any obligations in return.[166] Such an inequality would not be reconcilable with the principle of the sovereign equality of states, which is enshrined in Article 2(1) of the Charter.[167]

On the other hand, one could refute this statement on the basis that the protection offered by the Charter system to non-members is limited. It does not include an undertaking to come to their defence, for example, in the case of an armed attack. Thus, as the protection provided by the Charter does not include any obligation on members to instrumentalise Chapter VII in favour of a non-member state, their cannot be any legal claim on non-members to subject themselves to Chapter VII in return.

Moreover, the sovereign equality argument seems to beg the question, since it does not explain convincingly why this particular interpretation of sovereign equality has to be binding on non-member states. It imposes an interpretation of Article 2(1) on non-member states which is in direct contrast with the practice of former non-member states like the Federal Republic of Germany and Switzerland.[168] These states have continuously indicated that their decision to abide by Chapter VII decisions of the Security Council was purely on a voluntary basis and that they were not under any legal obligation to do so.[169] They were thus not willing to regard Chapter VII of the Charter as an exception to the principle of *pacta tertiis nec nocent nec prosunt*, according to which a treaty does not create obligations or rights for a third state without its consent.[170]

created for their implementation. By accepting the basic principles, non-members tacitly accepted the whole instrument. See also Christian Tomuschat, "Yugoslavia's Damaged Sovereignty over the Province of Kosovo", in GPH Kreijen *et al* (eds), *State, Sovereignty and International Governance* 336 (Oxford, Oxford University Press, forthcoming 2002).

[166] Note that Art 2(4) of the Charter also protects non-member states, in that member states are forbidden to use force against "any state". Art 2(4) reads as follows: "All Members shall refrain in their international relations from the threat or use of force against the territorial integrity or political independence of any state, or in any other manner inconsistent with the Purposes of the United Nations". See Verdross & Simma, above n 55, at 177.

[167] Fassbender (UN Security Council Reform), above n 165, at 111 ff.

[168] Before joining the United Nations in 1973 and 2002, respectively.

[169] Andreas Zimmermann & Carsten Stahn, "Yugoslav Territory, United Nations Trusteeship or Sovereign State? Reflections on the current and future legal status of Kosovo", 70 *Nordic Journal of International Law* 440 (2001). For the position of Germany before its admission to the United Nations, see U Beyerlin & W Strasser, "Völkerrechtliche Praxis der Bundesrepublik Deutschland im Jahre 1973", 35 *Zeitschrift für ausländisches öffentliches Recht und Völkerrecht* 806 (1975). See also Swiss Federal Council, above n 164, at 561–62. See also Mathias-Charles Krafft *et al*, "Chapter on Switzerland", in Vera Gowlland-Debbas (ed), *National Implementation of Non-Military Security Council Sanctions: A Comparative Study* 435 ff (Leiden, Martinus Nijhoff, forthcoming).

[170] Art 34 of the Vienna Convention, above n 134; see also Zimmermann & Stahn, above n 169, at 440.

Finally, one also has to keep in mind that Article 2(6) merely requires the organisation to ensure that non-members states act in accordance with the principles contained in Article 2(1) to 2(5) of the Charter.[171] It does not require members to ensure that non-members also subject themselves to the enforcement system provided for in Chapter VII.[172] In essence, therefore, it seems more accurate to limit the supremacy of the Charter vis-a-vis the international community to the fundamental principles embodied by it, than to extend it to the Chapter VII enforcement system as well.[173]

As far as the supremacy of normative principles is concerned, it seems logical that norms of such fundamental importance such as *ius cogens* would also apply to the international community as a whole.[174] This was indeed confirmed by the ICJ in the *Barcelona Traction* case, where it stated that there are obligations of a state towards the international community as a whole (*erga omnes*), which are the concern of all states and for whose protection all states have a legal interest.[175] Without expressly referring to *ius cogens* in this context, the ICJ implied it when mentioning examples of norms with *erga omnes* effect, namely the outlawing of aggression and genocide, and the principles concerning the basic rights of the human person, including protection from slavery and racial discrimination.[176] It could therefore be concluded that a norm from which no derogation is permitted because of its fundamental nature will normally be applicable *erga omnes*, ie all members of the legal community.[177]

As far as the supremacy of the international constitutional order is concerned, Article 103 of the Charter makes obligations under the Charter superior to every other treaty obligation that states may have incurred. Therefore, member states would have to respect binding decisions of organs of the United Nations which were adopted in accordance with the Charter, and which impose obligations on states that deviate

---

[171] Art 2(6) of the Charter reads as follows: "The Organization shall ensure that states which are not Members of the United Nations act in accordance with *these Principles* (emphasis added) so far as may be necessary for the maintenance of international peace and security."

[172] Zimmermann & Stahn, above n 169, at 440. For a different interpretation of Art 2(6), see Fassbender (UN Security Council Reform), above n 165, at 113; Verdross & Simma, above n 55, at 177.

[173] This matter is taken up again in ch 5, at s 1.

[174] See also Jochen A Frowein, "Obligations *Erga Omnes*", III *Encyclopedia of International Law* 757 (1995).

[175] *Barcelona Traction* case, above note 101 at 32. Frowein, (Obligations *Erga Omnes*), above n 174, at 757; Tomuschat (Obligations), above n 130, at 195.

[176] *Barcelona Traction* case, above n 101, at 32; Jochen A Frowein, "Collective Enforcement of International Obligations", 47 *Zeitschrift für Ausländisches Öffentliches Recht und Völkerrecht* 71 (1987).

[177] Frowein (Obligations *Erga Omnes*), above n 174, at 757.

from obligations incurred by a treaty.[178] It is also clear that member states cannot ratify treaties that violate *ius cogens*. Therefore obligations arising under the Charter, as well as (other) norms of *ius cogens* would pose limits to treaty law.[179]

The question arises whether there could be a conflict between the norms contained in the Charter and *ius cogens*, and if so, which law would prevail. Although the Charter is silent about the relationship between itself and customary international law, it seems logical that Charter norms will be in accordance with *ius cogens* norms. The main reason relates to the concept of the Charter as a matrix that links all past and future peremptory norms, as discussed above. At the time that the Charter was designed it served as comprehensive updating of previously established customs. Since it would also inspire future customary and peremptory norms, these rules would never be substantially incompatible with the norms established in the Charter.[180]

4.3. The Dynamic and Evolutionary Nature of the Charter

Like a national constitution, the Charter was intended to endure for succeeding generations, surviving times of political and social turbulence.[181] As a result it had to be framed in terms sufficiently open and flexible to allow for dynamic evolution through interpretation. In this way it can keep up with the community whose life it governs.[182] Like the constitutions of states, the Charter has been subjected to substantial social changes in the world since the days of its negotiation in San Francisco.[183]

---

[178] See Libya *v* United States, above n 7 at 3 ff. See also Gowlland-Debbas (State Responsibility), above n 157, at 88. She stated that this hierarchy among treaties and the predominance of Charter obligations reflected the constitutional character of the Charter. Cf Heribert F Köck, "UN-Satzung und allgemeines Völkerrecht—Zum exemplarischen Charakter von Art 103 SVN", in Konrad Ginther *et al* (eds), *Völkerrecht zwischen normativem Anspruch und politischer Realität. Festschrift für Karl Zemanek zum 65. Geburtstag* 69 ff (Berlin, Duncker & Humblot, 1994).

[179] Art 53 of the Vienna Convention, above n 134; see Geoffrey S Watson, "Constitutionalism, Judicial Review, and the World Court", 34 *Harvard International Law Journal* 37 (1993).

[180] Dupuy, above n 140, at 14; Watson, above n 179, at 37. Cf Georg Schwarzenberger, "The Problem of International Constitutional Law in International Judicial Perspective", in Jost Delbrück (ed), *Recht im Dienst des Friedens. Festschrift für Eberhard Menzel zum 65. Geburtstag am 21 Januar 1976* 249 (Berlin, Duncker & Humblot, 1975). He regarded the 7 principles formulated in Art 2 of the Charter as the consensual *ius cogens* of the United Nations.

[181] For arguments by the American Supreme Court to the effect that a constitution is intended to endure for ages to come, see *McCulloch v Maryland* 17 US (4 Wheat) 316 (1819); *Bell v Maryland*, 378 US 226, 315 (1964); *Martin v Hunter's Lessee* 14 US (1 Wheat) 304, 326 (1816). See also Sloan, above n 4, at 71.

[182] Sloan, above n 4, at 117; Tomuschat (Obligations), above n 130, at 251. Member states submit to a system which is in constant movement, not unlike a national constitution whose original texture will be unavoidably modified by thick layers of political practice and jurisprudence.

[183] BN Merish, "*Travaux Préparatoires* as an Element in the Interpretation of the Treaties", 11 *Indian Journal of International Law* 54 (1971).

The dynamic nature of the Charter in combination with its normative character makes it necessary to subject it to rules of interpretation comparable to those generally applying to municipal constitutions.[184] However, since the Charter is also a treaty, the question arises whether such a dynamic approach would be compatible with the Vienna Convention on the Law of Treaties of 1969. According to Article 5 of the Vienna Convention, it applies to the constitutive documents of international organisations. Although Article 4 of the Vienna Convention determines that the convention only applies to treaties concluded after its entry into force, the passages on interpretation contained in Articles 31 to 33 reflect customary international law.[185] Therefore the interpretation of the Charter will primarily be ascertained on the basis of the ordinary meaning of the terms, the context in which the they are used, as well as the object and purpose of the treaty.[186]

The fact that there is no hierarchy between these principles and that they are defined in abstract terms allows for the peculiarities of each treaty to be taken into account for the purposes of their interpretation.[187] With respect to the Charter, the object and purpose of the treaty as a criteria for interpretation opens the door for a dynamic interpretation.[188] Furthermore, Article 5 contains a qualification that justifies the treating of the Charter as a constitution. It states that the Vienna Convention is applicable to constituent instruments of international organisations, "without prejudice to any relevant rules of the organization". If this qualification also reflects customary international law (and would therefore be applicable to treaties concluded before its adoption), it would also strengthen a more constitutional-like interpretation of the Charter.[189]

The ICJ acknowledged the dynamic nature of the Charter early on and developed a functional method of interpretation which resembles the concept of implied powers in American constitutional interpretation, and the

---

[184] Lorinser, above n 4, at 85–86; Fraas, above n 6, at 13. According to Ress (Die Bedeutung der Rechtsvergleichung), above n 69, at 246, the constitutive document as well as the secondary (internal) law of the organisation are subjected to constitutional rules of interpretation. See also Zemanek, above n 65, at 455–56.

[185] Fassbender, above n 4, at 546; Rosenne, above n 137, at 256; Sloan, above n 4, at 61; Georg Ress, "The Interpretation of the Charter", in Bruno Simma (ed), *The Charter of the United Nations*, 30 (Oxford, Oxford University Press, 1995). See also the *Legality of the Use by a State of Nuclear Weapons in Armed Conflict*, Advisory Opinion, ICJ Rep 1996, at 75.

[186] This general rule of interpretation is contained in Art 31 of the Vienna Convention, above n 134. See Bernhardt (Encyclopedia), above n 72, at 324; Fraas, above n 6, at 13; Herbst, above n 6, at 83; Pollux, "The Interpretation of the Charter", 23 *British Yearbook of International Law* 67 (1946); Sloan, above n 4, at 115.

[187] See Ress (in Simma), above n 185, at 36; Bernhardt (Encyclopedia), above n 72, at 324; Herbst, above n 6, at 87, 83.

[188] Sloan, above n 4, at 119; see also Ress (in Simma), above n 185, at 35.

[189] Sloan, above n 4, at 116 .

teleological method in continental Europe.[190] It focused on the function of the relevant Charter provision in the context of the constituent instrument as a whole.[191] As a consequence the purpose of the organisation became decisive for the interpretation of the Charter.[192] Relatively recently, in the advisory opinion requested by the World Health Organization (WHO) on the *Legality of the Use by a State of Nuclear Weapons in Armed Conflict*,[193] the ICJ reaffirmed the dual nature (ie conventional versus normative) of constitutive documents of international organisations. It stressed that the organisation's very nature, its objectives and practice are all elements which deserve special attention during interpretation.[194] This emphasis on the elements representing the dynamic character of the Charter reaffirmed its capacity to evolve and endure over time.

The dynamic nature of the Charter is also reflected in the fact that the practice of organs of the United Nations, which tends to be evolutionary in itself, is an independent criteria for Charter interpretation.[195] This results from the fact that in the day to day functioning of the organisation, each organ is primarily responsible for interpreting its own functions as outlined in the Charter.[196] The principle of efficiency and the need for a

---

[190] Ress (Die Bedeutung der Rechtsvergleichung), above n 69, at 246; See in particular *Reparation for Injuries Suffered in the Service of the United Nations*, Advisory Opinion, ICJ Rep 1949, at 174–88; *Certain Expenses* opinion, above n 136, at 151–80. For later examples, see *Effect of Awards* opinion, above n 99, at 57, *Legal Consequence for States of the Continued Presence of South Africa in Namibia (South West Africa) Notwithstanding Security Council Resolution 276 (1970)*, Advisory Opinion, ICJ Rep 1972, at 31 (hereinafter the *Namibia* opinion); *Western Sahara*, Advisory Opinion, ICJ Rep 1975, at 32.

[191] Rosenne, above n 137, at 237; Sloan, above n 4, at 65–66; see also Fraas, above n 6, at 13 who referred to an *effet utile*. See also Ress (in Simma), above n 185, at 42.

[192] Ress (Die Bedeutung der Rechtsvergleichung), above n 69, at 246–47; Rosenne, above n 137, at 237. This also means that the importance of the intention of the original members as reflected in the *travaux préparatoires* is diminished. See also Fassbender, above n 4, at 595, who argues that a constitution typically emancipates itself from the forces that brought it about. An interpretation based on the original will of the parties would unduly subject the present and the future to whatever a bygone generation declared to be the law, and this would impede the solution of contemporary problems. But see Pollux, above n 186, at 74. To deny that the initial interpretation of the five permanent members of the Security Council is binding on everyone, is a denial of political reality, since any of the permanent members could prevent any modification of their interpretation by the veto.

[193] ICJ Rep 1996, at 75–76.

[194] Herbst, above n 6, at 81–82 saw this as a rejection of an unlimited application of the Vienna Convention, above n 134, to constitutive treaties of international organisations.

[195] See Rudolf Bernhardt, "Interpretation in International Law", 1 *Encyclopedia of Public International Law* 323 (1994); Herbst, above n 6, at 314.

[196] Herbst, above n 6, at 314; Pollux, above n 186, at 57. See also Michael C Wood, "The Interpretation of Security Council Resolutions", in 2 *Max Planck Yearbook of United Nations Law* 82 (1998). Subsidiary organs of the Security Council often need to interpret particular Security Council resolutions in carrying out their functions. These would include, inter alia, the International Criminal Tribunals for former Yugoslavia and Rwanda and the Sanctions Committees. The decisions of these subsidiary organs are binding to the extent provided for in the relevant Security Council resolution. Moreover, even if this is not explicitly provided for, they would still be highly persuasive.

realistic interpretation of the Charter thus elevates the practice of organs to an important point of departure during Charter interpretation.[197] This also seems to be the tenor of the *Namibia* opinion where the ICJ held that an organ's practice can be used to interpret the obligations in the Charter, where it was generally accepted by the members of the United Nations.[198]

The reference to general acceptance would imply that an organ's practice is not a valid criteria for Charter interpretation if it does not enjoy general support.[199] At first glance this requirement seems like a difficult barrier to overcome for a non-representative organ such as the Security Council.[200] However, in practice the threshold determining that consensus has been reached is not so high. In the *Namibia* opinion the ICJ accepted the Security Council's interpretation of Article 27(3), whereby the withholding of a vote by a permanent member is regarded as a concurring vote. Although this interpretation did not strictly correspond to the wording of the article,[201] the ICJ declared that it has consistently been followed by the Security Council and has been accepted by states in practice.[202] It further stated that South Africa, in particular, had never

---

[197] Heike Gading, *Der Schutz grundlegender Menschenrechte durch militärische Massnahmen des Sicherheitsrates—das Ende staatlicher Souveränität?* 92–93 (Berlin, Duncker & Humblot, 1996). Martin Lailach, *Die Wahrung des Weltfriedens und der internationalen Sicherheit als Aufgabe des Sicherheitsrates der Vereinten Nationen* 162 (Berlin, Duncker & Humblot, 1998).

[198] *Namibia* opinion above n 190, at 22. That such acceptance can indeed serve as a consensus amongst states in terms of Art 31(3)(b) of the Vienna Convention, above n 134, is also submitted by Matthias J Herdegen, *Die Befugnisse des UN-Sicherheitsrates: aufgeklärter Absolitismus im Völkerrecht?* 112 (Heidelberg, Müller, 1998). See also Jochen A Frowein, "The Internal and External Effects of Resolutions by International Organizations", 49 *Zeitschrift für ausländisches öffentliches Recht und Völkerrecht* 790 (1989).

[199] See also Herbst, above n 6, at 314; Lailach, above n 197, at 38. The Friendly Relations Declaration, above n 113, which was adopted without a vote, is one example where General Assembly practice was regarded as a criteria for interpreting the Charter. In *Nicaragua v United States*, merits, above n 152, at 102–03, the ICJ relied on the Friendly Relations Declaration to make a distinction between the most grave forms of the use of force that constitute an armed attack or aggression and less grave forms, such as acts of reprisal involving the use of force, and several other activities listed in the Declaration. See also Louis B Sohn, "The UN System as Authoritative Interpreter of its Law", in Oscar Schachter & Christopher C Joyner (eds), *United Nations Legal Order vol I* 177, 179 (Cambridge, Cambridge University Press, 1995).

[200] See Herdegen, above n 198, at 113. He stated that the more the interpretation of the Security Council deviates from the wording of the Charter or a generally accepted interpretation by member states, the more important the acceptance of the Security Council's practice by the other principal organs of the United Nations and members states will become. See also Gading, above n 197, at 54; Georg Nolte, "The Limits of the Security Council's Powers and its Functions in the International Legal System: Some Reflections", in Michael Byers (ed), *The Role of Law in International Politics* 325 (Oxford, Oxford University Press, 2000). See also Andreas Stein, above n 38, at 70 ff.

[201] Art 27(3) of the Charter reads as follows: "Decisions of the Security Council on all other matters shall be made by an affirmative vote of nine members including the concurring votes of the permanent members...".

[202] *Namibia* opinion, above n 190, at 22; Herbst, above n 6, at 304–05; Lorinser, above n 4, at 45; Sohn, above n 199, at 194; Stein, above n 38, at 97 ff.

before objected to this voting procedure and could therefore not now question its validity.[203]

This indicates that the onus would rest on states to voice their objection to a particular practice at an early stage in order not to be prevented from doing so by the principle of estoppel or acquiescence.[204] It would therefore not be convincing to argue that the Security Council's practice would only gain general acceptability where it is explicitly sanctioned by the General Assembly, which is representative of all the members of the United Nations.[205] This should not be understood as meaning that the practice of an organ is the only point of reference for interpreting its powers, since the Charter does not grant the Security Council the right of authentic (exclusive) interpretation of its powers.[206] Relying only on the practice of the organ could also result in a circular argument, where the practice of the organ is used as a method of interpretation, whilst at the same time the interpretation is used to determine whether the organ has remained within its competence.[207] Even so, the important point to be illustrated here is that the value of the practice of United Nations organs in the course of Charter interpretation underscores the latter's dynamic nature.

4.3.1.   *Charter Evolution and the Travaux Préparatoires*

A question that arises is what effect the Charter's capacity for evolutionary and dynamic interpretation would have on the importance of its

---

[203] *Namibia* opinion, above n 190, at 22–23; see also Herbst, above n 6, at 314.

[204] See Herbst, above n 6, at 313. But see Lorinser, above n 4, at 44, who claimed that there was disagreement as to the extent to which the Security Council interpretation had to be accepted by the members, since it was not clear what "generally acceptable" meant. See also Stein, above n 38, at 108–10 for a more cautious approach.

[205] General Assembly resolutions which expressed support for Security Council decisions include GA Res 46 of 25 August 1992 on Bosnia-Herzegovina, and GA Res 47 of 18 December 1992 on Somalia. The former resolution was adopted 2 weeks after the adoption of SC Res 770 of 13 August 1992 and urged the Security Council to adopt further appropriate measures in terms of Ch VII. In the case of Somalia the General Assembly adopted the mentioned resolution 2 weeks after the adoption of SC Res 794 of 3 December 1992. It showed itself to be deeply concerned about the tragic situation in Somalia and supported the idea of an international conference for a peaceful settlement of the conflict, after expressly referring to SC Res 794 (1992). See Lailach, above n 197, at 38, 215.

[206] Lorinser, above n 4, at 42; Martenczuk (Rechtskontrolle), above n 63, at 224; Gading, above n 197, at 53, 92; Lailach, above n 197, at 163; Nolte, above n 200, at 316. The Statement on Interpretation of the Charter, which was ultimately adopted by the Committee on Legal Problems during the drafting process of the Charter at San Francisco in 1945, also suggested that the Security Council would not have the power of authentic interpretation of its powers. It provided that each United Nations organ would, in the first instance, interpret the parts of the Charter applicable to its functions. In the event that two organs expressed or acted upon different interpretations of the Charter, they could ask for an advisory opinion of the Court, or set up an *ad hoc* committee of jurists to examine the question. See 13 *United Nation Conference on International Organization* 710 (1945).

[207] Lailach, above n 197, at 163; See Gading, above n 197, at 92.

negotiating history, as found in the *travaux préparatoires*.[208] Traditionally Article 32 of the Vienna Convention provides for recourse to the *travaux préparatoires* as a supplementary means of interpretation where the ordinary means provided for in Article 31 leave the meaning ambiguous, obscure or leads to a manifestly unreasonable result. Resorting to the *travaux préparatoires* under these circumstances is an accepted practice in international organisations,[209] as is also reflected in the jurisprudence of the ICJ. Already in the advisory opinion on *Conditions of Admission to Membership in the United Nations* did the ICJ indicate that it would resort to the negotiating history of the Charter where the text of the Charter was unclear.[210]

At the same time, however, the reliability or utility of the preparatory work in ascertaining the meaning of the Charter is restricted by several factors. First, the evolutionary nature of the Charter implies that its text assumes a life of its own, which separates itself progressively from what was discussed during negotiations.[211] This necessarily implies a reduced importance of the preparatory work with the passage of time. In addition, the text of a treaty is often deliberately ambiguous because the parties were unable to agree on a particular issue.[212] In such cases the *travaux préparatoires* usually contain material supporting all the different points of view in issue. This is witnessed by the fact that an appeal to the records by a supporter of one of the views seldom fails to produce an appeal to another part of the same records by a supporter of the opposite view.[213]

---

[208] The term *travaux préparatoires* is used rather loosely to indicate all the documents, such as memoranda, minutes of the conference, and drafts of the treaty under negotiation. See Merish, above n 183, at 63.

[209] According to Merish, above n 183, at 88, Art 32 of the Vienna Convention, above n 134, is a reflection of a customary rule of interpretation in the practice of international organisations. Pollux, above n 186, at 71; Leo Gross, "Treaty Interpretation: the Proper Role of an International Tribunal", 63 *Proceedings of the American Society of International Law* 117 (1969).

[210] Advisory Opinion, ICJ Rep 1948, at 63. In this opinion the ICJ did not consult the *travaux préparatoires*, since it regarded the text of the Charter as sufficiently clear. Nonetheless, from the opinion one can infer that if the Charter text had not been clear, the ICJ would have consulted the *travaux préparatoires*. See also the *Question of Reservations to the Convention on the Prevention and Punishment of the Crime of Genocide*, Advisory Opinion, ICJ Rep 1951, at 22–32. The ICJ supported its interpretation reached on the basis of other evidence by resorting to the *travaux préparatoires*. The majority of the judges examined the debates in the Sixth Committee of the General Assembly which adopted the Convention on the Prevention and Punishment of the Crime of Genocide of 1949. See also the approach of the International Criminal Tribunal for the former Yugoslavia (ICTY) in *Prosecutor v Zejnil Delalcic, Hazim Delic, Esad Landzo and Zdravko Mucic*, Judgment, case no IT–96–21, 20 February 2001, Appeals Chamber, at para 131, available at www.icty.org.

[211] Merish, above n 183, at 42.

[212] *Ibid*, at 41; Pollux, above n 186, at 68; Jose E Alvarez, "Theoretical Perspectives on Judicial Review by the World Court", 89 *ASIL Proceedings* 86 (1995).

[213] Gerald G Fitzmaurice, "The Law and Procedure of the International Court of Justice: Treaty Interpretation and Certain other Treaty Points", 28 *British Year Book of International Law* 15 (1951).

Furthermore, intentions reflected by the *travaux préparatoires* can sometimes be misleading. During the negotiation process the parties often manifest attitudes for bargaining purposes which do not represent their ultimate positions, or which they subsequently abandon in the light of the text agreed upon. Unfortunately it is not always clear that they were abandoned, and they may remain on the records as representing a view apparently maintained throughout.[214] This situation is aggravated by the fact that the preparatory documents do not contain the compromise behind the scenes or the private conversations of the heads of delegations.[215] It is not uncommon that some of the most important decisions taken, as well as the motivations from which they result, are the product of private meetings and discussions between delegations. The outcome appears as the actual text of some provision of the treaty, but the records will often give no indication of how or why it got there.[216] In such cases the earlier statements made by the participants are quite misleading, since the latter statements which reflect the actual intention of the parties were made in private and, so far as official records go, are non-existent.[217]

For the same reason one must be careful when inferring intentions from the silence of some delegations. As delegates have diverse motives for making or not making statements, silence does not always mean agreement and the records sometimes show an apparent unanimity that did not really exist.[218] At other times they often give an appearance of undue prominence to the view of the more vocal delegates. Some delegates are in the habit of making elaborate explanatory statements, while others for various reasons are not. Yet it does not follow that the former carried the greatest weight or represented the general view.[219]

It is worth noticing that several of the reasons forwarded here not only question the value of the preparatory documents as an instrument for Charter interpretation due to the Charter's evolutionary nature— although this is a an important factor—but also because of the way in which the *travaux préparatoires* are documented. This will necessarily also have implications for the value of records relating to the practice (ie decisions) of

---

[214] Fitzmaurice, above n 213, at 15; Merish, above n 183, at 42.
[215] Merish, above n 183, at 42.
[216] Fitzmaurice, above n 213, at 15.
[217] *Ibid.*
[218] *Ibid.*
[219] Fitzmaurice, above n 213, at 16. According to Pollux, above n 186, at 72, a less convincing argument is that the preparatory work could not be adduced against states which have subsequently adhered to an international treaty, in the drafting of which they did not participate. A state which accedes to a treaty or to a constitutive document of an international organisation accepts it as it stands. This would include any interpretation thereof that may be given on the basis of the records of the preparatory work when such records have already been made public. It is hard to see how a state, on being elected to membership of the United Nations, could claim to disregard the preparatory work which was fully accessible to it before it applied for membership.

organs such as the Security Council. As mentioned above, these decisions form an independent basis for Charter interpretation and it is likely that those interpreting them will apply the general principles of interpretation as they have been elaborated in relation to treaties.[220] As Security Council resolutions, like treaties, reflect a negotiated compromise between states, common sense would require that they are interpreted in good faith and that their terms be given their ordinary meaning, in the context and in the light of their object and purpose.[221] In addition, the discussions leading up to them can also be resorted to as a supplementary means of interpretation, to clarify the motivations of those states participating in the decision.[222]

Some authors claim that the preparatory work of Security Council resolutions would be of (even) greater significance than treaties, since the language used in Security Council resolutions does not reflect the same care and legal input as in the case of a treaty.[223] Security Council resolutions are often drafted by non-lawyers, in haste, under considerable political pressure and with a view to securing unanimity within the Security Council.[224] Inconsistencies in the use of terms and ungrammatical constructions are not uncommon and it would be misleading to pay the same amount of attention to these matters as one would do in the case of a carefully drafted treaty.[225] Consequently, the distinction between the general rule of interpretation and the supplementary means has less significance than in the case of treaties and less importance should be attached to the minutiae of language. Anything else would result in an over-extension of the similarities between treaties and Security Council resolutions.[226]

---

[220] Ie the principles contained in Art 31 and art 32 of the Vienna Convention, above n 134; See Wood, above n 196, at 95.

[221] Wood, above n 196, at 86, 88–89. Note that the ICTY adopted this approach in the *Prosecutor v Dusco Tadic*, Decision on the Defense Motion for Interlocutory Appeal and Jurisdiction, case no IT–94–1–T, 2 October 1995, Appeals Chamber, at para 10 ff, available at www.icty.org. hereinafter referred to as the *Tadic* decision. In interpreting the jurisdictional provisions of its Statute (which was adopted by a Security Council resolution), it first considered a literal and teleological interpretation, respectively, before finally launching into a logical and systematic interpretation.

[222] Herbst, above n 6, at 88–89. Wood, above n 196, at 93–94, stated that all Security Council documents referred to in the resolution, or referred to at the beginning of the Security Council meetings at which the resolution was adopted, would need to be considered as part of the *travaux préparatoires*. These would include reports of the Secretary-General, letters requesting the holding of the meeting, such drafts of the resolutions as are put forward formally as "S" documents, amendments that are put forward formally and accepted or rejected at the meeting, the verbatim records of the debate at the meeting, including statements made before or after the vote.

[223] Wood, above n 196, at 89.

[224] *Ibid*, at 82; Herbst, above n 6, at 89, noted that the lapse of time between the making of the decision and the consulting of the records was not as substantial in the case of Security Council resolutions as in the case of treaties.

[225] Wood, above n 196, at 89.

[226] *Ibid*, at 95.

However, even though the language of Security Council resolutions might not always be as carefully chosen as in the case of treaties, it is unlikely that any resulting ambiguities could be resolved by the *travaux préparatoires*. Most of the problems relating to the *travaux préparatoires* of treaties (ie of the Charter) also apply to that of Security Council resolutions.[227] First, the verbatim records usually reflect more than one view on the matter and even where there was no obvious disagreement, one should be careful to infer conclusions from the silence of delegates. Moreover, Security Council debates and decisions are very often a mere formality, since they confirm what has already been decided in secret consultations, for which no records are available.[228] Although the debates of the public and private meetings provided for in Rule 48 of the Provisional Rules of Procedure of the Security Council[229] are documented, the discussions during the many informal meetings remain unrecorded.[230] The net result is that the Security Council meets in public only to adopt resolutions already agreed upon in informal meetings, without giving any insight into the motives underpinning its decisions.[231]

In summary, therefore, whilst one should not reject outright the *travaux préparatoires* to the Charter or the records of Security Council decisions as a supplementary means of interpretation, one should not expect too much of them either. They will often not be able to yield answers exactly in those situations where answers are needed most, namely where the intentions of the parties are not clearly discernible from the text of the Charter

---

[227] This fact was completely ignored by Herbst, above n 6, at 98–99, who placed an excessive value on the practice of the Security Council (as reflected in the records), when interpreting the limits of its powers under the Charter.

[228] Bernhard Graefrath, "Die Vereinten Nationen im Übergang—Die Gratwanderung des Sicherheitsrates zwischen Rechtsanwendung und Rechtsanmassung", in Klaus Hüfner (ed), *Die Reform der Vereinten Nationen* 44 (Opladen, Leske & Budrich, 1994). This fact is also conceded by Wood, above n 196, at 94. See also Bardo Fassbender, "Uncertain Steps into a Post-Cold War World: The Role and Functioning of the UN Security Council after a Decade of Measures against Iraq", 13 *European Journal of International Law* 389 (2002).

[229] S/96/Rev 7 (1983), at www.uno.org.

[230] Tono Eitel, "The United Nations Security Council and its Future Contribution in the Field of International Law", 4 *Max Planck Yearbook of United Nations Law* 59 (2000). See also Frederic L Kirgis, "The Security Council's First Fifty Years", 89 *American Journal of International Law* 518 (1995).

[231] For example, there were various reports of the United States promising rewards and threatening punishment so as to influence the vote on SC Res 678 of 29 November 1990, authorising the use of force against Iraq. There were also alleged promises of or demands for financial help to/ by Colombia, Ivory Coast, Ethiopia and Zaire; an agreement with the Soviet Union not to include Estonia, Latvia, and Lithuania in the November 1990 Paris summit conference; and an agreement with China to lift trade sanctions in place since the Tiannamen Square incident and to support a World Bank loan of $114.3. Also, as result of Yemen's negative vote, the United States allegedly cut its substantial annual aid to that state. See David D Caron, "The Legitimacy of the Collective Authority of the Security Council", 87 *American Journal of International Law* 563–64 (1993); also see Eitel, above n 230, at 59; Graefrath, above n 228, at 44; Kirgis, above n 230, at 518.

or the Security Council resolution itself.[232] In the case of the Charter this is partly due to its dynamic character. Like municipal constitutions it is subjected to constant evolution which necessarily implies a diminished importance of the original intent of the drafters.

4.4.   The Separation of Powers

Another essential element of the legal framework provided by modern constitutions is that it provides for a system of law-making, administration and adjudication.[233] Such a separation of powers is a necessary prerequisite for rights of review amongst the different organs of state, because whenever the power is concentrated in one organ a system of checks and balances is automatically excluded.[234] The evident question that arises is whether the division of functions that exist within the United Nations[235] would amount to a separation of powers that paves the way for a system of checks and balances comparable to those in the constitutional orders of domestic jurisdictions.

Such a possibility is disputed by those who believe that there can be no separation of powers in a system that does not fulfil all the functions of the nation state. They argue that the separation of powers would presuppose an all-encompassing power, since its whole function is to serve as a barrier against this omnipotence of public organs and its over-concentration in one area.[236] The United Nations only exercises certain limited functions which do not amount to a complete set of competencies.[237] The Charter enumerates the purposes of the United Nations exactly and exhaustively and the organisation is obliged to respect the autonomy of the states as far as possible. Any limitation of the autonomy of its members needs specific grounds which must be found in the specific purposes defined in the Charter.[238]

They also submit that its political organs are not comparable to a legislature. Due to the limited competencies of the General Assembly, it cannot

---

[232] As a result, debates as to whether the *travaux préparatoires* should be consulted habitually or only in cases where the text of the Charter is ambiguous or unclear seem to be superfluous. For a discussion on the differences between the textual and intentions approach, see Merish, above n 183, at 41.

[233] Fassbender, above n 4, at 548, 554, 574; Tomuschat (Obligations), above n 130, at 216.

[234] Lorinser, above n 4, at 84.

[235] Fassbender, above n 4, at 574; Thürer, above n 140, at 457, 463.

[236] Lorinser, above n 4, at 97.

[237] *Ibid*; Karl Doehring, "Unlawful Resolutions of the Security Council and their Legal Consequences", 1 *Max Planck Yearbook of United Nations Law* 96 (1997).

[238] Doehring, above n 237, at 97. He argues that the rights and duties of states cannot be compared with fundamental rights within a constitutional system that can be limited as far as the common welfare requires it.

be compared to a national parliament.[239] In particular, it cannot make the Security Council accountable for its decisions. In municipal parliaments, on the other hand, such accountability is intrinsic to the relationship between the plenary organ and the executive.[240] Moreover, it is difficult to categorise the binding Security Council resolutions as being of a legislative or executory nature. The lines between the executive and legislative powers are therefore difficult to draw.[241] Additionally, no system exists to compel the members to give effect to binding decisions of the Security Council, or to render military assistance.[242] Under a national Constitution everyone can be forced to participate in common affairs and efforts when the community cannot otherwise be protected against perils.[243] Moreover, the Security Council could not be seen as a world government, because it is under no strict duty to act when the community of nations is endangered. Any action foreseen within the Security Council can be prevented by the veto. A national government, on the other hand, is always under the duty to exercise its competencies.[244]

One could point out that these arguments merely reaffirm that the separation of powers in the United Nations is of a rudimentary nature, but they do not serve as proof that no such separation exists, or that it has no potential for development. Stated differently, they would underline differences of degree, but not of principle and although these gradual differences are important, they should not be exaggerated. First, it is questionable whether the existence of a separation of powers presupposes a complete set of state competencies, since this would belie the existence of the European Union. Although the latter is not a state (nor does it necessarily have to become one), it possesses definite legislative, administrative and judicial powers.[245] Admittedly there are fundamental differences between the

---

[239] Lorinser, above n 4, at 97.

[240] Jost Delbrück, "Article 24", in Bruno Simma (ed), *The Charter of the United Nations. A Commentary* 405 (Oxford, Oxford University Press, 1994).

[241] *Ibid*, at 97–98; Herdegen, above n 198, at 151; see also Martenczuk (Rechtskontrolle), above n 63, at 65.

[242] Lorinser, above n 4, at 86; Arangio-Ruiz, above n 6, at 20–21.

[243] Doehring, above n 237, at 97; see also Tomuschat (Tyrannei), above n 4, at 278; *Ibid* (Obligations), above n 130, at 238.

[244] Doehring, above n 237, at 97; Verdross & Simma, above n 55, at 78.

[245] The European Union exercises competencies that have been transferred to it by the member states. Its main political organ is the Council of Ministers, which usually makes decisions on the basis of majority rule. The Treaty establishing the European Community (TEC) explicitly recognises the European Court of Justice as the guardian of Union legality vis-a-vis the other organs and the member states. This court possesses a clear cut constitutional authority to interpret the TEC and to annul measures adopted by other European Union organs. (See Art 220 ff of the TEC, available at www.europa.eu.int/.) Herdegen, above n 198, at 150–51; Ginther, above n 4, at 116; Fassbender, above n 4, at 558. Cf Koen Lenaerts, "Some Reflections on the Separation of Powers in the European Community", 28 *Common Market Law Review* 11 ff (1991).

European Union and the United Nations. The powers of the organs of the European Union are related to a process of legal and political integration explicitly foreseen in its constituent treaties, which is not the case with the United Nations. The example nonetheless remains relevant, since it illustrates that a separation of powers accompanied by a set of checks and balances would not only exist within states that possess the "complete responsibility" for the welfare of their subjects.[246] It also illustrates that a separation of powers does not necessarily imply a strong role for the most representative organ. The powers of the European Parliament have also been extended only gradually and its possibilities of holding the other organs accountable are still limited.

Furthermore, the competencies of the United Nations are quite broad, even though they are supposedly exhaustively enumerated in the Charter. First, there are the broad powers that flow from the maintenance of peace and security, which is a key function of governance in any community.[247] Second, the overall purposes of the organisation are very broad and the Charter sets forth a complete welfare programme for mankind, although in general and unspecified terms that needs concretisation.[248] This has enabled an increasing number of issues, ranging from demilitarisation to environmental protection and globalisation to be dealt with on the international plane.[249] As a result the Charter has provided extensive justification for the limitation of the sovereignty of member states over the last half century. State sovereignty could not prevent the increasing internationalisation of what have previously been perceived as domestic issues.[250]

Although the absence of an international enforcement system severely weakens the efficiency of the international order, it is incorrect to regard this as a problem peculiar to the international order. There are situations in domestic systems where enforcement of decisions cannot be guaranteed either. This is especially the case where municipal courts give decisions against state authorities such as the legislature, for example rulings on the unconstitutionality of legislation. Compliance is ultimately a function of the government's own sense of legality and legitimacy.[251] The same

---

[246] Fassbender, above n 4, at 558.

[247] *Ibid*, at 574. But see Martenczuk (Rechtskontrolle), above n 63, at 65, who found that the collective maintenance of international peace and security cannot be compared to the function of any organ within municipal jurisdictions. As a result, he questions whether analogies with national jurisdictions in the context of judicial control of the Security Council would be useful.

[248] Tomuschat (Obligations), above n 130, at 238.

[249] Tomuschat (Tyrannei), above n 4, at 278.

[250] Thürer, above n 140, at 457–58. See also Gading, above n 197, at 204–05, who referred to the growing inter-dependence between states in fields ranging from poverty alleviation, to environmental problems, to international terrorism etc.

[251] Sarah Wright Sheive, "Central and Eastern European Constitutional Courts and the Anti-majoritarian Objection to Judicial Review", 26 *Law and Policy in International Business* 1211 (1995); Shahabuddeen, above n 74, at 95.

accounts for the argument that a national government is under the duty to exercise its competencies. There is no guarantee that the government will indeed do so. It can refrain from taking action in a given situation, just as the Security Council can refrain from exercising its powers under Chapter VII.[252]

4.4.1. *Characterising the Powers of the Security Council*

Another argument against the acknowledgement of a separation of powers within the United Nations system is that the nature of the decisions of the Security Council is difficult to classify.[253] Apart from adopting binding decisions, the Security Council is also responsible for their enforcement in terms of Article 43 of the Charter. It would therefore function both as "legislature" and "executive".[254] If one compares this to municipal systems, it becomes apparent that this blurring of the lines is also not unique to the international order. Although the separation between the branches of government in national governments is clearer than that in the United Nations in that the one or the other branch is predominantly legislative, executive or judicial, the exact lines between them remain fluid. They develop through inter-action in accordance with the needs of the particular system. The division between the powers therefore cannot be regarded as complete from its inception. Moreover, the fluid lines between them would make it possible to (re)label a particular act as either legislative, executive or judicial.

An illuminating decision in this regard is that of the American Supreme Court in *Metropolitan Washington Airports Authority v Citizens for the Abatement of Aircraft Noise*.[255] In this case the state was to take over an airport which was formerly under federal control. The airport was to be operated under the control of an Oversight Authority in which 9 members of Congress were represented, who would retain a veto right against its decisions. In declaring this retention of a veto power in the hands of the members of Congress unconstitutional, Justice Stevens

---

[252]See Doehring, above n 237, at 98. He also argued that under a national constitution the right to exercise self-defence is an exception because one relies on protection by the government. With respect to the United Nations, however, the states keep their right to self-preservation under Art 51 of the Charter, if the Security Council remains inactive. This right is only restricted when the Security Council takes the measures necessary to maintain security. One can question this argument, since the system foreseen by the Charter envisages the exercise of the right to self-defence to be an exception as well.

[253]The issue of whether the General Assembly can engage in law-making activities will not be explored here. For a discussion of the normative effect of (unanimous) resolutions of the General Assembly, see Tomuschat (Tyrannei), above n 4, at 279–82. Cf Ginther, above n 4, at 111.

[254]Fassbender , above n 4, at 574.

[255]501 US 252 (1991).

indicated that the type of action at stake here could be characterised as executive or legislative. However, this characterisation was not decisive, since the action of the Oversight Authority would result in an unconstitutional aggrandisement of Congressional power, regardless of how one chose to label it. If the function of the oversight body were executive, it would violate the constitutional principle that Congress may not control a body that is executing the law.[256] If the function of the Oversight Authority were legislative, its actions would circumvent constitutional procedures such as bicameralism.[257]

The importance of this decision lies in the recognition that it is not so much the characterisation of the power that is important, since the power itself could often be re-characterised as something else. The decisive question is whether the power of an organ has been *aggrandised* unconstitutionally. In the context of the United Nations this rational would mean that one should not be side-tracked by arguments about whether the particular action of the Security Council would be of an executive or legislative nature. It suffices that it has the *potential* to be the one or the other. The question then becomes whether these executive or legislative powers are aggrandised at the expense of the constitutional structure provided for in the Charter. After all, the Charter does attribute different powers to different organs and in this way establishes a rudimentary system of checks and balances.[258]

This is reflected by the fact that the ICJ and the Security Council are functionally separate and independent from each other.[259] Although both organs are responsible for the peaceful settlement of disputes, the ICJ as principal judicial organ in terms of Article 92 of the Charter performs this function according to legal norms. The Security Council, on the other hand, as the primary guardian of peace and security in terms of Article 24 of the Charter, is a political organ. The nature of its proceedings is entirely different from that of a judicial body such as the ICJ and its conclusions can not attain the quality of a judicial decision which could replace the

---

[256] See *Bowsher v Synar*, 478 US 714 (1986).

[257] See *Immigration & Naturalization Service v Chadha*, 462 US 919 (1983). That the characterisation of power within the European Union could face similar problems, is indicated by Lenaerts, above n 245, at 13.

[258] See Fassbender, above n 4, at 576; also conceded by Lorinser, above n 4, at 98; Stein, above n 38, at 39 ff. Cf Gading, above n 197, at 55, 57. The more power the organs of international organisations have to adopt binding measures for member states and to enforce these decisions against them, the closer they resemble the national organs that have to observe the rule of law. This applies to the Security Council that can adopt and enforce binding decisions against the will of those affected. Just as the acts of national organs must be measured against their constitution, the acts of the Security Council have to be measured against the Charter.

[259] Lorinser, above n 4, at 91. See also Krzysztof Skubiszewski, "The International Court of Justice and the Security Council", in Vaughan Lowe & Malgosia Fitzmaurice (eds), *Fifty Years of the International Court of Justice* 606–10 (Cambridge, Cambridge University Press, 1996).

rulings of the ICJ or make them superfluous.[260] This means that decisions of the Security Council, whether taken under Chapter VII or otherwise, do not have *res judicata* effect, nor are they subjected to the principle *of lis pendens*.[261]

The flip-side of this functional separation is that simultaneous action by the Security Council and the ICJ with respect to the same issue is possible. In the *Nicaragua* case,[262] for example, Nicaragua brought a complaint and a draft resolution to the Security Council in an attempt to stop the mining of Nicaraguan harbours. The draft resolution failed due to the veto of the United States. Five days after the draft resolution was submitted, Nicaragua filed a request for provisional measures with the ICJ. The United States argued that the ICJ could not hear the case, because the adverse decision of the Security Council precluded the ICJ from examining the issue. The ICJ subsequently determined that the matter's presence before the Security Council did not prevent its own jurisdiction and that the proceedings before the two organs could be pursued *pari passu*.[263]

The ICJ reaffirmed these principles in the recent request for provisional measures in the *Case Concerning Armed Activities on the Territory of the Congo (Democratic Republic of the Congo v Uganda)*.[264] Uganda objected to the admissibility of the request and claimed that it was moot, as the substance of the request was essentially covered by Resolution 1304 (2000), which Uganda had accepted and was complying with.[265] The ICJ rejected this objection, recalling that whilst the Charter provided for a demarcation of functions between the General Assembly and the Security Council, it did not do so with respect to the Security Council and the ICJ. The Security Council had functions of a political nature assigned to it, whereas the ICJ exercised a purely judicial role. Both organs can therefore perform their separate but complementary functions with respect to the same events.[266]

---

[260] Graefrath, above n 32, at 204; Evans above n 20, at 60–61; Malanczuk, above n 42, at 90; Martenczuk, above n 13, at 533; Lorinser, above n 4, at 91–92; see also Delbrück (Art 24, in Simma), above n 240, at 403.

[261] See Malanczuk, above n 42, at 90.

[262] *Case Concerning Military and Paramilitary Activities in and against Nicaragua (Nicaragua v United States of America)*, Jurisdiction and Admissibility, ICJ Rep 1984, at 432, 435. Hereinafter referred to as *Nicaragua v United States*, jurisdiction and admissibility.

[263] *Ibid*, at 433. See also *Aegean Sea Continental Shelf (Greece v Turkey)*, Interim Measures, ICJ Rep 1976, at 28; *Case Concerning Application of the Genocide Convention, Bosnia and Herzegovina v Yugoslavia (Serbia and Montenegro)*, Provisional Measures, ICJ Rep 1993, at 18–19; Evans, above n 20, at 63.

[264] Reprinted in 39 *International Legal Materials* 1100 (2000).

[265] *Ibid*, at 1110.

[266] *Ibid*, at 1111. See also Fraas, above n 6, at 48–49. One should therefore not conclude that merely because the Security Council is under no obligation to refer a dispute before it to the ICJ, the latter may not deal with a dispute with respect to which the Security Council has taken action. See also Evans, above n 20, at 60–61; Lorinser, above n 4, at 93; Martenczuk, above n 13, at 531; Malanczuk (in Heere), above n 27, at 89, 90–91.

From the *Lockerbie* case[267] one can conclude that these principles would also apply in instances where these is a direct conflict between the ICJ and the Security Council. In the *Nicaragua* and *Congo* cases there was no such conflict, as the proceedings initiated in the one principal organ were not aimed at preventing parallel proceedings in another principal organ.[268] In the *Lockerbie* case, on the other hand, Libya introduced the claim before the ICJ to prevent the United States and the United Kingdom from instrumentalising the Security Council against itself, whilst the United States and the United Kingdom attempted to prevent Libya's claim before the ICJ by the adoption of Resolution 748 (1992).[269]

The majority of judges in the *Lockerbie* case did not regard this direct conflict between two principal organs as sufficient grounds for amending their position on the different roles of the respective organs. In rejecting the objections against jurisdiction, the majority focused on the temporal element, ie the fact that Libya had filed the claim before the Security Council resolutions had been adopted). By stressing this chronological order of events, one might come to the conclusion that the ICJ's jurisdiction would have been excluded if the order of events had been reversed. However, one could also argue that their conclusion was merely a consistent application of the ICJ's previous holding that the principles of *res judicata* and *lis pendens* do not apply to the Security Council.[270] Consequently, the adoption of a binding Security Council resolution does not in itself suffice to trump automatically the ICJ's ability to render a meaningful judgment in this case.[271] This is irrespective of whether the Security Council resolution was adopted before or after the filing of the claim with the ICJ, or whether it conflicted directly with the proceedings before the ICJ.

One should point out that the *Nicaragua*-case[272] is sometimes used to support the opposite submission, ie that the ICJ rejected the notion of a separation of powers in the United Nations.[273] But this rejection was first and foremost aimed at the attempt by the United States to introduce a political question doctrine in the jurisprudence of the ICJ—something which it has consistently refused to do.[274] Although it can also be read as a rejection of a blind transferral of municipal law concepts into international law, it should

---

[267] *Libya v United States*, preliminary objections, above n 18.

[268] See Evans, above n 20, at 64.

[269] *Ibid.*

[270] Martenczuk, above n 13, at 525, 533. See also Malanczuk (in Heere), above n 27, at 96.

[271] See in particular the joint declaration of Judges Bedjaoui, Ranjeva and Koroma in *Libya v United States*, preliminary objections, above n 18.

[272] *Nicaragua v United States*, jurisdiction and admissibility, above n 262, at 433.

[273] As is attempted by Herbst, above n 6, at 389–90; and Lorinser, above n 4, at 98.

[274] As was illustrated in ch 2 at s 3.1.2. See also *Nicaragua v United States*, jurisdiction and admissibility, above n 262, at 433; *United States v Iran*, above n 157, at 22. The ICJ stated that it is for the principal judicial organ of the United Nations to resolve any legal question that may be in issue between parties to a dispute. The resolution of such legal questions by the ICJ may be an important and sometimes decisive factor in promoting the peaceful settlement of the dispute.

not be read as a categorical rejection of the transferral of municipal elements of separation of power in all circumstances. The absence of a strict separation of powers would not mean that there is no separation at all.[275]

In conclusion therefore it is possible to regard the Charter of the United Nations as representing an embryonic international constitutional order—if one subscribed to the "relativist" approach outlined above.[276] Its normative and dynamic character, its supreme position in the international order and its rudimentary separation of powers give it a constitutional quality, not unlike that of municipal constitutions. The municipal constitutional orders and the Charter share a variety of common values and the qualitative differences between them would seem to be more a matter of degree than of principle. The gradual differences would affect the extent of the transferability of the municipal concepts to the international plane, but not necessarily the transferral *per se*.

Even so, one has to concede that the acceptance of this "relativist" approach depends on whether one is willing to regard as unimportant the difference between a decentralised international legal order premised on the notion of sovereign equality of independent states, and municipal legal orders that are composed of individuals. Many would argue that this is a fundamental difference which makes the "constitutional" character of the Charter and the duality of functions of its organs incomparable to seemingly similar phenomena in municipal orders. However, for the sake of argument these structural problems will not be regarded as an insurmountable obstacle. As a result, analogies between the Charter and domestic constitutions in relation to judicial review are regarded as permissible.[277] The next section of the chapter will first examine whether it has emerged as a general principle of law in municipal orders and, if so, whether it could be transferred to the embryonic constitutional order.

5.   THE GROWING SIGNIFICANCE OF JUDICIAL REVIEW IN MUNICIPAL ORDERS SINCE THE 1990S

Very few world wide comparative studies on constitutional review exist. However, on the basis of one study[278] to this extent, as well as a variety

---

[275] Consequently the decisions of the ICTY are too undifferentiated, in as far as they seem to reject the existence of any separation of powers within the United Nations. See *Tadic* decision, above n 221, at para 43. In determining whether the ICTY was established by law, the Appeals Chamber stated that this cannot refer to a legislature. For it is clearly impossible to classify the United Nations into the legislative, executive and judicial separation of powers which is largely followed in most municipal systems. Cf *Prosecutor v Tihomir Blaskic*, Judgement, case no IT–95–14, 2 March 2000, Trial Chamber, at para 40, at www.icty.org.
[276] Thürer, above n 140, at 457, 463); Sloan, above n 4, at 63; Dupuy, above n 140, at 30.
[277] Cf Fassbender, above n 4, at 527.
[278] See the website www.us-rs.si/en/revfr.html which is operated by the Constitutional Court of the Republic of Slovenia.

of regional and country studies,[279] it seems that at least 160 countries across the world currently recognise some form of judicial review, at least in theory. Although some Western European countries have already introduced judicial review since World War II,[280] its proliferation coincided with the world-wide democratisation process that intensified during the 1990s.

With respect to those countries that acknowledge constitutional review, the world-wide study divides the types of constitutional review into four major categories. The first is described as the European model which was introduced in Austria in 1920. According to this model, constitutional matters are either dealt with by specialised constitutional courts[281] with specially qualified judges, or by regular supreme courts or high courts or their special senates in special procedures.[282] The second is the American model, according to which constitutional matters are dealt with by all regular courts, under the regular court proceedings.[283] Third there is the mixed (American-European) model that combines the elements of the diffuse and concentrated systems. Despite the review power of the central constitutional or supreme court (or its special senate), all regular courts in the particular state are entitled not to apply the laws deemed as not in conformity with the Constitution.[284] The French *Conseil*

[279] Georg Brunner, "Die neue Verfassungsgerichtsbarkeit in Osteuropa", in 53 *Zeitschrift für ausländisches öffentliches Recht und Völkerrecht* 819 (1993); Young Hu, "Sechs Jahre Verfassungsgerichtsbarkeit in der Republik Korea", 45 *Jahrbuch des Öffentlichen Rechts* 535 (1997); Wright Sheive, above n 251, at 1201.

[280] Robert F Utter & David C Lundsgaard, "Judicial Review in the New Nations of Central and Eastern Europe: Some Thoughts from a Comparative Perspective", 3 *OSCE Bulletin (Office for Democratic Institutions and Human Rights)* 13 (1995).

[281] Countries (and regions) with this system include Albania, Andorra, Angola, Argentina (province of Tucuman), Armenia, Austria, Azerbaijan, Belarus, Benin, Bosnia and Herzegovina, Bulgaria, Burundi, Cambodia, Chile, Croatia, Cyprus, Czech Republic, Egypt, Gabon, Georgia, Germany, Hungary, Iraq, Italy, Kazakhstan, Kirghizia, Latvia, Lithuania, Macedonia, Madagascar, Mali, Malta, Moldavia, Mongolia, Montenegro, Palestine, Papua New Guinea, Poland, Romania, Russia, Rwanda, Serbia and Montenegro, Slovakia, Slovenia, South Africa, South Korea, Spain, Sri Lanka, Surinam, Syria, Tadjikistan, Thailand, Turkey, Ukraine, Uzbekistan. See www.us-rs.si/en/revfr.html. See also Lorinser, above n 4, at 82.

[282] Countries with this procedure are Belgium, Burkina Faso, Cameroon, Chad, Costa Rica, Eritrea, Iceland, Liechtenstein, Niger, Panama, Paraguay, Philippines, Senegal, Sudan, Uganda, Uruguay, Yemen, Zaire, Zambia. See www.us-rs.si/en/ revfr.html.

[283] Countries adhering to this procedure include Argentina, Bahamas, Bangladesh, Barbados, Bolivia, Botswana, Canada, Denmark, Dominican Republic, Fiji, Gambia, Ghana, Grenada, Guyana, Haiti, India, Ireland, Israel, Jamaica, Japan, Kenya, Kiribati, Malawi, Malaysia, Mexico, Namibia, Nauru, Nepal, New Zealand, Nigeria, Norway, Sierra Leone, Singapore, St Christopher/ Nevis, Sweden, Tanzania, Trinidad and Tobago, United States of America. See www.us-rs.si/en/revfr.html. See also Utter & Lundsgaard, above n 280, at 15; Lorinser, above n 4, at 81.

[284] Countries that adhere to this model and that have a specialised constitutional court include Colombia, Ecuador, Gautemala, Honduras, Peru, Portugal. Other countries which

Constitutionnel constitutes the fourth model. It envisages a process whereby constitutional matters are subject to review by special bodies of review, or by special senates of the regular Supreme Courts in special proceedings. The constitutional review is mainly of a preventative or consultative nature.[285] There is also a fifth category, concerning countries that acknowledge constitutional review in some form or another, but which do not seem to fit any of the former categories.[286]

Of the 25 or so remaining countries, it is not clear how many would actually reject judicial review on the national level,[287] since information about some of these legal systems is very difficult to obtain.[288] However, even if one accepted for the sake of argument that none of them recognised judicial review, this should not necessarily prevent the concept from being recognised as a general principle of law. First, one has to consider that more than two thirds of the world's states—representing all the major legal systems—recognise the principle of judicial review.

Second, it would be up to the few states not recognising judicial review on the national level to argue convincingly that it would be incompatible with the nature of its judicial system. As has been indicated in section 3 of this chapter, the issue of compatibility could serve as a minimum threshold when considering whether a particular principle could be regarded as a general principle of law. An argument of incompatibility would not be convincing when forwarded by any Western, Central or Eastern European state. All of these states—including traditional "non-reviewist" states such as the United Kingdom—indirectly acknowledge judicial review through their membership of the European Union and/or ratification of the European Convention on Human Rights.[289]

The judgments of the European Court of Human Rights are essentially declaratory, and it cannot itself annul or repeal inconsistent national law

---

adhere to the model, but which do not have a specialised Constitutional Court are Brazil, El Salvador, Greece, Indonesia, Switzerland, Taiwan, Venezuela. See www.us-rs.si/en/revfr.html. See also Lorinser, above n 4, at 82.

[285] Countries applying this procedure include Algeria, Djibouti, France, Ivory Coast, Morocco, Mozambique, The Netherlands. See www.us-rs.si/en/revfr.html.

[286] These countries include Afghanistan, Australia, Brunei, Burma, China, Congo, Cuba, Finland (based on long term practice), Guinea Bissau, Kuwait, Laos, Mauritius, Oman, Pakistan, Tunisia, Turkmenistan and Vietnam. www.us-rs.si/en/revfr.html. See also Utter & Lundsgaard, above n 2, at 15.

[287] Lesotho, Liberia, Libya, the UK do not recognise constitutional review on the national level.

[288] Such as Saudi-Arabia and Somalia.

[289] In discussing judicial review in common-law countries, it is often said that the mother country of the common law, the United Kingdom, does not have any form of judicial review. However, the indirect review provided by the European Court of Human Rights and the European Court of Justice indicates that this statement is too undifferentiated. See also Utter & Lundsgaard, above n 280, at 15.

or judgments.[290] It is up to the particular state to implement these decisions in accordance with the rules of its national system.[291] The situation is similar where the European Court of Justice determines that the actions of a member state are in violation of community law.[292] It is up to the particular member state in question to amend the measures constituting the violation, and the European Court of Justice cannot repeal the national measures by itself.[293]

Nonetheless, these courts provide an avenue through which independent judges review the decisions of democratically elected national bodies against the norms of "higher law".[294] Even though the member states have a certain leeway in implementing the decisions of these courts, they are bound by international law to do so and to amend their national laws and administrative practices where necessary.[295] Thus, by entering these international agreements the member states have made their legal systems receptive for judicial review. As a result, they could not argue that the concept of judicial review would be irreconcilable with their legal culture.

5.1. Legitimisation of Political Discretion as the Motivating Rational of Judicial Review

In seems that a main motivation for the expansion of judicial review in most of the above jurisdictions is that it strengthens the faith in the political organs and enhances legal certainty.[296] Stated differently, one can say that the common goal of judicial review is to legitimate political discretion. By subjecting the legality of actions of political organs to independent judicial review, they gain legitimacy and credibility.[297]

---

[290] *Marckx v Belgium*, Series A 31 (1979); see also DJ Harris *et al* (eds), *Law of the European Convention on Human Rights* 26 (London, Butterworths, 1995).

[291] *Vermeire v Belgium*, Series A 214–C (1991); Harris, above n 290, at 30.

[292] See for example Art 226 TEC and Art 227 TEC, available at www.europa.eu.int/.

[293] Art 228 TEC, *ibid*; see also Hans von der Groeben *et al* (eds), *Kommentar zum EU-/EG-Vertrag, Bd 4* 4/531–4/532 (Baden-Baden, Nomos, 1997).

[294] Ie the norms of the European Convention on Human Rights or of EC law.

[295] Harris, above n 290, at 26; Van der Groeben, above n 293, at 4/531 ff. This is, in principle, also the effect of the preliminary rulings procedure provided by Art 234 (former Art 177) of the EC Treaty. On receiving requests from national courts concerning the interpretation of EC law, the European Court of Justice is limited to interpreting EC law and may not give an opinion on the compatability of the national law with EC law. On the other hand, however, the European Court of Justice will formulate its opinion in such a way that the national court would be in a position to draw the necessary consequences for the national law with respect to the case at hand. For example, the national court would be able to determine that a particular national measure is not compatible with European Community Law and should therefore not be applied. Cf Paul Craig & Gráinne de Búrca, *EU Law: Text, Cases and Materials* 407 ff (Oxford, Oxford University Press, 1998).

[296] Lorinser, above n 4, at 83.

[297] Franck (International Legal Issues), above n 161, at 630; Alvarez (Theoretical Perspectives), above n 212, at 87.

The different forms of judicial review reflect a common desire to guarantee the respect of political organs for the balance of power between the different state structures.[298] There is a growing conviction that the constitutionality of acts of state organs cannot be guaranteed automatically, despite the fact that there is a division of state powers and that they are bound to the constitution.[299] Virtually all systems past and present of political, non-judicial control of the political branches have proved to be inefficient.[300] This results from the fact that limitations on power—unlike power itself—cannot be left to be nurtured by practice.[301] Even in the most democratic of societies legislative and executive officials have an incentive to manipulate limitations on their power, since they are inevitably motivated by their desire to remain in power and to employ the resources and prestige of their elected office to accomplish that goal.[302]

The limitations on power therefore need the protection of an organ with the prestige which is derived from principled impartiality, such as a court of law. Judges should be entrusted to umpire disputes about the constitutionality of political decisions, rather than leaving it to the wisdom and fairness of the political majority.[303] The suitability of the judiciary to exercise this control is questioned by those who regard judges as not (directly) elected and therefore unaccountable and uncontrollable. They regard the legislative and executive branches as being more democratic since they are directly responsible to the people.[304] They argue that decisions of legislators and executive branch officials can be overturned through the political process. Decisions of constitutional courts, on the other hand, are very difficult to overturn since it would imply a constitutional amendment.[305]

The supporters of judicial review counter these objections by underlining that this very independence of the judges, their traditional role of

---

[298] See Franck (International Legal Issues), above n 161, at 625.

[299] See Lorinser, above n 4, at 79, 84.

[300] Wright Sheive, above n 251, at 1222.

[301] Franck (International Legal Issues), above n 161, at 630–31.

[302] Wright Sheive, above n 251, at 1221.

[303] Franck (International Legal Issues), above n 161, at 630–31; Wright Sheive, above n 251, at 1221.

[304] Watson above n 179, at 28, 31; Roberts, above n 11, at 312–13. The criticism that judges are neither representative nor accountable to the electorate is less pronounced in the United Nations than in some national systems. ICJ judges are indeed elected by the Security Council and General Assembly. The ICJ is also a much more representative body than the Security Council. All the major regions of the world are represented and no state holds a veto in the decision-making process. Since judges also must step down or run for re-election every 9 years, they can be made accountable for irresponsible decisions by not being re-elected. See Art 13 of the Charter.

[305] Watson, above n 179, at 28; see also Lorinser, above n 4, at 80. Cf Wright Sheive, above n 251, at 1216. Abstract review allows courts to alter legislative outcomes and foreclose political initiatives that might otherwise be open to popularly elected legislatures and government.

determiners of rights, as well as their specialised knowledge make them well suited to function as guardians of the constitution.[306] It enables them to enforce and protect the "deeper" values expressed in a constitution from the vicissitudes of temporary majorities.[307] Furthermore, as was pointed out in section 3.1.3. of chapter 2, the ongoing arguments as to whether a question is predominantly political or legal and therefore justiciable are misdirected. Instead of attempting to distinguish between legal and political questions, one should distinguish between a political method and a legal method of solving disputes. A dispute that cannot be reduced to specific issues of fact or law between the parties would be purely political, whereas a legal dispute implies both a legal answer and a political answer.[308]

Moreover, even though the legal answers provided by the courts would have an impact on the political debate on the issue, this need not produce harmful results. Experience with constitutional review also indicates that it takes place within a layered institutional structure whose various constraints, for the most part, generate favourable perceptions about the results.[309] These constraints imply that the courts give the political organs a wide ambit of discretion and are reluctant to substitute their own judgment for that of the policy-experts.[310] Such reticence, in addition to a process of review grounded in principles of rationality and proportionality have secured many constitutional courts a measure of objectivity, which serves to insulate them from charges of arbitrariness.[311] As a result the risk of judicial self-aggrandisement would arguably be less than that of political self-aggrandisement where respect for the constitution is left entirely to political organs. The proliferation of judicial review in municipal law since the early 1990s can be interpreted as a growing consensus to this effect.

The same concern about political self-aggrandisement and the resulting illegitimacy of the decisions of political organs plagues the United Nations, notably the Security Council. As the global political system grows in power and acquires ever greater responsibilities in response to urgent new challenges, its need for legitimisation also becomes a matter

---

[306] Lorinser, above n 4, at 80; Wright Sheive, above n 251, at 1218. See also Heinz Klug, "Introducing the Devil: An Institutional Analysis of the Power of Constitutional Review", 13 *South African Journal on Human Rights* 191 (1997).

[307] See Utter & Lundsgaard, above n 280, at 22.

[308] Rosalyn Higgins, "Policy Considerations and the International Judicial Process", 17 *International & Comparative Law Quarterly* 63 (1968).

[309] Alvarez (Theoretical Perspectives), above n 212, at 88.

[310] Franck (International Legal Issues), above n 161, at 630. He referred in particular to the courts in the United States, Canada, Germany and Australia. Wright Sheive, above n 251, at 1218 mentioned a notion of "social accountability" on the part of the courts in this context.

[311] Alvarez (Theoretical Perspectives), above n 212, at 88.

of increasing urgency.[312] The Security Council was created to be an effective mechanism for the maintenance of international peace and security, and to that end was granted substantial authority. At the same time, other values such as representation and cohesion of the international community influenced the design of the institution that would use that authority.[313] Unfortunately the Security Council in the post Cold War era lacks legitimacy in that it does not represent the interests of the world community, but rather that of a very small minority of powerful countries, acting to some extent under pressure exercised by the only super-power.[314] Whereas the veto may have served as a guarantee against abuse of power and political self-aggrandisement of the Security Council in the past—albeit at the expense of laming the organisation—this is not the case anymore.[315] Controversial Security Council decisions imposing sanctions against Libya and refusing to amend the sanctions regime in place against Iraq are two well known examples.

In summary, it seems that the values underpinning the emerging general principle of judicial review in municipal orders, namely the importance of legitimacy in the exercise of political power and the undesirability of political self-aggrandisement, find some resonance in the international order. In addition, fears that the ICJ might have an over-zealous approach when testing the legality of Security Council decisions would seem unfounded. As was already illustrated in the context of advisory opinions, the ICJ attaches a presumption of legality to resolutions of United Nations organs.[316] Thus, even though the ICJ has consistently rejected a political question doctrine,[317] it nonetheless grants the political organs a wide ambit of discretion by departing from the presumption that they have acted within their powers. Stated differently, the restraint is not so much reflected in when the ICJ involves itself in a decision, but by how it goes about it.

---

[312] Franck (International Legal Issues), above n 161, at 631. But see TD Gill, "Legal and Some Political Limitations on the Power of the UN Security Council to Exercise its Enforcement Powers under Chapter VII of the Charter", 26 *Netherlands Yearbook of International Law* 121 (1995), who did not regard legitimacy as a judicial issue. He submitted that problems of political imbalance, or legitimacy in the way the Security Council carried out is responsibilities could not be remedied by giving the ICJ a *de facto* veto over the Council's actions.

[313] Caron, above n 231, at 561.

[314] Dupuy, above n 140, at 30; Caron, above n 321, at 561.

[315] See Dupuy, above n 140, at 30; Malanczuk (in Heere), above note 27, at 98. But see Lorinser, above n 4, at 100, who argued that the mere failure of this mechanism is no justification for introducing judicial review. She was not prepared to accept that a general principle of judicial review is emerging in municipal law. Cf Tomuschat (Obligations), above n 130, at 249.

[316] See ch 2, at s 3.1.3. See also Dugard, above n 34, at 90.

[317] See ch 2, at s 3.1.2.

These factors, coupled with the on-going expansion of judicial review could tempt one to recognise it as a general principle of law to be transposed to the international plane. Before doing so, however, one has to consider to what extent the differences in implementation of judicial review in the respective municipal systems would form an obstacle to this conclusion.

5.2.   Difference in Implementation of Judicial Review and its Consequences

The above description on the expansion of judicial review merely focuses on the general recognition of some kind of legal testing of political acts by an independent judicial body, without explaining how or to what extent this is done. It thus remains on a very abstract or general level of communality. If one takes a closer look at the implementation of judicial review in municipal systems, one notices that it differs greatly from state to state. The methods chosen are closely related to the legal, political and socio-economic experiences made with the exercise of state power within a particular state.[318]

First, there are differences with respect to the legal subjects who have standing during constitutional proceedings. It can vary from higher organs of state to parliamentary groups to individuals, or a combination of these. Second, the scope and subject matter of constitutional review may differ. Some systems, for example, only allow for the constitutional scrutiny of laws of general applicability, whereas others allow for scrutiny of general laws as well as acts of the executive.[319] Third, there are differences as to the timing of review. The French model, in particular, usually only practices *a priori* abstract review and considers legislation after it is adopted by parliament but before it is promulgated.[320] The systems following the European model, on the other hand, mostly practice only *a posteriori* abstract review.[321]

Another difference relates to the effects of judicial review. It does not automatically follow that the organ exercising the review can nullify or suspend the act, or refuse to apply it. In certain cases the reviewing organ would only give a (non-binding) opinion as to the issue of constitutionality. Whereas binding decisions usually apply *erga omnes*, declaratory opinions

---

[318] Lorinser, above n 4, at 80.
[319] *Ibid*, at 83. See generally Rudolf Bernhardt, "Normkontrolle", in Hermann Mosler, *Verfassungsrichtsbarkeit in der Gegenwart* 727 ff (Berlin, Springer, 1962). Also see www.us-rs. si/en/revfr.html for an overview of the different types of reviewing powers.
[320] See also Wright Sheive, above n 251, at 1209.
[321] Wright Sheive, above n 251, 175 at 1209; Utter & Lundsgaard, above n 280, at p 21.

often only apply *inter partes*. Also, a finding of unconstitutionality may sometimes not be applied retroactively but only *ex nunc* or *pro futuro*.[322] The question that now has to be answered, is to what extent these differences in implementation would prevent judicial review from emerging as a general principle of law that could be transferred to the United Nations system. It is submitted that the most important of these differences concerns the scope and subject matter of judicial review in the different jurisdictions. Other differences, especially those relating to the consequences of judicial review, would not seem to be of a decisive nature.

It is unclear from the available material how many of the countries would actually allow judicial organs to review the powers of political organs in matters of national security. In particular, more information is needed about the number of countries allowing judicial organs to review a determination that a situation constitutes a threat to national security. Even if one were to make allowances for differences as to how the courts go about reviewing matters of national security, there would have to be some general agreement that they can review this type of decision. As this goes to the heart of judicial review in contentious proceedings before the ICJ such as the *Lockerbie* incident, it would not suffice to argue that some sort of judicial review exists in most countries, as this is too a vague a conclusion.[323]

Some might also argue that not only the recognition of such review is required in a majority of jurisdictions, but that it also has to be enforced effectively. However, it is questionable whether effective enforcement should be a decisive criteria. It would imply the extremely arduous task of attempting to evaluate the actual implementation of a general principle in the different legal systems. This would render the exercise of comparative analysis meaningless from a practical point of view.[324] One should rather take the principled approach of focussing on the official recognition of the principle and the growing consensus about its motivating rational.

Criticism that there cannot be a transferral of judicial review since the ICJ has no power of annulment, or that its decisions has no *erga omnes* effect, would also not seem to be convincing. The differences in the consequences of judicial review in the municipal systems illustrate that it is a fallacy to believe that judicial review necessarily has to result in a binding

---

[322] Lorinser, above n 4, at 82–83; see also Herdegen, above n 198, at 151; Utter & Lundsgaard, above n 280, at 19–20.

[323] See Gill, above n 312, at 117 who argues that courts traditionally steer clear of reviewing issues relating to national security. On the other hand, one should keep in mind that the national security argument is very often abused by governments. For that very reason it would be advisable to subject it to judicial review.

[324] See Bernhardt (Eigenheiten und Ziele), above n 72, at 447. For an opinion that a link between formal state recognition and actual intra-state implementation is important, see Bothe & Ress, above n 45, at 51.

decision with *erga omnes* effect.[325] To the contrary, judicial review is an institution that can exist without a formal doctrine of judicial supremacy. Consequently it can be transferred to an institution such as the ICJ whose decisions formally only bind the parties, or whose advisory opinions are strictly speaking only of a declaratory nature.[326] The ICJ would also have the latitude to determine that its judgment in a particular case would only have prospective effect.[327] This could avoid legal uncertainty with respect to the consequences of state action taken on the basis of a Security Council resolution, prior to the ICJ's determination of its illegality.[328]

The fact that the ICJ remains under-developed compared to municipal courts would also not have to mean that it is unsuitable for such a transferral. In fact, it seems logical that the judicial branch within an embryonic constitutional order would be of a limited nature, since anything else would upset the delicate balance within the system.[329] One could even argue that it is exactly this limited jurisdiction which poses the most effective barrier against the danger that the municipal analogy would turn the United Nations into a quasi-state.[330] Even though judicial review could exist in the international legal order, its intensity and frequency could never be comparable to that of states, due to the special nature of the international order.[331]

Finally, a point worth mentioning is that most national jurisdictions provide for judicial review explicitly in the constitution or another legislative enactment. The United States model, which does not provide for it explicitly in the Constitution, but where it was regarded as inherent in the constitution in *Marbury v Madison*,[332] would be the exception rather than the rule.[333] If the ICJ were to regard judicial review in contentious proceedings as inherent to the Charter it would seem to be following a model which is not representative of most states. However, if one were

---

[325] See Rosenne, above n 137, at 226.

[326] Watson, above n 179, at 13.

[327] The consequences of a finding of illegality by the ICJ have already been illuminated in connection with advisory opinions in ch 2, at s 4.2. As they would be essentially the same where such a finding is made in the course of contentious proceedings, they will not be repeated here.

[328] Alvarez (Theoretical Perspectives), above n 212, at 89.

[329] See Shahabuddeen, above n 74, at 95. It would be incorrect to view the ICJ as if it were a court exercising judicial power on exactly the same basis as that on which a municipal court does. But that consideration, relating to differences in the basis of the power, is not a convincing reason for suggesting that no analogy exists as to the nature of the power itself.

[330] As is feared by Lorinser, above n 4, at 86.

[331] Franck (International Legal Issues), above n 161, at 625; Malanczuk (in Heere), above n 27, at 99.

[332] above n 9, at 177. Justice Marshall regarded it as the task of the court to say what the law is. Those who apply the rule to particular cases must of necessity expound and interpret that rule. If two laws conflict each other, the courts must decide on the operation of each, as this constitutes the very essence of judicial duty.

[333] Watson, above n 179, at 6; Sloan, above n 4, at 72.

willing to regard the *Marbury* model as a method for implementing a common principle and not as the principle itself, then its exceptionality would lose significance. As has been explained in section 3.1. above, it is merely the *rationale* or *principle* behind the legal concept that must have a universal character. The particular *method* chosen for its concretisation in the international order can be chosen from any (one) municipal system, whose structures most resemble those of the international order with respect to the issue at hand.

One might argue that in the United Nations, the *Marbury* model presents itself as a suitable method in the light of the Charter's silence on this issue. Just as the American Supreme Court could be regarded as the inherent guardian of the United States Constitution, the ICJ as principal judicial organ could be regarded as the inherent guardian of legality in the United Nations order.[334] Furthermore, in both the United States and the United Nations the issue of judicial review can be regarded as the natural outcome of an evolutionary process. In most of the other jurisdictions the introduction of judicial review marked a clear break from a former (oppressive) regime.[335] Thus, its explicit guarantee was to mark the explicit introduction of a new era. In the United States however, judicial review was the outcome of the evolutionary inter-action of its different organs of government[336]—as it should arguably be in the case of the United Nations.[337]

The ICJ has already paved the way for regarding itself as the inherent guardian of the UN Charter in the *Namibia opinion*.[338] As explained in chapter 2 at section 2.2, this opinion was aimed at clarifying the legal consequences for states of the continued presence of South Africa in Namibia, notwithstanding Resolution 276 of 30 January 1970. Since the Government of South Africa raised objections challenging the validity of this (and other preceding) resolutions, the question arose whether the

---

[334] See Peter Malanczuk (in Heere), above n 27, at 98–99; Sloan, above n 4, at 71–72; Franck (International Legal Issues), above n 161, at 662, Franck, above n 10, at 520.

[335] See Brunner, above n 279, at 865 with respect to Eastern Europe.

[336] See Alvarez (Theoretical Perspectives), above n 212, at 89. Judicial review emerged and continues to develop through long-term, evolutionary conversations between institutional organs. See also Michael J Glennon, "Protecting the Court's Institutional Interests: Why not the *Marbury* approach?", 81 *American Journal of International Law* 121–22 (1987). At the time of the *Marbury* decision, above n 9, the United States Supreme Court was still young and in need of establishing its legitimacy. It had not yet secured its position as final arbiter of the meaning of the United States Constitution.

[337] But see Lorinser, above n 4, at 78. She argued that the following of the *Marbury* model by the ICJ would enhance the perception of many countries that the organisation is dominated and manipulated by the United States. However, whether this really is be the case, is questionable. Until now it has been—ironically enough—mainly those countries who fear dominance by the United States which have argued in favour of judicial review within the United Nations, whereas as the United States has been one of its most vehement opponents.

[338] *Namibia* opinion, above n 190, at 3.

ICJ was in a position to determine their validity. It pointed out that it did not possess powers of judicial review or appeal in relation to the United Nations organs in question. Nor did the validity of the resolutions form the subject of the request for an advisory opinion. The ICJ nevertheless, "in the exercise of its judicial function", considered their validity before elaborating on the legal consequences arising from those resolutions.[339]

Some may reject the relevance of this example, arguing that judicial review in advisory opinions are not comparable to that in contentious proceedings. First, as was elaborated on in chapter 2 at section 3.1.1, there are textual justifications for exercising judicial review in advisory proceedings. Second, the role of the ICJ in advisory proceedings is different from its role in contentious proceedings. In the former it acts as principal judicial organ and legal adviser of the United Nations as a whole, whereas in the latter it has to resolve disputes between two (or more) individual states. This would make advisory opinions a more appropriate avenue for judicial review. Finally, others may even argue that it would be inappropriate to compare advisory opinions with contentious proceedings, since advisory opinions are non-binding.[340]

Nonetheless, the International Criminal Tribunal for the former Yugoslavia (ICTY) and the International Criminal Tribunal for Rwanda (ICTR) have used the *Namibia* opinion as authority for justifying their right to review the legality of the Security Council resolutions that created them.[341] The fact that the Security Council was not party to these disputes, or that the role of these tribunals are not comparable with the ICJ's advisory role, did not prevent them from doing so. Therefore it is possible that the ICJ would secure the power of judicial review in contentious proceedings with a similar argument.

6. CONCLUSION

The growth in the significance of judicial review in municipal orders in recent years reflects some movement towards its emergence as a general principle of law. Most countries now allow for the testing of the legality of decisions of political organs by an independent judicial organ in some

---

[339] *Ibid*, at 45.
[340] See *ibid*, for arguments that dispute the correctness of this position.
[341] See the *Tadic* decision, above n 221, at para 18. The ICTY determined that the competence to determine the legality of its own creation belonged to the essence of its jurisdiction, ie its judicial function to state what the law is. See also the decision of the ICTR, in *The Prosecutor v Kanyabashi*, Decision on the Defense Motion on Jurisdiction, Case No ICTR–96–15–T, Trial Chamber, 18 June 1997, at 6 ff, available at www.ictr.org; Herbst, above n 6, at 283–84, 290–91.

form or another. The motivating rationale for this development is the need to legitimate the exercise of political power—an issue which is also of considerable importance in the United Nations system. This common quest for political legitimisation could tempt one to recognise judicial review as a general principle of law in terms of 38(1)(c) of the ICJ statute. Such recognition would enable the ICJ to review Security Council decisions where their legality is questioned in contentious proceedings between states. In a dispute such as *Lockerbie*, this would provide the ICJ with the power to determine whether the Security Council has violated the Charter. Currently it is unclear whether the ICJ has this power, due to the silence of the Charter on this issue.

However, although the power of the ICJ to review decisions of the Security Council in contentious proceedings may be desirable, basing it on the general principles of law in terms of Article 38(1)(c) of the ICJ statute would be tenuous. On the one hand the above analysis has indicated that the quest for legitimacy is gaining importance both in municipal jurisdictions as well as in the international order. It also illustrated that several arguments against judicial review by the ICJ compared to those in municipal jurisdictions are too undifferentiated. These would include arguments relating to the absence of a separation of powers within the United Nations system, and the lack of annulment power of the ICJ.

On the other hand, some important difficulties in the recognition of judicial review as a general principle of law remain. First, it implies a "relativistic" approach to the structural differences between the decentralised international legal order and those existing within sovereign states. As many international lawyers regard these differences as fundamental, the comparison of the Charter with municipal constitutions for the purposes of judicial review will—at least for the present—continue to meet with considerable objection. Second, recognising a general principle of judicial review, based on the existence of some sort of legal testing of the actions of political organs in most countries, would be too general. It would not take account of the fact that the scope of this testing does not necessarily extend to decisions concerning national security. Since this is of direct relevance to the type of judicial review that the ICJ would exercise in contentious proceedings, more information as to the subject-matter of judicial review in municipal jurisdictions is needed.

It would thus seem that the impasse in the debate as to whether the ICJ could exercise judicial review in contentious proceedings can not yet be resolved satisfactorily by resorting to Article 38(1)(c) of the Statute. If the ICJ were eventually to decide that it had such power of review, it might very well follow the line of argument in the *Namibia* opinion and thus resort to a *Marbury* type solution.[342] It may also be motivated

---

[342] *Namibia* opinion, above n 190, at 45.

by the fact that the ICTY and ICTR resorted to a similar approach when determining that they had the power to review the legality of their own creation. Thus, if the ICJ refused to grant itself this power, it would have the strange consequence that the principle judicial organ of the United Nations did not have the power of review in contentious proceedings, whereas mere subsidiary organs of the Security Council indeed would possess this power.

Nonetheless, if the ICJ were to resort to this solution, it is unlikely to end the debate on the matter, as the meaning of its "judicial function" is bound to be interpreted differently by lawyers. It would be a pragmatic way of securing judicial review, that would not necessarily satisfy intellectually. This raises the question whether the uncertainties surrounding the ICJ's power of review in contentious proceedings can be answered satisfactorily at all without amending the Charter. It is submitted that this is unlikely, unless the obstacles surrounding the emergence of judicial review as a general principle of law lose significance with the passage of time. This would imply, inter alia, a broader acceptance of the "relativistic" approach outlined above and more clarity as to the scope of judicial review in municipal orders.

From these observations, combined with those in the previous chapter relating to advisory opinions as a mode for judicial review of Security Council decisions, one can draw the conclusion that the role of the ICJ in enforcing limitations to the Chapter VII powers of the Security Council is likely to remain limited in future. Consequently, one is confronted with the need to explore alternative (or rather complementary) modes of enforcement of these limitations in the decentralised international legal order. However, this question will only be addressed in the final chapter. For it is first necessary to identify the limitations of the Security Council when exercising its Chapter VII powers and it is this issue which will form the focal point in subsequent chapters.

Part II

Limitations to the Security Council's Chapter VII Powers

4

Limits to the Security Council's Discretion under Article 39 of the Charter

1. INTRODUCTION

WHEREAS THE PREVIOUS chapters focused on the mechanisms for facilitating judicial review within the United Nations system, attention now turns to the criteria to be applied during judicial review. Before the Security Council may impose coercive measures of an economic or military nature under Articles 40, 41 and 42 of the Charter, it must determine the existence of "threat to the peace, breach of the peace, or an act of aggression" within the meaning of Article 39 of the Charter.[1] This means that the Security Council has a discretion both in deciding when to act (Article 39) and how to act (Articles 40, 41 and 42).

The extent to which this discretion is subjected to limitation is a hotly debated issue. Some authors claim that both types of action fall within the absolute discretion of the Security Council.[2] Others argue that the decision as to when the Security Council should intervene in terms of Article 39 lies purely within its discretion,[3] but that general international law, in particular *ius cogens*, as well as the purposes and principles of the United Nations

---

[1] Jochen A Frowein, "Article 39", in Bruno Simma (ed), *Charter of the United Nations. A Commentary* 618 (Oxford, Oxford University Press, 1994); TD Gill, "Legal and Some Political Limitations on the Power of the UN Security Council to Exercise its Enforcement Powers under Chapter VII of the Charter", 26 *Netherlands Yearbook of International Law* 60 (1995); Ruth Gordon, "United Nations Intervention in Internal Conflicts: Iraq, Somalia, and Beyond", 15 *Michigan Journal of International Law* 563 (1993); Vera Gowlland-Debbas, "Security Council Enforcement Action and Issues of State Responsibility", 43 *International and Comparative Law Quarterly* 60 (1994); Angus M Gunn, "Council and Court: Prospects in Lockerbie for an International Rule of Law", 52 *University of Toronto Law Review* 228 (1993); Barbara Lorinser, *Bindende Resolutionen des Sicherheitsrates* 39 (Baden-Baden, Nomos, 1996); Bernd Martenczuk, "The Security Council, the International Court and Judicial Review: What Lessons from Lockerbie?", 10 *European Journal of International Law* 538 (1999).
[2] Gabriel H Oosthuizen, "Playing the Devil's Advocate: the United Nations Security Council is Unbound by Law", 12 *Leiden Journal of International Law* 521 (1999); Inger Österdahl, *Threat to the Peace* 98 (Uppsala, Iustus, 1998).
[3] Hans Kelsen, *The Law of the United Nations* 730 (London, Stevens, 1950); Benedetto Conforti, "The Legal effect of Non-Compliance with Rules of Procedure in the UN General Assembly and the Security Council", 63 *American Journal of International Law* 479 (1969).

would pose limits to the type of action that may be taken by the Security Council.[4] Yet others argue the exact opposite and state that once the Security Council is acting in terms of Article 39, there are no limits as to what it can do. However, whether it has passed the threshold constituted by Article 39 is something that can be measured by means of judicial criteria.[5]

The following chapter analyses which of these scenarios (if any) is the most accurate with respect to Article 39. It commences with an abstract analysis of the nature of the Security Council's determination under Article 39. This will include an attempt to define the concepts "threat to peace", "breach of the peace" and an "act of aggression" in legal terms by interpreting them according to their ordinary meaning, in context and with due consideration to the object and purpose of the Charter. Due to its dominant role in practice the term "threat to peace" forms the centre of the analysis, followed by a concise discussion of the concepts "breach of the peace" and "act of aggression". Thereafter the chapter concentrates on the practice of the Security Council, in order to determine if and to what extent it corresponds to any of the preliminary conclusions flowing from the abstract analysis of Article 39.

The present chapter is not concerned with the discretion of the Security Council contained in Articles 40, 41 and 42 of the Charter, ie determining the type of enforcement measures necessary to restore or maintain international peace and security. Instead, it is exclusively concerned with the threshold that triggers Chapter VII action, whereas the type of measures that can be resorted to once this threshold has been crossed are analysed in chapter 5 and subsequent chapters. Chapter 3 at section 4.2. indicated that it remains controversial whether the Security Council can adopt enforcement measures against non-member states, on the basis that the enforcement mechanism contained in Chapter VII has obtained customary international law status. The extent to which this controversy could affect the legality of enforcement measures is also discussed in chapter 5 and subsequent chapters, when analysing the Security Council practice in this regard. The matter will not, however, feature in the present chapter. Since an Article 39 determination remains an abstract decision that does not in itself produce any binding measures against non-members, the principle of *pacta tertiis nec nocent nec prosunt* would not prevent the Security Council from making such a determination.

2.   THE NATURE OF THE SECURITY COUNCIL'S DISCRETION UNDER ARTICLE 39

Supporters as well as opponents of an unlimited Security Council discretion under Article 39 of the Charter forward interesting arguments to

---

[4] Gill, above n 1, at 40.
[5] Bernd Martenczuk, *Rechtsbindung und Rechtskontrolle des Weltsicherheitsrates* 224 ff (Berlin, Duncker & Humblot, 1996); *ibid*, above n 1, at 517.

underpin their positions.[6] The supporters thereof point to the fact that the terms "threat to the peace", "breach of the peace" or an "act of aggression" are not defined anywhere in the Charter.[7] Second, the determination that one of these situations has occurred is a judgement based on factual findings and the weighing of political considerations which could not be measured by legal criteria.[8]

Third, the voting (veto) power attributed to the five permanent members in Article 27(3) of the Charter would be a reflection of the political nature of an Article 39 determination. This structural bias in favour of the major powers is a clear indication that decisions in the interest of peace and security will be based exclusively on (national) political considerations.[9] It is as an acknowledgement that the Security Council and in particular its five permanent members are the sole judges of the existence of the state of affairs which brings Chapter VII into operation.[10]

[6] Art 39 of the Charter reads: "The Security Council shall determine the existence of any threat to the peace, breach of the peace, or act of aggression and shall make recommendations, or decide what measures shall be taken in accordance with Articles 41 and 42, to maintain or restore international peace and security."

[7] Gowlland-Debbas (State Responsibility), above n 1, at 60; Gordon, above n 1, at 563. See also XII *United Nations Conference on International Organisation* 503–04 (1945). At San Francisco proposals to distinguish (in what was then Chapter VIII) between a threat to peace which resulted from the failure to arrive at a peaceful settlement of a particular dispute, and the presence of a general threat to the peace, breach of the peace or an act of aggression, was abandoned. This was done in order not to restrict unduly the broad discretion of the Security Council. However, as will be illustrated in s 2.3. below, fn 80, one can interpret these discussions relating to Art 39 as being more concerned with ensuring that the Security Council is in a position to take quick action, than with whether there should be limitations to its discretion to do so. See also Andreas Stein, *Der Sicherheitsrat der Vereinten Nationen und die Rule of Law* 27 (Baden-Baden, Nomos, 1999); Frowein (in Simma), above n 1, at 607.

[8] Separate opinion of Judge Weeramantry in *Case Concerning Questions of Interpretation and Application of the 1971 Montreal Convention Arising from the Aerial Incident at Lockerbie (Libyan Arab Jamahiriya v United States of America)*, Provisional Measures, ICJ Rep 1992, at 176. Hereinafter referred to as *Libya v United States*, provisional measures. Philip Alston, "The Security Council and Human Rights: Lessons to be Learned from the Iraq-Kuwait Crisis and its Aftermath", 13 *Australian Yearbook of International law* 138 (1990/ 1991); See also Yoram Dinstein, "The Legal Lessons of the Gulf War", 48 *Austrian Journal of Public and International Law* 4 (1995); *ibid*, "Humanitarian Intervention from Outside, in the face of Genocide, is Legitimate only when Undertaken by the Security Council", 27 *Justice* 6 (2001); See also Gowlland-Debbas (State Responsibility), above n 1, at 60.

[9] Derek Bowett, "The Impact of Security Council Decisions on Dispute Settlement Procedures", 5 *European Journal of International Law* 93 (1994). See also Heike Gading, *Der Schutz grundlegender Menschenrechte durch militärische Massnahmen des Sicherheitsrates— das Ende staatlicher Souveränität* 50–51 (Berlin, Duncker & Humblot, 1996). This bias reflected the conviction that international peace will not be served if coercive measures (and military power in particular) were used against the will of a major power. The net result was that such measures could only be adopted against smaller nations.

[10] David D Caron, "The Legitimacy of the Collective Authority of the Security Council", 87 *American Journal of International Law* 568, 565 (1993). See also Bowett, above n 9, at 94; Kelsen, above n 3, at 735. See also the separate opinion of Judge Weeramantry in *Libya v United States*, provisional measures, above n 8, at 176. In spite of these individual remarks by judges, the ICJ has to date not yet taken a position on the meaning of Art 39. The International Criminal Tribunal for the former Yugoslavia (ICTY) was confronted with the

Fourth, the exclusively political nature of an Article 39 determination is also underscored by the lack of any obligation on the part of the Security Council to decide whether a given situation falls within the terms of Article 39, or to take any enforcement action when it has made such a determination.[11] The Security Council does not have to act in all the situations that would seem to call for the exercise of its competence, but operates selectively and with discretion.[12]

Opponents of an unlimited discretion regard these arguments as flawed. First, the fact that the Security Council is under no obligation to act in terms of Chapter VII does not have to mean that when it does possess the political will to act in terms of this Chapter, it has an unlimited discretion to do so. The veto power is a minimum threshold, but the overcoming thereof is not in itself a justification for unlimited action in the context of Article 39.[13] Second, although it is undeniable that imprecision and vagueness surround the terms used in Article 39, these qualities are general features of law. The concretisation of vague terms is, in the first instance, a matter of legal interpretation.[14]

The application of vague legal terms on a particular set of facts is necessarily linked to a certain discretion, but the existence thereof neither has to be evidence of an unlimited political discretion of a preclusive nature, nor that no definition for these terms should be attempted at all.[15] There is nothing inherently special about the terms used in Article 39 that would *ab initio* remove them from the ambit of legal interpretation. On the contrary, the mere fact that Article 39 distinguishes between three criteria that trigger binding resolutions of the Security Council, implies that it does not have an unbound discretion.[16] If an unbound discretion had

---

question in the *Prosecutor v Tadic*, Decision on the Defence Motion on Jurisdiction, Case No IT–94–1, 10 August 1995, Trials Chamber, at para 23 and *ibid*, Decision on the Defence Motion for Interlocutory Appeal on Jurisdiction, Case No IT–94–1–AR72, 10 October 1995, Appeals Chamber, at para 29. Whereas the Trials Chamber determined that a threat to peace was a non-justiciable issue, the Appeals Chamber found that the Security Council did not have a completely unfettered discretion in this regard. It had to remain, at the very least, within the limits of the purposes and principles of the Charter. Both decisions are available at www.un.org/icty.

[11] Gill, above n 1, at 40. See Michael Reisman, "The Constitutional Crisis in the United Nations", 87 *American Journal of International Law* 95 (1993). Although the veto power is first and foremost with the permanent members, the non-permanent members can also block Chapter VII decisions. If a majority of them vote against a proposal, the Security Council cannot pass it, no matter how united and passionate the permanent five may be.

[12] Gill, above n 1, at 40; See Gaetano Arangio-Ruiz, Rapporteur to the International Law Commission, Fifth Report on State Responsibility, in A/CN.4/453/Add.3 16–17 (1993); Österdahl, above n 2, at 103–105.

[13] Martenczuk (Rechtskontrolle), above n 5, at 205–06; *ibid*, above n 1, at 542.

[14] Martin Lailach, *Die Wahrung des Weltfriedens und der internationalen Sicherheit als Aufgabe des Sicherheitsrates der Vereinten Nationen* 163 (Berlin, Duncker & Humblot, 1998); Lorinser, above n 1, at 39; Martenczuk, above n 1, at 543; Stein, above n 7, at 33.

[15] Lorinser, above n 1, at 40; Martenczuk, above n 1, at 543.

[16] Lorinser, above n 1, at 46; Stein, above n 7, at 124.

been intended, such a distinction would have been obsolete. The Charter would only have contributed to the Security Council the general power to adopt binding measures in the interest of international peace and security and nothing more.[17]

Stated differently, the criteria provided for in Article 39 should serve as (part of) a system of checks and balances that prevents the Security Council from becoming the world government which it was not intended to be, but which it could become if article 39 invested it with an unlimited discretion.[18] It could then, for example, determine that any social malaise in a society, such as the insufficient quality of foreign language facilities in a country, or its high rate of unemployment, constitutes a threat to international peace.[19] It is very unlikely that the members of the United Nations at any stage of its development intended an unrepresentative organ consisting of merely 16 countries should have the power to adopt binding obligations with such unforeseen consequences.[20] Some would argue that the Security Council would not be as unwise as to interpret its unlimited discretion in such a broad sense. However, it seems unconvincing to first argue that the Security Council has such wide competencies, but then to assume that it will not exercise it.[21]

Finally, an unlimited discretion of the Security Council under Article 39 would risk destroying the carefully crafted balance of competencies in the Charter. The Security Council's powers to impose binding sanctions and order other measures for the maintenance of international peace can only be exercised under Chapter VII.[22] In contrast, the Security Council's powers under Chapter VI, which relates to the peaceful settlement of disputes, are non-binding. For example, in the event of a dispute the continuance of which is likely to endanger the maintenance of international peace and security, the Security Council may merely recommend procedures for the settlement of the dispute.[23] These distinctions between Chapter VI and VII would become obsolete if the Security Council at any given time were free to declare the provisions of Chapter VII applicable.[24]

---

[17] Lorinser, above n 1, at 46; Stein, above n 7, at 124.
[18] Martenczuk (Rechtskontrolle), above n 5, at 206–07.
[19] Bowett, above n 9, at 92.
[20] Martenczuk (Rechtskontrolle), above n 5, at 205–06, 238; Bowett, above n 9, at 92; Lorinser, above n 1, at 42. Contra Dinstein, above n 8, at 4. He submitted that nothing prevented the Security Council from determining that the emergence of a political crisis in a particular state constituted a threat to peace, provided that the required majority is attained. As a result, anything under the sun could constitute a threat to peace.
[21] Lorinser, above n 1, at 46; Ian Brownlie, "The Decisions of Political Organs of the United Nations and the Rule of Law", in Ronald St John MacDonald (ed), *Essays in Honour of Wang Tieya* 96 (Dordrecht, Martinus Nijhoff, 1994).
[22] Martenczuk, above n 1, at 542.
[23] Arts 36 and 37(1) of the Charter.
[24] Martenczuk, above n 1, at 542.

At first glance, the arguments in favour of limiting the Security Council's discretion under Article 39 are very convincing. However, their ultimate weight will depend on whether the terms contained in Article 39 are indeed definable in legal terms. The weight of principled arguments for limiting the Security Council's discretion will be weakened considerably if it turns out that these terms are *de facto* "non-justiciable". The question is particularly pertinent with respect to a "threat to the peace", which is the most elastic and dynamic of the three terms contained in Article 39.

2.1   A Threat to Peace

The term peace can be defined either negatively (narrowly) or positively (widely). In accordance with the negative definition, "peace" is characterised by the absence of armed conflict between states.[25] According to the supporters of this view, a combined reading of Article 1(1) and Article 2(4) of the Charter reflects that the prevention of inter-state conflict is the primary purpose of the Charter. Whereas Article 1(1) elevates the maintenance of international peace and security to the most important goal of the United Nations, Article 2(4) outlaws the unilateral use of force by states against each other.[26] Therefore, in order to constitute a threat to peace, a situation has to have the potential of provoking armed conflict between states in the short or medium turn.[27] That it does not have to concern the actual outbreak of armed conflict follows from the term "threat", to which an element of flexibility is inherently attached. It also follows from the escalation of intensity implied by the terms of Article 39. As a "breach of the peace" and an "act of aggression" concern (different degrees of) the actual outbreak of hostilities,[28] a "threat to peace" has to amount to less.[29]

The supporters of positive peace reject the negative definition as too restricted. Instead, they embrace a definition that also includes

[25] Martenczuk (Rechtskontrolle), above n 5, at 224; *ibid*, above n 1, at 543; Frowein (in Simma), above n 1, at 608, Hans Peter Neuhold, "Threat to Peace", III *Encyclopedia of Public International Law* 937 (1997); Stein, above n 7, at 116.
[26] Martenczuk (Rechtskontrolle), above n 5, at 224, 228. He noted that the first part of the sentence constituting Art 39 refers to a threat to 'the peace' as a prerequisite for Security Council action. The second, part, however, states that measures to be taken should serve to maintain "international peace" and security. This gives the peace at stake an international (ie inter-state) character. See also Frowein (in Simma), above n 1, at 608. Cf Jost Delbrück, "Structural Changes in the International System and its Legal Order: International Law in the Era of Globalisation", 11 *Schweizerische Zeitschrift für Internationales und Europäisches Recht* 10 (2001); Gading, above n 9, at 70; Lailach, above n 14, at 46–47; Stein, above n 7, at 122.
[27] Lailach, above n 14, at 195–196; Martenczuk (Rechtskontrolle), above n 5, at 238–39, *ibid*, above n 1, at 544.
[28] See s 2.2. and s 2.3. below.
[29] Martenczuk, above n 1, at 544; Lailach, above n 14, at 194. For a supporter of the thesis that a threat to peace strictly correlates with the violation of the prohibition in Art 2(4), see Joachim Arntz, *Der Begriff der Friedensbedrohung in Satzung und Praxis der Vereinten Nationen* 44 ff (Berlin, Duncker & Humblot, 1975).

friendly relations between states and other economic, social, political and environmental conditions which are needed for a lasting, conflict free society.[30] Some support for this view was reflected in a 1992 statement of the President of the Security Council,[31] the then British Prime Minister John Major.[32] On behalf of the Security Council he stated that the absence of war and military conflicts amongst states did not in itself ensure international peace and security. The non-military sources of instability in the economic, social, humanitarian and ecological fields have become threats to peace and security. The United Nations membership as a whole, working through the appropriate bodies, needed to give the highest priority to the solution of the matters.[33] From this statement some have concluded a commitment on the part of the Security Council to maintain and restore the positive peace.[34]

These arguments have rightly been criticised for ignoring the limitations imposed on the Security Council by its structure and composition. In order to be effective, the Security Council can only react to those international crises which have the potential to spark international armed conflict in the short or medium term. It is a reactionary organ that is not equipped to attempt the prevention of all, possible long term tensions.[35] Using its Chapter VII powers to take decisions in these matters would also elevate the Security Council to the world government which it was not meant to be.[36] Instead, long-term structural elements necessary for the realisation of positive peace should be realised through recommendations of the General Assembly or the Economic and Social Council (ECOSOC) in accordance with Articles 14 and 60 of the Charter.[37]

This does not imply that these organs have exclusive jurisdiction over, for example, human rights issues and that the Security Council is precluded from dealing with them.[38] The Security Council should, however, not

---

[30] Martenczuk (Rechtskontrolle), above n 5, at 224; *ibid*, above n 1, at 543; Lailach, above n 14, at 32. See Rüdiger Wolfrum "Article 1", in Bruno Simma (ed), *The Charter of the United Nations. A Commentary* 50 (Oxford, Oxford University Press, 1994). Some textual support for this inclusive definition of peace can be found in the preamble of the Charter and Arts 1(2), 1(3), 55 and 73. These provisions refer to an evolutionary development in the state of international relations in order to reduce the issues likely to cause war. For example, Arts 1(2) and 1(3) speak of the strengthening of peace through the development of friendly relations and cooperation among nations. For their part, Arts 55 and 73 include human rights and self-determination, respectively, as elements of peace. See also Stein, above n 7, at 127 ff.

[31] S/23500 3 (1992).

[32] This was the first time in history that the Heads of State and Government represented the member states in the Security Council.

[33] *Ibid.*

[34] Matthias Herdegen, *Die Befugnisse des UN-Sicherheitsrates: aufgeklärter Absolitismus im Völkerrecht?* 12 (Heidelberg, Müller, 1998); see Lailach, above n 14, at 129.

[35] Lailach, above n 14, at 203–204; Martenczuk (Rechtskontrolle), above n 5, at 238–39.

[36] See Martenczuk (Rechtskontrolle), above n 5, at 202–03; Bowett, above n 9, at 92; Lorinser, above n 1, at 42.

[37] See Lailach, above n 14, at 30; Neuhold, above n 25, at 937.

[38] See Alston, above n 8, at 139.

invoke human rights violations and other structural problems as a trigger to Article 39 in situations which do not threaten negative peace, as this would lead to a duplication of the functions of ECOSOC and the General Assembly.[39] In this context it is also important to note that the 1992 Statement by the Presidency of the Security Council[40] explicitly attributed the task of countering the socio-economic threat to peace to the United Nations as a whole, and not to the Security Council *per se*.[41] This can be read as an awareness that the Security Council would not be the appropriate body for dealing with the long-term, structural causes of threats to peace.

This emphasis on the structural limitations is also not intended to deny the Security Council's need for flexibility when determining the existence of a threat to peace. After all, such flexibility is an essential pre-condition for an effective fulfilment of the obligation to "maintain" international peace, which is reiterated in Article 39.[42] The preventive component of this obligation would be undermined if the Security Council could not address threats to peace that originate from within states. The internal sources of a threat to peace can vary in nature and can include behaviour which is not illegal in itself.[43] The introduction of a massive armament programme would be one example. Since the national defence policy is a matter to be regulated by the states themselves, in as far as they are not bound by any international treaties,[44] increasing a country's military capacity is not *per se* illegal. However, a massive armament policy could under certain circumstances pose a threat to international peace and require Security Council action, as was the case with South Africa in 1977.[45]

---

[39] *Ibid*, at 139–40; Cf the Final Declaration of the Summit Meeting of the Non-Aligned Movement held in Jakarta in August 1992, NAC 10/Doc.1/Rev.1 para 31 (1992).

[40] S/23500 3 (1992).

[41] Dorothee Starck, *Die Rechtsmässigkeit von UNO-Wirtschaftssanktionen in Anbetracht ihrer Auswirkungen auf die Zivilbevölkerung* 168 (Berlin, Duncker & Humblot, 2000).

[42] Martenczuk, above n 1, at 544.

[43] Alston, above n 8, at 170; see also Lois E Fielding, "Taking a Closer Look at Threats to Peace: The Power of the Security Council to Address Humanitarian Crises", 73 *University of Detroit Mercy Law Review* 560 ff (1996); Jochen Herbst, *Rechtsbindung des UN-Sicherheitsrates* 331 (Frankfurt a/M, Peter Lang, 1999); Lailach, above n 14, at 194; Lorinser, above n 1, at 40; Martenczuk (Rechtskontrolle), above n 5, at 236.

[44] See *Military and Paramilitary Activities in and against Nicaragua (Nicaragua v United States of America)*, Merits, ICJ Rep 1986, at 135. Hereinafter referred to as the *Nicaragua v United States*, merits.

[45] See SC Res 418 of 4 November 1977:
    "*The Security Council,*
    Recalling its resolution 392 (1976) of June 1976, strongly condemning the South African Government for its resort to massive violence against and killings of the African people, including schoolchildren and students and others opposing racial discrimination, and calling upon the Government urgently to end violence against the African people and to take urgent steps to eliminate *apartheid* and racial discrimination,
    Recognizing that the military build-up by South Africa and its persistent acts of aggression against the neighbouring States seriously disturb the security of those States,
    ...
    Strongly condemning the South African Government for its acts of repression, its defiant continuance of the system of *apartheid* and its attacks against neighbouring independent States,

A similar situation could arise where a state is suppressing internal riots that threaten its territorial integrity. In terms of international law, states may use internal force for this purpose, as long as they respect certain basic norms of humanitarian law. At the same time, this does not prevent the Security Council from determining that a threat to peace exists where the internal turmoil has a destabilising ("spill-over") effect that stretches beyond the country's own borders.[46] The internal cause of the threat to peace can also be of a non-military nature, such as economic or social instability, or an ecological disaster.[47] However, in order to constitute a threat to peace the impact of the internal social or economic conditions must be such that it could result in international armed conflict.[48]

In essence, therefore, those who adhere to the "negative peace" acknowledge that almost any internal factor has the potential to constitute a threat to peace.[49] However, unlike those supporting a "positive peace" concept they do not regard the nature of the internal cause as decisive, but the impact that it has on international relations. In addition, they reject the notion that the prognosis as to whether internal instability could result in international armed conflict is a purely subjective judgement. Such an "impact prognosis" also contains a normative component which manifests itself in the predictability as to what the consequences of the internal source of conflict would be in the short or medium term.[50] The mere contingency or uncertainty of future events does not exclude a normative judgement. Also in the sphere of international relations can past experience facilitate a

Considering that the policies and acts of the South African Government are fraught with danger to international peace and security,

...
Acting under Chapter VII of the Charter of the United Nations,
1. *Determines*, having regard to the policies and acts of the South African Government, that the acquisition by South Africa of arms and related material constitutes a threat to the maintenance of international peace and security... " .
See also Gowlland-Debbas (State Responsibility), above n 1, at 63; Martenczuk (Rechtskontrolle), above n 5, at 249. But see Herdegen, above n 34, at 22–23, who argued that the development of a weapons arsenal—such as the development of the nuclear capacities of India and Pakistan—should not be interpreted as a threat to peace too easily. The protection of the territorial integrity of a state and the development of its weapons arsenal belongs to the core of state sovereignty. Consequently a military build-up would have to be directly related to armed conflict before posing a threat to peace (as was the case in Iraq).

[46] Herdegen, above n 34, at 21. Martenczuk (Rechtskontrolle), above n 5, at 178, 230, noted that the threat to peace did not have to be brought about by government forces, but can also result from the actions of rebel groups or freedom movements.
[47] Martenczuk (Rechtskontrolle), above n 5, at 224.
[48] Lailach, above n 14, at 186.
[49] Alston, above n 8, at 170, 172 noted that an abstract categorisation of the internal causes of threats to peace would not be useful. The extraordinary divergent range of situations likely to arise would make it very difficult to articulate such a list, let alone obtain agreement on it. For a different opinion, see Herdegen, above n 34, at 15 ff.
[50] Martenczuk (Rechtskontrolle), above n 5, at 245; see also Stein, above n 7, at 160.

judgement on the probability of the occurrence of a future risk such as armed conflict? Without this normative element the structure of the Charter will lose all contours and the Security Council would be elevated to the world government which it was never intended to be.[51]

Some authors suggest that a complete erosion of the Charter structure can be countered if the concept of positive peace is restricted to those situations causing extreme human suffering.[52] They justify this (limited) expansion of the threat to peace by means of a teleological interpretation of the Charter. In accordance with the preamble of the Charter, the underlying rationale for the maintenance of international peace and security is the prevention of extreme human suffering resulting from war.[53] This reflects the fact that the goals of the United Nations are not so much aimed at serving states but rather the people on their territory. If one takes the human condition as the Charter's point of departure, the linking of peace to the absence of international armed conflict would be too narrow.[54] Extreme suffering could also result from other means than international conflict, such as genocide, slavery, systematic torture, systematic and extensive racial discrimination, the collapse of state structures, as well as natural disasters such as famine.[55]

Thus, in order to do justice to the humanitarian undertone of the Charter, peace should also be interpreted as including the absence of extreme human suffering, meaning that the existence of such suffering would constitute a threat to peace.[56] By making the existence of a threat to peace dependent on whether the human suffering would lead to an international armed conflict, the prevention of extreme human suffering is reduced to a tool for preventing negative peace. This would do injustice to the philanthropic spirit of the Charter which is aimed at preventing extreme human suffering in all its forms.[57] Instead, the concretisation of extreme suffering, such as the examples mentioned above, would *per se* constitute a threat to peace.[58]

The supporters of this argument further argue that genocide, slavery, systematic torture, or systematic and extensive racial discrimination have *erga omnes* effect.[59] A logical outflow of the *erga omnes* effect would be that other states resort to counter-measures, especially since the persons directly affected by these violations would most often not be in a position

---

[51] Lailach, above n 14, at 195–96; Frowein (in Simma), above n 1, at 609; Martenczuk (Rechtskontrolle), above n 5, at 238–39.
[52] See Lailach, above n 14, at 240. See also Gading, above n 9, at 151.
[53] Lailach, above n 14, at 180.
[54] *Ibid*, at 180–81.
[55] Lailach, above n 14, at 181. See also Herdegen, above n 34, at 15 ff. He described the existence of such situations as a physical threat to internationally protected goods of high value.
[56] Lailach, above n 14, at 205.
[57] *Ibid*, at 135, 207. See also Gading, above n 9, at 76–77; Österdahl, above n 2, at 18.
[58] See extensively Gading, above n 9, at 125.
[59] Gading, above n 9, at 150; Herdegen, above n 34, at 17 ff.

to defend themselves and would thus have to rely on other states for assistance.[60] In such a situation it would be preferable that the Security Council take action, since it would act in the interest of the international community as a whole.[61] Individual states, on the other hand, might be tempted to abuse the violation of *erga omnes* obligations as a pretext to adopt measures that serve their national interest. This may even lead to military intervention by states, in spite of the prohibition of the unilateral use of force in Article 2(4) of the Charter.[62]

These arguments are not entirely convincing. First, using the *erga omnes* status of certain human rights obligations as a justification for de-linking the definition of peace from the absence of international armed conflict, would be a self-defeating argument.[63] Those forwarding the *erga omnes* argument concede that the violations of *erga omnes* human rights obligations within a state can enhance the possibility of unilateral military intervention by other states.[64] This would strengthen the claim that systematic and massive human rights violations would constitute a threat to (negative) peace, rather than weaken it.

Second, experience has shown that the violation of *erga omnes* obligations or other forms of extreme suffering within a country inevitably result in regional destabilisation, to a point where international armed conflict is likely if not imminent.[65] The destabilisation can be the result of, for example, refugee flows to neighbouring countries or the aligning of neighbouring or other countries with fighting factions for political or moral reasons.[66] The fear that the Security Council would be prevented from action in such cases[67] would therefore be unfounded. It is true that in such instances the prevention of extensive human suffering is reduced to an instrument for achieving a higher goal, as opposed to being recognised as a goal in itself. However, this is an unavoidable consequence if one strives to keep the definition of a threat to peace within definable terms. Once the link between peace and the absence of international

---

[60] *Ibid*, at 140, 142; Lailach, above n 14, at 231–33, 304. See also Antonio Cassese, "Ex iniuria ius oritur: Moving towards International Legitimation of Forcible Humanitarian Countermeasures in the World Community?", 10 *European Journal of International Law* 25 (1999); Bruno Simma, "NATO, the UN and the Use of Force: Legal Aspects", 10 *European Journal of International Law* 2 (1999).

[61] Gading, above n 9, at 142.

[62] *Ibid*, at 142.

[63] *Ibid*, at 78.

[64] *Ibid*, at 240–41.

[65] Frowein (in Simma), above n 1, at 611. Gading, above n 9, at 76; Österdahl, above n 2, at 19–20.

[66] Gordon above n 1, at 569; Frowein (in Simma), above n 1, at 612; Gading, above n 9, at 39. See also Thomas Bruha & Markus Krajewski, "Funktionswandel des Sicherheitsrats als Verfassungsproblem", *Vereinte Nationen* 16 (1998); Walter Kälin, "Humanitäre Intervention: Legitimation durch Verfahren? "Zehn Thesen zur Kosovo-Krise", 10 *Schweizerische Zeitshcrift für Internationales und Europäisches Recht* 161 (2000).

[67] As is feared by Lailach, above n 14, at 205.

armed conflict is severed, there is a concrete risk that the concept would become indefinable, which could eventually result in a complete erosion of the Charter structure.[68]

In summary therefore a threat to peace in terms of Article 39 of the Charter would only remain justiciable as long as one defines "peace" as the absence of armed conflict between states. If one embraced the positive definition of peace, the term would become non-justiciable, since any internal problem could constitute a threat to peace, regardless of its impact on international relations. This, in turn, would amount to an unlimited discretion of the Security Council in terms of Article 39. Such an unbound discretion would, however, ignore the structural limitations which are necessary for the efficient functioning of the Charter system. An uncurbed flexibility in determining whether Article 39 has been triggered could lead to an over-extension of the Security Council that would undermine its own efficiency and ultimately that of the organisation as a whole.

The next question that springs to mind is whether these structural reservations concerning a positive definition of peace and its implications for a "threat to peace" in Article 39 of the Charter find resonance in the Security Council's practice. Stated differently, one has to examine if and to what extent the Security Council itself has linked the existence of a threat to peace to the potential outbreak of an international armed conflict. This examination commences in section 3. Section 2.2. and section 2.3. will, however, first briefly outline the meaning of a "breach of the peace"and an "act of aggression" in order to give a complete picture of the terms contained in Article 39.

2.2.   A Breach of the Peace

The term breach of the peace would denote a serious outbreak of armed hostilities, but which is not so serious as to constitute an act of aggression.[69] To date the Security Council has determined the existence of a breach of the peace on only four occasions. These concerned the invasion of South Korea (the Republic of Korea) by North Korea (Democratic Popular Republic of Korea);[70] the Argentinean invasion of the Falklands/ Malvinas;[71] the war between Iran and Iraq;[72] and the Iraqi invasion and occupation of Kuwait.[73]

---

[68] *Ibid*, at 240. See also Gading, above n 9, at 151. She conceded that a restrictive notion of human rights with *erga omnes* effect is necessary. A broad definition would create considerable legal uncertainty, since it would allow the Security Council to intervene with respect to a wide variety of human rights abuses. Furthermore, the Security Council would not be able to act effectively if it had to intervene on a large scale.

[69] Frowein (in Simma), above n 1, at 609; Gill, above n 1, at 43.

[70] SC Res 82 of 25 June 1950.

[71] SC Res 502 of 3 April 1982.

[72] SC Res 598 of 20 July 1987.

[73] SC Res 660 of 2 August 1990.

It has been argued that only the latter three instances related to significant military operations of one country against another, as the Korean war entailed the use of force by a *de facto* regime which was not recognised as a state at the time.[74] This argument is only convincing if one accepts recognition as an additional criteria for state creation, which is not in accordance with the prevailing view in international law.[75] At the time of South Korea's invasion by North Korea, both territories fulfilled the criteria for statehood. In both areas there already existed a *de facto* government which exercised effective control, whilst the 38th North latitude effectively formed the border between the two regimes.[76] It is therefore fair to conclude that also in the case of the Korean conflict the breach of the peace related to the significant use of force by one state against another.

The Security Council has not yet determined that a civil war within a country constitutes a breach of the peace. Although some scholars claim that a civil war could constitute a breach of the peace,[77] the question remains academic in the light of the fact that any serious internal armed conflict (ie with "spill-over" potential) would constitute a threat to peace and in this way trigger the Article 39 threshold.[78]

2.3. An Act of Aggression

The term "act of aggression" was included in the text of Article 39 at the insistence of the Soviet Union. Although the United States and the United Kingdom ultimately agreed to its inclusion, they successfully resisted any attempts to define the term at that time.[79] They feared that a definition could be interpreted as having an exhaustive character and thus provide would-be aggressors with a loophole. Consequently it was decided to leave it to the Security Council to decide what constituted an

---

[74] Gill, above n 1, at 43; Herbst, above n 43, at 329; Lailach, above n 14, at 51; Josef L Kunz, "Legality of the Security Council Resolutions of June 25 and 27, 1950", 45 *American Journal of International Law* 139 (1951).

[75] See Peter Malanczuk, *Akehurst's Modern Introduction to International Law* 1998 (London, Routledge, 1998); John Dugard, *International Law: A South African Perspective* 81 (Kenwyn, Juta, 2000).

[76] Following elections which were held on 10 May 1948, South Korea adopted the Constitution of the Republic of Korea on 12 July 1948. During this time the Democratic Popular Republic of Korea was also proclaimed in the North. See Denise Bindschedler-Robert, "Korea", III *Encyclopedia of Public International Law* 88 (1997).

[77] According to Lailach, above n 14, at 246–47, extreme and systematic human suffering caused by internal armed conflict could *per se* constitute a breach of the peace. See also Frowein (in Simma), above n 1, at 609; Kelsen, above n 3, at 735; Kunz, above n 74, at 140.

[78] The border conflict that broke out between Eritrea and Ethiopia in 1998 could have qualified as a breach of the peace, but the Security Council preferred to describe it as a threat to peace. See SC 1227 of 10 February 1999; SC Res 1297 of 12 May 2000 and SC Res 1298 of 17 May 2000.

[79] Gill, above n 1, at 44.

act of aggression.[80] In the years that followed, the content of the term was intensely debated in the United Nations and legal literature[81]. Finally in 1974, the General Assembly reached a compromise in the form of Resolution 3314 (XXIX), the well-known Definition of Aggression.[82] Although the Security Council can use it as a point of departure, it is not obliged to make use of this resolution, as the preamble and Article 4 of the Definition of Aggression clearly indicate.[83]

Aggression has been described to include both the direct and indirect threat or use of force intended to induce a state to act in a certain way. The term "force", according to the prevailing view, does not cover all possible kinds of force, but is limited to armed force.[84] This is not only reflected in the general tenor of the Definition of Aggression,[85] but also follows from a teleological interpretation of Article 2(4) of the Charter. If this provision were to extend to other forms of force such as economic coercion, states would be left with no means of exerting pressure on other states that violated international law.[86] This conclusion is confirmed by General Assembly Resolution 2625 (XXV) of 24 October 1970, which is also known as the Friendly Relations Declaration and which contains an interpretation of the fundamental Charter principles.[87] When interpreting the principle

---

[80] See 12 *United Nations Conference on International Organisation* 341–421 (1945). Gill, above n 1, at 44, interpreted this discussion as providing the Security Council with an unlimited power to determine whether an act of aggression existed. Contra Martenczuk (Rechtskontrolle), above n 5, at 198; and *ibid*, above n 1, at 542. The discussion at the San Francisco Conference was not concerned with the question whether there were limits to the Security Council's power of determination under Art 39. Instead, in the light of the experiences of the pre-war period, it was merely concerned with ensuring that the Security Council would come to the help of the victims of aggression. It was therefore considered to define certain situations under which the intervention of the Security Council would be "automatic". However, in the end this idea was rejected and it was decided to let the Security Council itself determine whether it wanted to act in the event of such an act. The discussion did not, however, extend to whether there were limits to the Security Council's discretion under Art 39. Cf Bengt Broms, "The Definition of Agression", 154 *Recueil des Cours de l'académie de droit international de la Haye* 305–06 (1977 / I).
[81] For an overview, see Broms, above n 80, at 305 ff.
[82] GA Res 3314 (XXIX); See also Gill, above n 1, at 44.
[83] For example, GA Res 3314 (XXIX) of 14 December 1974, at Art 4 determines that: "The acts enumerated above are not exhaustive and the Security Council may determine that other acts constitute aggression under the provisions of the Charter". See also Gill, above n 1, at 45; Herbst, above n 43, at 325.
[84] Michael Bothe, "Die Erklärung der Generalversammlung der Vereinten Nationen über die Definition der Aggression", 18 *Jahrbuch für Internationales Recht* 130 (1975); Frowein (in Simma), above n 1, at 610.
[85] See, for example, GA Res 3314 (XXIX) of 14 December 1974, at Art 3(g).
[86] Albrecht Randelzhofer, "Article 2", in Bruno Simma (ed), *The Charter of the United Nations. A Commentary* 112 (Oxford, Oxford University Press, 1994). See Gading, above n 9, at 74, for the view that an act of aggression can also refer to non-military force such as extreme economic pressure, the rejection of a peaceful settlement or an attack with propagandistic and ideological methods.
[87] Declaration on Principles of International Law concerning Friendly Relations and Cooperation among States in accordance with the Charter of the United Nations, GA Res 2625 (XXV) of 24 October 1970.

that states shall refrain in their international relations from the threat or use of force, the Friendly Relations Declaration deals solely with military force.[88] Economic and other types of coercion, on the other hand, are referred to under the principle of non-intervention.[89]

Direct aggression is usually easily identified as an armed attack against the territorial integrity or political independence of another state, such as the invasion of Kuwait by Iraq.[90] More difficult, however, is defining and demonstrating an accepted notion of indirect aggression, which is sometimes referred to as low-intensity aggression. It refers to the participation of one state in the use of force by another state in a way that falls somewhere short of full-scale armed invasion across national borders. Examples would be to allow parts of a state's territory to be used for violent acts against another state, or external assistance to insurgents, mercenaries or rebels.[91]

This also follows from a closer scrutiny of the section of the Friendly Relations Declaration dealing with the prohibition of the use of force.[92] The references to the organisation of irregular forces, armed bands and the prohibition of participation in acts of civil strife or terrorist acts are characterised by the broadest possible wording. The terms "encouraging", "assisting" and "participating" could be interpreted to include any possible act of support, which would in fact extinguish the limits between armed and other types of force.[93] That such a broad interpretation was not intended is indicated by the fact that the Friendly Relations Declaration discusses economic and other types of non-military coercion in the context of non-intervention and not in connection with the use of force, as

[88] For example, it refers to the use of force in the context of a war of aggression, the organisation of irregular forces or armed bands, military occupation, etc. See also Bothe, above n 84, at 130; Randelzhofer (in Simma), above n 86, at 112.

[89] Randelzhofer (in Simma), above n 86, at 113. Gading, above n 9, at 73, argued that in the light of the Definition of Aggression, colonisation and racist regimes also constituted violations of the prohibition to use force.

[90] Scott S Evans, "The Lockerbie Incident Cases: Libyan-Sponsored Terrorism, Judicial Review and the Political Question Doctrine", 18 *Maryland Journal of International Law and Trade* 30 (1991).

[91] Evans, above n 90, at 31–32. The General Assembly has also used the concept of indirect aggression to describe terrorist acts, especially when they are state sponsored. For example, it employed this description in its resolution on measures to eliminate international terrorism. By recalling the definition of aggression in that resolution, it impliedly included terrorism as a form of aggression. See GA Res 46/51 of 9 December 1991. See also Bothe, above n 84, at 135–36; Lailach, above n 14, at 242; Randelzhofer (in Simma), above n 86, at 113–14.

[92] Paras 8 and 9 of that section states:
"Every state has the duty to refrain from organising or encouraging the organisation of irregular forces or armed bands, including mercenaries, for incursion into the territory of another state.
   Every state has the duty to refrain from organising, instigating, assisting or participating in acts of civil strife or terrorist acts in another state or acquiescing in organised activities within its territory directed towards the commission of such acts, when the acts referred to in the present paragraph involve a threat or use of force".

[93] Randelzhofer (in Simma), above n 86, at 115; see also Bothe, above n 84, at 135.

was mentioned above. A narrower interpretation of these terms also finds support in the *Nicaragua*-decision[94] of the ICJ, which found that not every act of assistance is to be qualified as indirect force. It characterised the arming and training of the contra rebels by the United States as the use of force, but not the mere supplying of funds to them. The ICJ did not, however, indicate any criteria for deciding what acts of assistance are to be considered as indirect force and the scope of the prohibition of the use of indirect force remains inconcrete.[95]

The debate concerning the content of the term "aggression" gained new momentum with the adoption of the Rome Statute of the International Criminal Court of 17 July 1998 (hereinafter the ICC Statute).[96] Article 5(1)(d) of the ICC Statute stipulates that the International Criminal Court (ICC) shall, apart from genocide, crimes against humanity and war crimes, also have jurisdiction with respect to the crime of aggression. The exercise of this jurisdiction is, however, contingent on the future inclusion of a definition for the crime of aggression in the ICC statute.[97] Article 5(2) determines that the ICC shall not exercise its jurisdiction with respect to the crime of aggression, unless agreement has been reached to amend the Statute in accordance with the regular amendment procedures.[98] Such an amendment shall then provide for both a definition of that crime and set out the conditions under which the ICC shall exercise its jurisdiction thereto.[99] In August 1999 a working group on the crime of aggression was set up for this purpose.[100] Until the working group reaches agreement on these issue and the ICC Statute is amendment accordingly, the act of aggression *de facto* remains a dead letter.[101]

It is very possible that the crime of aggression becomes as obsolete in practice to the functioning of the ICC Statute, as was the inclusion of an act of aggression in Article 39 to the functioning of the Charter. To date, the Security Council has never made a determination that the use of force by

---

[94] *Nicaragua v United States*, merits, above n 44, at 101.
[95] Randelzhofer (in Simma), above n 86, at 115.
[96] Available at www.un.org/law/icc/.
[97] Irina K Müller-Schieke, "Defining the Crime of Aggression under the Statute of the International Criminal Court", 14 *Leiden Journal of International Law* 409 (2001).
[98] Provided for in Arts 121 and 123 of the ICC Statute, above n 96.
[99] Andreas Zimmermann, "Article 5", in O Triffterer, *Commentary on the Rome Statute of the International Criminal Court* 102 (Baden-Baden, Nomos, 2000).
[100] Proceedings of the Preparatory Commission, PCNICC/1999/L.4/Rev.1 para 8 (1999); see also Müller-Schieke, above n 97, at 411 ff.
[101] Zimmermann, above n 99, at 102. See also Müller-Schieke, above n 97, at 423 ff. A primary problem with which the working group is confronted concerns the role of the Security Council in determining the existence of the crime of aggression. If one accepted that the Security Council had exclusive responsibility for establishing the existence of an act of aggression, the ICC could only exercise jurisdiction over individuals responsible for this crime once the Security Council has determined that an act of aggression has occurred. At the same time, such an order of events would place a question mark over the independence of the ICC, as the exercise of a judicial function would become dependent on the action of a political body.

any state constituted an act of aggression.[102] The invasion of South Korea by North-Korea and the Iraqi invasion of Kuwait were both determined to constitute a breach of the peace,[103] whilst the situation in Cyprus after the Turkish invasion in 1974 was described as a serious threat to international peace and security.[104]

One reason would be that the characterisation of a situation as a breach of the peace (or a threat to peace) does not necessarily apportion guilt or responsibility, nor does it automatically commit the Security Council to the taking of action aimed at reversing the situation. A determination that an act of aggression has occurred clearly denotes the aggressor as the guilty party and at least politically necessitates far-reaching coercive measures by the Security Council.[105] Members of the Security Council may, however, be unwilling to do so, due to domestic strategic interests or relations with neighbouring states. Such a condemnation might also undermine or contradict the Security Council's role in offering good offices, as it would not be able to come across as even-handed.[106]

3. THE EXISTENCE OF A THREAT TO PEACE ACCORDING TO SECURITY COUNCIL PRACTICE

The following section focuses on the Security Council's own practice in determining a threat to peace. It examines, in particular, if and to what extent the Security Council has linked a threat to peace to the potential outbreak of an international armed conflict. If it were to do so consistently, it would affirm that the Security Council has to maintain and restore negative peace, which would also imply that its discretion in terms of Article 39 is not unlimited. If, on the other hand, the Security Council interpreted the notion of a threat to peace in a fashion unrelated to international armed conflict, it could mean that the international community has, over time, attributed a positive content to the term peace in Article 39. It was explained above that the structure of the Charter would militate against a positive definition and the unlimited Security Council discretion that it entails. Even so, if there were a consistent and generally accepted Security Council practice to this effect, it would amount to an amendment of the Charter through practice that endowed the term peace in Article 39 with a positive content.[107]

---

[102] Gill, above n 1, at 45.
[103] SC Res 82 of 25 June 1950 and SC Res 660 of 2 August 1990, respectively.
[104] SC Res 353 of 20 July 1974.
[105] Gill, above n 1, at 45; see also Gowlland-Debbas (State Responsibility), above n 1, at 63; Herbst, above n 43, at 327.
[106] Müller-Schieke, above n 97, at 421.
[107] See the amendment of Art 27(3) of the Charter through practice in ch 3, at s 4.3.

3.1.   The Double Strategy

Ever since the determination that Southern Rhodesia's unilateral declaration of independence in 1965 constituted a threat to peace,[108] the Security Council has frequently made use of a double strategy whereby it utilised the impact of a situation within a country on international relations to address the internal situation itself under Chapter VII of the Charter.

In the case of Southern Rhodesia, for example, the Security Council determined that a continuation of the minority regime constituted a threat to peace.[109] According to some authors, the motivation for this determination was to be found in the denial of the right to self-determination and the extensive violations of human rights in the country.[110] They regard the internal situation as decisive, since no international conflict had actually broken out.[111] Others point to the danger of violent involvement with neighbouring states at the time.[112] A combination of these factors is probably the correct answer. The right to self-determination was prominent in the resolution, and its denial also implied human rights violations. This also lead to considerable tension in the region—a fact which was underlined by the United Kingdom, who sponsored the relevant resolutions.[113] Thus, even though racial policies were the motivation for the coercive measures, the volatile international tensions created in the region by the secession would prevent a conclusion that the oppressive racial policies *per se* constituted a threat to peace.[114]

Similarly, in the case of South Africa the Security Council followed a double strategy by connecting the apartheid policies in the country with the tensions in the region, the cumulative effect of which resulted in a

---

[108] In SC Res 217 of 20 November 1965.

[109] SC Res 217 of 20 November 1965. See also SC Res 221 of 9 April 1966; and SC Res 232 of 16 December 1966, which introduced and expanded a mandatory embargo.

[110] For example, Jordan stressed the denial of the right to self-determination, in S/1340 4 (1966); similarly Pakistan, in S/1335 18 (1966). The United States indicated that this could lead to tension in the country, in S/1333 5 (1966).

[111] Gading, above n 9, at 98. See also Gowlland-Debbas (State Responsibility), above n 1, at 64. In the case of Southern-Rhodesia, it was obvious that the policy of racial segregation embarked upon by the Ian Smith regime for the avowed purpose of perpetuating white minority rule and progressively enforced at all levels by legal, educational and other governmental policies, flouted elementary principles of human rights law.

[112] Frowein (in Simma), above n 1, at 612.

[113] United Kingdom in S/1331 6 (1966). Later resolutions placed a bigger emphasis on the danger of international armed conflict. See SC Res 326 of 2 February 1973; SC Res 423 of 14 March 1978 and SC Res 424 of 17 March 1978. See also Frowein (in Simma), above n 1, at 612; Lailach, above n 4, at 63, 65–66. Cf Myres M McDougal & W Michael Reisman, "Rhodesia and the United Nations: The Lawfulness of International Concern", 62 *American Journal of International Law* 10–11 (1968).

[114] Martenczuk (Rechtskontrolle), above n 5, at 168; Österdahl, above n 2, at 44; see also Stein, above n 7, at 151.

threat to peace.[115] In November 1977 the Security Council determined that the acquisition by South Africa of arms and related materials constituted a threat to international peace.[116] Even though the resolution was motivated by the apartheid policies, the threat to peace was explicitly connected to the arms build-up in South Africa.[117]

This double strategy was revived after the end of the Cold War, notably with the adoption of Resolution 688 of 5 May 1991. This Resolution was adopted in reaction to the Iraqi governments' massive oppression and expulsion of the Kurdish and Shiite minorities in the country, in the aftermath of the (first) Gulf War. The Security Council condemned the behaviour of the Iraqi Government and determined that the consequences thereof threatened international peace in the region.[118] Although the widespread human rights violations were a motivating factor, the resolution was also adopted against a backdrop of a massive exodus of refugees from an ethnic group that formed a large and restless minority in the surrounding states to which the refugees were fleeing.[119] In addition, border incursions had already taken place and tensions were high as large numbers of military personnel remained in the border areas in the aftermath of a devastating war.[120] A determination that the consequences of the oppression of the

---

[115] Frowein (in Simma), above n 1, at 609; Lailach, above n 14, at 69–70; Gowlland-Debbas (State Responsibility), above n 1, at 65; Gordon, above n 1, at 465; Gading, above n 9, at 100. The double strategy is also reflected in the Security Council debates. States referred to the violation of human rights by apartheid as well as the attacks on neighbouring states. See, for example, the United Kingdom in S/ PV.2046 4 (1977); Pakistan *ibid*, at 6; Rumania, *ibid*, at 3. See also Martenczuk (Rechtskontrolle), above n 5, at 169; Stein above n 7, at 154–55.

[116] See above, fn 45, for a citation of the preamble of SC Res 418 of 4 November 1977.

[117] Note also that South Africa had carried out sporadic military operations against Zambia after 1971. In 1975, it committed troops to fighting against Marxist-backed forces in the Angolan conflict. See David L Johnson, "Sanctions and South Africa", in 19 *Harvard International Law Journal* 917 (1978).

[118] SC Res 688 of 5 May 1991:

"*The Security Council,*

...

Gravely concerned by the repression of the Iraqi civilian population in many parts of Iraq, including most recently in Kurdish-populated areas, the consequences of which threaten international peace and security in the region;

...

Condemns the repression of the Iraqi civilian population in many parts of Iraq, including most recently in the Kurdish-populated areas, the consequences of which threaten international peace and security in the region ...".

[119] Gordon, above n 1, at 574: see also Alston, above n 8, at 132 ff.

[120] Gordon, above n 1, at 574; Alston, above n 8, at 135; Gading, above n 9, at 102; Herbst, above n 43, at 218; Lailach, above n 14, at 74. The Security Council debates also supported the view that the border incursions and refugee flows resulted in the threat to peace. Nobody attempted to define the human rights violations *per se* as constituting a threat to peace. See, for example, Belgium in S/PV 2982 67 (1991); Ivory Coast, *ibid*, at 41; Ecuador, *ibid*, at 36; Turkey *ibid*, at 6. Some countries submitted that the international impact of the refugee flows did not yet constitute a threat to peace, eg India, *ibid* at 62; Zimbabwe, *ibid*, at 32 Yemen, *ibid*, at 27. Cuba, *ibid*, at 46, also argued that the Security Council was not the appropriate organ to deal with the matter.

Kurdish population within Iraq posed a threat to peace in the region was therefore very plausible in the circumstances.[121]

With respect to the conflict in former Yugoslavia (Bosnia-Herzegovina and Croatia), the Security Council resolutions were punctuated by condemnations of the massive and systematic violations of human rights of ethnic minorities and violations of humanitarian law. [122] This included the practice of "ethnic cleansing" and the deliberate impeding of the delivery of food and medical supplies to the civilian population.[123] At the same time, the resolutions attributed an international dimension to the threat to peace by either directly referring to the impact of the conflict on neighbouring countries,[124] or by explicitly reaffirming those resolutions

---

[121] Alston, above n 8, at 132; Lailach, above n 14, at 74; Stein, above n 7, at 183. But see Martenczuk, above n 1, at 17,1 who regarded this as a Chapter VI resolution, due to its formulation and the fact that it did not contain any further Chapter VII measures.

[122] Gowlland-Debbas (State Responsibility), above n 1, at 65.

[123] Eg SC Res 824 of 6 May 1993, in which the Security Council created so-called safe havens:
"*The Security Council,*
Reaffirming all its earlier resolutions,
...
Reaffirming again its condemnation of all violations of international humanitarian law, in particular, ethnic cleansing and all practices conducive thereto, as well as the denial or the obstruction of access of civilians to humanitarian aid and services such as medical assistance and basic utilities,
Taking into consideration the urgent security and humanitarian needs faced by several towns in the Republic of Bosnia and Herzegovina as exacerbated by the constant influx of large numbers of displaced persons including, in particular, the sick and wounded,
...
Deeply concerned at the continuing armed hostilities by Bosnian Serb paramilitary units against several towns in the Republic of Bosnia and Herzegovina and determined to ensure peace and stability throughout the country, most immediately in the towns of Sarajevo, Tuzla, Zepa, Gorazde, Bihac, as well as Srebrenica,
Convinced that the threatened towns and their surroundings should be treated as safe areas, free from armed attacks and from any other hostile acts which endanger the well-being and the safety of their inhabitants,
...
Recalling the provisions of resolution 815 (1993) on the mandate of UNPROFOR and in that context acting under Chapter VII of the Charter,
3. *Declares* that the capital city of the Republic of Bosnia and Herzegovina, Sarajevo, and other such threatened areas, in particular the towns of Tuzla, Zepa, Gorazde, Bihac, as well as Srebrenica, and their surroundings should be treated as safe areas by all the parties concerned and should be free from armed attacks and from any other hostile act...".

[124] Eg the first resolution determining a threat to peace, ie SC Res 713 of 25 September 1991:
"*The Security Council,*
...
Deeply concerned by the fighting in Yugoslavia, which is causing a heavy loss of human life and material damage, and by the consequences for the countries of the region, in particular in the border areas of neighbouring countries,
Concerned that the continuation of this situation constitutes a threat to international peace and security...". See also SC Res 770 of 13 August 1992; SC Res 757 of 30 May 1992; SC Res 781 of 9 October 1992; SC Res 787 of 16 November 1992; SC Res 820 of 17 April 1993; SC Res 836 of 4 June 1993; SC Res 838 of 10 June 1993 and SC Res 1003 of 5 July 1995; S C Res of 827 25 May 1993.

containing such references.[125] One should also keep in mind that Croatia and Bosnia-Herzegovina were internationally recognised states by the time the Security Council adopted the respective resolutions. This would place the double strategy followed in the resolutions beyond doubt.[126] It was subsequently also identifiable in dealing with other crisis situations on the Balkans, notably in relation to Albania[127] and Kosovo.[128]

Since 1990 the Security Council has also instrumentalised the double strategy extensively on the African continent. For example, in the wake of the massive and systematic ethnically motivated killing of (predominantly) Tutsi civilians in Rwanda, Resolution 981 of 17 May 1994 described the situation in Rwanda as a threat to peace in the region.[129]

---

[125] The international dimension of the conflict was also emphasised during Security Council debates. For example, with the adoption of SC Res 713 of 25 September 1991, several states mentioned that they were not supporting the resolution on the basis of the internal situation in Yugoslavia. Instead, the support followed from the destabilising effects that refugees and other ensuing problems of the conflict had on a region with many ethnic minorities and severe economic problems. See Belgium in S/PV 3009 21 (1991); India *ibid*, at 46; United Kingdom in S/PV 3009 57 (1991); Russia, *ibid*, at 51; United States, *ibid*, at 58. See also Lailach, above n 14, at 90; Gading, above n 9, at 112.

[126] Frowein (in Simma), above n 1, at 611; Gading, above n 9, at 115–16; Cf S/25704 (1993).

[127] SC Res 1101 of 28 March 1997:

"*The Security Council,*

...

Reiterating its deep concern over the deteriorating situation in Albania,

...

Stressing the importance of regional stability, and in this context fully supporting the diplomatic efforts of the international community to find a peaceful solution to the crisis

...

Determining that the situation of crisis in Albania constitutes a threat to peace and security in the region,

...

Welcomes the offer made by certain Member States to establish a temporary and limited multinational protection force to facilitate the safe and prompt delivery of humanitarian assistance, and to help create a secure environment for the missions of international organisations in Albania, including those providing humanitarian assistance.. ".

[128] It is noteworthy that SC Res 1160 of 31 March 1998 imposed an arms embargo against Yugoslavia without first determining a threat to peace. That a finding of a threat to peace can be made implicitly was already indicated in ch 2 at s 2.2.1., during the discussion of the *Legal Consequence for States of the Continued Presence of South Africa in Namibia (South West Africa) Notwithstanding Security Council Resolution 276 (1970)*, Advisory Opinion, ICJ Rep 1971, at 12. However, as such a practice can lead to major legal uncertainty it is not to be encouraged. Subsequently, SC Res 1199 of 23 September 1998 removed any uncertainty in this regard by determining that the situation in Kosovo constituted a threat to peace in the region. See also SC Res 1244 of 10 June 1999; cf S/1998/834, at para 28; S/1998/912.

[129] SC Res 918 of 17 May 1994:

"*The Security Council,*

...

Having considered the report of the Secretary-General, dated 13 March 1994 (S/1994/565),

...

Whilst the preamble to this resolution combined references to the internal situation in Rwanda as well as its regional effects such as refugee flows, Resolution 929 of 22 June 1994 concentrated on the internal conditions such as the systematic killing of civilians, without explicitly mentioning the massive flows of refugees to neighbouring countries.[130] The international dimension did nonetheless find some recognition in the fact that Resolution 929 (1994) described the crisis in Rwanda as constituting a threat to peace "in the region".[131]

> *Deeply concerned* that the situation in Rwanda, which has resulted in the death of many thousands of innocent civilians, including women and children, the internal displacement of a significant percentage of the Rwandan population, and the massive exodus of refugees to neighbouring countries, constitutes a humanitarian crisis of enormous proportions,
>
> *Expressing* once again its alarm at continuing reports of systematic, widespread and flagrant violations of international humanitarian law in Rwanda, as well as other violations of the right to life and property,
>
> *Recalling* in this context that the killing of members of an ethnic group with the intention of destroying such a group, in whole or in part, constitutes a crime punishable under international law,
>
> ...
>
> B.　*Determining* that the situation in Rwanda constitutes a threat to peace and security in the region,
>
> *Acting* under Chapter VII of the Charter of the United Nations,
>
> 13.　*Decides* that all States shall prevent the sale or supply to Rwanda by their nationals or from their territories or using their flag vessels or aircraft of arms and related material of all types, including weapons and ammunition, military vehicles and equipment, paramilitary police equipment and spare parts.. " .

[130] SC Res 929 of 22 June 1994:
"*The Security Council,*

...

Deeply concerned by the continuation of systematic and widespread killings of the civilian population in Rwanda,

Recognizing that the current situation in Rwanda constitutes a unique case which demands an urgent response by the international community,

Determining that the magnitude of the humanitarian crisis in Rwanda constitutes a threat to peace and security in the region,

...

1.　*Welcomes* also the offer by Member States (S/1994/734) to cooperate with the Secretary-General in order to achieve the objectives of the United Nations in Rwanda through the establishment of a temporary operation under national command and control aimed at contributing, in an impartial way, to the security and protection of displaced persons, refugees and civilians at risk in Rwanda, on the understanding that the costs of implementing the offer will be borne by the Member States concerned;

2.　*Acting* under Chapter VII of the Charter of the United Nations, *authorises* the Member States cooperating with the Secretary-General to conduct the operation referred to in paragraph 2 above using all necessary means to achieve the humanitarian objectives set out in subparagraphs 4(a) and (b) of resolution 925 (1994)...".

[131] See also SC Res 925 of 8 June 1994; and also SC Res 955 of 8 November 1994, which created the International Criminal Tribunal for Rwanda. See Martenczuk, above n 1, at 179; Herbst, above n 43, at 249. Lailach, above n 14, at 107. But see Stein, above n 7, at 269.

The Security Council's double strategy was also identifiable in resolutions addressing the conflicts in Liberia;[132] Zaire (Democratic Republic of Congo);[133] Central African Republic;[134] and Sierra Leone.[135]

3.2.   (Possible) Deviations from the Double Strategy?

Despite this frequent utilisation of the double strategy, the Security Council has also adopted resolutions in which it seemed to regard a particular situation within a country as posing a threat to peace in and of itself—without paying attention as to whether it would also destabilise international relations. The following passages will examine those situations which have been described in literature as a deviation from the different manifestations of a negative definition of peace (including the double strategy). They will question, in particular, if and to what extent the respective Security Council resolutions have indeed attempted to de-link a threat to peace from the threat of an outbreak of international armed conflict.

3.2.1.   Somalia

The downfall in 1991 of the military regime of *Major-General Mohammed Siad Barre*, who had been in power in Somalia since October 1969, was accompanied by a general collapse of the Somalian state. Whilst civil war broke out between rivalling clans, state institutions ceased to operate and the economic and social infrastructure came to a halt.[136] The cumulative

---

[132] SC Res 788 of 19 November 1992; Liberia in S/PV 3138 13 (1992); Senegal, *ibid*, at 22, Sierra Leone, *ibid*, at 49, India, *ibid*, at 86; SC Res 813 of 26 March 1993; SC Res 1343 of 7 March 2001. See also Niels M Blokker & Marieke Kleiboer, "The Internationalisation of Domestic Conflict: The Role of the United Nations Security Council", 9 *Leiden Journal of International Law* 28 (1996); Lailach, above n 14, at 81, Martenczuk (Rechtskontrolle), above n 5, at 176. But see Österdahl, above n 2, at 57, who regarded the Liberian civil war in itself as constituting a threat to international peace, regardless of its impact on the region.

[133] SC Res 1078 of 9 November 1996; For fears that the situation in the refugee camps may spark a regional conflict, see the comments of Chile in S/PV 3713 23–24 (1996); Canada, *ibid*, at 10; United Kingdom, *ibid* at 12; Botswana, *ibid*, at 14, Guinea-Bissau, *ibid*, at 18. See also SC Res 1234 of 9 April 1999; SC Res 1234 of 9 April 1999; SC Res 1279 of 30 November 1999; SC Res 1291 of 24 February 2000; SC Res 1304 16 June 2000.

[134] SC Res 1125 of 6 August 1997; SC Res 1159 of 27 March 1998; SC Res 1230 of 26 February 1999; SC Res 1271 of 22 October 1999; S/1998/1203, at para 29, S/1998/61, at para 11; S/1998/61, at paras 2 ff; S/1998/1203, at para 29, S/1998/61, at para 11; S/1998/61, at paras 21 ff.

[135] SC Res 1132 of 8 October 1997; SC Res 1156 of 16 March 1998; SC Res 1171 of 5 June 1998; SC Res 1181 of 13 July 1998; SC Res 1231 of 11 March 1999; SC Res 1270 of 22 October 1999; SC Res 1306 of 5 July 2000; S/1998/486, at para 29; S/1999/237, at para 18; S/2000/20, at para 14. S/1999/20, at para 11.

[136] Nii Lante Wallace-Bruce, "Of Collapsed, Dysfunctional and Disoriented States: Challenges to International Law", 57 *Netherlands International Law Review* 61 (2000).

effect of these developments, which was characterised by anarchy, massive human rights abuses and wide-spread hunger (aggravated by drought), sparked the Security Council into action.[137] In Resolution 733 of 23 January 1992 it determined that the continuation of the situation constituted a threat to peace and security.[138] In doing so, the Security Council inter alia explicitly referred to the consequences of the conflict on the stability and peace in the region. Resolution 733 (1992) also adopted a mandatory arms embargo against Somalia.[139]

This was followed by the creation of a classic peace-keeping mission in Resolution 751 of 24 April 1992, the main task of which was to distribute humanitarian aid to the civilian population. As it became clear that the delivery of food, medicine and other relief supplies was severely impeded by attacks from armed gangs, the Security Council adopted Resolution 794 of 3 December 1992.[140] This resolution explicitly determined that the magnitude of the human tragedy in Somalia constituted a threat to peace and authorised the use of force in order to ensure the delivery of humanitarian aid.[141]

---

[137] Gordon, above n 1, at 572.
[138] SC Res 733 of 23 January 1992:
"*The Security Council,*

...

Gravely alarmed at the rapid deterioration of the situation in Somalia and the heavy loss of human life and widespread material damage resulting from the conflict in the country and aware of its consequences on stability and peace in the region,
Concerned that the continuation of this situation constitutes, as stated in the report of the Secretary-General, a threat to international peace and security....". See also Martenczuk (Rechtskontrolle), above n 5, at 174, who criticised this formulation of a threat to peace as too vague.
[139] At para 5.
[140] SC Res 794 of 3 December 1992:
"*The Security Council,*

Recognizing the unique character of the present situation in Somalia and mindful of its deteriorating, complex and extraordinary nature, requiring an immediate and exceptional response,
Determining that the magnitude of the human tragedy caused by the conflict in Somalia, further exacerbated by the obstacles being created to the distribution of humanitarian assistance, constitutes a threat to international peace and security,
Gravely alarmed by the deterioration of the humanitarian situation in Somalia and underlining the urgent need for the quick delivery of humanitarian assistance in the whole country,

...

Expressing grave alarm at continuing reports of widespread violations of international humanitarian law occurring in Somalia, including reports of violence and threats of violence against personnel participating lawfully in impartial humanitarian relief activities; deliberate attacks on non-combatants, relief consignments and vehicles, and medical and relief facilities; and impeding the delivery of food and medical supplies essential for the survival of the civilian population,

...

Sharing the Secretary General's assessment that the situation in Somalia is intolerable ....
Determined to establish as soon as possible the necessary conditions for the delivery of humanitarian assistance wherever needed in Somalia ...".
[141] At para 10 and para 12.

It is notable that the paragraphs leading up to the determination of a threat to peace did not explicitly refer to the cross-border refugee flows or its potentially destabilising effect on the region. It merely focused on the internal situation, which it described as unique.[142] The destabilising effect of the conflict on the countries in the region was mentioned during the preceding Security Council debates.[143] It was also indirectly referred to in Resolution 794 (1992), as it mentioned Resolution 733 (1992) in its preamble. Consequently some authors maintain that the threat to peace in Resolution 794 (1992) was not exclusively constituted by the internal situation, but also by its international dimension.[144]

However, if this were the case, it remains unclear why the Security Council explicitly determined that the internal humanitarian situation constituted a threat to peace, whilst not mentioning the cross-border effects of the conflict at all.[145] This fact gains significance if one takes into account that by refraining from such an explicit reference in the text, the Security Council rejected the Secretary-General's position that a threat to peace had to result from the repercussions of the Somali conflict on the entire region.[146] It therefore seems that the Security Council expanded the definition of a threat to peace by regarding the humanitarian crisis in Somalia in and of itself as such a threat.[147]

Whether this particular incident would be convincing evidence of a general acceptance of a positive definition of peace by the Security Council is questionable. The situation in Somalia was unique, since the immense suffering of the civilian population was accompanied by a complete collapse of government and other state structures.[148] This factor was not explicitly mentioned in Resolution 794 (1992),[149] but did gain significance

---

[142] See Martenczuk (Rechtskontrolle), above n 5, at 174. During the Security Council debates several countries underlined the uniqueness of the situation in Somalia and that it therefore required a unique solution. See for example Zimbabwe in S/ PV 3145 7 (1992); Belgium *ibid* at 34 ff; the United States *ibid*, at 36 and Ecuador *ibid*, at 14.

[143] Cape Verde in S/ PV3145 19–20 (1992), regarded it as a "second dimension" of the conflict. Hungary, *ibid*, at 44 and the United Kingdom, *ibid*, at 33, were also very concerned about the refugee flow. See also Venezuela, *ibid*, at 42 and the United States, *ibid*, at 38.

[144] Herbst, above n 43, at 242–43.

[145] Gordon, above n 1, at 572; Gading, above n 9, at 119; Lailach, above n 14, at 86; Österdahl, above n 2, at 53; Stein, above n 7, at 251.

[146] In S/24868 3 (1992) he stated: "At present no Government exists in Somalia that could request and allow such use of force. It would therefore be necessary for the Security Council to make a determination under Article 39 of the Charter that a threat to the peace exists, as a result of the repercussions of the Somali conflict on the entire region.. " .

[147] Gading, above n 9, at 119; Gordon, above n 1, at 572; Matthias Herdegen, "Der Wegfall effektiver Staatsgewalt im Völkerrecht: 'The Failed State'", 34 *Berichte der Deutschen Gesellschaft für Völkerrecht* (1995) at 66–67; Lailach, above n 14, at 86.

[148] Daniel Thürer, "The 'failed State' and international law", 81 *International Review of the Red Cross* 731 ff (1999). See also Gordon, above n 1, at 573; Lailach, above n 14, at 87; Wallace Bruce, above n 136, at 59; Stein, above n 7, at 260.

[149] The Secretary-General referred to the absence of a government in S/24868 3 (1992); as did Ecuador in S/PV 3145 13 (1992).

in later resolutions.[150] A consequence thereof was that there was no representative body which could represent the Somali people on the international level, or which could give consent to the intervention of international forces on its territory.[151] Stated differently, the Somali state lacked a government which could act as trustee of the rights and interests of the people(s) on its territory.[152] As a result, the Security Council took over this trusteeship role in a way that included the use of force to restore law and order.[153]

In conclusion, therefore, Resolution 794 (1992), which was widely supported internationally, would constitute evidence of an expanded definition of peace with respect to "failed" or "collapsed" states. In situations where there is a complete breakdown in government authority, the mere existence of a severe humanitarian crisis within a country can constitute a threat to peace.[154] Whether the resolution would be evidence of a complete de-linking of a threat to peace and the outbreak of international armed conflict is nonetheless doubtful. Subsequent resolutions on Somalia reaffirmed the international dimension of the conflict. For example, Resolution 814 of 26 March 1993 determined that the situation in Somalia continued to threaten peace and security "in the region". The same accounts for Resolution 837 of 6 June 1993 and Resolution 886 of 18 November 1993.[155]

3.2.2.   Haiti

On 1 October 1991, *Jean Betrand Aristide* was democratically elected as President of Haiti. Shortly afterwards he was brought down and expelled from the country by means of a military coup. In the aftermath of the political disruption that followed, a considerable number of refugees attempted to flee to the United States' military base in Guantanamo, Cuba.[156] In Resolution 841 of 16 June 1993 the Security Council determined that the

---

[150] In particular SC Res 923 of 31 May 1994:

   "*The Security Council,*

   ...

   Determining that the situation in Somalia continues to threaten peace and security and having regard to the exceptional circumstances, including in particular the absence of a government in Somalia, and acting under Chapter VII of the Charter of the United Nations.. " .
   See also SC Res 897 of 4 February 1994.
[151] Thürer (failed State), above n 148 at 13, 23.
[152] *Ibid*, at 15.
[153] *Ibid*, at 23, 28; see also Herdegen (Staatsgewalt), above n 147, at 67.
[154] See Thürer (failed state), above n 148, at 740.
[155] SC Res 954 of 4 November 1994, also explicitly referred to the impact of the situation in Somalia and the refugee flows on neighbouring countries.
[156] See Martenczuk (Rechtskontrolle), above n 5, at 252.

situation threatened peace and security in the region.[157] It also imposed a mandatory oil and military embargo until a settlement was reached on restoring President Aristide to power.

On 3 July 1993 the military leaders and President Aristide adopted the Governors Island agreement, which foresaw the return of President Aristide to Haiti by 30 October of that year. Consequently the Security Council suspended the sanctions against Haiti with Resolution 861 of 27 August 1993. However, when the military leaders failed to comply with the Governors Island Agreement and prevented the United Nations Mission in Haiti (UNMIH)[158] from entering the country, the Security Council reinstated the sanctions in Resolution 873 of 13 October 1993.[159]

---

[157] SC Res 841 of 16 June 1993:
"*The Security Council,*
Having received a letter from the Permanent Representative of Haiti to the President of the Council

...

requesting that the Council make universal and mandatory the trade embargo of Haiti recommended by the Organisation of American States,

...

Also recalling the statement of 16 February 1993 (S/25344), in which the Council noted with concern the incidence of humanitarian crises, including mass displacement of population, becoming or aggravating threats to international peace and security,
Deploring the fact that, despite the efforts of the international community, the legitimate Government of President Jean-Betrand Aristide has not been reinstated,
Concerned that the persistence of this situation contributes to a climate of fear of persecution and economic dislocation which could increase the number of Haitians seeking refuge in neighbouring Member States and convinced that a reversal of this situation is needed to prevent its negative repercussions on the region,

...

Considering that the above-mentioned request of the Permanent Representative of Haiti, made within the context of the related actions previously taken by the Organisation of American States, defines a unique and exceptional situation warranting extraordinary measures by the Security Council in support of the efforts undertaken within the framework of the Organisation of American States, and
Determining that, in these unique and exceptional circumstances, the continuation of this situation threatens international peace and security in the region,
Acting, therefore, under Chapter VII of the Charter of the United Nations,

...

3. *Decides* that the provisions set forth in paragraphs 5 to 14 below, which are consistent with the trade embargo recommended by the Organisation of American states, shall come into force at 00.01 EST on 23 June 1993 ...".
[158] Which was established in SC Res 867 of 23 September 1993.
[159] SC Res 873 of 13 October 1993:
"*The Security Council,*

...

Deeply disturbed by the continued obstruction of the arrival of the United Nations Mission in Haiti .... and the failure of the Armed Forces in Haiti to carry out their responsibilities to allow the Mission to begin its work,
Having received the report of the Secretary-General (S/26573), informing the Council that the military authorities of Haiti, including the police, have not complied in good faith with the Governor Island Agreement,

The Security Council measures reached their peak in Resolution 940 of 30 July 1994,[160] which authorised member states to use all necessary means to ensure the capitulation of the military regime. Consequently the military leaders relented and allowed the occupation of the country by American troops. Thereafter President Aristide returned to Haiti and the Security Council suspended all sanctions against the country.[161]

The enforcement measures adopted by the Security Council were predominantly motivated by the lack of respect for democracy by the military regime.[162] At the same time the potential destabilising effect of the refugee flows in the region gave the Security Council the opportunity to

---

Determining that their failure to fulfil obligations under the Agreement constitutes a threat to peace and security in the region,
Acting under Chapter VII of the Charter of the United Nations,
1. *Decides*, in accordance with paragraph 2 of resolution 861 (1993), to terminate the suspension of the measures set out in paragraph 5 to 9 of resolution 841 (1993) ...".

[160] SC Res 940 of 31 July 1994:
"The Security Council,
...
Condemning the continuing disregard of [the Governors Island Agreement and the related Pact of New York] by the illegal de facto regime, and the regime's refusal to cooperate with efforts by the United Nations and the Organisation of American States (OAS) to bring about their implementation,
Gravely concerned by the significant further deterioration of the humanitarian situation in Haiti, in particular the continuing escalation by the illegal de facto regime of systematic violations of civil liberties, the desperate plight of Haitian refugees and the recent expulsion of the staff of the International Civilian Mission (MICIVIH), which was condemned in its Presidential statement of 12 July 1994 (S/PRST/1994/32),
...
Reaffirming that the goal of the international community remains the restoration of democracy in Haiti and the prompt return of the legitimately elected President, Jean-Bertrand Aristide, within the framework of the Governors Island Agreement,
...
Determining that the situation in Haiti continues to constitute a threat to peace and security in the region....

    4. *Acting* under Chapter VII of the Charter of the United Nations, *authorises* Member States to form a multinational force under unified command and control and, in this framework, to use all necessary means to facilitate the departure from Haiti of the military leadership, consistent with the Governors Island Agreement, the prompt return of the legitimately elected President and the restoration of the legitimate authorities of the Government of Haiti, and to establish and maintain a secure and stable environment that will permit implementation of the Governors Island Agreement, on the understanding that the cost of implementing this temporary operation will be borne by the participating Member States.." .

[161] SC Res 944 of 29 September 1994 and SC Res 948 of 15 October 1994.
[162] According to Österdahl, above n 2, at 67, the references to arbitrary killings, illegal detentions, abductions, and continued denial of freedom of expression etc, confirmed that the Security Council was more concerned with the internal political situation in Haiti than with any international repercussions thereof. See also Gading, above n 9, at 161; Gordon, above n 1, at 573; Martenczuk (Rechtskontrolle), above n 5, at 179.

link the internal situation to a threat to negative peace.[163] Some authors question whether the situation did indeed pose a threat to stability in the region, as the exodus of refugees mainly affected the United States which was neither likely to invade Haiti for this reason, nor to experience instability from the influx.[164]

However, this point of view seems to disregard the United States' willingness to engage in unilateral military action in situations affecting its interests. Given its history of military interventions in the region, a unilateral military retaliation by the United States against the Haitian military regime could not have been excluded.[165] The determination that the consequences of the military coup in Haiti posed a threat to peace in the region was therefore justified.[166] The same would apply to the determination in Resolution 873 (1993), according to which the non-compliance with the Governors Island agreement resulted in a threat to the peace. The non-compliance could be seen as prolonging and thereby aggravating an already threatening situation.[167]

The Security Council action in Haiti illustrates that a military coup or the existence of a non-democratic system of government can pose a threat to international peace under certain circumstances. However, it would not support the submission that the lack of democracy within a country would in and of itself pose such a threat. One might be tempted to make this argument, in the light of the growing importance of the democratic legitimacy of governments since 1990.[168] This is clearly illustrated by a statement issued by the states that participated in the Conference on the Human Dimension of the Organisation for Security and Cooperation in Europe (OSCE)[169] in 1991 in Moscow. The statement affirmed that in case of an overthrow or attempted overthrow of a legitimately elected government of a participating state by undemocratic means, they will support

---

[163] Österdahl, above n 2, at 66, 68. During the Security Council debates leading up to SC Res 940 of 30 July 1994, China in S/PV 3413 10 (1994), regarded the impact on the region as a threat to international peace and security. It nonetheless did not regard the application of military measures as sufficiently founded. The United States, *ibid*, at 12, referred to the closeness of the conflict to its coast-line, whilst France, *ibid*, at 14 and the Czech Republic, *ibid*, at 24, expressed concern about the large refugee flows. Cuba, *ibid*, at 5, however, argued that this was a pretextual argument and that the refugee flows—albeit a humanitarian problem— would not pose a threat to peace in that particular geographical area; similarly Mexico, *ibid*, at 4.

[164] Gordon, above n 1, at 573; Martenczuk (Rechtskontrolle), above n 5, at 252; Stein, above n 7, at 298.

[165] Gerald P McGinley, "The ICJ's decision in the Lockerbie cases", 22 *Georgia Journal of International and Comparative Law* 597–98 (1992); Stefan Sohm, "Zur Bekämpfung des internationalen Terrorismus", 13 *Humanitäres Völkerrecht* 173 (1994).

[166] See Lailach, above n 14, at 114.

[167] *Ibid*, at 116–17. See also Österdahl, above n 2, at 68.

[168] See generally Thomas Franck, "The Emerging Right to Democratic Governance", 86 *American Journal of International Law* 46 ff (1992); Gading, above n 9, at 160.

[169] Then still known as the Conference for Security and Cooperation in Europe (CSCE).

vigorously, in accordance with the Charter of the United Nations, the legitimate organs of the state upholding human rights, democracy and the rule of law.[170]

In the same year the European Community also issued a Declaration on the Guidelines on the Recognition of New States in Eastern Europe and in the Soviet Union.[171] In this document the member states affirmed their readiness to recognise, subject to the normal standards of international practice and political realities, those new states which have constituted themselves on a democratic basis.[172] Examples of growing support for democratic forms of government outside Europe include the Commonwealth's decision to suspend Nigeria in 1995, after the annulation of the Nigerian elections in 1993.[173] The Commonwealth also condemned the unconstitutional overthrow of the democratically elected government in Pakistan in 1999 and called for the restoration of civilian democratic rule without delay.[174]

However, these developments still have not yet reached a level of consistency from which one can conclude that democracy is the only acceptable form of governance. Stated differently, democratic governance has not yet reached a stage where it has obtained *erga omnes* effect.[175] Once it has reached such a level of acceptance, dictatorships may become so offensive to the international conscience that their mere existence could trigger international intervention. That this is not yet the case is reflected in the international recognition, toleration and/ or support of many non-democratic governments in Africa, Asia and the Middle-East.[176]

3.2.3.   Angola

After gaining independence in 1975, Angola immediately went from a 15 year revolutionary war against Portugal to a civil war between the *Movimento Popular de Libertacao de Angola* (MPLA) and the *Uniao Nacional*

---

[170] Document of the Moscow Meeting of the Conference on the Human Dimension of the CSCE of 3 October 1991, Art II, at para 17.2, reprinted in *30 International Legal Materials* 1670 (1991). See also Herdegen (Staatsgewalt), above n 147, at 54.

[171] Reprinted in 31 *International Legal Materials* 1486–87(1992).

[172] *Ibid,* see also Sean D Murphy, "Democratic Legitimacy and the Recognition of States and Government", 48 *International and Comparative Law Quarterly* 558–59 (1999).

[173] However, it was not expelled and no comprehensive economic sanctions were imposed. Most states also did not sever diplomatic relations with the new government or refuse to recognise it. See Murphy, above n 172, at 576.

[174] Durban Communiqué of the Commonwealth Head of Government Meeting held in Durban, South Africa from 12–15 November 1999, at para 18, available at www.thecommonwealth.org/.

[175] Gading, above n 9, at 164; Martenczuk (Rechtskontrolle), above n 5, at 253, Österdahl, above n 2, at 117; see also Stein, above n 7, at 293.

[176] The international community also fully accepted the transfer of governance of Hong Kong from the democratic United Kingdom to non-democratic China in 1997. See Murphy, above n 172, at 572.

para a Independência Total de Angola (UNITA). During the civil war UNITA received outside support from South Africa, the United States and Zaire, whereas the MPLA was backed by the Soviet Union, Eastern European countries and Cuba.[177] In 1991 a peace agreement was signed between the two sides, which was followed by elections in 1992.

After suffering defeat against the MPLA during the first round of the elections, UNITA rejected the results although the elections were declared fair and free by international monitors.[178] Subsequently there was renewed violence between the Government (MPLA) and UNITA, with devastating effects for the civilian population. Negotiations between the representatives of the Secretary-General and the parties brought to light that UNITA in particular was not willing to honour its obligations resulting from the peace agreement. In Resolution 864 of 15 September 1993, the Security Council determined that as a result of UNITA's military actions, the situation in Angola constituted a threat to international peace.[179] In addition, the resolution determined that from then on oil and weapons

---

[177] See Blokker & Kleiboer, above n 132, at 28; Lailach, above n 14, at 123; Österdahl, above n 2, at 57.
[178] See Martenczuk, above n 1, at 178.
[179] SC Res 864 of 15 September 1993:
  "*The Security Council,*
  Reaffirming its resolutions 696 (1991) of 30 May 1991, 747 (1992) of 24 March 1992, 785 (1992) of 30 October 1992, 793 (1992) of 30 November 1992, 804 (1993) of 29 January 1993, 811 (1993) of 12 March 1993, 823 (1993) of 30 April 1993; 834 (1993) of 1 June 1993 and 851 (1993) of 15 July 1993,

  ...

  Expressing grave concern at the continuing deterioration of the political and military situation, and noting with consternation the further deterioration of an already grave humanitarian situation,

  ...
  A.
  ...
  7. *Condemns* UNITA for continuing military actions, which are resulting in increased suffering to the civilian population of Angola and damage to the Angolan economy and *again demands* that UNITA immediately cease such actions;
  ...
  13. *Strongly condemns* the repeated attacks carried out by UNITA against United Nations personnel working to provide humanitarian assistance and reaffirms that such attacks are clear violations of international humanitarian law;
  14. *Takes note* of statements by UNITA that it will cooperate in ensuring the unimpeded delivery of humanitarian assistance to all Angolans and *demands* that UNITA act accordingly;
  ...
  B. *Strongly condemning* UNITA and holding its leadership responsible for not having taken the necessary measures to comply with the demands made by the Council in its previous resolutions,
  Determined to ensure respect for its resolutions and the full implementation of the 'Acordos de Paz',
  Urging all States to refrain from providing any form of direct or indirect assistance, support or encouragement to UNITA,
  Determining that, as a result of UNITA's military actions, the situation in Angola constitutes a threat to international peace and security… " .

were only to be delivered to places authorised by the Angolan government. In this way oil deliveries to UNITA were to be prevented.[180]

Resolution 864 (1993) was unique in that it was the first time that the Security Council took sides in a domestic conflict, by imposing mandatory sanctions against a specific group within a state, as opposed to against the state itself. As a result, some authors interpreted this resolution as being exclusively concerned with the internal situation in Angola and lacking any international dimension.[181] However, even though Resolution 864 (1993) was motivated by internal humanitarian considerations, the international dimension of the conflict was undeniable. The preamble of Resolution 864 (1993) explicitly mentioned the involvement of other states in the conflict. In addition, it reaffirmed a variety of previous resolutions in which the Security Council urged member states to take all necessary steps to stop immediately and effectively any direct or indirect military or paramilitary interference from their territories.[182]

It is therefore not unreasonable to conclude that the international involvement in the conflict was one of the dimensions to UNITA's military actions that formed the basis of the threat to international peace.[183] In essence, the Security Council resolutions on Angola amount to an affirmation of the intertwining of the internal humanitarian situation with regional instability.

3.2.4. *East Timor*

A week after the FRETILIN political party in East Timor declared its unilateral independence from Portugal on 28 November 1975, Indonesian naval, air and land forces invaded the territory.[184] Soon afterwards the Indonesian Foreign Minister announced the establishment of a "provincial

---

[180] Other targeted sanctions such as travel restrictions were adopted in SC Res 1127 of 28 August 1927. See also SC Res 1295 of 18 April 2000; SC Res 1336 of 23 January 2001; SC Res 1348 of 19 April 2001; SC Res 1404 of 18 April 2002. The targeted sanctions were ultimately suspended for a period of 90 days in SC Res 1412 of 17 May 2002, in order to facilitate travel by UNITA members in the interest of the peace process and national reconciliation.

[181] Blokker & Kleiboer, above n 132, at 31; Österdahl, above n 2, at 57.

[182] See SC Res 785 of 30 October 1992, at para 4; SC Res 793 of 30 November 1992, at para 8; SC Res 804 of 29 January 1993, at para 9; SC Res 834 of 1 June 1993, at para 10; SC Res 851 of 15 July 1993, at para 11.

[183] In the debates leading up to SC Res 864 of 15 September 1993, the humanitarian situation was of a major concern for states. See, for example, the statements of the United States in S/PV 3277 42 (1993); Pakistan, *ibid*, at 51; Djibouti, *ibid*, at 36; Japan *ibid*, at 43. However, China and Egypt also referred to the consequences for the neighbouring countries in *ibid*, at 28 and 16, respectively. The Reports of the Secretary-General also reflected concern about ongoing foreign involvement in the conflict. S/1994/202, at para 15; S/1994/282, at para 16; S/1997/438, at para 8; S/1998/838, at para 7; S/1998/931, at para 10; S/1998/1110, at para 11; S/2000/23, at para 12.

[184] J Purnawanty, "Various Perspectives in Understanding the East Timor Crisis", 14 *Temple International and Comparative Law Journal* 65 (2000); Roger S Clark, "East Timor, Indonesia, and the International Community", *ibid*, at 79–80.

government" in East Timor and the Indonesian parliament approved a bill for the incorporation of East Timor as Indonesia's twenty-seventh province on 17 July 1976.[185] However, in December 1976 the General Assembly rejected the claim that East Timor had been integrated into Indonesia, since the people in the territory had not been able to exercise freely their right to self-determination.[186] The General Assembly continued to regard East Timor as a non-self-governing territory and in United Nations documents Portugal continued to be named as the administering authority.[187] The Security Council, for its part, voiced a similar response in Resolution 384 of 22 December 1975 and Resolution 389 of 22 April 1976, in which it reaffirmed East Timor's right to self-determination and called for Indonesian withdrawal.[188]

For more than 20 years negotiations on the situation in East Timor made slow progress, until the fall of the Indonesian *President Suharto* in May 1998 added new momentum to the possibility of a negotiated settlement.[189] A year later Portugal, Indonesia and the United Nations Secretary-General concluded a set of agreements for a popular consultation in East Timor. In essence, it requested the Secretary-General to assist the East Timorese people in determining whether the territory would become an autonomous area of Indonesia, or whether it would be granted independence.[190] To fulfil this request, the Security Council established the United Nations Mission in East Timor (UNAMET)[191] that proceeded to organise and conduct a popular consultation.[192]

When it became clear that 78 per cent of the population expressed themselves in favour of independence, large scale violence broke out.[193] Hundreds of people were killed as houses and public buildings were looted, the infrastructure destroyed and hundreds of thousands of people driven from their homes, many across the border into West Timor.[194] Most of this violence was blamed on pro-Indonesian militias and the Indonesian Military, that had been accused of arming, funding and preparing local militias for a guerrilla movement in case the outcome of the referendum favoured independence.[195]

---

[185] Clark, above n 184, at 81.
[186] GA Res 31/53 of 1 December 1976; Clark, above n 184, at 81.
[187] Clark, above n 184, at 81. The General Assembly continued to adopt annual resolutions until 1982. Thereafter, the matter was debated annually in its Special Commission on Decolonisation and sporadically in the Commission on Human Rights and its Sub-Commission on Prevention of Discrimination and Protection of Minorities.
[188] SC Res 384 of 22 December 1975; SC Res 389 of 22 April 1976.
[189] Purnawanty, above n 184, at 65. See also Clark, above n 184, at 80–81.
[190] Clark, above n 184, at 83; Purnawanty, above n 184, at 66–67.
[191] SC Res 1246 of 11 June of 1999, at para 1.
[192] See also Purnawanty, above n 184, at 67.
[193] Clark, above n 184, at 85, Purnawanty, above n 184, at 66.
[194] Clark, above n 184, at 85.
[195] Human Rights Watch, "Indonesia and East Timor", *Human Rights Watch World Report* (2000), at www.hrw.org; see Purnawanty, above n 184, at 67, who was reluctant to accept the involvement of the Indonesian military.

The Security Council reacted by adopting Resolution 1264 of 15 September 1999, that authorised a multinational force under Chapter VII of the Charter to restore peace and security in East Timor.[196] In Resolution 1272 of 25 October 1999, the Security Council also established a United Nations Transitional Administration in East Timor (UNTAET),[197] which effectively administered the territory until it gained independence on 20 May 2002.[198]

The determination that the situation in East Timor constituted a threat to peace was motivated by humanitarian considerations. This is clearly reflected by the Security Council's condemnation of the large scale, systematic and massive human rights violations in East Timor. At the same

---

[196] SC Res 1264 of 15 September 1999:
"The Security Council,

...

Reiterating its welcome for the successful conduct of the popular consultation of the East Timorese people of 30 August 1999 and *taking note* of its outcome, which it regards as an accurate reflection of the views of the East Timorese people,
Deeply concerned by the deterioration in the security situation in East Timor, and in particular by the continuing violence against and large-scale displacement and relocation of East Timorese civilians,

...

Appalled by the worsening humanitarian situation in East Timor, particularly as it affects women, children and other vulnerable groups,
Reaffirming the right of refugees and displaced persons to return in safety and security to their homes,

...

Expressing its concern at reports indicating that systematic, wide-spread and flagrant violations of international humanitarian and human rights law have been committed in East Timor, and stressing that persons committing such violations bear individual responsibility,
Determining that the present situation in East Timor constitutes a threat to peace and security...".
[197] SC Res 1272 of 25 October 1999:
"The Security Council,

...

Reiterating its welcome for the successful conduct of the popular consultation of the East Timorese people of 30 August 1999, and *taking note* of its outcome through which the East Timorese people expressed their clear wish to begin a process of transition under the authority of the United Nations towards independence, which it regards as an accurate reflection of the views of the East Timorese people,

...

Deeply concerned by the grave humanitarian situation resulting from violence in East Timor and the large-scale displacement and relocation of East Timorese civilians, including large numbers of women and children,

...

noting the importance of ensuring the security of the boundaries of East Timor,

...

Expressing its concern at reports indicating that systematic, widespread and flagrant violations of international humanitarian and human rights law have been committed in East Timor, *stressing* that persons committing such violations bear individual responsibility, and *calling* on all parties to cooperate with investigations into these reports,
Determining that the continuing situation in East Timor constitutes a threat to peace and security,...".
[198] See SC Res 1338 of 31 January 2001, SC 1392 of 31 January 2002; SC Res 1410 of 17 May 2002.

time the conflict had an international dimension as it involved Indonesian armed forces, whose presence in the territory had been regarded as illegal by the international community ever since Indonesia's invasion of East Timor. It would therefore not be accurate to interpret the threats to peace contained in Resolution 1264 (1999) and Resolution 1272 (1999) as being underpinned exclusively by large scale violations of human rights and humanitarian law.

3.2.5. *Threats to Peace Relating to International Terrorism*

Resolution 748 of 31 March 1992 and Resolution 883 of 11 November 1993 determined that Libya's refusal to extradite the subjects suspected of the *Lockerbie* bombings constituted a threat to peace.[199] At first glance, several arguments seem to support the legality of what was, at that time, a novel interpretation of a threat to international peace. First, the mere fact that the Security Council had never before determined that the refusal to extradite suspected terrorists constitute a threat to peace, did not make the determination illegal *per se*. As has been illustrated in section 2.1. above, the notion of a threat to peace is a dynamic concept that can be developed by the subsequent practice of the organs of the United Nations.[200]

A conclusion of illegality can also not be based on the fact that the refusal to extradite is within international law,[201] since the existence of a threat to the peace does not presuppose the violation of international law. Section 2.1. also explained that in a particular set of circumstances legal acts which would not normally disrupt international relations in any severe way, could constitute a threat to peace. With respect to the *Lockerbie* incident one has to bear in mind that the suspects were also members of the Libyan intelligence services and that the Libyan government had a history of involvement in international terrorism.[202] Since this established a special link with the Libyan government, the question thus became one of state-sponsored terrorism in violation of Article 2(4) of the Charter and not merely one of extradition.[203] Under these circumstances a refusal to extradite the suspects could pose an imminent threat to international peace, as it may provoke unilateral military action against Libya by the United States and the United Kingdom.[204]

---

[199] See extensively ch 1, at s 2.1.
[200] Nigel White, "To Review or Not to Review? The Lockerbie Cases Before the World Court", 12 *Leiden Journal of International Law* 403, 418 (1999), submitted that the Security Council has entrenched this position by subsequent practice as regards Sudanese and Afghan support for terrorism.
[201] As is argued by Bernhard Graefrath, "Leave to the Court what Belongs to the Court: The Libyan Case", 4 *European Journal of International Law* 199 (1993).
[202] Lailach, above n 14, at 78; White, above n 200, at 403.
[203] Martenczuk, above n 1, at 261; Cf Sohm, above n 165, at 173.
[204] Sohm, above n 165, at 173.

The United States' previous bombardment of Tripoli when suspecting Libya of terrorist activities against it, illustrates that this was a concrete possibility.[205]

Libya's history of involvement in international terrorism would also rebut the argument that it is highly unlikely that a refusal to extradite the suspects could pose a threat to peace almost four years after the bombing.[206] The argument would assume that the causality between the threat to peace and Libya's behaviour was limited to the latter's omission in the form of a refusal to grant extradition.[207] This assumption loses sight of the context in which the refusal to grant extradition occurred. The refusal on Libya's part did not so much mark the beginning of a threat to peace, but the aggravation thereof as Libya passed up on the opportunity to act in a concrete fashion on its promise to put an end to support for international terrorism.[208] Furthermore, a lapse of four years would not necessarily mean that the threat to peace has abated. It is possible that the responsible state could repeat the terrorist attack, especially where it has a history of state-sponsored terrorism.[209]

These arguments would have been convincing, had they not overlooked the fact that by requesting the extradition of the *Lockerbie* suspects, the Security Council itself acted as a judicial forum. Chapter 9 at section 2.2. will illustrate how this behaviour violated Article 1(1) of the Charter, according to which the United Nations has to bring about the settlement of disputes in accordance with justice and international law. Section 2.4. of chapter 9 will further explain how the Security Council could have prevented this violation by creating an independent judicial sub-organ to deal with the issue of the extradition. Here it will suffice to say that the Security Council's request for extradition of the *Lockerbie* suspects was illegal as it was not adopted in accordance with Charter principles.

Other situations in which the Security Council requested the extradition of suspected terrorists in terms of Chapter VII concerned Sudan and Afghanistan. In Resolution 1044 of 31 January 1996, the Security Council condemned the terrorist assassination attempt on the life of the Egyptian President in Addis Ababa, Ethiopia and called on Sudan to

---

[205] *Ibid*; McGinley, above n 165, at 597–98.

[206] See Graefrath, above n 201, at 199; Alfred P Rubin, "Libya, Lockerbie and the Law", 4 *Diplomacy and Statecraft* 8 (1993). The lapse of time was also a source of concern for Judge Bedjaoui in his dissenting opinion in *Libya v United States*, provisional measures, above n 8, at 153.

[207] As is attempted by Graefrath, above n 201, at 196, who claimed that it would be very difficult to prove causality between an omission and a threat to peace. See also Rubin, above n 206, at 11.

[208] Lailach, above n 14, at 78. See also White, above n 200, at 418.

[209] Martenczuk, above n 1, at 262. He also noted that terrorism is a hidden problem. States involved in such attacks would hardly ever admit it and uncovering their involvement requires time-consuming and extensive inquiries.

extradite the suspects to Ethiopia.[210] Although this was a non-binding Chapter VI resolution, the Security Council thereafter adopted Resolution 1054 of 26 April 1996,[211] determining that the non-compliance with Resolution 1044 (1996) constituted a threat to international peace and

---

[210] SC Res 1044 of 31 January 1996:
"The Security Council,
Deeply disturbed by the world-wide persistence of acts of international terrorism in all its forms which endanger or take innocent lives, have a deleterious effect on international relations and jeopardize the security of States,

...

Convinced that the suppression of acts of international terrorism, including those in which States are involved, is an essential element for the maintenance of international peace and security,
Gravely alarmed at the terrorist assassination attempt on the life of the President of the Arab Republic of Egypt, in Addis Ababa, Ethiopia, on 26 June 1995, and *convinced* that those responsible for that act must be brought to justice,
Taking note that the Third Extraordinary Session of the Organisation of African Unity (OAU) Mechanism for Conflict Prevention, Management and Resolution of 11 September 1995, considered that attack as aimed, not only at the President of the Arab Republic of Egypt, and not only at the sovereignty, integrity, and stability of Ethiopia, but also at Africa as a whole,

...

4. *Calls upon* the Government of the Sudan to comply with the requests of the Organisation of African Unity without further delay to:
   (a) *Undertake* immediate action to extradite to Ethiopia for prosecution the three suspects sheltering in the Sudan and wanted in connection with the assassination attempt on the basis of the 1964 Extradition Treaty between Ethiopia and the Sudan;
   (b) *Desist* from engaging in activities of assisting, supporting and facilitating terrorist activities and from giving shelter and sanctuaries to terrorist elements and act in its relations with its neighbours and with others in full conformity with the Charter of the United Nations and with the Charter of the Organisation of African Unity... " .
[211] SC Res 1054 of 26 April 1996:
"The Security Council,

...

Gravely alarmed at the terrorist assassination attempt on the life of the President of the Arab Republic of Egypt, in Addis Ababa, Ethiopia, on 26 June 1995, and *convinced* that those responsible for that act must be brought to justice,
Taking note that the Third Extraordinary Session of the Organisation of African Unity (OAU) Mechanism for Conflict Prevention, Management and Resolution of 11 September 1995, considered that attack as aimed, not only at the President of the Arab Republic of Egypt, and not only at the sovereignty, integrity, and stability of Ethiopia, but also at Africa as a whole,
Regretting the fact that the Government of Sudan has not yet complied with the requests of the Central Organ of the OAU set out in those statements,

...

Reaffirming that the suppression of acts of international terrorism, including those in which States are involved is essential for the maintenance of international peace and security,
Determining that the non-compliance by the Government of Sudan with the requests set out in paragraph 4 of Resolution 1044 (1996) constitutes a threat to international peace and security,
Determined to eliminate international terrorism and to ensure effective implementation of resolution 1044 (1996) and to that end acting under Chapter VII of the Charter of the United Nations,

...

security. Consequently it ordered diplomatic sanctions against Sudan under Chapter VII of the Charter, which were to remain in effect until the latter had extradited the suspects to Ethiopia.[212]

The first explicit Chapter VII resolution on Afghanistan, namely Resolution 1267 of 15 October 1999, was adopted after the bombing of the United States embassies in Kenya and Tanzania in August 1998.[213] In Resolution 1267 (1999), the Security Council determined that the *Taliban's* failure to stop providing sanctuary and training for international terrorists and their organisations constituted a threat to international peace. The Chapter VII measures adopted in response to this threat did not explicitly demand for *Usama bin Ladin's* extradition to the United States. Instead, it left the *Taliban* the choice of turning him over to appropriate authorities in a country where he had been indicted, which effectively meant the United States.[214]

> 3.   *Decides* that all States shall:
> (a)   *Significantly* reduce the number and the level of the staff at Sudanese diplomatic missions and consular posts and restrict or control the movement within their territory of all such staff who remain;
> (b)   *Take steps* to restrict the entry into or transit through their territory of members of the Government of Sudan, officials of that Government and members of the Sudanese armed forces;
> *Calls upon* all international and regional organisations not to convene any conference in Sudan.." .

[212] Subsequently, in SC Res 1070 of 16 August 1996, the Security Council introduced a resolution that would have banned the take-off, landing or over-flight of planes operated by Sudan Airways or any Sudanese government agency. The date of entry of the resolution was still to be determined. After receiving a report by the United Nations Office for the Coordination of Humanitarian Affairs (OCHA) on the expected humanitarian impact, the Security Council decided not to implement the resolution. See United Nations Department of Humanitarian Affairs, *Note Concerning the Possible Humanitarian Impact of the International Flight Ban Decided in Security Council Resolution 1070 (1996)*, 18 February 1997; see also Starck, above n 41, at 59.

[213] SC Res 1214 of 8 December 1998 was ambivalent, in that it expressed concern about the conflict "causing a serious and growing threat to regional and international peace and security".

[214] SC Res 1267 of 15 October 1999:
> "*The Security Council*,
> *Reaffirming* its previous resolutions, in particular resolutions 1189 (1998) of 13 August 1998, 1193 (1998) of 28 August 1998 and 1214 (1998) of 8 December 1998, and the statements of its President on the situation in Afghanistan,
> *Reiterating* its deep concern over the continuing violations of international humanitarian law and human rights, particularly discrimination against women and girls, and over the significant rise in the illicit production of opium, and stressing that the capture by the Taliban of the Consulate-General of the Islamic Republic of Iran and the murder of Iranian diplomats and a journalist in Mazar-a-Sharif constituted flagrant violations of established international law,
> *Recalling* the relevant international counter-terrorism conventions and in particular the obligations of parties to those conventions to extradite or prosecute terrorists,
> *Strongly condemning* the continuing use of Afghan territory, especially areas controlled by the Taliban, for the sheltering and training of terrorists and planning of terrorist acts, and reaffirming its conviction that the suppression of international terrorism is essential for the maintenance of international peace and security,

The Security Council also imposed an air embargo against the *Taliban* and the freezing of its financial resources until it complied with the extradition request. In Resolution 1333 of 19 December 2000, the Security Council reaffirmed Resolution 1267 (1999). In addition, it determined that the *Taliban's* refusal to stop providing sanctuary and training for international terrorists, as well as its refusal to turn over *Usama bin Ladin* constituted a threat to international peace and security.[215] In the subsequent paragraphs it introduced an arms and air embargo against the *Taliban*. It also extended the financial embargo (ie the freezing of financial resources) to *Usama bin Ladin* and individuals and entities associated with him and the *Al-Quaida* movement.[216]

Chapter 9 at section 2.2. will elaborate upon why the resolutions requesting the extradition of the terrorist suspects from the Sudan and of *Usama bin Ladin* suffered from similar legal deficits as Resolution 748 (1992)

> *Deploring* the fact that the Taliban continues to provide safe haven to Usama bin Laden and to allow him and others associated with him to operate a network of terrorist training camps from Taliban-controlled territory and to use Afghanistan as a base from which to sponsor international terrorist operations,
> *Noting* the indictment of Usama bin Laden and his associates by the United States of America for, inter alia, the 7 August 1998 bombings of the United States embassies in Nairobi, Kenya, and Dar es Salaam, Tanzania and for conspiring to kill American nationals outside the United States, and noting also the request of the United States of America to the Taliban to surrender them for trial (S/1999/1021),
> *Determining* that the failure of the Taliban authorities to respond to the demands in paragraph 13 of resolution 1214 (1998) constitutes a threat to international peace and security,
> ...
> *Acting* under Chapter VII of the Charter of the United Nations,
> 1. *Insists* that the Afghan faction known as the Taliban, which also calls itself the Islamic Emirate of Afghanistan, comply promptly with its previous resolutions and in particular cease the provision of sanctuary and training for international terrorists and their organisations, take appropriate effective measures to ensure that the territory under its control is not used for terrorist installations and camps, or for the preparation or organisation of terrorist acts against other States or their citizens, and cooperate with efforts to bring indicted terrorists to justice;
> 2. *Demands* that the Taliban turn over Usama bin Laden without further delay to appropriate authorities in a country where he has been indicted, or to appropriate authorities in a country where he will be returned to such a country, or to appropriate authorities in a country where he will be arrested and effectively brought to justice..." .

[215] SC Res 1333 of 19 December 2000:
"*The Security Council,*
...
Determining that the failure of the Taliban authorities to respond to the demands in paragraph 13 of resolution 1214 (1998) and in paragraph 2 of resolution 1267 (1999) constitutes a threat to international peace and security...". These demands referred to the termination of protecting international terrorists and the surrendering of Usama bin Laden, respectively.
[216] These additional measures were to be applicable for a period of 12 months. However, following the terrorist attacks in the United States on 11 September 2001, the Security Council extended these economic measures (with the exception of the air embargo) for an indefinite period. See SC Res 1388 of 15 January 2002; and SC Resolution 1390 of 16 January 2002.

and Resolution 883 (1993), despite the fact that the terrorist activities in themselves constituted a threat to international peace and security.[217]

Subsequent to the attacks in the United States on 11 September 2001, the Security Council adopted Resolution 1373 of 28 September 2001, which described any act of international terrorism as constituting a threat to international peace and security.[218] The resolution further imposed extensive mandatory measures for the suppressing and financing of international terrorism, which effectively incorporated existing international treaties aimed at combating international terrorism.[219] This particular determination of a threat to the peace constituted a novelty in that it was not merely directed at a particular terrorist act, but at all (future) acts of terrorism. However, despite the broad and abstract nature of the determination, it would remain within the negative definition of peace. This follows from the explicit reference to the international (ie inter-state) dimension of such attacks, combined with the fact that the use of force against a state would be inherent to terrorist attacks of any kind.[220]

In essence therefore, whilst the above mentioned Security Council resolutions relating to international terrorism may constitute a novelty in certain ways and are not free from controversy, neither their novelty nor their controversy relates to a de-linking of a "threat to peace" from the potential outbreak of international armed conflict.

3.2.6.   *HIV/AIDS as a threat to peace*

The discussion devoted to HIV/AIDS during the Security Council's opening session on 10 January 2000, marked the first time that this organ debated a health issue in the context of international peace and security. In his address to the Security Council Mr Al Gore, the then Vice-President

---

[217] Since the terrorist attacks in the United States on 11 September 2001, the Security Council has condemned the threat to peace posed by international terrorism in several resolutions. See, for example, the preambles to SC 1368 of 12 September 2001 and SC 1373 of 28 September 2001; see also SC Res 1377 of 12 November 2001, Annex.
[218] SC Res 1373 of 28 September 2001:
"The Security Council,
...
   Reaffirming also its unequivocal condemnation of the terrorist attacks which took place in New York, Washington, DC and Pennsylvania on 11 September 2001, and expressing its determination to prevent all such acts,
   Reaffirming further that such acts, like any act of international terrorism, constitute a threat to international peace and security...".
[219] SC Res 1373 of 28 September 2001, at paras 1 and 2. See also Jurij Daniel Aston, "Die Bekämpfung abstrakter Gefahren für den Weltfrieden durch legislative Massnahmen des Sicherheitsrats—Resolution 1373 (200) im Kontext", 62 *Zeitschrift für ausländisches öffentliches Recht und Völkerrecht* 262–63 (2002).
[220] See Aston, above n 219, at 277. Even though the international actors involved in these attacks sometimes are non-state actors, the attacks themselves remain directed at a state.

of the United States, suggested that the Security Council's security agenda should not be limited to resisting aggression and preventing armed conflict. As the heart of this agenda was aimed at protecting lives, it should also address the global environmental challenge, the global challenge to defeat drugs and corruption, the global challenge of terror magnified by the availability of new weapons of mass destruction, and the new HIV/AIDS pandemic.[221]

The fact that he described these issues as a "security threat" and not a "threat to peace" raises the question whether this choice of words was deliberate. If this were the case, the Security Council would only be able to take binding action in terms of Chapter VII if the "threat to security" would simultaneously amount to a "threat to peace", since it is this latter term that forms the threshold for an Article 39 determination. However, it is more likely that he regarded a "threat to security" as a synonym for a "threat to peace", as the language with which he described parts of the security agenda (ie references to aggression and armed conflict), traditionally describes situations that constitute a threat to peace. Other speakers, such as the Argentinean representative openly stated that a threat to peace should include a threat to human security and need not relate to the absence of war.[222]

Some statements were more ambivalent and seemed to interpret the consequences of HIV/AIDS in the context of a threat to negative peace.[223] The Secretary-General of the United Nations noted that about 10 times more people in Africa died of HIV/AIDS in 1999 than in armed conflict, and that the resulting social and economic crisis threatened political stability. He specifically referred to the high infection rates in the police and armed forces which left African states ill-equipped to face security threats.[224] The same concern was reflected by the Canadian representative,

---

[221] Vice President Al Gore, Opening Statement in the Security Council Meeting on AIDS in Africa, SC/6781 (2000), of 10 January 2000, at www.un.org/News/Press/docs/. The number of people who will die of AIDS in the first decade of the 21st century will rival the number that died in all the wars throughout the 20th century. Cf Commission on Global Governance, *Our Global Neighbourhood* 71 (Oxford, Oxford University Press, 1995).

[222] Argentina, SC/6781 (2000), above n 221. See also the Chairman of the Economic Community of West African States (ECOWAS), *ibid*. He stated that peace and security did not mean the absence of military conflict, but depended upon the socio-economic realities of nations. See also Marcella David, "Rubber Helmets: The Certain Pitfalls of Marshalling Security Council Resources to Combat Aids in Africa", 23 *Human Rights Quarterly* 560 ff (2001). Cf Kenneth Manusama, "HIV/AIDS-discussie in de VN-Veiligheidsraad: een kwestie van competentie", *VN-Forum* 27 (2000).

[223] For scepticism about the Security Council's authority to deal with AIDS, see Namibia in SC/6781 (2000), above n 221. The representative noted that AIDS was not under the purview of the Security Council. However, by effectively addressing conflict situations on the continent, the Security Council would enable African governments to devote more resources to addressing socio-economic problems.

[224] SG/SM/7275 (2000), at www.un.org/News/Press/docs/. See also the Netherlands in SC/6781 (2000), above n 221. The representative stated that AIDS was a health problem, but

who stated that the ministries of defence in sub-Saharan African countries estimated the infection rate in the armed services at between 20 and 40 per cent. As the disease progressed, it would mean a loss of continuity at the command level and within the ranks, as well as a reduction in the effectiveness of prior peace-keeping training.[225]

Although the above debate reflected a clear attempt on the part of some states to irrevocably sever the link between a threat to peace and the absence of armed conflict, the debate in itself would not be conclusive evidence that the Security Council has indeed done so. Apart from the fact that several of the statements were too ambivalent to give convincing support to such a conclusion, the Security Council has not (yet) determined that the HIV/AIDS pandemic constitutes a threat to peace in terms of Article 39 of the Charter. Until now the Security Council has limited itself to welcoming the sensitising of peacekeeping personnel to the prevention and control of HIV/AIDS in some of its resolutions.[226]

4.   CONCLUSION

The vast majority of Security Council determinations in terms of Article 39 of the Charter resulted from the consequences of an internal armed conflict

---

one that devastated whole economies, overwhelmed entire public health systems, and ultimately tended to destroy the very fabric of societies. As such, it was responsible for an unprecedented degree of doom and despair, which, in itself, was one of the most virulent seeds of conflict.

[225] Canada in SC/6781(2000), above n 221.
[226] See in particular SC Res 1308 of 17 July 2000:
> *The Security Council,*
> *Deeply concerned* by the extent of the HIV/AIDS pandemic worldwide, and by the severity of the crisis in Africa in particular,
> ...
> *Emphasizing* the important roles of the General Assembly and the Economic and Social Council in addressing HIV/AIDS,
> ...
> *Recognizing* that the spread of HIV/AIDS can have a uniquely devastating impact on all sectors and levels of society,
> ...
> Stressing that the HIV/AIDS pandemic, if unchecked, may pose a risk to stability and security,
> ...
> *Bearing in mind* the Council's primary responsibility for the maintenance of international peace and security,
> 1. *Expresses concern* at the potential damaging impact of HIV/AIDS on the health of international peacekeeping personnel, including support personnel,
> ...
> 3. *Requests* the Secretary-General to take further steps towards the provision of training for peacekeeping personnel on issues related to preventing the spread of HIV/AIDS and to continue the further development of pre-deployment orientation and ongoing training for all peacekeeping personnel on these issues ..." .

and, in particular, from the systematic and large scale violations of human rights and humanitarian law that accompanied these conflicts. In addressing these issues, the Security Council consistently used a double strategy by means of which the internal (humanitarian) situation was regarded as a threat to regional stability. An objective assessment of the different situations in which this strategy was followed leads to the conclusion that the potential involvement of neighbouring countries in the conflict was a concrete risk in all instances. It would therefore not be correct to describe the link between the internal humanitarian situation and its regional consequences as an artificial or pretextual ground for Security Council intervention. To the contrary, the evolution of the above mentioned civil conflicts illustrated that large scale and systematic violations of human rights and humanitarian law within a country will almost inevitably lead to a destabilisation of the region.

The double strategy implemented by the Security Council also reflects the reluctance of states to accept that the existence of a humanitarian crisis within a country would in and of itself constitute a threat to peace. Resolution 794 (1992) on Somalia constitutes the only exception in this regard. As this resolution enjoyed general support and acceptance by the international community, it can serve as an indication that the mere existence of a humanitarian crisis can constitute a threat to peace in situations where it is accompanied by a complete breakdown of government. However, as it remains an isolated incident surrounded by unique circumstances, it would not serve as convincing evidence that the Security Council and the international community in general have accepted that any large scale humanitarian crisis constitutes a threat to peace in and of itself.

Support for this conclusion can also be found in Resolution 1296 of 19 April 2000, which concerned the protection of civilians in armed conflict. The Security Council stated that the deliberate targeting of civilian populations or other protected persons and the committing of systematic, flagrant and widespread violations of international humanitarian law and human rights in situations of armed conflict *may* constitute a threat to international peace and security.[227] This cautious formulation can be read as an affirmation that the threat to peace would flow from the international consequences of such violations, rather than from the violations themselves.

In addition, the double strategy followed by the Security Council supports the conclusion that the term peace in Article 39 (still) possesses a negative content. Although the threats to peace in the post Cold War era predominantly originate within states, it is still their impact on international relations rather than their source of origin that is decisive for

---

[227] SC Res 1296 of 19 April 2000, at para 5, emphasis added.

determining whether a threat to peace exists. This would mean that the discretion of the Security Council to determine that a threat to peace exists is not unlimited. If it were to determine that a particular social problem in a country constituted a threat to peace, irrespective of whether the impact thereof had a destabilising effect on the region, states could protest against this determination as being *ultra vires*. This could be the case, for example, if the Security Council determined that HIV/AIDS in and of itself constituted a threat to peace.

However, if states refrained from objecting to such a determination, it would in effect mean that they embraced an expanded notion of peace. It would be a decisive step in attributing a positive content to the term peace in Article 39, which would simultaneously provide the Security Council with an unlimited discretion to determine the existence of a threat to peace.[228] Whether this would be a wise development is highly doubtful, as it could confront the Security Council with situations that it is not equipped to deal with. For example, if the Security Council were to determine that HIV/AIDS constituted a threat to peace, it remains unclear what role it could play in implementing the strategies required to combat the disease. These strategies would include, inter alia, the reducing of vulnerability through information about infection and behavioural change, the development and distribution of vaccines, and the provision of care for those infected.[229] Within the United Nations system the institutions best equipped to deal with these long term socio-economic strategies would include UNAIDS, the United Nations Development Program (UNDP), the World Health Organisation (WHO) and the World Bank.[230]

It is difficult to see what the role of the Security Council should be with respect to these goals, apart from requiring that peace-keepers or peace-enforcers under its authority be sensitised to HIV/AIDS prevention and control. Surely, it cannot be expected that the Security Council adopt a binding resolution requiring a particular country to adopt a specific policy for the purposes of combating HIV/AIDS, or to commit a certain percentage of its budget to this purpose? If this is indeed what states are striving for, there would be no turning back from placing the Security

---

[228] David, above n 222, at 563.

[229] See Peter Piot, Executive Director of UNAIDS in SC/6781 (2000), above n 221, who regarded these issues as the essence of the strategy to combat the disease. See also Mark Malloch Brown, Administrator, UNDP, Chairman of the Committee of Co-sponsoring Organisations of UNAIDS, *ibid*. He stated that the pandemic cannot be seen in isolation from the broader development context. Weak government, poor services and economic failure translate directly into failed vaccine and contaminated blood supply chains. Cf Manusama, above n 222, at 26–27.

[230] As was conceded by the Director of UNAIDS, in SC/6781 (2000), above n 221; see also David, above n 222, at 572 ff.

Council in the role of world government. As neither the Security Council nor the Charter system is structured to accommodate such a role,[231] it should come as no surprise when it eventually leads to an over-extension of the Security Council that would ultimately lead to the demise of the United Nations as a whole.

---

[231] David, above n 222, at 566, 575.

5

An Overview of the Substantive Limits to the Security Council's Discretion Under Articles 40, 41 and 42 of the Charter

1.   INTRODUCTION

ONCE THE SECURITY Council has legitimately determined that a threat to peace exists, the question arises whether there are limits to the Security Council's discretion in resorting to enforcement measures in order to restore or maintain international peace and security. The answer to this question is closely related to the nature of the enforcement measures under consideration. The following chapters will illustrate that different types of limitations are at play, depending on whether the Security Council is resorting to military enforcement measures or non-military enforcement measures.[1] Whereas the authority to resort to

---

[1] The relevant part of Chapter VII of the Charter reads as follows:
"Article 40

In order to prevent an aggravation of the situation, the Security Council may, before making recommendations or deciding upon the measures provided for in Art 39, call upon the parties concerned to comply with such provisional measures as it deems necessary or desirable. Such provisional measures shall be without prejudice to the rights, claims, or position of the parties concerned. The Security Council shall duly take account of failure to comply with such provisional measures."

"Article 41

The Security Council may decide what measures not involving the use of armed force are to be employed to give effect to its decisions, and it may call upon the Members of the United Nations to apply such measures. These may include complete or partial interruption of economic relations and of rail, sea, air postal, telegraphic, radio, and other means of communication, and the severance of diplomatic relations."

"Article 42

Should the Security Council consider that measures provided for in Art 41 would be inadequate or have proved to be inadequate, it may take such action by air, sea or land forces as may be necessary to maintain or restore international peace and security. Such action may include demonstrations, blockade, and other operations by air, sea, or land forces of Members of the United Nations."

military measures primarily flows from Article 42 of the Charter, the authority to adopt non-military coercive measures is predominantly anchored in Article 41.[2]

The nature and scope of the provisional measures that can be adopted under Article 40 of the Charter is the subject of some debate. These measures are intended to act as a "holding operation" or "cooling-off measures" without prejudice to the rights, claims or position of the parties concerned.[3] Since the object of these measures is to prevent an aggravation of the situation, they would typically have as their subject matter the suspension of hostilities, troop withdrawal, and the conclusion of or adherence to a truce.[4] For example, in Resolution 660 of 2 August 1990, the Security Council acted under Article 40 when demanding that Iraq withdraw immediately and unconditionally all its forces to the position in which they were located on 1 August 1990.

On the one hand, it seems clear that these measures presuppose an Article 39 determination and can be binding in nature. This is clearly supported by the systematic positioning of Article 40 in Chapter VII, as well as the situations in which the Security Council has explicitly resorted to Article 40.[5] On the other hand, it is not clear whether provisional measures could also include military measures. For example, some argue that peace-enforcement units for restoring and maintaining a cease-fire may find their basis in Article 40.[6] Others question this by claiming that it would evade Article 42, which exclusively regulates coercive military measures.[7]

Although this latter view seems to be more accurate, the scope of Article 40 will not be examined in any of the following chapters.

---

[2] Yoram Dinstein, "The Legal Lessons of the Gulf War", 48 *Austrian Journal of Public and International Law* 6 (1995).

[3] The *Prosecutor v Dusco Tadic*, Decision on the Defence Motion for Interlocutory Appeal and Jurisdiction, Case No IT–94–1–T, 2 October 1995, Appeals Chamber, at para 34, available at www.un.org/icty. Hereinafter referred to as the *Tadic* decision.

[4] See Jochen A Frowein, "Art 40", in Bruno Simma (ed), *The Charter of the United Nations. A Commentary* 618–19 (Oxford, Oxford University Press, 1994). In this context the function of the "without prejudice" clause would be, for example, to reassure parties that troop withdrawal from an occupied territory in response to provisional measures would not amount to a settlement of a territorial dispute regarding that territory. See Gaetano Arangio-Ruiz, "On the Security Council's 'Law-Making'", 83 *Rivista di Diritto Internazionale* 648–49 (2000).

[5] See also SC Res 598 of 20 July 1987, in which the Security Council adopted provisional measures in response to the breach of the peace between Iran and Iraq. For earlier examples, see SC Res 54 of 15 July 1948 and SC Res 62 of 16 November 1948 on Palestine. See Frowein (Art 40), above n 4, at 618–20. For a different opinion, see the Appeals Chamber of the ICTY in the *Tadic* decision, above n 3, at para 33. It questioned the mandatory character of the provisional measures and suggested that these measures were subjected to the limitation provided in Art 2(7) of the Charter. The ICTY based this assumption on the language of Art 40, ie the phrase "before making the recommendations or deciding upon the measures provided for in Art 39".

[6] Secretary-General, *An Agenda for Peace*, S/24111 para 44 (1992).

[7] Frowein (Art 40), above n 4, at 619.

Instead, they will focus on the nature of the limitations at stake when the Security Council resort to military measures on the one hand, and to non-military measures, on the other. Stated differently, they depart from the premise that the limitations applicable with respect to non-military enforcement measures will apply regardless of whether they stem from Article 40 or 41 of the Charter. Similarly, the limitations applicable to military enforcement measures will not be affected if they were to stem from Article 40 rather than from Article 42. The Security Council would thus not be able to go any further in terms of Article 40, than it would be able to under Article 41 or 42 of the Charter. The reason for this approach lies in the fact that the Security Council usually only refers to Chapter VII in general terms when resorting to enforcement action, without indicating the specific Article under which it is acting.[8] From a practical point of view it therefore seems more useful to identify the limitations to Security Council action in connection with the type of enforcement measure (military versus non-military) at stake, rather than in connection with the exact Article.

The current chapter concentrates on identifying substantive limitations to the discretion of the Security Council in choosing the type of enforcement measures for maintaining or restoring international peace and security. The term "substantive" is used to describe peremptory norms of international law (*ius cogens*), as well as those limits that flow from the purposes and principles of the Charter, notably fundamental human rights norms and basic norms of international humanitarian law (the law of armed conflict). These "substantive" limits can be distinguished from the "structural" limits inherent in the Charter and which affect, in particular, the power of the Security Council to delegate certain powers to sub-organs or other entities. The implications of these structural limits for the Security Council are examined as of chapter 7.

This chapter commences its analysis by inquiring whether the Charter intended the Security Council's broad discretion to be limited by substantive norms at all. After answering this question in the affirmative, it examines where these limitations can be found. It subsequently identifies the norms of *ius cogens*, as well as the purposes and principles of the Charter as the main substantive limits to the Security Council's discretion during enforcement action. In doing so, it pays particular attention to the limits flowing from the principle of good faith and its interaction with fundamental human rights norms and the basic norms of international humanitarian law. The analysis remains general in that it does not engage

---

[8] For example, among the 12 resolutions adopted after the Iraqi invasion of Kuwait and before the hostilities ended, only SC Res 660 of 2 August 1990 referred to specific provisions of Chapter VII, ie Art 39 and Art 40. Cf Ruth Lapidoth, "Some Reflections on the Law and Practice Concerning the Imposition of Sanctions by the Security Council", 30 *Archiv des Völkerrechts* 118 (1992).

in an application of any of the substantive limits identified in Security Council practice. Such an application is undertaken in chapters 6, 8 and 9 in particular (albeit not exclusively) in relation to the human rights limitations identified in this chapter. The current chapter thus constitutes the principled foundation on which the subsequent evaluation of the conformity of Security Council practice with substantive (human rights) limitations is based.

Although the current chapter also identifies the core elements of international humanitarian law to which the Security Council remains bound during military enforcement action, an evaluation of the extent to which United Nations (authorised) forces have acted in accordance with these norms falls outside the scope of this study.[9] Since this is the only chapter in the study dealing with the basic norms of international humanitarian law, some effort is made to identify the core content of these norms. In the case of fundamental human rights, the core content of the norms at stake is at issue in subsequent chapters and therefore is not explored in the current chapter.

Finally, when discussing the Security Council's broad discretion to adopt enforcement measures, one has to bear in mind that it remains controversial whether this competence extends to non-member states. According to chapter 3 at section 4.2., the argument that the Chapter VII enforcement mechanism is applicable against non-members by means of customary international law, is not completely convincing.[10] As a result, all references to states in the following paragraphs should be understood as referring to members of the United Nations only. Similarly, references to non-state entities relate to those located in member states. Even though these entities are not members of the United Nations themselves, they are subjected to its Chapter VII enforcement mechanism by means of their presence in a member state. The Chapter VII enforcement mechanism applies to member states in an all-inclusive manner, ie both with respect to their territory and those located in it. Since this entitles the Security Council to subject the entire state to enforcement measures, it seems only

---

[9] As will be indicated in s 4.3.1, a settled practice has developed by means of which troop-contributing countries take primary and direct responsibility for humanitarian law violations committed by their contingents. Cf Judith G Gardam, "Proportionality and Force in International Law", 87 *American Journal of International Law* 407 ff (1993), for a discussion of the potential eroding effect of high altitude bombing such as occurred in the (first) Gulf War on the proportionality principle. See also Natalia Lupi, "Report by the Inquiry Commission on the Behaviour of Italian Peace-Keeping Troops in Somalia", 1 *Yearbook of International Humanitarian Law* 375 ff (1998); Robert M Young & Maria Molina, "IHL and Peace Operations: Sharing Canada's lessons learned from Somalia", 1 *Yearbook of International Humanitarian Law* 362 ff (1998).

[10] This point will be taken up again when discussing the enforcement measures against (former) non-member states, ie North Korea, Southern Rhodesia, the Federal Republic of Yugoslavia and East Timor, respectively, in ch 6 and ch 7.

logical that it also entitles the Security Council to adopt more limited enforcement measures that only affect part of the member state's territory and/or certain entities located therein.[11]

2.   THE NATURE OF THE SECURITY COUNCIL'S DISCRETION UNDER ARTICLE S 40, 41 AND 42 OF THE CHARTER

That the Security Council has a wide discretion to deviate from customary international law or treaty law when resorting to enforcement measures already flows from the nature of these measures.[12] An enforcement measure such as a trade embargo, for example, will inevitably have an impact upon the legal rights of those states or entities against which the measures are directed, as well as other states which have any trade relations with them.[13] For example, it could have an impact on their use of rail, sea, air, postal telegraphic, radio and other means of international communication.[14] States and those on their territory would nonetheless be obliged to accept these infringements of their rights, if the enforcement measures are to have any effect at all. Without the ability to impose on these rights, the Security Council would not be able to act efficiently in the interests of international peace and security.[15]

---

[11] This is also in accordance with the general principle of *a maiore ad minimus*. See, for example, SC Res 864 of 15 September 1993, at para 19, which imposed an oil embargo against the UNITA rebel movement in Angola.

[12] Dapo Akande, "The International Court of Justice and the Security Council: is there Room for Judicial Control of Decisions of the Political Organs of the United Nations?", 46 *International and Comparative Law Quarterly* 320 (1997).

[13] Jochen A Frowein, "Art 42", in Bruno Simma (ed), *The Charter of the United Nations. A Commentary* 633 (Oxford, Oxford University Press, 1994); TD Gill, "Legal and Some Political Limitations on the Power of the UN Security Council to Exercise its Enforcement Powers under Chapter VII of the Charter", 26 *Netherlands Yearbook of International Law* 62 (1995); Bernd Martenczuk, "The Security Council, the International Court and Judicial Review: What Lessons from Lockerbie?", 10 *European Journal of International Law* 546 (1999); Nigel White, "To Review or Not to Review? The Lockerbie Cases Before the World Court", 12 *Leiden Journal of International Law* 418 (1999).

[14] Arangio-Ruiz, above n 4, at 625.

[15] Akande, above n 12, at 318, 320; Gill, above n 13, at 62. See also Jochen A Frowein, "Art 39", in Bruno Simma (ed), *The Charter of the United Nations. A Commentary* 615 (Oxford, Oxford University Press, 1994). He qualified this argument by submitting that deviations from obligations under international law would only be acceptable in so far as they result from binding enforcement measures under Art 40, Art 41 or Art 42. Where the Security Council merely recommends (non-binding) measures in the wake of an Art 39 determination, they would have to remain within the limits of international law. Anything else would unduly restrict the rights of the addressee state. This would mean that a non-mandatory trade embargo could only be enforced in so far as it did not violate trade agreements or norms of customary international law. One could counter this argument, however, by claiming that the decisive difference between binding and non-binding enforcement measures relates to their impact on the *implementing* states rather than the *addressee* states. Whereas binding Security Council decisions oblige the implementing states to give effect to the enforcement

This would not only relate to rights under customary international law, but also to rights enjoyed under treaty law. Article 103 of the Charter explicitly provides that obligations under the Charter prevail over any other international agreements. Since obligations of member states under the Charter include the obligation to accept and carry out binding decisions of the Security Council, obligations flowing from enforcement measures will prevail over treaty obligations.[16] Although Article 103 of the Charter only refers to "obligations" under the Charter prevailing over "obligations" under other treaties, the same principle must also apply to rights arising under other treaties. If a treaty obligation is extinguished or suspended by a binding Security Council decision, this will necessarily imply that the rights stemming from those obligations are extinguished or suspended as well.[17]

The other side of this coin is that the Security Council is not obliged to limit the enforcement measures to those states from which the threat to peace, breach of the peace or an act of aggression originates.[18] This would require the Security Council to do extensive fact-finding in each case before acting, which would prevent it from acting quickly and thus compromise its efficiency.[19] After all, the complexity of international relations and the political delicacies involved are often such that it is difficult to determine who is actually responsible for the threat to peace.[20] This also means that enforcement measures are not necessarily of a punitive nature, directed at states or entities who violated international law.[21] Although the situation causing a threat to peace will often entail an illegal act, the upholding of international law is not the Security Council's primary concern. Instead, it is the maintenance or restoration of international peace

measures—including those requiring a deviation from existing international law—non-binding recommendations merely permit this. This permission nonetheless implies that the addressee state has to accept a limitation of its rights under international law, to the extent that the implementing state decides to give effect to the Security Council recommendation. If this were not the case, the non-binding Security Council measures would have no added value and would therefore be pointless.

[16] Akande, above n 12, at 319; Gill, above n 13, at 63; Christopher Greenwood, "The Impact of Decisions and Resolutions of the Security Council on the International Court of Justice", in Wybo P Heere, *International Law and The Hague's 750th Anniversary* 84 (The Hague, TMC Asser, 1999); Gabriel H Oosthuizen, "Playing the Devil's Advocate: the United Nations Security Council is Unbound by Law", 12 *Leiden Journal of International Law* 521 (1999).

[17] Greenwood (in Heere), above n 16, at 84.

[18] Martin Lailach, *Die Wahrung des Weltfriedens und der internationalen Sicherheit als Aufgabe des Sicherheitsrates der Vereinten Nationen* (Berlin, Duncker & Humblot, 1998); Frowein (Art 40), above n 4, at 620; Barbara Lorinser, *Bindende Resolutionen des Sicherheitsrates* 49 (Baden-Baden, Nomos, 1996).

[19] Lorinser, above n 18, at 54. See also Bernd Martenczuk, *Rechtsbindung und Rechtskontrolle des Weltsicherheitsrates* 214 (Berlin, Duncker & Humblot, 1996).

[20] Lorinser, above n 18, at 55.

[21] Arangio-Ruiz, above n 4, at 630; Lailach, above n 18, at 191.

and security, which is not necessarily synonymous with the maintenance of international law.[22]

The need for efficient action further implies that the Security Council has a wide discretion in deciding how to make use of the enforcement measures provided for in Chapters VI and VII of the Charter. On the one hand, it is not obliged to adopt any enforcement measures after having determined that an Article 39 situation exists, as Articles 40, 41 and 42 are merely of a permissive nature. On the other hand, if the Security Council does decide to resort to enforcement measures, it does not have to exhaust the mechanisms for the peaceful settlement of disputes provided for in Chapter VI, before adopting coercive measures under Chapter VII. Once it has made a determination in terms of Article 39, it can immediately resort to the measures provided for in Articles 40, 41 and 42 of the Charter.[23]

The Security Council also does not have to adopt the measures in Articles 40, 41 and 42 in any particular order, even though the measures listed there are in themselves graduated.[24] In other words, the Security Council is not required to postpone military action for a prolonged period of time in order to convince itself that provisional measures or sanctions have no possibility of achieving the desired objective. If this were the case, the Security Council could be forced to wait for months or even years before resorting to military enforcement measures.[25] This would rob the enforcement provisions in Chapter VII of their effectiveness and undermine the entire purpose of the collective security system provided for in the Charter.[26]

This freedom of the Security Council to choose a (combination of) measures under Chapters VI and/ or VII to be adopted for the maintenance of international peace and security already indicates that it is not bound by a

---

[22] Gill, above n 13, at 46; Martenczuk (Rechtskontrolle), above n 19, at 217–18. See also Lailach, above n 18, at 192–93. If the Security Council had only adopted measures against states that violated international law, it would have acted as a criminal tribunal as opposed to a political organ.

[23] The Security Council could also combine Chapter VII measures with non-binding recommendations in terms of Chapter VI. See Martenczuk (Rechtskontrolle), above n 19, at 234; Vera Gowlland-Debbas, "Security Council Enforcement Action and Issues of State Responsibility", 43 *International and Comparative Law Quarterly* 62 (1994).

[24] SC Res 661 of 6 August 1990 and SC Res 665 of 25 August 1990 were examples of a combination of the enforcement measures provided for in Art 41 and Art 42 of the Charter. Whereas the former resolution imposed sanctions against Iraq after its invasion of Kuwait, the latter permitted countries cooperating with Kuwait to adopt the necessary measures to halt inward and outward maritime shipping, in order to ensure strict implementation of the sanctions. See Dinstein, above n 2, at 7–8; see also Derek Bowett, "The Impact of Security Council Decisions on Dispute Settlement Procedures", 5 *European Journal of International Law* 94 (1994); Frowein (Art 42), above n 13, at 631; Gill, above n 13, at 48; Gowlland-Debbas (State Responsibility), above n 23, at 62; Lapidoth, above n 8, at 117; Lorinser, above n 18, at 55.

[25] Gill, above n 13, at 53.

[26] *Ibid*, at 51 ff.

general principle of proportionality.[27] This principle requires that there be a rational link between the means and the end pursued and that the damage inflicted by the means should not be disproportionate to that end.[28] This usually implies that the end should be achieved by the least restrictive means.[29] However, applying this principle to the Security Council would force it to exhaust all non-binding or non-military enforcement measures before authorising the use of force. As was indicated above, this would not be reconcilable with the flexibility that the Security Council needs in order to engage in quick and efficient action. It also does not pay due consideration to the interest of the world community in preventing war, or the uncertainty as to how those states or entities subjected to enforcement measures will react.[30]

In essence therefore the question is not so much whether the Security Council can impinge on existing international law when adopting enforcement measures, but to what extent it can do so. Some authors claim that the Security Council's discretion in this regard is unlimited and that it does not have to pay any regard to international law when acting to maintain or restore international peace and security.[31] They find support for this argument in the omission of any reference to "justice or international law" in the first part of Article 1(1) of the Charter.[32] Whereas the Article explicitly refers to "justice and international law" in its second part, ie in connection with the settlement of international disputes, it contains no such reference when referring to collective measures for the prevention and removal of threats to the peace, and for the suppression of acts of aggression or other breaches of the peace.[33] They submit that this was a

---

[27] Lorinser, above n 18, at 53, Oosthuizen, above n 16, at 555.

[28] In international law the principle of proportionality was recognised first in the customary international law of reprisal and self-defence. See Jost Delbrück, "Proportionality", III *Encyclopedia of Public International Law* 1141 (1994).

[29] Martenczuk, above n 19, at 276, 279. Matthias Herdegen, *Die Befugnisse des UN-Sicherheitsrates: aufgeklärter Absolutismus im Völkerrecht?* 30–31 (Heidelberg, Müller, 1998), submitted that the differentiation between military and non-military measures implied a proportionality principle. He nonetheless conceded that the broad discretion of the Security Council watered it down considerably. Similarly, Nicolas Angelet, "International Law Limits to the Security Council", in Vera Gowlland-Debbas (ed), *United Nations Sanctions and International Law* 73 (The Hague, Kluwer, 2001).

[30] Martenczuk (Rechtskontrolle), above n 19, at 280; Lorinser, above n 18, at 53; Gowlland-Debbas (State Responsibility), above n 23, at 62.

[31] Notably Hans Kelsen, *The Law of the United Nations* 294 (London, Stevens, 1950); see Akande, above n 12, at 318.

[32] Art 1(1) of the Charter reads: "[The Purposes of the United Nations are:] To maintain international peace and security, and to that end: to take effective collective measures for the prevention and removal of threats to peace, and for the suppression of acts of aggression, or other breaches of the peace, and to bring about by peaceful means, and in conformity with the principles of justice in international law, adjustment or settlement of international disputes or situations which might lead to a breach of the peace; ...."

[33] Kelsen, above n 31, at 294. See also Akande, above n 12, at 318. Martenczuk, above n 13, at 545.

deliberate omission on the part of the drafters at San Francisco, since the committee charged with preparatory work on the preamble, purposes and principles of the Charter rejected all proposed amendments which aimed at subjecting the exercise of collective enforcement measures to the principles of international law.[34] This would be a clear indication that the drafters of the Charter did not intend to curtail the relevant powers of the Security Council when adopting measures to restore or maintain international peace and security.[35]

However, these submissions do not give a full picture of the discussion at San Francisco, as the issue also arose in the committee on the structure and procedure of the Security Council.[36] In that committee, Norway had proposed an amendment which would have required that no solution should be imposed upon a state that would impair its confidence in its future security or welfare. This proposal resulted from its belief that the phrase "justice and international law" in Article 1(1) of the Charter only applied to the pacific settlement of disputes, as opposed to coercive action.[37] The United Kingdom and the United States then indicated that the reference to "justice and international law" did indeed bind the Security Council, as a result of which the Norwegian proposal was unnecessary.[38]

The only way in which to reconcile these two seemingly opposing views, is to interpret the omission of the terms "justice and international law" in the first part of Article 1(1) as a mechanism for enabling the Security Council to deviate to some extent from international law when acting in the interest of peace and security. This deviation would not be possible if the phrase "international law and justice" had been explicitly included. At the same time, however, it was not meant to free the Security

---

[34] See 6 *United Nations Conference on International organisation* 1 ff (1945). During the debates, the delegates in favour of the amendments made frequent references to the dangers of smaller nations being sacrificed in the context of expediency or appeasement—with references to the fate of Czechoslovakia in 1938—and the necessity of peace being based on justice and international law. The delegates opposed to the amendments all pointed to the necessity of providing the Security Council with maximum flexibility and power in the application of collective enforcement measures. They also stressed the potential pitfalls of conditioning such action on considerations of international law or "justice". These terms were considered to be too open-ended and capable of conflicting interpretation. See also Gill, above n 13, at 66; Akande, above n 12, at 315.

[35] Oosthuizen, above n 16, at 552–53. See also the dissenting opinion of Judge Schwebel in *Case Concerning Questions of Interpretation and Application of the 1971 Montreal Convention Arising from the Aerial Incident at Lockerbie (Libyan Arab Jamahiriya v United States)*, Preliminary Objections, 37 *International Legal Materials* 627 (1998).

[36] 11 *United Nations Conference on International organisation* 378 (1945).

[37] *Ibid*, Akande, above n 12, at 319.

[38] 11 *United Nations Conference on International organisation* 378 (1945). See Akande, above n 12, at 319. Also see Martenczuk (Rechtskontrolle), above n 19, at 270, who acknowledged these statements, even though he claimed that the purposes and principles did not provide any workable limits to the Security Council's discretion.

Council completely from the obligation to respect international law when adopting enforcement measures under Chapter VII.[39] Stated differently, the explicit inclusion of the phrase "international law and justice" in the second part of Article 1(1) is merely meant to reaffirm that no deviation from international law is possible when the Security Council is involved in the settlement of disputes. It is not, however, meant to affirm that no *adherence* to international law is required when the Security Council takes enforcement measures in the interest of peace and security. That some adherence is indeed required, will be illuminated in the following passages. They will illustrate that collective enforcement measures are subjected to the norms of justice and international law to the extent that they constitute norms of *ius cogens* and/or core elements of the principles and purposes of the United Nations.

3. *IUS COGENS* AS A SUBSTANTIVE LIMIT TO SECURITY COUNCIL DISCRETION

Although the Security Council may impinge on customary international law or treaty law when maintaining international peace and security, most authors agree that these impingements find their limits in peremptory norms of international law, otherwise known as *ius cogens*.[40] The first question that comes to mind is whether this approach would result in an over-extension of the role and purpose of the notion of *ius cogens*, which was initially developed in the context of treaty law.[41]

---

[39] See Arangio-Ruiz, above n 4, at 644; Akande, above n 12, at 320; Heike Gading, *Der Schutz grundlegender Menschenrechte durch militärische Massnahmen des Sicherheitsrates—das Ende staatlicher Souveränität?* 48 (Berlin, Duncker & Humblot, 1996).

[40] Akande, above n 12, at 323; Dinstein, above n 2, at 9; Michael Fraas, *Sicherheitsrat der Vereinten Nationan und Internationaler Gerichtshof* 77–78 (Peter Lang, Frankfurt a/M, 1998); Thomas M Franck, "The Political and the Judicial Empires: Must there be a Conflict over Conflict-Resolution?", in Najeeb Al-Naumi & Richard Meese, *International Legal Issues Arising under the United Nations Decade of International Law* 662 (The Hague, Martinus Nijhoff, 1995); Lorinser, above n 18, at 53; Dorothee Starck, *Die Rechtsmässigkeit von UNO-Wirtschaftssanktionen in Anbetracht ihrer Auswirkungen auf die Zivilbevölkerung* 222–23 (Berlin, Duncker & Humblot, 2000); Geoffrey S Watson, "Constitutionalism, Judicial Review, and the World Court", 34 *Harvard International Law Journal* 38 (1993); White, above n 13, at 418.

[41] Art 53 of the Vienna Convention on the Law of Treaties of 1969, reprinted in 8 *International Legal Materials* (1969) 679 ff. Hereinafter referred to as the Vienna Convention. See Andreas Zimmermann, "Sovereign Immunity and Violations of International Jus Cogens—Some Critical Remarks", 16 *Michigan Journal of International Law* 438 1995). He noted that during the preparatory discussion of the International Law Commission (ILC) leading to the Vienna Convention, no attempts were made to extend this notion beyond the invalidation of incompatible treaties. However, it is doubtful that any conclusion could be drawn from this fact alone, since the mandate of the drafters of the Vienna Convention was limited to issues of treaty law. It could thus not have been expected of them to deliberate on the possible role of *ius cogens* outside the treaty context.

In accordance with the principles of treaty law, a treaty is null and void if it is concluded in conflict with a peremptory norm of general international law (ie *ius cogens*).[42] States parties have to eliminate as far as possible the consequences of acts performed in reliance on provisions in conflict with the peremptory norm, and should bring their mutual relations in conformity with the peremptory norm.[43] If one were to use the prohibition against torture as an example, it would mean that any treaty that provides for the transfer of detainees from one country to another in order to facilitate torture practices during questioning, would be null and void.[44] Where a treaty itself does not violate a *ius cogens* norm, but the execution of certain obligations under the treaty would have such effect, the state is relieved from giving effect to the obligation in question. The treaty itself would, however, remain valid. Thus, the obligations existing under an extradition treaty would fall away if it resulted in the extradition of a person to a country where he or she faced torture. The treaty itself would nonetheless remain intact.[45]

As the Charter also is a treaty, it seems logical that a similar rational should apply. Thus, where the execution of an obligation under the Charter such as a binding Security Council decision would result in a violation of a *ius cogens* norm, member states would be relieved from giving effect to the obligation in question. The fact that the Charter is also the constitutive document of an international organisation with separate legal personality would not justify a deviation from this conclusion. The mere fact that the organisation itself can act independently from the member states does not change the fact that the obligations imposed by the organisation result from a treaty and may therefore not conflict with the norm of *ius cogens*. Any other conclusion would effectively allow states to

---

[42] Art 53 of the Vienna Convention, above n 41.

[43] Art 71 of the Vienna Convention, above n 41; see also AJJ de Hoogh, "The Relationship between Jus Cogens, Obligations Erga Omnes and International Crimes: Peremptory Norms in Perspective", 42 *Österreichische Zeitschrift für öffentliches Recht und Völkerrecht* 190 (1991).

[44] After the terrorist attacks in the United States on 11 September 2001, the United States were accused of sending detainees suspected of involvement with the Al-Quaida network to countries in the Middle-East, where they were tortured during questioning. See Jan Ross, "Daumenschrauben gefällig?", *Die Zeit*, 27 February 2003, at 8; see also Amnesty International Report, AMR 51/170/2001, available at www.amnesty.org.

[45] A series of decisions of the Swiss Federal Supreme Court may be illuminating in this regard. In the first of these decisions in 1982 (BGE 108 Ib 412), the Court refused to give effect to an extradition request by Argentina, despite an existing extradition agreement between the two countries, for fear that the persons affected might be subjected to torture or inhumane or degrading treatment. Although mainly relying on Art 3 of the European Convention of Human Rights and Fundamental Freedoms of 1950, it also described the prohibition of torture as a "general principle of law" that had to be taken into account during extradition proceedings. By 1985 (BGE 111 Ib 142) when considering an extradition request by Tunisia, the Federal Supreme Court explicitly stated that the prohibition of torture and *refoulement* constituted elements of the *ordre public international*, which is a synonym for *ius cogens*. See also Eva Kornicker, *Ius Cogens und Umweltvölkerrecht* 105 (1997).

circumvent their most fundamental international obligations by creating an international organisation. This, in turn, would undermine the logic that states cannot confer more powers to organs of international organisations than they can exercise themselves. For if states may not conclude an agreement in accordance with which they can deviate from peremptory norms of international law themselves, they would also not be able to conclude an agreement that invests an international organisation with the power to do so.

This line of argument does, however, presuppose that the delegation of powers by member states to the organisation is not a once-only event that coincides with its creation. Instead, it is an ongoing interaction as a result of which the powers delegated to the organisation are afterwards limited by the development of *ius cogens*.[46] An organ such as the Security Council therefore has to take into account the evolution of new *ius cogens* norm when adopting enforcement measures.[47] If the delegation of powers consisted of a single action that did not provide for any ongoing interaction (ie "progressive limitation"), the Security Council would not be bound to those *ius cogens* norms which developed after the entering into force of the Charter. These norms would only limit the powers of member states when acting individually and would not affect the powers previously conferred on the Security Council.

Since the concept of *ius cogens* was only introduced in the Vienna Convention in 1969, it would effectively mean that none of the *ius cogens* norms that are currently recognised under international law would be applicable to the Security Council. As a result, states could instrumentalise the collective security system in order to engage in slavery, apartheid or even genocide, provided that the requisite majority in

---

[46] According to Jost Delbrück, "Art 24", in Bruno Simma (ed), *The Charter of the United Nations. A Commentary* 404 (Oxford, Oxford University Press, 1994), one cannot describe the conferral of powers on the Security Council as a "delegation" of powers. The Security Council is an organ of the United Nations which acts on behalf of the organisation and not on behalf of the member states. Its actions and decisions are attributed to the United Nations organisation as a whole and not to individual members, such as the members of the Security Council. However, even if one accepted this argument, it would not alter the fact that the member states vested powers in the Security Council by means of a treaty. The Charter can neither grant the Security Council more powers than the member states intended it to have, nor can it enable the Security Council to do anything which the member states cannot do themselves. See Gill, above n 13, at 68; See Danesh Sarooshi, *The United Nations and the Development of Collective Security* 27 (Oxford, Oxford University Press, 1999). See also *Legality of the Use by a State of Nuclear Weapons in Armed Conflict*, ICJ Rep 1996, at 9; *Tadic* decision, above n 3, at para 29; Franck (International Legal Issues), above n 40, at 662.

[47] See Vera Gowlland-Debbas, Judicial Insights into Fundamental Values and Interests of the International Community', in Alexander S Muller *et al* (eds), *The International Court of Justice. Its Future Role after Fifty Years* 363 (The Hague, Martinus Nijhoff, 1997). *Ius cogens* is a dynamic concept, the content of which evolves in accordance with the changing requirements of the international community.

the Security Council can be secured.[48] In order to avoid such a clearly unacceptable situation, the conferral of powers on the Security Council has to be regarded as an ongoing interaction, to the extent that these powers are afterwards limited by the development of *ius cogens*.[49]

Although most authors agree that *ius cogens* binds states acting individually (unorganised) as well as collectively within the United Nations, some have submitted that the latter is not the case.[50] According to this line of argument the Security Council, if bound by *ius cogens*, would have to intervene against a party responsible for the violation of a *ius cogens* norm. This, in turn, implies that the Security Council would have to allocate responsibility for the violations of a *ius cogens* norm before resorting to enforcement measures. Such an obligation would run counter to the flexibility inherent to Chapter VII of the Charter, which does not require a legal evaluation of the positions of the parties by the Security Council before taking action.[51] This argument is flawed in that it focuses on *ius cogens* in connection with the *subjects* against which Security Council action is taken, instead of the *type* of action to be undertaken by the Security Council. Section 2 of this chapter has already outlined that the Security Council neither has to resort to enforcement measures, nor does it—where it does decide to adopt such measures—first have to determine

---

[48] Akande, above n 12, at 320; Fraas, above n 40, at 78; Jochen Herbst, *Rechtskontrolle des UN-Sicherheitsrates* 377 (Frankfurt a/M, Peter Lang, 1999); Lorinser, above n 18, at 53.

[49] This conclusion would also be in line with the growing recognition of the normative superior quality of *ius cogens* in other areas of international law that even extend beyond the treaty context. An illuminating example of state practice of this type is The Swiss Federal Constitution of 1999. According to Art 139(3), Art 193(4) and Art 194(2) a People's Initiative (*Volksinitiative*) aimed at constitutional amendment may not be in conflict with *ius cogens*. Any initiative that is in violation of *ius cogens* has to be invalidated by the Swiss authorities. This approach echoes the *obiter dictum* statement of the ICTY, according to which a peremptory norm of international law serves to de-legitimise any conflicting legislative, administrative or judicial act. See the *Prosecutor v Anto Furundzija*, Case No IT–95–17/1–T10, Judgment, 10 December 1998, Trial Chamber, at para 155, available at www.icty.org. Another example is that of *John Doe I v Unocal Corporation*, 2002 US App (9th Cir 2002) Lexis 19263, which was initiated under the United States Alien Tort Claims Act (28 USC § 1350) and involved, inter alia, allegations of forced labour. In deciding the law to be applied to the cause of action, the Court determined that in light of the *jus cogens* nature of the alleged violations, it would be preferable to apply international law rather than the law of any particular state. The superior normative quality of *ius cogens* norms was also, in principle, recognised in a variety of cases dealing with sovereign immunity. See *Princz v The Federal Republic of Germany*, 26 F 3d 1168 (DC Cir 1994); *Siderman v De Blake*, 965 F 2d 715 (9th Cir 1992); *Federal Republic of Germany v Prefecture of Voiotia*, Judgment, Greek Supreme Court, 20 January 2001, discussed in Bernhard Kempen, "Der Fall *Distomo*: griechische Reparationsforderungen gegen die Bundesrepublik Deutschland", in Hans-Joachim Cremer *et al* (eds), *Tradition und Weltoffenheit des Rechts. Festschrift für Helmut Steinberger* 179 (Berlin, Springer, 2002); *Germany v Margellos*, Case No 6/17–9–2002, Greek Special Supreme Court, Judgment, 17 September 2002, at para 14; *Al-Adsani v United Kingdom*, European Court of Human Rights, Judgment, 21 November 2001, at para 3, available at www.coe.int.

[50] In particular Martenczuk (Rechtskontrolle), above n 19, at 272; *ibid*, above n 12, at 546.

[51] Martenczuk (Rechtskontrolle), above n 19, at 272.

the substantive legal position of the parties, or limit the enforcement measures to those parties responsible for violations of international law. This does not change the fact, however, that in choosing the *type* of enforcement measures for maintaining or restoring international peace, the Security Council is bound by the norms of *ius cogens*.[52]

Although there is no clarity as to all the norms that would belong to *ius cogens*,[53] a core of such norms has been identified by authors. It includes the prohibition of the unilateral use of force, the right to self-defence, the prohibition of genocide, the prohibition of the violation of basic norms of international humanitarian law, the prohibition of racial discrimination and slavery, and the right to self-determination.[54] Chapter 6 at section 2.2. and chapter 9 at section 2.1.2., respectively, will argue that the right to life and the right to a fair trial during criminal proceedings (due process) can now also be considered as elements of *ius cogens*.[55]

4. THE PURPOSES AND PRINCIPLES OF THE CHARTER AS A SUBSTANTIVE LIMIT TO SECURITY COUNCIL DISCRETION

A separate but closely related category of limits to the discretion of the Security Council when adopting enforcement measures flows from the purposes and principles of the United Nations, as contained in Articles 1 and 2 of the Charter.[56] This follows from Article 24(2), which explicitly states that the Security Council shall act in accordance with the purposes

---

[52] *Ibid*, at 281–82, acknowledges that the Security Council is obliged to respect humanitarian law and very basic human rights such as the right to life. Since these norms form elements of *ius cogens*, he seems to contradict his own argument.

[53] As is underlined by Oosthuizen, above n 16, at 559, who argued that at this stage in the development of international law, *ius cogens* did not present a limit to the Security Council's enforcement powers.

[54] Akande, above n 12, at 320, 322; Karel Doehring, "Self-Determination", in Bruno Simma (ed), *The Charter of the United Nations. A Commentary* 70 (Oxford, Oxford University Press, 1994); Lailach, above n 18, at 230; White, above n 13, at 421. See also Ian D Seiderman, Hierarchy in International Law: The Human Rights Dimension 86 (Antwerp, Intersentia, 2001). Note also the separate opinion of Judge *ad hoc* Elihu Lauterpacht in *Application of the Convention on the Prevention and Punishment of the Crime of Genocide (Bosnia and Herzegovina v Yugoslavia (Serbia and Montenegro)*, Further Request for the Indication of Provisional Measures, ICJ Rep 1993, at 440–44. Hereinafter referred to as *Bosnia and Herzegovina v Serbia and Montenegro*, provisional measures II. He stated that the prohibition of genocide has long been accepted as a norm of *jus cogens*.

[55] See also Seiderman, above n 54, at 85.

[56] Akande, above n 12, at 317; Angelet, above n 29, at 75; Herbst, above n 48, at 298; Gill, above n 13, at 41; Starck, above n 40 at 141 ff; See also Doehring (in Simma), above n 54, at 57, who stated that the purposes of the organisation were directly applicable law and not a non-binding, political prescription. See also David Schweigman, *The Authority of the Security Council under Chapter VII of the United Nations Charter* 167–68 (The Hague, Kluwer, 2001); Mary Ellen O'Connell, "Debating the Law of Sanctions", 13 *European Journal of International Law* 70–71 (2002).

and principles of the organisation when discharging its duties.[57] In addition
to the primary goal of peace and security,[58] the purposes include respect
for the self-determination of peoples,[59] the solving of socio-economic and
humanitarian problems and the promotion of human rights.[60] The principles of the United Nations include the sovereign equality of member
states[61]; the obligation to act in good faith[62]; the obligation of members to
settle disputes peacefully[63]; the prohibition of the unilateral threat or use
of force by member states[64]; the obligation of members to assist the
United Nations in action it takes in accordance with the Charter[65]; the
obligation of the organisation to ensure that non-members act in accordance with the purposes and principles of the United Nations[66]; and the
obligation of the organisation not to intervene in the domestic jurisdiction
of members.[67]

Since these purposes and principles are broad and vague, several
authors question their utility in serving as limits to the Security Council's
enforcement powers. It has been argued that Article 24(2) refers to the
purposes and principles of the organisation collectively, as a result of
which the behaviour of the Security Council would only violate them if it
does not correspond to any one of these purposes and principles.[68] This
seems unlikely in the light of their breadth, as well as the fact that they
are not static, but should reflect the changes which have taken place in the
international legal order since 1945.[69] A reliance on the purposes and principles would therefore broaden the powers of the Security Council, rather
than limit them.[70]

These arguments are not convincing. The collective reference to the
purposes and principles in Article 24(2) relates to the fact that they are

---

[57] See also the dissenting opinion of Judge Weeramantry in *Case Concerning Questions of
Interpretation and Application of the 1971 Montreal Convention Arising from the Aerial Incident at
Lockerbie (Libyan Arab Jamahiriya v United States of America)*, Provisional Measures, ICJ
Rep 1992, at 171. He noted that the duty of the Security Council to act in accordance with the
purposes and principles of the United Nations was imperative and categorical. Similarly, the
separate opinion of Judge *ad hoc* Lauterpacht in *Bosnia and Herzegovina v Serbia and
Montenegro*, provisional measures II, above n 54, at 440.
[58] Art 1(1).
[59] Art 1(2).
[60] Art 1(3).
[61] Art 2 (1).
[62] Art 2(2).
[63] Art 2(3).
[64] Art 2(4).
[65] Art 2(5).
[66] Art 2(6).
[67] Art 2(7).
[68] Martenczuk (Rechtskontrolle), above n 19, at 208. For a similar concern, see Matthew
Craven, "Humanitarianism and the Quest for Smarter Sanctions", 13 *European Journal of
International Law* 51 (2002).
[69] Gowlland-Debbas (State Responsibility), above n 23, at 91.
[70] Oosthuizen, above n 16, at 562.

listed individually in Articles 1 and 2 of the Charter, which would make any repetition unnecessary. Acting in accordance with the purposes and principles would therefore mean that the Security Council may not maintain peace and security at the complete expense of any of them. The Security Council has to balance the realisation of its primary goal with the realisation of the secondary goals contained in the Charter. This is a typical feature of constitutional interpretation, as constitutions often contain a variety of different goals which can only be harmonised by a balancing of the different interests involved. Although this implies a limitation of the secondary goals contained in the Charter, it may not lead to an erosion of their core content.

Similarly, such a complete negation of the core content of the Charter purposes and principles could also not be justified on the basis of the Security Council's implied powers. The implied powers enable the Security Council to take measures which were not specifically provided for in the Charter, but which are necessary to carry out its primary responsibility for the maintenance of peace and security.[71] Thus, where the Charter leaves gaps in providing for specific Security Council authority it may rely on its implied powers. The implied powers do not, however, enable the Security Council to override specific limitations provided for in the Charter as such an open-ended power would effectively make every other Charter principle redundant.[72]

As far as the purposes of the Charter in Article 1 is concerned, enforcement measures under Chapter VII may thus not undermine the essence of self-determination, basic human rights or norms of international humanitarian law.[73] In addition, it may not result in the imposition of a settlement on parties, as Article 1(1) clearly states that international

---

[71] See Fraas, above n 40, at 51. He explained that it was not very helpful to look at Art 24(2) when examining whether Art 24(1) would provide for implied powers, since the latter did not contain the complete set of competencies of the Security Council. The chapters mentioned there, ie VI, VII, VIII and XII, are not the only ones that convey powers on the Security Council. Chapter VI (in Art 26) and Chapter XIV (in Art 94(2)), for example, also attribute certain competencies to it. See also Delbrück (in Simma), above n 46, at 403–04; Kelsen, above n 31, at 292.

[72] Arangio-Ruiz, above n 4, at 653–54; Gill, above n 13, at 72; Fraas, above n 40, at 52; Delbrück (in Simma), above n 46, at 403, 410. See also Krzystof Skubiszewski, "Implied Powers of International organisations", in Yoram Dinstein (ed), *International Law at a Time of Perplexity. Essays in Honour of Shabtai Rosenne* 856 ff (Dordrecht, Martinus Nijhoff, 1989).

[73] During the debates of the Committee on the Structure and Procedure of the Security Council at San Francisco, the delegate of the United States, in particular, stressed that the Security Council was bound by the purposes and principles of the Charter. In his opinion the principles of equal rights, self-determination and the promotion and encouragement of respect for human rights and fundamental freedoms for all without respect to race, language, religion or sex, constituted the highest rules of conduct. If the Security Council violated the principles and purposes of the Charter it would be acting *ultra vires*. See 11 *United Nations Conference on International Organisation* 378 (1945); see also, Akande, above n 12, at 319; Lorinser, above n 18, at 54; Starck, above n 40, at 169 ff.

disputes have to be settled in accordance with the principles of justice and international law.[74]

With respect to the principles contained in Article 2 of the Charter, the main limitations for Security Council action flow from Articles 2(1), 2(2) and 2(7).[75] As far as Article 2(1) and 2(7) are concerned,[76] it is well recognised that the respect for state sovereignty commanded by these Articles can be limited by enforcement measures under Chapter VII of the Charter. This is not only inherent in the nature of the enforcement measures provided for in that chapter, but is also explicitly provided for in the last part of Article 2(7). In addition, the notions of state sovereignty and domestic jurisdiction have decreased as the organisation's jurisdiction has steadily increased in the years since its foundation.[77] For example, it was illustrated in chapter 4 that grave and systematic violations of human rights and international humanitarian law cannot be regarded as purely internal matters anymore. As a result, some authors submit that the concept of sovereignty contained in Article 2(1) is without significance and would not pose a limitation to Security Council action.[78]

This interpretation comes across as too extreme, if one considers that the concept of the sovereign equality of member states still forms a corner stone of the United Nations and international relations in general.[79] The Security Council will therefore have to respect the core elements of state

---

[74] This is not affected by the fact that Art 94(2) of the Charter authorises the Security Council to enforce a decision of the ICJ, where any of the parties to the dispute fails to comply with the ICJ's judgment. This (in practice never utilised) power of the Security Council does not in itself bring about any modification of the rights or obligations of the states involved in the dispute. Instead, the modification is brought about by a binding judgment, which resulted from a judicial settlement procedure which the parties consented to. The Security Council can merely enforce this modification if and to the extent that it is required by the binding judgment. See Arangio-Ruiz, above n 4, at 624.

[75] The nature of the remaining obligations contained in Art 2(3), Art 2(4) and Art 2(5) are such that they can only be fulfilled by the individual member states, rather than the organs of the United Nations. Although Art 2(6) is directed at the organisation, it is difficult to see how it could serve as a limitation to Security Council action, apart from the fact that it does not facilitate the application of the Chapter VII enforcement mechanism against non-member states. See also ch 3, at s 4.2.

[76] Art 2(1) reads as follows: "The organisation is based on the principle of the sovereign equality of all its Members". Art 2(7) determines that: "Nothing contained in the present Charter shall authorise the United Nations to intervene in matters which are essentially within the domestic jurisdiction of any state or shall require the Members to submit such matters to settlement under the present Charter; but this principle shall not prejudice the application of enforcement measures under Chapter VII."

[77] Ruth Gordon, "United Nations Intervention in Internal Conflicts: Iraq, Somalia, and Beyond", 15 *Michigan Journal of International Law* 524 (1993); see Martenczuk (Rechtskontrolle), above n 19, at 212.

[78] Martenczuk (Rechtskontrolle), above n 19, at 210; Oosthuizen, above n 16, at 553.

[79] Felix Ermacora, "Art 2(7)", in Bruno Simma (ed), *The Charter of the United Nations. A Commentary* 142 (Oxford, Oxford University, 1994); Albrecht Randelzhofer, "Art 2", *ibid*, at 73; Gading, above n 39, at 190.

sovereignty when resorting to enforcement measures.[80] These would typically include territorial sovereignty, in the sense that the Security Council may not change the borders of a state against its will, or transfer one part of a state territory to another.[81]

4.1. The Meaning of the Principle of Good Faith

Article 2(2) obliges members to fulfil their obligations under the Charter in good faith.[82] At first glance it seems as if this obligation is addressed to the individual member states rather than the organisation.[83] However, when one reads it together with the first sentence of Article 2,[84] it becomes clear that the members have to act in good faith both when acting individually and as an organ of the United Nations.[85] This introductory sentence explicitly states that the organisation and its members shall act in accordance with the principles contained in that Article.[86]

In the United Nations system the obligation of the organisation to act in good faith is closely related to the concept of equitable (promissory) estoppel, which had initially been developed in inter-state relations. Equitable estoppel implies that where one party has reason to believe, based on the actions or words of another party, that a situation or occurrence would or would not in future change in a particular manner, the other party may not change the situation in that manner.[87] It is an important outgrowth of the doctrine of good faith, as it protects the belief of the party invoking estoppel. In this sense equitable estoppel attributes an objective character to good faith, as it implies that the belief in question

---

[80] Doehring (in Simma), above n 54, at 57; see also Schweigman, above n 56, at 173.

[81] Bowett, above n 24, at 93; Gill, above n 13, at 70.

[82] Art 2(2) of the Charter reads as follows: "All members, in order to ensure to all of them the rights and benefits resulting from membership, shall fulfil in good faith the obligations assumed by them in accordance with the Charter."

[83] As is argued by Martenczuk (Rechtskontrolle), above n 19, at 210; Oosthuizen, above n 16, at 560.

[84] The first sentence of Art 2 determines that: "The organisation and its Members, in pursuit of the Purposes stated in Art 1, shall act in accordance with the following Principles:"

[85] *Conditions of Admission of States to Membership in the United Nations,* Advisory Opinion, ICJ Rep 1948, at 57; see also Herbst, above n 48, at 359–61; Jörg P Müller, "Art 2(3)", in Bruno Simma (ed), *The Charter of the United Nations* 96 (Oxford, Oxford University Press, 1994); Randelzhofer, above no 79, at 73; Frederic L Kirgis, "Security Council Governance of Post Conflict Societies: A Plea for Good Faith and Informed Decision Making", 95 *American Journal of International Law* 581 (2001); Schweigman, above n 56, at 174; Starck, above n 40, at 176.

[86] See also Elisabeth Zoller, *La bonne foi en droit international public* 190 ff (Paris, Pèdonne, 1977).

[87] Thomas Cottier & Krista N Scheffer, "Good Faith and the Protection of Legitimate Expectations in the WTO", in Marco Bronckers & Reinhard Quick (eds), *New Directions in International Economic Law* 172 (The Hague, Kluwer, 2000); Christopher Brown, "A Comparative and Critical Assessment of Estoppel in International Law", 50 *University of Miami Law Review* 381 (1996).

has to be fair, honest and reasonable.[88] From the presence of good faith in the form of a legitimate expectation on the part of the party invoking estoppel, one could simultaneously deduce the absence of good faith on the part of the party creating the expectation. As a result, the non-realisation of a legitimate expectation would amount to an act of bad faith.[89]

A more controversial question is whether the legitimate expectation created, must have resulted in detriment or advantage to one of the parties, as the case may be.[90] According to one (narrower) line of international jurisprudence, equitable estoppel is based on the law's desire to vindicate those who rely upon others to their own detriment. This element generally requires that the promisee suffers a detriment or loss as a result of the expectation created, or that that the promisor gains an advantage from it.[91] At the same time, however, another (broader) line of international jurisprudence merely focuses on the reliance on the expectation created, without examining whether any detriment was suffered.[92]

This line of argument culminated in the *Nuclear Test* case, in which the ICJ regarded the unilateral declaration by France that it would terminate its nuclear testing program in Polynesia, as legally binding.[93] The ICJ

---

[88] JF O'Connor, *Good Faith in International Law* 110 (Aldershot, Dartmouth, 1991); Cottier & Scheffer, above n 87, at 50–51; Robert Kolb, "Aperçus sur la bonne foi en droit international public", 54 *Revue Hellénique de Droit International* 38–39 (2001).

[89] But see Zoller, above n 86, at 294–95. Whilst accepting that estoppel protects the good faith of the promisee, she rejected the notion that it sanctioned the absence of good faith of the promisor. The latter's good faith would not enter into play, as it is being held responsible for the consequences of its acts, regardless of whether those consequences were intended or accompanied by bad faith motives. Similarly, Brown, above n 87, at 382.

[90] Ian Sinclair, "Estoppel and acquiescence", in Vaughan Lowe & Malgosia Fitzmaurice (eds), *Fifty Years of the International Court of Justice. Essays in Honour of Sir Robert Jennings* 106 (Cambridge, Cambridge University Press, 1996); Jörg Paul Müller & Thomas Cottier, "Estoppel", II *Encyclopedia of Public International Law* 119 (1994).

[91] *Payment of Various Serbian Loans Issued in France (Serbia v France)*, Judgment, PCIJ 1929 (Series A) Nos 20/21, at 38. *Tinoco (UK v Costa Rica)*, Arbitration, 18 *American Journal of International Law* 149 (1923); *Barcelona Traction, Light & Power Co (Belgium v Spain)*, ICJ Rep 1964, at 24; *North Sea Continental Shelf (Federal Republic of Germany v The Netherlands)*, ICJ Rep 1969, at 25; *Land, Island and Maritime Frontier Dispute (El Salvador v Honduras)*, ICJ Rep 1990, at 118. See also Bin Cheng, *General Principles of Law as applied by International Courts and Tribunals* 143–44 (London, Stevens, 1953).

[92] See *Legal Status of Eastern Greenland*, PCIJ 1933 (Series A/B), No 53, at 62. The reliance of Denmark on the Norwegian (Ihlen) declaration that recognised Danish sovereignty over Greenland sufficed for the purposes of invoking equitable estoppel by Denmark. No indication of detriment suffered by Denmark because of such reliance was required or demonstrated A comparable example is that of the *Temple of Preah Vihear (Cambodia v Thailand)*, ICJ Rep 1962, at 6. Thailand (Siam) was precluded from disputing the validity of the map that was used for drawing up the border between Cambodia and Siam, as it had never questioned its validity during the period that expired between the time it was drawn up and the time the dispute arose. As noted in the dissenting opinion of Judge Spender, *ibid* at 144, there was no discussion or indication of the detriment suffered by Cambodia in reliance upon Thailand's acceptance of the purported border. See also Brown, above n 87, at 396–97; O'Connor, above n 88, at 92.

[93] *Nuclear Tests (Australia v France)*, Judgment, ICJ Rep 1974, at 26.

effectively accepted a promissory estoppel claim without requiring that the party invoking it suffer any detriment or harm.[94] It was motivated by the fact that one of the basic principles governing the creation and performance of legal obligations, whatever their source, is the principle of good faith.[95] This principle implied the protection of the confidence and trust which are essential for the stability of international relations, in particular in relation to expectations created *erga omnes*.[96] The ICJ thus seemed to regard the consistency in the behaviour of international actors and the stability resulting from it as worthy of legal protection, to the extent that it could be reasonably expected.[97]

Although the concept of equitable estoppel mainly applies to inter-state relations, it is a general principle of law and can as such also be used to bind organs of international organisations to the legitimate expectations created by their actions.[98] As in the case of inter-state relations, it would imply an objective assessment of whether an organ of the United Nations acted in accordance with a legitimate expectation it had created and, in turn, whether the organ acted in accordance with the meaning and spirit of good faith.[99] It is further submitted that within the United Nations it would be justifiable to adhere to the broader notion of equitable estoppel,

---

[94] Brown, above n 87, at 409; Kolb, above n 88, at 39. See also International Law Commission, *Report on the work of its fifty-first session* para 532 (1999), available at www.un.org.

[95] *Nuclear Test* case, above n 93, at 268.

[96] See the *Nuclear Test* case, above n 93, at 269; see also Kolb, above n 88, at 39–40.

[97] For a different opinion see Brown, above n 87, at 410. He claimed that this broad interpretation might undermine the very stability it seeks to create. It would allow for wild fluctuations in legal rulings depending on the whims of the parties and judges in a given dispute. See also Zoller, above n 86, at 341 ff; See also the dissenting opinion of Judge Barwick and Judge De Castro, in the *Nuclear Test* case, above n 93, at 268 and 374–75, respectively, who questioned the legal character of the French unilateral declarations.

[98] See Jörg P Müller, *Vertrauensschutz im Völkerrecht* 228 (Cologne, Heymann, 1971); Herbst, above n 48, at 363. Cf International Law Commission, *Report on the work of its fifty-first session* para 530 (1999), available at www.un.org; *ibid, Report on its fifty-second session* paras 541 ff (2000).

[99] Müller (in Simma), above n 85, at 93; Müller (Vertrauensschutz), above n 98, at 229–30. Contra White, above n 13, at 419. He argued that a lack of good faith would only be a justifiable limit to Security Council action if it can be explained why all its members went along with the resolution, in spite of them being aware that it was in bad faith. This argument cannot be accepted, since determining the subjective motives for state action is a virtually impossible task based on speculation. See also the cautious approach of Herbst, above n 48, at 363. He observed that the principle was applied restrictively in that it did not protect a future expectation of an abstract nature. For example, in para 2 of SC Res 984 of 11 April 1995, the Security Council stated that its permanent members which were in possession of nuclear weapons would act immediately in accordance with the relevant provisions of the Charter, in the event that non-nuclear weapon states, who were parties to the Treaty on the Non-Proliferation of Nuclear Weapons, were the victim of an act of aggression in which nuclear weapons were used. One could be tempted to read this as a self-imposed, binding obligation to intervene in the case of a nuclear attack on a non-nuclear state. However, Herbst suggested that due to the general and abstract nature of the declaration, it was unlikely that states could rely on the estoppel principle if the Security Council refrained from intervening under the circumstances so described.

which would not depend on the demonstration of detriment suffered or advantage gained, as the case may be.[100] This relates to the need for ensuring consistency with regard to the actions of an organisation which, whilst effectively having *erga omnes* effect, could only be subjected to judicial review with great difficulty.[101] Without such consistency the trust and confidence of member states in the organisation responsible for the maintenance of international peace would be eroded, with detrimental effects for its long term efficiency and the stability of international relations in general.[102]

The relevance of equitable estoppel as a concretisation of good faith in serving as a limit to the enforcement powers of the Security Council gains significance when one examines the interaction between this principle and the obligation of the Security Council to respect fundamental human rights norms and basic norms of international humanitarian law.

4.2. The Interaction between the Principle of Good Faith and Respect for Fundamental Human Rights

As pointed out above in section 4, the Security Council's obligation to respect the core content of fundamental human rights when resorting to enforcement measures already follows from Article 1(3) of the Charter. The type of enforcement measures that are bound by the core content of human rights norms concerns non-military enforcement measures, for example economic sanctions. When the Security Council resorts to military measures, the limits to its powers are primarily provided by the

---

[100] However, even if one adhered to the narrower concept of equitable estoppel, it is arguable that the Security Council would be estopped from violating fundamental human rights. For by doing so, it would be securing a benefit in the form of an aggrandisement of its powers, in contradiction of Art 1(3) of the Charter.

[101] See ch 2 and ch 3.

[102] It is noteworthy that equitable estoppel in the European Community (EC) is still strongly linked to the notion of unreasonable (non-foreseeable) economic damage. See, for example, Case 344/85, *Ferriere San Carlo SpA v Commission*, [1987] ECR 4435; Case 120/86, *Mulder v Minister van Landbouw en Visserij*, [1988] ECR 2321; Case 170/86, *Von Deetzen v HZA Hamburg-Jonas*, 1988 [ECR] 2355; Case 203/86, *Spain v Council* [1998] ECR 4563; Case T–203/96, *Embassy Limousines v Parliament* [1998], at para 75–para 76. This can be explained by the fact that the EC system of trade liberalisation is inherently linked to rapidly changing economic conditions and "hard business luck". This factor combined with the legal certainty provided by a centralised judiciary in the form of the ECJ, would justify adherence to the more restrictive concept of equitable estoppel in the EC context. Cf John Temple Lang, "Legal Certainty and Legitimate Expectations as General Principles of Law", in Ulf Bernitz & Joakim Nergelius (eds), *General Principles of European Community Law* 170 ff (Kluwer, The Hague, 2000); Eleanor Sharpston, "European Community Law and the Doctrine of Legitimate Expectations: How Legitimate and for Whom?", 11 *Northwestern Journal of International Law & Business* 90–91 (1990). For a discussion of the emerging doctrine of equitable estoppel in the World Trade Organisation (WTO), see Cottier & Scheffer, above n 87, at 60 ff.

basic norms of the law of armed conflict,[103] which are elaborated on in section 4.3.

In spite of the broad language of Article 1(3) of the Charter, the core content of the human rights norms at stake can be drawn from the human rights instruments developed under the auspices of the organisation.[104] Although the Security Council is not a party to these treaties by means of ratification, they represent an elaboration upon the Charter's original vision of human rights found in Article 1(3) and Articles 55 and 56.[105] The human rights contained in these documents thus constitute the human rights that, under Article 1(3), the United Nations have to promote and respect.

The obligation to promote and respect human rights is strengthened by the interaction between Article 1(3) and the principle of good faith (equitable estoppel) contained in Article 2(2) of the Charter. This principle implies that the United Nations have to conform to the human rights standards developed within the framework of the organisation. In this context one has to bear in mind that the organisation created an extensive system for monitoring the implementation of the human rights instruments developed by it.[106] By promoting human rights in this manner,

---

[103] This is not to be interpreted as implying that the protection granted by human rights norms are automatically suspended by the outbreak of armed conflict. After all, in the preamble of SC Res 237 of 14 June 1967, the Security Council itself stated that essential and inalienable human rights should be respected even during the vicissitudes of war. However, to the extent that there are differences between human rights standards and standards of humanitarian law, the latter will be determinative during an armed conflict, as it constitutes the *lex specialis*. The different standards gain particular importance with respect to the legality of the deprivation of life, as will be illustrated in ch 6. See also *Legality of the Threat or Use of Nuclear Weapons*, Advisory Opinion, ICJ Rep 1996, at 230. Hereinafter referred to as *Nuclear Weapons* opinion; Human Rights Committee, *General Comment No 29, State of Emergency* para 3 (2001); Theodor Meron, "The Humanization of Humanitarian Law", 94 *American Journal of International Law* 266 (2000).

[104] These include the Universal Declaration of Human Rights of 10 December 1948; the International Covenant on Civil and Political Rights of 16 December 1966 and the Protocols thereto; the International Covenant on Economic, Social and Cultural Rights of 16 December 1966; the Convention on the Elimination of All Forms of Racial Discrimination of 21 December 1965; the Convention on Elimination of All Forms of Discrimination Against Women of 17 December 1979; the Convention Against Torture and Other Cruel, Inhumane or Degrading Treatment or Punishment of 17 December 1984; and the International Convention on the Rights of the Child of 20 December 1989. The text of these and all other United Nations human rights documents cited in this chapter, are available at www.unhchr.ch/.

[105] See also Roger Normand, "A Human Rights Assessment of Sanctions: The Case of Iraq, 1990–1997", in Willem JM van Genugten & Gerard A de Groot (eds), *United Nations Sanctions. Effectiveness and Effects, Especially in the Field of Human Rights. A Multi-disciplinary Approach* 23 (Antwerp, Intersentia, 1999); Hans-Peter Gasser, "Collective Economic Sanctions and International Humanitarian Law", 56 *Zeitschrift für ausländisches öffentliches Recht und Völkerrecht* 880 (1996); Andrew K Fishman, "Between Iraq and a Hard Place: The Use of Economic Sanctions and Threat to International Peace and Security", 13 *Emory International Law Review* 712 (1999).

[106] Fraas, above n 40, at 82–83; See Akande, above n 12, at 324.

the United Nations created the expectation of respect for these rights on the part of the organisation itself. The obligation to act in good faith obliges member states, when acting in the context of an organ of the United Nations, to fulfil legally relevant expectations that are raised by their conduct with regard to human rights standards accepted in the framework of the organisation.[107]

On the basis of the principle of good faith, one can therefore argue that organs of the United Nations, including the Security Council, will be estopped from behaviour that violates the essence of the rights protected in these treaties, as this would constitute an act of bad faith on the part of the organisation. The flip-side of this argument would imply that those members of the United Nations which have not yet ratified the major United Nations human rights instruments would nonetheless be bound to the core content (essence) of the rights contained in these instruments when serving as a member of the Security Council. When participating in the decision-making process of an organ of the United Nations, these members will have to act in accordance with those obligations that the majority of members created for the organisation as a whole.

The following chapters (notably chapters 6, 8 and 9) will be mostly concerned with the implications of the "expectation of respect" for certain human rights standards contained in the International Covenant on Civil and Political Rights of 1966 (ICCPR) and the International Covenant on Economic, Social and Cultural Rights of 1966 (ICESCR). Together with the United Nations Declaration of Human Rights of 1948 (UDHR), these covenants form the Universal Bill of Human Rights, which constitute the foundation of the United Nations system for the protection of human rights. This implies that these treaties serve as the primary point of departure when analysing the Security Council's good faith obligation to respect human rights standards. The implications of a similar "expectation of respect" in relation to the norms contained in the other United Nations human rights treaties are only referred to in passing, or in a supplementary fashion.

4.2.1.   The Limitation of Human Rights by the Security Council

The next question that springs to mind is whether the Security Council would be allowed to limit human rights when adopting non-military enforcement measures under Article 41 of the Charter. In answering this question one has to distinguish between non-derogable rights, and those

---

[107] Fraas, above n 40, at 82. See Akande, above n 12, at 323. He claimed that it would be anachronistic if an organ of the United Nations were itself empowered to violate human rights, when the whole tenor of the Charter is to promote the protection of human rights by and with in states.

human rights that can be subjected to limitation. Article 4(2) of the ICCPR contains the non-derogable human rights which have to be respected by states even in times of emergency. The non-derogable rights include the right to life[108]; the prohibition of torture or cruel and degrading treatment[109]; the prohibition of slavery and servitu de[110] or civil imprisonment[111]; the impermissibly of retroactive punishment[112]; the right of recognition before the law[113]; and freedom of thought, religion and conscience.[114]

The protected status of these rights implies that the obligation on the part of the Security Council to act in good faith towards human rights norms would be stronger in relation to the non-derogable rights and that it may not limit these rights when adopting enforcement measures under Article 41 of the Charter. In addition, most of the non-derogable human rights have arguably gained *ius cogens* status, which constitutes a separate reason why the Security Council may not limit these rights when adopting enforcement measures,[115] regardless of whether (all of its) members have actually ratified the ICCPR.

As far as the derogable rights in the ICCPR are concerned, Article 4(1) allows states to derogate from their obligations in times of emergency. This derogation is, however, subjected to a strict principle of proportionality, since states may only derogate from their obligations to the extent strictly required by the exigencies of the situation.[116] That states are also allowed to limit the rights in the ICESCR follows from states parties' obligation to take steps, to the maximum of their available resources, to achieve progressively the full realisation of the rights in the ICESCR.[117] This formulation acknowledges limits to economic, social and cultural rights necessitated by limited resources.[118] However, although this is a flexible criteria for limitation, it does not relieve states parties from a minimum core obligation with respect to each right. Even in times of

---

[108] Art 6(1) ICCPR. An exception is provided for in relation to the death penalty in Art 6(2).
[109] Art 7 ICCPR.
[110] Art 8(1) and (2) ICCPR.
[111] Art 11 ICCPR.
[112] Art 15 ICCPR.
[113] Art 16 ICCPR.
[114] Art 18(1) ICCPR.
[115] See *General Comment No 29*, above n 103, at para 11, which described the proclamation of certain rights as being of a non-derogable nature as a recognition, in part, of their peremptory nature.
[116] Art 4(1) ICCPR. See also Human Rights Committee, *General Comment No 5, Derogation of Rights* para 3 (1981). It opined that measures taken under Art 4 were of an exceptional and temporary nature. They may only last as long as the life of the nation concerned is threatened. Also, in times of emergency the protection of human rights becomes all the more important, particularly those rights from which no derogation can be made. This was reaffirmed in *General Comment No 29*, above n 103, at para 2 and para 4.
[117] Art 2(1) ICESCR.
[118] See Committee on Economic, Social and Cultural Rights, *General Comment No 3, The Nature of States Parties Obligations* para 1 and para 9 (1990).

economic hardship minimum essential levels of each of the rights are incumbent upon every state party.[119]

The question that arises is what the right of derogation in Article 4(1) of the ICCPR and the flexible nature of the rights in the ICESCR imply for enforcement measures imposed by the Security Council. Since the situations in which the Security Council resorts to Article 41 of the Charter would amount to an emergency, it should have the right to limit the derogable rights protected by the ICCPR.[120] Moreover, in order for economic sanctions to achieve their objections, they will almost always have a significant impact on economic, social and cultural rights.[121] It therefore seems logical that the Security Council has the right to limit the rights protected by the ICESCR.

This still leaves unanswered whether the Security Council would be subjected to a proportionality principle when limiting the derogable rights in the ICCPR and the rights in the ICESCR and if so, what the nature of this proportionality principle should be. After all, the Security Council is a unique institution with authority and responsibilities that differ from those of individual states.[122] When responding to a threat to international peace and security, the Security Council is reacting to situations that threaten international peace as opposed to the security of one single state. The gravity of the situation coupled with the Security Council's need to act efficiently may therefore question whether it should be subjected to a (strict) proportionality principle when limiting human rights in terms of Articles 41 of the Charter.[123]

As will be illustrated in chapter 6, this question gains particular significance with respect to economic and social rights, since they are the most likely to be affected by economic sanctions. Certain statements of the Committee on Economic, Social and Cultural Rights (hereinafter the Committee), lead to the conclusion that the Security Council has to respect some notion of proportionality when limiting human rights in the context of an economic embargo. According to the Committee, the provisions of the ICESCR cannot be considered to be inoperative or in

---

[119] *Ibid*, at para 10. It continues by stating that a state party in which any significant number of individuals is deprived of essential foodstuffs, or essential primary health care, or basic shelter and housing, or of the most basic forms of education is, prima facie, failing to discharge its obligations under the Covenant.

[120] Fraas, above n 40, at 83.

[121] Human Rights Committee, *General Comment 8, Right to liberty and security of persons* para 3 (1982). For example, sanctions often cause significant disruption in the distribution of food, pharmaceuticals and sanitation supplies. They also jeopardise the quality of food and the availability of clean drinking water, severely interfere with the functioning of basic health and education systems and undermine the right to work. See also Anna Segall, "Economic sanctions: legal and policy constraints", 81 *International Review of the Red Cross* 37 (1999).

[122] Normand, above n 105, at 28.

[123] See Normand, above n 105, at 28, who stated that the Security Council moved in a grey area between war and peace.

any way inapplicable, solely because a decision has been taken that considerations of international peace and security warrant the imposition of economic sanctions.[124] The state targeted with sanctions and the international community itself must do everything possible to protect at least the core content of the economic, social and cultural rights of the peoples of that state.[125]

The Committee derives this obligation from the commitment in the Charter to promote respect for all human rights.[126] This conclusion of the Committee can be interpreted as a reaffirmation of the expectation that the Security Council will act in accordance with the core content of human rights norms that were developed within the framework of the United Nations. It also implies that the leeway granted to the Security Council to limit economic, social and cultural rights may not be interpreted as an authorisation to suspend these rights and that some notion of proportional limitation needs to be maintained. For the same reason coercive measures under Article 41 of the Charter may also not suspend the derogable rights in the ICCPR or limit them beyond any proportion.[127]

In chapters 6, 8 and 9 the leeway of the Security Council in limiting human rights, as well as the type of proportionality principle applicable when doing so, will be developed in more detail. As will be illuminated in those chapters, these questions are closely related to the nature of the right at stake (eg the right to health, the right to a fair hearing) and the nature of the enforcement measures (eg broad economic sanctions, quasi-judicial measures etc) involved.

These chapters will also illustrate that the Security Council's obligation to act in good faith towards human rights norms further implies the obligation to monitor the impact of enforcement measures on the civilian population on a regular basis. This follows from the fact that the regular monitoring of human rights forms a central obligation of states parties to the

---

[124] *General Comment No 8*, above n 121, at para 7.

[125] *Ibid*, at para 7. At para 10 it stressed that the imposition of sanctions did not in any way nullify or diminish the relevant obligations of that state party. While sanctions will inevitably diminish the capacity of the affected state to fund or support some of the necessary measures, the affected state remains under an obligation to ensure the absence of discrimination in relation to the enjoyment of these rights, and to resort to all possible measures, including negotiations with other states and the international community, to reduce to a minimum the negative impact upon the rights of vulnerable groups within the society. See also Human Rights Committee, *General Comment No 12, The right to adequate food* para 28 (1999). Even where a state faces severe resource constraints, whether caused by a process of economic adjustment, economic recession, climatic conditions or other factors, measures should be undertaken to ensure that the right to adequate food is especially fulfilled for vulnerable population groups and individuals.

[126] *General Comment No 8*, above n 121, at para 8. It also underlined that every permanent member of the Security Council has signed the ICESCR, although China and the United States have yet to ratify it, and that most of the non-permanent members at any given time are parties to the ICESCR.

[127] Cf Seiderman, above n 54, at 84.

ICCPR and ICESCR.[128] In the process they have to pay special attention to any worse-off regions or areas and to any specific groups or sub-groups which appear to be particularly vulnerable or disadvantaged. This is to ensure that states parties are aware of the extent to which the various rights are enjoyed by all individuals within its territory or under its jurisdiction.[129] By emphasising the importance of monitoring in such a fashion, the United Nations has created the legitimate expectation that it would monitor the impact of its own actions on human rights as well, notably when these rights are limited by Security Council enforcement action.

4.3.   The Interaction between the Principle of Good Faith and Respect for Basic Norms of International Humanitarian Law

In addition to the promotion of respect for human rights norms, Article 1(3) of the Charter also outlines the solving of international problems of a humanitarian character through international cooperation as a purpose of the United Nations.[130] From this it follows that the basic rules of international humanitarian law, otherwise known as the law of armed conflict, constitutes a further limitation on the enforcement powers of the Security Council under Chapter VII of the Charter. For it is difficult to see how the United Nations could realise this aim if its own forces did not respect the basic rules of international humanitarian law in situations of armed conflict.[131]

This conclusion is also underpinned by the United Nations' own behaviour. During peace-keeping operations the organisation has consistently requested troop contributing countries to ensure that their respective

---

[128] Committee on Economic, Social and Cultural Rights, *General Comment No 1, Reporting by States Parties* para 3 (1989). General Comment No 12, above n 125, at para 31; Human Rights Committee, *Consolidated Guidelines for State Reports under the ICCPR* para D (1999).

[129] *General Comment No 1*, above n 128, at para 3.

[130] Art 1(3) of the Charter; Gasser, above n 105, at 880. This can also be concluded from the *Legal Consequence for States of the Continued Presence of South Africa in Namibia (South West Africa) Notwithstanding Security Council Resolution 276 (1970)*, advisory opinion, ICJ Rep 1971, at 55–56. The ICJ affirmed that Resolution 276 (1970) obliged states to refrain from entering treaties with South Africa, where the latter acted on behalf of Namibia. However, this obligation did not extend to treaties of a humanitarian character, the non-respect of which would have negative consequences for the people of Namibia. See Herbst, above n 48, at 381; Gowlland-Debbas (State Responsibility), above n 23, at 92; Gill, above n 13, at 83.

[131] Richard D Glick, "Lip Service to the Law of War: Humanitarian Law and United Nations Armed Forces", in 17 *Michigan Journal of International Law* 62 (1995). See also Starck, above n 40, at 157 ff. She underlined that human rights and the norms of humanitarian law are two sides of the same coin, as both categories of norms are underpinned by the necessity of respect for and protection of the dignity of the human person. See also Andreas Stein, *Der Sicherheitsrat der Vereinten Nationen und die Rule of Law* 6 (Baden-Baden, Nomos, 1999).

contingents respect the four 1949 Geneva Conventions,[132] and has itself requested these forces to respect the "principles and spirit" of these Conventions.[133] It has followed this practice with respect to enforcement operations authorised under Chapter VII of the Charter, as well as (classic) peace-keeping operations where the United Nations forces could become involved in hostilities in self-defence.[134] For example, in the Korean conflict, the Unified Command announced that it would be guided by the humanitarian principles of the 1949 Geneva Conventions and, in particular, the principles in common Article 3.[135] During the (first) Gulf War, the United Nations authorised forces also left no doubt as to the applicability of international humanitarian law to the military operations.[136]

A clause stating that the United Nations force shall observe the "principles and spirit" of the general international conventions applicable to the conduct of military personnel was also included in the regulations for UNEF and ONUC, as well as the United Nations Forces in Cyprus (UNFICYP).[137] By 1991, a similar clause was included in the model status-of-forces agreement for peace-keeping operations, which codified customary practices and principles applicable to United Nations peace-keeping operations.[138] In accordance with this clause, the United Nations

---

[132] The conventions in question concern the Geneva Convention for the Amelioration of the Condition of the Wounded and Sick in Armed Forces in the Field of 12 August 1949; the Geneva Convention for the Amelioration of the Condition of Wounded, Sick and Shipwrecked Members of Armed Forces at Sea of 12 August 1949; the Geneva Convention Relative to the Treatment of Prisoners of War of 12 August 1949; the Geneva Convention Relative to the Protection of Civilian Persons in Time of War of 12 August 1949, available at www.icrc.org.

[133] Legal Opinion of the Secretariat of the United Nations, "Question of the Possible Accession of Intergovernmental Organisations to the Geneva Conventions for the Protection of War Victims", *United Nations Juridical Yearbook* 153–54 (1972). Hereinafter referred to as Legal Opinion.

[134] The Rules for United Nations (authorised) forces are developed for each specific force. The specific rights and responsibilities for contingents are agreed upon between the United Nations and troop-contributing states in participation agreements. The relation with the host state is regulated in a status of forces agreement (SOFA). Where no such agreements have been concluded, it may be assumed that informal agreements referring to established practice exists. Most of this practice is contained in the model agreements drafted by the Secretary-General. See Marten Zwanenburg, "Compromise or Commitment: Human Rights and International Humanitarian Law Obligations for UN Peace Forces", in 11 *Leiden Journal of International Law* 238 (1998).

[135] S/233 (1951); Le Comité international de la Croix Rouge et le conflit de Corée, 1 *Recueil des documents* 8–11 (1952); Finn Seyersted, *United Nations Forces in the Law of Peace and War* 183–84 (Leyden, Sitjhoff, 1966); see also Christopher Greenwood, "International Humanitarian Law and United Nations Military Operations", 1 *Yearbook of Humanitarian Law* 18–19 (1998).

[136] See United States Department of Defence, "Report to Congress on Conduct of Persian Gulf War", 31 *International Legal Materials* 612 (1992); Akande, above n 12, at 324.

[137] ST/SGB/UNEF/1 Reg 44 (1957); ST/SGB/ONUC/1 Reg 43 (1963); UNFICYP, ST/SGB/UNFICYP/1 Reg 40 (1964). See also; JG Fleury, "The Plea of Ignorance", *War, Peace and Security WWW Server*, at www.cfcsc.dnd.ca/irc/amsc/amsc1/011.html.

[138] Fleury, above n 137.

has to observe and respect the "principles and spirit" of the four Geneva Conventions of 12 August 1949, the Additional Protocols of 8 June 1977[139] and the UNESCO Convention of 14 May 1954 on the Protection of Cultural Property in the event of armed conflict during peace-keeping operations.[140]

By expressing its support in this manner, the United Nations created the expectation of respect for core humanitarian principles on the part of the organisation itself. One can therefore argue that the organs of the United Nations, including the Security Council, would be estopped from behaviour that violated core principles of international humanitarian law, as this would constitute an act of bad faith on the part of the organisation. The good faith obligation to respect basic norms of international humanitarian law has been significantly reinforced by the United Nations' own contribution to the development and concretisation of the core elements of international humanitarian law. This has been effected, in particular, by the Secretary-General's Bulletin of 6 August 1999,[141] which sets out the fundamental principles and rules of international humanitarian law applicable to forces under United Nations command and control.[142]

---

[139] Ie Protocol Additional to the Geneva Conventions of 12 August 1949, and relating to the Protection of Victims of International Armed Conflicts of 8 June 1977 (hereinafter referred to as Additional Protocol I); Protocol Additional to the Geneva Conventions of 12 August 1949, and relating to the Protection of Victims of Non-International Armed Conflicts of 8 June 1977 (hereinafter referred to as Additional Protocol II), available at www.icrc.org.

[140] A/46/185 para 28 (1991). This clause has subsequently been included, inter alia, in the Agreement between the United Nations and the Government of the Republic of Rwanda on the Status of the United Nations Assistance Mission for Rwanda (UNAMIR) of 5 November 1993. See S/26927 para 7 (1997); see also Greenwood, above n 135, at 21; Fleury, above n 137

[141] ST/SGB/1999/13. Hereinafter referred to as the Bulletin.

[142] The Bulletin is applicable to United Nations forces conducting peace-keeping and peace enforcement operations under United Nations command and control, but not to forces authorised but not commanded by the United Nations. See ST/SGB/1999/13, at s 1.1. It is therefore narrower in scope than the Safety Convention, above n 153, which would also apply to forces under national command and control that were authorised by the United Nations to become involved in an internal armed conflict. However, this should not be interpreted to mean that the latter category would not be bound by the core principles of humanitarian law. Art 20(a) of the Safety Convention determines that "nothing in the Convention shall affect the applicability of international humanitarian law and universally recognised standards of human rights as contained in international instruments in relation to the protection of United Nations operations and United Nations associated personnel *or the responsibility of such personnel to respect such laws and standards.*" (Emphasis added). This clearly implies that the protection granted to United Nations (authorised) forces by the Safety Convention does not free them from their responsibility to respect core elements of humanitarian law. For further discussion see Daphna Shraga, "UN Peace-keeping Operations: Applicability of International Humanitarian Law and Responsibility for Operations-Related Damage", 94 *American Journal of International Law* 408 (2000); Paolo Benvenuti, "Le Respect du Droit International Humanitaire par les Forces des Nations Unies: La Circulaire du Secretaire Général", 105 *Revue Générale de Droit International* 361 (2001); Marten Zwanenburg, "The Secretary-General's Bulletin on Observance by United Nations Forces of International Humanitarian Law: Some Preliminary Observations", in 5 *International Peace-keeping* 137 (1999).

In spite of any ambiguities concerning its official legal status,[143] this Bulletin creates a clear expectation that United Nations forces will act in accordance with the principles concretised therein.[144]

The same applies to the jurisprudence of the International Criminal Tribunal for the former Yugoslavia (ICTY) and the International Criminal Tribunal for Rwanda (ICTR), which have significantly contributed to the clarification of core humanitarian standards since the mid 1990s. Although their decisions are not formally binding on the United Nations itself, it would not be in accordance with the principle of good faith if the Security Council authorised military forces to deviate from core humanitarian principles concretised by its very own sub-organs. The combined effect of the Bulletin and the ICTY/ICTR jurisprudence—which shows a clear overlap in their concretisation of the core elements of international humanitarian law, as will be indicated in section 4.3.2—therefore clearly strengthens the expectation that the United Nations (including the Security Council) would observe and respect these norms under all circumstances.

4.3.1. *The Limitation of International Humanitarian Law by the Security Council*

The question that now has to be answered is how to deal with the organisation's own, official point of view that it is not bound by the 1949 Geneva Conventions.[145] It has supported this position with the argument that some of the obligations contained therein can only be discharged by the exercise of judicial and administrative powers which the organisation does not possess. This includes, in particular, the authority to exercise criminal jurisdiction over members of the forces who act in violation of international humanitarian law.[146] This factor, combined with the

[143] One could, for example, argue that the Bulletin—being an internal administrative issuance—would not be strictly binding on the members of the national contingents, as they do not constitute members of the United Nations secretariat. For a discussion, see Zwanenburg, above n 142, at 135.

[144] The Bulletin was the result of several attempts to give greater content to the undertaking to respect the principles and spirit of the international humanitarian conventions. In 1995 the United Nations Special Committee on Peace-keeping Operations requested the Secretary-General to draw up a code of conduct for peace-keeping personnel consistent with applicable international humanitarian law, so as to ensure the highest standards of conduct (A/50/230 (1995)). The ICRC took the lead in the discussion that ensued and in 1996 submitted to the Secretary-General a set of draft guidelines, which ultimately resulted in the current Bulletin (ST/SGB/1997/1). See also International Committee of the Red Cross, Report of a Meeting of Experts on the Applicability of International Humanitarian Law to United Nations Forces (Geneva, ICRC, 1995); Greenwood, above n 135, at 29; Benvenuti, above n 142, at 356 ff. Cf Linos-Alexandre Sicilianos, "L'autorisation par le Conseil de Sécurité de Recourir a la Force: Une Tentative d'Évaluation", 106 *Revue Générale de Droit International Public* 34 ff (2002).

[145] Legal Opinion, above n 133, at 153; see also Zwanenburg, above n 142, at 134.

[146] Legal Opinion, above n 133, at 153.

settled practice of troop-contributing states to take primary and direct responsibility for international humanitarian law violations committed by their contingents,[147] has been used to substantiate the position that the international humanitarian law obligations of contributing states would relieve the United Nations from any obligations in this regard.[148]

It is submitted that in light of the analysis in section 4.3., the United Nations' own position cannot be understood as meaning that it is not bound by the norms of the 1949 Geneva Convention at all. It could only be understood as meaning that it is not bound by these norms in exactly the same manner as states and that the Security Council may authorise some limitation of the norms of international humanitarian law if the circumstances so require.[149] This follows not only from the nature of some of the obligations at stake (eg those concerning the exercise of criminal jurisdiction), but also from the special role of the United Nations—and the Security Council in particular—in maintaining and restoring international peace and security.

For example, it has been suggested that a Security Council authorised operation, including a military offensive in terms of Chapter VII of the Charter, would constitute an act of law enforcement on behalf of the entire international community and would therefore not possess the character of war. Consequently, the United Nations could not be regarded as a belligerent for the purposes of international humanitarian law.[150] This argument is closely linked to the notion that the need for impartiality during a United Nations (authorised) operation would prevent it from becoming a party to an armed conflict.[151] These factors may explain why neither the

---

[147] See, for example, UNMIK/REG/2000/47, at s 2.4., available at ww.un.org/peace/kosovo. This regulation subjected the KFOR personnel to the exclusive criminal jurisdiction of their respective sending states. John Cerone, "Minding the Gap: Outlining KFOR Accountability in Post-Conflict Kosovo", 12 *European Journal of International Law* 486 (2001); see also ch 8, at s 3.1.

[148] Glick, above n 131, at 96.

[149] The general view amongst authors is that the United Nations, as a subject of international law, is subject to the norms of humanitarian law when engaged in a situation of armed conflict, to the extent that they constitute customary international law. However, as explained above, at s 2, the Security Council may deviate from customary law. The norms which have acquired customary status include the four 1949 Geneva Conventions, above n 132; The Hague Convention (IV) Respecting the Laws and Customs of War on Land and the Regulations annexed thereto of 18 October 1907; as well as certain parts of the two Additional Protocols to the 1949 Geneva Conventions, above n 139. See S/25704 para 35 (1993); *Nuclear Weapons* opinion, above n 103, at 257; Greenwood, above n 135 at 16–17. See also the conclusions of the Institut de Droit International, "Conditions of Application of Humanitarian Rules of Armed Conflict to Hostilities in which the United Nations Forces may Be Engaged", 54 (II) *Annuaire de l'Institut de Droit International* 465 ff (1971); Benvenuti, above n 142 at 360; Luigi Conforti, "La Compatabilité des Sanctions du Conseil de Securité avec le Droit International Humanitaire—Commentaire", in Vera Gowlland-Debbas, *United Nations Sanctions and International Law* 236–37 (The Hague, Kluwer, 2001).

[150] Greenwood, above n 135, at 14.

[151] See also Glick, above n 131, at 70.

United Nations, nor the states involved in the NATO operations in Bosnia-Herzegovina, regarded themselves as parties to an armed conflict, despite the NATO air attacks during 1994 and 1995 and UNPROFOR's increasingly severe bouts of fighting with the Bosnian Serbs.[152]

Moreover, in the context of international armed conflicts the matter is complicated by the Convention on the Safety of United Nations and Associated Personnel of 9 December 1994,[153] which treats the terms of this convention and those of the law of international armed conflict as mutually exclusive regimes. The Safety Convention, which criminalises attacks on United Nations and associated personnel, applies to all operations established by the Security Council and conducted under United Nations authority and control.[154] The only exception concerns a United Nations operation authorised by the Security Council as an enforcement action under Chapter VII of the Charter, in which any of the personnel of a United Nations force are engaged as combatants against organised armed forces and to which the law of international armed conflict applies.[155] This means that the threshold for the application of the law of international armed conflict becomes the ceiling for the application of the Safety Convention.[156]

The Safety Convention has been regarded as an important and necessary step in increasing the protection afforded to peace-keepers. Therefore it is to be expected that the United Nations and those states which contribute large numbers of personnel to United Nations operations will be extremely reluctant to accept that United Nations forces have become parties to an international armed conflict and thereby forfeited the protection granted by the Safety Convention.[157] It is most likely that only those Chapter VII operations under unified command and control which relate to conflicts with a clear international character, such as Korea and the (first) Gulf War, would be excluded from the scope of the Safety Convention. Chapter VII operations under national command and control conducted in a context of an internal armed conflict, such as those undertaken in Somalia, Rwanda, Haiti and possibly even the NATO operations in Bosnia-Herzegovina and Kosovo, would still fall under the

---

[152] Greenwood, above n 135, at 24; Evan T Bloom, 'Protection of Peace-keepers: The Convention on the Safety of United Nations and Associated Personnel', 89 *American Journal of International Law* 625 (1995).

[153] A/49/742 (1994). Hereinafter referred to as the Safety Convention. It has entered into force on 15 January 1999.

[154] *Ibid*, at Art 1(c)(i); Bloom, above n 152, at 622–23.

[155] Art 2(2) of the Safety Convention, above n 153; Greenwood, above n 135, at 25.

[156] Greenwood, above n 135, at 25; see also *ibid*, "Protection of Peace-keepers: The Legal Regime", 7 *Duke Journal of Comparative & International Law* 199 ff (1996), Bloom, above n 152, at 625 ff.

[157] Greenwood, above n 135, at 25; see also Bloom, above n 152, at 624.

protective regime of the Safety Convention.[158] This conclusion is supported by the fact that Article 1 of the Safety Convention covers operations under United Nations "authority and control",[159] which is broad enough to include the latter type of operations.[160]

These examples illustrate that some deviation from well established international humanitarian law principles may be called for during United Nations (authorised) operations. However, this should not be interpreted as meaning that forces acting under the authority of the United Nations could also deviate from the core obligation of international humanitarian law. After all, the question whether the United Nations could become a party to an armed conflict in the formal sense cannot be the only determinative factor in deciding whether the norms of international humanitarian law are applicable. From the perspective of those affected by the armed conflict, the triggering of the rules of international humanitarian law will rather depend on whether hostilities are occurring, as the legal character of the force's mandate is hardly likely to mitigate the effect of its actual participation in an armed conflict.[161] In addition, and as is illuminated above in section 4.3., a negation of the core norms of international humanitarian law would also violate the expectation to respect these norms resulting from Article 1(3) in combination with Article 2(2) of the Charter.

Consequently, the Security Council does not have the competence to authorise the United Nations command to deviate from the core norms of international humanitarian law, nor is it allowed to authorise member states (acting under unified command and control) or regional organisations to do so during a military offensive. One could even argue that the Security Council would not be allowed to delegate a military mandate to member states or a regional organisation, unless it has the assurance that they would respect the basic norms of international humanitarian law during a military offensive. If this were not the case, the organisation

---

[158] Daphna Shraga, "The United Nations as an Actor Bound by International Humanitarian Law", 5 *International Peace-keeping* 76 (1998).
[159] As opposed to "Command and Control".
[160] See Shraga, above n 158, at 76; Greenwood, above n 135, at 25. In Somalia, for example, the United Nations and the United States characterised their involvement in the conflict against rebel groups and dissident factions as internal. Although the Safety Convention was not yet in force at the time, the example illustrates that the submission that any third-party intervention in an internal conflict would internationalise the conflict, would not be consistent with United Nations practice. Cf *Her Majesty the Queen v Private DJ Brocklebank*, Court Martial Appeal Court of Canada, Court File No CMAC–383; 2 April 1996, at www.dnd.ca/. The Court, inter alia, determined that neither the 1949 Geneva Conventions nor Additional Protocol II applied to the Canadian Force in Somalia. It found that there was no evidence of an armed conflict in Somalia and that the Geneva Conventions and Additional Protocols did not apply to peace operations. For criticism of this decision, see Young & Molina, above n 9, at 365 ff.
[161] Zwanenburg (Compromise), above n 134, at 239; see also Greenwood, above n 135, at 17, 22.

could circumvent its obligations under international law by delegating its enforcement powers to member states. However, since a presumption of legality is attached to Security Council resolutions, one will then have to assume that this assurance has been given unless evidence to the contrary is provided.

As has been mentioned above, the supervision of respect for international humanitarian law by United Nations (authorised) forces primarily rests with the national authorities[162] and an analysis of the extent to which they have given effect to this duty falls outside the scope of this study. It is nonetheless worth noting that the United Nations' obligation to observe core principles of international humanitarian law carries with it the expectation that the organisation would also provide its own monitoring mechanism. Although the United Nations Secretariat has started tracking individual cases of misconduct and inquired about follow-up actions at the national level, it has thus far refrained from institutionalising these procedures by, for example, creating a humanitarian Ombudsperson.[163]

One could attempt to justify this absence of an institutionalised monitoring mechanism with the argument that the main applicable treaties, namely the 1949 Geneva Conventions and their Additional Protocols, were not developed under the auspices of the United Nations. The organisation would therefore not fulfil the same oversight role as it does with respect to human rights treaties such as the ICCPR and the ICESCR. As a result, it would also not be under a similar obligation to monitor its own adherence to international humanitarian law. On the other hand, one has to bear in mind that the progressive involvement of the United Nations in the concretisation of core humanitarian principles combined with its own commitment to respect these norms, can indeed result in an expectation that the organisation will provide its own mechanism for monitoring their observance by United Nations (authorised) forces. The creation of such a mechanism would also increase the political legitimacy of peace enforcement mandates.

4.3.2. Core Elements of International Humanitarian Law

The core elements of international humanitarian law that are applicable to all forms of armed conflict[164] concern the rules designed to protect the

---

[162] This well established practice is also reaffirmed in ST/SGB/1999/13, at s 4, which subjects members of the military personnel of a United Nations force to prosecution in their national courts in case of violations of humanitarian law.

[163] See Zwanenburg, above n 142, at 139.

[164] An international armed conflict exists where there are hostilities involving the use of armed force between two or more states. An internal armed conflict is constituted by protracted armed violence between governmental authorities and organised groups, or between such groups within a state. The internal armed conflict distinguishes itself from cases of civil unrest or terrorist activities (to which international humanitarian law does not apply),

civilian population as well as the rules governing means and methods of warfare.[165] The essence of these rules is personified by common Article 3 of the 1949 Geneva Conventions, which aims to protect persons taking no active part in hostilities. These include civilians, members of the armed forces who have laid down their arms, and those placed *hors de combat* by sickness, wounds, detention, or any other course.[166] The International Court of Justice (ICJ), ICTY and ICTR considered this Article to represent the minimum humanitarian standards applicable to all forms of armed conflict.[167]

by means of the protracted nature of the armed violence and the extent of organisation of the parties involved. See *Prosecutor v Zejnil Delalcic, Hazim Delic, Esad Landzo and Zdravko Mucic*, Judgment, Case No IT–96–21, 16 November 1998, Trial Chamber, at para 184. Hereinafter referred to as the *Celebici* judgment; *Prosecutor v Dusco Tadic*, Opinion and Judgment, Case No IT–94–1–T, 7 May 1997, Trial Chamber, at para 561 ff; *Prosecutor v Alfred Musema*, Judgment, Case No ICTR–96–13, 27 January 2000, Trial Chamber, at para 257 ff. See also E/CN4/1998/87, at para 70; Sonja Boelaert-Suominen, "The Yugoslavia Tribunal and the Common Core of Humanitarian Law Applicable to all Armed Conflicts", 13 *Leiden Journal of International Law* 632 ff 2000); Meron, above n 103, at 260.

[165] *Nuclear Weapons* opinion, above n 103, at 257; *Prosecutor v Milan Martic*, Review of the Indictment Pursuant to Rule 61, Case No IT–95–11–R61, 8 March 1996, Trial Chamber, at para 12. Hereinafter referred to as *Martic* Rule 61 proceeding; *Prosecutor v Dario Kordic & Mario Cerkez*, Motion to Dismiss the Amended Indictment for lack of Jurisdiction based on the Limited Jurisdictional Reach of Art 2 and Art 3, Case No IT–95–14/2–PT, 2 March 1999, Trial Chamber, at para 30; Boelaert-Suominen, above n 164, at 644.

[166] Common Art 3 reads as follows: 'In the case of armed conflict not of an international character occurring in the territory of one of the High Contracting Parties, each Party to the conflict shall be bound to apply, as a minimum, the following provisions:

(1)   Persons taking no active part in the hostilities, including members of armed forces who have laid down their arms and those placed *hors de combat* by sickness, wounds, detention, or any other cause, shall in all circumstances be treated humanely, without any adverse distinction founded on race, colour, religion or faith, sex, birth or wealth, or any other similar criteria. To this end, the following acts are and shall remain prohibited at any time and in any place whatsoever with respect to the above-mentioned persons:
    (a)   violence to life and person, in particular murder of all kinds, mutilation, cruel treatment and torture;
    (b)   taking of hostages;
    (c)   outrages upon personal dignity, in particular humiliating and degrading treatment;
    (d)   the passing of sentences and the carrying out of executions without previous judgment pronounced by a regularly constituted court, affording all the judicial guarantees which are recognized as indispensable by civilized peoples.
(2)   The wounded and sick shall be collected and cared for.
An impartial body, such as the International Committee of the Red Cross, may offer its services to the Parties to the conflict.
The Parties to the Conflict should further endeavour to bring into force, by means of special agreements, all or part of the other provisions of the present Convention.

The application of the preceding provisions shall not affect the legal status of the Parties to the conflict.'

[167] *Military and Paramilitary Activities in and against Nicaragua (Nicaragua v United States of America)*, Merits, ICJ Rep 1986, at 113–1; *Tadic* decision, above n 3, at para 102; *Prosecutor v*

In accordance with these standards, parties may never make civilians the object of attack[168] and may consequently never use weapons that are incapable of distinguishing between civilian and military targets.[169] In the area of operation military forces have to avoid, to the extent feasible, locating military objectives within or near densely populated areas. They also have to take all necessary precautions to protect the civilian population, individual civilians and civilian objects against the dangers resulting from military operations.[170] The absolute prohibition of unlawful attacks on civilians also outlaws reprisals, even if they were a response proportionate to a similar violation perpetrated by the other party.[171]

The distinction between combatants and civilians also implies that the collateral damage to civilians caused by a military offensive has to be proportional, in that it may not cause damage and harm to the civilian population disproportionate to the concrete and direct military advantage anticipated.[172] The military forces thus have to take all feasible precautions to avoid and minimise incidental loss of civilian life, injury to

---

Zejnil Delalcic, Hazim Delic, Esad Landzo and Zdravko Mucic, Judgment, Case No IT–96–21, 20 February 2001, Appeals Chamber, at para 143; *Prosecutor v Jean Paul Akayeshu,* Judgment, Case No ICTR–96–4, 1 June 2001, Appeals Chamber, at para 442. See also the *Prosecutor v Tihomir Blaskic,* Judgment, Case No IT–95–14, 2 March 2000, Trial Chamber, at para 170. The Trial Chamber stated that the provisions of Additional Protocol 1 and Additional Protocol 2 prohibiting attacks against civilians were sufficiently covered by common Art 3 of the Geneva Conventions. See Boelaert-Suominen above n 164, at 620.

[168] The prohibition concerns attacks on the civilian population as such, as well as individual circumstances. See *Martic* Rule 61 proceeding, above n 165, at para 12.

[169] *Nuclear Weapons* opinion, above n 103, at 257; ST/SGB/1999/13, at s 5.1. See the Report of the Special Rapporteur on the Situation of Human Rights in Kuwait under Iraqi Occupation, E/CN 4/1992/26, at para 36, that also based these principles on the so-called Martens Clause. A modern form of this clause (which dates from 1899) can be found in Art 1(2) of Additional Protocol 1 to the 1949 Geneva Conventions, above n 139. It states that in cases not covered by this protocol, or by other international agreements, civilians and combatants remain under the protection and authority of the principles of international law derived from established custom, from the principles of humanity and from dictates of public conscience. See also Theodor Meron, "The Martens Clause, Principles of Humanity, and Dictates of Public Conscience", 94 *American Journal of International Law* 82–83 (2000); Zwanenburg, above n 142, at 137.

[170] ST/SGB/1999/13, at s 5.4. Military installations and equipment of peace-keeping operations, as such, shall not be considered military objectives. This is a deviation from Art 58(b) and Art 58 (c) of Additional Protocol I, above n 139, that do not include this exception for United Nations installations and equipment. See Zwanenburg, above n 142, at 137; Benvenuti, above n 142, at 363.

[171] *Prosecutor v Zoran Kupreskic, Mirjan Kupreskic, Vlatko Kupreskic, Drago Josipovic and Vladimir Santic,* Judgment, Case No IT–95–16, 14 January 2000, Trial Chamber, at paras 521 ff; *Martic* Rule 61 proceeding, above n 165, at para 15; ST/SGB/1999/13, at s 5.6; see also Meron (Martens Clause), above n 169, at 82.

[172] See the *Nuclear Weapons* opinion, above n 103, at 257; *Martic* Rule 61 proceeding, above n 165, at para 18; ST/SGB/1999/13, at s 5.5; Boelaert-Suominen, above n 164, at 649. See also William J Fenrick, "Targeting and Proportionality during the NATO Bombing Campaign against Yugoslavia", in 12 *European Journal of International Law* 498 (2001); Delbrück, above n 28, at 1142.

civilians or damage to civilian property. These include attacks which employ a method or means of combat which cannot be directed at a specific military objective.[173]

Persons no longer taking part in military operations, including civilians, members of armed forces who have laid down their weapons and persons placed *hors de combat* by reasons of sickness, wounds or detention, shall in all circumstances be treated humanely without any adverse distinction based on race, sex, religious convictions or any other ground.[174] Acts such as violence to life or physical integrity; murder as well as cruel treatment such as torture, mutilation or any form of corporal punishment; collective punishment; the taking of hostages; rape (of both male and female victims); enforced prostitution; any form of sexual assault and humiliation and degrading treatment; enslavement and pillage against any of the above mentioned persons are prohibited at any time and in any place.[175]

As far as an offensive against legitimate military targets are concerned, parties are not permitted to use weapons that cause superfluous injury or unnecessary suffering to combatants.[176] These include, in particular, the prohibition of the use of asphyxiating, poisonous or other gases and biological methods of warfare; bullets which explod, expand or flatten easily in the human body and certain explosive projectiles. The use of certain conventional weapons, such as non-detectable fragments, anti-personnel mines, booby traps and incendiary weapons, is also prohibited.[177]

The provision declaring that the protections guaranteed under common Article 3 are to be applied at all times and all places,[178] regardless of whether the conflict is of an international character, constitutes strong evidence for considering these norms to be of a *jus cogens* nature.[179] This conclusion is strengthened by the fact that both the Bulletin as well as the ICTY and ICTR jurisprudence refer to these norms as fundamental and

---

[173]ST/SGB/1999/13, at s 5.3; see *Martic* Rule 61 proceeding, above n 165, at para 18. See also Gardam, above n 9, at 407. In accordance with state practice during the Gulf War, this criteria will be violated where there was negligent behaviour in ascertaining the nature of a target or the conduct of the attack itself, so as to amount to the direct targeting of civilians.

[174]ST/SGB/1999/13, at s 7.1. ff. S 8 explicitly refers to the humane treatment of detainees, whilst s 9.1. provides that the sick and wounded shall be treated humanely and receive the medical care and attention required by their condition.

[175]ST/SGB/1999/13, at s 7.2; *Furundzija* judgment, above n 49, at paras 143 ff and para 476; See *Celebici* case, above n 164, at paras 442 ff. See also Boelaert-Suominen, above n 164, at 638; Zwanenburg, above n 142; Benvenuti, above n 142, at 367.

[176]*Nuclear Weapons* opinion, above n 103, at 257. ST/SGB/1999/13, at s 6.4; see also Benvenuti, above n 142, at 364–65.

[177]ST/SGB/1999/13, at s 6.2.

[178]Common Art 1 determines that: The High Contracting Parties undertake to respect and to ensure respect for the present Convention in all circumstances.'

[179]Seiderman, above n 54, at 96. Note that in the *Celebici* case, above n 164, at paras 442 ff, the Trial Chamber explicitly referred to the prohibition of torture as a norm of *jus cogens*.

constituting the core principles of international humanitarian law.[180] The ICJ, for its part, explicitly refrained from determining that the fundamental rules of international humanitarian law would constitute elements of *jus cogens*.[181] Yet, at the same time, it did refer to these norms as "intransgressible principles of international customary law".[182] This would arguably come very close to a determination that one is dealing with *ius cogens*, as the term "intransgressible" does indicate that no circumstance would justify any deviation.[183]

In essence therefore, the United Nations and its organs are bound by the core principles of international humanitarian law for three separate, albeit closely related reasons. First, it concerns norms which constitute elements of the purposes of the United Nations. In addition, the United Nations has committed itself to these norms in a fashion that has created a legal expectation that it will honour them when authorising a military operation for the restoration or maintenance of international peace and security. Any behaviour to the contrary would violate the principle of good faith to which the organisation is bound in terms of Article 2(2) of the Charter. Finally, one could also argue that these norms now concern elements of *ius cogens* which have to be respected by states and organs of the United Nations alike.

5.   CONCLUSION

The foregoing analysis reflect that the Security Council's powers to adopt enforcement measures are limited by two categories of norms which are closely related. First, the norms of *ius cogens* prevent the Security Council from adopting measures that would result in genocide, or that would violate the right to self-defence, the right to self-determination, or certain basic norms of human rights and international humanitarian law. The principles and purposes of the United Nations, for their part, oblige the Security Council to refrain from imposing a settlement on parties and to respect the core elements of self-determination, human rights, international humanitarian law and state sovereignty. It also requires the Security Council to act in good faith and to fulfil legal expectations previously created by its own actions, when resorting to enforcement measures under Chapter VII.

---

[180] In the *Akayeshu* case, above, n 167, at para 442, the ICTR even described common Art 3 as the "quintessence" of humanitarian law.
[181] *Nuclear Weapons* opinion, above n 103, at 258.
[182] *Ibid*, at 257.
[183] Conforti, above n 149, at 238. For the Security Council's obligation to respect norms of *ius cogens*, see ch 5, at s 3.

These two categories thus overlap with respect to certain purposes of the United Nations, notably the right to self-determination and basic norms of human rights and international humanitarian law. This does not mean, however, that the contents of these two categories are identical in as far as the overlap is concerned. The following chapters will illuminate that, on the one hand, those human rights norms which constitute elements of *ius cogens* also form part of the purposes of the United Nations. At the same time, however, not all human rights norms that qualify as core elements of the purposes of the United Nations constitute *ius cogens*. This relates to the fact that the activities of the United Nations in recent decades, in particular in the field of human rights, have contributed to the evolution of the core contents of these norms. This, in turn, has lead to an expansion of the core content of the purposes of the organisation.

The following chapters will further examine the consequences for Security Council enforcement measures of the inter-action between the purpose to promote human rights in Article 1(3) of the Charter and the principle of good faith in Article 2(2). The interaction between socio-economic rights and the principle of good faith forms a focal point of the analysis of the Security Council's power to impose economic sanctions in chapter 6. This chapter will also illustrate how the right to self-defence can limit the power of the Security Council to impose an arms-embargo in a situation of inter-state armed conflict.

The role of self-determination as a limitation on Security Council enforcement measures is illuminated in chapter 8, in connection with the competence of the Security Council to authorise the civil administration of a territory. Chapter 9 examines whether the Security Council has respected the principles of justice and international law (including the principle of the right to a fair trial) when adopting quasi-judicial measures as a mechanism for restoring or maintaining international peace and security. This analysis will also illustrate how the imposition of a settlement on parties can violate the territorial integrity of a state.

As indicated above in section 1, chapter 7 identifies additional, structural limitations to the Security Council's enforcement powers. It concerns limitations to the competence of the Security Council to authorise member states or regional organisations to use military force. Chapter 7 will illustrate that the Security Council's ability to delegate military powers is limited by the structure of the Charter as a whole, rather than by any particular purpose, principle or norm of *ius cogens*. Although chapter 7 is exclusively concerned with the delegation of military powers, chapters 8 and 9 will build on this delegation model when examining situations in which the Security Council delegated its power to take binding decisions to the Secretary-General and judicial sub-organs, respectively.

6

Limits to the Security Council's Discretion to Impose Economic Sanctions

1. INTRODUCTION

I N CHAPTER 5 at Section 4 it was determined that the Security Council's powers to adopt enforcement measures can be limited by basic human rights norms, as they constitute core elements of the purposes of the United Nations and to some extent even norms of *ius cogens*. The purpose of the current chapter is to identify in a more concrete fashion the extent to which human rights norms can limit the Security Council's discretion to impose non-military measures in the form of economic sanctions. In addition, it will analyse the limitations following from the right to self-defence—which was also identified as an outer limit for Security Council enforcement action—for economic sanctions in inter-state armed conflicts.

The chapter commences by elaborating on the nature of the particular human rights which pose a limitation to economic enforcement measures. In doing so, it concentrates on the (non-derogable) right to life and the (derogabe) right to health, as practice has shown that these rights are the most likely to be affected by broad economic embargoes. The chapter also underlines the importance of an effective monitoring mechanism for determining the impact of the sanctions regime on civilians.

The yardsticks identified during this inquiry are then applied to the three most controversial economic sanctions regimes which the Security Council has adopted during the existence of the United Nations. These include the economic embargoes against Iraq, former Yugoslavia, and Haiti, respectively. The only other comprehensive economic embargoes in the history of the United Nations were those against Southern Rhodesia after its unilateral declaration of independence in 1965, and Libya after its refusal to extradite the *Lockerbie* suspects in 1992. In both instances, however, the human rights impact was much less severe.

In the case of Southern Rhodesia,[1] the limited economic impact of the embargo was mainly due to the continued economic support and oil exports from South Africa throughout the entire period of the embargo.[2] In the case of Libya,[3] both the Libyan Government and the Organisation of African Unity (OAU) expressed concern about the impact of the sanctions on the well-being of the Libyan population.[4] However, since Libya was still able to sell oil abroad and to attract foreign investment in oil-related projects, it is unlikely that the human rights impact was of a disproportionate nature.[5]

The controversy surrounding the legality of the embargoes against Southern Rhodesia and Libya, respectively, arguably lies elsewhere. With respect to Southern Rhodesia, the non-membership in the United Nations at the time of the embargo may constitute a point of controversy. For the question arises whether the Security Council could have adopted such a regime against the territory at all, as it still remains debatable whether the enforcement mechanism envisaged by Chapter VII of the Charter applies to non-member states by means of customary law.[6] Moreover, even if one accepted the customary law status of Chapter VII in the post Cold War era, it still remains questionable whether it had already obtained customary status by 1965. Thus, if the Security Council were entitled to adopt mandatory enforcement measures against Southern Rhodesia, it is unlikely that customary international law provided the basis for doing so.

---

[1] Mandatory sanctions were first introduced by SC Res 232 of 16 December 1966, which prohibited the export of petroleum, armaments, vehicles and aircraft to Southern Rhodesia, as well as the import of Rhodesian agricultural products and minerals. The sanctions were extended in later years by SC Res 253 of 29 May 1968; SC Res 277 of 15 March 1970 and SC Res 388 of 6 April 1976. It was officially terminated by the SC in SC Res 460 of 21 December 1979, after agreement had been reached between the *de facto* Rhodesian government and the national liberation movements about transition to African majority rule. See Alan J Kreczko, "The Unilateral Termination of UN Sanctions Against Southern Rhodesia by the United Kingdom", 21 *Virginia Journal of International Law* 99–100 (1981); W Michael Reisman & Douglas L Stevick, "The applicability of International Law Standards to United Nations Economic Sanctions Programmes", 9 *European Journal of International Law* 98 (1998); Peter F Hurst, "Economic Sanctions: The Lifting of Sanctions against Zimbabwe-Rhodesia by the United States", 21 *Harvard International Law Journal* 104 (1980).

[2] David L Johnson, "Sanctions and South Africa", 19 *Harvard International Law Journal* 908 (1978).

[3] The economic sanctions included an air and arms embargo, the freezing of assets of the government or Libyan public authorities and undertakings, as well as an embargo against the sale and maintenance of specified equipment used in the oil refining and petrochemicals production process. See SC Res 748 of 31 March 1992; SC Res 883 of 11 November 1993. The sanctions were ultimately suspended by SC Res 1192 of 27 August 1998, after Libya surrendered the two *Lockerbie* suspects for trial in the Netherlands.

[4] S/PV 3312 29 (1993); S/1995/596 paras 7–8 (1995); Reisman & Stevick, above n 1, at 109.

[5] The embargo did not require the freezing of assets derived from the sale or supply of Libyan petroleum, natural gas or agricultural products. See also Reisman & Stevick, above n 1, at 110.

[6] See ch 3 at s 4.2.

A legal basis for the Security Council embargo could, however, be found in the fact that Southern Rhodesia's unilateral secession was never recognised internationally.[7] The territory remained under the *de iure* sovereignty of the United Kingdom,[8] who had consented to the enforcement measures against the territory. This consent of the *de iure* administering power, who also happens to be a permanent member of the Security Council, provided a sufficient legal basis for the adoption of the mandatory sanctions regime against Southern Rhodesia. The issue of the legality of Security Council action against a non-member of the United Nations will be taken up again in section 3.2.1. below, in connection with the economic embargo against the Federal Republic of Yugoslavia.

In the case of Libya, chapter 9 at section 2.2. challenges the legality of the sanctions regime on the basis that it was adopted in violation of basic due process principles entrenched in Article 1(1) of the Charter and Article 14(1) of the International Covenant on Civil and Political Rights (ICCPR). As a result, every limitation of human rights resulting from this sanctions regime would arguably be disproportionate and therefore illegal. However, as the cause of the illegality would relate to due process issues, it has to be distinguished from the impact of the Libyan sanctions regime in and of itself on the right to life and the right to health of the civilian population.

The final part of the current chapter deals with the role of self-defence as an outer limit to economic sanctions. Section 4 illustrates that this right becomes particularly relevant in situations where the Security Council imposes an arms embargo upon states involved in an inter-state conflict that involves an armed attack. In doing so, it pays particular attention to the implications of the arms embargo adopted against the former Yugoslavia in Resolution 713 of 25 September 1991.

2. HUMAN RIGHTS LIMITATIONS TO ECONOMIC SANCTIONS

2.1. The Right to Life

In addition to economic and social rights such as the right to health, the right most likely to be affected by economic sanctions is the right to life.[9]

---

[7] See eg, the preambles to SC Res 221 of 9 April 1966 and SC Res 232 of 16 December 1966.
[8] See GA Res 1747 (XVI) of 28 June 1962, which affirmed that Southern Rhodesia was a non-self-governing territory under the administering Authority of the United Kingdom. See also GA Res 1755 (XVII) of 12 October 1962 and GA Res 1760 (XVII) of 31 October 1962.
[9] Roger Normand, "A Human Rights Assessment of Sanctions: The Case of Iraq, 1990–1997", in Willem JM van Genugten & Gerard A de Groot (eds), *United Nations Sanctions. Effectiveness and Effects, Especially in the Field of Human Rights. A Multi-disciplinary Approach* 28 (Antwerpen, Intersentia, 1999).

This non-derogable right, which is protected in Article 6 ICCPR, is regarded as the supreme right basic to all human rights.[10] Although the right to life in the first instance provides protection against arbitrary killing, its scope has gradually been expanded to include a broader range of aspects such as protection against malnutrition and epidemics. For example, in its General Comment No 6 which was adopted in 1982, the Human Rights Committee considered that the "inherent right to life" cannot be understood in a restrictive manner. States parties should take all positive measures to reduce infant mortality and to increase life expectancy, especially by adopting measures to eliminate malnutrition and epidemics.[11]

This obligation is reinforced by the Convention on the Right of the Child (CRC), which recognises the right to life of every child and calls on states to ensure, to the maximum extent possible, the survival and development of the child.[12] It also calls on states to take appropriate measures to diminish infant and child mortality.[13] This would reinforce the expectation that a sanctions regime imposed by the Security Council should at the very least not result in denying children access to the basic goods and services essential to sustain life.[14] Even though there may be varied interpretations of the positive obligations under the right to life, its core minimum would oblige those imposing a sanctions regime to refrain from policies that lead to the deterioration of malnutrition, infant mortality or epidemics amongst children.[15]

---

[10] Art 6(1) and Art 6(2) of the ICCPR read as follows:

"1.　Every human being has the inherent right to life. This right shall be protected by law. No one shall be arbitrarily deprived of his life.

2.　In countries which have not abolished the death penalty, sentence of death may be imposed only for the most serious crimes in accordance with the law in force at the time of the commission of the crime and not contrary to the provisions of the present Convention and to the Convention on the Prevention and Punishment of the Crime of Genocide. This penalty can only be carried out pursuant to a final judgement rendered by a competent court."

See also Human Rights Committee, *General Comment No 6, The Right to Life* para 1 (1982). See also Brigit C A Toebes, *The Right to Health as a Human Right in International Law* 261 (Antwerp, Intersentia, 1999).

[11] General Comment No 6, above n 10, at para 5; see also Toebes, above n 10, at 160–61, Anna Segall, "Economic sanctions: legal and policy constraints", 81 *International Review of the Red Cross* 32 (1999). For a restrictive interpretation, see Yoram Dinstein, "The right to life, physical integrity and liberty, in Louis Henkin" (ed), *The International Bill of Rights* 115 (New York, Columbia University, 1981).

[12] Art 6(1) and Art (2) CRC.

[13] Art 24(2)(a) CRC.

[14] Segall, above n 11, at 33. She submits that a sanctions regime should contain mechanisms for combating infant mortality, malnutrition and epidemics amongst children.

[15] Human Rights Watch, Explanatory Memorandum Regarding the Comprehensive Embargo on Iraq. Humanitarian Circumstances in Iraq para 17 (2000) at www.hrw.org/. Hereinafter referred to as Explanatory Memorandum. Normand, above n 9, at 33. Cf Dorothee Starck, *Die Rechtsmässigkeit von UNO-Wirtschaftssanktionen in Anbetracth ihrer Auswirkungen auf die Zivilbevölkerung* 343 ff (Berlin, Duncker & Humblot, 2000).

As far as the rest of the population is concerned, the Security Council would be prohibited from deliberately acting in a way which actively deprives individuals of food and causes hunger and/ or starvation.[16] The Committee on Economic, Social and Cultural Rights (hereinafter the Committee) has stressed that the right to food is indispensable for the fulfilment of other human rights enshrined in the International Bill of Human Rights.[17] As a result, it would not be permitted to adopt a food embargo or similar measures which endanger conditions for food production and access to food in other countries.[18]

The only permissible limitation to the right to life[19] is provided by international humanitarian law during times of armed conflict. According to the standards of humanitarian law, an attack which may be expected to cause incidental loss of civilian life which would be excessive in relation to the concrete and direct military advantage anticipated, is illegal.[20] It is widely accepted that this and other basic norms of humanitarian law are applicable to all military operations of an enforcement nature which are carried out by forces of the United Nations, or by the forces of member states acting under Security Council authorisation.[21] Like human rights law, the rules of humanitarian law form part of the purposes and principles of the organisation.[22] Furthermore, it is arguable that the core elements of humanitarian law, which include the principle of proportional collateral damage to civilian life and property, have acquired *ius cogens* status.[23]

Thus, where the loss of civilian life resulted from a lack of access to food incidental to a legitimate armed attack by United Nations (authorised) forces, this would arguably not constitute a violation to the right to life. However, the Security Council may never authorise forces to deprive civilians deliberately of access to supplies essential to their survival, as starvation is a prohibited method of warfare.[24] Civilian loss of

---

[16] Segall, above n 11, at 34. Cf Rene Provost, "Starvation as a Weapon: Legal Implications of the United Nations Food Blockade Against Iraq and Kuwait", 30 *Columbia Journal of Transnational Law* 577 ff (1992).

[17] Committee on Economic, Social and Cultural Rights, *General Comment No 12, The Right to Adequate Food* paras 1, 4 (1999).

[18] *Ibid*, at para 37; Segall, above n 11, at 42. One could also argue that the right to food obliges states to supply essential foodstuffs to those in need. See also the last sentence of Art 1(2) of the ICESR, according to which a people may in no case be deprived of its own means of subsistence; see also Hans Köchler, *Etische Aspekte der Sanktionen im Völkerrecht: die Praxis der Sanktionspolitik und die Menschenrechte* 24 (Vienna, International Progress Organisation, 1994).

[19] Apart from the imposition of the death penalty, see above n 10.

[20] See ch 5, at s 4.3.2.

[21] *Ibid*, at s 4.3.

[22] *Ibid*, at s 4.3.2.

[23] *Ibid*, at s 3.2.

[24] See Art 54, Art 69 and Art 70 Protocol Additional to the Geneva Conventions of 12 August 1949, and relating to the Protection of Victims of International Armed Conflicts of

life resulting from lack of access to food would only be legal if it were collateral to the military attack and remain proportional to the purpose of the military target.

Moreover, this type of collateral damage would only be permissible during times of armed conflict. Where the Security Council "only" resorts to economic sanctions (whether before or after a period of armed conflict), this may not result in the loss of civilian life due to lack of access to food. The purpose of economic sanctions as opposed to military measures is exactly that it should apply economic and political pressure without endangering civilian lives. This presupposes a recognition of the non-derogable and supreme nature of the right to life in all circumstances short of war.[25]

2.2.   The Right to Health

The "expectation to respect" the core content of the right to health[26] obliges the Security Council, at the very least, to structure its economic embargoes in a way that does not undermine the availability and accessibility of basic health facilities, goods and services on a non-discriminatory basis. This presupposes, in particular, that the embargo may not undermine the accessibility of minimum essential food which is nutritionally adequate and safe; the accessibility to basic shelter, housing and sanitation, as well as an adequate supply of safe and potable water; the accessibility of essential drugs as from time to time defined under the WHO Action

---

8 June 1977, at www.crc.org. See also Art 14 and Art 18(2) of the Protocol Additional to the Geneva Conventions of 12 August 1949, and relating to the Protection of Victims of Non-International Armed Conflicts of 8 June 1977, at www.icrc.org. For the *ius cogens* nature of the prohibition against starvation as a method of warfare, see extensively Starck, above n 15, at 282 ff; See also Segall, above n 11, at 27–28; Hans-Peter Gasser, "Collective Economic Sanctions and International Humanitarian Law", 56 *Zeitschrift für ausländisches öffentliches Recht und Völkerrecht* 882 (1996); Manfred Kulessa, "Von Märchen und Mechanismen", 43 *Vereinte Nationen* 92 (1995).

[25] For a comparable argument see Gasser, above n 24, at 900–01.
[26] Art 12 of the ICESCR reads as follows:

> "1.   The States Parties to the present Covenant recognize the right of everyone to the enjoyment of the highest attainable standard of physical and mental health.
>
>   2.   The steps to be taken by the States Parties to the present Covenant to achieve the full realization of this right shall include those necessary for:
>   (a)   The provision for the reduction of the still-birth rate and of infant mortality and for the healthy development of the child;
>   (b)   The improvement of all aspects of environmental and industrial hygiene;
>   (c)   The prevention, treatment and control of epidemic, endemic, occupational and other diseases;
>   (d)   The creation of conditions which would assure to all medical service and medical attention in the event of sickness."

Programme on Essential Drugs; and the equitable distribution of all health facilities, goods and services.[27]

Such respect for the core content of the right to health simultaneously implies that the Security Council has to maintain some notion of proportionality when adopting economic sanctions. This can also be concluded from a statement of the Committee according to which it was essential that economic sanctions distinguished between the basic objective of applying political and economic pressure upon the governing elite, and the collateral infliction of suffering upon the most vulnerable groups within the targeted country.[28] This seems to introduce a proportionality principle akin to the one recognised by the rules of international humanitarian law, that was already referred to above in section 2.1.

The problem with this criteria is that the norms of humanitarian law are intended to apply during times of armed conflict. This makes it unclear whether one could apply a proportionality test derived from it in situations where the Security Council resorts to non-military measures (ie economic sanctions), outside the context of armed conflict.[29] This was the case, for example, after the first Gulf War in Iraq follwoing the adoption of the cease-fire agreement in Resolution 687 of 3 April 1991. It is submitted, however, that there are several reasons for arguing that the Security Council is also bound to such a proportionality principle when resorting to economic sanctions instead of military action.

First, the notion of collateral damage to civilians, especially with respect to their economic, social and cultural rights, is inherent in both types of measures. Broad economic sanctions strike indiscriminately and fail to make a distinction between those responsible for the threat to peace and innocent civilians.[30] Second, it is a more flexible proportionality principle

---

[27] The core obligations were formulated by the Committee on Economic and Social Rights, *General Comment No 14, The Right to the Highest Attainable Standard of Health* para 43 (2000). At para 44, the Committee formulated additional obligations of a comparable nature. These include accessibility to ensure reproductive, maternal and child health care; immunisation against the major infectious diseases occurring in the community; the prevention treatment and control of epidemic and endemic diseases; the availability and accessibility of education and information concerning the main health problems in the community, including methods of preventing and controlling them; and of training for health personnel, including education on health and human rights.

[28] Committee on Economic, Social and Cultural Rights, *General Comment No 8, The Relationship between Economic Sanctions and Respect for Economic, Social and Cultural Rights* para 4 (1997).

[29] Normand, above n 9, at 28. See also Matthew Craven, "Humanitarianism and the Quest for Smarter Sanctions", 13 *European Journal of International Law* 58 (2002); Mary Ellen O'Connell, "Debating the Law of Sanctions", *Ibid*, at 74.

[30] Normand, above n 9, at 31; Gasser, above n 24, at 883; see also Hadewych Hazelzet, "Assessing the Suffering form 'Successful' Sanctions: An Ethical Approach", in Willem JM van Genugten & Gerard A de Groot (eds), *United Nations Sanctions. Effectiveness and Effects, Especially in the Field of Human Rights. A Multi-disciplinary Approach* 88 (Antwerpen, Intersentia, 1999); Köchler, above n 18, at 32; Reisman & Stevick, above n 1 at 92.

than that provided in Article 4(1) of the ICCPR which permits a derogation only to the extent strictly required by the situation. In the light of the leeway that the Security Council needs to act effectively, a more flexible principle for measuring the proportionality of its actions would be justifiable.[31] At the same time the proportionality could not have a lower threshold than that required for military measures. For this would have the extraordinary result that the Security Council were not bound to proportionality when limiting human rights where there exists a "mere" threat to peace, although it would be bound to do so during a full-scale war.[32]

If one accepted this principle of proportional collateral damage in the context of economic sanctions, it would mean that the sanctions must be aimed at the regime and limitations imposed on the human rights of the civilian population may not be disproportionate compared to the purpose served thereby.[33] With respect to the right to health, the sanctions would arguably be disproportionate where a sanctions regime deprived a significant segment of the population from the core elements of this right and/ or systematically undermined the quality of the health care system. In this context it is important to point out that the Committee has explicitly stated that states should refrain at all times from imposing embargoes or similar measures restricting the supply of another state with adequate medicines and medical equipment. Restrictions of such goods should never be used as an instrument of political or economic pressure.[34]

In assessing whether this is the case, one has to consider the impact of shortages of medical supplies and the deterioration of the public health system and infrastructure.[35] One would also have to determine whether efforts have been made to reduce the impact, particularly on the most vulnerable such as the young and the elderly.[36] These type of

---

[31] Some argued that the Security Council, having the power and moral authority of United Nations member states acting together, should be held to a higher standard of human rights protection than individual states. See Andrew K Fishman, "Between Iraq and a Hard Place: The Use of Economic Sanctions and Threat to International Peace and Security", 13 *Emory International Law Review* 713 (1999). But this argument does not take into account the special nature of the Security Council.

[32] Segall, above n 11, at 34.

[33] Normand, above n 9, at 31; Hazelzet, above n 30, at 88. See also Jochen Herbst, *Rechtskontrolle des UN-Sicherheitsrates* 380–81 (Frankfurt a/M, Peter Lang, 1999), who supported the proportionality principle provided for in Art 4(2) of the ICCPR. Cf TD Gill, "Legal and Some Political Limitations on the Power of the UN Security Council to Exercise its Enforcement Powers under Chapter VII of the Charter", 26 *Netherlands Yearbook of International Law* 7 (1995); Reisman & Stevick, above n 1, at 128 ff.

[34] Committee on Economic and Social Rights, in *General Comment No 14*, above n 27, at para 41. At para 12 it also emphasised the essentiality of the availability and equal accessibility of public health care facilities (including goods and services) that are of sufficient quantity, medically appropriate, of good quality and also culturally acceptable.

[35] See Committee on Economic, Social and Cultural Rights, General Comment 14, above n 26, at paras 18 ff; Segall, above n 11, at 27, 37.

[36] Segall, above n 11, at 37.

assessments require a certain passage of time, since the extent of the impact of a sanctions regime on the civilian population, as well as the effects of countering measures may not become apparent for some time.[37]

2.3. Monitoring Human Rights Obligations

Since comprehensive economic sanctions would almost by definition have a limiting effect on the economic, social and cultural rights of the civilian population in the targeted country, the Security Council has to monitor the civilian impact of its sanctions regime on a regular basis. Otherwise it would not be able to determine whether the economic sanctions were having a disproportionate impact on these rights. Moreover, it would not be able to determine whether the sanctions might violate the right to life, by depriving civilians of basic foodstuffs or contributing to infant mortality or malnutrition amongst children.[38]

The absence of a monitoring mechanism in a Security Council resolution that imposes economic enforcement measures would thus mean that potential violations of *ius cogens* norms such as the right to life might go unnoticed. Stated differently, the likeliness of violations of basic human rights by economic sanctions would be significantly reduced if effective monitoring procedures were provided for. The provision of a monitoring mechanism in an enforcement resolution would also strengthen faith in the Security Council's legitimacy. It would be tangible evidence of its commitment to legal norms that constitute *ius cogens* norms and/ or core elements of the purposes and principles of the United Nations.

One could therefore conclude that the absence of a monitoring mechanism in a Security Council resolution that imposes economic sanctions would directly contribute to the continuation or aggravation of a situation that violates the most basic human rights. The more extensive the sanctions, the greater this risk would be. Consequently, the absence of a monitoring mechanism under such circumstances can be seen as a fundamental deficit that would render the Security Council resolution invalid.

[37] Gasser, above n 24, at 902.

[38] The importance of the monitoring of the consequences of economic sanctions was underlined by the Committee on Economic, Social and Cultural Rights, General Comment No 8, above n 28, at para 13; See also International Conference of the Red Cross and Red Crescent, *Resolution 4: Principles and Action in International Humanitarian Assistance and Protection* para F4(b) (1995), in 36 *International Review of the Red Cross* 73–74 (1996). Hereinafter referred to as Res 4. See also the Secretary-General, *Supplement to the Agenda for Peace*, A/50/60 17–18 (1995); Margaret Doxey, *United Nations Sanctions: Current Policy Issues* 45 (Halifax, Dalhousie, 1999), Eric Hoskins, *The Impact of Sanctions: A Study of UNICEF's Perspectives* 7 (New York, UNICEF, 1998).

This conclusion is not as radical as it might seem at first sight. It does not prevent the Security Council from adopting extensive coercive measures in a situation that threatens the peace. The Security Council still retains its very wide discretion as to which type of economic measures it will adopt, as long as it provides for monitoring. It would also have considerable leeway in deciding the nature of the monitoring system, as long as it reflects a commitment to procedures which are necessary to ensure the substantive protection of basic human rights. These would include monitoring on a regular basis throughout the period of sanctions, and steps to respond effectively to any disproportionate suffering by vulnerable groups within the targeted country.[39]

Moreover, even if one did not generally accept an obligation on the Security Council to provide a monitoring mechanism in its enforcement resolutions, such an obligation would exist in those particular instances where the Security Council has given a unilateral undertaking to monitor effectively the impact of sanctions on the civilian population. In such cases the principle of good faith would prevent (ie estop) it from not executing its undertaking to do so.[40] For example, on 29 January 1999, the President of the Security Council presented a note to members of the Security Council, setting out practical proposals to improve the work of Sanctions Committees.[41] One of these were that Sanction Committees should monitor, throughout the sanctions regime, the humanitarian impact of sanctions on vulnerable groups, including children.[42] This statement would oblige the Security Council to provide for such monitoring in future sanctions regimes, as its explicit undertaking to do so creates a legal expectation that it will indeed execute its intentions.[43]

3.   IMPLICATIONS FOR SECURITY COUNCIL PRACTICE

3.1.   Iraq

After Iraq's invasion of Kuwait in August 1990, the Security Council imposed the most extensive trading and financial embargo in the history of the United Nations that lasted from 6 August 1990 to 22 May 2003. The adoption of Resolution 661 of 6 August 1990 resulted in the suspension of Iraq's customary trade and financial relations, including restrictions on

---

[39] General Comment No 8, above n 28, at paras 13–14; Res 4, above n 38, at para F4(c); Normand, above n 9, at 25–26; Hazelzet, above n 30, at 89; Fishman, above n 31, at 715. Cf Reisman & Stevick, above n 1, at 132.
[40] See ch 5 at s 4.1.
[41] S/1999/92; Segall, above n 11, at 43.
[42] S/1999/92, at para 11.
[43] See ch 5 at s 4.1.

the sale of Iraqi oil and the freezing of the country's assets.[44] Resolution 661 (1990) also instituted an arms embargo, and provisions requiring verification that Iraq destroy or dispose of its chemical and biological weapons of mass destruction.[45]

The following assessment of the impact of the sanctions regime on human rights in Iraq mainly concerns the period which followed the formal recognition of the cease-fire in Resolution 687 (1991)[46] until the outbreak of the second Gulf War in March 2003.[47] During the two Gulf Wars, the limits to the Security Council's enforcement measures were primarily provided by the law of armed conflict (humanitarian law).[48]

3.1.1. The Impact on the Right to Life and the Right to Health

Despite the inclusion of various humanitarian exemptions in the sanctions regime,[49] of which the oil for food programme that was introduced in 1995 formed the most prominent element,[50] the impact of the sanctions regime on the basic needs of civilians were increasingly severe. By the turn of the century the deteriorating living conditions made people's everyday lives a continuing struggle, while food shortages and the lack of medicine and clean drinking water threatened their very survival.[51]

According to the United Nations Children's Fund (UNICEF), infant mortality in most of Iraq had more than doubled in the first nine years since the United Nations sanctions were imposed. In the government

---

[44] SC Res 661 of 6 August 1990, at para 20.
[45] *Ibid*, at para 19; see also Fishman, above n 31, at 702. See also SC Res 687 of 3 April 1991, at paras 7–10, which included a more detailed listing of proscribed items including conventional arms, weapons of mass destruction, ballistic missiles and services related to technical support and training. See also Report of the International Committee of the Red Cross, *Iraq: A Decade of Sanctions* 2–3 (1999) at www.icrc.org. Hereinafter referred to as ICRC Report.
[46] At para 33.
[47] The sanctions were terminated soon after the termination of hostilities during the second Gulf War in SC Res 1483 of 22 May 2003, at paras 10 ff.
[48] For a different approach that prefers to apply the norms of humanitarian law as a limit to the Security Council's powers even after the recognition of the cease-fire see Starck, above n 15, at 291 ff.
[49] Eg SC Res 661 of 6 August 1990, at para 4 excluded payments and foodstuffs exclusively for medical or humanitarian purposes from the sanctions regime. SC Res 687 of 3 April 1991, at para 4 also broadened the humanitarian exemptions in order to provide "essential civilian needs". SC Res 706 of 15 August 1991, at para 2 allowed for limited oil sales for the same purpose. The amount nonetheless remained below what was proposed in an inter-agency mission report (S/22799 (1991)) that estimated the cost of restoring Iraq's key sectors to pre-war levels at $22 million.
[50] SC Res 986 of 14 April 1995, at para 4, authorised Iraq to sell up to $2 billion worth of oil under United Nations auspices every six months. Of this amount 66 % were to fund humanitarian imports.
[51] ICRC Report, above n 45, at 2. Fishman, above n 31, at 687; Reisman and Stevick, above n 1, at 101–03.

controlled central and southern Iraq,[52] home to 85 per cent of the population, the death rate for children under five rose from 56 per 1000 live births in the period between 1984 to 1989, to 131 per 1000 during 1994 to 1999. During these same periods, infant mortality also increased from 47 to 108 deaths per 1000 live births.[53]

Furthermore, almost all younger children were affected by a shift in their nutritional status towards malnutrition. A third of all children under five were chronically malnourished, which represents a 72 per cent rise since 1991.[54] Since 1997 the extent of chronic infant and child malnutrition had stabilised in the more populous centre and south, while in the northern governorates the situation had slightly improved.[55] However, the situation was unlikely to improve substantially unless the water and sanitation infrastructure was repaired. It had been in constant decline since the country's power system—which was central for water and sewage treatment—was crippled during the air campaigns of the Gulf War.[56]

Together with food and medicine shortages, the degradation of the water and sanitation sectors, which lacked the necessary funds for improving infrastructure, were direct causes of malnutrition.[57] It also contributed to epidemics such as cholera and diarrhoea, which had

---

[52] In accordance with the Memorandum of Understanding that was signed by Iraq and the United Nations on 20 May 1996, the Iraqi government would be responsible for the implementation of the oil for food programme in the 15 governorates in the centre and south of the country. The United Nations, for its part, would implement the programme on behalf of the Iraqi government in the three northern (Kurdish) governorates. See S/1996/356; SC Res 986 of 14 April 1995, at para 8; Human Rights Watch, Explanatory Memorandum, above n 15, at para 3.

[53] UNICEF survey of 27 August 1999 with updated statistics, at www.unicef.org/; ICRC Report, above n 45, at 2; S/1999/356, Annex II, at paras 88 ff (hereinafter referred to as Annex II). See also Eric Hoskins, "The Humanitarian Impacts of Economic Sanctions and War in Iraq", in Thomas G Weiss *et al* (eds), *Political Gain and Civil Pain. Humanitarian Impacts of Economic Sanctions* 120 (Lanham, Rowman & Littlefield, 1997).

[54] UNICEF survey, above n 53, ICRC Report, above n 45, at 3.

[55] S/1999/4, at paras 70 ff; S/2001/1089, at para 63; ICRC Report, above n 45, at 3; Annex II, above n 53, at paras 29 ff; See also Human Rights Watch, Explanatory Memorandum, above n 15, at para 6 fn 7. From these documents it appears that there are several reasons why the north of Iraq is doing better than the south. Amongst others, the per capita allocation of funds under the oil-for-food programme is higher, due to the north's historic vulnerability. The distribution of food and medicine through the United Nations agencies is also comparatively more efficient than distribution by the Iraqi government, and the northern border is more permeable to embargoed commodities than the rest of the country. Other factors include a relatively larger and more varied rain-fed agricultural sector, which made this area less dependent on food rations and lowered the market cost of food.

[56] Human Rights Watch, Explanatory Memorandum, above n 15, at para 8.

[57] Annex II, above n 53, at para 20 and para 39. The most vulnerable groups have been the hardest hit, especially children under the age of five who are being exposed to unhygienic conditions, particularly in urban centres. Human Rights Watch, Explanatory Memorandum, above n 15, at para 6. See also Hoskins (Humanitarian Impacts), above n 53, at 116–17. See also S/2001/1089, at para 61.

reappeared for the first time in decades as the major killer of children.[58] This progressive worsening of infant mortality, epidemics and malnutrition amongst Iraqi children leads one to the conclusion that their right to life was systematically violated for more than a decade.[59] As these consequences could not be dissociated from the impact of the sanctions regime,[60] the Security Council had made itself guilty of violating a core element of the purposes and principles of the United Nations, which also constitutes a *ius cogens* norm. As the first Gulf War officially ended with the cease-fire agreement of Resolution 687 (1990), the loss of innocent life thereafter could not be justified under the principle of collateral damage of the law of armed conflict. The economic sanctions regime was bound by basic human rights norms, including first and foremost the right to life of Iraqi children.

Similarly, the Security Council had made itself guilty of the violation of the right to health of the population at large. Iraq's 130 former modern hospitals, many of them built by foreign companies between the sixties and eighties, had not received the necessary repairs or maintenance since the imposition of sanctions. The buildings were in an advanced state of disrepair and even basic equipment was no loner being replaced. As a result, standards of health care had reached exceptionally low levels.[61] Primary health centres, which served the widest sector of the population, could not function properly owing to the shortage of even the most basic equipment such as stethoscopes, sterilizers and writing paper.[62]

The oil-for-food programme introduced by Resolution 986 (1995) brought some relief to the situation, as it increased the availability of food, medical supplies and other commodities to the population. As a result, the humanitarian situation in the northern part of the country started to improve, whilst in the south further deterioration was stopped or slowed down.[63] However, even in the absence of further deterioration,

---

[58] ICRC Report, above n 45, at 2–3. Given the gravity of the nutritional situation, the World Food Program (WFP) in February 1999 launched an appeal of $21 million to help more than one million people in Iraq suffering from the effects of food shortages and poor water supply. This included 200,000 acutely malnourished children, of whom most were under the age of five. These children have not had proper drinking water or sanitation since they were born.
[59] Segall, above n 11, at 33.
[60] Annex II, above n 53, at para 46; ICRC Report, above n 45, at 4; Human Rights Watch, Letter to the United Nations Security Council, 4 January 2000, at paras 9 ff, at www.hrw.org/. Hereinafter referred to as Letter; HC Graf Sponeck, "Sanctions and Humanitarian Exemptions: A Practitioner's Commentary 2, 13 *European Journal of International Law* 83 (2002).
[61] ICRC Report, above n 45, at 3; Annex II, above n 53, at para 43; Human Rights Watch, Letter, above n 60, at para 8.
[62] *Ibid.* Standards of treatment were also falling as doctors could not keep their knowledge up to date. Hardly any medical literature had entered the country during the first decade of sanctions, as the importation of scientific literature was prohibited under the embargo. See also Hoskins (Humanitarian Impacts), above n 53, at 118–19.
[63] Annex II, above n 53, at para 32; Human Rights Watch, Explanatory Memorandum, above n 15, at para 4; S/1999/4, at para 87; S/2001/1089, at paras 51 ff.

the situation continued to have lethal consequences for the civilian population. The limited available funds had not allowed for significant improvement in the infrastructure necessary for the provision of health care. It did not halt the collapse of the health system or the deterioration of water supplies, which together posed one of the gravest threats to the health and well-being of the civilian population.[64]

By the turn of the century it became increasingly difficult to justify this limitation of the right to health as proportional, if the anticipated constructive consequences of the sanctions had been the Iraqi government's compliance with Security Council demands for disarmament.[65] The reality of a decade of sanctions had shown that the Security Council could not reasonably expect that the Iraqi government would comply with these demands, even at the price of gravely damaging Iraqi society.[66] By the year 2000 it was clear that the continuation of the embargo in this form prolonged disproportionate suffering amongst the civilian population. It also meant that the Security Council was acting in bad faith by violating a core obligation under the ICESCR, namely not to engage in policies that undermine the right of the Iraqi people to the highest attainable standard of physical and mental health.[67]

Accusing the Security Council of violating the right to life of the Iraqi children and the right to health of the Iraqi society as a whole, is not an attempt to deny the Iraqi government's own callous and manipulative disregard for its human rights obligations towards its people throughout the period of sanctions.[68] It is undisputed that the Iraqi government greatly compounded and magnified the humanitarian crisis by, for example, failing to comply fully with Resolution 687 (1991) and refusing between 1991 and 1996 to implement any oil-for-food arrangement.[69]

---

[64] Annex II, above n 53, at para 21; ICRC Report, above n 45, at 4; Human Rights Watch, Explanatory Memorandum, above n 15, at para 25; S/1999/4, at para 55; S/2001/1089, at para 65 ff; Fishman, above n 31, at 705.

[65] Human Rights Watch, Explanatory Memorandum, above n 15, at para 24; Cf Starck, above n 15, at 361–62. Tono Eitel, "The United Nations Security Council and its Future Contribution in the Field of International Law", 4 *Max Planck Yearbook of United Nations Law* 66 (2000); Bardo Fassbender, "Uncertain Steps into a Post Cold War World: The Role and Functioning of the UN Security Council after a Decade of Measures against Iraq", 13 *European Journal of International Law* 295 (2002); Robert Howse, "The Road to Baghdad is Paved with Good Intentions", *Ibid*, at 90.

[66] Fishman, above n 31, at 688.

[67] Human Rights Watch, Explanatory Memorandum, above n 15, at para 13.

[68] For a detailed overview of Iraq's failure to comply with its obligations under international human rights law during the first decade of sanctions, see the reports of the Special Rapporteur of the United Nations Commission on Human Rights on the situation of Human Rights in Iraq. These include A/54/466 (1999); E/CN.4/1999/37; E/CN.4/1998/67; E/CN.4/1997/57; E/CN.4/1996/61; and E/CN.4/ 1995/ 56. Cf Human Rights Watch, World Report, (1999), at www.hrw.org/.

[69] See Human Rights Watch, Explanatory Memorandum, above n 15, at para 12. The Iraqi government has also been criticised for excessive warehousing of medicines and failure to order foods specially designed for the nourishment of infants, small children, and nursing mothers. Cf S/1999/4, at para 84; Reisman & Stevick, above 1, at 105–06.

At the same time, however, it would be an over-simplification to place the blame for the high child malnutrition and mortality rate and the precarious state of health of the civilian population squarely on the Iraqi government. Deficiencies in the sanctions regime and in particular shortages of revenue, directly contributed to the situation as well.[70] For even if all humanitarian supplies had been provided in a timely fashion and better cooperation of the Iraqi government had been secured, the magnitude of the humanitarian need was such that it could not be met by the parameters set forth in resolution 986 (1995) and the subsequent measures preceding the termination of the sanctions regime in May 2003.[71] These measures were, at best, of a stopgap nature which could neither meet all the basic needs of 22 million people, nor ensure the maintenance of a whole country's collapsing infrastructure.[72]

Moreover, given the expectation that the Security Council's obligation to act in good faith will result in a respect for human rights, it had to acknowledge its obligation not to undermine the right to life and the right to health of the Iraqi civilian population.[73] The Security Council therefore had to design its economic enforcement system in a way that minimised its impact on civilians, in particular on vulnerable groups such as children. This would, inter alia, require the taking into account of predictable strategies of the targeted government to minimise the impact of the economic embargo on itself. By the turn of the century (ie after nine years of sanctions) it was clear and predictable that the Iraqi government would not hesitate to use the civilian population as a shield to deflect the impact of the sanctions away from itself in order to ensure its own survival.[74] Ignoring this fact would amount to nothing less than an act of bad faith and an abdication of responsibility on the part of the Security Council.

---

[70] Annex II, above n 53, at para 54; Human Rights Watch, Explanatory Memorandum, above n 15, at para 8.

[71] SC Res 1153 of 20 February 1998, at para 2, expanded the oil export ceiling to $5.2 billion every six months. SC Res 1175 of 19 June 1998 at paras 1 ff, authorised the use of $300 million for rehabilitation of the oil sector, recognising that this was essential in order to sustain funding for the entire humanitarian programme. SC Res 1284 of 17 December 1999, at paras 15 ff, also implemented some of the key recommendations of the humanitarian panel which was established by the Security Council and involved a range of United Nations expertise (see Annex II, above n 53). Eg it removed any dollar ceiling on oil exports and accelerated the procedure exempting humanitarian items from the sanctions. It also allowed for a cash component to be utilised for rehabilitation of the oil sector. Additional measures for the rehabilitation of (oil) infrastructure followed in SC Res 1293 of 31 March 2000; SC Res 1330 of 5 December 2000; See SC Res 1352 of 1 June 2001; SC Res 1360 of 3 July 2001; SC Res 1382 of 29 November 2001. For the implications of SC Res 1409 of 14 May 2002, see below at (text leading up to) fn 80.

[72] Human Rights Watch, Explanatory Memorandum, above n 15, at para 46; S/1999/4, at para 116; ICRC Report, above n 45, at 5; Human Rights Watch, Letter, above n 60, at paras 9 ff.

[73] See Human Rights Watch, Explanatory Memorandum, above n 15, at para 13.

[74] *Ibid*, at paras 4–5. See also Normand, above n 9, at 31; Starck, above n 15, at 124, 132–33. John Mueller & Karl Mueller, "Sanctions of Mass Destruction", *Foreign Affairs* 52 (1999).

This state of affairs is not mitigated by the argument that the Iraqi opposition was in support of the sanctions regime. It is quite possible that (certain members) of the Iraqi opposition might have supported some type of sanctions against the Hussein government. Since the opposition could not protest openly, it is difficult to determine to what extent this was the case. However, even if there was significant support amongst opposition members for a sanctions regime, this would not justify a sanctions system that violated the right to life and the right to health in the fashion described above. Like the Security Council, the Iraqi opposition as a "government in waiting" would have been bound to respect the right to life and the core content of the right to health of the Iraqi people.[75] Therefore the opposition's potential support for sanctions against the Hussein regime could not be interpreted as permitting the international community to disregard the legal limits provided by international human rights law.

In order to ensure that its actions lay well within the parameters established by basic human rights, the Security Council should, at the very least, have implemented the recommendations forthcoming from within the United Nations without any conditions or delay.[76] Although Resolution 1284 (1999) had incorporated some of these recommendations, it was in a form that required further action by the Security Council or the Sanctions Committee, which severely delayed their implementation. Moreover, the Security Council should have acknowledged that these recommendations only addressed the immediate threats to the right to life and health of ordinary Iraqis. It did not contain elements of comprehensive planning and economic revival that were essential in order to reverse the dangerously degraded state of the country's civilian infrastructure and social services.[77] Stated differently, it did not contain a lasting strategy for addressing the Security Council's violations of the right to life of the Iraqi children and its disproportionate limitation of the right to health of the population.

---

[75] Iraq has been party to the ICCPR and the ICESCR since 1971. See Status of Ratifications, available at www.unhchr.ch .
[76] Such as the recommendation of the humanitarian panel, above n 71. The same applies to the inter-agency mission report, above n 49. It suggested limited oil sales to fund the humanitarian needs, commencing with a sum of $6.9 billion for the first year with an initial four-month sale of $2.65 billion. After several weeks of debate in July 1991, SC Res 706 of 15 August 1991 and SC Res 712 of 19 September 1991 were adopted, allowing Iraq to sell $1.6 billion over six months. This was lower than the $2.65 billion over four months, suggested by the report. The Security Council resisted efforts of the Secretary-General to raise the allocation to $2.4 billion. Cf Lutz Oette ‚Die Entwicklung des Oil for Food-Programs und die gegenwärtige humanitäre Lage in Irak", 59 *Zeitschrift für ausländisches öffentliches Recht und Völkerrecht* 856 ff (1999); Human Rights Watch, Explanatory Memorandum, above n 15, at para 25; Human Rights Watch, Letter, above n 60, at para 6.
[77] Human Rights Watch, Letter, above n 60, at para 7.

In principle, it remained within the discretion of the Security Council to determine how to restructure the embargo in order to limit its impact on the Iraqi population. However, given the level of deterioration of the infrastructure, it was difficult to see how this could be done without permitting some import of civilian goods and investments in the civilian economy.[78] One proposal that was put forward concerned the removal of restrictions on the imports of commodities that were not of a dual-use nature and on financial transactions involving civilian sectors of the economy, including foreign investments. At the same time there should be a continued prohibition of all imports and exports of a clearly military nature and scrutiny of import contracts concerning items of a dual-use nature.[79]

The Security Council ultimately adopted a seemingly similar solution in Resolution 1409 of 14 May 2002. Although it did not remove restrictions on foreign investments, this resolution did allow for the controlled import of all civilian goods. However, given the cumbersome procedures attached to the processing of applications for exporting commodities to Iraq and the implied delays, it remains doubtful whether this restructured system would have restored the necessary element of proportionality which has been lacking in the Iraqi sanctions regime over the last decade.[80] Given the short-lived nature of this amended regime, which only lasted until 22 May 2003,[81] this question will most likely remain unanswered.

3.1.2. Monitoring

If one subscribed to the notion that the Security Council is under a general obligation to provide for a monitoring mechanism when adopting economic sanctions, one can conclude that it fulfilled this obligation formally in the case of Iraq. Already in Resolution 666 of 13 September 1990, the Security Council decided that the Sanctions Committee created under Resolution 660 (1990)[82] had to keep the situation in Iraq and Kuwait

---

[78] *Ibid*; Annex II, above n 53, at para 58.
[79] Human Rights Watch, Letter, above n 60, at para 15.
[80] SC Res 1409 of 14 May 2002, at paras 2 ff. All applications for the sale or supply of commodities to Iraq first had to be registered with the Office of the Iraq Program (OIP). Thereafter these applications were scrutinised by experts of the United Nations Monitoring, Verification and Inspection Commission (UNMOVIC) and the International Atomic Energy Agency (IAEA), who could also request further information. If UNMOVIC and/ or the IAEA determined that the application contained any military products, the application became ineligible. In instance, where they found the application to contain dual-use items (S/2002/515 (2002), the application was forwarded to the Sanctions Committee which could approve or deny the application or place it on hold.
[81] SC Res 1483 of 22 May 2003.
[82] SC Res 661 of 6 August 1990, at para 6, provided for a Sanctions Committee which had to oversee the implementation of sanctions. These Sanctions Committees (which proliferated after 1990), are set up as subsidiary organ of the Security Council under Art 29 of the Charter and replicate Security Council membership. See Doxey, above n 38, at 41; Eitel above n 65, at 67; Starck, above n 15, at 86 ff.

under constant review to determine whether humanitarian circumstances had arisen.[83]

The subsequent resolutions reflect the fact that the Sanctions Committee did concern itself with the situation in Iraq on an ongoing basis. In the process it consulted with specialised United Nations agencies in the field and created the United Nations Office of the Iraq Program, as well as a humanitarian panel. It expanded the humanitarian exemptions to the embargo and the oil-for-food programme on several occasions. One would therefore not be able to accuse the Security Council of formally violating its monitoring obligation.

However, the fact that the Security Council formally provided for a monitoring mechanism does not mean that it actually engaged in effective monitoring.[84] Even if one does not accept a general obligation on the Security Council to engage in effective monitoring, it did create such an obligation for itself in the case of Iraq. The formal commitment to monitoring in Resolution 661 (1990) and subsequent resolutions created the concrete expectation that the sanctions regime would be structured in a way that minimises its impact on the civilian population. The principle of good faith implies that this monitoring system, at the very least, ensures that the basic human rights of the population are respected. As has been illustrated above, the monitoring system in place for more than a decade had neither prevented the violation of the right to life of infants and children, nor of the right to health of the civilian population in general.

A major contributing factor has been the lack of transparency of decisions of the Sanctions Committee, since it functions behind closed doors.[85] For example, the Sanctions Committee has systematically refrained from explaining why it refused to implement all the proposals of the Secretary-General, the humanitarian panel or other United Nations missions to Iraq concerning expansion of the oil-for-food programme. The need for insight into the deliberations of the Sanctions Committee becomes especially important in the light of the fact that it functions by consensus, which means that each member effectively has a veto power.[86] This gives a single member the power to prevent the exemption

---

[83] SC Res 666 of 13 September 1990, at para 1. See SC Res 706 of 15 August 1991, at paras 1(d) and 5, for a reaffirmation of the Security Council's commitment to reviewing regularly whether the payments authorised for humanitarian purposes actually met the needs. See also SC Res 712 of 19 September 1991, at para 2.

[84] See Human Rights Watch, Letter, above n 60, at para 22.

[85] Michael P Scharf & Joshua L Dorosin, "Interpreting UN Sanctions: The Rulings and Role of the Yugoslavia Sanctions Committee", 19 *Brooklyn Journal of International Law* 774 (1993); see also Oette, above n 76, at 842.

[86] Scharf & Dorosin, above n 85, at 774; Oette, above n 76, at 842.

of specific goods from the sanctions regime for humanitarian purposes.[87] As a result, a high number of exemption applications have been placed on hold, with serious implications for the implementation of the humanitarian programme, not to mention its politicisation.[88] Whether the lack of transparency of a sanctions-monitoring mechanism would in itself render it *mala fides*, is debatable. It has been argued, for example, that the veil of confidentiality is necessary to protect the members of the Security Council from undue political pressure. If it were lifted, the members responsible for negative decisions regarding humanitarian exemptions could be subjected to unjustified or excessive political pressure from affected countries, businesses or persons.[89] Even though there is merit in this argument, the case of Iraq has illustrated that the harm resulting from such confidentiality can outweigh the advantages. In this particular instance it has contributed to the Sanctions Committee's persistent refusal to expand the humanitarian programme to the extent proposed by technical experts within the United Nations.[90] In the light of the severe consequences that this has had for the right to life and the right to health within Iraq, the lack of transparency has ultimately contributed to a monitoring mechanism which could not protect core human rights and was therefore in bad faith.[91]

One could summarise the above analysis by stating that the sanctions regime in place against Iraq had become illegal by the turn of the century. By that time it was clear that it violated certain core elements of the purposes and principles of the United Nations which to some extent also constitute *ius cogens* norms. Almost a decade of sanctions combined with extensive information about the deterioration of the humanitarian crisis in Iraq had given the Security Council ample opportunity to restructure its sanctions regime. Even though the Security Council had subsequently introduced and expanded the oil-for-food programme and had undertaken some monitoring of the sanctions' impact on civilians, this did not prevent the sanctions regime from directly aggravating violations of the right to life of the Iraqi children, and the right to health of the population

---

[87] The Secretary-General has suggested that for items placed on hold, the Sanctions Committee should provide written and explicit explanations within 48 hours. This would enable the applicants to provide any additional information required by the Sanctions Committee. See S/1999/4, at para 122.

[88] S/1999/986, at para 101; S/2001/1089, at paras 6 and 127; see also Human Rights Watch, Letter, above n 60, at paras 7 and 23; Human Rights Watch, Explanatory Memorandum, above n 15, at para 20; S/1999/4, at para 127. Cf Oette, above n 76, at 853–54; Gian Luca Burci, "Interpreting the Humanitarian Exceptions through the Sanctions Committees", in Vera Gowlland-Debbas (ed), *United Nations Sanctions and International Law* 150 (The Hague, Kluwer, 2001).

[89] Hans-Peter Kaul, "Sanktionsausschüsse des Sicherheitsrates: Ein Einblick in Arbeitsweise und Verfahren", 44 *Vereinte Nationen* 98 (1996).

[90] S/1999/4, at paras 20 and 44.

[91] Fishman, above n 31, at 689.

at large. This justifies the conclusion that the sanctions regime became illegal by the turn of the century and was in bad faith of the very principles that it was supposed to enhance.

3.2.   Former Yugoslavia

The first coercive measures adopted in response to the conflict in the former Yugoslavia consisted of a mandatory arms embargo against the territory,[92] which was to be monitored by a Sanctions Committee created for this purpose.[93] These measures were followed by an extensive trade embargo against the Federal Republic of Yugoslavia (FRY),[94] as well as a prohibition of fuel shipments for industrial inputs through the FRY.[95] Thereafter the Security Council also ordered the freezing of the FRY's financial assets and overseas property and extended the sanctions regime to those areas of Bosnia-Herzegovina controlled by the Bosnian Serbs.[96] The Dayton Peace Accord of 21 November 1995 ultimately provided for the lifting of the economic embargo after the holding of free and fair elections in Bosnia-Herzegovina.[97]

Before turning to the human rights impact of the sanctions regime, it is necessary to focus on the implications of the FRY's (non-)continuation of membership in the United Nations for the legality of the Security Council embargo. One of the important consequences of the dissolution of the Socialist Federal Republic of Yugoslavia (SFRY) in 1992 was uncertainty regarding the continued membership of the FRY (Serbia and Montenegro) in the United Nations. This uncertainty could have serious consequences for the legality of all subsequent Security Council decisions regarding the FRY, as it is not beyond doubt that the Security Council could subject a non-member state to coercive measures in terms

---

[92] SC Res 713 of 25 September 1991, at para 6.
[93] SC Res 724 of 15 December 1991, at par 5(b).
[94] SC Res 757 of 30 May 1992 prohibited exports to and imports from the FRY; banned foreign financial assistance to enterprises in the FRY; severed its air links to the rest of the world; and severed scientific, technical, cultural cooperation and sporting exchanges with the FRY. See also Reisman & Stevick, above n 1, at 112; Julia Devin and Jaleh Dashti-Gibson, "Sanctions in the Former Yugoslavia: Convoluted Goals and Compilated Consequences", in Thomas G Weiss *et al* (eds), *Political Gain and Civil Pain. Humanitarian Impacts of Economic Sanctions* 158 (Lanham, Rowman & Littlefield, 1997).
[95] SC Res 787 of 16 November 1992, at paras 9 ff; See also Reisman & Stevick, above n 1, at 112.
[96] SC Res 820 of 17 April 1993. SC Res 942 of 23 September 1994 subsequently expanded the sanctions against the Bosnian Serb territory to include a ban on all commercial, financial and industrial activities and transactions with Bosnian Serb persons and entities, as well as a freeze of Bosnian Serb assets held abroad. See also Reisman & Stevick, above n 1, at 113; Devin & Dashti-Gibson, above n 94, at 159.
[97] SC Res 1022 of 22 November 1995. After elections took place on 14 September 1996, the Security Council terminated the sanctions in SC Res 1074 of 1 October 1996.

of Chapter VII—unless the non-member has voluntarily subjected itself to the Charter system.[98]

The FRY insisted that it automatically continued the statehood and legal personality of the SFRY, which included continued membership in the United Nations.[99] This claim was, however, contested by the other former republics of the SFRY who all sought admission to the United Nations as new states. The FRY's assertion also met with a mixed and ambiguous response from the United Nations itself.[100] In Resolution 777 of 19 September 1992, the Security Council affirmed that the former SFRY had ceased to exist and that the FRY could not automatically continue its membership in the United Nations. In addition, it recommended to the General Assembly that the FRY should apply for membership in the United Nations and that it should not participate in the work of the General Assembly.[101] The General Assembly gave effect to this recommendation in Resolution 47/1 of 22 September 1992. After reaffirming that the FRY could not continue automatically the membership of the SFRY in the United Nations, it decided that the FRY should apply for membership in the United Nations and that it should not participate in the work of the General Assembly.[102]

These ambiguous statements by the Security Council and the General Assembly are a reflection of the deep divisions that existed within the United Nations on the issue and which were also mirrored in the interpretations given to the resolutions. For example, in the Security Council the United States and France interpreted them as meaning that the FRY was not a member of the United Nations anymore.[103] The Russian Federation and China, on the other hand, drew the conclusion that the FRY continued to be a member of the United Nations and was merely prevented from participating in the work of the General Assembly.[104]

---

[98] See s 1 above and ch 3 at s 4.2. This problem did not exist with respect to the other territories of the former Yugoslavia such as Bosnia-Herzegovina and Croatia, as they were already admitted to the United Nations by 22 May 1992.

[99] See the Declaration adopted on 27 April 1992 at a joint session of the Assembly of the SFRY (the National Assembly of the Republic of Serbia) and the Assembly of Montenegro, in A/46/915, Annex II (1992). See also *Case Concerning Application of the Convention of the Prevention and Punishment of the Crime of Genocide (Bosnia and Herzegovina v Yugoslavia)*, Application of 23 April 2001 for Revision of the Judgment of 11 July 1996, at www.icj-cij.org. Hereinafter referred to as *Bosnia- Herzegovina v Yugoslavia*, revision. For a detailed analysis on the issue of state succession and its consequences for the former Yugoslav republics, see Andreas Zimmermann, *Staatennachfolge in völkerrechtliche Verträge* 599 ff (Berlin, Springer, 2000).

[100] *Bosnia-Herzegovina v Yugoslavia*, revision, above n 99.

[101] At para 1.

[102] See also Andreas Zimmermann & Carsten Stahn, "Yugoslav Territory, United Nations Trusteeship or Sovereign State? Reflections on the current and future legal status of Kosovo, 70 *Nordic Journal of International Law* 439 (2001).

[103] S/PV 3116 12 (1992).

[104] *Ibid*, at 2, 12; Zimmermann, above n 99, at 602.

Similar divisions became apparent within the ICJ during the FRY's request for provisional measures against Belgium, Canada, the Netherlands, Portugal and Spain for the violation of the obligation not to use force.[105] Although the majority avoided the question of the FRY's continued membership in the United Nations on the basis that it was not decisive for the issue at hand,[106] the separate and dissenting opinions did indicate considerable disagreement in this regard. Whereas Judges Kooijmans[107] and Oda[108] regarded Yugoslavia's membership of the United Nations as having terminated during 1992, Judge *ad hoc* Kreca[109] was of exactly the opposite opinion.

The United Nations Secretariat seemed to have regarded the FRY as the automatic successor to the SFRY's membership in the United Nations, if albeit in a limited form. It took the view that the General Assembly Resolution 47/1 (1992) had neither terminated nor suspended Yugoslavia's membership of the United Nations, because it had not been adopted pursuant to Article 5 (suspension) or Article 6 (expulsion) of the Charter. Consequently, the seat and nameplate of Yugoslavia remained as before and the Secretariat continued to fly the old flag of Yugoslavia.[110] The Secretariat also allowed the permanent mission of the SFRY to continue to operate and had accredited officials of the FRY as representatives of the SFRY mission.[111] In that capacity, these representatives have circulated documents, participated in the work of various United Nations

---

[105] *The application of the Federal Republic of Yugoslavia against the Kingdom of Belgium [and others] for Violation of the Obligation not to Use Force*, Provisional Measures, Order of 2 June 1999, available at www.icj-cij.org. Hereinafter referred to as the *Case concerning the Legality of the Use of Force*. See also Zimmermann, above n 99, at 603.

[106] *Case concerning the Legality of the Use of Force*, above n 105, at para 33. The ICJ took a similar approach in *Case Concerning Application of the Convention on the Prevention and Punishment of the Crime of Genocide (Bosnia and Herzegovina v Yugoslavia (Serbia and Montenegro)*, Provisional Measures, ICJ Rep 1993, at 14.

[107] Separate opinion of Judge Kooijmans in *Case concerning Legality of the Use of Force*, above n 105, at para 5.

[108] Separate Opinion of Judge Oda in *Case concerning Legality of the Use of Force*, above n 105, at para 4.

[109] Dissenting opinion of Judge *ad hoc* Kreca in *Case concerning Legality of the Use of Force*, above n 105, at para 8 ff; see also Zimmermann, above n 99, at 603.

[110] *Consequences for Purposes of Membership in the United Nations of the Disintegration of a Member-State—General Assembly Resolution 47/1 and Practical Consequences of its Adoption*, Legal Opinion of 29 September 1992, in *United Nations Juridical Yearbook 1992*, at 428. The General Assembly reacted to this position by adopting GA Res 48/88 of 20 December 1993, in which it urged member states and the Secretariat to fulfil the spirit of GA Res 47/1 of 22 September 1992, to end the *de facto* working status of the FRY. In GA Res 47/229 of 29 April 1993, the General Assembly further decided that the FRY should not participate in the work of ECOSOC. See also *Bosnia-Herzegovina v Yugoslavia*, revision, above n 99; Zimmermann & Stahn, above n 102, 439.

[111] See Sean D Murphy, "Contemporary Practice of the United States Relating to International Law", in 94 *American Journal of International Law* 677–78 (2000).

committees and attended Security Council meetings as observers.[112] The FRY was also still included on the list of member states that were called upon to bear the expenses of the United Nations.[113]

For its part, the FRY consistently and repeatedly endeavoured to gain access to the United Nations on the assumption of automatic continuity of the SFRY membership.[114] This included the paying of the membership dues apportioned to it as late as September 1998.[115] It was only after the fall of the *Milosevic* regime in 2000 that the FRY reconsidered its position, which eventually resulted in its request for and admission to the United Nations on 1 November 2000 as a "new" member. Whilst this admission clarifies the membership of the FRY in the United Nations as of 1 November 2000, it also tends support to the conclusion that the FRY along with the international community had acquiesced in the notion that it was not a member of the United Nations between September 1992 and November 2000.[116]

If this indeed were the case, it becomes imperative to determine whether the FRY can be regarded as having subjected itself voluntary to the Charter system between 1992 and 2000, as any coercive measures of the Security Council in the absence of such acceptance would rest on an uncertain legal basis. It is submitted that the FRY's consistent attempts to be recognised as the automatic successor to the SFRY's membership would constitute sufficient proof of a voluntary acceptance of the Charter system within its territory. Even though the FRY's actions (such as payment of membership dues) might not in themselves have sufficed to

---

[112] The attendance of Security Council meetings was allowed until 23 June 2000, when the Security Council barred the FRY representative from attending its meeting by a vote of 7 to 4. See S/PV 4164 (1993); see also Murphy, above n 111, at 678.

[113] See eg, GA Res 52/215 of 22 December 1997. The General Assembly thus acted in a contradictory fashion in that it first requested the termination of the *de facto* working status of the FRY in the United Nations, but then still continued to request membership dues from the FRY.

[114] As openly acknowledged by the FRY Government in *Bosnia-Herzegovina v Yugoslavia*, revision, above n 99.

[115] Voucher confirming the payment made by the Government of the FRY in the amount of $588 476, value date 16 September 1998, annexed to *Bosnia and Herzegovina v Yugoslavia*, revision, above n 99.

[116] *Bosnia and Herzegovina v Yugoslavia*, revision, above n 99; Zimmermann & Stahn, above n 102; at 440. For a slightly different opinion, see *Prosecutor v Milan Multinovic et al*, Decision on Motion Challenging Jurisdiction, Case No IT–99–37–PT, 6 May 2003, Trial Chamber, at paras 37 ff, available at www.icty.org. It submitted that GA Res 47/1 of 22 September 1992 did not deprive the FRY of all attributes of United Nations membership. Whilst it prevented the FRY from participating in the work of the General Assembly, the FRY retained sufficient indicia of United Nations membership to make it amenable to the Chapter VII regime of the Charter. Moreover, since the FRY was a member of the United Nations at the time the conflict broke out, it remained subjected to the Chapter VII regime of the Charter afterwards—even if its membership of the United Nations subsequently ceased. This follows from the centrality of the goal of the maintenance of international peace and security within the international legal order.

prove the country's membership in the United Nations, it was a clear indication of its subjection to and acceptance of the legal framework and enforcement system enshrined in the Charter. As a result, the FRY would be estopped from claiming that any coercive measures by the Security Council against the FRY between 1992 and 2000 were illegal, on the basis that they were taken against a non-member of the United Nations.

3.2.1.   The Impact on the Right to Life and the Right to Health

The crisis in former Yugoslavia had a significant impact on the right to life and the right to health of the civilian population of the FRY, which possessed a well-developed and accessible health care system before the war.[117] Even though medical supplies and other commodities essential for civilian needs were excluded from the embargo,[118] the availability of medicines declined by more than 50 per cent between 1991 and 1995. Physicians faced a critical shortage of certain vaccines, including those for measles, mumps and rubella.[119] As a result, the number of children vaccinated dropped and epidemics of diseases that were formerly almost eradicated, increased.[120] Water-borne and water-related diseases also increased significantly during this period, due to the deterioration in water quality resulting from the scarcity of water purifying chemicals.[121]

After dropping continuously from 1971 to 1991, the infant mortality rate increased from 21.7 to 21.9 per 1000 live births during 1992 and 1993. This represents an increase from 1991 to 1993 of one additional infant death in every 1000 births. A growing food shortage contributed to widespread malnutrition of under-school aged children and every second hospitalised child was reported to be anaemic.[122] Mental health services also deteriorated, with international observers reporting a tripling of the

---

[117] Devin & Dashti-Gibson, above, n 94, at 171; see also Starck, above n 15, at 113 ff.

[118] SC Res 757 of 30 May 1992, at paras 4 (c), 5 and 7(a); SC Res 942 of 23 September 1994 at paras 7(b), 11(a) and 13; SC Res 820 of 17 April 1993, at paras 12, 22 and 27. See Scharf & Dorosin, above n 85, at 781; Doxey, above n 38, at 19.

[119] The Sanctions Committee, after several rounds of negotiations, excluded pharmaceutical supplies and materials from the humanitarian exemptions to the embargo. Devin & Dashti-Gibson, above, n 94, at 166, 172; Hoskins, above n 38, at 7.

[120] Eg in 1992 and 1993, the number of patients suffering from polio in Kosovo rose significantly, with the risk of a more wide-spread epidemic. Devin & Dashti-Gibson, above, n 94, at 172.

[121] Devin & Dashti-Gibson, above, n 94, at 176. Eg, an outbreak of about 1500 cases of shigella, mostly among children, was reported in Macedonia in October 1993. A study at the end of 1992 by the health institute of Novi Sad showed that the number of water-borne diseases had increased ten-fold in Vojvodina since 1991.

[122] Devin & Dashti-Gibson, above, n 94, at 172; Reisman & Stevick, above n 1, at 114, 116. The FRY finally introduced a food rationing programme in September 1994 for the first time since 1948.

mortality rate in mental institutions in less than one year.[123] The blocking of oil and gas imports limited the provision of health services and hospitals reported having insufficient heating and a limited capacity to perform necessary medical services.[124]

Although economic sanctions contributed to the deteriorating socio-economic situation in the FRY after 1991, the extent to which it affected the basic human rights of the population remains difficult to determine. Other factors such as the mismanagement of the economy and the dislocations produced by the war seemed to be the key factors in the country's overall economic decline.[125] During the time sanctions were imposed, the Serbian economy was also experiencing the impact of a severe and long standing economic crisis that commenced in 1979 and continued over the following 10 years, as the country transitioned to a market economy.[126]

This crisis gained new momentum after the collapse of socialism in Eastern Europe in 1989 and the subsequent break-up of Yugoslavia. Before the war, the former Yugoslav republics accounted for 40 per cent of trade with Serbia and Montenegro. After the break-up of the country, this trade almost disappeared. Due to the economic inter-dependency of the republics, the loss of these markets probably had a greater impact on the economy of the FRY than the loss of foreign trade that resulted from sanctions.[127] In addition, the war in Croatia and Bosnia played a major role in the collapse of the FRY's economic and social structure. For example, the influx of more than 700, 000 refugees and their need for food, shelter and health care placed a heavy burden on the economic and social system.[128]

Economic and social decline within the FRY thus clearly resulted from a variety of complex factors, which makes it difficult to determine the extent to which the sanctions regime in itself caused or aggravated the hardship endured by the population.[129] In addition, the coercive pressure of sanctions contributed to the stimulation of peace talks that ultimately resulted in the Dayton Agreement, even if it could not be said that sanctions alone forced the warring parties to accept a negotiated settlement.[130] These factors would caution against a conclusion that the impact of the sanctions regime in the FRY amounted to a disproportionate limitation of

---

[123] Reisman & Stevick, above n 1, at 116.
[124] Devin & Dashti-Gibson, above, n 94, at 166.
[125] Reisman & Stevick, above n 1, at 113; Doxey, above n 38, at 18; Devin & Dashti-Gibson, above n 94, at 161–62.
[126] V Bojicic & D Dyker, *Sanctions on Serbia: Sledgehammer or scalpel?* 3 ff (Sussex, Sussex European Institute, 1993); Devin & Dashti-Gibson, above, n 94, at 162.
[127] Devin & Dashti-Gibson, above n 94, at 162.
[128] *Ibid*, at 162.
[129] *Ibid*, at181–82.
[130] *Ibid*, at 182–83.

human rights norms and thus to a violation of the purposes and principles of the United Nations.[131]

3.2.2. Monitoring

Although the primary task of the Sanctions Committee was to monitor violations of the arms and economic embargo,[132] it also provided some monitoring of its humanitarian impact throughout the existence of the economic sanctions regime. For example, Resolution 757 (1992) also permitted the Sanctions Committee to promulgate guidelines for sanctions interpretation and to receive notifications from states that intended shipments of foodstuffs and medical commodities to Serbia and Montenegro.[133] Two weeks later, Resolution 760 of 18 June 1992 also authorised the Sanctions Committee to use the no-objection procedure for permitting export to Serbia and Montenegro of products other than food and medical commodities for essential humanitarian needs.[134] When the Security Council extended sanctions to the Bosnia Serb territory, it affirmed the Sanctions Committee's right to approve the export of commodities for essential needs.[135]

As in the case of Iraq, the Sanctions Committee functioned behind closed doors, which makes it difficult to assess the efficiency with which it monitored the impact of the embargo on the civilian population. As mentioned in section 3.1.2. above, the lack of transparency in itself can be interpreted as a sign of insufficient monitoring. However, in the case of the FRY it would be difficult to argue that the monitoring process was deficient to the extent that it constituted an act of bad faith by the Security Council. Such a conclusion would only be justified where it is clear that the Security Council was not effectively addressing core human rights violations flowing from or aggravated by the sanctions regime itself. In the case of the FRY this could not be concluded as the extent to which the

---

[131] Reisman & Stevick, above n 1, at 113; see also Doxey, above n 38, at 18; Starck, above n 15, at 362.

[132] SC Res 724 of 15 December 1991, at para 5(b); SC Res 757 of 30 May 1992, at para 13; SC Res 820 of 17 April 1993, at para 18; SC Res 942 of 23 September 1994, at para 19.

[133] At paras 4(c), 13(e) and 13(f).

[134] At para 1. This resolution was adopted at British insistence, due to a difference of opinion within the Sanctions Committee as to whether the exemptions provided for in SC Res 757 of 30 May 1992, also applied to emergency relief assistance provided by the inter-governmental and non-governmental humanitarian agencies. The United States, Belgium, Austria, Japan and France expressed the view that the Sanctions Committee could include such a provision in its guidelines without waiting for Security Council action. The United Kingdom, on the other hand, took the position that a new Security Council resolution to this effect was needed. See S/AC.27/SR.12 (1992); Scharf & Dorosin, above n 85, at 781–82; Doxey, above n 38, at 43; Reisman & Stevick, above n 1, at 112.

[135] SC Res 820 of 17 April 1993, at paras 22 and 27; SC Res 942 of 23 September 1994, at paras 7(b) and and 13. See also Doxey, above n 38, at 44.

sanctions regime affected the basic human rights of the population remained unclear.

3.3. Haiti

In June 1993 the Security Council adopted a mandatory embargo on the sale and supply of oil and arms to Haiti and obliged states to freeze the funds of the Haitian government and its officials.[136] This embargo was adopted almost two years after the military coup against *President Aristede* in October 1991.[137] Resolution 917 of 6 May 1994 extended these sanctions to a complete trade embargo that also banned imports to or exports from Haiti, including the import of oil products.[138] The sanctions were terminated after the Security Council's authorisation of the use of force against the military government[139] resulted in the latter's capitulation and the return of *President Aristede*.[140]

3.3.1. *The Impact on the Right to Life and the Right to Health*

Before the outbreak of the crisis in Haiti, child mortality and nutritional status trends had shown steady improvement over several decades, in spite of the country's stagnant economy and persistent poverty.[141] However, after the outbreak of the crisis and the imposition of sanctions these positive trends came to an end. For example, in 1993 the data collected from 42 health facilities across the country showed that 50 per cent of children under the age of five were malnourished. By September 1994, the same 42 health facilities indicated that 61 per cent of children under

---

[136] SC Res 841 of 16 June 1993.

[137] It was preceded by an extensive regional trade embargo, instituted by the Organisation of American States (OAS) only days after the military coup. The embargo was, however, never consistently applied by member states. The Haitian military government also minimised its impact by trading with countries from outside the OAS region. See OAS Res 1/91, OEA/Ser.F/V.1, MRE/RES.1/91; OAS Res 2/91, OEA/Ser.F/V.1; MRE/RES.2/91; OAS Res 3/92, OEA/Ser.F/V.1, MRE/RES.3.92. See also Reisman & Stevick, above n 1, at 118.

[138] SC Res 861 of 27 August 1993 briefly suspended the sanctions after the adoption of the Governors Island Agreement in July 1993, as it was expected that President Aristede would return to power by October 1993. When his reinstatement failed to materialise, SC Res 873 of 13 October 1993 reinstated the sanctions.

[139] SC Res 940 of 30 July 1994.

[140] SC Res 944 of 29 September 1994, at para 4; SC Res 948 of 15 October 1994, at para 10. See also Reisman & Stevick, above n 1, at 118

[141] Harvard Centre for Population and Development Studies, *Sanctions in Haiti: Crisis in Humanitarian Action* 5 (Cambridge MA, Harvard School of Public Health, 1993). Hereinafter referred to as the Harvard Report; Felicia Swindells, "UN Sanctions in Haiti: A Contradiction under Articles 41 and 55 of the UN Charter", 20 *Fordham International Law Journal* 1207 (1997).

five suffered from malnutrition.[142] Between 1991 and 1993 the rate of infant mortality was estimated to have increased by 32 per cent, resulting in up to 1000 additional deaths per month.[143]

It is widely accepted that these developments were, to some extent, brought about by the sanctions regime.[144] Although medical supplies and foodstuffs were exempt from the embargo,[145] the lack of fuel in particular contributed to the decline in health by curtailing the distribution of food, water and vaccination programmes.[146] Water provision was impeded as there was insufficient fuel to generate the power required for pumping water.[147] The lack of fuel also caused delays in the transportation of supplies to rural areas and prevented patients from reaching rural health clinics. In addition, it impeded the use of generators to supply electricity for health clinics and made it very difficult to maintain refrigerating facilities ("cold chain") in field sites around the country.[148] Doctors attributed a measles epidemic that swept through Haiti from July 1991 to the end of 1993 directly to the low immunisation coverage.[149]

In the light of these developments, one could be tempted to conclude that the sanctions regime in place in Haiti violated the right to life of children and were therefore not in accordance with the purposes and principles of the United Nations.[150] However, the extent to which the

---

[142] Elizabeth D Gibbons, *Sanctions in Haiti. Human Rights and Democracy under Assault* 23 (Westport, Praeger, 1999). But see Sarah Zaidi, "Humanitarian Effects of the Coup and Sanctions in Haiti", in Thomas G Weiss *et al* (eds), *Political Gain and Civilian Pain. Humanitarian Impacts of Economic Sanctions* 203 (Lanham, Rowman & Littlefield, 1997). She submitted that sanctions had little impact on the nutritional status of Haitian children, who already suffered from unprecedented high levels of malnutrition compared with other children of the Western Hemisphere. One third of all children were malnourished and these levels remained more or less constant throughout the crisis.

[143] Harvard Report, above n 141, at 10; Reisman & Stevick, above n 1, at 120.

[144] Harvard Report, above n 141, at 20; Reisman & Stevick, above n 1, at 120; Swindells, above n 141, at 1931.

[145] The export of food, medicine and fuel for humanitarian purposes to the country could be authorised by the Sanctions Committee through a no-objection procedure. See SC Res 841 of 16 June 1993, at para 7; SC Res 917 of 6 May 1994, at paras 7(a)–7(d).

[146] Swindells, above n 141, at 1931, 1935; Hoskins, above n 38, at 7, Gibbons, above n 142, at 23.

[147] Gibbons, above n 142, at 26. The supply of spare parts for pumping facilities and water purification products were cut off during the sanctions regime, which further restricted water provision. A study by the Pan American Health Organisation (PAHO) and the World Health Organisation (WHO) estimated that in the first 18 months of the crisis, potable drinking water output declined by 30% to 50%. See also Zaidi, above n 142, at 200.

[148] The situation was further aggravated by the fact that the sanctions regime prohibited the relief agencies from delivering any resources from the international community through state structures or by public sector personnel. Consequently, those Haitians who were dependent on public services, generally the poorest, were discriminated against in the delivery of humanitarian assistance. See Gibbons, above n 142, at 25–56; Harvard Report, above n 141, at 13; Swindells, above n 141, at 1934.

[149] See Gibbons, above n 142, at 26, 68; Swindells, above n 141, at 1932, 1938; Zaidi, above n 142, at 190.

[150] See Reisman & Stevick, above n 1, at 120, who regarded the suffering inflicted on the civilian population as disproportionate. Whilst the impoverished majority suffered the brunt of

sanctions in themselves were responsible for these conditions remains controversial, as a variety of factors contributed to the precarious humanitarian situation in the country.[151] For example, the immunisation programme was also impeded by the reluctance of the population to assemble for immunisations out of fear of violence and attacks. Mountainous areas were difficult to research due to the absence of passable roads.[152] The shifting of the population during the crisis also made it difficult to identify and reach out to eligible women and children. In addition, hoarding and price manipulation by the 18 Haitian drug import companies could have contributed to the marked price increase and unavailability of some essential drugs.[153]

In essence, the sanctions regime was superimposed upon a military coup, the *de facto* government's mismanagement, an atmosphere of political violence and repression and black-market activities by the private business community. As such, it became very difficult to desegregate any single element of the situation as being responsible for any particular human rights violation.[154] Some legitimacy for the sanctions regime also flowed from its support by *President Aristede* and many of his followers from the time of the coup to the day the multinational force was deployed in Haiti.[155] These factors, combined with the relatively short period of 16 months during which the Security Council sanctions were in place, would make a conclusion that the sanctions regime in itself violated the right to life of Haitian children premature. It would be more accurate to describe the sanctions regime as a borderline case which was likely to have become illegal if it had continued in an unaltered form beyond 1994.

3.3.2. *Monitoring*

Although Resolution 841 (1993) and Resolution 917 (1994) did not explicitly request the Sanctions Committee[156] (or any other body) to monitor

the sanctions, the Haitian economic and military elite avoided their impact by controlling the black market in food and fuel.

[151] Swindells, above n 141, at 1931; Zaidi, above n 142, at 190. However, she also noted that neither the UN specialised agencies nor NGOs conducted any new research between 1991 to 1994. As a result, no reliable statistics exist for this period.

[152] See Zaidi, above n 142, at 205.

[153] Harvard Report, above n 141, at 13; Hoskins, above n 38, at 7; Gibbons, above n 142, at 25; Zaidi, above n 142, at 200.

[154] Harvard Report, above n 141, at 20.

[155] Zaidi, above n 142, at 201. See also Reisman & Stevick, above n 1, at 123. However, as was mentioned in s 3.1.1. above, the legitimate "government in waiting" would also be bound to respect the right to life of its people. Their potential support for sanctions against the military regime cannot be interpreted as permitting the Security Council to disregard the limits provided for in the Charter itself.

[156] Created by SC Res 841 of 16 June 1993, at para 10.

the impact of the sanctions regime on the civilian population, the Sanctions Committee was mandated to decide expeditiously on requests for humanitarian exemptions to the embargo and to promulgate guidelines for the implementation of sanctions.[157] Moreover, after extensive news coverage of the dire impact of sanctions on the civilian population, the Security Council adopted a Presidential Statement in November 1993, in which it expressed its determination to minimise the impact of the present situation on the most vulnerable groups. It also called upon member states to continue and to intensify their humanitarian assistance to the people of Haiti.[158] These measures would, at least formally, fulfil the Security Council's obligation to monitor the impact of sanctions on the basic rights of the population.

One manifestation of the monitoring process was the establishment of a humanitarian fuel programme in December 1993. This programme, established by the United Nations and the OAS, was to be operated by the Pan American Health Organisation (PAHO) and the World Health Organisation (WHO), in collaboration with an executive management committee, known as the *Programme D'approvisionnement en Combustible pour les Activités Humanitaires* (PAC). The objective of this programme was to minimise repercussions of the embargo on the health and nutrition of the most vulnerable segments of the Haitian population, by permitting non-profit making organisations to maintain their essential humanitarian activities through a minimal allocation of petroleum.[159]

Whether these efforts amounted to effective monitoring is difficult to ascertain, in the light of the short time-frame during which the sanctions were implemented. That the monitoring was not optimal, is inter alia reflected in the lack of transparency of the workings of the Sanctions Committee.[160] At the same time it would be premature to conclude that the monitoring was insufficient to the point of constituting an act of bad faith on the part of the Security Council. As was already mentioned in connection with the embargo against the FRY, such a conclusion would only

---

[157] SC Res 841 of 16 June 1993, at paras 7(d) and 7(f); SC Res 917 of 6 May 1994, at paras 14(e) and 14(f).
[158] S/26747 (1993). In a Presidential Statement issued two weeks earlier, the Security Council attributed responsibility for the suffering directly to the refusal of the military authorities to comply with the Governors Island Process, see S/26668 (1993). See also Doxey, above n 38, at 18; Reisman & Stevick, above n 1, at 120.
[159] Swindells, above n 141, at 1926; Gibbons, above n 142, at 68.
[160] Another complication resulted from the vague language used to exempt foodstuffs and medical supplies from the embargo in SC Res 917 of 6 May 1994, at para 7(a). Due to protracted consultations between humanitarian agencies and the Sanctions Committee regarding the scope of the exemptions, the latter only finalised guidelines on the matter during July of that year. Meanwhile, shipments into Haiti were delayed or cancelled by wary suppliers. This fate befell a UNICEF ordered shipment of 24,000 vials of measles vaccines. See Gibbons, above n 142, at 26 ff; Swindells, above n 141, at 1932 ff.

be acceptable where it is clear that the Security Council is not effectively addressing core human rights violations flowing from or aggravated by the sanctions regime itself. It is unlikely that the short period of time (nine months) that passed between the introduction of the humanitarian fuel programme and the termination of sanctions in October 1994 facilitated such an assessment. As was mentioned above, it would be more accurate to describe the sanctions regime in Haiti—including the monitoring system—as a borderline case, which would have needed serious adjustment, had it remained in force beyond 1994.

3.4. Summary

The preceding paragraphs have illustrated that the presumption of legality attached to Security Council decisions, as well as the need for an effective collective security system imply that it has considerable discretion in limiting human rights when imposing a mandatory sanctions regime. States claiming the illegality of an economic sanctions regime will have to provide convincing evidence that the sanctions regime in itself caused or aggravated the violation of basic human rights norms of the targeted population. In addition, they will have to prove that the Security Council had either refused to take steps to remedy these violations, or that the steps taken were insufficient. Although a certain passage of time is required to determine the impact of economic sanctions and/ or the impact of any adjustments to the sanctions regime, the case of Haiti has illustrated that a sanctions regime could border on illegality within a relatively short time. It is therefore essential that the Security Council constantly monitors the impact of the sanctions regime on the civilian population.

In all instances where the Security Council has adopted an economic sanctions regime, it has provided for (rudimentary) monitoring by the Sanctions Committee. The fact that the Sanctions Committees (inter alia) have to administer humanitarian exemptions to the economic embargo, does reflect some awareness on its part of the possible disproportionate consequences of economic sanctions. In the light of the presumption of legality attached to Security Council resolutions, this should be regarded as *prima facie* evidence of the Security Council's willingness to comply with its monitoring obligations in good faith. The mere fact that this type of monitoring is inadequate would not suffice to constitute an act of bad faith on the part of the Security Council. It is only in situations such as Iraq, where the monitoring system was clearly unable to prevent the sanctions regime from violating the basic rights of the Iraqi population, that it would be deficient to the point of constituting an act of bad faith by the Security Council.

4.   THE RIGHT TO SELF-DEFENCE AS A LIMITATION TO ECONOMIC
SANCTIONS

The role of the inherent right to self-defence as an outer limit to Security
Council action features in those situations where the Security Council
imposes an arms embargo upon states involved in an inter-state conflict
that involves an armed attack. This became evident during the war in the
former Yugoslavia, when the Security Council adopted an arms embargo
against the country in Resolution 713 of 25 September 1991[161] and maintained it against the entire territory, even though Bosnia-Herzegovina was
admitted to the United Nations as a separate state on 25 May 1992.[162]

In the meantime, the FRY continued to transfer units of the Yugoslav
People's Army (JNA) to the Bosnian Serb forces and to provide material
and logistical support to these forces, (at least) until the sealing of the border between Serbia and Bosnia-Herzegovina in 1994.[163] This continued
forceful intervention by the FRY constituted an armed attack against
Bosnia-Herzegovina,[164] which engaged the right to individual and collective self-defence as recognised by Article 51 of the Charter.[165] In principle,
this entitled Bosnia-Herzegovina to take necessary and proportionate
measures—including the reception of arms and other military aid from
third states—to secure its territorial integrity and political independence.[166]
However, at that time this was not possible, due to the restrictions imposed
in this regard by Resolution 713 (1991) and subsequent resolutions.

---

[161] At para 6.

[162] See eg SC Res 752 of 15 May 1992 and SC Res 757 of 30 May 1992, that explicitly reaffirmed SC Res 713 of 25 September 1991 in their preambles. See also separate opinion of
Judge *ad hoc* Lauterpacht in *Case Concerning Application of the Convention on the Prevention
and Punishment of the Crime of Genocide (Bosnia and Herzegovina v Yugoslavia (Serbia and
Montenegro))*, Further Requests for the Indication of Provisional Measures, ICJ Rep 1993, at
438. Hereinafter referred to as *Bosnia-Herzegovina v Serbia and Montenegro*, provisional
measures II.

[163] As a result, the Security Council demanded that Bosnia-Herzegovina's neighbours immediately cease all forms of interference in Bosnia-Herzegovina and that those units of the JNA
within Bosnia-Herzegovina be withdrawn, placed under the control of the Bosnian
Government, or be disbanded and disarmed. See SC Res 752 of 15 May 1992, at paras 3 ff.
This demand was repeated in SC Res 757 of 30 May 1992, at paras 1 ff. See also Craig Scott *et
al*, "A Memorial for Bosnia: Framework of Legal Arguments Concerning the Lawfulness of
the Maintenance of the United Nations Security Council's Arms Embargo on Bosnia and
Herzegovina", 16 *Michigan Journal of International Law* 20 (1994). They stated that the agreement to close the borders can in itself be interpreted as a recognition by the United Nations
and by Serbia that material support for the Bosnian Serb military had been reaching the
Bosnian Serbs from Serbia despite the arms embargo.

[164] In accordance with the decision concerning *Military and Paramilitary Activities in and
against Nicaragua (Nicaragua v United States of America)*, Merits, ICJ Rep 1986, at 101, it would
(at least) constitute indirect aggression. See also Art 3(g) of GA Res 3314 (XXIX) of
14 December 1974. See ch 4, at s 3.

[165] Scott *et al*, above n 163, at 41–42, 49.

[166] *Ibid*, at 50.

Chapter 7 at section 2.1. elaborates on the fact that the primacy of the Security Council's decisions concerning peace and security implies that they take precedence over the right to self-defence. However, since the inherent right of states to defend themselves against an armed attack is a peremptory norm of international law,[167] this primacy is not unconditional. Instead, it requires the Security Council to adopt measures that are effective or likely to be effective against the armed attack within a reasonable period of time.[168] Stated differently, the balancing of the primacy of the Security Council within the Charter system with the inherent right to self-defence of states results in an obligation on the Security Council to take effective action, if it decides to respond to an armed attack against a member of the United Nations and thereby prevent it from exercising self-defence in a decentralised fashion.[169]

The decision as to whether the measures chosen are or will be effective primarily rests with the Security Council itself, as auto-interpretation by states regarding the adequacy of the measures would vitiate the collective security system contemplated by the Charter.[170] Thus, where the Security Council imposes a mandatory arms embargo on all parties involved in an inter-state conflict, states will not (initially) be able to claim that such an embargo unduly limits their right to individual or collective self-defence. The Security Council may limit the attacked state's right to receive assistance from third states in an effort to prevent the widening or aggravation of the conflict.[171]

However, if it becomes clear that the embargo has a severely unequal effect which is significantly weakening the position of the attacked state in maintaining its territorial and political integrity, the Security Council would be obliged to amend the embargo.[172] This point had arguably been reached in Bosnia-Herzegovina by the time it initiated legal proceedings against the FRY in 1993, under Chapter IX of the Convention on the Prevention and Punishment of the Crime of Genocide of 1948.[173] The situation in the country was aggravated by the fact that the arms embargo had also lead to a situation where it was unable to defend itself sufficiently against the Serbian policy of "ethnic cleansing". Viewed in this light, the arms embargo had the effect that members of the United Nations tolerated,

---

[167] Gill, above n 33, at 102.
[168] *Ibid*, at 103; Scott *et al*, above n 163, at 57.
[169] Gill, above n 33, at 103; Scott *et al*, above n 163, at 61, 68.
[170] As explained below in (the text leading up to) fn 179 ff.
[171] Gill, above n 33, at 103; see also Bernd Martenczuk, *Rechtsbinudng und Rechtskontrolle des Weltsicherheitsrats* 268 (Duncker & Humblot, Berlin, 1996).
[172] Scott *et al*, above n 163, at 57. Cf Barbara Lorinser, *Bindende Resolutionen des Sicherheitsrates* 56 (Baden-Baden, Nomos, 1996), who submitted that the Security Council may not actively contribute to the demise of a state.
[173] See ch 1, at s 3.

to some degree, the genocidal activity of the Serbs and in this manner contribute to the violation of a *ius cogens* norm.[174]

Resolution 713 (1991) thus arguably lead to the violation of two *ius cogens* norms, as the inability of Bosnia-Herzegovina to defend itself ultimately contributed to the genocide of a part of its population.[175] In spite of this situation, the Security Council lacked the political will to lift the arms embargo against Bosnia-Herzegovina, or adopt extensive military measures to protect its population.[176] This remained the case until the adoption of Resolution 1031 of 15 December 1995, which authorised IFOR to use force in implementing its obligations under the Dayton Accords in Bosnia-Herzegovina.[177] The Security Council eventually provided for a lifting of the arms embargo in Resolution 1074 (1996).[178]

5.   CONCLUSION

The controversies surrounding the arms embargo against former Yugoslavia and certain protracted economic embargoes such as the sanctions regime

---

[174] Separate opinion of Judge Lachs in *Bosnia-Herzegovina v Serbia and Montenegro*, provisional measures II, above n 162, at 439 ff; see the preamble of GA Res 47/121 of 18 December 1992. The General Assembly cited with approval the findings of the United Nations Commission on Human Rights Special Rapporteur, stating that the marked imbalance between the weaponry in the hands of the Serbian and the Muslim population of Bosnia-Herzegovina in areas under Serbian control was a contributing factor in the intensity of the ethnic cleansing. See also Scott *et al*, above n 163, at 14–15; Kulessa, aboven n 24 at 91–92; Ken Roberts, "Second-Guessing the Security Council: the International Court of Justice and its Powers of Judicial Review", 7 *Pace International Law Review* 311 (1995).

[175] However, in order to hold the Security Council responsible for (being an accomplice to) genocide, one would have to prove that it had the intent to do so. In the case of SC Res 713 of 25 September 1991, this would be extremely difficult, especially in the light of the presumption of legality attached to Security Council resolutions. The mere fact that that the arms embargo contributed to genocide would not suffice to prove intent. See extensively Starck, above n 15, at 370 ff. The leading judgments of the International Criminal Tribunal for the Former Yugoslavia (ICTY) and the International Criminal Tribunal for Rwanda (ICTR) on genocide include *Prosecutor v Goran Jelesic*, Judgment, Case No IT–95–10–A, 5 July 2001, Appeals Chamber; *Prosecutor v Jean Paul Akayeshu*, Judgment, Case No ICTR–96–4, 1 June 2001, Appeals Chamber; *Prosecutor v Clément Kayishema and Obed Ruzindana*, Judgment, Case No ICTR–95–1–A, 1 June 2001, Appeals Chamber. These decisions are available at www.icty.org and www.ictr.org, respectively.

[176] An initiative by six Security Council members on 29 June 1993 to lift the arms embargo against Bosnia-Herzegovina failed, due to the abstaining vote of the other nine members. Para 3 of the rejected resolution determined that the Security Council "decide(d) to exempt the Government of the Republic of Bosnia and Herzegovina from the arms embargo imposed on former Yugoslavia by its resolution 713 (1991) with the sole purpose of enabling the Republic of Bosnia and Herzegovina to exercise its inherent right to self-defence…". The text of the draft resolution can be found in S/25997 (1993). See also S/PV 3247 148 (1993); separate opinion of Judge *ad hoc* Lauterpacht, in *Bosnia-Herzegovina v Serbia and Montenegro*, provisional measures II, above n 162, at 438.

[177] At para 14.

[178] At para 2.

against Iraq underline the risks inherent in embargoes which are adopted for an indefinite period. In both instances the absence of a time limit to the embargoes directly contributed to their becoming illegal over time. This is mainly due to the combined effect of two characteristics of the procedures by means of which sanctions are imposed.

The first is that as a general rule, member states do not have the power to terminate binding enforcement measures imposed under Chapter VII of the Charter on their own accord.[179] This follows from the principle of the "parallelism of competence", which is a general principle of administrative law. It determines that when a constitution invests a certain decision-making competence in a given organ, without expressly stipulating how such a decision may be revoked, the power of revocation lies with the same organ.[180] If one applies this principle to the Charter, it would mean that only the Security Council can terminate enforcement measures under Chapter VII, since the Charter does not provide any other procedure for doing so.[181] Furthermore, if member states had a general right to determine for themselves whether the aim of the enforcement measures had been achieved, they would most likely come to very different conclusions depending on their geo-political interests. This would lead to major legal uncertainty which would undermine the effective functioning of the United Nations collective security system.[182]

Second, the Security Council is not obliged to determine when and how sanctions will end when adopting them and in practice they are often adopted without a particular time limit attached to them.[183] This means that a separate Security Council decision is needed to terminate economic sanctions which will also have to be taken under Chapter VII. This follows from the principle of the "parallelism of forms", which is well established

---

[179] For exceptions to this rule, see extensively ch 10 at s 3.

[180] See Eric Suy, "Some Legal Questions Concerning the Security Council", in Ingo von Münch (ed), *Festschrift für Hans-Jürgen Schlochauer zum 75. Geburtstag* 684 (Walter de Gruyter, Berlin, 1981). See also David D Caron, "The Legitimacy of the Collective Authority of the Security Council", 87 *American Journal of American Law* 578 (1993); Hurst, above n 1, at 253; Kreczko, above n 1, at 104; Brigitte Reschke, "Der aktuelle Fall: Die Aufhebung der Sanktionen gegen Haiti", 3 *Humanitäres Völkerrecht* 136 (1994).

[181] See Reschke, above n 180, at 136.

[182] This reasoning was also reflected in the reaction of the General Assembly and the Security Council to the United Kingdoms" unilateral termination of the mandatory sanctions against Southern Rhodesia on 12 December 1979 (S/13688 (1979). The General Assembly responded by adopting GA Res 192 of 18 December 1979, which affirmed that it was within the exclusive authority of the Security Council to revoke mandatory sanctions imposed by that organ and that a unilateral termination of sanctions violated states" obligation under Art 25 of the Charter. The Security Council, for its part, still considered it necessary to terminate sanctions in SC Res 460 of 21 December 1979 See also Reschke, above n 180, at 136–37; Suy, above n 180, at 685–86.

[183] See Reschke, above n 180, at 136.

in the Charter system.[184] This is problematic to the extent that a Chapter VII resolution can only be adopted if there is consensus amongst the five permanent members to this effect. As a result, the termination of the embargo can be blocked by the "reverse veto" of a permanent member.

The preferred solution to this dilemma would be for the Security Council to subject its sanctions regimes to a time limit. Since the Security Council would then need an additional Chapter VII decision to extend the sanctions regime—as opposed to terminating it—there is less chance that a sanctions regime which violates basic human rights or the right to self-defence, as the case may be, would be perpetuated.[185] Recently, the Security Council has shown itself willing to follow this approach when it limited the ban on the import of rough diamonds from Sierra Leone to 18 months,[186] whilst a similar ban on rough diamonds from Liberia was subjected to a limitation of 12 months.[187] The Security Council has also started to follow this approach with respect to arms embargoes. It did so for the first time in Resolution 1298 of 17 May 2000, which subjected the arms embargo against Eritrea and Ethiopia to a time-limit of 12 months.[188] Similarly, the arms embargo adopted against the Taliban in Resolution 1333 of 19 December 2000 was limited to a period of 12 months,[189] whereas Resolution 1343 of 7 March 2001 subjected the arms embargo against Liberia to a limitation of 14 months.[190]

A different point of concern, particularly in the context of broad economic embargoes, is the inadequate monitoring of sanctions regimes.

---

[184] This principle, which normally supplements the rule of the "parallelism of competencies", determines that the same type of act by the same organ is required to revoke the decision that had been taken. The Security Council has, since 1990, consistently terminated its enforcement measures by means of Chapter VII resolutions. In fact, SC Res 460 of 21 December 1979, which terminated the sanctions against Southern Rhodesia, constituted the only instance in which the terminating resolution was not explicitly adopted under Chapter VII of the Charter.

[185] Eitel, above n 65, at 66; See also Lutz Oette "A Decade of Sanctions against Iraq: Never Again! The End of Unlimited Sanctions in the Recent Practice of the UN Security Council", 13 *European Journal of International Law* 97 (2002). At 101–02 he noted that some countries fear that time limits would undermine the effectiveness of sanctions. According to this argument, the limitation of the duration of sanctions might encourage the target to endure short-term damage and attempt to prevent the renewal of sanctions at the end of the period, without having complied with the demands of the Security Council. (For arguments to this effect, see the statements of the United States and the Netherlands in S/PV.4168 5 ff (2002). However, in the absence of time limits, members of the Security Council may not be willing to vote for the initial imposition of sanctions at all. In addition, the inclusion of a time limit does not, of itself, create a presumption against the renewal of sanctions.

[186] SC Res 1306 of 5 July 2000, at para 6.

[187] SC Res 1342 of 7 March 2001, at paras 6 and 10.

[188] At paras 6 and 16.

[189] At paras 23–24.

[190] At para 9. This embargo was extended for an additional 12 months in SC Res 1408 of 6 May 2002, at para 5.

Even though deficiencies in the monitoring of the impact of such an embargo on the human rights of the civilian population would not in and of itself have any (immediate) legal consequences, it severely undermines the political legitimacy of the sanctions regime. The lack of transparency in the decision-making process of the Sanctions Committees combined with the fact that they rarely give reasons for their decisions, creates the impression that the Security Council is insulated from accountability and is indifferent towards human rights.[191] The situation is aggravated by a lack of continuity within the different Sanctions Committees. These committees, which have all been established on an *ad hoc* basis, draw their representatives from the permanent missions in New York that are subjected to constant personnel change. In addition, five new permanent members take their seats on the Security Council every year.[192] This lack of continuity frustrates attempts to develop a coherent human rights policy within and amongst the different Sanctions Committees. The net result is a perception of inconsistency towards human rights monitoring which, in turn, creates the image of a Security Council that is indifferent towards the human rights of the very population that it claims to protect.

For these reasons the Security Council has much to gain from replacing the current sanctions monitoring system by a single, permanent body that is responsible for planning and monitoring sanctions.[193] This monitoring system should review the human rights implications of economic embargoes on a regular basis, with particular emphasis on its impact on vulnerable groups. In addition, it should introduce some form of transparency into the sanctions monitoring system by, for example, providing detailed reports to the Secretary-General and the General Assembly.[194] In this context one should mention that since 1999 the Security Council's report to the General Assembly includes a report of the work of each Sanctions Committee.[195] Although these are modest measures that cannot substitute a complete overhaul of the current sanctions monitoring system, they do reflect a greater awareness of the need for a transparent and human rights oriented monitoring system and are therefore to be welcomed.

A permanent monitoring body that is involved in the planning and administering of sanctions from the outset may also enhance the effective

---

[191] Scharf & Dorosin, above n 85, at 823; see also Doxey, above n 38, at 44; Burci, above n 88, at 145; Starck, above n 15, at 90 ff.

[192] Doxey, above n 38, at 41. See also Eitel, above n 65, at 68. Cf Mariano J Aznar-Gómez, "A Decade of Human Rights Protection by the UN Security Council: a Sketch of Deregulation?", 13 *European Journal of International Law* 229 (2002).

[193] Doxey, above n 38, at 40.

[194] Gasser, above n 24, at 903.

[195] The Security Council suggested these reports as a method for making the work of the Sanctions Committees more transparent in S/1995/234, at para 1. In S/1996/54, at para 1, the Security Council also encouraged the Chairperson of each Sanctions Committee to give an oral briefing to interested member states after each meeting. See also Doxey, above n 38, at 45.

targeting of sanctions. The potential disproportionate impact of sanctions is often related to the fact that the type of sanctions chosen by the Security Council is more likely to harm the civilian population than those entities responsible for the threat to international peace. The sanctions regimes against Iraq and Haiti are clear examples of situations where the aim of bringing about political change by means of economic pressure were thwarted by regimes that insulated themselves from the impact of the sanctions at the expense of the civilian population. Had the type of measures that the Security Council resorted to been more carefully targeted from the outset, these results might have been avoided.

In some instances the Security Council has indeed adopted more carefully tailored measures. For example, after UNITA failed to accept the result of the 1991 elections in Angola, the Security Council did not impose sanctions on the country as a whole. Instead, it adopted an arms embargo and a ban on oil sales against UNITA;[196] restricted the travelling of its senior members; banned UNITA flights and the insuring and servicing of UNITA aircraft;[197] froze UNITA funds within other countries;[198] and banned the import of diamonds and the provision of mining services to areas which are not under the control of the Angolan government.[199] Such more carefully targeted measures combined with subsequent monitoring of their impact on the civilian population could both enhance the efficiency of sanctions as a tool for political pressure, as well as reduce the risk of limiting the basic rights of the civilian population in an illegal fashion.

At the same time, however, one should bear in mind that the tailoring of sanctions are not an automatic guarantee that the basic rights of individuals will not be disproportionately limited. This is illustrated by Resolution 1333 of 19 December 2000 and Resolution 1390 of 16 January 2002, which authorised the freezing of assets of *Usama bin Ladin* and individuals and undertakings "associated" with him and the *Al-Quaida* movement.[200] These resolutions further authorised the relevant Sanctions Committee to maintain an updated list, based on information received from member states and regional organisations, of the individuals and undertakings

---

[196] SC Res 864 of 15 September 1993, at para 19.
[197] SC Res 1127 of 28 August 1997, at para 4.
[198] SC Res 1173 of 12 June 1998, at para 11.
[199] SC Res 1173 of 12 June 1998, at para 12. A similar measure was adopted against the Revolutionary United Front in Sierra Leone in SC Res 1306 of 5 July 2000. Earlier, SC Res 1171 of 5 June 1998 adopted an arms embargo and travel restrictions against the rebel forces in Sierra Leone. See also Doxey, above n 38, at 28.
[200] SC Res 1333 of 19 December 2000, at para 8(c) and SC Res 1390 of 16 January 2002, at para 2(a).

designated as being "associated" with *Usama bin Ladin* and the *Al-Quaida* organisation.[201]

Chapter 9 at section 2.3. will illuminate that the targeting of individuals and undertakings in such a broad and vague fashion entails the risk of a violation of the basic right to a fair hearing of those concerned. It is therefore essential that in each situation in which the Security Council imposes a sanctions regime, it carefully considers the type of human rights that may be disproportionately affected in the process and provides for a mechanism that would prevent this from happening.

In summary, the Security Council should develop a consistent practice of subjecting economic sanctions to (renewable) time limits. This type of self-restraint combined with better targeting and monitoring of sanctions would significantly strengthen the efficiency and legitimacy of collective enforcement measures, whilst simultaneously reducing the risk that they violate the basic rights of the affected population. Although recent Security Council practice reflects some steps in this direction, it is premature to talk of the emergence of a more human rights oriented sanctions policy. This is reflected, inter alia, in some of the resolutions adopted by the Security Council in response to international terrorism, such as Resolution 1333 (2000) and 1390 (2002).

Finally, it is important to emphasise that the mere exercise of the "reverse veto" against the termination of an economic embargo is not in itself illegal. Such an interpretation would negate the fact that the rule of "parallelism of forms" (of which the "reverse veto" is a logical if not necessarily welcome consequence), is well established within the United Nations. This conclusion may seem to contradict that of chapter 7, that examines the legality of the delegation of military enforcement measures by the Security Council to member states. There it is argued that the delegated mandate becomes illegal when its termination is prevented by the "reverse veto" of a single permanent member. However, that argument is closely related to the fact that the Security Council action involves a *delegation* of enforcement measures, which should have been exercised by the Security Council itself. The following chapter will illustrate that such a delegation of powers that are centralised with the Security Council under the Charter structure justifies an *exception* to the rule of "parallelism of forms", to the extent that the termination of the delegated powers will not necessarily be prevented by the "reverse veto".

---

[201] SC Res 1333 of 19 December 2000, at para 8(c) and SC Res 1390 of 16 January 2002, at para 5(a).

7

Limits to the Security Council's Discretion to Authorise States and Regional Organisations to Use Force

1. INTRODUCTION

ACCORDING TO ARTICLE 43 and 47 of the Charter, the Security Council is responsible for the implementation of military measures provided for in Article 42 of the Charter. Article 43(1) of the Charter intended member states to make armed forces available to the Security Council on its call, whereas Article 47 intended for the Military Staff Committee, consisting of the Chiefs of Staff of the five permanent members of the Security Council or their representatives, to assist the Security Council with respect to the employment and command of such forces.[1] In practice, however, these intentions did not materialise, as Article 43(1) subjects any obligation to make forces available to the Security Council to a voluntary agreement between the latter and member states.[2] The qualification in Article 43(2) that the agreement(s) shall be negotiated "as soon as possible" reflects that their actual conclusion are contingent on political circumstances. This is also reflected in Article 43(3), that explicitly subjects the agreement to ratification by the national parliaments of the signatory states. In the absence of such an agreement, no state can be forced to provide military troops against its will.[3]

---

[1] See also Heike Gading, *Der Schutz grundlegender Menschenrechte durch militärische Massnahmen des Sicherheitsrates—das Ende staatlicher Souveränität?* 24 (Berlin, Duncker & Humblot, 1996).

[2] Nigel D White & Özlem Ülgen, "The Security Council and the Decentralized Military Option: Constitutionality and Function", 44 *Netherlands International Law Review* 385 (1997).

[3] Art 43(3) was included to counter the fears of the Americans that their forces might be forced to participate in military measures without the express consent of Congress. This would have prevented them from joining the United Nations. Gading, above n 1, at 24 ff; Christian Walter, *Vereinte Nationen und Regionalorganisationen* 270 (Berlin, Springer, 1996).

Since no such agreement has materialised unto this day,[4] the United Nations was forced to look for alternative ways to implement military enforcement measures. It found a solution in the authorisation of "willing and able" states or regional organisations to execute military measures on its behalf. The authorisation model—which could also be described as a model of delegated enforcement[5]—was used for the first time during the Korean war in 1950. Due to the absence of the Soviet Union in protest against Taiwan's membership in the United Nations, the Security Council was able to determine that a breach of the peace had occurred and recommended the United Nations member states to make such forces and other assistance available to a unified command under the USA.[6] The return of the Soviet Union to the Security Council prevented it from further use of this instrument. The only exception was Resolution 221 of 9 April 1966 which was adopted against Southern Rhodesia.[7] It is only since 1990 that this model has been reinvented, in particular since Resolution 678 of 29 November 1990. This resolution authorised member states cooperating with the Government of Kuwait to use all necessary means to uphold and implement the Resolution 660 of 2 August 1990, and all subsequent relevant resolutions and to restore international peace and security in the area.[8]

The following chapter focuses on whether the Security Council has the legal authority to authorise such action and, if so, to what extent. It does so by drawing a distinction between the authorisation of states, on the one hand, and regional (defence) organisations, on the other, to engage in military action. In both instances it follows the same methodology. It first identifies the Charter requirements for such an authorisation and then applies them to the Security Council practice. When analysing the authorisations to states to engage in military action, special attention is paid to the controversial military mandates, namely the (alleged) authorisations to use force in Iraq and Korea. Similarly, when examining the authorisations to regional organisations to engage in military action, the (questionable)

---

[4] On 30 April 1947 the Military Staff Committee presented a document of 41 Articles of which 25 were accepted by all the members of the Military Staff Committee. The remaining differences related to technical issues which played an important role in the consequent escalating political conflict between the Soviet Union and the United States. See "General Principles Governing the Organisation of the Armed Forces Made Available to the Security Council by Member Nations of the United Nations", *United Nations Yearbook* 424–43 (1946–47); See also Gading, above n 1, at 25.

[5] Niels M Blokker, "Is the Authorisation Authorised? Powers and Practice of the United Nations Security Council to Authorise the Use of Force by Coalitions of the 'Able and Willing'", 11 *European Journal of International Law* 542 (2000).

[6] SC Res 82 of 25 June 1950; Blokker (Authorisation), above n 5, at 543.

[7] Blokker (Authorisation), above n 5, at 543.

[8] John Quigley, "The United Nations Security Council: Promethean Protector or Helpless Hostage?", 35 *Texas International Law Journal* 157 (2000).

legality of the military action of the Economic Community in West Africa (ECOWAS) in Liberia and Sierra Leone, respectively, and of the North Atlantic Treaty Organisation (NATO) in Kosovo forms a focal point.

The chapter does not focus on the legality of military intervention against a state *outside* the provisions of the Charter. For example, it does not engage in an analysis of the legality of a military intervention on humanitarian grounds in the absence of a Security Council mandate.[9] Instead, it departs from the premise that the central role of the Security Council with respect to the use of force combined with the highly inconsistent nature of state practice regarding so-called humanitarian intervention, renders claims that such a right would exist highly questionable at this point in time.[10] In essence therefore the question whether and/ or to what extent the Security Council can delegate its military enforcement powers to states and regional (defence) organisations is central to this Chapter.

Before commencing with the analysis, it has to be clarified that the terms "authorisation" and "delegation" are treated as synonymous, as both will refer to the transfer of power by the Security Council to (a) member state(s), or a regional (defence) organisation. At first glance it does seem to be more accurate to speak of a "delegation" when an organ of the United Nations transfers one of its own powers to another entity. This follows from the advisory opinion of the ICJ regarding the *Application for*

---

[9] Humanitarian intervention has to be distinguished from an intervention on invitation by the legitimate government, which will be referred to below, at s 5.1. and s 5.2. For a discussion of humanitarian intervention see, inter alia, Martha Brenfors & Malene Maxe Petersen, "The Legality of Unilateral Humanitarian Intervention—A Defence", 69 *Nordic Journal of International Law* 449 ff (2000); Ian Brownlie & CJ Apperley, "Kosovo Crisis Inquiry: Memorandum on the International Law Aspects", 49 *International and Comparative Law Quarterly* 878 ff (2000); Antonio Cassese, "Ex iniuria ius oritur": Are We Moving towards International Legitimation of Forcible Humanitarian Countermeasures in the World Community?", 10 *European Journal of International Law* 23 ff (1999); Bruno Simma, "NATO, the UN and the Use of Force: Legal Aspects", *ibid*, at 1 ff; Jonathan I Charney, "Anticipatory Humanitarian Intervention in Kosovo", 93 *American Journal of International Law* 835 ff (1999); Louis Henkin, "Kosovo and the law of Humanitarian Intervention", *ibid*, at 824 ff; Ruth Wedgewood, "NATO's Campaign in Yugoslavia", *ibid*, at 828 ff; Christine M Chinkin, "Kosovo, a 'Good' or 'Bad' War?", *ibid*, at 841 ff; *ibid*, "The Legality of NATO's Action in the Former Republic of Yugoslavia (FRY) under International Law", 49 *International and Comparative Law Quarterly* 910 ff (2000); Christopher Greenwood, "International Law and the NATO Intervention in Kosovo", *ibid*, at 926 ff; Walter Kälin, "Humanitäre Intervention: Legitimation durch Verfahren? Zehn Thesen zur Kosovo-Krise", 10 *Schweizerische Zeitschrift für internationales und europäisches Recht* 157 ff (2000); Daniel Thürer, "Der Kosovo-Konflikt im Lichte des Völkerrechts: Von drei—echten und scheinbaren—Dilemmata", *Archiv des Völkerrechts* 38 ff (2000).

[10] See also Michael Bothe, "Die NATO nach dem Kosovo-Konflikt und das Völkerrecht", 10 *Schweizerische Zeitschrift für internationales und europäisches Recht* 182 (2000); Cassese, above n 9, at 26; Kälin, above n 9, at 168; Simma, above n 9, at 6; Thürer, above n 9, at 38. See also Yoram Dinstein, "Humanitarian Intervention from Outside, in the face of Genocide, is Legitimate only when Undertaken by the Security Council", in 27 *Justice* 5–6 (2001).

Review of Judgement No 158 of the United Nations Administrative Tribunal[11] (hereinafter the *Application for Review* opinion). The ICJ had to opine on whether the United Nations Committee on Applications for Review of Administrative Tribunal Judgements had the competence to request advisory opinions of the ICJ. This Committee was a United Nations subsidiary organ established by the General Assembly to review decisions of the United Nations Administrative Tribunal (UNAT).[12]

In determining whether the Committee has the power to request an advisory opinion, the ICJ determined that this was not an instance where the General Assembly delegated its own powers to request an advisory opinion from the ICJ in terms of Article 96(1) of the Charter. This was not possible, as the Committee was performing a function that the General Assembly could not, ie the reviewing of decisions of the Administrative Tribunal.[13] Instead the General Assembly endowed a subsidiary organ, created for a particular task, with the powers to request advisory opinions in the performance of that task. This the General Assembly could do in terms of Article 96(2) of the Charter. Consequently, the ICJ found that the Committee was "duly authorised" under Article 96(2) of the Charter to request advisory opinions of the ICJ.[14]

From this statement of the ICJ one can conclude that the term "delegation" should be reserved for situations where a United Nations organ such as the Security Council empowers another entity such as a subsidiary organ or member states to exercise one of its own functions. The term authorisation, on the other hand, should be reserved for situations where the organ creates subsidiary organs and "authorises" them to perform functions which it may not perform itself, but which it may nonetheless authorise under the Charter.[15] This would apply, for example, to the creation of the two *ad hoc* war crimes tribunals, ie the International Criminal Tribunal for the former Yugoslavia (ICTY) and the International Criminal Tribunal for Rwanda (ICTR).[16]

At the same time one has to bear in mind that the Security Council itself resorts to the term "authorisation" when transferring its power to

---

[11] ICJ Rep 1973, at 166.
[12] See also Danesh Sarooshi, *The United Nations and the Development of Collective Security* 12 (Oxford, Oxford University Press, 1999).
[13] *Application for Review* opinion, above n 11, at 174; see also Sarooshi, above n 12, at 12.
[14] *Application for Review* opinion, above n 11, at 174–75.
[15] See Sarooshi, above n 12, at 12. He regarded the *Application for Review* opinion, above n 11, as support for the conclusion that an authorisation is more limited than a delegation regarding its objective and with respect to the nature of the powers transferred. This would follow from the fact that the General Assembly's powers under Art 96(1) of the Charter is much broader than the authorisation given to the Committee to request advisory opinions in term of Art 96(2) of the Charter. Whereas the General Assembly has the power to request an advisory opinion of the ICJ on any legal question, the Committee can only request an advisory opinion on legal questions arising within the scope of its activities.
[16] The legality of the creation of ICTY and ICTR is discussed in ch 9 at s 2.1.

engage in military operations to member states. Therefore the term "authorisation" can be regarded as synonymous with the delegation of powers, at least as far as it concerns the transferral of the Security Council's military power to member states or regional organisations.[17] Moreover, as will be illustrated below, the legality of the transferral of Security Council powers will ultimately not depend on the formal description of the transferred power as an "authorisation" as opposed to a "delegation". Instead, it will be determined by the nature of the power at stake and whether the ultimate control over the exercise of the power remains with the Security Council.

2.   AUTHORISING INDIVIDUAL STATES TO ENGAGE IN MILITARY ENFORCEMENT OPERATIONS

2.1.   Legal Basis for the Mandate

Article 43 of the Charter does not give an answer to the question whether the Security Council can authorise member states or groups of member states to execute military measures on its behalf where they are willing to do so. This Article only regulates the extent to which member states are *obliged* to participate in military operations of the United Nations. It does not deal with the issue whether the Security Council can authorise *consenting* states to undertake military measures on its behalf. Stated differently, Article 43 cannot be interpreted as implying that the Security Council is prevented from deploying any troops if and as long as no agreement in terms of Article 43(1) exists.[18]

An answer to whether the Security Council can authorise consenting states to engage in military operations on its behalf can be found in Article 42 of the Charter. The prevailing opinion is that the existence of an Article 43 agreement is not a pre-requisite for the Security Council to resort to Article 42 of the Charter, as this would severely limit the discretion of the Security Council under this Article.[19] Consequently, Article 42 implies that the Security Council can authorise member states to undertake military measures for the restoration or maintenance of international

---

[17] See also Sarooshi, above n 12, at 13, who submits that although the Security Council is using the term "authorisation", it is in fact delegating its Chapter VII powers to members.
[18] As is argued by Bernhard Graefrath, "Die Vereinten Nationen im Übergang—Die Gratwanderung des Sicherheitsrates zwischen Rechtsanwendung und Rechtsanmassung", *Die Reform der Vereinten Nationen* 45 (Opladen, Leske & Budrich, 1994). Cf Quigley, above n 8, at 160.
[19] Niels M Blokker, "Grenzen aan de macht(iging)?", 33 *Nederlands Juristenblad* 1551 (1997); Gading, above n 1, at 26; Sarooshi, above n 12, at 144; White & Ülgen, above n 2, at 386.

peace and security, where they are willing to do so.[20] This argument gains strength if one reads Article 42 in conjunction with Article 48(1) of the Charter.[21] The latter concretises states' obligation to carry out binding measures of the Security Council, in that it provides the latter with a discretion to determine who will participate in enforcement action.[22] If one regards Article 48(1) as an extension of Article 25, it would provide the Security Council with the formal possibility to determine that the action required for the execution of Security Council decisions is undertaken by all or only some United Nations members. This would complement the material basis for authorising member states to undertake military measures on behalf of the Security Council, provided in Article 42.[23]

A further possible basis for such authority could be found in Article 106 of the Charter.[24] It determines that in order to enable the Security Council to exercise its responsibilities under Article 42—pending the coming into force of the Article 43 agreement(s)—the five permanent members shall consult with each other on joint action on behalf of the United Nations, as may be necessary for maintaining international peace and security. Although this Article has fallen into disuse and is by now regarded as obsolete,[25] it does lend support to the notion that the Charter foresees that the need for military action may arise before any Article 43(1) agreement has been concluded.

One should point out that Articles 42 and 48(1) do not enable the Security Council to force members to contribute troops for military operations. If one reads these Articles together with Article 2(5) of the Charter, it can seem as if Chapter VII measures of the Security Council can oblige

---

[20] See also Jochen A Frowein, "Article 42", in Bruno Simma (ed), *The Charter of the United Nations* 633 (Oxford, Oxford University Press, 1994). He found support for this view in the *Certain Expenses of the United Nations*, Advisory Opinion, ICJ Rep 1962, at 167. Hereinafter referred to as *Certain Expenses* opinion. The ICJ rejected the notion that the Security Council could not take action in a situation threatening the peace, in the absence of an Art 43 agreement. However, one should bear in mind that this opinion was given in relation to peacekeeping measures which were taken under Chapter VI of the Charter. It does not give any direct answer to the question whether the Security Council can authorise the armed forces of a member state to undertake military measures under Art 42 of the Charter.

[21] Art 48(1) of the Charter reads as follows: "The action required to carry out the decisions of the Security Council for the maintenance of international peace and security shall be taken by all the Members of the United Nations or by some of them, as the Security Council may determine."

[22] Gading, above n 1, at 26–27.

[23] Blokker (Grenzen), above n 19, at 1551; see also Matthias Herdegen, *Die Befugnisse des UN-Sicherheitsrates: aufgeklärter Absolitismus im Völkerrecht?* 3 (Heidelberg, Müller, 1998).

[24] Albrecht Randelzhofer, "Article 2(4)", in Bruno Simma (ed), *The Charter of the United Nations* 120 (Oxford, Oxford University Press, 1994).

[25] Rudolf Geiger, "Art 106", in Bruno Simma (ed) *The Charter of the United Nations. A Commentary* 1151 (Oxford, Oxford University Press, 1994).

states to provide positive assistance, including making troops available.[26] However, a systematic interpretation of the Charter does not lead to this result. Article 43 makes the conclusion of the agreement(s) mentioned therein a pre-condition for obliging states to provide troops. Consequently, Article 2(5) in combination with Articles 42 and 48(1) cannot lay down a more far-reaching requirement of positive assistance, as this would undermine the purpose and meaning of Article 43.[27]

Some authors argue that the Security Council can also authorise states to use force on the basis of the right to self-defence contained in Article 51 of the Charter,[28] as this Article is also located in Chapter VII.[29] This argument is not convincing, as Article 51 is not intended to be used by the Security Council itself, but rather by states (either individually or collectively) when falling victim to an armed attack, *pending* Security Council action.[30] As a result, a state facing an armed attack can defend itself with the support of other states so inclined, without prior request or authorisation by the Security Council.[31] In such a situation the defending states are bound by the principles of necessity and proportionality and may only undertake measures necessary to repel the armed attack.[32]

Once the Security Council authorises the use of force it does so on the basis of Articles 42 and 48(1). This relates to the fact that its primary responsibility to maintain international peace and security allows it to adopt measures which extend beyond what is permitted in terms of

[26] Art 2(5) of the Charter reads as follows: "All Members shall give the United Nations every assistance in any action it takes in accordance with the present Charter, and shall refrain from giving assistance to any state against which the United Nations is taking preventive or enforcement action." See also Jochen A Frowein, "Article 2(5)", in Bruno Simma (ed), *The Charter of the United Nations. A Commentary* 130 (Oxford, Oxford University Press, 1994).

[27] Frowein (Article 2(5)), above n 26, at 130.

[28] The first sentence of Art 51 of the Charter reads as follows: "Nothing in the present Charter shall impair the inherent right of individual or collective self-defence if an armed attack occurs against a Member of the United Nations, until the Security Council has taken measures necessary to maintain international peace and security... ."

[29] TD Gill, "Legal and Some Political Limitations on the Power of the UN Security Council to Exercise its Enforcement Powers under Chapter VII of the Charter", 26 *Netherlands Yearbook of International Law* 92 (1995).

[30] Quigley, above n 8, at 144; Burns H Weston, "Security Council Resolution 678 and Persian Gulf Decision Making: Precarious Legitimacy", 85 *American Journal of International Law* 520 (1991). See also Nico Schrijver, "Responding to International Terrorism: Moving the Frontiers of International Law for 'Enduring Freedom?'", in 48 *Netherlands International Law Review* 281 (2001).

[31] Hans Kelsen, "Collective Security and Collective Self-Defence under the Charter of the United Nations", in 42 *American Journal of International Law* 792 (1948); Markus Krajewski, "Selbstverteidigung gegen bewaffnete Angriffe nicht-staatlicher Organisationen—Der 11 September 2001 und seine Folgen", in 40 *Archiv des Völkerrechts* 211–12 (2002).

[32] See *Military and Paramilitary Activities in and against Nicaragua (Nicaragua v United States of America)*, Merits, Judgement, ICJ Rep 1986, at 94. Hereinafter referred to as *Nicaragua v United States*, merits. See also Antonio Cassese, *International Law* 305 (Oxford, Oxford University Press, 2001); Keith Harper, "Does the United Nations Security Council have the Competence to Act as a Court and Legislature?", in 27 *New York University Journal of International Law and Politics* 113–14 (1994); see also Gill, above n 29, at 93–94.

self-defence. Not only can it authorise military measures in a situation which does not yet constitute an armed attack, but it could also combine military measures with extensive sanctions, in order to restore or maintain international peace.[33] In addition, states are obliged in terms of Article 2(5) of the Charter to give the Security Council every assistance in any action it takes in accordance with the present Charter. This obligation is conditioned by the existence of preventive or enforcement action in terms of Article 41 or 42.[34] The purpose of these broad powers and obligations are to enable the Security Council to fulfil its responsibility for maintenance peace and security effectively. As it would not be able to do so when acting under the more limited scope of Article 51 of the Charter, it would in effect undermine its own purpose if attempting to authorise the use of force on the basis of that Article.

The word "until" in Article 51 does not necessarily imply an automatic suspension of the exercise of the right to self-defence, once the Security Council has adopted a resolution. For example, a resolution merely calling on an aggressor to withdraw would still allow the victim state to defend itself militarily, as anything else would be severely detrimental to it if the aggressor ignored the Security Council's call.[35] Moreover, the right to self-defence could also continue to be exercised when the response of the Security Council to an armed attack does not include an authorisation to use force and also does not call for a cease-fire, or demand a cessation of military action by all parties involved.[36] In the case of Iraq, for example, the Security Council explicitly affirmed Kuwait's inherent right of individual or collective self-defence, when it adopted economic sanctions in Resolution 661 of 6 August 1990.[37]

Similarly, in the wake of the terrorist attacks in the United States on 11 September 2001, the Security Council explicitly recognised the inherent right of individual or collective self-defence, but refrained from authorising military measures to restore or maintain international peace and security.[38] Several weeks after the adoption of this resolution, the

---

[33] See ch 5, at s 2.

[34] See also Frowein (Article 42), above n 20, at 635.

[35] During the Falkland Island crisis in 1982, the United Kingdom also argued that the right of self-defence under Art 51 continued after SC Res 502 of 1982 had demanded the immediate withdrawal of all Argentine forces from the Falkland Islands. See Letter from the Permanent Representative of the United Kingdom to the President of the Security Council, S/15016 (1982). Roger K Smith, "The legality of coercive arms control", 19 *Yale Journal of International Law* 497 (1994); see also Craig Scott *et al*, "A Memorial for Bosnia: Framework of Legal Arguments Concerning the Lawfulness of the Maintenance of the United Nations Security Council's Arms Embargo on Bosnia and Herzegovina", in 16 *Michigan Journal of International Law* 64 (1994).

[36] See also Gill, above n 29, at 100; Smith, above n 35, at 498; Cassese, above n 32, at 305.

[37] See also Gill, above n 29, at 99; Smith, above n 35, at 497.

[38] See the preamble of SC Res 1368 of 12 September 2001. The Security Council merely expressed its readiness to take all necessary steps to respond to the terrorist attacks, without authorising any concrete measures in this regard.

United States launched air attacks in the territory of Afghanistan. If one accepted that the terrorist attacks constituted an armed attack for which Afghanistan could be held responsible,[39] this military response constituted a Security Council endorsed exercise of the right to self-defence.[40]

However, once the Security Council authorises the use of force in order to restore international peace and security, the exercise of the right to self-defence is subsumed into the Security Council's right to authorise the use of military enforcement measures under Article 42 of the Charter.[41] In view of the primacy of the Security Council's authority in this respect and its broad powers in the context of international peace and security, this Article combined with Article 48(1) form the legal basis for the collectively authorised military enforcement action.[42]

For example, as far as Afghanistan is concerned, the Security Council eventually adopted Resolution 1386 of 20 December 2001, which authorised member states to use all necessary means to maintain security in Kabul and its surrounding areas. This authorisation has since been extended to areas outside Kabul in Resolution 1510 of 13 October 2003.[43] Since the adoption of these resolutions, the legality of the use of force in the described areas stems from Articles 42 and 48(1) of the Charter. Within these areas states could not engage in any (additional) military activity on the basis of Article 51 of the Charter. This Article could nonetheless still be used as a basis for military action in the rest of Afghanistan, since the Security Council neither authorised the use of force in those areas, nor did it call for a cessation of the military action.[44] This continued military

---

[39] Although an analysis of this issue falls outside the scope of this chapter, it is noteworthy that the 19 NATO countries viewed these attacks as an armed attack. They based their decision on information provided by the United States government, indicating that the attacks were carried out by the Al-Quaida network, which was headed by Usama bin Laden and protected by the Taliban regime in Afghanistan. See NATO Press release No 124, 2 October 2001, at www.nato.int/terrorism. See also Schrijver, above n 30, at 281 ff. Sean D Murphy, "Terrorism and the Concept of 'Armed Attack' in Art 51 of the UN Charter", 43 *Harvard International Law Journal* 43 ff (2002). For a more critical approach, see Krajewski, above n 31, at 202 ff

[40] Following the initiation of military action, the United States and the United Kingdom reported to the Security Council, invoking the right of individual and collective self-defence. See S/2001/946 and S/2001/947; see also Schrijver, above n 30, at 283.

[41] Gill, above n 29, at 100. See also ch 6, at s 4, which explains that the primacy of the Security Council action over the right to self-defence may not result in extinguishing this right. Cf Friederike Böhmer, *Die Ermächtigung zu militärischer Gewaltanwendung durch den Sicherheitsrat* 129 ff (Baden-Baden, Nomos, 1997), for a discussion of the parallel existence of the right to self-defence and the collective security system contained in the Charter.

[42] *Ibid.*

[43] SC Res 1386 of 20 December 2001, at paras 1 and 3. See also SC Res 1510 of 13 October 2003, at para 1.

[44] *Ibid.* Since the right to self-defence is exercised by a permanent member of the Security Council, it cannot be expected that it would adopt a resolution explicitly calling for the cessation of hostilities.

action on the basis of Article 51 does, however, have to remain within the boundaries of the principles of necessity and proportionality.[45]

2.2. The Necessity of Overall Command and Control by the Security Council

The fact that the Security Council may authorise member states to exercise military power on its behalf does not mean that it could also delegate ultimate control of the military operation to those states engaged in the military operation. That would amount to a complete abdication of powers that would undermine the centralised nature and institutional structure of the Charter in the context of international peace and security.[46] This is not to deny the reality that the authorisation to undertake military measures necessarily implies some discretionary decision-making power concerning the day-to-day military operations by those states engaged in the military action. In fact, the Security Council is obliged to consult on military strategy with those forces who undertake the military operation. This follows from Article 44 of the Charter, according to which the Security Council must, before calling on member states to provide military contingents under Article 43, invite these states to participate in the Security Council's decision to send those contingents into combat.[47] Since no Article 43 agreements have been concluded Article 44 does not apply directly to situations where the Security Council authorise member states to undertake military action. Even so, the guarantee provided in Article 44 must still apply by analogy since the object and purpose of that Article, namely that there should be no military action without representation, would also apply in situations where states are authorised to use force.[48]

What is important, however, is that overall control of the operation remains with the Security Council.[49] The centralisation of control over military action embodies the centralisation of the collective use of force,

---

[45] See Richard L Griffiths, "International Law, the Crime of Aggression and the Ius Ad Bellum", 2 *International Criminal Law Review* 324 (2002). The (internationally recognised) interim administration, which was established in Afghanistan after the fall of the Taliban, also invited the United States and other countries to remain in Afghanistan for the purpose of combating the Al-Quaida terrorist organisation. Such intervention by invitation can form an additional legal basis for the presence of foreign troops in a country, as illuminated below in s 5.1. and 5.2.

[46] Sarooshi, above n 12, at 5, 33.

[47] See also Sarooshi, above n 12, at 34.

[48] Sarooshi, above n 12, at 34–35.

[49] White & Ülgen, above n 2, at 387, Blokker (Grenzen), above n 19, at 1551, Frederick L Kirgis, "Book Review", 93 *American Journal of International Law* 973 (1999). Gading, above n 1, at 34–35, described this as a co-control between the Security Council and the commanders of the countries from which the troops are stemming.

which forms the corner stone of the Charter.[50] A complete delegation of command and control of a military operation to a member state or a group of states, without any accountability to the Security Council, would lack that degree of centralisation constitutionally necessary to designate a particular military action as a United Nations operation.[51] It would undermine the unique decision-making process within an organ which was the very reason states conferred to it the very power which that organ would now seek to delegate. This concern is encapsulated in the maxim *delegates non potest delegare*: a delegate cannot delegate.[52]

Stated differently, the authorisation of one single state by the Security Council to use force can reflect the collective will of the Security Council only if and to the extent that the Security Council as a collective entity retains overall control of the military operation.[53] Anything less would allow the Security Council to absolve itself from its collective responsibility and in effect allow member states to decide individually how and when to use military force—a decision which is not allowed under the Charter. This would also open the door to abuse by states who claim to be acting on behalf of the United Nations whilst (exclusively) pursuing their own national interests.[54] This is a real risk if one bears in mind that the military operation is often executed by the very states who initiated the authorisation at Security Council level. Since they do so for reasons closely related to their national interest, the Security Council could be called into action for domestic purposes as opposed to restoring or maintaining international peace.[55]

This conclusion is further supported by the argument that the prohibition of a total delegation of powers is a general principle of the law of international organisations.[56] This argument has its origins in the decision

---

[50] White & Ülgen, above n 2, at 386; see also Sarooshi, above n 12, at 155, 250; Quigley, above n 8, at 159.

[51] See also Thomas Bruha & Markus Krajewski, "Funktionswandel des Sicherheitsrats als Verfassungsproblem", 46 *Vereinte Nationen* 17 (1998). See also Sarooshi, above n 12, at 155, 250. For the same reason, the Security Council may not delegate the power to determine when there has been a threat to peace, breach of the peace or an act of aggression.

[52] Sarooshi, above n 12, at 15–16.

[53] White & Ülgen, above n 2, at 383, 386. The greater the multi-lateral component of the force authorised by the United Nations and the greater the international consensus behind the operation, the bigger its political legitimacy. For example, the political legitimacy of such operations will be increased if they also have the support of the General Assembly. At the same time, one has to remember that the lack of political legitimacy does not *per se* render the operation unlawful.

[54] Blokker (Grenzen), above n 19; at 1551; Quigley, above n 8, at 159, 161. See also Sarooshi, above n 12, at 22–23. He noted that the entity that has initially been endowed with a power, has a legal responsibility to exercise the power for the purpose stipulated by the delegator. This is the rationale behind the *delegatus non potest delegare* maxim.

[55] Bruha & Krajewski above n 51, at 17.

[56] Sarooshi, above n 12, at 7.

of *Meroni v High Authority* of the European Court of Justice (ECJ).[57] In this decision the ECJ distinguished between a delegation that merely amounts to the execution of a function or circumscribed powers, and a delegation that involves the actual transfer of responsibility.[58] In the case at hand the High Authority of the European Coal and Steel Community had attempted to delegate the power to collect a levy to two subsidiary organs. They had been specifically created to administer a scheme designed to control the price of iron ore on the international market, the so called Imported Ferrous Scrap Equalization Fund.[59] One of the preliminary questions the ECJ had to address, was whether the High Authority had actually delegated certain responsibilities, or whether it had only granted to its subsidiary organs the competence to make resolutions whose application still belonged to the High Authority.[60]

According to the ECJ, the difference between these two situations concerned the degree to which the discretionary decision-making power had been transferred. The consequences resulting from a delegation of powers are very different depending on whether it involves clearly defined executive powers, or whether it involves a wide margin of discretion which facilitates policy choices.[61] In the former instance the transfer of powers can be reviewed in the light of objective criteria determined by the delegating authority. Such a delegation would not alter the consequences involved in the exercise of the powers concerned. In the latter instance, however, the choices of the delegator could be replaced by that of the delegate, which brings about an actual transfer of responsibility.[62] In the *Meroni* case the terms of establishment of the subsidiary organ did not permit the High Authority to exercise direct authority and control over it, in the sense that the High Authority could change the subsidiary body's decisions.[63] This amounted to an actual transfer of responsibility to the subsidiary which constituted an unlawful delegation.[64] In essence

---

[57] Case 9/56, [1958] ECR 133. Hereinafter referred to as the *Meroni* decision.
[58] Blokker (Grenzen), above n 19, at 1552; Sarooshi, above n 12, at 10.
[59] See also Sarooshi, above n 12, at 11; Blokker (Authorisation), above n 5, at 532.
[60] *Meroni* decision above n 57, at 147; Sarooshi, above n 12, at 11.
[61] *Meroni* decision, above n 57, at 152; Blokker (Authorisation), above n 5, at 553; Sarooshi, above n 12, at 36.
[62] *Meroni* decision, above n 57, at 152; Sarooshi, above n 12, at 10; see also Blokker (Authorisation), above n 5, at 553.
[63] Sarooshi, above n 12, at 37.
[64] See *Meroni* decision, above n 57, at 149 ff. In addition, the High Authority had delegated powers which were more extensive than its own. Had the High Authority itself exercised the powers delegated to the two subsidiary bodies, it would have been obliged to state reasons for its decisions and publish an annual report, as well as other data that could be useful to governments or other parties concerned. This followed from the rules laid down in the Treaty establishing the European Coal and Steel Community. In contrast, the delegation by the High Authority to the subsidiary bodies did not make the exercise of the powers by the latter subject to any similar conditions. See also Sarooshi, above n 12, at 36–37; Blokker (Grenzen), above n 19, at 1152; *ibid* (Authorisation), above n 5, at 552–53.

therefore the question of the legality of the delegation depends on the degree to which the delegator remains involved in the decision-making process. If it can exercise substantive control and in this way still directs its own mind to the particular situation, the delegation would be lawful.[65]

To the extent that this principle can be regarded as a general principle of the law of international organisations,[66] it could be applied by analogy to the Security Council, despite the structural differences between the European Union and the United Nations.[67] In the context of the Security Council it would mean that an illegal delegation of powers had not occurred where the Security Council had already decided on the way in which a particular action is to be carried out and only the implementation of the decision is delegated.[68] Neither has it occurred where a certain amount of discretionary power or responsibility has been transferred, but where the Security Council retains control over that decision in the sense that it can alter or terminate it.[69] However, the thesis that these principles are general to international institutions would only be a supplementary argument, since with respect to the Security Council they first and foremost follow from the Charter as the blueprint for the centralisation of the use of force.

2.3.   The Meaning of Overall Command and Control by the Security Council

In order for the Security Council to remain in control of a military operation, the use of force must be explicitly recognised in a Security Council resolution.[70] This flows from the principle underlying Article 42 that armed force should be used as a last resort.[71] Even though it is up to the Security Council to decide if and when to move from Article 41 to Article 42 of the Charter,[72] the substantive principle that force be used only as a last resort carries with it a procedural requirement that the deliberative body authorising force do so explicitly.[73]

---

[65] Sarooshi, above n 12, at 11; see also Blokker (Authorisation), above n 5, at 553.
[66] A fact that is questioned by Bardo Fassbender, "Quis Judicabit? The Security Council, Its Powers and Its Legal Control", 11 *European Journal of International Law* 231 (2000).
[67] See also Blokker (Grenzen), above n 19, at 1152.
[68] Sarooshi, above n 12, at 11.
[69] *Ibid*, at 37.
[70] Jules Lobel & Michael Ratner, "Bypassing the Security Council: Ambiguous Authorisations to use force, Cease-Fires and the Iraqi Inspection Regime", 93 *American Journal of International Law* 125 (1999), White & Ülgen, above n 2, at 387.
[71] Lobel & Ratner, above n 70, at 129, 134.
[72] See ch 5, at s 2., for an explanation as to why the Security Council is not bound to a proportionality principle when moving from Art 41 to Art 42 of the Charter.
[73] Lobel & Ratner, above n 70, at 129.

This argument gains strength if one considers that the means for determining the implied intention of the Security Council are limited. Apart from the text of the resolution, states will only be able to rely on the records of Security Council meetings for this purpose. However, in the light of the increasing number of unrecorded, informal Security Council discussions these records would most likely be inconclusive.[74] Consequently, implicit authorisation would result from nuanced interpretations of ambiguous state actions rather than from the clear authorisation of the Security Council, which in turn would create major legal uncertainty.[75] The practice of the Security Council in the post Cold War era also lends support to the view that military enforcement action has to be authorised explicitly. As will be illustrated below, it has explicitly referred to Chapter VII when adopting military enforcement measures in a consistent manner since the adoption of Resolution 660 (1990).[76]

The second prerequisite for ensuring that overall command and control remains with the Security Council concerns the terms of the authorising Security Council resolution. It should specify clearly the extent, nature and objective of the military action, since broad and indeterminate language provides states with an opportunity to employ force for potentially limitless objectives.[77] Defining the mandate clearly may not be as easy as it seems, as the Security Council cannot, in advance, prescribe the military tactics of the authorised states, if they are to react effectively to unpredictable situations.[78] These decisions have to be taken in the field in the light of rapidly changing circumstances. As a result, ambiguous and broad language cannot be avoided completely.[79]

To ensure that the Security Council remains in control of such an authorisation, the broad or vague language should be interpreted restrictively

[74] For other problems related to the preparatory records of the Security Council when determining the intention of the parties, see ch 3, at s 4.3.1.

[75] Lobel & Ratner, above n 70, at 133–34. In the *Meroni decision*, above n 57, at 9, the ECJ also stated that a delegation of powers cannot be presumed. Even when empowered to delegate its powers, the delegating authority must take an express decision transferring them. If one is willing to regard this as a general principle of the law of international organisations, it would add further strength to the argument that any authorisation of a member state by the Security Council has to be explicit. See Sarooshi, above n 12, at 8–9; Henry G Schermers & Niels M Blokker, *International Institutional Law* 153 (1995).

[76] Philip Alston, "The Security Council and Human Rights: Lessons to be Learned from the Iraq-Kuwait Crisis and its Aftermath", 13 *Australian Yearbook of International Law* 146 (1992).

[77] Lobel & Ratner, above n 70, at 125 ff; see also Sarooshi, above n 12, at 41, 155; White & Ülgen, above n 2, at 38.

[78] Lobel & Ratner, above n 70, at 127; Blokker (Grenzen), above n 19, at 1553.

[79] Sarooshi, above n 12, at 218, 159. Bruha & Krajewski, above n 51, at 17, suggested that the mandate should also provide guidelines with respect to the number of troops and the type of weapons to be used. However, Sarooshi, above n 12, at 159 pointed out that it would not be particularly helpful to require the Security Council to specify the level of the use of force to be undertaken. As command and control over the military operation is delegated to states, they should also have the discretion to decide which degree of force should be used to attain the Security Council's objectives. Cf Blokker (Authorisation), above n 5, at 566.

by those executing the military mandate.[80] This is of particular importance for mandates which are not subjected to an explicit time limit. In such instances one should attempt to draw a "functional limitation" from the purpose of the authorising resolution.[81] If, for example, the purpose was to establish a permanent cease-fire the authorisation should automatically cease once this has been achieved, unless it is explicitly continued by the Security Council. This amounts to a "presumption of expiration" once the purpose of the mandate has been achieved. In the absence of such a presumption the authorisation to use force will continue after the purpose of the mandate has been achieved. This would mean that the termination of the use of force would require an affirmative decision by the Security Council. This could be prevented by the "reverse veto" of any of the permanent members, which is a real risk when the authorised states include a permanent member that has a direct interest in blocking the terminating Security Council resolution.[82]

For this reason a clause in the authorising resolution according to which the Security Council has to make a future determination on the termination of the mandate would be of little use. Its net result would be to shift the control over the military operation from the Security Council to the permanent member(s) with a direct interest in its continuation and to facilitate its indefinite continuation.[83] The essence of the "presumption of expiration" is thus to ensure that the Security Council as a collective entity determines when a mandate is terminated, as opposed to one or a few states exclusively pursuing their own national interests.[84]

In instances where a functional limitation cannot be drawn from the purpose of the authorising resolution, the authorisation to use force will cease when it becomes clear that it does not enjoy the support of the majority of Security Council members anymore, including a majority of the permanent members. This will first be the case where a draft resolution aimed at terminating the military mandate is only opposed by one or two permanent members. It will also be the case where the terminating resolution is blocked by one or two permanent members and a minority of the non-permanent members. A third possibility is where a majority of the permanent members are in favour of its continuation, but no overall majority in favour of continuation exists within the Security Council.[85]

---

[80] Lobel & Ratner, above n 70, at 125, 127; see also Sarooshi, above n 12, at 41.
[81] A term used by Blokker, above n 5, at 563.
[82] Lobel & Ratner, above n 70, at 145; Sarooshi, above n 12, at 158.
[83] Lobel & Ratner, above n 70, at 145; Sarooshi, above n 12, at 151.
[84] Lobel & Ratner, above n 70, at 144–45; Sarooshi, above n 12, at 158; White & Ülgen, above n 2, at 387; Quigley, above n 8, at 159.
[85] Theoretically this means that a mandate can cease even if all five permanent members are in favour of its continuation. However, in practice it is highly unlikely that such a situation will ever occur.

Finally it is, in principle, possible that an overall majority for the continuation of the mandate exists, which does not include a majority of the permanent members.

The moment any of these situations occur, the overall control over the operation shifts from the Security Council as a collective entity to the (permanent) member(s) who have a direct interest in its continuation. As this would in effect amount to an illegal delegation of power, the authorisation of the use of force will cease automatically.[86] This implies that the delegation of a competence which is centralised within the Security Council (ie the use of force) justifies an exception to the rule of parallelism of forms, to the extent that the termination of the delegation cannot necessarily be prevented by the reverse veto.[87]

At this point it is necessary to acknowledge that currently this line of argument is neither supported by state practice, nor has it received any attention by legal writers. Even so, it would not be void of authority to those accepting the logical consequences of the structural limitations inherent in a concept of delegation that requires the delegating power to remain in overall control of the delegated mandate. In fact, a "pure" application of this logic would imply that an open-ended Security Council authorisation would already become illegal when one single permanent member of the Security Council withdraws it support from the mandate. For if the legality of the *initiation* of an open-ended Security Council mandate requires consensus amongst the five permanent members, it is only logical that the legality of the *continuation* of such a mandate would depend on consensus as well.

However, the practical consequence of such a "purist" view would be that an open-ended mandate would already become illegal if, for example, one permanent member withdrew its support by submitting a draft resolution requesting the termination of the mandate in question. This would clearly open the door to political abuse by permanent members whose request for termination of a particular authorisation would be based on pretextual grounds. It would also not do justice to the presumption of legality attached to a Security Council authorised mandate, nor to the doctrine of efficiency that underpins the Charter regime. Therefore, in order to give recognition to these considerations, it seems more appropriate to regard the Security Council mandate as legal, as long as it enjoys

---

[86] One should also keep in mind that Security Council resolutions are underpinned by a presumption of legality. Therefore, instead of rejecting broad military mandates as invalid, they should be construed in a way that would make them valid. This would mean a narrow interpretation that leads to the automatic expiration of the authorisation in the circumstances outlined above. For the presumption of legality of Security Council resolutions, see the *Certain Expenses opinion*, above n 20, at 168. See also chapter 2, at s 5.2.2.

[87] See ch 6 at s 5.

the support of the majority of Security Council members, including a majority of its permanent members. In this way recognition is given to the special role attributed to the permanent members by the Charter regime, whilst also recognising that overall control by the Security Council as a collective entity would not be possible once an open-ended mandate is no longer supported by a majority of its members.

Finally, overall control implies that the Security Council oversees the military action on an ongoing basis by means of a reporting procedure.[88] This follows from the analogy with Article 54 of the Charter. This Article requires a regional organisation that has used force in the maintenance of peace and security to report to the Security Council, including full notification of planned military enforcement action. The purpose of this provision is to ensure that the Security Council has the information that it needs for exercising overall authority and control over enforcement action by the regional arrangement or agency.[89] Since a similar need exists in instances where individual states are authorised to use force, they should be subjected to a similar reporting obligation.[90]

In practice the Security Council resolutions generally require the authorised states to submit periodic reports. Even though the resolutions only "request" states to report on the military operation, states seem to regard themselves as obliged to give effect to this request. Reporting has therefore become an established procedural practice for monitoring a military operation in terms of Chapter VII of the Charter.[91] However, the *formal* submission of reports to the Security Council does not in itself constitute *effective* and meaningful monitoring of the military operation.[92] First, states may be inclined to submit reports merely stating that the operation is going smoothly, without providing the Security Council with information about the nature and extent of the measures already undertaken.[93] Reporting states would be particularly reluctant to divulge any information

---

[88] White & Ülgen, above n 2, at 387; see also Sarooshi, above n 12, at 155; Quigley, above n 8, at 159.

[89] Sarooshi, above n 12, at 161–62.

[90] *Ibid*. The existence of a reporting obligation also flows from the object and purpose of the reporting requirement in Art 51 of the Charter. Art 51 imposes a legal obligation on states to report back to the Security Council on any measures they may have taken in exercise of their right to individual or collective self-defence. Thus, the Charter imposes an obligation on states who are lawfully using force not under the direct operational control of the Security Council to report on a regular basis back to the Security Council.

[91] Sarooshi, above n 12, at 160–61; White & Ülgen, above n 2, at 410. See also Blokker (Authorisation), above n 5, at 564. He draws a parallel with the European Communities where the ECJ feels strongly about obligations on the member states to report to the European Commission. This is seen by the ECJ as a prerequisite for the Commission to carry out its watch-dog tasks. Eg Case 96/81, *Commission v Netherlands* [1982] ECR 1791 at 1803; Case C–237/90, *Commission v Germany* [1992] I–5973 at I–6016.

[92] Kirgis, above n 49, at 973.

[93] See Blokker (Authorisation), above n 5, at 564.

on having acted outside their mandate.[94] Furthermore, states may be withholding important information on planned, future military operations. Even though they would be required to report on these matters in terms of (the analogy with) Article 54 of the Charter, states would most likely refuse to do so on the premise that the effectiveness of military operations depends on their secrecy.[95]

Although this latter problem is unlikely to be overcome in practice, the Security Council can enhance more effective monitoring of what has already been done by requiring states to specify clearly the parameters and modalities of the military operation. In addition, it should request the Secretary-General to submit reports which would supplement those submitted by states. The perspective of the Secretary-General is different from that of the authorised states, since he represents the interests of the United Nations as a whole and not those of the individual states participating in the military operation.[96]

3. SECURITY COUNCIL PRACTICE VIS-À-VIS INDIVIDUAL STATES

The practice of the Security Council reflects that it has maintained overall control over most of the military mandates that involved the use of force by individual member states. The two main exceptions in this regard remain the authorisations of the use of force against North Korea and Iraq, as will be illuminated below in sections 3.1. and 3.2., respectively.

With respect to the remaining mandates, the Security Council frequently effected overall control by explicitly subjecting the authorisations to a time-limit.[97] In those instances where the Security Council has authorised an open-ended mandate, it subsequently terminated the mandate by the adoption of a Chapter VII resolution.[98] If this had not been the case,

---

[94] Blokker (Authorisation), above n 5, at 564.
[95] Sarooshi, above n 12, at 162. Cf Linos-Alexandre Sicilianos, "L'autorisation par le Conseil de Sécurité de Recourir a la Force: Une Tentative d'Évaluation", in 106 *Revue Générale de Droit International Public* 20–21 (2002).
[96] Blokker (Authorisation), above n 5, at 565; Sarooshi, above n 12, at 160.
[97] See SC Res 918 of 17 May 1994, at para 4 (Rwanda); SC Resolution 1080 of 15 November 1996, at para 8 (Eastern Zaire/ Democratic Republic of Congo); SC Res 1078 of 9 November 1996, at para 11 (Eastern Zaire/ Democratic Republic of Congo); SC Res 1291 of 24 February 2000, at para 3 (Democratic Republic of Congo); SC Res 1101 of 28 March 1997, at para 6 (Albania); SC Res 1125 of 6 August 1997, at para 4 (Central African Republic); SC Res 1272 of 25 October 1999, at para 17 (East Timor); SC Res 1410 of 17 May 2002, at para 1 (East Timor); SC Res 1386 of 20 December 2001, at para 1 (Afghanistan).
[98] In Somalia, for example, SC Res 814 of 26 March 1993, provided for the transition of UNITAF to UNOSOM II. The latter's mandate was ultimately terminated by SC Res 954 of 31 March 1995. See also SC Res 975 of 30 January 1995, that terminated the authorisation to use force in Haiti, which was granted in SC Res 940 of 31 July 1994. In East Timor SC Res 1272 of 25 October 1999, replaced the multi-national force that was established by SC

attempts to draw a functional limitation from the purposes of the mandates would more often than not have proved futile.[99] Even though the authorising resolutions sometimes described the purpose of the military mandates in some detail, the complexity and/ or breadth of the nature of the tasks involved would have made a functional limitation difficult to administer.[100]

This is not affected by the fact that some of these military operations (especially those operating under the command and control of the Secretary-General),[101] were of a low intensity.[102] A reduction of the degree of the force used is not in itself a guarantee that the purposes for which it is authorised is clear enough to accommodate a functional limitation. Therefore, had these mandates not been explicitly terminated by the Security Council, they would have existed only as long as they enjoyed the support of the majority of Security Council members, including a majority of the permanent members.[103] Fortunately, however, such a situation did not arise, as non of the permanent members had a direct interest in the unlimited prolongation of any of the mandates in question. As a result, it was possible to generate the consensus necessary to terminate the authorisation to use force by means of a Chapter VII resolution.

Res 1264 of 15 September 1999, with the United Nations Transitional Administration in East Timor (UNTEAT). In accordance with SC Res 1410 of 17 May 2002, UNTAET was replaced by the United Nations Mission of Support in East Timor (UNMISET), whose mandate is subjected to a time-limit.

[99] The authorisation against Southern-Rhodesia forms one of the few examples where an automatic expiration indeed was possible. SC Res 221 of 9 April 1966, at para 5, called upon the Government of the United Kingdom to prevent, by the use of force if necessary, the arrival at Beira of vessels reasonably believed to be carrying oil destined for Southern Rhodesia. This authorisation automatically expired when its purpose had been achieved, ie when it was clear that the Joanna V would not be discharging her cargo in Beira. See also Sarooshi, above n 12, at 200; Elina Kalkku, "The United Nations Authorisation to Peace Enforcement with the Use of Armed Forces in the Light of the Practice of the UN Security Council", 9 *Finnish Yearbook of International Law* 360–61 (1998).

[100] See, for example, SC Res 794 of 3 December 1992, at para 1, that authorised the use of all necessary means to establish a "secure environment" for humanitarian relief operations in Somalia. The breadth and complexity of this mandate would have made a functional limitation futile. See also SC Res 940 of 31 July 1994, at para 4 (Haiti); SC Res 1264 of 15 September 1999, at para 3 (East Timor).

[101] Whereas Arts 42 and 48(1) of the Charter form the legal basis for delegating the operational command and control to the member states, such a delegation to the Secretary-General can be based on Art 98. It explicitly provides for the Security Council (and other principal organs) to delegate functions to the Secretary-General. See, for example, SC Res 794 of 3 December 1992 at paras 10 and 12. The resolution extended the authorisation to use force to ensure a secure environment for humanitarian relief operations in Somalia to member states, as well as the Secretary-General.

[102] SC Res 1291 of 24 February 2000, at paras 4 ff (Democratic Republic of Congo); SC Res1101 of 28 March 1997, at para 2 (Albania); SC Res 1125 of 6 August 1997, at para 2 (Central African Republic).

[103] See above s 2.3.

Finally, the Security Council practice also indicates that the reporting requirement formed a consistent feature of the Security Council's overall control and would by now constitute a settled practice within the delegation model.[104] At the same time, the reporting requirement remains an under-developed element of the overall control by the Security Council, as it has not yet attempted to develop any significant substantive criteria in this regard. Even though the absence of such criteria would not affect the legality of the military mandate, the presence of substantive reporting requirements would enhance the transparency of the military operation and strengthen its political legitimacy.[105]

As was mentioned at the outset of this section, there have also been situations in which the Security Council was unable to maintain overall control over military authorisations directed at individual states. The following paragraphs will examine the two instances where such control was lacking, namely North Korea and Iraq. Whereas the lack of overall control over the North Korean mandate was closely related to the country's non-membership of the United Nations at the time (as well as certain conditions pertinent to the Cold War period), the Iraqi mandate epitomises the dangers inherent in a broad, open-ended mandate that directly affects the interest of a permanent member.

3.1. North Korea

3.1.1. The Implications of North-Korea's Non-Membership of the United Nations

The model of delegated enforcement action was used for the first time in 1950 during the Korean conflict.[106] On 25 June 1950 armed forces from North Korea pushed south across the 38 parallel, invading the Republic of Korea. The Security Council (in the absence of the Soviet Union) responded that very day by passing resolution 82 of 25 June 1950,

---

[104] See, for example, SC Res 794 of 3 December 1992, at para 18 (Somalia); SC Res 940 of 31 July 1994, at paras 13 and 14 (Haiti); SC Res 918 of 17 May 1994, at para 11 (Rwanda); SC Res 1291 of 24 February 2000, at para 4 (Democratic Republic of Congo); SC Res 1101 of 28 March 1997, at para 2 (Albania); SC Res 1125 of 6 August 1997, at para 6 (Central African Republic); SC Res 1264 of 15 September 1999, at para 12 (East Timor); SC Res 1272 of 25 October 1999, at para 18 (East Timor/ UNTAET); SC Res 1410 of 17 May 2002, at para 13 (East Timor/ UNMISET); SC Res 1386 of 20 December 2001, at para 9 (Afghanistan).

[105] The military mandate relating to Albania constituted the only attempt to introduce more substantive reporting requirements. SC Res 1101 of 28 March 1997, at para 9, required the periodic reports to specify the parameters and modalities of the operation on the basis of consultations between the participating member states and the government of Albania.

[106] Blokker (Authorisation), above n 5, at 543.

determining that this armed attack constituted a breach of the peace.[107] Subsequently, in Resolution 83 of 27 June 1950, the Security Council recommended that members furnish such assistance as may be necessary in order to repel the armed attack and to restore international peace and security in the area. In addition, it recommended that the assistance be placed under the unified command of the United States.[108] The United States was also requested to report to the Security Council on the course of the action taken.[109]

The resolution did not explicitly base the authorisation to use force on Article 42 and Article 48(1) of the Charter. The fact that the objective of military mandate was to "restore international peace and security in the area", nonetheless affirms that these Articles were meant to underpin the authorisation.[110] This immediately raises a question as to whether the Security Council may authorise the use of force against a country which was not a member of the United Nations at the time. Chapter 3 at section 4.2. indicated that it remains controversial whether the Security Council can apply the Chapter VII enforcement mechanism against non-member states by means of customary international law.[111] Moreover, even if one accepted that such a customary international law rule existed in the post Cold War era, it is highly unlikely that it existed in 1950, when Chapter VII resolutions were few and far between. It is therefore unlikely that the Security Council had the legal competence to authorise the use of force against North Korea in terms of Article 42 and 48(1) of the Charter.

---

[107] See also Sarooshi, above n 12, at 169; Kalkku, above n 99, at 356–57.

[108] SC Res 84 of 7 July 1950, at para 3.

[109] *Ibid*, at para 6. The Secretary-General proposed the establishment of a subsidiary organ in the form of a Committee on Co-ordination for the Assistance of Korea to assist in the command and control of the forces involved. This Committee would have been composed of the Republic of Korea and the states who had contributed troops, ie Australia, France, India, New Zealand, Norway, the United Kingdom and the United States. This was strongly opposed by the United States, who wanted sole operational command and control over its own forces and was reluctant to have the decisions by its designated commander reviewed by a United Nations subsidiary organ. Sarooshi, above n 12, at 171–72; see also Blokker (Authorisation), above n 5, at 555, 561; Finn Seyersted, *United Nations Forces in the Law of Peace and War* 41 (Leyden, Sijthoff, 1966).

[110] According to the Secretary-General, the forces were fighting on behalf of the United Nations to assist the Republic of Korea to repel the attack and to restore international peace and security in Korea. See A/1287 (1950). See also the statement of the United States Ambassador to the United Nations to this effect in 23 *Department of State Bulletin* 579 (1950). See also Lobel & Ratner, above n 70, at 138. But see Jochen A Frowein, "Art 39", in Bruno Simma (ed), *The Charter of the United Nations. A Commentary* 614–15 (Oxford, Oxford University Press, 1994). He submitted that the measures were based on Art 51 of the Charter, since they followed a "recommendation" by the Security Council to engage in military action. However, since the Security Council cannot oblige states to engage in military force, all authorisations to do so are, in a sense, mere recommendations. The use of the term "recommends" as opposed to "authorises" would therefore not be decisive in this instance.

[111] See ch 3, s 4.2.

This does not, however, mean that the use of force against North Korea was necessarily illegal. Since South Korea was subjected to an armed attack.[112] A military response was justifiable in terms of the right to individual and collective self-defence.[113] This is not affected by the fact that South Korea was not a member of the United Nations either, as the right to self-defence also exists outside of the Charter framework.[114] Therefore, the collective military action against North Korea that was necessary to repel the attack was legal, in spite of the fact that the Security Council could not act under Article 42 and 48(1) of the Charter. This included the military action necessary to push back the North Korean forces across the 38 parallel. It did not, however, include the military pursuit of the North Koreans beyond the 38 parallel towards the end of 1950. These measures extended beyond what was allowed in terms of collective self defence and could only have been authorised under Article 42 and 48(1) of the Charter.[115] Since the Security Council did not have the power to apply the Chapter VII enforcement mechanism against North Korea, the legality of these measures remain a point of controversy.

At this point it is necessary to mention that there were also other controversies regarding the Security Council's action in connection with North Korea. Even if one accepted, for the sake of argument, that the Security Council could have based a military mandate against North Korea on Articles 42 and 48(1), several other questions still have to be answered. The first is whether the absence of the Soviet Union during the adoption of the above-mentioned resolutions affected their legality. It is submitted that this question should be answered in the negative. Article 28 of the Charter determines that the Security Council shall be organised to function continuously, and that each of its members shall for this purpose be represented at all times. If a (permanent) member does not participate in a meeting it would be violating Article 28.[116] If the permanent member were allowed to claim the illegality of a resolution on the basis that it was adopted in its absence, it would be profiting from its own illegal behaviour and, in the process, undermine the efficiency of the Charter system. For this reason the absence of a (permanent) member

---

[112] Seyersted, above n 109, at 33.
[113] See also ch 4, at s 2.2. Both South Korea and North Korea constituted states at the time of South Korea's invasion. Consequently, both states were entitled to the rights and subjected to the obligations of international law. In this instance, North Korea's invasion of South Korea triggered the latter's right to self-defence. Cf John Dugard, *International Law: A South African Perspective* 81 (Kenwyn, Juta, 2000).
[114] *Nicaragua v United States*, merits, above n 32, at 94; See also ch 3, at s 4.1.
[115] See also White & Ülgen, above n 2, at 394.
[116] Jochen Herbst, *Rechtskontrolle des UN-Sicherheitsrates* 315 (Frankfurt am Main, Peter Lang, 1999).

during the voting procedure should—as was done in practice—be treated as an abstention.[117]

3.1.2.   The Transferral of the Overall Control to the General Assembly

Another problem with the mandate concerned the fact that the authorisation to use force was not subjected to a time limit and the broad purpose of restoring peace and security in the area could have lead to an open-ended mandate. The matter was also complicated by the fact that the Soviet Union had returned to the Security Council on 1 August 1950, after which consensus within the Security Council was no longer possible.[118] From then on political decision-making was transferred to the General Assembly. For example, when North Korea had been driven back to the 38 parallel in October 1950, the question arose whether they should be pursued into North Korean territory. The United Nations Unified Command put this question to the General Assembly, which responded affirmatively with Resolution 376 (V) of 7 October 1950.[119]

The General Assembly also attempted to secure a cease-fire by its Resolution 384 (V) of 14 December 1950 and by subsequent direct exchange of communications with the Government of the People's Republic of China.[120] However, this initiative failed and when armistice negotiations commenced on 10 July 1951, this was brought about by direct contact between the United Nations Command and the Commander of the opposing side.[121] The Armistice Agreement was eventually signed on 27 July 1953 between the Commander-in-Chief of the United Nations Command, on the one hand, and the Supreme Commander of the Korean People's Army and the Commander of the Chinese People's Volunteers, on the other. After the Armistice Agreement was signed and had entered into force, it was submitted to the General Assembly that approved it in Resolution 711 (VII) of 28 August 1953.[122]

The extent of the involvement of the General Assembly in the Korean war gives the impression that the overall command and control was transferred from the Security Council to the General Assembly. This especially relates to the termination of the authorisation, which it seemed to

---

[117] Herbst, above n 116, at 315; This would correspond to the Roman law principles of *nemo turpitudinem in suam allegans auditur* and *protestatio facto contrario*. See also Josef L Kunz, "Legality of the Security Council Resolutions of June 25 and 27, 45 *American Journal of International Law* 141–42 (1950).
[118] See Seyersted, above n 109, at 34.
[119] *Ibid*, at 37.
[120] *Ibid*, at 38.
[121] *Ibid*.
[122] *Ibid*, at 39.

have effected through the official acceptance of the Armistice Agreement in Resolution 711 (VII) (1953). Given the central role of the Security Council with regard to enforcement action, the legality of this transfer of overall control is highly questionable. It was, however, an emergency measure that resulted from the unique circumstances when the Soviet Union first departed from the Security Council and then returned at a time when the latter had already authorised enforcement action.

In this context it is also important to keep in mind that the Security Council itself initiated the military enforcement action. Had it not done so, the General Assembly would not have been able to initiate such action on its behalf. This would have constituted a clear violation of Article 11(2) of the Charter, according to which the General Assembly may not engage in enforcement action.[123] For the same reason it is also questionable whether the General Assembly would have been able to authorise measures that extended beyond what had initially been authorised by the Security Council. For example, if the crossing of the 38 parallel had not also been covered by the initial Security Council authorisation, it is doubtful whether the General Assembly could have authorised it. As it was, the authorisation to restore peace and security in the region contained in Security Council Resolution 83 (1950) was broad enough to include such action. The General Assembly Resolution 376 (V) (1950) thus merely reaffirmed what had already been determined by the Security Council.

Finally, it is worth noting that even if the General Assembly had not adopted Resolution 711 (VII) (1953), one could still have regarded the Armistice Agreement as a functional limitation to the military mandate. In the negotiations leading to up to it, the South Korean Government took the position that an automatic resumption of force should follow if North Korea violated the armistice, or if Korean unification could not be achieved at the political conference proposed in the armistice.[124] However, this position was consistently rejected by the United States and the United Nations coalition force.[125] This supports the conclusion that the armistice in practice constituted a functional limitation to the military mandate.

---

[123] As was later affirmed in *the Certain Expenses* opinion, above n 20, at 178. But see Inger Österdahl, "The Continued Relevance of Collective Security Under the UN: The Security Council, Regional Organisations and the General Assembly", 10 *Finnish Yearbook of International Law* 133 (1999), who encourages the General Assembly to disregard the legal constraints and start a new practice in line with the Uniting for Peace resolution. For a comparable argument, see also Nigel White, "The Legality of Bombing in the Name of Humanity", *Journal of Conflict and Security Law* 10–11 (2000).

[124] Lobel & Ratner, above n 70, at 147.

[125] See Letter of 7 August 1953 from the Acting United States Representative to the United Nations, addressed to the Secretary-General, transmitting a special report of the Unified Command on the armistice in Korea in accordance with the SC Res of 7 July 1950 (S/1588), in S/2079 (1953). See also Lobel and Ratner, above n 68, at 147.

In essence therefore neither the absence of the Soviet Union during the adoption of the relevant Security Council resolutions, nor the breadth of the Security Council mandate, nor the extent of the General Assembly's involvement in the termination of the military operation constituted the primary source of the illegality with which the military operation in North Korea was tainted. Most of the questions raised by these issues could be answered in a plausible fashion—if one assumed that the Security Council had the right to authorise the use of force in terms of Article 42 and 48(1) of the Charter in this particular instance.

However, as was illustrated above, it remains questionable whether the Security Council could indeed have done so, as North Korea was not a member of the United Nations at the time. It is this lack of a competence to resort to Article 42 and 48(1) that renders illegal those military measures that could only have been exercised on the basis of these Articles. These included the initial authorisation to pursue the North Korean forces beyond the 38 parallel in Resolution 83 (1950), since these measures could not be justified in terms of the right to self-defence. This also implies that General Assembly Resolution 376 (V) (1950), which "reaffirmed" the right of the United Nations forces to cross the 38 parallel, was illegal. As the Security Council did not have the competence to authorise these measures in Resolution 83 (1950), the General Assembly was in no position to reaffirm them either.

3.2.   Iraq

3.2.1.   The Basis and Scope of the Mandate

In Resolution 660 of 2 August 1990 the Security Council determined that the Iraqi invasion of Kuwait constituted an international breach of the peace and demanded that Iraq immediately withdrew all its forces from Kuwait. This demand was explicitly based on Articles 39 and 40 of the Charter.[126] The authorisation to use force for the purpose of liberating Kuwait followed in Resolution 678 of 29 November 1990. After recalling and reaffirming Resolution 660 (1990) and all subsequent resolutions, the Security Council authorised the member states cooperating with the Government of Kuwait to "use all necessary means" to uphold and implement Resolution 660 (1990) and all subsequent relevant resolutions and to restore international peace and security in the area.[127] The Security Council adopted this resolution under Chapter VII, but did not specify the Articles on which it based the authorisation.

---

[126] SC Res 660 of 2 August 1990, at para 2.
[127] SC Res 678 of 29 November 1990, at para 2.

In the light of the above analysis, one can conclude that this authorisation to individual states to engage in military action would have to follow from Articles 42 and 48(1) of the Charter. Some have argued, instead, that this military action was a manifestation of self-defence as provided for in Article 51 of the Charter.[128] Section 2.1. above explained that such an interpretation would ignore the text and purpose of Article 51, which provides for states to act on their own, pending Security Council action. Moreover, the objective specified in Resolution 678 (1990) to restore international peace and security in the region is considerably broader than the objectives which would be allowed by the law of self-defence.[129]

The object of the authorisation—which did not contain a time limit—was to uphold and implement resolution 660 (1990) and all subsequent relevant resolutions and to restore international peace and security in the area.[130] While this language was motivated by the goal of expelling Iraq from Kuwait, its breadth could justify any force used any time in the future against Iraq, in response to acts by Iraq that might threaten the peace.[131] This is particularly problematic as the broad authorisation could be interpreted as permitting the individual states to determine when force had to be used in future. This would constitute an illegal delegation of powers, as it would shift the overall control of the operation to the individual states and away from the Security Council as a collective entity. The latter would not be able to terminate the authorisation by a resolution in future, since this could be prevented by the reverse veto of a permanent member. Overall control by the Security Council would be limited to a vague request to the states concerned to keep it regularly informed of the progress of its actions.[132] This would be of little use,

---

[128] See Quigley, above n 8, at 143. See Weston, above n 30, at 517. SC 678 of 29 November 1990 embraced Art 51 by recalling and reaffirming SC Res 661 of 6 August 1990, in which the Security Council affirmed the inherent right to individual or collective self-defence. However, this was an indirect reference which did not elevate the latter resolution to the legal basis for the authorisation to use force. For a different opinion see Smith, above n 35, at 497–98.

[129] At the Security Council meeting during which SC Res 678 of 29 November 1990 was adopted, the United Nations secretary of state James Baker and the British Foreign Secretary Douglas Hurd spoke in terms of authorising the enforcement of collective security, not in terms of legitimating the exercise of collective self-defence. See S/2963 (1990); see also Harper, above n 32, at 114; White & Ülgen, above n 2, at 396; Sarooshi, above n 12, at 176.

[130] Blokker (Grenzen), above n 19, at 1552.

[131] Lobel & Ratner, above n 70, at 126; Sarooshi, above n 12, at 179; Quigley, above n 8, at 147; Rex Zedalis, "The Quiet, Continuing Air War Against Iraq: An Interpretive Analysis of the Controlling Security Council Resolutions", 55 *Zeitschrift für Öffentliches Recht* 192–93 (2000). See also Christine Gray, "From Unity to Polarisation: International Law and the Use of Force against Iraq", in 13 *European Journal of International Law* 7 (2002).

[132] SC Res 678 of 29 November 1990, at para 4. The lack of detailed reporting requirements in the resolution was criticised during Security Council debates. Malaysia submitted that when the United Nations Security Council authorised countries to use force, these countries had to be fully accountable for their actions to the Security Council through a clear system of reporting and accountability, which was not adequately covered in SC Res 678 of 29 November 1990. See S/PV 2963 76 (1990). See also Yemen, *ibid*, at 33.

however, if the Security Council was in no position to terminate the military mandate.[133]

In order for the authorisation to be legal despite the broad language, one would have to attribute a functional limitation to it that takes account of the central role of the Security Council in initiating and terminating enforcement action. This would mean that the authorisation to use force to "restore international peace and security in the region" existed only in the context of ousting Iraq from Kuwait. Similarly, the authorisation to enforce "subsequent resolutions" only concerned those resolutions adopted after Resolution 660 (1990) up to the adoption of Resolution 678 (1990).[134] Consequently the authorisation automatically terminated with the cease-fire agreement that was formally recognised in Resolution 687 (1991), after Iraq's withdrawal from Kuwait. Thus, military action undertaken to weaken Iraq's military capacity and/ or government in order to prevent a subsequent invasion of its neighbouring countries could only be based on Resolution 678 (1991) up to the point where the cease-fire was formerly recognised by the Security Council. Any further military action directed at enforcing the obligations imposed on Iraq in Resolution 687 (1991) and subsequent resolutions would need an additional Security Council resolution to that effect.[135]

This functional limitation to the authorisation to use force also finds support in the text of Resolution 687 (1991). Although paragraph 1 does affirm that all 13 prior resolutions survived the cease-fire, only paragraph 4 of Resolution 687 (1991) contains language authorising the use of force where the Security Council finds this appropriate.[136] This was expressed

---

[133] Although there were, for the most part, detailed reports on the military operation, some of the reports submitted during the Gulf War were very brief and merely stated that things were going according to plan. For a compilation of the reports made to the Security Council, see Marc Weller (ed), *Iraq and Kuwait: The Hostilities and their Aftermath* (Cambridge, Grotius, 1993). See also Bruha & Krajewski, above n 51, at 16–17; Blokker (Grenzen), above n 19, at 1550, 1553; *ibid* (Authorisation), above n 5, at 555–56; Gading, above n 1, at 34; Sarooshi, above n 12, at 184.

[134] See also Lobel & Ratner, above n 70, at 140, 148; Zedalis, above n 131, at 195.

[135] Support for this interpretation can also be drawn from statements of states, some of whom participated in the Gulf War, and who declared that their sole purpose was to liberate Kuwait. See the statement of the United Kingdom, in S/PV 2977 (Part II) (closed) 39 (1991); the Soviet Union, *ibid*, at 45; Australia, *ibid* at 51 and Malaysia, *ibid*, at 55. See also Lobel & Ratner, above n 70, at 129, 140; Quigley, above n 8, at 146–47; Peter Hulsroij, "The Legal Function of the Security Council", 1 *Chinese Journal of International Law* 82 (2002).

[136] SC Res 687 of 3 April 1991:
"*The Security Council*,
...
Conscious of the need to take the following measures acting under Chapter VII of the Charter,
...

4. *Decides* to guarantee the inviolability of the above-mentioned international boundary and to take as appropriate all necessary measures to that end in accordance with the charter of the United Nations.. " . See also Lobel & Ratner, above n 70, at 148; Zedalis, above n 131, at 196–97.

in the context of guaranteeing the inviolability of the Iraq-Kuwait border. In addition, paragraph 34 of Resolution 687 (1991) determined that the Security Council remained seized of the matter and would take such further steps as may be required for the implementation of that resolution and to secure peace and security in the area. These paragraphs reflect that, with the possible exception of the guaranteeing of the inviolability of the Iraqi-Kuwait border, the Security Council as a collective entity and not individual member states had to decide whether the use of force was necessary to implement the conditions imposed by Resolution 687 (1991).[137]

Moreover, one can argue that even with respect to the Iraq-Kuwait border, a decision of the Security Council as a collective entity will be required. Paragraph 4 of Resolution 687 (1991) authorised the Security Council—and not individual member states—to take as appropriate all necessary measures to guarantee the inviolability of the international boundary.[138] This argument gains strength if one reads Resolution 687 (1991) together with Resolution 686 of 2 March 1991, which regulated the provisional cease-fire that was adopted after the suspension of hostilities. In paragraph 4 it explicitly recognised that the authorisation to use force in Resolution 678 (1990) remained valid during the period required for Iraq to comply with the terms of the provisional cease-fire.[139] Resolution 687 (1991) in contrast did not explicitly state that Resolution 678 (1990) would remain valid until Iraq complied with its detailed terms. The crux of Resolution 687 (1991) would therefore be the transformation of the temporary cessation of hostilities into a permanent cease-fire, accompanied by a termination of the authorisation to use force.[140]

As a result the question whether the cease-fire in terms of Resolution 687 (1991) has been broken in any material way, has to be taken by the Security Council collectively. The same applies for whether such a breach would result in a revival of Resolution 678 (1990), or whether a subsequent resolution authorising the use of force is required.[141]

---

[137] Lobel & Ratner, above n 70, at 149–50; Quigley, above n 8, at 141; Zedalis, above n 131, at 197. Cf Michael Byers, "The Shifting Foundations of International Law: A Decade of Forceful Measures against Iraq", in 13 *European Journal of International Law* 25 (2002).

[138] Lobel & Ratner, above n 70, at 149.

[139] SC Res 686 of 2 March 1991:
"*The Security Council,*

...

Acting under Chapter VII of the Charter,

...

4. *Recognizes* that during the period required for Iraq to comply with paras 2 and 3 above, the provisions of para 2 of Resolution 678 (1990) remain valid.. ."

[140] See also Lobel & Ratner, above n 70, at 148; Sarooshi, above n 12, at 180, 182; cf Zedalis, above n 131, at 201–02.

[141] See also Lobel & Ratner, above n 70, at 150.

3.2.2.　The Absence of a Mandate for the Military Interventions Following Resolution 687 (1991)

The question that now has to be answered, is to what extent the military interventions in Iraq following the adoption of Resolution 687 (1991) were legal. Two days after its adoption, the Security Council adopted Resolution 688 of 5 April 1991, in which it expressed its concern about the repression of the Kurdish population in Iraq. Consequently it demanded that Iraq end this repression as a contribution to removing the threat to international peace and security in the region.[142] Shortly afterwards, the United States, the United Kingdom and France introduced and enforced so-called "safe havens" and "no-fly zones" in northern Iraq on the basis of Resolution 688 (1991). The rationale was that these zones were necessary to prevent the Iraqi repression of the Kurds and Shia and the resulting outflow of refugees, which constituted a threat to international peace and security in the region.[143]

Although Resolution 688 (1991) determined that a threat to the peace existed, it did not contain any specific follow-up measures in the event that the Iraqi Government did not cease its repression of certain parts of the population.[144] Since resolution 678 (1990) expired with the adoption of Resolution 687 (1991), it would be unconvincing to argue that Resolution 678 (1990) read together with Resolution 688 (1991) would provide a legal basis for the military action.[145] The argument that

[142] SC Res 688 of 5 April 1991:
"The Security Council,

...

Gravely concerned by the repression of the Iraqi civilian population in many parts of Iraq, including most recently in the Kurdish populated areas, which led to a massive flow of refugees towards and across international frontiers and to cross-border incursions, which threaten international peace and security in the region,

...

  1. *Condemns* the repression of the Iraqi civilian population in many parts of Iraq, including most recently in Kurdish population areas, the consequences of which threaten international peace and security in the region;
  2. *Demands* that Iraq, as a contribution to remove the threat to international peace and security in the region, immediately end this repression and expresses the hope in the same context that an open dialogue will take place to ensure that the human and political rights of all Iraqi citizens are respected;
  3. *Insists* that Iraq allows immediate access by international humanitarian organisations to all those in need or assistance in all parts of Iraq and make available all necessary facilities for their operations.. ."

[143] Quigley, above n 8, at 149.

[144] Alston, above n 76, at 148; Quigley, above n 8, at 146; Zedalis, above n 131, at 188. Gray, above n 131, at 9.

[145] The United States government asserted that the authorisation to use force granted in SC Res 678 of 29 November 1990 remained in effect. See Letter from President Bush to the Speaker of the House of Representatives and President Pro-Tem of the Senate, 27 *Weekly Compilation of Presidential Documents* 16 September 1991, at 1284; Lobel and Ratner, above n 68, at 151.

Resolution 688 (1991) combined with Resolution 687 (1991) required Iraq to allow all those in need in Iraq access to humanitarian organisations,[146] is equally unconvincing. Resolution 687 (1991) did not authorise the use of military force where Iraq refused to grant such access, but left it to the Security Council to decide whether enforcement action was needed to secure Iraq's compliance with the resolution.[147] The 1991 attacks also enjoyed little support from traditional United States allies and earned criticism from Russia and most of the members of the Security Council.[148]

Early in 1993 the United States, the United Kingdom and France launched air strikes against Iraq in response to various violations of the Iraqi cease-fire agreement. One of these included a crossing of the Kuwaiti border without permission and a failure to remove six police posts from the Kuwaiti side of the demilitarised zone. In addition, Iraqi authorities refused to guarantee the safety and free movement of United Nations aircraft transporting United Nations weapons inspectors, who had to monitor the compliance with Resolution 687 (1991).[149] Those strikes were undertaken only after the Security Council stated in a Presidential Statement that the Iraqi actions constituted an unacceptable and material breach of the relevant provisions of Resolution 687 (1991).[150] This has been interpreted as a revival of Resolution 678 (1990).[151] However, even

---

[146] The United Kingdom mainly argued that that this was a humanitarian intervention, which did not require a Chapter VII mandate. See *Parliamentary Papers*, House of Commons, Paper 235–iii, at 85 ff (1992–93). However, the existence of a right to humanitarian intervention was earlier disputed by the United Kingdom Foreign and Commonwealth Office, in *Foreign Policy Document No 148*, reprinted in 57 *British Yearbook of International Law* 614–15 (1986). See also "Memorandum of the United Kingdom Foreign and Commonwealth Office submitted to the House of Commons Foreign Affairs Committee in respect of Operation Provide Comfort", in 63 *British Yearbook of International Law* 824 (1992). According to this Memorandum, SC Res 688 of 5 April 1991 was not adopted under Chapter VII and the intervention in northern Iraq was not specifically mandated by the United Nations. See Brownlie & Apperley, above n 9, at 149.

[147] Alston, above n 76, at 147, also noted that SC Res 688 of 5 April 1991, unlike many of the earlier Gulf-related resolutions, did not explicitly refer to previous resolutions in either the pre-ambular or operative parts. Therefore it would be tenuous to regard it as an extension of SC Res 687 of 3 April 1991. See also Quigley, above n 8, at 149; Zedalis, above n 31, at 197.

[148] See Lobel & Ratner, above n 70, at 132–33. Alston, above n 76, at 152, stated that one could attempt to justify the establishment of the safe havens and no-fly zones on the basis that Iraq acquiesced in them. In a letter to the Secretary General of 21 April 1991, the Iraqi Foreign Minister noted, inter alia, that while opposing the steps taken by the United States and other foreign forces, Iraq has not hindered these operations, because it is not opposed to the provisions of humanitarian assistance to those who are in need of it. It also wished to avoid any complication that may prevent the return of all Iraqi citizens in security to their places of residence. See S/22513, Annex 2 (1991). Alston acknowledged, however, that this may also be interpreted as laying the foundation for having acted under duress throughout the period following the surrender of the forces and that any legal agreements entered into under such circumstances were null and void As a result, it would be unwise to draw any conclusion with respect to acquiescence from this statement.

[149] Lobel & Ratner, above n 70, at 150.

[150] S/25081 (1993).

[151] Lobel & Ratner, above n 70, at 150–51.

though the Security Council as a collective entity decided that there was a material breach of the cease-fire agreement, it did not explicitly authorise the use of force, as a result of which the legality of this military operation is open to question. It merely warned Iraq of the serious consequences which would ensue from failure to comply with these obligations.[152]

In June 1993, the United States launched a missile attack at downtown Baghdad, targeting the headquarters building of the Iraqi intelligence service. In this instance the United States informed the Security Council that it acted in self-defence under Article 51 of the Charter, in response to a failed attempt by the Iraqi intelligence services to assassinate former United States President George Bush, whilst he was visiting Kuwait in April 1993.[153] The United States regarded the assassination attempt as a direct armed attack, which was an unprecedented interpretation of the right to self-defence in the Charter era.[154] Although the fact that it was unprecedented does not in itself render the interpretation illegal, it does seem a disproportionate interpretation in the light of the fact that the plot was thwarted two months before the armed attack was launched.[155]

In September 1996 the United States launched missile attacks on air defence installations in Southern Iraq and thereby extended the southern no-fly zone from the 32nd to the 33rd parallel.[156] The United States cited Resolution 949 of 15 October 1994 as authority for this military intervention.[157] This resolution was adopted in response to Iraq's aggressive troop movement towards the border of Kuwait at that time.[158] After

---

[152]S/25081 (1993).
[153]Quigley, above n 8, at 137
[154]*Ibid*, at 138.
[155]Quigley, above n 8, at 138–39. Cf Christine Gray, *International Law and the Use of Force* 117 (Oxford, Oxford University Press, 2000).
[156]See also Zedalis, above n 131, at 203.
[157]Letter of President Clinton on Military Force Against Iraq Resolution, news-wire of 5 November 1996; cited in Zedalis, above n 131, at 203.
[158]SC Res 949 of 15 October 1994:
"*The Security Council,*
Recalling all its previous relevant resolutions, and reaffirming resolutions 678 (1990) of 29 November 1990, 686 (1991) of 2 March 1991, 687 (1991) of 3 April 1991, 689 (1991) of 9 April 1991 and 833 (1993) of 27 May 1993, and in particular para 2 of resolution 678 (1990),
Recalling that Iraq's acceptance of resolution 687 (1991) adopted pursuant to Chapter VII of the Charter of the United Nations forms the basis of the cease- fire,
Noting past Iraqi threats and instances of actual use of force against its neighbours,
Recognizing that any hostile or provocative action directed against its neighbours by the Government of Iraq constitutes a threat to peace and security in the region,
....
Noting that Iraq has affirmed its readiness to resolve in a positive manner the issue of recognizing Kuwait's sovereignty and its borders as endorsed by resolution 833 (1993), but *underlining* that Iraq must unequivocally commit itself by full and formal constitutional procedures to respect Kuwait's sovereignty, territorial integrity and borders, as required by resolutions 687 (1991) and 833 (1993),
...."

reaffirming paragraph 2 of Resolution 678 (1990), it compelled Iraq not to utilise its military or other forces in a hostile or provocative manner that threatens either its neighbours or United Nations operations in Iraq.

The question arises whether the mere affirmation of an expired resolution in the preamble of a subsequent resolution could justify the use of force against Iraq, as the operative part of the subsequent resolution contained no authorisation to use force if Iraq were to behave in a recalcitrant manner.[159] Moreover, even if Resolution 949 (1994) did revive Resolution 678 (1990), it could only do so in the context of the purpose for which Resolution 678 (1990) was originally adopted, namely the ousting of Iraq from Kuwait. A revival of the authorisation of the use of force would therefore be plausible if Iraq were to re-enter Kuwait territory. It would not, however, be justification for the extension and enforcement of a no-fly zone which was unrelated to resolution 678 (1990), as it was instituted for the protection of the Iraqi civilian population after Iraq's withdrawal from Kuwait and the subsequent expiration of resolution 678 (1990).[160]

Early in 1998 the United States sent armed forces into the Persian Gulf to pressure Iraq to permit greater access to United Nations weapons inspectors, who had to monitor Iraq's compliance with Resolution 687 (1991).[161] During December of 1998, and regularly thereafter, the United States carried out missile and air attacks in the no-fly zones, firing at air defence installations they identified as having fired on them or having threatened them.[162] By this time only the United Kingdom supported the use of force against Iraq, as opposed to the other (permanent) members of the Security Council.[163]

The United States and the United Kingdom once again put forward the argument of implied authorisation. They relied on the previously adopted

Acting under Chapter VII of the Charter of the United Nations,

1. *Condemns* recent military deployments by Iraq in the direction of the border with Kuwait;
2. *Demands* that Iraq immediately complete the withdrawal of all military units recently deployed to southern Iraq to their original positions;
3. *Demands* that Iraq not again utilise its military or any other forces in a hostile or provocative manner to threaten either its neighbours or United Nations operations in Iraq;
4. *Demands* therefore that Iraq not re-deploy to the south the units referred to in para 2 above or take any other action to enhance its military capacity in southern Iraq... ."

[159] See also Zedalis, above n 131, at 204.
[160] *Ibid*, at 204–05.
[161] Quigley, above n 8, at 141.
[162] *Ibid*, at 151; White, above n 123, at 1.
[163] According to Russia, the action violated international law and the cease-fire regime of SC Res 687 of 3 April 1991, did not provide for the unilateral use of force without further Security Council resolutions. See UN Press Release, SC/6683 (1991); see also Gray (International Law), above n 155, at 192; Quigley, above n 8, at 141–42.

Resolution 1205 of 5 November 1998, and submitted that it implicitly revived Resolution 678 (1990). Resolution 1205 (1998) condemned the decision of Iraq to cease co-operation with the weapons inspectors and demanded that Iraq rescind its decision.[164] It did not, however, contain any explicit mandate to use force or to revive Resolution 678 (1990). In addition, it could not revive Resolution 678 (1990) for the purpose of enforcing weapons inspections, as the enforcement power granted in that resolution was never intended for such a purpose. Consequently, this argument is deficient for the same reason as the reliance on Resolution 949 (1994) to justify a revival of the authorisation to use force.[165] Self-defence would not provide a convincing argument either, since it only enters into play if the United States aircraft had a right to be in the no-fly zone in the first place—something which it could not do on the basis of the above-mentioned resolutions.[166] For similar reasons the military response by the United States and the United Kingdom against increased surface-to-air missile attacks on its pilots in and around the no-fly zones in February 2001, were illegal.[167]

From these arguments it also follows that neither the principle of self-defence, nor Resolution 678 (1990) in combination with Resolution 687 (1991) provided a legal basis for the full scale invasion of Iraq by the United States and the United Kingdom on 17 March 2003. Such a legal basis could only have been provided by an explicit authorisation to use all necessary means to disarm Iraq. The last Resolution adopted before the invasion, ie Resolution 1441 of 8 November 2002, was limited to the setting-up of an enhanced inspection regime, with the aim of bringing to full and verified completion the disarmament process established by resolution 687 (1991).[168]

---

[164] At para 2.

[165] Note that SC Res 1154 of 2 March 1998, at para 3, did not contain implied authorisation to use force either. This resolution stressed that the compliance by Iraq with its obligations to accord immediate and unrestricted access to the weapons inspectors was necessary for the implementation of SC Res 687 of 3 April 1991. Although it determined that any violation would have severest consequences for Iraq, it did not authorise the use of force. See Lobel & Ratner, above n 70, at 133; Zedalis, above n 131, at 192–93; Gray, above n 131, at 11–12.

[166] See Quigley, above n 8, at 151–52; Sarooshi, above n 12, at 232.

[167] Gray, above n 131, at 9. The Secretary-General also implicitly rejected the legality of these attacks. In response to calls from Iraq for condemnation of the air attacks, he emphasised that only the Security Council was competent to determine whether its resolutions were of such a nature and effect as to provide a lawful basis for the no-fly zones and for the acts that have been taken in their enforcement. See also www.un.org/News/dh/latest/page2.html.

[168] SC Res 1441 of 8 November 2002, at para 2. See also Rainer Hoffmann, "International Law and the Use of Military Force against Iraq", 45 *German Yearbook of International Law* 21 ff (2002). The United Kingdom and the United States nonetheless relied on the combined effect of SC 678 of 29 November 1990, SC Res 687 of 3 April 1991 and SC Res 1441 of 8 November 2002. See the Statement of the Attorney-General Goldsmith in *The Times* (London), 18 March 2003, at A2; and See Letter of Ambassador John Negroponte to Ambassador Mamady Traore, President of the Security Council, 20 March 2003, reprinted in Harold H Koh, "On American Exceptionalism", 61 *Stanford Law Review* 1521 fn 131 (2003).

Neither the determination that Iraq remained in material breach of its obligations under Security Council resolutions and that this resolution afforded a final opportunity for compliance, nor the warning that serious consequences would result if Iraq continued to violate its obligations, constituted an authorisation to use force.[169] This clearly follows from the fact that consent for the use of force was withheld by three permanent members. In a joint statement China, France and Russia stated that Resolution 1441 (2002) excluded any automaticity in the use of force. In case of failure by Iraq to comply with its obligations, it would be for the Security Council to take a position on how to proceed.[170] The Statement by the United States that a failure by the Security Council to act decisively in the event of a further Iraqi violation would not constrain any member state to act in self-defence,[171] once again disregarded the fact that self-defence could not, under the circumstances, form a legal basis for military action.

Finally, it is worth noting that the military invasion could also not be justified on the basis of an *ex post facto* authorisation on the basis of Resolution 1483 of 22 May 2003. This Resolution recognised the United States and United Kingdom as the occupying "Authority" and authorised their administration of Iraq under Chapter VII of the Charter.[172] As the extent to which *ex post facto* authorisations of military mandates can be accommodated within the Charter system is illuminated in section 4.2. below, it will suffice to say that in order to amount to such, the *ex post facto* Security Council resolution must be explicit and unambiguous. Resolution 1483 (2003) makes no mention of an *ex post facto* approval of the military invasion.[173] In addition, several permanent members explicitly mentioned that this resolution was exclusively directed at the future administration of Iraq and could not be read as an *ex post facto* legitimisation of the war as such.[174] It would therefore not be possible to claim that the necessary consensus amongst the five permanent members that is a pre-requisite for any Security Council authorisation to use force, developed subsequent to the attack on Iraq.

---

[169] SC Res 1441 of 8 November 2002, at para 1, paras 2 and 13. See also Koh, above n 168, at 1523.

[170] *Joint Statement by China, France and Russia Interpreting UN Security Council Resolution 1441 (2002)*, available at www.staff.city.ac.uk/p.willetts/IRAQ/INDEX.HTM; See also Daniel Thürer, "Der Krieg gegen Sadam als Testfall. Ist das Völkerrecht wirklich am Ende?", *Neue Zürcher Zeitung Online*, 23 May 2003, available at www.nzz.ch; Hoffmann, above n 168 at 24.

[171] See the *United States Explanation of Vote on UN Security Council Resolution 1441 (2002)*, available at www.staff.city.ac.uk/p.willetts/IRAQ/INDEX.HTM; Hofmann, above n 168 at 29 ff.

[172] SC 1483 of 22 May 2003, at para 4.

[173] Frederic L Kirgis, "Security Council Resolution 1483 on the Rebuilding of Iraq", *ASIL Insights* (2003) available at www.asil.org/insights.htm.

[174] Notably the representatives of France and Russia. See *Neue Zürcher Zeitung Online*, 23 May 2003, at www.nzz.ch/; Robert van de Roer, "Resolutie Irak is zege voor VS", *NRC Handelsblad*, 23 May 2003, at 5.

A major concern regarding the mandate authorised in Resolution 1483 (2003), is its open-ended nature. Given the breadth and complexity of a mandate that implies complete military and civil occupation,[175] any attempt at defining a functional limitation would be futile. Overall control by the Security Council over the mandate could therefore only have been ensured by subjecting it to a time limit. As it stands, however, the mandate was effectively adopted for an unlimited period of time. This open-endedness was not altered by Resolution 1511 of 16 October 2003. This resolution inter alia reaffirmed that the mandate of the Authority, as well as that of the multinational stabilisation force created by Resolution 1511 (2003), will cease when an internationally recognised and democratically elected Iraqi government assumes the responsibilities of the Authority. It is submitted, however, that this does not provide an administrable functional limitation to the mandate, which remains open-ended.[176] As a result, any of the veto powers can prevent a termination of the authorisation and in this way extend it indefinitely. If this were to happen, the Security Council will potentially relinquish overall control over the operation to those (permanent) members with a direct interest in prolonging the international presence in Iraq.

This would constitute an illegal delegation of powers that is not in conformity with the Charter principle of the centralisation of the use of force. Therefore the "Authority"s mandate in Iraq would remain legal only as long as these is support amongst the majority of Security Council members, including a majority of the permanent members, that such a presence is justified. It is the Security Council as a collective entity that has to decide if and to what extent the presence of the "Authority" is legitimate and not (potentially) one single Council member. Stated differently, the only way of ensuring that the Security Council remains in overall control of the mandate granted in Resolution 1483 (2003), is to regard it as terminated at that moment in which a majority of permanent members withdraw their support for the mandate, or these is no overall majority within the Security Council for the continuation of the mandate anymore.

4.   AUTHORISING REGIONAL (DEFENCE) ORGANISATIONS TO
ENGAGE IN MILITARY ENFORCEMENT OPERATIONS

4.1.   The Legal Basis for the Mandate

Apart from authorising individual states in terms of Article 42 and 48(1) to enforce military measures, the Security Council can also utilise regional

---

[175] For a discussion of the implications of the mandate in the context of the civil administration of Iraq, see ch 8 at s 2.
[176] In accordance with SC Res 1483 of 22 May 2003, at para 25. See also SC Res 1511 of 16 October 2003, at paras 1 and 15.

organisations for this purpose. This follows from Article 53(1) of the Charter, which determines that the Security Council shall, where appropriate, utilise regional arrangements or agencies for enforcement action under its authority.[177] If one reads this Article together with Article 43 of the Charter, it becomes clear that the Article 43 agreements referred to above could also be concluded between the Security Council and regional organisations. This follows from the reference to "groups of states" in Article 43(3), that would be wide enough to include such organisations. However, as in the case of individual states, such organisations cannot be forced to provide troops unless a binding agreement to this effect is in place.[178]

The first question that has to be answered in the context of Article 53(1), is which organisations would qualify as regional organisations, sometimes also referred to as Chapter VIII organisations. This question gains particular relevance with respect to the North Atlantic Treaty Organisation (NATO) and its involvement in former Yugoslavia. Doubts have been raised as to whether an organisation such as NATO, which was originally adopted for the purpose of collective self-defence, can be regarded as a regional organisation that can be utilised for enforcement action.[179]

The only Article in the Charter that sheds light on the meaning of "regional organisation", is Article 52(1).[180] From this Article once can deduce that a regional organisation should have the task of taking care of the peaceful settlement of disputes within its own region.[181] The term "regional" implies a distinctive feature about the members of the organisation, which is generally understood to be of a ageographic nature.[182] It can either relate to the geographic region from which all the member states come, or to the geographic area in which the organisation will operate, or a combination of these factors.[183] Whatever the combination, the activities of the regional organisation are limited to its own region and amongst its own members.[184] Examples of regional organisations include

---

[177] Gading, above n 1, at 31.

[178] Walter, above n 3, at 269 and 273. Such an agreement could also be contained in the constitutive document of the regional organisation. However, at present, none of the constitutive documents of regional organisations contains a binding commitment to provide troops to the Security Council.

[179] Gading, above n 1, at 32.

[180] Walter, above n 3, at 276.

[181] Ige F Dekker & Eric PJ Myjer, "Air Strikes on Bosnian Positions: Is NATO Also Legally the Proper Instrument of the UN?", 9 *Leiden Journal of International Law* 413 (1996); Walter, above n 3, at 276.

[182] Walter, above n 3, at 40.

[183] *Ibid*, at 40–41. The distinctive geographic factor can also be accompanied by cultural and historical ties such as those between the members of the Commonwealth. In all instances, however, it is important that the regional organisation is of a long term nature, since it is unlikely that an *ad hoc* organisation would be able to contribute to the settlement of disputes more effectively than the United Nations.

[184] Walter, above n 3, at 276–77; Dekker & Myjer, above n 181, at 416; Hartmut Körbs, *Die Friedenssicherung durch die Vereinten Nationen und Regionalorganisationen nach Kapitel VIII der Satzung der Vereinten Nationen* 186–87 (Bochum, Brockmeyer, 1997).

the Organisation of American States (OAS) and the League of Arab States.[185]

Regional organisations are thereby distinguished from a regional *defence* organisation, which has as its sole purpose the offering of protection against external aggression.[186] Whereas regional organisations are governed by Chapter VIII of the Charter, defence organisations are governed by Article 51 of the Charter.[187] NATO was established as a collective defence organisation in the sense of Article 51 of the Charter and not as a regional organisation under Chapter VIII.[188] Its purpose was to deter a Soviet military attack in Western Europe and to defend Europe from an attack should deterrence fail.[189] From NATO's activity in former Yugoslavia one can conclude that the organisation's functions have expanded to include conflict and crisis management within neighbouring countries. This evolution of NATO's mandate has been questioned by some, who find it too informal in the light of the way the organisation came into being in 1949 and its political importance.[190]

This argument presents an unnecessarily static image of the possibilities offered by the constitution of an international organisation, which is a living instrument that must be capable of adapting to changes occurring in practice.[191] The evolution of the Charter itself has already been elucidated in the context of peace-keeping measures, which has no explicit base in the Charter.[192] The ICJ has nonetheless condoned these measures and has consistently acknowledged the dynamic nature of the constitution of an international organisation.[193] It has also recognised the right of the members of the international organisation to interpret its powers in practice, which could lead to the expansion of power through usage.

---

[185] Mary Ellen O'Connell, "The UN, NATO, and International Law After Kosovo", 22 *Human Rights Quarterly* 66 (2000); Gading, above n 1, at 32.
[186] Dekker & Myjer, above n 181, at 413; Körbs, above n 184, at 186–87.
[187] Walter, above n 3, at 58.
[188] Dekker & Myjer, above n 181, at 414, Walter, above n 3, at 51; Körbs, above n 184, at 225 ff.
[189] Celeste A Wallander, "Institutional Assets and Adaptability: NATO After the Cold War", 54 *International Organisation* 712 (2000).
[190] Dekker & Myjer, above n 181, at 414–15. The implication thus is that until its founding Treaty is explicitly amended to provide for an expanded mandate, the Security Council cannot authorise NATO to enforce a military mandate in terms of Chapter VIII of the Charter.
[191] Niels Blokker & Sam Muller, "NATO as the UN Security Council's Instrument: Question Marks from the Perspective of International Law?", 9 *Leiden Journal of International Law* 419 (1996).
[192] See ch 2, at s 2.1., see also Blokker & Muller, above n 191, at 420.
[193] See the *Certain Expenses* opinion, above n 20, at 151 ff. For later examples, see *Legal Consequence for States of the Continued Presence of South Africa in Namibia (South West Africa) Notwithstanding Security Council Resolution 276 (1970)*, Advisory Opinion, ICJ Rep 1972, at 31; and *Legality of the Use by a State of Nuclear Weapons in Armed Conflict*, Advisory Opinion, ICJ Rep 1996, at 75–76.

The amendment of Article 27(3) of the Charter through consistent state practice is a classic example.[194] Thus, what is at issue here is the grey area between the acceptability of an extensive, evolutionary interpretation and practice, and the necessity of amending the constitutive instrument of the organisation in accordance with that practice for the purposes of legal certainty.[195] In the case of NATO, its members have unanimously accepted that the risks to its security should be more broadly defined. The core purpose of the alliance remained collective defence, but the security threat was not related to a monolithic, massive military attack anymore.[196] Instead, it now arose from the adverse consequences of instabilities that may arise from serious economic, social and political difficulties, including ethnic rivalries and territorial disputes which were faced by many countries in central and eastern Europe.[197] As a result, the military concept of the organisation will serve a broad concept of collective security that will include defence and crisis management.[198] In the light of this clear and unanimous agreement within the organisation regarding its expanded role, one can conclude that member states have amended the NATO constitution through practice.[199]

However, in spite of its expanded security mandate, it is questionable whether NATO has evolved into a regional organisation in terms of Chapter VIII of the Charter. Whereas a regional organisation's activities are limited to its own members, NATO's expanded notion of its security role has predominantly crystallised in activities beyond the borders of its members. In spite of their geographical proximity, none of the successor states to the former Yugoslavia in which NATO troops are currently deployed are members of the organisation. Stated differently, the NATO presence in these countries would only serve as evidence of a broader definition of its security role, but not as evidence of its evolution into a regional organisation.[200]

Moreover, even if one were to regard NATO as a regional organisation in terms of Chapter VIII of the Charter, the Security Council would still not be able to rely on Article 53(1) when deploying NATO troops "out of area".

---

[194]See also ch 3, at s 4.3.; cf Krystof Skubiszewski, "Implied Power of the International Organisations", in Yoram Dinstein (ed), *International Law at a Time of Perplexity. Essays in Honour of Shabtai Rosenne* 857 (Dordrecht, Martinus Nijhoff, 1989).

[195]Blokker & Muller, above n 191, at 419.

[196]See the "Declaration on Peace and Cooperation issued by the Heads of State and Government participating in the meeting of the North Atlantic Council (including decisions leading to the creation of the North Atlantic Cooperation Council (NACC)) of 8 November 1991", at www.nato.int. Hereinafter referred to as the Rome Declaration. See also Wallander, above n 189, at 718.

[197]Rome Declaration, above n 196, at para 4.

[198]*Ibid*, at para 5.

[199]Blokker & Muller, above n 191, at 421.

[200]See also Körbs, above n 184, at 247 ff But see Blokker & Muller, above, n 191, at 420, who regarded NATO's evolution as sufficient for its qualifying as a regional organisation.

The Security Council can only rely on Article 53(1) of the Charter where it authorises the regional organisation to engage in military action within its own region *and* against (a) member state(s).[201] For the NATO mandate to be legal in an instance such as the former Yugoslavia, the Security Council would have to rely on Articles 42 and 48(2) of the Charter. As has already been indicated in section 2.1. above, Article 42 allows the Security Council to designate the member states who will participate in the military action. Article 48(2) allows for these decisions of the Security Council to be carried out by the members of the United Nations directly and through their action in the appropriate international agencies of which they are members. Although this Article first and foremost relates to the United Nations specialised agencies, its wide formulation makes it applicable to all types of international organisations whose members are also members of the United Nations, such as NATO.[202]

In summary therefore Article 53(1) of the Charter should be understood as the clause facilitating enforcement action between the regional organisation and its members. Article 42 in conjunction with 48(2) of the Charter, on the other hand, enables the military utilisation of a regional organisation outside of its territory and/ or against non-members, as well as the military utilisation of other organisations such as regional defence organisations.[203]

4.2.   The Necessity of Prior Authorisation by the Security Council

It was outlined above that the authorisation of individual states to use force is legal only and to the extent that overall control of the operation remains with the Security Council. This follows from the principle of the centralisation of the use of force which is a cornerstone of the Charter system. The same arguments apply where regional organisations are authorised to use military force. This means that the Security Council has to remain in control over both the initiation and termination of the mandate.[204]

---

[201] Walter, above n 3, at 278.
[202] *Ibid*, at 277; See also Bothe, above n 10, at 183; Körbs, above n 184, at 255.
[203] Walter, above n 3, at 278.
[204] However, as in the case of authorisations to individual states, the overall control does not necessitate direct involvement of a United Nations official in the military chain of command. Such involvement is to be discouraged, as it undermines efficiency. One example was the so called "dual key" arrangements in Bosnia-Herzegovina, provided for in SC Res 816 of 31 March 1993, at para 4 and SC Res 836 of 4 June 1993. It effectively authorised the use of force by NATO in "close co-ordination" with the Secretary-General. The Security Council and the Secretary-General interpreted this phrase as meaning that the initial decision to resort to military air power had to be taken by the Secretary-General in consultation with the members of the Security Council. This approach undermined the ability of the military operation to respond to an emergency operation and was ultimately abandoned. See also S/25935 4 (1993); Sarooshi, above n 12, at 74 ff.

The initiation of the military mandate is dependent on an explicit, prior authorisation to this effect. Where no such authorisation exists, the regional intervention would be illegal, unless it concerns a situation of self-defence.[205] Arguments that regional organisations would have a residual power to adopt military measures where the Security Council fails to act in situations of gross and systematic human rights violations,[206] or that they could act more efficiently than the Security Council, would undermine the notion of centralised use of force that is inherent in the Charter.[207] For the same reason the Security Council could not grant a regional organisation a general (open-ended) mandate to adopt binding measures. This would in effect mean that it cedes its right to adopt military measures to a regional organisation.[208]

It has been attempted to base a residual power for regional organisations to adopt military measures on a "right of emergency" that would flow from an analogy between Article 51 and Article 53 of the Charter.[209] Just as states can rely on the right to self-defence in a case of an armed attack, unless or until the Security Council takes action, regional organisations would have the power to intervene where the Security Council remains inactive in situations of gross and systematic human rights violations.[210] This argument is underpinned by the rationale that the chances for abuse of the military mandate by a regional organisation is unlikely, due to the institutional and collective control provided within the regional body, as well as by the higher degree of disinterest and objectivity within an organisation composed of mutually independent states.[211]

This line of thinking would clearly violate the second sentence of Article 53(1), which explicitly states that no enforcement action shall be taken by regional organisations without authorisation by the Security Council.[212] Moreover, it also negates the fact that the Security Council may be deliberately refraining from action, because the major powers cannot agree on whether a threat to peace exists, or whether military action is called for. The counter argument that the Security Council

---

[205] White & Ülgen, above n 2, at 388, Sarooshi, above n 12, at 33.

[206] As is suggested by Walter, above n 3, at 260–61.

[207] Gading, above n 1, at 32; see also Bruha & Krajewski, above n 51, at 17, O'Connell, above n 185, at 63.

[208] Gading, above n 1, at 33.

[209] Walter, above n 3, at 261.

[210] *Ibid.* See also Matthias Herdegen, "Der Wegfall effektiver Staatsgewalt: 'The Failed State'", 34 *Berichte der Deutschen Gesellschaft für Völkerrecht* 76 ff (1995), who supported a humanitarian intervention by regional organisations without prior Security Council authorisation in the case of a failed state.

[211] Walter, above n 3, at 262, 264; see also Georg Nolte, "Restoring Peace by Regional Action", 53 *Zeitschrift für ausländisches öffentliches Recht und Völkerrecht* 635 (1993), White & Ülgen, above n 2, at 388, 406.

[212] Sarooshi, above n 12, at 33–34.

could, prevent the regional organisation from intervening by adopting a Chapter VII resolution to that affect,[213] is not convincing. First, it turns the Charter system on its head as it forces the Security Council to explain why it is not adopting military measures. In this way the Security Council is required to do exactly the opposite from what is envisaged by the Charter system which is based on an "opt-in procedure" in the case of enforcement action, as opposed to an "opt-out" procedure. The Security Council only has to justify its engagment in military action and cannot be forced into a situation where it has to justify its inaction. This is clearly reflected in the veto provided for in Article 27(3), as well as Article 39 of the Charter.

Second, any Chapter VII resolution intended to terminate the regional organisation's military action could be frustrated in practice by a veto of a permanent member who is silently condoning the illegal military operation.[214] This is a real risk where the interests of a permanent member of the Security Council coincides with those of a regional (defence) organisation. It is also aggravated where the institutional structures and controls exerted by regional organisations are rudimentary in practice, enabling the enforcement action to be dominated by the interests of the more powerful nations within the regional organisation.[215] For this reason it is essential that the Security Council authorises the military operation by the regional organisation prior to its initiation (unless the organisation acts in self-defence).

One has to consider that an illegal military intervention can in practice be legalised *ex post facto* by the Security Council.[216] Even though this would not find any textual basis in the Charter, it cannot be excluded that the Security Council could develop a practice of *ex post facto*, retroactive authorisation.[217] As in the case of a prior authorisation, the retroactive authorisation will have to be given in unambiguous terms under Chapter VII of the Charter. Unless and until such a resolution is adopted by the Security

---

[213] As is suggested by Walter, above n 3, at 261.

[214] See also Henkin, above n 9, at 827; Körbs, above n 184, at 539.

[215] White & Ülgen, above n 2, at 388. Walter, above n 3, at 262, 264, further argued that although the structure of the regional organisations and the collective decision-making procedure would lessen the possibility of abuse of power, it could never be completely excluded—not even within the Security Council itself. Therefore the possible abuse of power by a regional organisation should be tolerated, since it may also occur within the Security Council. This conclusion seems twisted, for in instance of abuse of power—whether within the United Nations or a regional organisation—the reactions of states should be to reject the particular behaviour as invalid, instead of justifying it on the basis that it could never be excluded.

[216] Herdegen (Staatsgewalt), above n 210, at 76; See also Bothe, above n 10, at 183; Kälin, above n 9, at 162; Inger Österdahl, *Threat to the Peace* 57 (Uppsala, Iustus, 1998); Walter, above n 3, at 308; Wedgewood, above n 9, at 832; Sicilianos, above n 95, at 38 ff.

[217] Herdegen (Staatsgewalt), above n 210, at 76; See also Bothe, above n 10, at 183; Kälin, above n 9, at 162; Österdahl, above n 216, at 57; Walter, above n 3, at 308; Wedgewood, above n 9, at 832; Sicilianos, above n 95, at 38 ff.

Council, the military intervention remains unauthorised. Anything less would invite states to intervene unilaterally and then claim implicit authorisation from obscure language in subsequent Security Council resolutions, or on the basis that the subsequent resolutions did not explicitly condemn the intervention.[218] This once again turns the Security Council into an "opt out" organ, which is not reconcilable with its Charter role.

Some have argued that the withholding of an *ex post facto* authorisation of an intervention by a regional organisation can constitute an act of bad faith where the United Nations subsequently sends its own peace-keeping troops.[219] It would allow the United Nations to send peace-keeping forces only at a time when the more risky and dangerous groundwork had already been laid by a regional organisation. Thus, without a retroactive authorisation of the use of force, the Security Council would be profiting from the illegally gained advantages of the regional organisation and in this way perpetuate the illegality of the situation.[220] This argument is not convincing, for if a regional organisation intervenes without a clear mandate of the Security Council, it has to take into account the negative consequences of its own illegal action such as a possible "exploitation" of its military successes by the United Nations. In fact, this is to be expected in situations where it presents the Security Council with a *fait accompli* and where the latter has to make the best of a situation which it had not authorised.[221]

5. SECURITY COUNCIL PRACTICE VIS-À-VIS REGIONAL (DEFENCE) ORGANISATIONS

The practice of the Security Council reflects that it has encountered considerable difficulty to maintain overall control over the military mandates of regional (defence) organisations such as the Economic Community of West African States (ECOWAS) and NATO. The interventions of ECOWAS in Liberia and Sierra Leone in the 1990s were accompanied by questions concerning the absence of a prior Security Council authorisation and the possibility of an *ex post facto* authorisation of the respective interventions. With respect to NATO, similar questions arose in the context of the conflict in former Yugoslavia, notably with respect to NATO's military intervention in Kosovo in 1999. This situation was further complicated by the fact that the Security Council resolution which

---

[218] See also Ugo Villani, "The Security Council's Authorisation of Enforcement Action by Regional Organisations", 6 *Max Planck Yearbook of International Law* 55 (2002). He submitted that in the presence of a prior authorisation by the Security Council, it may be presumed that the military action by the regional organisation is lawful. In the absence of such an authorisation, the military action is presumed wrongful until proven otherwise.

[219] Walter, above n 3, at 308.

[220] *Ibid*, at 308.

[221] See also Körbs, above n 184, at 537.

subsequently authorised the (future) NATO presence in Kosovo was of an open-ended nature. This could undermine the Security Council's ability to exercise control over the termination of the NATO mandate in Kosovo.

5.1. ECOMOG in Liberia

ECOWAS qualifies as a regional organisation which could be utilised by the Security Council in terms of Article 53(1) of the Charter. This follows from the founding treaty of the organisation in conjunction with additional protocols regulating mutual defence assistance. According to its founding treaty,[222] ECOWAS is an organisation dedicated to promoting economic integration between its member states. In addition to the founding treaty, the ECOWAS member states signed a Protocol on Non-Aggression on 22 April 1978 which is based, inter alia, on the consideration that the organisation could not attain its objectives without the establishment of a peaceful atmosphere and harmonious understanding between the member states. It also contains a clause on the peaceful settlement of disputes.[223]

The security dimension of ECOWAS was extended by an additional Protocol Relating to the Mutual Assistance on Defence, signed on 29 May 1981.[224] This treaty provides for the establishment of a multinational ECOWAS defence force with an elaborate command structure. The force was to provide mutual assistance and defence in any case of external aggression, or conflict between member states that could not be settled in terms of the non-aggression protocol, or internal armed conflict engineered and supported actively from outside that would be likely to endanger security and peace in the whole region.[225] Since the force can render assistance in conflict situations between member states, ECOWAS's regional character in terms of Article 52 of the Charter seems to be beyond doubt.[226] However, the extent to which it can become involved in member states was the subject of some controversy. In particular, it has been questioned whether the force could intervene in situations

---

[222] Treaty establishing the Economic Community of West African States of 28 May 1975, in 14 *International Legal Materials* 1200 (1975).
[223] Protocol on Non-Aggression of ECOWAS of 22 April 1978, reprinted in PF Gonidec, *Les organisations internationales africaines* 275–76 (Paris, L'Harmattan, 1987); see also Nolte (Restoring Peace), above n 211, at 613.
[224] A/SP3/5/81, in 4 *Nigeria's Treaties in Force* 898 (1970–1990).
[225] *Ibid*; see also Anthony C Ofodile, "The Legality of ECOWAS' Intervention in Liberia", 32 *Columbia Journal of Transnational Law* 411 (1994).
[226] Körbs, above n 184, at 368, nonetheless raised a formal doubt in this regard, as the Protocol on Non-Aggression, above n 213, had not yet been ratified by the ECOWAS members during its military interventions in Liberia and Sierra Leone. He did not regard the fact that ECOWAS members in practice regarded themselves as bound by the Protocol as sufficiently compensating for the absence of a formal ratification of the Protocol.

such as Liberia, where the conflict was predominantly or exclusively of an internal nature, as this was not provided for explicitly in the Protocol.[227]

ECOWAS clearly assumed that it had the power to render assistance in the case of Liberia, for on 7 August 1990, it created the ECOWAS Cease-fire Monitoring Group (ECOMOG), with a mandate to restore law and order and create the necessary conditions for free and fair elections in Liberia.[228] These forces landed in Liberia on 27 August 1990.[229] There was no prior Security Council resolution that authorised this intervention. Instead, it has been attempted to see this intervention as evidence of an *ex post facto* Security Council authorisation.[230] Even if one were to accept the possibility of a retroactive authorisation, it is doubtful whether the ECOMOG intervention would be of precedential value in this regard, as the legal basis of the intervention remains controversial.

Some justify the ECOMOG intervention on invitation by the Liberian government.[231] The fact that President Doe had issued an invitation to representatives of ECOWAS states to intervene militarily does not figure in official texts, but has been reported in the serious press and not officially contradicted.[232] Those who argue in favour of *ex post facto* Security Council authorisation dispute the legitimacy of the invitation, due to the lack of effective control by President Doe at the time the invitation was extended. At the time of the ECOMOG intervention there had been a complete collapse of the effective government. There were five different people claiming to be President and President Doe's control was limited to an area around Monrovia.[233] Thus, rather than legitimating the intervention on the basis of this invitation, they read a

---

[227] Nolte, above n 211, at 613, affirmed the power of the force to do so in the case of Liberia, whereas Ofodile, above n 225, at 411, was more cautious. See also Brownlie & Apperley, above n 9, at 915.

[228] Nii Lante Wallace-Bruce, "Of Collapsed, Dysfunctional and Disoriented States: Challenges to International Law", 47 *Netherlands International Law Review* 62 (2000).

[229] Ofodile, above n 225, at 384.

[230] Greenwood, above n 9, at 929; Herdegen (Staatsgewalt), above n 210, at 76; Österdahl, above n 216, at 57; Sicilianos, above n 95, at 40.

[231] Nolte, above n 211, at 634.

[232] *Ibid*, at 621–22. He noted that both prevailing scholarly opinion and state practice support the view that military action by third states which is undertaken within a country upon the request of its lawful government, is not prohibited by Art 2(4) of the Charter. Also, since such military action is not undertaken against the will of the state concerned, it would not qualify as enforcement action, which would necessitate an authorisation by the Security Council. See also R Jennings & A Watts (eds), *Oppenheim's International Law*, Vol 1 438 9th edn (London, Harlow, 1992); L Doswald-Beck, "The Legal Validity of Military Intervention by Invitation of the Government", 56 *British Yearbook of International Law* 251 (1985). See also *Nicaragua v United States*, merits, above n 32, at 116.

[233] Herdegen (Staatsgewalt), above n 210, at 75–76; Österdahl, above n 216, at 57; Walter, above n 3, at 237. But see Nolte (Restoring Peace), above n 211, at 625, who regarded a

retroactive authorisation into subsequent Security Council statements and resolutions.[234]

The statements issued by the President of the Security Council on 22 January 1991 and 7 May 1992, respectively, "recognised" the ECOMOG action.[235] Thereafter the Security Council adopted Resolution 788 of 19 November 1992, which determined that the situation in Liberia constituted a threat to peace and security in West Africa as a whole. It also imposed an arms embargo on Liberia in terms of Chapter VII of the Charter.[236] In addition, it "commended" ECOWAS for its efforts to restore peace, security and stability in Liberia.[237] According to the preamble of Resolution 866 of 22 September 1993, ECOMOG had the primary responsibility for supervising the implementation of the military provisions of the peace agreement. The United Nations Observer Mission in Liberia (UNOMIL), on the other hand, was to verify and monitor this process.[238] This division of powers between ECOMOG and the UNOMIL combined with the fact that the latter would not be engaging in enforcement measures,[239] have been interpreted as implying that ECOMOG was engaged in enforcement action.[240] This conclusion was also supported with the argument that the Security Council resolutions were all adopted unanimously and the military action was also supported by the Secretary-General and the General Assembly.[241]

It is unlikely that the vague language used in the presidential statements and Security Council resolutions would amount to an *ex post facto* authorisation of military enforcement action. First, the language is broad and vague enough to apply only to those aspects of the intervention that

---

President Doe's degradation to a minor contender for power irrelevant. International recognition is usually not withdrawn from an established regime, even if it has lost control over large portions of the country, if no successor regime has taken its place.

[234] See also Walter, above n 3, at 299; Herdegen (Staatsgewalt), above n 210, at 76; see also Villani, above n 218, at 543.
[235] See S/22133 (1991) and S/23886 (1992).
[236] At para 8.
[237] At para 1; see also SC Res 813 of 26 March 1993, at para 2; SC Res 856 of 10 August 1993, at para 6.
[238] At para 3. See also Brownlie & Apperley, above n 9, at 908.
[239] SC Res 866 of 2 September 1993:
  "*The Security Council,*
  ....
  3. *Decides* that UNOMIL (...) shall have the following mandate:
  ....
  (h) Without participation in enforcement operations, to co-ordinate with ECOMOG in the discharge of ECOMOG's separate responsibilities both formally, through the Violations Committee, and informally... ."
[240] Walter, above n 3, at 304.
[241] *Ibid*, see also S/25402 (1993).

constituted classic peace-keeping. After all, it has been argued that at the time of the presidential statements in 1991, the rebels under Charles Taylor also accepted the ECOWAS peace plan and cease-fire, as a result of which no authorisation for enforcement action was required.[242] Admittedly, this situation had changed by the time of the adoption of Resolution 788 (1992), which was the first resolution regarding the situation in Liberia. Since October 1992 heavy fighting that exceeded the limits of self-defence had broken out between Charles Taylor's rebel forces (the NPFL) and ECOMOG.[243]

Even so, the vague formulation of the Security Council resolutions leaves the question to what extent or degree it had supported the ECOMOG involvement unanswered. In addition, the fact that UNOMIL, was not to engage in enforcement action does not necessarily lead to the conclusion that ECOMOG was indeed authorised to do so. Neither can this be concluded from the unanimous support for the Security Council resolutions, as one could also argue that such support resulted from the very fact that *no* enforcement operation was authorised. One could argue that states voted in favour of the resolutions exactly because they supported classic peace-keeping action as opposed to military intervention, or even that they recognised this as an intervention on invitation by the government.[244] One should also keep in mind that in the post Cold War era the Security Council has always referred explicitly to Chapter VII when intending to act under it.[245] In essence therefore the language of the resolutions, combined with the ambiguous circumstances under which they were adopted, do not lend convincing support to an argument of *ex post facto* ratification of the ECOMOG intervention.

5.2. ECOMOG in Sierra Leone

The involvement of ECOMOG in Sierra Leone was to some extent surrounded by similar ambiguities to the case in Liberia. The ECOMOG involvement followed a military coup in Sierra Leone on 25 May 1997, during which the democratically elected Government of President Kabbah was overthrown. By 20 June 1997 the Foreign Ministers of the ECOWAS countries had agreed to work towards the reinstatement of the legitimate Government by a combination of dialogue, the imposition of sanctions and

---

[242] Walter, above n 3, at 298; see also Brownlie & Apperley, above n 9, at 908. But see Ofodile, above n 225, at 412, who submitted that ECOWAS did not receive the consent of all the contending parties in Liberia.

[243] See also Walter, above n 3, at 299; Ofodile, above n 225, at 413.

[244] If the Security Council resolutions did indeed contain an implied authorisation to ECOMOG to engage in enforcement action, it is also possible that it related only to military action engaged in *after* their adoption.

[245] Nolte (Restoring Peace), above n 211, at 633–34.

the use of force.[246] On 29 August 1997 the ECOWAS countries adopted an oil and arms embargo and authorised its troops to use all necessary means to ensure its enforcement.[247] In the wake of this decision there were several violent incidents between ECOMOG troops and others that attempted to undermine the embargo.[248]

Although the Security Council supported the mediation efforts initiated by ECOWAS and supported their objectives to reinstate the legitimate Government in a Presidential Statement,[249] it did not authorised them to use force to realise these objectives. The only such authorisation concerned the enforcement of a United Nations arms and petroleum embargo against Sierra Leone, which was imposed by Resolution 1132 of 8 October 1997.[250] After determining that the situation in Sierra Leone constituted a threat to international peace and security in the region, the Security Council adopted the embargo in order to persuade the military junta to relinquish power and make way for the restoration of the democratically elected Government. Accordingly, the Security Council intended to terminate the embargo once this goal had been achieved.[251]

In addition, the Security Council authorised ECOWAS (ie ECOMOG) under Chapter VIII to ensure a strict implementation of the embargo. This included the halting of inward shipping where necessary in order to inspect and verify the cargoes.[252] ECOWAS also had to report to the Security Council on a monthly basis through the Sanctions Committee established in the same resolution.[253] This reference to Chapter VIII clarified that the Security Council authorised the regional organisation to use force for limited purposes, ie to prevent the inward maritime shipping of arms and petroleum.

The duration of the authorisation was not subjected to a time limit, but a functional limitation could be deducted from its purpose of enforcing the embargo. As the embargo itself was aimed at restoring the democratically elected Government in Sierra Leone, the authorisation to enforce it would expire once this goal had been achieved. After the return of the democratically elected President on 10 March 1998, the Security Council terminated the petroleum embargo in Resolution 1156 of 16 March 1998.[254] It finally terminated the arms embargo against the Government in

---

[246] See their final communiqué of the meeting in S/1997/499, Annex, at 3. See also Georg Nolte, *Eingreifen auf Einladung* 427 (Berlin, Springer, 1999).
[247] S/1997/695, Annex I and Annex 2; see also Nolte (Eingreifen), above n 246, at 428.
[248] Nolte (Eingreifen), above n 246, at 428.
[249] S/PRST/1997/36; see also Nolte (Eingreifen), above n 246, at 427; cf Sicilianos, above n 95, at 41.
[250] SC Res 1132 of 8 October 1997, at para 6.
[251] *Ibid*, at para 1 and para 19.
[252] *Ibid*, at para 8.
[253] *Ibid*, at para 9.
[254] SC Res 1156 of 16 March 1998, at para 2.

Resolution 1171 of 5 June 1998.[255] This meant that the purpose of the authorisation to use force by ECOMOG had ceased to exist, as a result of which the authorisation itself had ceased.[256]

The ECOMOG enforcement action that extended beyond this mandate—and which effectively continued until early 2000—was not authorised by the Security Council. The Security Council praised the ECOMOG action on several occasions. For example, in Resolution 1162 of 17 April 1998 it commended ECOMOG on its important role in support of the objectives to restore peaceful conditions in the country.[257] This was reiterated in Resolution 1181 of 13 July 1998, in which the Security Council also noted the role of ECOMOG in assisting the implementation of disarmament[258] and welcomed its commitment to ensure the security of United Nations personnel in Sierra Leone.[259] Subsequent resolutions also commended the role of ECOMOG for its role in restoring security and stability in Sierra Leone, the protection of civilians and the promotion of a peaceful settlement of the conflict.[260] However, none of these statements were made under Chapter VIII, or contained language that would *ex post facto* authorise ECOMOG to engage in enforcement action.[261]

As in the case of the ECOMOG intervention in Liberia, it has been argued that a Security Council mandate was superfluous, as the ECOMOG intervention in Sierra Leone occurred on the invitation of the democratically elected government.[262] Even though this government had been overthrown and was not in effective control of the country, it was still almost universally recognised as the legitimate Government of Sierra Leone, which could invite military support from ECOMOG.[263] This would also explain why the Security Council limited itself to authorising the use of force only in order to halt inward maritime shipping in violation of the United Nations embargo.[264] As this enforcement action affected international waters over which Sierra Leone had no jurisdiction, its invitation for military support could not cover military action in that area. Consequently Sierra Leone and ECOWAS needed a Security Council resolution to authorise enforcement action in international waters.[265]

---

[255] SC Res 1171 of 5 June 1998, at para 1.
[256] *Ibid*, at para 2, also imposed an arms embargo against non-governmental forces. However, it did not grant ECOMOG any authorisation to enforce it.
[257] SC Res 1162 of 17 April 1998, at para 2.
[258] *Ibid*, at para 6.
[259] *Ibid*, at para 9.
[260] SC Res 1260 of 20 August 1999, at para 3; see also SC Res 1231 of 11 March 1999, at para 10; SC Res 1270 of 22 October 1999, at para 7; SC Res 1289 of 7 February 2000, at para 2.
[261] As was asserted by Villani, above n 218, at 555.
[262] Nolte (Eingreifen), above n 246, at 427.
[263] *Ibid*, at 429–30.
[264] *Ibid*; at 428.
[265] *Ibid*; at 428–29.

An in depth analysis of the validity of this argument falls outside the scope of this Chapter. For present purposes it suffices to point out that the vagueness of the Security Council statements concerning the ECOMOG involvement in Sierra Leone, as well as other circumstances surrounding it, would weaken claims that it is evidence of an *ex post facto* authorisation by the Security Council to use force.

5.3.   NATO in Former Yugoslavia

From the discussion in section 4 above, it follows that Article 42 in combination with Article 48(2) of the Charter provided the legal basis for the Security Council resolutions mandating military enforcement action in former Yugoslavia. The military mandates relating to Bosnia-Herzegovina tended to cause confusion on this point, by sometimes (indirectly) referring to both Chapter VII and VIII of the Charter.[266] In doing so, these resolutions made it unclear as to whether the Security Council was acting in terms of Article 53(1) of the Charter, or Article 42 combined with Article 48(2). However, as none of the successor states to the former Yugoslavia are members of NATO, the Security Council could not base the mandate on Article 53(1) of the Charter, despite their regional proximity to the NATO members. The authorisations therefore had to be based on Articles 42 and 48(2) of the Charter.[267]

In Bosnia-Herzegovina the military mandates commenced with the authorisation to use force to secure the delivery of humanitarian aid,[268] followed by the enforcement of the no-fly zone,[269] the arms embargo[270] and the protection of the safe havens,[271] respectively. Although none of these authorisations were subjected to a time-limit, they were explicitly terminated by Resolution 1031 of 15 December 1995.[272] This resolution also created IFOR, which was to operate under NATO command and which was authorised to use force in implementing its obligations under

---

[266] In several resolutions the Security Council authorised states to take all necessary means "nationally or through regional agencies or arrangements", which could give the impression that it was acting under Chapter VIII of the Charter. See SC Res 781 of 9 October 1992, at para 5; SC Res 787 of 16 November 1992, at para 12; SC Res 836 of 4 June 1993, at para 10; SC Res 816 of 31 March 1993, at para 5; SC Res 820 of 17 April 1993, at para 29; SC Res 1031 of 15 December 1995, at para 14. See also See also White & Ülgen, above n 2, at 389; O' Connell, above n 185, at 66.

[267] To Walter, above n 3, at 278 ff; cf O' Connell, above n 185, at 67.

[268] SC Res 770 of 13 August 1992.

[269] SC Res 781 of 9 October 1992; SC Res 816 of 31 March 1993.

[270] SC Res 787 of 16 November 1992; SC Res 820 of 17 April 1993.

[271] SC Res 836 of 4 June 1993. Under SC Res 819 of 16 April 1993 and SC Res 824 of 6 May 1993, the so-called "safe havens" were established in Sarajevo, Srebrenica, Tuzla, Zepa, Gorazde and Bihac.

[272] SC 1031 of 15 December 1995, at para 19.

the Dayton Accords in Bosnia and Herzegovina.[273] These included the separation of the warring parties and the supervision of the cease-fire, which amounted to an extensive military mandate.[274] The mandate authorised in Resolution 1031 (1995) was initially limited to a period of 12 months.[275] Reporting obligations (either addressed to member states,[276] or to the Secretary-General[277]), were also a common feature of the authorising resolutions.

In essence therefore, the NATO authorisations to use force in Bosnia-Herzegovina were legally unproblematic, as they had a legal basis in the Charter and remained under the overall control of the Security Council from beginning to end. The matter is different, however, with respect to NATO's air campaign in Kosovo. The following passages will reveal that the legal controversy surrounding this military action relates to the absence of a Security Council authorisation at the time the air-strikes ensued, as well as to the open-endedness of the military mandate that was ultimately adopted.

5.3.1. The Absence of a Security Council Mandate for the Kosovo Air-Campaign

Chapter 6 at section 3.2. has already elaborated on the fact that the consistent attempts of the Federal Republic of Yugoslavia (FRY) to be recognised as the automatic successor to the former Socialist Federal Republic of Yugoslavia in the United Nations, amounted to a voluntary acceptance of the Charter system within the FRY's territory. As a result, the FRY would be estopped from claiming that any coercive measures by the Security Council against the FRY between 1992 and 2000 were illegal on the basis that they were taken against a non-member of the United Nations. This, in turn, means that the Security Council could have authorised NATO enforcement action in Kosovo during this period in terms of Articles 42 and Article 48(2) of the Charter. However, as in the case of other authorisations to use force, this authorisation had to be explicit and had to be

---

[273] In essence, it adopted the mandate that was proposed in the General Framework Agreement for Peace in Bosnia and Herzegovina, which was signed on 14 December 1995 in Paris. This document, which consists of a general framework and 11 annexes, is generally referred to as the Dayton Accords. It is available at www.ohr.int.

[274] SC Res 1031 of 15 December 1995, at paras 15 ff. See also the Dayton Accords, Annex 1–A, above n 369, at Art I2(b) and Art IV4(b).

[275] SC Res 1088 of 12 December 1996, replaced IFOR with SFOR after the expiration of the former's 12 months mandate. SFOR's mandate has been extended on an ongoing basis.

[276] Eg SC Res 770 of 13 August 1992, at para 4; SC Res 787 of 16 November 1992, at para 14; SC Res 816 of 31 March 1993, at paras 7–8; In terms of SC Res 1031 of 15 December 1995, at para 25; SC Res 1088 of 12 December 1996, at para 26.

[277] Eg SC Res 781 of 9 October 1992, at para 4; SC Res 836 of 4 June 1993, at paras 12–13; SC Res 1174 of 15 June 1998, at para 25; SC Res 1247 of 18 June 1999, at para 25; SC Res 1305 of 21 June 2000, at para 25.

obtained prior to any enforcement action. In the case of Kosovo, the Security Council authorised the establishment of KFOR in Resolution 1244 of 10 June 1999. However, it did not authorise the NATO air campaign preceding the establishment of this force.

In March 1998, in the wake of the escalating crisis in Kosovo, the Security Council imposed a mandatory arms embargo against the Federal Republic of Yugoslavia (FRY) and the Kosovar Albanians. Resolution 1160 of 31 March 1998 adopted these measures under Chapter VII of the Charter[278] and stated that the failure to make constructive progress towards the peaceful resolution of the situation in Kosovo would lead to the consideration of additional measures.[279] However, there was no authorisation to use "all necessary means", ie to resort to force for its implementation.[280]

The Security Council next adopted Resolution 1199 of 23 September 1998, which explicitly determined that the situation in Kosovo constituted a threat to peace and security in the region. The operative part of the resolution demanded the cessation of hostilities, a cease-fire, as well as immediate steps by both parties to improve the humanitarian situation and enter into negotiations with international involvement. The FRY was also requested to implement a series of measures aimed at achieving a peaceful solution to the crisis. Once again, however, there was no authorisation for a military intervention. The resolution merely determined that if these measures and those of Resolution 1160 (1998) were not implemented, the Security Council would consider additional measures to maintain or restore peace and stability in the region.[281]

Resolution 1203 of 24 October 1998 repeated the substance of the foregoing resolutions and may have authorised limited use of force when endorsing NATO and OSCE agreements with Belgrade for the deployment of verifiers within Kosovo.[282] This follows from the statement that in the event of an emergency, action may be needed to ensure their safety and freedom of movement.[283] However, this wording would only have authorised force in order to protect the Verification Mission and not a comprehensive air campaign.[284] Resolution 1207 of 17 November 1998 also contained no language justifying the use of force. It is thus clear that when the NATO air campaign was launched on 24 March 1999, there was no prior Security Council authorisation to this effect.[285]

---

[278] At para 8.
[279] At para 19.
[280] Simma, above n 9, at 6; Chinkin, above n 9, at 842; Kälin, above n 9, at 164.
[281] At para 16; see also Simma, above n 9, at 6–7; Brownlie & Apperley, above n 9, at 895.
[282] SC Res 1203 of 24 October 1998, at para 1.
[283] *Ibid*, at para 9.
[284] Chinkin (Legality), above n 9, at 912.
[285] Brownlie & Apperley, above n 9, at 895; Gray, above n 131, at 14.

Consequently, the NATO air-strikes in Kosovo and the FRY were in violation of the Charter.

After a period of intensive diplomacy and the cessation of the bombing, the Security Council adopted Resolution 1244 of 10 June 1999. This resolution authorised the deployment of an international civil and security presence in Kosovo.[286] The security presence had to include substantial NATO participation and was to be established under unified command and control.[287] It was authorised to use force for a broad variety of tasks. These ranged from the deterring of renewed hostilities to the establishing of a secure environment in which refugees and displaced persons could return home, the international civil presence could operate, a transitional administration could be established and humanitarian aid could be delivered.[288]

The military authorisation granted in Resolution 1244 (1999) only had prospective effect and cannot be interpreted as a retroactive, *ex post facto* legitimisation of the NATO air campaign. During the debates leading up to Resolution 1160 (1998) and Resolution 1199 (1998), it became clear that the Russian Federation and China would veto any Security Council resolution authorising the use of force against the FRY.[289] In fact, on 26 March 1999 Russia submitted a draft resolution that would have condemned the NATO action as a breach of international law.[290] Although this draft resolution was vetoed by the western permanent members and only received support from China and Namibia, it does confirm that two permanent members were not in support of the air campaign. Since they maintained these positions up to the adoption of Resolution 1244 (1999), there could be no question of an *ex post facto* authorisation.[291]

The military mandate granted in Resolution 1244 (1999) was very broad, as is reflected by the fact that, amongst other things, it concerned the facilitation of conditions under which the international civil presence could operate and a transitional administration could be established.[292] As was explained in connection with Resolution 1483 (2003) on Iraq,[293]

---

[286] SC Res 1244 of 10 June 1999, at para 5.
[287] *Ibid*, at para 7 and annex 2, pt 4.
[288] SC Res 1244 of 10 June 1999, at para 7 ff.
[289] Kälin, above n 9, at 164; Simma, above n 9, at 7.
[290] S/1999/328.
[291] See Russia in S/PV 4011 7 (1999); and China in *ibid*, at 8. Brownlie & Apperley, above n 9, at 895; Charney, above n 9, at 11; Simma, above n 9, at 11; Sicilianos, above n 95, at 42 ff; Villani, above n 218, at 548. But see Wedgewood, above n 9, at 830, who regarded SC Res 1244 of 10 June 1998, as an *ex post facto* ratification. She (inter alia) submitted that it was implausible that the Security Council would ratify the result of an allied military campaign if it considered the means wholly illicit or tantamount to aggression.
[292] SC Res 1244 of 10 June 1999, at para 10 and para 11 ; The legal implications of the civil aspects of the mandate are discussed in ch 8, at s 2 and s 3.2.1.
[293] See above, at s 3.2.3.

the need to subject a military mandate to a time limit acquires special importance in such circumstances, as a functional limitation would be inadministrable in practice. Unfortunately, however, the mandate granted under Resolution 1244 (1999) is of an open-ended nature.[294] This, in turn, implies that its termination could be prevented by the veto of a permanent member. In such a case, the mandate would remain legal if and to the extent that it is supported by a majority of Security Council members, including a majority of the permanent members. Anything else would imply a shifting of the overall control over the mandate from the Security Council as a collective entity to those permanent member(s) with a direct interest in the prolongation of the mandate, which would amount to an illegal delegation of powers.[295]

6.   CONCLUSION

From the above analysis one can conclude that the authorisation model is not only authorised by the Charter, but has also in practice become a firmly established substitute for the Article 43 agreements foreseen in the Charter. In the post Cold War era it provides a pragmatic and affordable way to legitimate military operations in a fashion that also takes account of the military complexities surrounding military intervention, such as the need for unified command and control. At the same time, the central role of the Security Council in maintaining international peace and security requires that it has to maintain overall control over an authorised military operation at all times. The fact that the military mandate is delegated to a regional (defence) organisation as opposed to individual member states does not alter this essential element of a legal authorisation to use force. Regional (defence) organisations do not have any residual right to engage in military operations in the absence of a clear, prior mandate from the Security Council.

The initiation of a military operation is, however, only one of the elements which are essential for ensuring Security Council control over the military mandate. The control of the termination of the mandate by the Security Council as a collective entity is equally important in this regard. The clearest and most reliable way for doing so is to subject the military mandate to a time limit in the authorising resolution. In instances where the Security Council refrains from doing so, states can attempt to infer a functional limitation from the purposes of the authorising resolution. The military mandate would then be regarded as expired once the purposes for which it was authorised have been fulfilled.

---

[294] At para 19; See also Blokker (Authorisation), above n 5, at 563 fn 95.
[295] See above at ss 2.3. and 3.2.3.

However, one has to concede that such a "presumption of expiration" would only provide an administrable solution where the military mandate is of a limited nature and attached to a single or clear goal. This would be the case, for example, where the enforcement of a limited naval embargo is authorised in order to effect the reinstatement of the democratically elected government. Unfortunately the "presumption of expiration" would be of little use in instances where the military mandate is extensive and its purposes multifarious. In such an instance the delegation would remain legal as long as it is supported by an overall majority within the Security Council, including a majority of the permanent members. Without such support the Security Council, as a collective entity, will not be able to claim consistent overall control over the military operation. This implies that the delegation of the competence to use force justifies an exception to the rule of parallelism of forms, as the termination of the delegation will not necessarily be prevented by the "reverse veto".

In this context one may also consider whether there could be a role for the General Assembly in determining the termination of the military mandate. It could, for example, adopt a resolution affirming the functional expiration of the military mandate, or that its termination was necessitated by the disintegration of support within the Security Council regarding its continuation. At first sight, such a resolution would seem to constitute a clear violation of Article 11(2) of the Charter, which reserves (all aspects of) enforcement action exclusively to the Security Council. One could, however, attempt to justify this with the argument that the General Assembly would be exercising an emergency role for which it had already set a precedent during the Korean war. At the time, the General Assembly action resulted from the unique circumstance that the Security Council first initiated a military operation but was then prevented from terminating it, due to a disagreement amongst its permanent members. Even though the weight of this precedent is weakened by the questionable legality of the Korean military operation as a whole, it does illustrate how the General Assembly could develop a residual role in terminating military mandates in future situations where the necessary consensus within the Security Council to do so is lacking. In addition, one should also bear in mind that the General Assembly would, strictly speaking, merely be *reaffirming* that the mandate has terminated, as actual termination follows automatically from the structure and purpose of the Charter. The reaffirming role of the General Assembly would mainly serve to strengthen legal certainty regarding termination.

Finally, it needs to be emphasised that any residual role for the General Assembly in this regard should be seen as an *ultima ratio*. The purpose and structure of the Charter, as well as the efficiency and legitimacy of the United Nations would be better served by a clear mandate that is subjected to a (renewable) time limit and that remains under the overall control of the Security Council from beginning to end. However, whether this is a realistic expectation remains doubtful in the light of past Security Council practice. It has revealed that such overall control remains elusive exactly in those situations in which it is needed the most, ie where a military intervention directly affects the interests of powerful permanent members. In such situations the permanent members are prone to justify unilateral interventions on the basis of dubious *ex post facto* or implied authorisations, which neither enhances the political legitimacy of the Chapter VII mechanism, nor contributes to its long term endurance and efficiency.

8

Limits to the Security Council's Discretion to Authorise the Civil Administration of Territories

1. INTRODUCTION

THE MILITARY MANDATES authorised by the Security Council in Kosovo and East Timor, respectively, were complemented by civil mandates, which effectively placed the respective territories under complete United Nations administration. Although Resolution 1244 of 10 June 1999 explicitly determined that Kosovo remained a part of the territory of the Federal Republic of Yugoslavia (FRY),[1] the resolution left the FRY with very little effective authority over the area. The Yugoslav military, police and paramilitary forces were required to withdraw from the territory,[2] as they were replaced by an international security presence under NATO command.[3] In addition, the civil administration was transferred to an international civil presence (UNMIK), that functioned under the control of a Special Representative of the Secretary-General.[4]

Since this included the transfer of the legislative and executive authority, as well as the administration of the judiciary, it effectively placed the complete system of governance in Kosovo under the auspices of the United Nations.[5] For example, the Special Representative may change, repeal or suspend existing laws which are incompatible with the mandate, aims or purposes of UNMIK.[6] He is also entitled to issue new

---

[1] The preamble of SC Res 1244 of 10 June 1999 explicitly affirms the sovereignty and territorial integrity of the Federal Republic of Yugoslavia. See also SC Res 1160 of 31 March 1998 at para 13; and SC Res 1199 of 23 September 1998, at para 7.
[2] SC Res 1244 of 10 June 1999, Annex 2, at para 2.
[3] SC Res 1244 of 10 June 1999, at para 7 and Annex 2, at para 4.
[4] SC Res 1244 of 10 June 1999, at para 6.
[5] See SC Res 1244 of 10 June 1999, at paras 10–11. See also Andreas Zimmermann & Carsten Stahn, "Yugoslav Territory, United Nations Trusteeship or Sovereign State? Reflections on the current and future legal status of Kosovo", 70 *Nordic Journal of International Law* 442–43 (2001); Carsten Stahn, "International Territorial Administration in the former Yugoslavia: Origins, Developments and Challenges ahead", in 61 *Zeitschrift für ausländisches öffentliches Recht und Völkerrecht* 134 ff (2001).
[6] S/1999/779, at 39.

legislative acts in the form of regulations, which remain in force until repealed by UNMIK or superseded by rules subsequently issued by the future political institutions of Kosovo.[7] In addition, he may appoint any persons to perform functions in the civil administration of Kosovo, including the judiciary, and may remove them from office.[8]

A similar situations prevails in East Timor where the United Nations Transitional Administration in East Timor (UNTAET) was established by Resolution 1272 of 25 October 1999,[9] in the aftermath of the territory's referendum on independence. UNTAET, which was headed by a Special Representative of the Secretary-General,[10] included a military and civil component and was endowed with overall responsibility for the administration of East Timor. This included the power to exercise all legislative and executive authority, as well as the administration of justice.[11] Subsequently, the Special Representative adopted a variety of far-reaching laws regulating, inter alia, the establishment of a national consultative council,[12] a judicial service commission,[13] a central fiscal authority[14] and a national defence force.[15]

When East Timor gained independence on 20 May 2002, UNTAET was replaced by the so-called United Nations Mission of Support in East Timor (UNMISET).[16] Although the civilian component (like the military component) is significantly reduced compared to that of UNTAET, it still yields considerable power over the civil administration. UNMISET, which is headed by a Special Representative of the Secretary-General, is authorised under Chapter VII of the Charter to take all necessary action to provide assistance to core administrative structures critical to the viability and political stability of East Timor.[17] This includes decision-making power with regard to the financial and central services; the internal systems in the Council of Ministers, the Chief Minister's office and various ministries; essential services such as water and sanitation and the judicial system.[18] UNMISET also remains responsible for interim law

---

[7] UNMIK/REG/1/1999 of 23 July 1999, at s 4. This and all other regulations adopted by the Special Representative are available at www.un.org/peace/kosovo/.
[8] *Ibid*, at s 1(2); Stahn, above n 5, at 112.
[9] At para 1.
[10] SC Res 1272 of 25 October 1999, at para 6.
[11] *Ibid*, at paras 1 and 6, which explicitly stated that the Special Representative will have the power to enact new laws and regulations and to amend, suspend or repeal existing ones; see also Matthias Ruffert, "The Administration of Kosovo and East-Timor by the International Community", 50 *International & Comparative Law Quarterly* 623 (2001).
[12] UNTAET/REG/1999/2 of 2 December 1999, s 1 ff. This and other regulations adopted by the Special Representative are available at www.un.org/peace/etimor/untaetR/UntaetR.htm.
[13] UNAET/REG/1999/3 of 3 December 1999, at ss 1 ff.
[14] UNTAET/REG/2000/1 of 14 January 2000, at ss 1 ff.
[15] UNTAET/REG/2001/1 of 31 January 2001, at ss 2 ff.
[16] SC Res 1410 of 17 May 2002, at para 1.
[17] SC Res 140 of 17 May 2002, at para 2(a).
[18] S/2002/432, at para 70.

enforcement and public security, assistance in developing the East Timor Police Service (ETPS) and contributing to the maintenance of the new country's external and internal security.[19]

Following the invasion of Iraq in March 2003 and the capitulation of the Hussein regime, the Security Council authorised the civil administration of Iraq under Chapter VII of the Charter by the United States and the United Kingdom (ie the Authority).[20] In addition, the Special Representative of the Secretary-General was authorised under Chapter VII to work intensively with the Authority in a variety of areas related to civil administration. These included activities for the restoration and establishment of national and local institutions for representative governance; the reconstruction of key infrastructure; the rebuilding of the civilian police and legal and judicial reform.[21] On the one hand this mandate differs from those in East Timor and Kosovo, since the civil administration is effectively carried about by (two) member states rather than the Secretary-General, whose Special Representative has more of a coordinating role. At the same time, however, there is a common denominator in the form of a Chapter VII resolution that authorised the "external" civil administration of the territory in question.

Whilst chapter 7 concentrated on the legality of the military mandates authorised by the Security Council, this chapter examines the extent to which the Security Council is empowered to authorise the civil administration of territories under Chapter VII of the Charter. In the process it builds on limitations to Security Council powers already introduced in previous chapters. These include the conditions attached to a delegation of Chapter VII powers, as will be reflected in the section dealing with the nature of the mandates for civil administration. Thereafter, the chapter once again draws attention to the Security Council's obligation to respect human rights norms, which has already been illuminated in chapter 5 at section 4.2.

In doing so, this chapter merely outlines the general obligation of the Security Council to respect human rights and provide a suitable monitoring mechanism when authorising a mandate for civil administration. It does not attempt to analyse the concrete obligations flowing from each specific right in the International Bill of Rights. The only exception concerns the right to self-determination, as it may arguably turn out to be the right most severely affected by the long term civil administrations in the respective territories. Since the right to self-determination is a vast and complex subject in itself, section 3 only concentrates on the main

---

[19] At para 2(b) and 2(c); S/2002/432, at paras 79 ff.
[20] SC Res 1483 of 22 May 2003, at para 4. See also SC Res 1511 of 16 October 2003, at para 1.
[21] SC Res 1483 of 22 May 2003, at para 8. See also SC Res 1511 of 16 October 2003, at para 8.

characteristics of the right and its implications for the powers of the Security Council.

Finally, it is worth mentioning that the only other instance in which the Security Council has authorised the direct, comprehensive administration of a territory in terms of its Chapter VII powers, concerned the United Nations Transitional Administration for Eastern Slavonia (UNTAES).[22] This region was the last remaining part of the Serb controlled Republika Srpska Krajina (RSK), which during the war in Croatia used to control one third of Croatia's territory. After the war, the RSK ceased to exist and UNTAES was created in order to provide for a peaceful reintegration of the territory into Croatia.[23] The UNTAES mission had a military and civil component which were both concentrated in the hands of a United Nations Transitional Administrator.[24]

Although this mandate effectively granted UNTAES complete governmental control over the territory,[25] it was explicitly agreed with the parties from the outset that the mandate would last no longer than two years.[26] At the end of this period, Croatia resumed full control over the area.[27] As a result, those limitations to Security Council powers that become pertinent during an extended mandate for civil administration, notably the right to self-determination, did not obtain the same relevance in the case of UNTAES. For this reason the UNTAES mandate will not form a subject of discussion in the following passages.

For similar reasons this chapter will also not focus on the High Representative for Bosnia-Herzegovina, whose appointment was authorised when the Security Council endorsed the Dayton Accords.[28] Although his mandate is authorised under Chapter VII of the Charter, it does not amount to a comprehensive mandate for civil administration

---

[22] For an overview of situations in which the United Nations has administered territories on a different legal basis (ie outside of Chapter VII of the Charter), see Stahn above n 5, at 107 ff; Ralph Wilde, "From Danzig to East Timor and Beyond: The Role of International Territorial Administration", 95 *American Journal of International Law* 583 ff (2001).

[23] *Basic Agreement on the Region of Eastern Slavonia, Baranja and Western Sirmium*, S/1995/951, Annex. This agreement, which is hereinafter referred to as Basic Agreement, entered into force on 22 November 1995; Zimmermann & Stahn, above n 5, at 433.

[24] SC Res 1037 of 15 January 1996, at para 2.

[25] The military component consisted of the supervision and facilitation of the demilitarisation as agreed to by the parties; the monitoring of the voluntary and safe return of refugees and displaced persons to their home of origin; and to contribute to the maintenance of peace and security in the region. The civilian component included the establishment and training of a temporary police force; the undertaking of tasks relating to civil administration and public services; the facilitating of the return of refugees and the organising and conducting of elections. See SC Res 1037 of 15 January 1996, at paras 10–11; Basic Agreement, above n 23, at paras 3–4.

[26] Basic Agreement, above n 23, at para 1.

[27] See also Zimmermann & Stahn, above n 5, at 433.

[28] See SC Res 1031 of 15 December 1995, at para 27; the General Framework Agreement for Peace in Bosnia and Herzegovina, Annex 10, at Art 5, available at www.ohr.int.

comparable to those in Kosovo, East Timor or Iraq.[29] Instead, the High Representative is mainly responsible for the removal from office of public officials who violate legal commitments contained in the Dayton Accords, as well as for imposing interim legislation in situations where Bosnia-Herzegovina's national institutions failed to do so.[30] The powers of the High Representative are also limited by the fact that the Constitutional Court of Bosnia-Herzegovina can review whether his decisions are in accordance with international human rights norms.[31] Consequently, the potential for an uncontrolled exercise of power by the Security Council (through the High Representative) is not as acute as in Kosovo or East Timor.

2. THE LEGAL BASIS OF THE MANDATES

In Kosovo and East Timor the Security Council established the respective civil administration on the basis of its implied powers under Chapter VII of the Charter. The implied power to establish a civil administration would flow from the Security Council's express powers in Article 41 to take non-military measures for the maintenance or restoration of international peace and security.[32] In addition, it delegated to them the power to take binding decisions in the form of civil regulations. As these civil administrations were effectively established through the Secretary-General,[33] Article 98 of the Charter constituted the basis for the delegation of powers.[34]

In the case of Iraq, the authorisation of the Authority to administrate the territory would also stem from the Security Council's implied powers flowing from Article 41 of the Charter. However, since the delegation of the Chapter VII power to take binding decisions in this regard was directed towards those member states constituting the Authority rather

---

[29] See Michael Bothe & Thilo Marhaun, "UN Administration of Kosovo and East Timor: Concept, Legality and Limitations of Security Council Mandated Trusteeship Administration", in Christian Tomuschat (ed), *Kosovo and the International Community* 224 (The Hague, Kluwer, 2001).

[30] Conclusions of the Peace Implementation Conference in Bonn of 10 December 1997, at paras XI 2(a) to XI 2(c), available at www.ohr.int; SC Res 1144 of 19 December 1997, at para 2; see also Stahn, above n 5, at 112.

[31] See *Request for Evaluation of Constitutionality of the Law on State Border Service*, Decision, No U 9/00 of 3 November 2000, available at www.ustavnisud.ba.

[32] This line of argument was also followed with respect to the establishment of the International Criminal Tribunal for the former Yugoslavia in *The Prosecutor v Tadic*, Decision on the Defence Motion for Interlocutory Appeal and Jurisdiction, Case no IT–94–1–AR72, 2 October 1995, Appeals Chamber, at para 28, at www.un.org/icty. See also ch 9, at s 2.1.

[33] See SC Res 1244 of 10 June 1999, at para 6; SC Res 1272 of 25 October 1999, at para 6 and SC Res 1410 of 17 May 2002, at para 3.

[34] See also ch 7, at s 3.

than the Secretary-General, the basis for the delegation would be Article 41 in combination with Article 48(1) of the Charter.[35] If one accepts that Article 42 combined with Article 48(1) serves as a basis for the delegation of military power to individual member states,[36] it seems plausible and consistent that Article 41 combined with Article 48(1) could provide a similar basis for the delegation of non-military powers to individual member states.

UNTAET initially received a mandate of 15 months[37] which was eventually extended until 20 May 2002.[38] UNMISET currently has a mandate that is limited to 12 months.[39] In Kosovo the mandate for civil administration (like the military mandate) was granted for an indefinite period of time.[40] This means that an affirmative Chapter VII resolution will be required to terminate the Special Representative's authority. A similar situation prevails in Iraq, where the Authority's authorisation for civil administration has not been subjected to a time limit.[41]

Chapter 7 at section 2.3. explained that in the case of military authorisations, such an open ended mandate would only remain legal as long as it enjoyed the support of the majority of the members of the Security Council, including a majority of the permanent members. Since the mandate concerns delegation of a power that is centralised with the Security Council under the Charter structure, it has to be accompanied by sufficient overall control by the Security Council. If this is not the case, the delegation would lack that degree of centralisation constitutionally necessary to designate a particular military action as a United Nations operation.

Chapter 7 at section 2.3. also explained that this degree of overall control can only be present as long as the Security Council as a collective entity is in favour of the continuation of the military mandate. The moment this collective support collapses the delegation becomes illegal and expires automatically, as it implies a shift of the overall control over the military operation from the Security Council to the (permanent) member(s) that have a direct interest in its continuation. It was further acknowledged in that chapter that this line of argument is not yet supported by state practice, or by legal writers. Even so, it would not be void of authority to those accepting the logical consequences of the structural limitations inherent to a concept of delegation that requires the delegating power to remain in overall control of the delegated mandate.

---

[35] Art 48(1) determines that: "The action required to carry out the decisions of the Security Council for the maintenance of international peace and security shall be taken by all the Members of the United Nations or by some of them, as the Security Council may determine."
[36] See ch 7 at s 2.1.
[37] SC Res 1272 of 25 October 1999, at para 17.
[38] See SC Res 1338 of 31 January 2001, at para 2 and SC 1392 of 31 January 2002, at para 2.
[39] SC Res 1410 of 17 May 2002, at para 1; SC Res 1480 of 19 May 2003, at para 1.
[40] SC Res 1244 of 10 June 1999, at para 19.
[41] SC Res 1483 of 22 May 2003, at para 25. See also SC Res 1511 of 16 October 2003, at para 15.

The question now becomes whether one could apply the same reasoning to an open-ended mandate for civil administration. As this mandate also concerns a delegation of a competence that is centralised with the Security Council under the Charter structure, it seems plausible to do so. In this instance the delegation relates to the power to issue binding decisions of a non-military nature in the interest of peace and security. As this power is first and foremost to be exercised by the Security Council itself, any delegation thereof must be accompanied by sufficient overall control by the Security Council. Where this is not the case, the binding decisions—whether in the form of regulations adopted by the Special Representative in Kosovo or decrees or decisions adopted by the Authority in Iraq—would lack that degree of centralisation which they need to qualify as decisions taken on behalf of the United Nations.

In light of this similar need for overall control over the delegated mandate, the delegation model that was developed in the context of authorisations to use force can also be applied to delegations involving other Chapter VII powers. The fact that this model gains particular significance with respect to military mandates, given that the centralisation of the use of force forms a cornerstone of the Charter, would thus not mean that it can only be applied to those mandates. If applied to an open-ended mandate for civil administration, it would imply that the mandate will only remain legal as long as an overall majority within the Security Council is in favour of its continuation, including a majority of the five permanent members. The moment this support disintegrates, the delegation becomes illegal and the mandate expires automatically.

This would be the case, for example, where the adoption of a draft resolution aimed at the termination of the mandate is prevented only by the "reverse veto" of one or two permanent members. It will also be the case where the terminating resolution is opposed by one or two permanent members and a minority of the non-permanent members. A third possibility is where a majority of the permanent members are in favour of its continuation, but no overall majority in favour of continuation exists within the Security Council. Finally it is theoretically possible that an overall majority for the continuation of the mandate exists, which does not include a majority of the permanent members.[42]

It is important to point out that the trusteeship system provided for in Chapter XII could not have served as a legal basis for the Security Council action in any of the above territories, even though the type of administration provided for by UNMIK, UNTAET and UNMISET closely resemble the trusteeship system.[43] Chapter XII limits the applicability of the

---

[42] For an elaboration of this argument, see ch 7, at s 2.3.
[43] See also Zimmermann & Stahn, above n 5, at 436–37.

trusteeship system to three different categories of territories, namely those formerly held as mandates under the mandates system of the League of Nations, territories detached from enemy states as a result of World War II, and territories voluntarily placed under the trusteeship system by states responsible for their administration.[44] As none of these categories apply to UNMIK, any attempt of the Security Council to place it within the mandate system would most likely directly contravene an express Charter provision.[45] Similarly, the Security Council could also not bestow the status of a trust territory in terms of Chapter XII on East-Timor. Even though East-Timor was listed as a non-self governing territory under Portuguese control in 1960, no agreement was ever concluded by means of which it was to be placed within the trusteeship system.[46]

At the same time, however, this does not mean that the Security Council could not utilise Chapter VII to place these territories under United Nations administration, or (as in the case of Iraq) under the temporary administration of (a) member state(s). The inclusion of Chapter XII in the Charter does not imply that this constitutes a conclusive set of rules precluding the exercise of administrative authority in any other form.[47] Such an interpretation would not take sufficient account of the unique role of the Security Council in the maintenance of international peace and security and the broad powers granted to it under Chapter VII of the Charter for that purpose.[48]

Finally, it might be necessary to draw attention to the fact that East Timor was not a member of the United Nations at the time Resolution 1272 (1999) was adopted, whilst the status of the Federal Republic of Yugoslavia (FRY) at the time of the adoption of Resolution 1244 (1999) is still disputed. As far as the FRY is concerned, chapter 6 at section 3.2. has already elaborated on the fact that the consistent attempts of the Federal Republic of Yugoslavia (FRY) to be recognised as the automatic successor

---

[44] See Art 77(1) of the Charter.

[45] In addition, Art 78 explicitly determines that the trusteeship system shall not apply to territories which have become members of the United Nations, as this would not be consistent with the principle of sovereign equality. As the FRY has been a member of the United Nations (at least) since 1 November 2000, its territory could not be subjected to the trusteeship system. See also Zimmermann & Stahn, above n 5, at 436; Stahn, above n 5, at 119.

[46] The agreement between Indonesia and Portugal of 5 May 1999 (S/1999/513), which provided for the voluntary transfer of authority in East Timor to the United Nations during the transitional period towards independence, did provide a legal basis for subsequent Security Council action in the territory. It did not, however, amount to a trusteeship agreement in terms of Art 77(1)(c) of the Charter. See also Ruffert, above n 11, at 621.

[47] Stahn, above n 5, at 130.

[48] The qualification contained in Art 78 of the Charter above n 40, would not apply where the Security Council is acting under Chapter VII. The preservation of national sovereignty (which lies at the heart of Art 78), may be overcome in situations constituting a threat to peace. See Stahn, above n 5, at 130; Zimmermann & Stahn, above n 5, at 438; see also Ruffert, above n 11, at 620–21.

to the former Socialist Federal Republic of Yugoslavia in the United Nations, amounted to a voluntary acceptance of the Charter system within the FRY's territory. As a result, the FRY would be estopped from claiming that any coercive measures by the Security Council against the FRY between 1992 and 2000 were illegal on the basis that they were taken against a non-member of the United Nations.[49]

With respect to East Timor it is also fair to assume that the territory was under the legitimate authority of the United Nations at the time of the adoption of Resolution 1272 (1999). On 5 May 1999, Indonesia and Portugal agreed that if the results of the popular consultation in East Timor favoured independence, the authority in East Timor would be transferred to the United Nations for the duration of the transitional period until independence.[50] This consent by, in particular, the *de iure* administration (Portugal) to transfer the authority to the United Nations constituted a clear legal basis for the adoption of subsequent Chapter VII resolutions.[51] Consent to United Nations action in the post-independence phase was reflected, inter alia, by the presentation of a request from East Timor to the Secretary-General to join the United Nations during the first session of the East Timorese parliament on 20 May 2002.[52]

3. THE OBLIGATION OF THE UNITED NATIONS (AUTHORISED) CIVIL ADMINISTRATION TO RESPECT HUMAN RIGHTS

The obligation resting on the organs of the United Nations to respect the human rights norms that are rooted in the Charter and which were developed under the auspices of the United Nations[53], gains particular significance in cases where it is responsible for the administration of territories. In these situations, the actions of those acting on behalf of the organisation have the potential for directly violating a broad spectrum of human rights.

---

[49] See ch 3 at s 4.2. for a discussion of the implication of non-membership for Chapter VII resolutions.

[50] Agreement between Indonesia and Portugal on the question of East Timor of 5 May 1999 (S1999/513), at Art 6.

[51] See also ch 3, at s 4.2. See also André JJ de Hoogh, "Attribution or Delegation of (Legislative) Power by the Security Council? The Case of the United Transnational Administration in East Timor (UNTAET)", 7 *Yearbook of International Peace Operations* 11 (2001). He emphasised the necessity for the consent of all parties concerned.

[52] Unite Nations Press Briefing, 20 May 2002, available at www.un.org/peace/timor/set-200502.htm. The Secretary-General responded that he would be honoured to pass on the request to the General Assembly and that he did not anticipate any obstacles to East Timor's membership. The Security Council subsequently recommended to the General Assembly that the Democratic Republic of East Timor be admitted to membership in the United Nations in SC Res 1414 of 23 May 2002. The General Assembly admitted East Timor to the United on 27 September 2002. See Press Release GA/ 10069 of 27 November 2002, available at www.un.org.

[53] As discussed in ch 5, at s 4.2.

In addition, it would clearly constitute an act of bad faith if an international administration undertaken in the interest of the local people did not pay due respect to the human rights norms developed by the very same organisation that is executing the administration.[54]

In Kosovo the United Nations recognised its human rights responsibilities with the adoption of UNMIK Regulation 1999/24. This regulation required all persons undertaking public duties or holding public office in Kosovo, to observe international human rights standards as recognised in the United Nations human rights treaties.[55] A similar clause was included in UNTEAT Regulation 1999/1, which made these standards applicable to all persons undertaking public duties or holding public office in East Timor.[56] At the time of writing UNMISET had not yet adopted a similar regulation. Resolution 1410 (2002) does nonetheless require UNMISET to respect human rights, as it states that internationally accepted human rights principles should form an integral part of training and capacity-building carried out by UMISET in the execution of its mandate.[57] At this point it is important to note that although the explicit recognition of the applicability of international human rights standards by UNMIK, UNTAET and UNMISET adds to legal certainty, it should not be considered as the primary source of the human rights obligations resting on the United Nations and its organs. These obligations stem from the Charter itself[58] and will bind the organisation when undertaking the civil administration of a territory, regardless of whether there was an explicit resolution or regulation to this effect.[59]

---

[54] Stahn, above n 5, at 117. Cf Frédéric Mégret & Florian Hoffmann, "The UN as a Human Rights Violator? Some Reflections on the United Nations Changing Human Rights Responsibilities", 25 *Human Rights Quarterly* 334 (2003).
[55] These include the Universal Declaration of Human Rights of 10 December 1948; the International Covenant on Civil and Political Rights of 16 December 1966 (ICCPR) and the Protocols thereto; the International Covenant on Economic, Social and Cultural Rights of 16 December 1966 (ICESCR); the Convention on the Elimination of All Forms of Racial Discrimination of 21 December 1965; the Convention on Elimination of All Forms of Discrimination Against Women of 17 December 1979; the Convention Against Torture and Other Cruel, Inhumane or Degrading Treatment or Punishment of 17 December 1984; and the International Convention on the Rights of the Child of 20 December 1989. See UNMIK/REG/1999/24 of 12 December 1999, at s 3. The text of these treaties are available at www.unhchr/ch. See also Stahn, above n 5, at 150.
[56] UNTAET/REG/1999/1 of 27 November 1999, at s 2.
[57] At para 5.
[58] As illuminated in ch 5, at s 4.2.
[59] The only exception would be where the Security Council (or those acting under its authority) declare themselves bound by norms which would provide human rights protection that extends beyond what is required by the International Bill of Rights. This was the case in Kosovo, where UNMIK/REG/1999/24 of 12 December 1999, at para 3, also subjected UNMIK to the European Convention for the Protection of Human Rights and Fundamental Freedoms of 4 November 1950 (ECHR) and its Protocols. However, although this form of self-limitation is to be welcomed, it is not a pre-condition for the legality of the Special Representative's mandate, as a result of which the implications of the ECHR for the Special Representative's powers falls outside the scope of this analysis.

The duty to observe human rights norms would also extend to situations where the Security Council delegates certain aspects of the civil administration to entities which do not function under its direct control, such as KFOR.[60] If this were not the case, the Security Council would be able to circumvent its obligations under international law by delegating its enforcement powers to member states.[61] This means that where the Security Council does not explicitly require these entities to respect human rights, the delegation can only be legal if it is presumed that it entails an obligation to this effect.[62] As a result, the authorisation granted to KFOR in Resolution 1244 (1999) to participate in the civil administration, necessarily implied that the countries acting on behalf of the Security Council would do so in accordance with human rights norms. KFOR would therefore be required to act in accordance with basic human rights norms when engaging in policing and other civil activities, as opposed to military combat.[63]

For the same reason, Resolution 1483 (2003) implied that the countries constituting the Authority in Iraq will administer the territory in accordance with human rights norms. A reaffirmation of this obligation can also be drawn from the text of the Resolution, which calls upon the Authority to administer the authority "in accordance with the Charter of the United Nations".[64] Given the reference to human rights norms in Articles 1(3) and 55 of the Charter, this reference to Charter norms would simultaneously constitute a reference to human rights norms.[65]

At the same time one has to bear in mind that the Security Council is allowed to derogate from (derogable) human rights in a state of national emergency, to the extent strictly required by the exigencies of the situation.[66] Where states take the latter course of action, they are required to give express notice to other states parties, through the intermediary of

---

[60] In the case of UNTEAT this problem did not arise, as both the civil and military components of the mandate functioned under the control of the Security Council (in the form of the Special Representative); see SC 1272 of 25 October 1999, at para 6.

[61] See ch 5 at s 4.3.1., where this argument was formulated in connection with the Security Council's obligation to respect basic rules of humanitarian law. See also John Cerone, "Minding the Gap: Outlining KFOR Accountability in Post-Conflict Kosovo", in 12 *European Journal of International Law* 472–73 (2001).

[62] See ch 5, at s 4.3.1.

[63] It would also imply that UNMIK/REG/2000/47 of 18 August 2000, at s 2.2, according to which KFOR shall respect applicable law and UNMIK regulations only in so far as they do not conflict with the fulfilment of the mandate given under SC Res 1244 (1999), cannot be interpreted as meaning that it is not bound by basic human rights norms when ensuring public safety and order in Kosovo. See Zimmermann & Stahn, above n 5, at 446–47; Stahn, above n 5, at 151.

[64] SC Res 1483 of 22 May 2003, at para 4.

[65] See also Frederic L Kirgis, "Security Council Resolution 1483 on the Rebuilding of Iraq", *ASIL Insights* (2003), available at www.asil.org/insights.htm.

[66] See Art 4(1) of the ICCPR.

the Secretary-General.[67] As far as the Security Council is concerned, a determination that the situation in the administered territory constitutes a threat to international peace, would suffice to indicate the existence of a state of emergency. To argue that (those acting on behalf of) the Security Council may not derogate from derogable human rights under these conditions, unless it has also proclaimed a state of emergency in the respective territory,[68] would unduly restrict the Security Council's flexibility. It would also not give due effect to the presumption of legality attached to its decisions. Consequently, UNMIK and KFOR in Kosovo, UNTAET/ UNMISET in East Timor, as well as the Authority in Iraq are—on the basis of the threat to peace existing in the respective regions—entitled to derogate from the derogable human rights in the ICCPR to the extent strictly required by the exigencies of the situation.[69]

In this context it is worth remembering that chapter 5 at section 4.2.1. and chapter 6 at section 2.2., illustrated the Security Council's need for flexibility when derogating from human rights norms in the context of an economic embargo. As a result, it also proposed the application of a proportionality principle to economic sanctions regimes that is comparable to the one acknowledged by international humanitarian law. The question thus arises why the Security Council and those acting on its behalf need to adhere to a stricter proportionality principle when derogating from human rights norms in the context of the civil administration of a territory. The reason can be found in the different natures of the Chapter VII measures at stake. Economic embargoes by their very nature imply a certain amount of collateral damage to economic and social rights in order to achieve the primary goal, ie pressuring the government into changing its behaviour. The purpose of a civil administration, on the other hand, is not to exercise pressure, but to advance the well-being of the people in the affected territory. As this cannot be done without due respect for human rights norms, derogation therefrom could only be justified in accordance with a strict proportionality principle.

3.1. The Monitoring of Human Rights Obligations

In practice it is difficult to determine the extent to which any of the above mentioned civil administrations derogate from human rights norms, as the broad scope of immunity provided to UNMIK/ KFOR, UNTEAT/

---

[67] See Art 4(3) of the ICCPR.
[68] As is implied by Stahn, above n 5, at 153.
[69] For a different opinion, see Stahn, above n 5, at 153, who claims that no explicit declarations of derogation have been made for KFOR or UNMIK.

UNMISET,[70] as well as the Authority in Iraq shields them from the legal scrutiny of local judicial fora. If the scope of immunity awarded to the administrators of these territories were to result in a complete absence of a judicial forum where the conformity of their acts with international human rights standards could be challenged, it would violate the notion of accountability inherent in a system of administration aimed at serving the well-being of the administered population,[71] as well as the principle of good faith. Since the obligation to provide extensive monitoring forms a focal point of the United Nations human rights system,[72] there is a clear expectation that the organisation itself would provide for human rights monitoring in situations where it fulfils functions comparable to those of a government, or authorises entities to do so on its behalf.[73]

In Kosovo the Special Representative has responded to this obligation by establishing the Ombudsperson in Regulation 2000/ 38 of 30 June 2000. The Ombudsperon has jurisdiction to receive and investigate complaints from any person or entity in Kosovo, concerning human rights violations and actions constituting an abuse of authority by the civil administration or any emerging central or local institution.[74] Although this procedure does not provide for the extensive protection of a fully fledged court system, it does introduce some accountability. In light of the presumption of legality attached to UNMIK's mandate, this would constitute *prima facie* evidence that the United Nations is fulfilling its obligation to monitor the human rights obligations of UNMIK in good faith.

It is doubtful, however, whether a similar argument could be made in the case of KFOR. The jurisdiction of the Ombudsperson with regard to KFOR is limited, as the Ombudsperson can only deal with cases involving the international security presence with the consent of

---

[70] With respect to UNMIK see UNMIK/REG/2000/47 of 18 August 2000, at s 2 and s 3. In the case of East Timor, UNTEAT/ UNMISET considered itself immune from local jurisdiction, even though no legal instrument relating to such immunity was adopted. See Ralph Wilde, "Accountability and Internatinonal Actors in Bosnia and Herzegovina, Kosovo and East Timor", 7 *ILSA Journal of International and Comparative Law* 456 (2001); Zimmermann & Stahn, above n 5, at 448; Marcus G Brand, "Institution-Building and Human Rights Protection in Kosovo in the Light of UNMIK Legislation", 70 *Nordic Journal of International Law* 477–78 (2001).

[71] See also Bothe & Marhaun, above n 29, at 236; Zimmermann & Stahn, above n 5, at 448; Stahn, above n 5, at 153.

[72] See ch 5 at s 4.2.1.

[73] Support for this statement can also be found in *Effects of Awards of Compensation made by the United Nations Administrative Tribunal*, Advisory Opinion, ICJ Rep 1954, at 57. The ICJ opined that it would hardly be consistent with the expressed aim of the Charter to promote freedom and justice for individuals, if it did not offer a judicial remedy to its own staff for the settlement of any disputes which may arise between them and the organisation. Although this opinion concerned the relation between the United Nations and its staff, the rationale should also apply in a situation where it claims to administer a territory according to international human rights standards.

[74] At s 3.1.

KFOR's Commander.[75] This factor, combined with the immunity that
KFOR enjoys in municipal courts, mean that individuals can be left without a remedy in situations where KFOR violates human rights whilst
maintaining civil law and order. This has typically occurred in a number
of situations where persons were arrested and held by order of the KFOR
commander without opportunity to challenge their detention.[76]

It is unlikely that this situation would be reconcilable with the right of
liberty and security of the person, according to which anyone who is
deprived of his or her liberty by arrest or detention shall have access to a
court in order to dispute the legality of the detention.[77] Even if one were
to make allowances for the fact that the situation in Kosovo constituted a
state of emergency which required a derogation from this right, the complete absence of a legal remedy against an act that constitutes a severe
limitation of personal liberty would seem excessive to what is "strictly
required by the exigencies of the situation". Support for this conclusion
can be drawn from statements of the Human Rights Committee, which
recently described the provision of remedies for any violation of the provisions of the ICCPR as inherent in the Covenant as a whole—even in
times of emergency.[78]

The example illustrates the need for the extension of the (mandatory)
jurisdiction of the Ombudsperson to KFOR policing actions, or the creation of an alternative United Nations forum where the legality of such
actions can be tested. As long as no such mechanism exists, the United
Nations is not complying with the obligation to monitor the human rights
obligations of KFOR in good faith. This is not altered by the fact that
members of KFOR can be prosecuted for serious human rights violations

---

[75] UNMIK/REG/2000/38 of 30 June 2000, at s 3.4; Zimmermann & Stahn, above n 5, at 446;
Brand, above n 70, at 483.
[76] Stahn, above n 5, at 153; Zimmermann & Stahn, above n 5, at 448; Megret & Hoffmann,
above n 54, at 335.
[77] Art 9 ICCPR. See also the Human Rights Committee, General Comment 8, *Right to liberty
and security of persons* para 1 (1982), available at www.unhchr.ch, according to which this
right applies to all persons deprived of their liberty by arrest or detention. Stahn, above n 5,
at 157.
[78] Human Rights, Committee, *General Comment No 29, State of Emergency* para 14 (2001). It is
also unlikely that this situation is in accordance with Art 14(1) ICCPR, which provides that
in the determination of any criminal charges against individuals, or of their rights and obligations in a law suit, everyone should be entitled to a fair and impartial hearing by a competent, independent and impartial tribunal established by law. Ch 9 at s 2.3. illustrates that this
right does not only protect procedural guarantees in relation to judicial proceedings, but
also the right of *access* to a fair hearing (at least) with respect to criminal proceedings. Those
deprived of their liberty by means of arrest should therefore be granted access to a legal
forum for the purposes of contesting the arrest. See also Stahn, above n 5, at 153 ff; the
*Syracuse Principles on the Limitation and Derogation Provisions in the International Covenant on
Civil and Political Rights*, at para 70, reprinted in 7 *Human Rights Quarterly* 12 (1985);
cf Ian D Seiderman, *Hierarchy in International Law: The Human Rights Dimension* 81 ff
(Antwerp, Intersentia, 2001).

in their home countries.[79] Such a (decentralised) form of supervision cannot relieve the United Nations from its own responsibility to ensure that those who are administering a territory on its behalf observe the human rights norms they are bound by.

It is unclear to what extent similar deficits plague the civil administration in East Timor. On the one hand, no comprehensive international monitoring mechanism is in place that could compensate for the immunity which the UNTAET/ UNMISET officials enjoy(ed) from proceedings in local courts.[80] The Special Representative did not provide for the establishment of an Ombudsperson or any other international institution that oversees the compatibility of UNTAET/ UNMISET regulations or the actions of its personnel (which include both the civil and the security presence) with United Nations human rights standards. At the same time, however, the Special Representative did provide for some human rights monitoring on the national level. For example, he guaranteed regular review of pre-trial detention, as well as a *habeus corpus* procedure for challenging unlawful arrest or detention.[81] In addition, some UNTAET regulations determined that executive decisions taken by the organs of the UNTAET administration in accordance with those regulations may be challenged before the local courts.[82] UNTAET therefore did, to some extent, give effect to the obligation to monitor whether human rights violation had been committed under its administration.

The administration of Iraq would form a greater concern, given the United Nations' limited control over the administration as a whole. According to Resolution 1483 (2002), the coordinating tasks of the Special Representative include that of promoting and protecting human rights.[83] This enables him to take a stand on the implementation of safeguards needed for the protection of human rights.[84] However, the extent to which

---

[79] According to UNMIK/REG/2000/47 of 18 August 2000, at s 2.4.; KFOR personnel are subject to the exclusive criminal jurisdiction of their respective sending states. As was mentioned in ch 5 at s 4.3.1., this has become established practice during peace-keeping or peace-enforcement operations.
[80] See Jarat Chopra, "The UN's Kingdom of East Timor", in 42 *Survival* 2000, at 29.
[81] UNTAET/REG/2000/30, sd 20.9 an 47.
[82] See eg UNTAET/REG/2000/17 of 8 June 2000, s 6 (regulating the logging and export of wood); and UNTAET/REG/2000/19 of 30 June 2000, at 8 (regulating protected places). During such proceedings against UNTAET or a servant of UNTAET, the court applies the same substantive norms as would be applicable under the procedures for administrative matters. As UNTAET/REG/1999/1 of 27 November 1999, at s 2 determined that all applicable law in East Timor had to conform to international human rights standards, this review would simultaneously imply some measure of human rights protection. See also UNTAET/REG/2000/10 of 6 March 2000, at s 42, that provided for review of decisions taken by the UNTAET procurement policy body before a court of competent jurisdiction. See Carsten Stahn, "The United Nations Transitional Administrations in Kosovo and East Timor: A First Analyis", in 5 *Max Planck Yearbook of United Nations Law* 162 (2001).
[83] SC Res 1483 of 22 May 2003, at para 8(g).
[84] See also Kirgis, above n 65.

this will result in, for example, the creation of an ombudsperson or other mechanism for effective human rights monitoring of the Authority, still remains to be seen. At the time of writing, the Authority effort's to administer the territory had only been underway for several months, as a result of which any conclusion in this regard would be premature. But given the limited power of the Special Representative in Iraq compared to his counterparts in Kosovo and East Timor, it is not unreasonable to fear that any efforts on his part to introduce a human rights monitoring mechanism might be marginalised by the Authority. If this were to happen, the Authority would effectively be shielded from any measure of international accountability for human rights violations, which, in turn, would taint its mandate for administration with an element of illegality.

3.2. The Implications of the Right to Self-Determination for United Nations Civil Administrations

In terms of Article 1(2) of the Charter, the purposes and principles of the United Nations include the duty to respect the self-determination of peoples. This principle, which was later concretised as a collective human right in Article 1 of the ICCPR an ICESCR respectively,[85] is now widely recognised by authors as a norm of *ius cogens* that would constitute an outer limit to Security Council action.[86]

Although neither the Charter nor any of the other United Nations instruments distinguishes between external and internal forms of self-determination, this distinction has evolved through political debate, scholarly writing and practice.[87] The latter constitutes the more extreme

---

[85] Art 1 of the ICCPR and ICESCR reads as follows: "All peoples have the right to self-determination. By virtue of that right, they freely determine their political status and freely pursue their economic, social and cultural development."
[86] See Manfred Nowak, *UN Covenant on Civil and Political Rights* 7 (Kehl, Engel, 1993). TD Gill, "Legal and Some Political Limitations on the Power of the UN Security Council to Exercise its Enforcement Powers under Chapter VII of the Charter", 26 *Netherlands Yearbook of International Law* 74 (1995); Dorothee Starck, *Die Rechtsmässigkeit von UNO-Wirtschaftssanktionen in Anbetracht ihrer Auswirkungen auf die Zivilbevölkerung* (Berlin, Duncker & Humblot, 2000), at 38; Zimmermann & Stahn, above n 5, at 453; Christian Tomuschat, "Yugoslavia's Damaged Sovereignty over the Province of Kosovo", in GPH Kreijen *et al* (eds), *State, Sovereignty and International Governance* 341 (Oxford, Oxford University Press, 2002). For a different opinion, see Bernd Martenczuk, *Rechtsbinudng und Rechtskontrolle des Weltsicherheitsrats* 271 (Duncker & Humblot, Berlin, 1996). He questioned whether the content of the right to self-determination would be clear enough to provide any limits to Security Council action. For a discussion of the development of the right to self-determination into customary international law in the context of decolonisation, see Daniel Thürer, *Das Selbstbestimmungungsrecht der Völker* 126 (Stämpfli, Bern, 1976).
[87] Karl Doehring, "Self-Determination", in Bruno Simma (ed), *The Charter of the United Nations* 62 (Oxford, Oxford University Press, 1994); Gudmundur Alfredsson, "The Right of Self-Determination and Indigenous Peoples", in Christian Tomuschat (ed), *Modern Law of Self-Determination* 50 (Dordrecht, Martinus, Nijhoff, 1993). Cf Thürer, above n 72, at 53 ff.

form that can result in the establishment of a sovereign and independent state, the free association or integration with an independent state, or the emergence into any other political status freely determined by a people.[88]

Internal self-determination, on the other hand, concerns a people's pursuit of its political, economic, social and cultural development within the framework of an existing state.[89] This first implies that the people in its entirety, having organised into a state, is free to decide on a form of government.[90] Any outside pressure designed to enforce the installation of a particular form of government, or to enforce the maintenance of an existing form of government would constitute an internationally prohibited intervention.[91] In addition, the internal right to self-determination implies that minority groups within a state may claim a certain respect for their situation. This relates to the fact that "a people" can be composed of a portion of the population of an existing state, where the members of this group are united by common characteristics such as a race, religion and language and where they identify themselves as "a people".[92]

At the same time, a people is bound to exercise their right to self-determination in a fashion that respects the integrity of the state within which they reside. The various international documents that support the existence of a people's right to self-determination contain parallel statements, indicating that the exercise of such a right must be sufficiently limited to prevent threats to an existing state's territorial integrity, or the

---

[88] See the General Assembly's *Declaration on Principles of International Law Concerning Friendly Relations and Co-operation Among States in Accordance with the Charter of the United Nations*, in GA Res 2625 (XXV) of 24 October 1970. Hereinafter referred to as the Friendly Relations Declaration. See also *Western Sahara*, Advisory Opinion, ICJ Rep 1975, at 12 ff; Supreme Court of Canada, *Reference Re Secession of Quebec*, 20 August 1998, reprinted in 37 *International Legal Materials* para 126 (1998). Hereinafter referred to as *Re Secession of Quebec*.

[89] *Re Secession of Quebec*, above n 88, at para 127. See also Alfredsson, above n 87, at 50, who stated that within the context of United Nations debates, internal self-determination usually mainly refers to democratic government and group autonomy. Cf Doehring (in Simma), above n 87, at 69.

[90] Doehring (in Simma), above n 87, at 64.

[91] *Ibid*, at 65; Thürer, above n 72, at 111.

[92] *Interpretation of the Convention between Greece and Bulgaria Respecting Reciprocal Emigration singed at Neuilly-sur-Seine on November 27th 1919 (Question of the "Communities")*, Advisory Opinion, PCIJ 1930, (Series B) No 17, at 21; *Re Secession of Quebec*, above n 88, at para 124 ff. The right to self-determination has developed largely as a human right, and is generally used in documents that simultaneously contain references to nation and state. The juxtaposition of these terms is indicative that the reference to people does not have to include the entire population of a state. To restrict the definition of the term to the population of existing states would render the granting of a right to self-determination largely duplicative, given the parallel emphasis within the majority of the source documents on the need to protect the territorial integrity of existing states. It would also frustrate its remedial purpose. See also Doehring (in Simma), above n 87, at 63; Thürer, above n 72, at 160, Zimmermann & Stahn, above n 5, at 454.

stability of relations between sovereign states.[93] The outcome of this qualification is that a people constituting only a portion of the population normally has to fulfil its right to self-determination internally. External self-determination in the form of secession has traditionally only been recognised with respect to colonial peoples breaking away from the colonial powers, or where a people is subject to alien subjugation, domination or exploitation outside a colonial context.[94] No general right of a (minority) people to secede has yet been recognised in international law.[95]

However, according to the influential advisory opinion (reference) of the Canadian Supreme Court *Re Secession Quebec*, the right to external self-determination might also exist, as a last resort, when a people is blocked from a meaningful exercise of its internal self-determination.[96] Determining factors would include whether the people is a victim of attacks on its physical integrity or of massive violations of its fundamental rights; whether its members have access to government; whether they can freely make political choices and pursue their economic, social and cultural development; and whether they are equitably represented in legislative, executive and judicial institutions.[97] The Court acknowledged, however, that it remains unclear whether a right to secession in such a case would already reflect an established international law standard.[98]

If one applies these norms to the Security Council, it would first of all mean that it would not be allowed to authorise unilateral secession outside the colonial context. The only potential exception might be where a (minority) people within a state is completely prevented from exercising

---

[93] Friendly Relations Declaration, above n 74, *Vienna Declaration and Program of Action*, in A/Conf 157/24 (1993); at Art 1; the *General Assembly's Declaration on the Occasion of the Fiftieth Anniversary of the United Nations*, GA Res 50/6 of 9 November 1995; Doehring (in Simma), above n 87, at 64–65; Tomuschat (Damaged Sovereignty), above n 86, at 341–42.

[94] *Re Secession of Quebec*, above n 88, at para 133; See also the General Assembly's *Declaration on the Granting of Independence to Colonial Countries and Peoples'*, in GA Res 1514 of 14 December 1960; Doehring (in Simma), above n 87, at 61; Thürer, above n 72, at 154.

[95] See Tomuschat (Damaged Sovereignty), above n 86, at 342.

[96] *Re Secession of Quebec*, above n 88, at para 134; Zimmermann & Stahn, above n 5, at 455–56; Tomuschat (Damaged Sovereignty), above n 86, at 343.

[97] *Re Secession of Quebec*, above n 88, at para 135 ff. See also Communication No 75/92, *Katangese Peoples' Congress v Zaire*, available at www.up.ac.za/chr/, in which the claimants requested the African Commission on Human and Peoples' Rights to recognise their right to secede from Zaire. They based their claim on Art 20(1) of the African Charter of Human and Peoples' Rights, according to which all peoples have the right to self-determination. Although the Commission declared the Katangese claim inadmissible, its reasoning indicated that groups within a state who are persecuted, whose rights are consistently violated and who are denied a meaningful participation in government may have the right to secede from the state of which they are nationals. Part of the problem with the Katangese communication, however, was that it lacked factual evidence indicating oppression or human rights abuses by the Zairian government directed at the Katangese people. See Frans Viljoen, "Overview of the African Regional Human Rights System", in Christof Heyns (ed), *Human Rights Law in Africa 1998* 145–46 (The Hague, Kluwer, 2001).

[98] *Re Secession of Quebec*, above n 88, at para 134.

any meaningful internal self-determination. In addition, the Security Council and those acting on its behalf would be precluded from imposing a particular form of government on the population of a state in the long term.[99] Consequently, a United Nations civil administration in terms of Chapter VII of the Charter would only be reconcilable with the right to internal self-determination, if and to the extent that it consistently and progressively involves all peoples within the territory in all aspects of the governmental process. By means of such active participation the transitional administration acquires an element of consent necessary to prevent it from deteriorating into a form of "new-colonialism", which would not be reconcilable with the principle of internal self-determination.[100]

3.2.1. Implications for Kosovo

When considering the situation in Kosovo, one can argue that at the time of adoption of Resolution 1244 (1999), secession by the Kosovo Albanians would have been justified on the basis that the Kosovo Albanian people could not exercise their right to self-determination internally in any meaningful way.[101] By that time they had been subjected to gross and systematic human rights violations by the Federal (Serbian) government, which had been condemned both by the General Assembly and the Security Council.[102] In addition, the violation of basic human rights was supported by a systematic denial of access to and representation in the governmental structures of Kosovo. This is reflected in the abolition of Kosovo's autonomous status through amendments to the Serbian Constitution during and after 1988.[103]

The amendments transferred both the control over the Kosovar security forces and the Kosovo judicial system to the government of Serbia and effectively prohibited the use of Albanian as an official language in Kosovo. Other discriminatory decrees prohibited the sale of property to Albanians, caused the shut down of Albanian newspapers and created

---

[99] Gill, above n 86, at 75.

[100] *Ibid*, at 75–76.

[101] The Kosovo Albanians can be considered as a "people". They constitute 90 per cent of the population of Kosovo, speak their own language, and share a Muslim religious identity differing from the Serb orthodox religion. In *Re Secession Quebec*, above n 88, at para 125, the Canadian Supreme Court considered common language and culture as factors necessary in determining whether a certain group is a "people". See also Zimmermann & Stahn, above n 5, at 454; Tomuschat (Damaged Sovereignty), above n 86, at 326. He noted that SC Res 1244 of 10 June 1999 lacked conceptual clarity as it referred to the "population" of Kosovo (para 5 of the preamble), as well as "people", and "inhabitants" of Kosovo (para 10).

[102] See GA Res 49/204 of 23 December 1994 and GA Res 50/190 of 22 December 1995; see also SC Res 1160 of 31 March 1998 and SC Res 1199 of 23 September 1998.

[103] See Art 110 of the Constitution of the Republic of Serbia of 1995, available at www.serbia-info.com/index.html.

municipalities reserved for Serbian citizens.[104] By 1991, these conditions had resulted in a secret referendum in Kosovo in which a clear majority of Kosovars expressed the wish to secede.[105] In the light of these factors one could argue that the inclusion in Resolution 1244 (1999) of an authorisation to the Kosovo Albanians to secede, would have been reconcilable with the right to self-determination.[106]

The Security Council, however, did not follow this route, but sanctioned the right of self-determination of the Kosovo Albanians in the form of substantial autonomy within the FRY instead.[107] In doing so, it also reaffirmed the commitment of the United Nations to the sovereign and territorial integrity of the FRY and acknowledged that Kosovo's final future status had to be determined by a political process.[108] On the one hand, one could interpret this reticence as an acknowledgement on the part of the Security Council that it did not have the power to authorise a secession, even in cases where the threat to international peace was brought about by the severe oppression of a minority people. On the other hand, one could argue that this self-limitation resulted from a political compromise amongst the five permanent members that would not have any significance for the Security Council's legal competence to authorise the secession of a people that is prevented from exercising any meaningful internal self-determination.[109]

---

[104] See Zimmermann & Stahn, above n 5, at 425; Tomuschat (Damaged Sovereignty), above n 86, at 342–43; cf Noel Malcolm, *A Short History of Kosovo* (London, Macmillan, 1998), at 343 ff.

[105] See Zimmermann & Stahn, above n 5, at 425–26, who described Kosovo's failed attempt to secede from the FRY after the results of the referendum became known. By means of secret elections on 24 May 1992, a parliament and a president were elected. However, due to the presence of Serbian military and police forces in Kosovo, the newly elected institutions were incapable of governing Kosovo. In addition, the state "Kosova", which was proclaimed by representatives of the Kosovo Albanians in 1991, was never recognised internationally (with the exception of Albania).

[106] *Ibid*, at s 6.

[107] SC Res 1244 of 10 June 1999, at para 10; see Tomuschat (Damaged Sovereignty), above n 86, at 344–45.

[108] SC Res 1244 of 10 June 1999, at para 11(e). This commitment is reaffirmed in the statement of the G–8 Foreign Ministers adopted at the Petersburg Centre on 6 May 1999 (S/1999/516) and the list of principles agreed by the Serbian Parliament and the Belgrade government on 3 June 1999 (S/1999/649). These documents were annexed to SC Res 1244 of 10 June 1999 and endorsed in its preamble. Para 11(e) of the resolution also takes into account the Rambouillet Accords of 23 August 1999 (S/1999/648), which contained an interim agreement for peace and self-government in Kosovo. These accords, which were rejected by FRY before the NATO military intervention, provided for the extensive self-government of Kosovo within the FRY, pending negotiations on its final status. See also Zimmermann and Stahn, above n 5, at 455.

[109] See Tomuschat (Damaged Sovereignty), above n 86, at 344, who stated that one can only speculate regarding the reasons that prompted the Security Council to refrain from a clear stance. Obviously, to state that a state has forfeited its right to control over a given part of its national territory inhabited by an ethnic group suffering massive discrimination, is a decision replete with delicate consequences. To set such a precedent might be harmful to certain members of the Security Council.

If one preferred the latter interpretation, one would nonetheless have to concede that political developments within the FRY since the adoption of Resolution 1244 (1999), have significantly reduced the threat that the federal (Serbian) government once posed for the right to internal self-determination of the Kosovo Albanians. Since the fall of the Milosevic regime the federal government has signalled a willingness to safeguard and protect the minority rights of the Albanian population of Kosovo.[110] Thus, even if a right to unilateral secession had existed before, it would have ceased to exist, as internal self-determination would now take precedence over external self-determination.[111] Similarly, the Security Council would not be able to authorise the secession of Kosovo anymore, unless it was with the full consent of the federal Yugoslavian government.

As far as internal self-determination is concerned, Resolution 1244 (1999) foresaw the transfer of administrative responsibilities by the civil presence to the provisional institutions for democratic and autonomous self-government, once these had been established. It also determined that in a final stage, the civil presence must oversee the transfer of authority from Kosovo's provisional institutions to institutions established under a political settlement.[112]

In practice, the most significant development regarding the transfer of administrative responsibility concerned the promulgation of the Constitutional Framework for Provisional Self-Government in Kosovo on 15 May 2001 (hereinafter the Constitutional Framework).[113] This document, which entered into force one day later, was the result of intensive debates between UNMIK and the Kosovo political leaders, involving the Kosovo Albanian, Kosovo Serb and the Kosovo Turkish community.[114] The Constitutional Framework established an Assembly which provided for broad political participation by the so called "national Communities", defined as communities of inhabitants belonging to the same ethnic or religious or linguistic group.[115] The Constitutional Framework also provided for the transfer of legislative powers to the Assembly in areas such

---

[110] Zimmermann & Stahn, above n 5, at 456.

[111] *Ibid.*

[112] SC Res 1244 of 10 June 1995, at paras 11(d) and 11(f).

[113] UNMIK/REG/2001/9 of 15 May 2001.

[114] See S/2001/565, at para 20 ff; Carsten Stahn, "Constitution without a State? Kosovo under the United Nations Constitutional Framework for Self-Government", 14 *Leiden Journal of International Law* 542–43 (2001). The document was elaborated by a Joint Working Group, composed of representatives of the three major Kosovo Albanian political parties, a Kosovo Serb member, a Bosniac member representing Kosovo's other minorities, a representative of civil society and an independent expert, as well as seven international members.

[115] See Constitutional Framework, above n 99, at ch 9, which (inter alia) reserves 20 of the 120 seats of the Assembly for non-Albanian minorities. The remaining 100 seats are to be distributed on the basis of proportional representation amongst all the registered parties in Kosovo. The Assembly was elected on 17 November 2001. See also Stahn (Constitution), above n 114, at 555.

as economic and financial policy, fiscal and budgetary issues, education, culture, health, environmental protection, transport and agriculture.[116]

At the same time, the Special Representative retained authority over key areas such as the maintenance of law and order, the supervision of local municipal administration and the supreme authority in judicial affairs.[117] The Constitutional Framework also still assigned to the Special Representative and KFOR the powers which typically rest with a federal government, such as treaty-making powers, cross-border control, monetary policy, civil aviation, defence and emergency powers.[118] Moreover, the Special Representative retained the authority to veto laws adopted by the Kosovo Assembly. Each law adopted by the Assembly shall be forwarded to the Special Representative for promulgation.[119] One must assume that he is entitled to deny promulgation on the basis of chapter 12 of the Constitutional Framework, which authorises the Special Representative to take "appropriate measures" whenever the actions of the provisional institutions for self-government are inconsistent with Resolution 1244 (1999) or the Constitutional Framework. It is therefore fair to conclude that despite the transfer of administrative responsibility effected by the Constitutional Framework, the Special Representative retains the overall decision-making power in Kosovo.[120]

All things considered, however, the above-mentioned measures constitute *prima facie* evidence of the progressive transfer of administrative responsibilities from the United Nations to the transitional institutions. Given the complexity of the situation as well as the absence of institutional infrastructure, it would be premature to expect a more comprehensive transfer of power to the people of Kosovo at this point in time. Similarly, the political difficulties surrounding the final status of Kosovo would presently also prevent a transfer of the "federal powers" to either the federal government or the autonomous interim government of Kosovo.[121]

3.2.2.   Implications for East Timor

As far as East Timor is concerned, the relationship with the United Nations is somewhat different, as the former Portuguese colony had been entitled to the right to external self-determination ever since it was listed

---

[116]Constitutional Framework, above n 99, at ch 5.1.
[117]*Ibid*, at chs 6 and 8.1.
[118]Constitutional Framework, above n 99; ch 8.1.; Zimmermann & Stahn, above n 5, at 428.
[119]Constitutional Framework, above n 99, at ch 9.1.44.
[120]Stahn (Constitution), above n 114, at 547.
[121]Note that the Constitutional Framework refrains from making any determination which could be interpreted as an anticipation of Kosovo's future status. The preamble of the Constitutional Framework leaves sufficient leeway for various scenarios by referring to a process which shall, in accordance with Resolution 1244 (1999), take full account of all relevant factors, including the will of the people. See Zimmermann & Stahn, above n 5, at 456 ff.

as a non-self governing territory in 1960.[122] This was not affected by Indonesia's illegal occupation and integration of East Timor in 1976, as the United Nations never recognised Indonesia's *de iure* sovereignty over the territory.[123] The referendum that was held in 1999 and which paved the way for East Timor's independence was the logical consequence of the (long overdue) exercise by a people of its right to external self-determination.[124] Once the East Timorese had expressed their wish to become independent, the authority in the territory was transferred to the United Nations for the duration of the period leading up to independence.[125]

UNTAET and UNMISET thus had to facilitate the realisation of both the external and internal dimensions of the East Timorese people's right to self-determination. The former was effected by a variety of measures that culminated in East Timor's independence on 20 May 2002. First important steps on the way to realising both elements of self-determination included the establishment by UNTAET of a National Council with 36 members from parties and municipal social groups.[126] The National Council was competent to initiate or modify regulations by simple majority, as long as this also met with the approval of the Special Representative.[127] The latter had also established an executive cabinet including representatives from East Timorese groups which functioned as a kind of government under his leadership.[128]

In March 2001, the Special Representative further promulgated a regulation on the election of a Constituent Assembly to prepare a Constitution for an independent and democratic East Timor.[129] The members of the Constitutional Assembly were elected on 30 August 2001 and sworn in on 15 September 2001. Soon afterwards, the Special Representative appointed a Council of Ministers in consultation with the Constitutional Assembly, which replaced the above-mentioned executive cabinet.[130] The Constitutional Assembly's Systemisation and Harmonisation Committee also commenced the drafting of the Constitution which was adopted on 22 March 2002.[131]

---

[122] GA Res 1542 (XV) of 15 December 1960, at para 1(i).
[123] GA Res 31/53 of 1 December 1976; SC Res 384 of 22 December 1975; SC Res 389 of 22 April 1976; Tomuschat (Damaged Sovereignty), above n 86, at 338; Chopra, above n 80, at 29.
[124] See Tomuschat (Damaged Sovereignty), above n 86, at 338.
[125] S/1999/513.
[126] UNTAET/REG/2000/24 of 14 July 2000, at s 3.
[127] UNTAET/REG/2000/24 of 14 July 2000, at s 2, s 4 and s 10.
[128] UNTAET/REG/2000/23 of 14 July 2000, at s 2; see also Ruffert, above n 11, at 625.
[129] UNTAET/REG/2001/2 of 16 March 2001, at s 1. The Constituent Assembly comprises 88 representatives, of whom 13 represent the 13 administrative districts and 75 were elected on the basis of one single nationwide constituency.
[130] UNTAET/REG/2001/28 of 19 September 2001, at s 1.3. s 3 and s 14.1.
[131] UNTAET Press Office, Fact Sheet 4, April 2002, available at www.un.org/peace/etimor/. The Constitution of the Democratic Republic of East Timor of 22 March 2002 [hereinafter referred to as the Constitution] is available at www.etan.org.

The Constitution provided for the transfer of government to a directly elected President and a directly elected Parliament on independence.[132] As part of the transitional provisions, the Constitution further determined that the President elected under UNTAET Regulation 2002/01 of 16 January 2002,[133] would take on the competencies attached to this position in the Constitution.[134] The Constituent Assembly was to be transformed into a National Parliament with the entering into force of the Constitution.[135] The National Parliament would then designate the Prime Minister who, in turn, was responsible for proposing the remaining members of government. Until such a time as the first constitutional Government could be appointed and sworn in by the President, the Council of Ministers appointed by the Special Representative remained in office.[136]

Apart from facilitating the formal independence of East Timor, this systematic development of local democratic institutions, to which the administrative responsibilities were transferred, formed an important element in the realisation of the internal self-determination of the East Timorese people. The complete realisation of this right may still prove to be a challenge to UNMISET, since the Special Representative retains considerable power over the country. As indicated above in section 1, Resolution 1410 (2002) grants the Special Representative the ability to take all necessary "actions" to assist in issues ranging from the functioning of ministries, to fiscal matters, as well as law and order and security.[137] As these "actions" would include the adoption of legislation, it is clear that that the powers of UNMISET could still have a considerable impact on the internal right to self-determination of the East Timorese people.

However, at present the above mentioned steps constitute *prima facie* evidence that the Security Council and those acting under its authority are honouring the obligation to transfer progressively the responsibility of governance to the East Timorese people. If one considers the fragility of the newly independ state and its governmental structures, the termination of the extensive powers of the Special Representative at this point in time would be premature. It is also important to note that the Security Council has indicated that UNMISET will, over a period of two years, fully devolve all operational responsibilities to the East Timorese authorities

---

[132] See in particular the Constitution, above n 131, at ss 74, 76, 85–88, 95–98 and 170. In accordance with a recommendation of the Constitutional Assembly which was endorsed by the Security Council on 31 October 2001, the independence of East Timor was to be declared on 20 May 2002. See S/PRST/2001/32, at para 1 and S/PRST/2002/13, at para 2.
[133] Mr Xanana Gusmão was elected as President on 14 April 2002 by more than 82 per cent of the vote. UNTAET Press Office, Fact Sheet 4, April 2002, above n 131.
[134] Constitution, above n 131, at s 169.
[135] Ibid, at s 167(1).
[136] Ibid, at s 168.
[137] SC Res 1410 of 17 May 2002, at paras 2 and 6.

as soon as is feasible and without jeopardising stability.[138] In the light of these developments, it is fair to conclude that the Security Council has thus far given due consideration to the internal self-determination of the East Timorese people.

3.2.3. Implications for Iraq

Although Iraq still continues to remain a state as a matter of international law, the people of Iraq are currently subjected to the complete control of the states constituting the Authority.[139] As a result, the internal self-determination of the Iraqi people is effectively suspended, until such a time as they can freely determine their own political future.

A formal commitment to respect and realising the right to internal self-determination is however, clearly present in Resolution 1483 (2003). The text of the resolution stresses the right of the Iraqi people to freely determine their own political future and control their own national resources and to realise this goal as soon as possible.[140] In addition, it calls on the Authority and the United Nations (in the form of the Special Representative) to cooperate in restoring and establishing national and local institutions for representative governance, including the facilitation of a process leading to an internationally recognised, representative government of Iraq.[141]

A first and crucial step for initiating the process of self-government, was the formation of an interim Iraqi administration consisting of Iraqis, that could function as a transitional administration under the auspices of the Authority, until an internationally recognised government is in place that could assume the responsibilities of the Authority.[142] The formation of the interim administration took the form of a Governing Council that came together for the first time on 13 July 2003. The Governing Council, which represents a variety of religious and ethnic groups,[143] has the power to appoint and dismiss ministers, adopt a budget, as well as initiate the

---

[138] *Ibid*, at para 8. See also S/PRST/2001/32, at 2. For earlier commitments to this effect, see SC Res 1272 of 25 October 1999, at para 8.

[139] See Kirgis, above n 65.

[140] SC Res 1483 (2003), at para 4.

[141] *Ibid*, at para 8(c). See also Kirgis, above n 65. These commitments are reaffirmed in SC Res 1511 of 16 October 2003, at paras 1ff.

[142] The formation of such an interim administration with the assistance of the Authority and the Special Representative is foreseen in SC Res 1483 of 22 May 2002, at para 9.

[143] See "Erste Session des irakischen Regierungsrats", in *NZZ Online*, 13 July 2003, available at www.nzz.ch/. The 25 members of the Governing Council were made up of 13 Shiite Muslims, 5 Arab Sunni Muslims, 5 Kurds, one Turkoman and one Assyria Christian. The composition of the Governing Council also reflected the presence of all major political parties. See also Paul Haven, "US-Backed Iraqi Governing Council Meets", *HeraldTribune.com*, 14 July 2003, availabe at www.heraldtribune.com.

process of drafting a constitution.[144] At the same time, all issues of national security remain with the (representative of) the Authority, who also has a veto power against all decisions of the Governing Council.[145]

This formation of a Governing Council with some decision-making powers within three months after the end of hostilities in Iraq can serve as *prima facie* evidence of the Authority's commitment to the progressive transfer of administrative responsibilities to the Iraqi people. Whether this will ultimately result in the full realisation of the Iraqi people's right to self-determination will depend on the Authority's willingness and ability to continue the transfer of all aspects of governance on an ongoing basis.

4.   CONCLUSION

In authorising the civil administrations for Kosovo, East Timor and Iraq the Security Council has remained within the boundaries of its Chapter VII powers, as these administrations were necessary for the restoration and maintenance of peace and security in the respective regions. In principle, these administrations have also acknowledged their obligation to respect international human rights norms, although the mechanisms in place for monitoring the fulfilment of these obligations leave much to be desired. The absence of an independent United Nations forum for reviewing the conformity of UNTAET/ UNMISET and KFOR's (non-military) actions with international human rights standards is not in accordance with the notion of accountability inherent to their respective human rights mandates. A similar deficit plagues the mandate of the Authority in Iraq, where there has not yet been any attempt to provide an independent human rights monitoring system. Unless the Security Council remedies these deficits within a reasonable time, it may very well taint the respective mandates for civil administration with an element of illegality.

As far as self-determination is concerned, all three administrations have thus far remained within the limitations flowing from this right. Whether this will remain the case in the long run will depend on whether the Security Council and those acting on its behalf continue to transfer the powers of government to local institutions that represent all the peoples' of Kosovo, East Timor and Iraq, respectively. In the case

---

[144] *NZZ Online*, above n 143. The Governing Council will also appoint a committee of 8 to 10 jurists for the drafting of a new, democratic Constitution for Iraq. In accordance with SC Res 1511 of 16 October 2003, at para 7, the Governing Council has to provide the Security Council with a timetable and programme for the drafting of a new constitution and for the holding of democratic elections by 15 December 2003.

[145] NZZ online, above n 143.

of Kosovo, the ultimate decision regarding a transfer of the "federal powers of government" will also require the consent of the Yugoslav federal government.

Although it may still take some time before a complete transfer of power can be facilitated, the civil administrations remain under an obligation to do so as soon as the local institutional structures and political climate allow for it. The longer the overall decision-making power remains in the hands of the respective Special Representative in Kosovo and East Timor, and with the Authority in Iraq, the more difficult it will become to reconcile their positions with the right to self-determination of the peoples affected. The risk of undermining the right to internal self-determination is particularly acute in Kosovo and Iraq, as the mandate for civil administration in both territories is of an open-ended nature. It is less so in East Timor, since UNMISET's mandate is subjected to a time-limit. The possibility that the Security Council may not be willing to extend the mandate may prove to be a useful tool for accelerating the transfer of power.

If the Special-Representative in Kosovo were to retain the overall decision-making power for several years to come, it is imaginable that some of the inhabitants of Kosovo will attempt to file a complaint with the Ombudsperson, claiming that the situation violates their right to self-determination guaranteed in the ICCPR and ICESCR. It is unlikely, however, that the Ombudsperson would be willing to consider such a complaint. Other United Nations monitoring bodies, notably the Human Rights Committee, has exercised considerable judicial self-restraint in dealing with claims relating to self-determination.[146] It can be expected that the Ombudsperson would follow a similar approach, considering the political sensitivities involved.

It is therefore unrealistic to expect the Ombudsperson to provide a vehicle for overseeing the observance of the right to self-determination. This illustrates that whilst a human rights monitoring mechanism is an essential element of a mandate for civil administration, it does not by itself suffice to guarantee the long term legality of the mandate. It needs to be complemented by the attachment of a time limit to the mandate, as well as an awareness of and respect for the limits of the mandate on the part of the Security Council itself and those acting on its behalf.

---

[146] For a discussion see Nowak, above n 86, at 25 ff.

9

Limits to the Security Council's Discretion to Adopt (Quasi-) Judicial Measures

1. INTRODUCTION

THE QUESTION WHETHER principal organs of the United Nations could create subsidiary bodies exercising judicial functions first arose in 1954, during the *Effects of Awards of Compensation Made by the United Nations Administrative Tribunal.*[1] The ability of the principal organs to create subsidiary organs was, as such, uncontroversial, as this is explicitly provided for in Article 7(2) of the Charter.[2] In addition, Article 22 provides the General Assembly with the power to establish such subsidiary organs as it deems necessary for the performance of its functions. The real issue to be determined is the extent to which the General Assembly could invest a subsidiary organ with judicial powers that it could not exercise itself.[3]

The ICJ indicated that the creation of such a subsidiary organ would be legal to the extent that it is necessary for the effective exercise by the principal organ of its powers in an area in which it has the competence to operate.[4] The legality of the establishment of the subsidiary body would thus depend on whether it falls within the implied powers of the principal

---

[1] Advisory Opinion, ICJ Rep 1954, at 46 ff. Hereinafter referred to as the *Effects of Awards of Compensation* opinion.

[2] Art 7(2) of the Charter reads as follows: "Such subsidiary organs as may be found necessary may be established in accordance with the present Charter."

[3] See also *Effects of Awards of Compensation* opinion, above n 1, at 56.

[4] *Ibid*, at 57. In this instance the ICJ concluded that since the Charter contained no provision which authorised any of the principal organs of the United Nations to adjudicate upon disputes between the United Nations and its staff members, and Art 105 secured for the United Nations jurisdictional immunities in municipal courts, the power to establish a tribunal to do justice between the organisation and its staff members was essential to ensure the efficient working of the Secretariat.

organ.[5] In addition, the subsidiary organ will ultimately remain subordinate to its creator, in that the latter can abolish the subsidiary organ or amend the terms under which it is to function.[6]

These criteria could be applied to the Security Council by analogy as it is also endowed with implied powers,[7] as well as with the power to establish such subsidiary organs as it deems necessary for the performance of its functions.[8] The first question then becomes whether the creation of the particular judicial body in question was necessary to give effect to the Security Council's primary responsibility for the maintenance of international peace and security. Second, one will have to ask whether the judicial body remains subordinate to the Security Council. However, in doing so one should bear in mind that a subsidiary judicial body will reflect a certain degree of independence, in that it will exercise its powers and functions in a manner which is distinct from the internal workings of the principal organ.[9] This is a natural consequence of the fact that the subsidiary organ performs functions that the principal organ cannot itself exercise.

Moreover, where a subsidiary organ exercises judicial functions, such independence is mandated by basic standards of procedural justice. This follows from Article 1(1) of the Charter that explicitly requires the United Nations to bring about the settlement of international disputes in conformity with the principles of justice and international law.[10] As the Security Council is bound by Article 1(1),[11] it will have to respect basic principles of procedural justice such as independence, impartiality and

---

[5] *Effects of Awards of Compensation* opinion, above n 1, at 56; see also Danesh Sarooshi, *The United Nations and the Development of Collective Security* 93–94 (Oxford, Oxford University Press, 1999).

[6] *Effects of Awards of Compensation* opinion, above n 1, at 61.

[7] See ch 5, at s 4.

[8] Art 29 of the Charter.

[9] As also reflected in the discussion in GAOR, 2nd Ses, 6th Comm, 57th mtg 143 (1947); see also Sarooshi, above n 5, at 90–91. This requirement of independence means that the establishment of sessional committees, sub-committees and working groups of United Nations principal organs does not represent the establishment of subsidiary organs. See also Susan Lamb, "The Powers of Arrest of the International Criminal Tribunal for the Former Yugoslavia", 75 *British Yearbook of International Law* 196 (1999); Georg Nolte, "The limits of the Security Council's Powers and its Functions in the International Legal System: Some Reflections", in Michael Byers (ed), *The Role of Law in International Politics* 322 (Oxford, Oxford University Press, 2000).

[10] Ian Brownlie, "The Decision of Political Organs of the United Nations and the Rule of Law", in Ronald St John MacDonald (ed), *Essays in Honor of Wang Tieya* 102 (Dordrecht, Minus Nijhoff, 1994); *ibid*, "Changing Relations between the International Court of Justice and the Security Council of the United Nations", 31 *Canadian Yearbook of International Law* 25 (1993); Gerald P McGinley, 22 *Georgia Journal of International and Comparative Law* 599 (1992).

[11] See ch 5, at s 4.2.

even-handedness when creating a subsidiary body which will exercise a judicial function. This obligation is strengthened when read together with Article 2(2) of the Charter which requires the United Nations to respect the principle of good faith, and—in disputes pertaining to individuals—Article 1(3), that obliges it to promote human rights such as the right to a fair hearing.[12]

Finally, where the Security Council delegates to the judicial sub-organ its own power to issue binding decisions to member states, it has to retain the overall control of the delegation. This means, in particular, that the Security Council as a collective entity has to retain control over the initiation and termination of the delegated mandate. As was explained in chapter 8 at section 2, the delegation of the power to issue decisions which are binding on states concerns the delegation of a power that is centralised with the Security Council under the Charter structure. If such a delegation is not accompanied by sufficient accountability to the Security Council, it would lack that degree of centralisation constitutionally necessary to designate a particular binding order issued on the basis of the delegation as a United Nations decision. It would also open the door for abuse by member states which could seek to instrumentalise the subsidiary organ in its own interest, as opposed to that of the international community.[13]

The following passages will examine the extent to which the Security Council has respected these requirements in situations where adjudication in one form or another proved to be necessary to restore or maintain international peace and security. The analysis will first focus on the adoption of measures that relate to criminal prosecution of individuals. In doing so, it will focus on the establishment of the ICTY and the International Criminal Tribunal for Rwanda (ICTR), as the jurisprudence and principles relating to these tribunals form an important point of reference for determining the legality of other Security Council decisions that concerns the criminal prosecution of individuals. This includes, in particular, the Security Council resolutions demanding the extradition of suspected international terrorists, as well as those requiring the freezing of assets of individuals associated with international terrorism. Thereafter the analysis concentrates on the legality of quasi-judicial bodies whose decisions were directed against states rather than individuals, namely the United Nations Compensation Commission for Iraq and the Iraq-Kuwait Boundary Demarcation Commission.

---

[12] *Ibid*. This point is taken up again below, at s 2.1.2.
[13] Note that this question did not arise in the *Effects of Awards of Compensation* opinion, above n 1, as the General Assembly merely created a tribunal whose decision was binding upon itself. See also Sarooshi, above n 5, at 106–07.

2.   (QUASI-) JUDICIAL MEASURES PERTAINING TO INDIVIDUAL CRIMINAL PROCEEDINGS

2.1.   The Creation of the ICTY and the ICTR

2.1.1.   The Legal Basis of the Mandates

The Security Council created the ICTY[14] and ICTR[15] as subsidiary organs in terms of Article 29 of the Charter,[16] for the prosecution of individuals responsible for serious violations of international humanitarian law in the former Yugoslavia and Rwanda, respectively. The Security Council regarded such prosecution as a necessary measure for restoring and maintaining peace in the regions.[17] At the time of their creation the question arose whether the Security Council had the competence to take such unprecedented measures in the interest of peace and security, especially since the Charter did not provide any explicit legal basis for doing so.[18]

When confronted with this question in the *Tadic* decision,[19] the Appeals Chamber of the ICTY determined that in establishing the ICTY the Security Council neither delegated to it some of its own functions, nor did it usurp for itself part of a judicial function which the Charter had attributed to other organs of the United Nations. Instead, the Security Council had resorted to the establishment of an international criminal tribunal as an instrument for the exercise of its own principal function of the maintenance of peace and security.[20] The Appeals Chamber thus followed the line of argument of the ICJ in the *Effects of Awards of Compensation* opinion.

---

[14] The ICTY was established in SC Res 827 of 25 May 1993, at paras 1 ff.

[15] The ICTR was established in SC Res 955 of 8 November 1994, at paras 1 ff.

[16] See S/25704 28 (1993).

[17] Whilst the ICTY was established when the conflict was still underway, the ICTR was established shortly after the civil war. The Security Council did not, however, regard this as an obstacle, as SC Res 955 of 8 November 1994 determined that the situation in Rwanda continued to constitute a threat to international peace. See also Daphna Shraga & Ralph Zacklin, "The International Criminal Tribunal for Rwanda", 7 *European Journal of International Law* 505 (1996). Karl Josef Partsch, "Der Sicherheitsrat als Gerichtsgründer", 42 *Vereinte Nationen* 11 (1994).

[18] See also the reservations expressed by China in S/PV 3217 (1993) and S/PV 3453 (1994), although it did not veto the establishment of the two *ad hoc* tribunals. Cf Heike Gading, *Der Schutz grundlegender Menschenrechte durch militärische Massnahmen des Sicherheitsrates—das Ende staatlicher Souveränität* 196–97 (Berlin, Duncker & Humblot, 1996); Lamb, above n 9, at 196; Shraga & Zacklin, above n 17, at 505.

[19] *The Prosecutor v Tadic*, Decision on the Defence Motion for Interlocutory Appeal and Jurisdiction, Case No IT–94–1–AR72, 2 October 1995, Appeals Chamber, at paras 27 ff, available at www.un.org/icty. Hereinafter referred to as the *Tadic* decision. The same issue also arose with respect to the ICTR in *The Prosecutor v Kanyabashi*, Decision on the Defence Motion on Jurisdiction, Case No ICTR–96–15–T, 18 June 1997, Trial Chamber, at paras 17, available at www.ictr.org. Hereinafter referred to as the *Kanyabashi* decision.

[20] *Tadic* decision, above n 19, at para 38; *Kanyabashi* decision, above n 19, at para 39.

In effect it determined that the Security Council possessed an implied power to establish the ICTY from its express powers in Article 41, since it was a measure necessary for the effective exercise of its powers to maintain or restore international peace and security.[21]

The Security Council also delegated the power to take decisions binding on member states to the *ad hoc* tribunals when establishing them under Chapter VII of the Charter.[22] In paragraph 4 of Resolution 827 (1993), the Security Council obliged states to lend cooperation and judicial assistance to the ICTY. At the same time, Article 29 of the ICTY Statute (which was adopted during the same resolution)[23] outlined the ICTY's right to issue binding orders on states in this regard. Similarly, paragraph 2 of Resolution 955 (1994) and Article 28 of the ICTR Statute secured similar obligations and rights with respect to the ICTR.[24]

The competence of the Security Council to delegate its power to make binding decisions to its subsidiary organ flows from Article 29 of the Charter, which explicitly allows the Security Council to establish subsidiary organs for the performance of its functions. Article 29 thus has a dual function. On the one hand, it facilitates the creation of subsidiary bodies which exercises powers that the Security Council itself cannot exercise, but which are necessary for the maintenance of international peace and security. On the other hand, it also facilitates the delegation of the Security Council's power to take binding decisions to the subsidiary organ, where this is necessary for the latter's efficient functioning in the interest of peace and security.[25]

2.1.2.   The Procedural Fairness Guaranteed by the Mandates

As the ICTY and ICTR are subsidiary organs of the Security Council, the Security Council has the ultimate right to terminate their existence or amend the terms of their Statutes.[26] At the same time, the fact that the ICTY and the ICTR are exercising a judicial power which the Security Council does not itself possess, ascribes to them a degree of independence which prohibits the Security Council from interfering in their conduct of

---

[21] Sarooshi, above n 5, at 97; see also Frederic L Kirgis, "The Security Council's First Fifty Years", 89 *American Journal of International Law* 522 (1995); Georg Nolte (in Byers), above n 9, at 322. But see also André JJ de Hoogh, "Attribution or Delegation of (Legislative) Power by the Security Council? The Case of the United Transnational Administration in East Timor (UNTAET)", 7 *Yearbook of International Peace Operations* 37 (2001), who relied on the implied powers of the Security Council, rather than Art 41 of the Charter.
[22] Sarooshi, above n 5, at 107.
[23] See above n 30.
[24] See also Lamb, above n 9, at 197; Sarooshi, above n 5, at 107–08.
[25] See Sarooshi, above n 5, at 107, who argues that the Security Council has a general competence to delegate its powers.
[26] Sarooshi, above n 5, at 104.

individual cases.[27] Consequently, the Security Council may not instruct the *ad hoc* tribunals with respect to the outcome of cases, nor can it review final and binding decisions handed down by them. For if it were to do so, the Security Council would in effect be acting like a judicial forum.[28]

Moreover, any interference by a political body such as the Security Council with the conduct of individual cases would violate Article 1(1) of the Charter, in that it would be contrary to the principle of independence. Since the dispute settlement procedure envisaged by the ICTY and ICTR concern the criminal prosecution of individuals, such interference would also violate the obligation of the Security Council in Articles 1(3) and 2(2) to promote human rights norms.[29] Of the human rights binding on the United Nations, the one that is of particular relevance to procedural justice is Article 14(1) of the ICCPR. It provides that in the determination of any criminal charges against individuals, or of their rights and obligations in a suit at law, everyone should be entitled to a fair and impartial hearing by a competent, independent and impartial tribunal established by law.

The terms "competent" and "established by law" are effectively synonyms, aimed at ensuring that the jurisdictional power of a tribunal or other judicial body is determined generally and independent of the given case, ie not arbitrarily or by a specific administrative act.[30] Courts and tribunals must also be independent and judges may not be subjected to political directives.[31] Impartiality, for its part, relates to the personal neutrality of a judge towards a particular case. Judges are not impartial where they are biased, ie where they have a personal interest in the case before them.[32] In addition to these institutional principles, the principle of equality of arms between the parties constitutes the most important element of

---

[27] *Tadic* decision, above n 19, at paras 37–38; *Kanyabashi* decision, above n 19, at paras 40 ff. See also Sarooshi, above n 5, at 103; Kirgis (First Fifty years), above n 21, at 523.

[28] Lamb, above n 9, at 197; Roy S Lee, "The Rwanda Tribunal", in 9 *Leiden Journal of International Law* (1996), at 45; Sarooshi, above n 5, at 103–04. See also Partsch, above n 17, at 13.

[29] See ch 5, at s 4.2.

[30] *Ibid*, at 245; Nihal Jayawickerama, "The Right to a Fair Trial under the International Covenant on Civil and Political Rights", in Andrew Byrnes (ed) *The Right to Fair Trial in International & Comparative Perspective* 39 (Hong Kong, Centrum for Comparative and Public Law, 1997).

[31] See Human Rights Committee, *Oló Bahamonde v Equatorial Guinea*, Comm No 468/1991, CCPR/C/49/D/468/1991 (1993). A situation where the functions and competencies of the judiciary and the executive are not clearly distinguishable, or where the latter is able to control or direct the former is incompatible with the notion of an independent and impartial tribunal within the meaning of Art 14(1) of the ICCPR. See also David Weissbrodt, *The Right to a Fair Trial under the Universal Declaration of Human Rights and the International Covenant on Civil and Political Rights* 142 (New York, United Nations, 2001). Manfred Nowak, *UN Covenant on Civil and Political Rights: CCPR Commentary* 245 (Kehl, Engel, 1993); Jayawickerama, above n 30, at 41.

[32] Nowak, above n 31, at 245.

a fair hearing.[33] One example thereof would be that the inspection of records or submission of evidence must be dealt with in a manner equal to both parties.[34]

At this point it is worth remembering that the Security Council may derogate from Article 14 on the basis that its decisions presuppose the existence of an emergency situation in the form of an international threat to peace and security. This is the logical conclusion to be drawn from Article 4(1) ICCPR, which allows states to derogate from the right to a fair trial (and other derogable rights contained in the ICCPR) in times of emergency in accordance with a strict proportionality principle.[35] However, there is increasing support for the proposition that the core elements of the right to a fair hearing in Article 14(1) are to be considered as non-derogable.[36] In its recent General Comment on States of Emergency, the Human Rights Committee noted that in situations of armed conflict, common Article 3 of the Geneva Conventions of 1949 explicitly guarantees the core elements of the right to a fair trial and there would be no justification for derogation from these guarantees during other emergency situations.[37] It is submitted that the non-derogable nature of these core elements would also constitute an outer limit for Security Council action. Even if one were to allow the Security Council more leeway than member states in derogating from the rights in the ICCPR, a deviation that affected the core (non-derogable) elements of Article 14 ICCPR would violate the principle of good faith.[38]

---

[33] *Ibid*, Jayawickerama, above n 30, at 39–40.

[34] *Ibid*, see also Human Rights Committee, *Fei v Colombia*, Comm No 514/1992, CCPR/C/57/1 (1996); Alfred de Zayas, "The United Nations and the Guarantees of a Fair Trial in the International Covenant on Civil and Political Rights and the Convention Against Torture and Other Cruel, Inhuman or Degrading Treatment or Punishment", in David Weissbrodt & Rüdiger Wolfrum (eds), *The Right to a Fair Trial* 683 (Berlin, Springer, 1997).

[35] See ch 5 at s 4.2.1.

[36] In 1993, the UN Sub-Commission on Prevention of Discrimination and Protection of Minorities proposed to states parties to the ICCPR the adoption of a Third Optional Protocol which would have elevated Art 14 to the level of non-derogability. However, the Human Rights Committee noted that it would not be feasible to expect that all provisions of Art 14 can remain fully in force in any kind of emergency. The inclusion of Art 14 as such into the list of non-derogable provisions would not be appropriate. This has not, however, prevented the core elements of this right to acquire non-derogable status in practice. See also E/CN.4/Sub.2/1994/26, at 13; De Zayas, above n 34, at 676–78.

[37] Human Rights Committee, General Comment No 29, *States of Emergency* para 16 (2001). See also Human Rights Committee, General Comment No 24, *Issues Relating to Reservations Made upon Ratification or Accession to the Covenant or the Optional Protocol thereto, or in Relation to Declarations under Art 41 of the Covenant* para 8 (1994). The Human Rights Committee noted that while particular reservations to particular clauses of Art 14 may be acceptable, a general reservation to the right to a fair trial would not be. See also the *Siracusa Principles on the Limitation and Derogation Provisions in the International Covenant on Civil and Political Rights* para 67 (1985), in 7 *Human Rights Quarterly* 11 (1985); De Zayas, above n 34, at 674.

[38] See ch 5, at s 4.2.

Furthermore, the *de facto* non-derogable status of the principles of independence, impartiality and even-handedness would also support the conclusion that these guarantees have acquired *ius cogens* status.[39] While the categories of *ius cogens* and non-derogable rights are not identical,[40] there exists a close relationship between them. This was explicitly acknowledged by the Human Rights Committee, which described the proclamation of certain rights as being of a non-derogable nature as a recognition, in part, of their peremptory nature.[41] The Human Rights Committee also stated that the category of peremptory norms extended beyond the list of non-derogable provisions as given in Article 4(2) ICCPR. States parties may in no circumstances invoke this Article as justification for, inter alia, deviating from fundamental principles of a fair trial.[42]

Further support for the *ius cogens* nature of the core elements of Article 14 ICCPR (at least in the context of criminal proceedings) can be drawn from certain statements of the International Criminal Tribunal for the former Yugoslavia (ICTY). In the *Tadic* decision,[43] the Appeals Chamber regarded it as "essential" that the principles of fairness and even-handedness as provided for in Article 14 of the ICCPR, are guaranteed by a judicial forum such as the ICTY.[44] The Secretary-General also hinted at the peremptory nature of these norms, when stating that full respect for the internationally recognised rights of the accused as contained in Article 14 ICCPR would be "axiomatic" at all stages of the ICTY's proceedings.[45] Any measure by the Security Council that would undermine the principles of

---

[39] General Comment No 29, above n 37, at para 16. See also De Zayas, above n 34, at 674, who observed that this sentiment was reflected in the confidential summary records of discussions of the Human Rights Committee with respect to communications under the First Optional Protocol to the ICCPR. See also Human Rights Committee, *Gonzalez del Rio v Peru*, Comm No 263/1987, CCPR/C/46/D/263/1987 (1992). The Human Rights Committee described the right to be tried by an independent and impartial tribunal as an absolute right that may suffer no exception.

[40] Ian D Seiderman, Hierarchy in International Law: *The Human Rights Dimension* 84–89 (Antwerp, Intersentia, 2001).

[41] Human Rights Committee, General Comment No 29, above n 37, at para 11. Seiderman, above n 40, at 85.

[42] *Ibid.*

[43] *Tadic* decision, above n 19, at para 42 ff.

[44] A similar conclusion was reached in the *Kanyabashi* decision, above n 19, at para 43. See also the Human Rights Committee, General Comment No 13, *Equality Before the Courts and the Right to a Fair and Public Hearing by an Independent Court Established by Law* para 4 (1984), available at www.unhchr/. It emphasised that whilst the ICCPR did not prohibit the establishment of special tribunals for the trying of civilians, such tribunals should be very exceptional and take place under conditions which afford the full guarantees stipulated in Art 14 ICCPR.

[45] S/25704 27 (1993); see also Arts 40, 41, 66 and 67 of the Rome Statute of the International Criminal Court of 17 July 1998, available at www.un.org/law/icc/; Dapo Akande, "The Role of the International Court of Justice in the Maintenance of International Peace", 8 *African Journal of International and Comparative Law* 323 (1996); Keith Harper, "Does the United Nations Security Council Have the Competence to Act as Court and Legislature?", *New York University Journal of International Law and Politics* 128 (1995).

independence, impartiality and even-handedness in international judicial proceedings would therefore arguably violate a *ius cogens* norm.

The Security Council showed itself well aware of the importance of these principles when it adopted the Statute of the ICTY and the ICTR. Article 21(1) to Article 21(4) of the ICTY Statute[46] guarantees, inter alia, the presumption of innocence, the principle of independence and the principle of equality of arms. The principle of impartiality is also guaranteed in Rule 15 of the ICTY's Rules of Procedure and Evidence. The Security Council secured these rights in a similar fashion with respect to the ICTR, by guaranteeing them in Article 20(1) to Article 20(4) of the ICTR Statute and Rule 15 of the ICTR's Rules of Procedure and Evidence, respectively.[47] The Security Council thus created the two *ad hoc* tribunals with due respect for the principle of independence which is inherent in the functioning of a subsidiary organ, as well as the basic elements of a fair hearing which are mandated by Article 1(1) of the Charter in combination with the *ius cogens* norms contained in Article 14 of the ICCPR.[48]

2.1.3. *The Scope of the Mandates*

The delegation of the power to take binding decisions is limited in scope, as it only relates to state cooperation required for the prosecution of individuals responsible for serious violations of international humanitarian law in the former Yugoslavia and Rwanda, respectively.[49] In addition to outlining the subject matter jurisdiction, the ICTR and ICTY Statutes also define the personal and territorial jurisdiction of the tribunals.[50] As far as the temporal jurisdiction is concerned, it is noteworthy that in the case of the ICTR it is explicitly limited to serious violations of humanitarian law

---

[46] The Statute and Rules of Procedure and Evidence of the ICTY are available at www.icty.org.

[47] *Ibid*, see also Partsch, above n 17, at 12–13. He underlined the fact that the Prosecutor is an independent organ of the ICTY/ICTR. In addition, the Security Council can only nominate 22 to 33 persons from whom the Secretary-General elects 11 judges. See also Arts 13 and 15 of the ICTY Statute, and Arts 12 and 15 of the ICTR Statute, respectively.

[48] See also the *Tadic* decision, above n 19, at para 46 and the *Kanyabashi* decision, above n 19, at para 44.

[49] These include the grave breaches of the four Geneva Conventions of 1949, ie the Geneva Convention for the Amelioration of the Condition of the Wounded and Sick in Armed Forces in the Field of 12 August 1949; the Geneva Convention for the Amelioration of the Condition of Wounded, Sick and Shipwrecked Members of Armed Forces at Sea of 12 August 1949; the Geneva Convention Relative to the Treatment of Prisoners of War of 12 August 1949; the Geneva Convention Relative to the Protection of Civilian Persons in Time of War of 12 August 1949; and—in the case of Rwanda—the Protocol Additional to the Geneva Conventions of 12 August 1949, and relating to the Protection of Victims of Non-International Armed Conflicts of 8 June 1977, all available at www.icrc.org. Other violations covered by the statutes included violations of the laws or customs of war (in the case of the former Yugoslavia), genocide and crimes against humanity. See Arts 1–5 of the ICTY Statute and Arts 1–4 of the ICTR Statute.

[50] See Arts 1–8 of the ICTY Statute and Arts 1–7 of the ICTR Statute, respectively.

in the territory of Rwanda and neighbouring states committed between 1 January 1994 and 31 December 1994.[51] As a result, it should be possible to draw a functional limitation to the ICTR's delegated powers, even though there is no explicit time-limit within which it has to fulfil its substantive mandate.[52]

This might be more difficult in the case of the ICTY, as its temporal jurisdiction is of an open-ended nature. The ICTY has jurisdiction with respect to individuals who committed serious violations of humanitarian law in the territory of the former Yugoslavia since 1 January 1991 and until peace is restored in the area.[53] Since the question whether peace has been restored is a highly complex issue, it would not serve as an administrable functional limitation to the duration of the mandate. This means that the Security Council has to take a Chapter VII decision to determine the cut-off date with respect to the ICTY's temporal jurisdiction. Since this decision could be blocked by the veto of a single permanent member, it means that the temporal jurisdiction of the ICTY could, in principle, continue for an indefinite period.

As was explained in chapter 7 at section 2.3. and chapter 8 at section 2, such a sequence of events would mean that the Security Council could relinquish overall control over the delegation to the permanent member with a direct interest in prolonging the ICTY's temporal mandate. This would amount to an illegal delegation of powers, as it is the Security Council as a collective entity that should retain the overall responsibility for a delegation of its powers to a subsidiary organ, as opposed to one single Security Council member. Therefore the ICTY's ongoing temporal mandate will remain legal only as long as a majority within the Security Council, including a majority of the permanent members, support this continuation. This means that the cut-off date for the ICTY's temporal jurisdiction would be determined at that moment in which a majority of the permanent members withdrew their support for its further continuation, or when no general majority exists within the Security Council regarding such continuation.[54] Serious violations of humanitarian law committed on the territory of the former Yugoslavia after this date would not fall under the ICTY mandate anymore.[55]

---

[51] Art 7 of the ICTR Statute.
[52] For a discussion of the functional limitation to delegated powers, see ch 7, at s 2.3. and ch 8, at s 2.
[53] See Art 8 of the ICTY Statute; SC Res 827 of 25 May 1993, at para 2; S/25704 para 28 (1993). As a result of this open-ended mandate, the serious violations of humanitarian law committed in Kosovo during 1998 and 1999 could be included in the ICTY mandate. See, inter alia, SC Res 1160 of 31 March 1998, at para 17; SC Res 1199 of 23 September 1998, at para 13; SC Res 1207 of 17 November 1998, at para 1 ff.
[54] See extensively ch 7, at s 2.3.
[55] In the case of judicial subsidiary organs, reporting to the Security Council has a different function than in the case of peace-keeping or peace-enforcement mandates. Art 34 of the

Finally, it is important to remember that the Security Council could not delegate more powers to the *ad hoc* tribunals than it possesses itself. In the context of cooperation and judicial assistance between the tribunals and states, this limitation gains significance with respect to the relationship between the ICTY and SFOR or KFOR. In particular, it implies that the ICTY cannot oblige SFOR or KFOR to use force in assisting the ICTY in arresting, detaining and transferring indicted persons to The Hague.[56] As the Security Council itself merely has the power to permit states to use military force (as opposed to obliging them),[57] a subsidiary body deriving its power to issue binding decisions from the Security Council would not be able to do so either. As a result, the ICTY could request (the states comprising) SFOR and KFOR to utilise their Chapter VII authorisation to use force to arrest indicted persons,[58] but it could not oblige them to take military action against their will.[59]

2.2.   The Extradition of Suspected Terrorists

From the above analysis one can conclude that Security Council resolutions authorising individual criminal prosecution as a method for restoring international peace and security are legal only if and to the extent that

ICTY Statute and Art 32 of the ICTR Statutes oblige the *ad hoc* tribunals to submit annual reports to the Security-Council. However, in the *Kanyabashi* decision, above n 19, at para 45, the ICTR described the obligation to report to the Security Council as an administrative and not a judicial act. The reason is that it may not in any way impinge upon the impartiality of its judicial decision.

[56] Sarooshi, above n 5, at 279.

[57] See ch 7, at ss 1 and 2.1.

[58] Although the power of arrest is not specifically mentioned in SC Res 1031 of 15 December 1995, its para 5 can be read as authorising IFOR to arrest ICTY indictees, if necessary by means of the use of force:

"*The Security Council,*

....

Acting under Chapter VII of the Charter of the United Nations,

....

7.   *Reminds* that the parties shall cooperate fully with all entities involved in the implementation of the peace settlement, as described in the [Dayton] Peace Agreement, or which are otherwise authorised by the Security Council, including the International Criminal Tribunal for the Former Yugoslavia, and that parties have in particular authorised the multinational force referred to in particular 14 below [IFOR] to take such action as required, including the use of necessary force, to ensure compliance with Annex 1–A of the [Dayton] Peace Agreement ...*".

In their explanatory statements before the Security Council the United States, the United Kingdom and France interpreted this resolution as authorising IFOR to arrest and detain indictees, see S/PV 3607 20–21 (1995). SC Res 1088 of 12 December 1996, which replaced IFOR with SFOR, contained similar language at paras 7 and 8. Cf Lamb, above n 9, at 186 ff.

[59] Sarooshi, above n 5, at 279–80; Lamb, above n 9, at 194.

they give due effect to the principles of independence, impartiality and even-handedness that underpin Article 1(1) of the Charter, as well as Article 14 of the ICCPR. This would also apply to Security Council resolutions requesting extradition, as it represents an important preliminary legal act in a criminal prosecution. Moreover, even though the extradition in itself does not constitute a determination of the guilt of the person to be extradited, it can effectively amount to such if it facilitates the prosecution of that person in a forum where his or her right to a fair trial cannot be guaranteed. It is therefore imperative that the independence, impartiality and even-handedness of the judicial body granting the extradition is beyond doubt. If one considers the Security Council's binding requests for the extradition of suspected terrorists in this light, their legality comes across as highly questionable.

With respect to the *Lockerbie* suspects,[60] the respective resolutions totally disregarded the principle of impartiality in relation to the two individuals whose extradition was demanded.[61] During the adoption of Resolution 731 of 22 January 1992, the countries that requested the extradition (the United Kingdom and the United States) participated in the voting procedure, which clearly violated the principle of impartiality.[62] It also violated Article 27(3) of the Charter, which determines that a party to a dispute shall abstain from voting when the Security Council takes a decision under Chapter VI of the Charter (as was the case with Resolution 731 (1992)).[63]

The impact of these flaws inherent to Resolution 731 (1992) was softened by the fact that it was a non-binding resolution in terms of Chapter VI of the Charter. Consequently Libya was not bound to give effect to it. However, the situation was different with respect to Resolution 748 of 31 March 1992, as it was adopted under Chapter VII of the Charter. This resolution suffered from the same deficits as Resolution 731 (1992), since the contents of the resolutions were essentially the same. Resolution 748 (1992) determined that Libya's refusal to extradite the suspects constituted a threat to international peace and repeated the requests for their

---

[60] For a discussion of the *Lockerbie* incident, see extensively ch 1, at s 2 ff.

[61] Brownlie, above n 10, at 100.

[62] See also the similar concern reflected in the dissenting opinion of Judge Ajibola, in *Case Concerning Questions of Interpretation and Application of the 1971 Montreal Convention Arising from the Aerial Incident at Lockerbie (Libyan Arab Jamahiriya v United States of America)*, Provisional Measures, ICJ Rep 1992, at 193. This decision is hereinafter referred to as *Libya v United States*, provisional measures. See also Harper, above n 45, at 140 who submitted that many international tribunals have accepted this as a general principle of law.

[63] See Bernhard Graefrath, "'Leave to the Court what Belongs to the Court'": The Libyan Case', 4 *European Journal of International Law* 188 (1993); Marcella David, "Passport to Justice: Internationalising the Political Question Doctrine for Application in the World Court", 40 *Harvard International Law Journal* 135, 142 (1999); Mark Weller, "The Lockerbie Case: A Premature End to the 'New World Order'", 4 *African Journal of International and Comparative Law* 315 (1992).

extradition.[64] Some authors have justified this behaviour with the argument that Article 27(3) of the Charter does not require states that are a party to a dispute to refrain from voting where it concerns a Chapter VII decision.[65] This argument negates the fact that Article 1(1) does apply to the Security Council, as do the core elements of Article 14 ICCPR. The effect of the violation of these norms was that the suspects faced extradition to jurisdictions where a fair trial would have been very difficult to guarantee, due to the extreme politicisation of the *Lockerbie* incident.[66]

An additional flaw in the *Lockerbie* resolutions concerned the fact that both Resolution 731 (1992) and Resolution 748 (1992) demanded Libya pay compensation.[67] This amounted to a determination of the Libyan state's responsibility for the *Lockerbie* incident by means of a procedure in which several members of the Security Council acted as judges in their own case. This violated Article 1(1) of the Charter, in that it disregarded the principle of impartiality and effectively imposed the terms of a judicial settlement on Libya.[68] In essence therefore the illegality of the *Lockerbie* resolutions resulted from two separate (if closely related) reasons. The first concerned the absence of due process in the adoption of the binding requests for extradition, whilst the second related to the biased way in which Libya's responsibility for the *Lockerbie* incident was determined.

Similar flaws affected the respective resolutions requesting the extradition of *Usama Bin Ladin* from Afghanistan,[69] as well as those suspected of the terrorist attack on the Egyptian President from the Sudan.[70] The procedures followed during their adoption were not in accordance with the basic standards of independence, impartiality and even-handedness,

---

[64] SC Res 748 of 31 March 1992, at para 1; See also SC Res 883 of 11 November 1993, at para 1.
[65] Michael Reisman, "The Constitutional Crisis in the United Nations", 87 *American Journal of International Law* 93, 96 (1993).
[66] See also Brownlie, above n 10, at 99–100. In the light of the public statements made by senior officials in the United Kingdom and in the United States, there was substantial doubt as to whether the two suspects could receive a fair trial either in the United States or in Scotland. See also the dissenting opinion of Judge *ad hoc* El-Kosheri, *Libya v United States*, provisional measures, above n 62, at 106; McGinley, above n 10, at 599.
[67] SC Res 748 of 31 March 1992, at para 1, incorporated the joint declaration of the United States and the United Kingdom requesting Libya to pay compensation by reference to SC Res 731 of 22 January 1992. It also explicitly mentioned the statements of the United Kingdom and the United States calling for extradition and compensation (S/23309 (1992)). See also Graefrath, above n 63, at 189; ch 1, at s 2.1.
[68] Graefrath, above n 63, at 193; Ken Roberts, "Second-Guessing the Security Council: the International Court of Justice and its Powers of Judicial Review", 7 *Pace International Law Review* 24 (1995). See also G Arangiou-Ruiz, Rapporteur to the International Law Commission, Fourth Report on State Responsibility, A/CN.4/SR.2277 3 (1992); McGinley, above n 10, at 599; Brownlie, above n 10, at 189.
[69] SC Res 1267 of 15 October 1999 and SC Res 1333 of 19 December 2000.
[70] SC Res 1044 of 31 January 1996; SC Res 1054 of 26 April 1996; and SC Res 1070 of 16 August 1996.

which are required during criminal proceedings.[71] In the case of *Usama Bin Ladin*, the United States participated in the voting of the relevant resolutions. Similarly, Egypt was a member of the Security Council in 1996 when the resolutions against the Sudan were adopted.[72] In the case of *Bin Ladin*, the impact of these procedural flaws has gained new significance since the terrorist attacks in the United States on 11 September 2001. In the light of the very strong prevailing perception that he was responsible for those attacks,[73] the question whether he could receive a fair trial in the United States has become particularly pertinent.

In essence therefore, all the above mentioned Security Council resolutions requesting the extradition of suspected terrorists violated basic principles of due process. In the case of the *Lockerbie* resolutions this fact (combined with the demand that Libya pays compensation), rendered the economic embargo imposed against the country illegal. As the embargo was exclusively underpinned by Libya's non-compliance with these two illegal demands,[74] it was void of a legal basis. In the case of the Sudan, however, the sanctions were partly underpinned by its refusal to extradite suspected terrorists, and partly by the fact that the country provided shelter and support for international terrorist elements.[75] Since this latter act objectively constituted a threat to international peace, the Security Council was entitled to adopt enforcement measures in response. As a result, the diplomatic embargo against the Sudan would in itself be illegal.

Similarly, the adoption of economic sanctions against the *Taliban* was, in itself, legally justified, despite the illegality of the extradition request. The sanctions were imposed not only due to the *Taliban's* refusal to extradite *Usama bin Ladin*, but also as a response to the fact that the *Taliban* regime provided sanctuary and training for international terrorists.[76] The criticism raised against this sanctions regime in the following section is therefore not directed at the fact that it was adopted in the absence of the existence of a valid threat to international peace. Instead, it is directed at the consequences of the type of sanctions adopted for the right to procedural fairness of those affected.

---

[71] Note that in these instances the Security Council did not request the respective countries to pay compensation. It thus did not instrumentalise a Security Council resolution to determine state responsibility for specific terrorist acts.

[72] See 50 *Yearbook of the United Nations* 1468 (1996).

[73] See, for example, *International Herald Tribune*, 14 December 1 (2001); *NRC Handelsblad*, 14 December 1 (2001). Note that the Security Council has affirmed its request for his extradition in subsequent resolutions. See the preamble of SC Res 1378 of 14 November 2001; see also SC Res 1390 of 16 January 2002, at para 1.

[74] SC Res 748 of 31 March 1992, at para 1; SC Res 883 of 11 November 1993, at para 1. See also ch 1, at ss 2.1. and 2.2.

[75] SC Res 1054 of 26 April 1996.

[76] SC Res 1267 of 15 October 1999; SC Res 1333 of 19 December 2000.

2.3.   The Freezing of Assets of Individuals Associated with International Terrorism

The sanctions regime established by Resolutions 1267 (1999) and 1333 (2000) authorised the freezing of the assets and resources of the (then) *de facto Taliban* regime in Afghanistan, as well as the assets of individuals and undertakings listed by the Sanctions Committee as being "associated" with the *Taliban, Usama bin Ladin* and *Al-Qaida*.[77] By targeting individuals and undertakings in such a broad and vague fashion, Resolution 1333 (2000) was bound to violate basic principles of procedural fairness.

Admittedly, such direct targeting of individuals can be regarded as justifiable in the light of the serious threat that terrorism constitutes to international peace and security. At the same time, they oblige the Security Council to provide those individuals and undertakings affected with a fair hearing by means of which they can challenge the allegations against them. After all, the listing by the Sanctions Committee presupposes the weighing of evidence, which is a legal act with legal consequences. This, in turn, necessitates access to an independent, impartial and even-handed procedure during which the evidence against potentially innocent victims of the listing procedure can be challenged. The more drastic the measures foreseen by the Security Council (in this case it concerned the freezing of all assets and economic resources of the affected individuals, except those needed for basic expenses)[78] the stronger this obligation will be.

At this point one needs to emphasise that Article 14(1) ICCPR should not be interpreted as merely containing procedural guarantees in relation to judicial proceedings, as it also includes the right of access to a fair hearing.[79] This would certainly be the case with respect to the determination of any criminal charges against a person.[80] Were this not the case, a state could do away with its criminal courts, or transfer their jurisdiction to determine certain categories of criminal charges to bodies which do not possess the minimum attributes of a judicial tribunal.[81] It would be

---

[77] SC Res 1333 of 19 December 2000, at para 8(c) and SC Res 1390 of 16 January 2002, at paras 2(a) 5(a).

[78] SC Res 1452 of 20 December 2002, at paras 1(a) 1(b), eventually excluded funds necessary for basic expenses such as foodstuffs, rent, medical expenses etc from the scope of the sanctions.

[79] Carsten Stahn, "International Territorial Administration in the former Yugoslavia: Origins, Developments and Challenges Ahead", 61 *Zeitschrift für ausländisches öffentliches Recht und Völkerrecht* 143–44 (2001). Cf in the European system *Golder v United Kingdom*, App No 4451/70, Judgment, 21 February 1975, at para 36. This and other decisions of the European Court of Human Rights cited here are available at www.echr.coe.int/.

[80] Sarah Joseph *et al*, *The International Covenant on Civil and Political Rights. Cases, Materials, and Commentary* 286 (Oxford, Oxford University Press, 2002).

[81] Jayawickrama, above n 30, at 38.

inconceivable that this Article should describe in detail the procedural guarantees afforded to parties facing criminal charges without protecting that which alone makes it possible for the parties to benefit from such guarantees.[82]

It is noteworthy that the Human Rights Committee has not yet interpreted the concept of "criminal charge".[83] As this term corresponds literally with that in Article 6 of the European Convention for the Protection of Human Rights and Fundamental Freedoms of 1950, the Strasbourg jurisprudence may serve as guidance in this regard. According to the European Court of Human Rights the nature and severity of the threatened sanction, as well as the type of sanctioned offence is to be drawn upon in evaluating whether a criminal charge exists.[84] For Article 6 to apply in virtue of the words "criminal charge", it suffices that the offence in question should have made the person concerned liable to a sanction which, due to its nature and degree of severity, places it within the "criminal" sphere.[85]

The freezing of assets undertaken in accordance with Resolution 1333 (2000) was a response to the alleged involvement of the affected individuals in international terrorism. In addition, it would constitute a sanction belonging to the criminal sphere, in light of its punitive nature, severity, as well as the stigmatisation resulting from it. The listing by the Sanctions Committee may also directly be the basis for criminal charges at the national level.[86] It is therefore fair to conclude that the freezing of the assets of the individuals concerned can qualify as a punitive sanction and the underlying decision as a criminal charge.[87] It would therefore be essential that the individuals affected have access to a fair hearing where they receive the opportunity to refute the claims against them.

Unfortunately, neither the respective Security Council resolutions nor the Sanctions Committee itself provided for such a legal remedy.

---

[82] *Ibid*. See also Nowak, above n 31, at 241; *Oló Bahamonde v Equatorial Guinea*, above n 31, at 286. With regard to non-criminal proceedings ("suit at law"), Art 14(1) would, at the very least, guarantee equal access to courts. The Human Rights Committee has observed that a situation in which an individual's attempts to seize the competent jurisdictions of his or her grievances are systematically frustrated, runs counter to the guarantees of Art 14(1), as the notion of equality before the courts encompasses the very access to the courts. See also Weissbrodt, above n 31, at 120.

[83] Jayawickrama, above n 30, at 39; Nowak, above n 31, at 243.

[84] Eg *Lauko v Slovakia*, App No 26138/95, Judgment, 2 September 1998, at para 56.

[85] *Lutz v Germany*, App No 9912/82, Judgment, 25 August 1987, at para 55.

[86] With regard to the Swedish individuals that featured on the list of the Sanctions Committee, the Swedish authorities considered the institution of criminal proceedings against the individuals concerned, but ultimately refrained from doing so due to lack of evidence.

[87] See also Ove Bring *et al*, "Chapter on Sweden", in Vera Gowlland-Debbas (ed), *National Implementation of Non-Military Security Council Sanctions: A Comparative Study* 316 (The Hague, Martinus Nijhoff, forthcoming), who noted that the freezing of assets clearly had a punitive character from the perspective of the individuals concerned.

According to the Guidelines of the Sanctions Committee for the Conduct of its Work,[88] affected individuals or undertakings can submit requests for de-listing to the Sanctions Committee via their respective government.[89] These requests are, however, not reviewed by an independent and impartial legal organ, but by the Sanctions Committee itself.[90] This political organ thus has to act as judge in its own case, as the same members who initially suspected individuals or undertakings of involvement in international terrorism also have to consider the accuracy of that judgment.

In addition, the procedure by means of which the Sanctions Committee reviews the request for removal from the list could hardly be described as even-handed. Once the requests are circulated to the members of the Sanctions Committee, they have to communicate any objections to the Chair within two working days.[91] Since the Sanctions Committee reaches decisions by consensus,[92] it means that the removal from the list can be prevented by the objection of one single member. The meetings are further held behind closed doors and members do not have to give reasons for their objections.[93] As a result, potentially innocent individuals can remain on the sanctions list and be deprived of all their material resources for an indefinite period of time,[94] without any evidence having been presented against them. This, in turn, would effectively amount to a conviction of involvement with international terrorism without trial. This situation clearly constitutes a violation of the basic due process principles that underpin Article 1(1) of the Charter and Article 14 ICCPR.

2.4.   Creating an *ad hoc* Tribunal for Investigating Persons Suspected of Involvement in International Terrorism

The next point to consider is that it is highly unlikely that the Security Council (or any of its Sanctions Committees) could ever act as a fair and effective adjudicator itself. It is a political body with no rules of procedure for fair, adjudicative hearings.[95] Unlike a court of law it does not contain the procedural mechanisms to weigh evidence, distinguish between

---

[88] Adopted on 7 November 2002, available at www.un.org. Hereinafter referred to as Guidelines.

[89] Guidelines, above n 88, at para 6(d).

[90] *Ibid*, at para 6(e).

[91] *Ibid*, at paras 6(d) and 8(b).

[92] *Ibid*, at para 6(e).

[93] *Ibid*, at paras 3(b) and 9(b).

[94] SC Res 1333 of 19 December 2001, at paras 23 and 24, initially imposed these measures for 12 months. However, thereafter SC Res 1390 of 16 January 2002, at para 3, extended these measures for an indefinite period of time.

[95] Kirgis (First Fifty Years), above n 21, at 532.

findings of fact and law, make determinations in an unbiased fashion, ensure unbiased access to information, or permit all parties in a dispute to be heard and to be presented by counsel. The Security Council is also not required to explain any of its holdings in a published opinion.[96] As it is also unlikely that the Security Council will adopt any procedural rules guaranteeing these standards in future, it will remain ill-suited as a forum for (criminal) adjudication. These factors may explain why the ICTY and ICTR concluded that the Security Council could not function as a judicial organ itself, but had to create an independent sub-organ for this purpose in situations where the restoration or maintenance of international peace and security required criminal prosecution.[97]

If one applies this reasoning to the Security Council measures discussed above in sections 2.2. and 2.3. it implies that the Council should have created an independent body for investigating persons suspected of involvement with international terrorism. The Security Council could then have invested this organ with the power to request the extradition of the suspects and to try them according to internationally accepted standards of due process.[98] This would have precluded the risk of a biased decision on extradition which, in turn, confronted the suspects with extradition to a forum where it would have been very difficult to guarantee a free trial under the circumstances. This means that the Security Council could have created a body similar to the ICTY or the ICTR, but with the purpose of extraditing and prosecuting the perpetrators of those acts of international terrorism defined in its statute. As international terrorism constitutes a threat to peace, the creation of such an *ad hoc* body can be regarded as a measure necessary to remove the threat and restore international peace.

Moreover, it is also plausible that the Security Council could authorise the independent *ad hoc* body to determine whether the particular terrorist attack constituted an act of *state sponsored* terrorism, which is an issue separate from the determination of individual criminal responsibility for such acts. In this context it is important to keep in mind that such an *ad hoc* organ might be able to engage in fact-finding in a more timely and efficient fashion than the International Court of Justice (ICJ). Although Article 36(2)(b) of the ICJ Statute theoretically provides the ICJ with jurisdiction to decide questions of fact which constitute a breach of an international obligation, it would have considerable practical difficulties in doing so in cases involving state-sponsored terrorism. First, it would have to

---

[96] Harper, above n 45, at 138.

[97] See *Tadic* decision, above n 19, at para 37; *Kanyabashi* decision, above n 19, at para 40 ff.

[98] See also Graefrath, above n 63, at 191; see also Derek Bowett, "The Impact of Security Council Decisions on Dispute Settlement Procedures", 5 *European Journal of International Law* 96 (1994).

establish jurisdiction over the case, which is contingent on the cooperation of the parties involved in the dispute.[99]

Second, comprehensive fact-finding by the ICJ in a case concerning state sponsored terrorism would be very difficult, as it includes on-the-spot examinations, cross-examination of evidence provided by states and cross examination of state officials.[100] Although the ICJ could attempt to do so under Article 50 of its Statute,[101] it is very likely that it would come across considerable resistance from the respective states and their intelligence services where it concerned the exposing of evidence.[102] As the ICJ itself has no means of forcing states to give effect to its requests, this obstacle would be very difficult to overcome. A body created under Chapter VII of the Charter, on the other hand, could more easily rely on the intelligence services of the member states for information, as the Security Council could adopt binding measures requesting parties to cooperate in the investigation.[103]

Finally, the Security Council could also have invested such a body with the power to review the evidence against those persons whose assets are to be frozen due to their suspected association with international terror- ism. By providing those affected with an impartial, independent and even-handed review mechanism, the Security Council would have pre- vented the current controversy concerning the illegality of the sanctions regime flowing from Resolution 1267 (1999) and 1333 (2000).[104]

---

[99] Bernd Martenczuk, *Rechtsbindung und Rechtskontrolle des Weltsicherheitsrates*, (Berlin, Duncker & Humblot, 1996); at 242.

[100] *Ibid*; Inger Österdahl, *Threat to the Peace* 111 (Uppsala, Swedish Institute of International Law, 1998).

[101] According to Art 50 of the ICJ Statute: "The Court may, at any time, entrust any individ- ual, body, bureau, commission, or other organisation that it may select, with the task of carrying out an inquiry or giving an expert opinion."

[102] Martenczuk (Rechtskontrolle), above n 99, at 242–43. Akande, above n 45, at 604–05. The reluctance of states to cooperate with the ICJ is also reflected in the large numbers of chal- lenges to jurisdiction in most cases where the ICJ has been seized other than by special agree- ment. In addition, the number of states accepting the compulsory jurisdiction of the ICJ remains low and many states who have done so have added reservations. See Jochen A Frowein, "The Internal and External Effects of Resolutions by International Organisations", 49 *Zeitschrift für ausländisches öffentliches Recht und Völkerrecht* 783 (1989). Karin Oellers- Frahm, "Die 'obligatorische' Gerichtsbarkeit des Internationalen Gerichtshofs," 47 *Zeitschrift für ausländisches öffentliches Recht und Völkerrecht* 260 (1987).

[103] See Martenczuk (Rechtskontrolle), above n 99, at 241–42. As an alternative, the Security Council could also refer the dispute to the International Civil Aviation Organisation (ICAO), a possibility which is also foreseen by Art 13 of the Montreal Convention. This would in effect amount to resorting to the procedures for pacific settlement of disputes in terms of Chapter VI of the Charter. However, since the Security Council is not obliged to resort to Chapter VI procedures before taking action under Chapter VII, it would be within the Security Council's discretion to pursue this avenue or not. For criticism of the Security Council for not pursuing this option during the *Lockerbie* incident, see David above n 63, at 120, 123.

[104] The Security Council could also opt for a more decentralised solution, ie by authorising member states to provide such a review mechanism in their own courts. This approach was

In essence therefore, the particular nature of the crime of international terrorism would entitle the Security Council to create an independent, impartial and even-handed judicial body for prosecuting the individual perpetrators of such acts, determining whether the acts in questions concerned state-sponsored terrorism, as well as providing judicial review for those persons whose assets were frozen on the demand of the Sanctions Committee due to their suspected involvement with international terrorism. On the one hand, such a body could be regarded as necessary for removing the threat to peace that international terrorism undoubtedly poses. At the same time, it would give recognition to the quasi-judicial nature of the measures involved, as well as the requirements flowing from Article 1(1) of the Charter and Article 14(1) ICCPR.

3.   (QUASI-) JUDICIAL MEASURES PERTAINING TO THE RIGHTS OF STATES

3.1.   The United Nations Compensation Commission for Iraq

3.1.1.   The Nature and Scope of the Mandate

The Compensation Commission was established as a subsidiary organ[105] of the Security Council with the purpose of dealing with the liability of Iraq for any direct loss or damage, including environmental damage and the depletion of natural resources, or injury to foreign governments, nationals and corporations, as a result of Iraq's unlawful invasion and occupation of Kuwait.[106] This process was to be financed by a levy on oil exported from Iraq after 3 April 1991, as well as oil exported earlier but not delivered or not paid for due to the economic sanctions regime.[107] The money generated in this fashion was to be placed in a United Nations Compensation Fund, from where it would be distributed to pay, inter alia,

---

followed in SC Res 1373 of 28 September 2001, which obliged member states to criminalise the financing of international terrorism. Whilst this resolution imposed far-reaching obligations on member states in the field of criminal law, it did so in terms which were broad enough to allow for their implementation in accordance with the principles of Art 14 ICCPR. See Bring *et al*, above n 87, at 321 ff.

[105] S/22559 para 4 (1991).
[106] SC Res 687 of 3 April 1991, at para 16; see also Peter Malanczuk, "International Business and New Rules of State Responsibility?—The Law Applied by the United Nations (Security Council) Compensation Commission for Claims Against Iraq", in Karl-Heinz Böckstiegel (ed), *Perspectives of Air Law, Space Law and International Business Law for the Next Century* 117 (Cologne, Carl Heymanns, 1996); Harper, above n 45, at 118; Frederick L Kirgis, "Book Review", 93 *American Journal of International Law* 973 (1999).
[107] See SC Res 705 of 15 August 1991, at para 2; SC Res 712 of 19 September 1991, at para 1 ff.

the compensation claims against Iraq.[108] After Iraq refused to export oil on these terms, the Security Council requested states that had frozen proceeds owed to the Government of Iraq from the sale of oil products on or after 6 August 1990, to transfer a certain amount of those proceeds into a United Nations administered escrow account. By means of this procedure, the Security Council effectively seized $800 million in Iraqi assets, of which 30 per cent were to be transferred to the compensation fund.[109]

In creating the Compensation Commission the Security Council relied for the first time on its implied powers to create a subsidiary body for the performance of a judicial function,[110] ie the determination of the extent of Iraq's liability for damages resulting from the Gulf war, as well as the validity of the claims submitted against it.[111] Normally, claims for compensation arising out of an internationally wrongful act would be regulated by an agreement between the states concerned, or a dispute settlement mechanism agreed upon by the parties.[112] However, in the aftermath of the Gulf War the Security Council regarded the creation of a Compensation Commission for adjudicating claims for compensation against Iraq in a binding fashion as necessary for the restoration and maintenance of peace in the region.[113] If one keeps in mind that Security Council resolutions are supported by a presumption of legality,[114] this seems to have been a

---

[108] The Compensation Commission and the Compensation Fund were established by SC Res 692 of 20 May 1991, at para 3, See also S/22559 (1991). Other activities to be funded from the compensation fund included the destroying of Iraq's military arsenal, half of the cost of the demarcation of the Iraq-Kuwait border, as well as the provision of humanitarian relief to the Iraqi people. See also Harper, above n 45, at 120; Vera Gowlland-Debbas, "Security Council Enforcement Action and Issues of State Responsibility", 43 *International and Comparative Law Quarterly* 81 (1994); Sean D Murphy, "The Security Council, Legitimacy, and the Concept of Collective Security After the Cold War", 32 *Columbia Journal of Transnational Law* 237 (1994).

[109] Decision taken by the Governing Council of the Compensation Commission during its second session in S/AC.26/1991/6 (1991). This and other decisions of the Governing Council cited hereinafter are available at http://www.unog.ch/uncc/decision.htm. See also SC Res 778 of 2 October 1992, at paras 1 2; Malanczuk, above n 106, at 120; Murphy, above n 108, at 238.

[110] Kirgis, (First Fifty Years), above n 21, at 525; Harper, above n 45, at 120. See also Andrea Gattini, "The UN Compensation Commission: Old Rules, New Procedures on War Reparations", 13 *European Journal of International Law* 160 (2002).

[111] The Secretary-General attempted to argue that the claims process against Iraq was not, in essence, of a judicial nature. However, he conceded that some claims could be disputed and that the resolution of such claims would be quasi-judicial. See S/22559 8–9 (1991). This seems to be a rather limited perception of the extent of the judicial nature of the process. After all, the determination of whether any given loss, damage or injury was direct and resulted from Iraq's invasion and occupation of Kuwait, would involve causation questions which are clearly legal in nature. See Frederic L Kirgis "Claims Settlement and the United Nations Legal Structure", in Richard B Lillich (ed), *The United Nations Compensation Commission* 111 (Irvington, Transnational, 1995).

[112] Bernhard Graefrath, "Iraqi Reparations and the Security Council", 55 *Zeitschrift für ausländisches öffentliches Recht und Völkerrecht* 52 (1995).

[113] Kirgis (in Lillich), above n 111, at 104; Harper, above n 45, at 120.

[114] As is also pointed out by Kirgis (in Lillich), above n 111, at 104.

reasonable conclusion under the circumstances. The Iraqi regime could not have been trusted to negotiate and adhere to a dispute settlement mechanism for this purpose voluntarily and the absence of such a mechanism would have aggravated the tense situation in the region.[115]

The delegation of Chapter VII powers to the Compensation Commission was limited in scope by subsequent decisions of the Governing Council.[116] In essence, the Compensation Commission could take binding decisions regarding claims submitted for losses resulting from the military operations or threat of military action by either side during the period 2 August 1990 to 2 March 1991; the departure of persons from or their inability to leave Iraq or Kuwait during that period; actions by officials, employees or agents of the Government of Iraq or Kuwait, or its controlled entities during that period in connection with the invasion or occupation; the breakdown of civil order in Kuwait or Iraq during that period, or hostage-taking or other illegal detention during that period.[117] By outlining the Compensation Commission's jurisdiction in this fashion and explicitly limiting its temporal jurisdiction to the period between 2 August 1990 and 2 March 1991, the Security Council prevented an open-ended mandate which could have expanded the Compensation Commission's jurisdiction for an indefinite period.[118]

3.1.2. The Lack of Independence of the Compensation Commission

The next question that arises is whether the Security Council, in creating the Compensation Commission, paid due regard to the principles of

---

[115] See also Kirgis, (First Fifty Years), above n 37, at 525. For a different opinion, see Graefrath (Reparations), above n 112, at 22. He rejected the notion that the enforcement of the payment of debts after the hostilities have ended constitutes a mechanism for maintaining or restoring international peace. Consequently he regarded the establishment of the Compensation Commission as falling outside the Security Council's (implied) powers under Chapter VII of the Charter.

[116] See below, at s 3.1.2., for a clarification of the role of the Governing Council.

[117] Claims for losses suffered as a result of the trade embargo and related measures following form SC Res 661 (1991), later resolutions and steps taken by individual states on that basis are excluded. An exception exists where such loss is a direct result of Iraq's unlawful invasion and occupation. Guidelines issued by the Governing Council attempted to clarify under which conditions a particular loss was attributable to the embargo and stated that losses directly resulting from the embargo and the economic situation caused thereby will not be compensated. See *Criteria for Expedited Processing of Urgent Claims*, in S/AC.26/1991/1, paras 16 and 18 (1991); *Criteria for Additional Categories of Claims*, in S/AC.26/1991/7/Rev1 paras 6, 21 and 34 (1992); *Propositions and Conclusions on Compensation for Business Losses: Types of Damages and their Valuation*, in S/AC.26/1992/9 para 6 (1992); *Compensation for Business Losses Resulting from Iraq's Unlawful Invasion and Occupation of Kuwait where the Trade Embargo and Related Measures were also a Cause*, in S/AC.26/1992/15, at paras 1, 3 and 5; See also Malanczuk, above n 106, at 122.

[118] The Governing Council also limited the time-frame within which claims could be submitted. See *Criteria for Additional Categories of Claims*, above n 117, at paras 15, 19 and 42; see also S/AC.26/1992/12 (1992); S/AC.26/Dec.30 (1995).

impartiality and even-handedness that underpin Article 1(1) of the Charter.[119] An examination of the mandate and procedure of the Compensation Commission leads to some doubts in this regard, as it is highly questionable whether the Compensation Commission enjoys the amount of independence that a body involved in claims adjudication requires.

The Compensation Commission consists of a Governing Council, a Secretariat and Commissioners. The Governing Council is the policy-making body of the Commission and consists of representatives from the 15 members of the Security Council. It meets periodically and issues decisions regarding, inter alia, the type of claims that are eligible for compensation, the procedures for filing and proving claims and the appointment of Commissioners.[120] The Secretariat (headed by the Executive Secretary) consists of United Nations employees responsible for providing administrative support to the Governing Council and the Commissioners, as well as for administering the fund from which claims are paid.[121]

The Commissioners are independent experts in finance law, accounting, insurance, environmental damage assessment, oil, trade and engineering drawn from around the world.[122] Sitting in panels of three, they review claims assigned to them by the Secretariat based on criteria established by the Governing Council.[123] These panels conduct their work in private and all records remain confidential.[124] The outcome of their reviews is forwarded in the form of recommendations[125] to the Governing

---

[119] See also TD Gill, "Legal and Some Political Limitations on the Power of the UN Security Council to Exercise its Enforcement Powers under Chapter VII of the Charter", 26 *Netherlands Yearbook of International Law* 67 (1995).

[120] Murphy, above n 108, at 226; Malanczuk, above n 106, at 120. Except for decisions on the method of ensuring that payments are made to the Compensation Fund (which require consensus), decisions of the Governing Council are taken by a majority of 9 members, excluding the right of veto.

[121] Malanczuk, above n 106, at 121.

[122] See the Commission's *Provisional Rules for Claims Procedure*, in S/AC.26/1992/10 Art 19(2) (1992); Murphy, above n 108, at 236; Malanczuk, above n 106, at 121.

[123] Graefrath (Reparations), above n 112, at 52.

[124] *Provisional Rules for Claims Procedure*, above n 122, at Art 30; Graefrath (Reparations), above n 112, at 52; Malanczuk, above n 106, at 126.

[125] The Compensation Commission deals with the claims on a consolidated basis requiring governments to group the claims of their nationals in six categories. Category A concerns departure claims for individuals who departed from Iraq or Kuwait during the period between 2 August 1990 and 2 March 1991 (capped at $5000 per family); Category B concerns claims for serious personal injury or death (capped at $10,000 per family); Category C concerns claims up to $100,000 for death, personal injury or actual loss; Category D concerns claims of individuals above $100,000; Category E concerns larger claims by corporate and other legal entities; whilst Category F concerns claims of governments and international organisations for damage to their property and for losses incurred by a government in evacuating its nationals from Iraq and Kuwait. See *Criteria for Expedited Processing of Urgent Claims*, above n 117, at paras 10 ff; *Criteria for Additional Categories of Claims*, above n 117, at paras 6 ff; see also Malanczuk, above n 106, at 123.

Council who can approve, alter or send back the recommendations to the Commissioners.

Although the Commissioners themselves are independent experts, the judicial process is ultimately controlled by the Governing Council who supervises the work and procedure of the panels. This political body has the final say over the disposal of claims and its decisions are not subject to appeal or review.[126] Moreover, there are questions surrounding the even-handedness in the proceedings of the Compensation Commission, resulting from Iraq's lack of standing before it.[127] Although being the defendant state, Iraq is not represented on the Governing Council or in the panels.[128] In addition, Iraq has no access to the Compensation Commission's confidential files or panels dealing with individual claims, which means that it does not receive any documented information concerning any of the individual claims.

Instead, Iraq's participation is limited to receiving the Executive Secretary's quarterly reports on which it may comment within a limited period of time.[129] These reports only contain statistical information regarding the type and number of claims received, as well as general information on factual and legal issues which have been raised in order to establish general guidelines for the work of the panels.[130] In addition, the panels of commissioners may request further written or oral submissions from Iraq in unusually larger or complex cases.[131] The extent to which this latter procedure is utilised remains within the discretion of the panel concerned and it is not a procedure that is accessible to Iraq as of right.[132] It is therefore fair to conclude that the Compensation Commission has invented a procedure which allows a compensation claim to be presented

---

[126] *Provisional Rules for Claims Procedure*, above n 122, at Art 40. The political nature of the Governing Council is not (as is implied by Gattini, above n 110, at 161,) altered by the fact that it usually decides by majority voting without the possibility of a veto. See also Murphy, above n 108, at 237; Gowlland-Debbas (State Responsibility), above n 108, at 81; Graefrath (Reparations), above n 112, at 53; Kirgis (First Fifty Years), above n 21, at 525; Malanczuk, above n 106, at 121; Martenczuk, above n 99, at 264.

[127] Malanczuk, above n 106, at 125; Murphy, above n 108, at 238.

[128] Iraq was also denied observer status in the Governing Council. See Malanczuk, above n 106, at 125.

[129] *Provisional Rules for Claims Procedure*, above n 122, at Art 16. See Graefrath (Reparations), above n 112, at 52; Malanczuk, above n 106, at 125; Gattini, above n 110, at 163.

[130] *Provisional Rules for Claims Procedure*, above n 122, at Art 16(1); Graefrath (Reparations), above n 112, at 53; Malanczuk, above n 106, at 126.

[131] *Provisional Rules for Claims Procedure*, above n 122, at Art 36(a).

[132] Malanczuk, above n 106, at 126–27. But see Gattini, above n 110, at 164. He submitted that this deficit is compensated for in practice, as all panels entrusted with unusually large or complex cases have requested Iraq to express its views in written form. Since 2001 Iraq has also been allowed to present its views during oral proceedings. See also *Report and Recommendations Made by the Panel of Commissioners Concerning the First Instalment of F4 Claims*, in S/AC 26/2001/16 para 24 (2001). See also David D Caron & Brian Morris, "The UN Compensation Commission: Practical Justice, not Retribution", 13 *European Journal of International Law* 192–93 (2002).

against a state without informing that state of the details of the claim, or to challenge its validity.[133] This, in turn, seems hardly reconcilable with the principle of equality of arms or the *audi alteram partem* rule that underpins Article 1(1) of the Charter.

It is also worth stating that these irregularities could not be justified with the argument that Iraq had officially accepted the terms of Resolution 687 (1991), including the creation of the procedure for compensation.[134] First, the weight of a consent effectuated by the devastation of the Gulf War is questionable.[135] Moreover, the fact that Iraq in principle accepted its liability under international law for damages resulting from the Gulf War, does not mean that it actually consented to a particular procedure which was imposed on it at a later time.[136] Stated differently, the acceptance of the obligation to make reparations cannot be interpreted as an advance recognition or acceptance of any individual reparation claim put forward afterwards by Kuwait or its allies, or a procedure which negates basic elements of procedural fairness.[137] In addition, it would not be acceptable that the Security Council instrumentalise the (coerced) consent of a country in a fashion that enables it to circumvent clear limitations on its powers contained in Article 1(1) of the Charter.

In essence therefore, the illegality of the Compensation Commission is not to be found in a lack of overall control by the Security Council over its mandate, but in the Security Council's excessive control over the exercise of the Compensation Commission's adjudicative function. The lack of independence that the Compensation Commission enjoys in this regard, combined with Iraq's lack of standing before it are in violation of the principles of justice as outlined in Article 1(1) of the Charter.

3.2. The Iraq-Kuwait Boundary Demarcation Commission

3.2.1. *The Implications of the Territorial Integrity of States for the Powers of the Security Council*

The limits to the powers of the Security Council in changing the territorial boundaries of states became a pertinent issue with the establishment of

---

[133] Graefrath (Reparations), above n 112, at 52–53; Malanczuk, above n 106, at 126.
[134] As is claimed by Jeremy P Carver, "Dispute Resolution or Administrative Tribunal: A Question of Due Process", in Richard B Lillich (ed), *The United Nations Compensation Commission*, (Irvington, Transnational, 1996), at 70; John R Crook, "The UNCC and its Critics: Is Iraq Entitled to Judicial Due Process?", in *ibid*, at 89.
[135] Kirgis (in Lillich), above n 111, at 106.
[136] SC 686 of 2 March 1991, at para 2(b), demanded that Iraq "accept *in principle* [emphasis added] its liability under international law for any loss, damage or injury arising in regard to Kuwait and third States, and their nationals and corporations, as a result of the invasion and illegal occupation of Kuwait by Iraq." Iraq agreed to fulfil this obligation in a *Letter to the Secretary General dated 3 March 1991*, in S/22320 (1991).
[137] Graefrath (Reparations), above n 112, at 29; Kirgis (in Lillich), above n 111, at 106–07.

the United Nations Iraq-Kuwait Boundary Demarcation Commission[138] (hereinafter Demarcation Commission), for the purpose of demarcating the border between Iraq and Kuwait in accordance with an agreement between the two states dating from 1963.[139] The Demarcation Commission was established under the auspices of the Secretary-General and consisted of three independent experts appointed by the Secretary-General, as well as one representative from Iraq and Kuwait, respectively.[140] Iraq discontinued its participation in the Demarcation Commission's work after the first five sessions due to dissatisfaction with its way of operating.[141] Thereafter the Demarcation Commission continued to operate without Iraqi participation.[142] and completed its task of determining the Iraq-Kuwait border in geographical coordinates of latitude and longitude by May 1993.[143] These coordinates were accepted by the Security Council as the final demarcation of the international boundary between Iraq and Kuwait.[144]

Iraq, for its part, rejected all conclusions of the Demarcation Commission on the basis that the Security Council had imposed a border in the absence of an agreement to this effect between the states affected.[145] Iraq consistently questioned the validity of the 1963 agreement, arguing that it was never subjected to the constitutional procedures required for ratification by the legislative branch and President of Iraq.[146] In addition (one might

---

[138] SC Res 687 of 3 April 1991, at para 3; S/22558 (1991), at para 3.

[139] See *Agreed Minutes between Kuwait and Iraq Regarding the Restoration of Friendly Relations, Recognition and Related Matters, signed at Baghdad on 4 October 1963*, in 30 *International Legal Materials* 855 para 1 (1991). Iraq recognised the boundaries as specified in the letter of the Prime Minister of Iraq of 2 July 1932 and which was accepted by the ruler of Kuwait in his letter of 10 August 1932. This letter described the border as "From the intersection of the Wadi-el-Audja with the Batin and thence northward along the Batin to a point just south of the latitude of Safwan; thence eastwards passing south of Safwan Wells, Jebel Sanam and Um Qasr leaving them to Iraq and so on to the junction of the Khor Zoberi with the Khor Abdulla. The islands of Warbah, Bubiyan, Maskan (or Mashjan), Failakah, Auha, Kubbar, Quaru and Umm-el-Maridam appertain to Kuwait." Both letters are reprinted in "The United Nations and the Iraq-Kuwait Conflict 1990–1996", IX *United Nations Blue Books Series* 165 (1996). See also Murphy, above n 108, at 243; Gill, above n 119, at 88.

[140] S/22558 para 3 (1991); *Letter dated 21 May 1992 from the Permanent Representative of Iraq to the United Nations addressed to the Secretary General*, in S/24044 paras 1 ff (1992).

[141] S/25811 (1993) Annex, at 21.

[142] Harry Post, "Adjudication as a Mode of Acquisition of Territory? Some Observations on the Iraq-Kuwait Boundary Demarcation in the Light of the Jurisprudence of the International Court of Justice", in Vaughan Lowe & Malgosia Fitzmaurice (eds), *Fifty Years of the International Court of Justice* 253 (Cambridge, Cambridge University Press, 1995).

[143] Murphy, above n 108, at 243. *Final Report of the Boundary Demarcation Commission* in S/25811 paras 8 ff (1993).

[144] SC Res 833 of 27 May 1993, at para 4; see also S/22558 paras 3 and 7 (1991).

[145] *Letter dated 7 June 1993 from the Permanent Representative of Iraq to the Secretary-General transmitting a letter dated 6 June 1993 from the Minister for Foreign Affairs of Iraq concerning the work of the Iraq-Kuwait Boundary Demarcation Commission*, in S/25905 (1993); See also Harper, above n 45, at 115.

[146] See *Identical letters dated 6 April 1991 from the Deputy Prime Minister and Minister for Foreign Affairs of Iraq to the President of the Security Council and the Secretary-General*, in S/22456 para 1

say in the alternative), Iraq questioned the Demarcation Commission's interpretation and application of the 1963 agreement. For example, it claimed that a map of British origin used by the Demarcation Commission could not find any legal basis in the 1963 agreement. It also submitted that the demarcation of the eastern side of the border went beyond the provisions of the 1963 agreement in a fashion that allocated Iraqi territory to Kuwait.[147] However, since the Demarcation Commission took its decision by majority vote, the Iraqi objections were overruled.[148]

By assuming the validity of the 1963 agreement and demarcating the border in a fashion that was not accepted by Iraq,[149] the Demarcation Commission (and ultimately the Security Council) implicitly determined that Iraq's version of the facts were without legal merit. This amounted to a legal conclusion which effectively imposed a settlement on Iraq with respect to a territorial dispute between itself and Kuwait.[150] Consequently it becomes difficult to accept the Security Council's position that the Demarcation Commission merely executed a technical exercise necessary to clarify and define an existing boundary, which could not be equated with the delimitation of a new boundary that affected the territorial rights of the states concerned.[151]

(1991); *Letter dated 23 April 1991 from the Permanent Representative of Iraq to the United Nations addressed to the Secretary-General*, in S/22558 Annex II, para 1 (1991); *Letter dated 16 August 1991 from the Permanent Representative of Iraq to the United Nations Addressed to the President of the Security Council*, in S/22957 (1991); *Letter dated 7 June 1993 from the Permanent Representative of Iraq to the Secretary-General transmitting a letter dated 6 June 1993 from the Minister for Foreign Affairs of Iraq concerning the work of the Iraq-Kuwait Boundary Demarcation Commission*, in S/25905 (1993). See also Post, above n 142, at 250.

[147] See *Letter dated 21 May 1992 from the Permanent Representative of Iraq to the United Nations addressed to the Secretary General*, in S/24044 paras 1 ff (1992); *Letter dated 7 June 1993 from the Permanent Representative of Iraq to the Secretary-General transmitting a letter dated 6 June 1993 from the Minister for Foreign Affairs of Iraq concerning the work of the Iraq-Kuwait Boundary Demarcation Commission*, in S/25905 (1993). See also Gill, above n 119, at 88.

[148] Note that Iraq also questioned the even-handedness of the Demarcation Commission. As Iraq could only appoint one of the five members of the Demarcation Commission and had no say in the selection of the three independent expert members, it felt severely under-represented. See *Letter dated 23 April 1991 from the Permanent Representative of Iraq to the United Nations addressed to the Secretary-General*, in S/22558 Annex II, para 2 (1991). See also MH Mendelson & SC Hulton, "The Iraq-Kuwait Boundary", 64 *British Yearbook of International Law* 150 (1993), who conceded that according to general practice demarcation commissions are set up by the states concerned and on the basis of parity.

[149] Whether Iraq's arguments would suffice to convince an impartial arbitrator or judge is a different matter altogether. It does not, however, change the fact that it constituted a dispute as to whether a valid boundary agreement existed and, if so, how it was to be interpreted. See also Gill, above n 119, at 89–99.

[150] See also Kirgis (First Fifty Years), above n 21, at 532; Brownlie, above n 10, at 97; Gill, above n 119, at 88; Peter Hulsroij, "The Legal Function of the Security Council", 1 *Chinese Journal of International Law* (2002), at 72.

[151] See the preambles to; SC Res 773 of 26 August 1992 and SC Res 833 of 27 May 1993; *Statement by the President of the Security Council concerning the Iraq-Kuwait Boundary Demarcation Commission* in S/24113 (1992). See also the *Letter dated 30 April 1991 from the Secretary-General addressed to the Minister for Foreign Affairs of Iraq*, in S/22558 Annex III (1991).

This raises the question whether the Security Council may determine the territorial boundaries of states in order to restore or maintain international peace in terms of Chapter VII of the Charter. On the one hand, it seems very plausible that the Security Council could impose a boundary on parties as a provisional measure in terms of Article 40 of the Charter.[152] For example, it could call on the parties to acknowledge temporarily a particular border and withdraw their troops behind it accordingly.[153] In accordance with the provisional character of Article 40, such measures would leave unaffected the rights of the parties concerned with respect to any disputed territory. Consequently, they would only be bound by the imposed boundary until they have reached an agreement about the final determination of the border, whether through negotiation or by means of a dispute settlement procedure to which they have both consented.[154]

On the other hand, it is very unlikely that the Security Council could impose any final settlement on countries regarding a territorial dispute between them. The Security Council itself seemed to concede as much by persistently claiming that it was not reallocating territory between Kuwait and Iraq, but simply carrying out the technical task of border demarcation.[155] This relates to the fact that the territorial integrity of states constitutes a fundamental element of state sovereignty, as a result of which the means for determining territorial boundaries have to stem from an agreement between the affected states.[156] Any binding decision of the Security Council that would effectively transfer territory from one state to another against the will of any of the affected parties would undermine the principle of the sovereign equality of states in Article 2(1) of the Charter.[157]

This would remain to be the case even where the decision was taken by an independent tribunal that was created in terms of Chapter VII of the Charter and that safeguarded all the elements of procedural fairness—if and to the extent that such a tribunal is operating against the will of (one of) the states affected.[158] The illegality of the Security Council's decision

---

[152] See also ch 5, at s 1.

[153] Jochen A Frowein, "Article 39", in Bruno Simma (ed), *The Charter of the United Nations. A Commentary* 619 (Oxford, Oxford University Press, 1994); Martenczuk, above n 90, at 265.

[154] Frowein (in Simma), above n 153, at 619.

[155] During the discussions leading up to the adoption of SC Res 687 (1991), India found it necessary to stress that the Security Council's actions merely recognised a boundary that Iraq and Kuwait had already agreed to. See S/PV 3108 7 (1992). See also Kirgis (First Fifty Years), above n 21, at 532; Brownlie, above n 10, at 97; Gill, above n 119, at 88.

[156] Harper, above n 45, at 144; Kirgis (First Fifty Years), above n 21, at 531; Nolte (in Byers), above n 9, at 322; see also the dissenting opinion of Judge Fitzmaurice in *Legal Consequence for States of the Continued Presence of South Africa in Namibia (South West Africa) Notwithstanding Security Council Resolution 276 (1970)*, ICJ Rep 1971, at 294. Hereinafter referred to as the *Namibia* opinion.

[157] Gill, above n 119, at 85; Bowett, above n 98, at 96.

[158] This solution was suggested by Harper, above n 45, at 147, who mainly objected to the lack of procedural fairness in the determination of the Iraq-Kuwait border.

in this case does not, in the first place, relate to the non-observance of due process elements, but to the nature of the dispute that formed the object of the Security Council decision. The implied powers of the Security Council would not extend so far as to allow it to create a dispute settlement mechanism that could take binding decisions on territorial disputes against the will of any state.[159] It would result in a violation of Article 2(1) of the Charter, that applies to all members of the United Nations in equal fashion, including states that posed a threat to the peace or committed a breach of the peace or an act of aggression.[160]

3.2.2.   The Implications of the Territorial Integrity of States for the Decisions of the Demarcation Commission

The question that remains to be answered is how these limitations to the power of the Security Council could be reconciled with the presumption of legality attached to its determination that the decisions of the Demarcation Commission constitute the final demarcation of the Iraq-Kuwait border. It seems that this would only be possible if this determination were regarded as a provisional measure in terms of Article 40 of the Charter. This would mean that the concept of "final demarcation" was understood as a "final provisional" demarcation. Stated differently, it would imply that the Security Council, in an act of self-limitation, had agreed not to engage in any future attempts to demarcate a provisional border between Iraq and Kuwait.

As indicated above, it is clearly within the power of the Security Council to determine a provisional border for the purposes of guaranteeing a cease-fire and troop withdrawals. Moreover, these measures do not need to follow the rules of procedural fairness, as they do not intend to affect the territorial rights of the parties concerned in any final fashion.[161] The Security Council could also rely on Article 98 of the Charter to delegate the determination of a provisional border to the Secretary-General, as long as it remains in overall control of the decision. In the case of the Demarcation Commission, the Security Council executed this control by

---

[159] See also Gill, above n 119, at 86; Bowett, above n 98, at 96; Dissenting opinion of Judge Fitzmaurice in the *Namibia* opinion, above n 156, at 294; Akande, above n 45, at 321. For a different opinion, see Mendelson & Hulton, above n 148, at 146 ff, who regarded this as falling within the powers of the Security Council to maintain international peace and security. See also the Matthias Herdegen, *Die Befugnisse des UN-Sicherheitsrates: aufgeklärter Absolitismus im Völkerrecht?* 33 (Heidelberg, Müller, 2000).

[160] Gill, above n 119, at 89. Furthermore, it would potentially violate the right to self-determination, which the population of an aggressor state would continue to possess. This issue is elaborated on in ch 8, at s 3.2.

[161] In addition, the provisional measures will often have to be taken without any delay, which would not be possible if they had to be taken in accordance with extensive due process measures.

initially outlining the mandate in Resolution 687 (1991)[162] and ultimately terminating it by adopting the final report of the Demarcation Commission in Resolution 833 (1993).[163]

This provisional boundary remains binding under Chapter VII of the Charter until such a time as the parties themselves come to a final agreement regarding the border between them. This can typically be achieved through negotiation, or by means of a dispute settlement procedure to which both parties have consented. In addition, it is also possible that the two states over time acquiesce in the provisional border between them and come to accept it as final. In the case of the Iraq-Kuwait boundary, this indeed seems to have happened over time. Kuwait expressed its acceptance of the conclusions of the Demarcation Commission and Resolution 833 (1993) within weeks of the latter being adopted.[164] Iraq, for its part, only took this step by the end of the following year. In a letter dated 12 November 1994, it communicated to the President of the Security Council Iraq's recognition of the sovereignty, territorial integrity and political independence of Kuwait, and of the international boundary between the two countries as demarcated by the Demarcation Commission and endorsed in Resolution 833 (1993).[165] Unlike its previous communiqués, this letter did not reiterate the objections regarding the work of the Demarcation Commission and thus constituted clear evidence of the country's acquiescence in the border as established by the Demarcation Commission and the Security Council.[166] However, it is important to keep in mind that had there not been clear acquiescence on the part of both countries, Iraq and Kuwait would have remained free to come to a boundary agreement other than that established under the Demarcation Commission, as the Security Council does not have the power to alter the territorial rights of states against their will.

---

[162] At paras 2 and 3.

[163] At paras 1 and 4.

[164] *Letter dated 16 June 1993 from the Permanent Representative of Kuwait to the Secretary-General transmitting a statement issued by the Kuwait Council of Ministers concerning the completion by the Iraq-Kuwait Boundary Demarcation Commission of its work*, in S/25963 (1993).

[165] *Letter dated 13 November 1994 from the Permanent Representative of Iraq transmitting the declaration of the National Assembly (10 November 1994) and decree of the Revolution Command Council No 2000 (10 November 1994) affirming Iraq's recognition of the sovereignty, territorial integrity and political independence of Kuwait and of its international boundaries as endorsed by the Security Council in its resolution 833 (1994)*, in S/1994/1288 (1994).

[166] Already when establishing the Demarcation Commission, the Secretary-General claimed that Iraq had accepted the terms of SC Res 687 of 3 April 1991, in S/22558, Annex III (1991). However, such claims ignored the fact that this acceptance had been expressed under considerable protest and whilst claiming that Iraq had no choice but to accept the resolution. See, for example, the penultimate paragraph of the *Identical letters dated 6 April 1991 from the Deputy Prime Minister and Minister for Foreign Affairs of Iraq to the President of the Security Council and the Secretary-General*, in S/22456 (1991). As far as the Demarcation Commission was concerned, this attitude only changed by 12 November 1994. See also Mendelson & Hulton, above n 148, at 148–49; Post, above n 142, at 260.

4. CONCLUSION

The above analysis reflects the fact that the Security Council has experienced considerable difficulties in remaining within the limits of its powers when establishing judicial organs. Unlike the case of military mandates or mandates for civil administration, the illegality does not relate to a lack of overall control over the mandate, but rather to the Security Council's excessive control in this regard. Due to the judicial nature of the mandate at stake, the Security Council's overall control has to be limited to decisions regarding the continuation of the mandate. It may not, however, influence the day to day functioning or the individual decisions of the (quasi-) judicial organ.

The only instances in which the Security Council proved itself capable of remaining within these limits concerned the establishment of ICTY and ICTR, whose statutes shield them from undue political influence. This forms a stark contrast with the Security Council's resolutions on the extradition and sanctioning of suspected terrorists, in which the Security Council acted as a judicial forum itself in violation of Article 1(1) of the Charter, as well as the core content of Article 14 ICCPR.

The illegal usurpation of judicial power has also occurred in instances affecting states' rights, notably in the case of the Iraq-Kuwait Boundary Demarcation Commission and the United Nations Compensation Commission for Iraq. Whereas Iraq ultimately acquiesced in the decisions of the former, it still remains to be seen whether it would also do so with regard to the decisions of the latter. However, given the fact that the Compensation Commission has developed a life of its own and has made numerous awards during the last decade, it seems that from the perspective of *Realpolitik*, Iraq would be left with no other choice than to acquiesce in these decisions, regardless of the controversies surrounding their legality.

The reference of acquiescence touches on the question of the consequences of illegal Security Council decisions which are not acquiesced in by states, or where there cannot be acquiescence due to the fact that the violation at stake concerns a *ius cogens* norm. This issue is addressed in the concluding chapter, which explores the extent to which the ICJ and/or member states could enforce limitations on the powers of the Security Council identified in the current and preceding chapters.

10

Conclusion

1.   RECAPTURING THE LIMITATIONS TO THE SECURITY COUNCIL'S CHAPTER VII POWERS

THE LIMITATIONS TO the powers of the Security Council identified in the foregoing analysis relate both to the threshold question of when the Security Council may act, as well as to the type of measures it can adopt once this threshold has been crossed.

The determination that a particular situation constitutes a threat to international peace still recognises the link between such a threat and the absence of armed conflict between states. This means that the current state of development of the law of the United Nations does not yet acknowledge a positive definition of peace that provides the Security Council with an unlimited discretion in determining whether a threat to peace exists. Such an all-inclusive definition would undermine the structure of the Security Council, which would be incapable of effectively restoring or maintaining an all-inclusive concept of peace. This view is also still supported by the practice of the Security Council, which reflects that whilst the threats to peace in the post Cold War era predominantly originate within states, it is still their impact on international relations rather than their source of origin that is decisive for determining whether a threat to peace exists.

At the same time, one has to bear in mind that the dynamic and evolutionary element inherent in the concept of a "threat to peace" may ultimately carry more weight than the structural arguments against the adoption of a positive threat to peace. If the Security Council were to embrace such a definition and member states were to acquiesce therein, it would amount to an amendment of the traditional negative definition through practice. Once this has occurred, it would be impossible to return to the more restricted definition that could be subjected to legal criteria. An over-extension of the Security Council could then only be prevented by political self-restraint within the Security Council itself, when considering whether or not to describe a particular situation as a threat to international peace.

However, even if the Security Council (and member states) eventually embraced an all-inclusive definition of peace, this would not alter the fact that the Security Council is also bound to limitations once the Article 39 threshold has been crossed. The discretion of the Security Council in choosing the type of enforcement measures available to it under Articles 40 to 42 of the Charter is limited by the norms of *ius cogens* and the principles and purposes of the Charter, as well as the interaction amongst these norms. This means that the Security Council would not be allowed to adopt measures that result in genocide, or that would violate the right to self-defence, or the right to self-determination. Furthermore, the enforcement measures have to remain within the boundaries provided by core human rights norms, the core rules of humanitarian law and core elements of state sovereignty. The Security Council may also not impose a settlement on parties and has to act in good faith by fulfilling legal expectations previously created by its own actions.

In addition, when the Security Council authorises the use of force or delegates its power to take binding decisions, this has to be done in accordance with the limitations flowing from the Charter structure. The delegation of military and other powers centralised in the Security Council is legal if and to the extent that the Security Council maintains overall control over the delegated mandate. This implies that an open-ended delegation without any clear functional limitation will only remain legal as long as it is supported by a majority within the Security Council, including a majority of the permanent members. The moment this support disintegrates, the overall control over the delegation shifts from the Security Council as a collective entity to the (permanent) member(s) with a direct interest in its continuation. As this amounts to an illegal delegation of power, the mandate will expire automatically. It further implies that an open-ended delegation of powers that are centralised within the Security Council justifies an exception to the rule of the parallelism of forms, as the termination of the delegation will not necessarily be prevented by the "reverse veto".

The application of these criteria to the non-military enforcement measures that the Security Council have adopted over the years reflects several instances of illegal behaviour on the part of the latter, notably in connection with economic embargoes. The comprehensive economic embargo against Iraq had, by the turn of the century, clearly resulted in the violation of the non-derogable right to life of Iraqi children and has had a disproportionate impact on (in particular) the right to health of the population as a whole. As in the case of other human rights norms, the Security Council is bound to respect the right to life and the core content of the right to health as a matter of good faith. It is also fair to conclude that the non-derogable nature of the right to life has elevated this right to a norm of *ius cogens*. Protracted economic embargoes also risk a violation of the right to self-defence, where it concerns an arms embargo in an inter-state armed conflict. The arms embargo against all parts of the former Yugoslavia in the 1990s ultimately resulted in the inability of Bosnia-Herzegovina to exercise its right to self-defence and to protect its people against genocide—both of which constitute norms of *ius cogens*.

In all instances where the Security Council requested the extradition of suspected terrorists (Libya, Sudan and Afghanistan), the respective resolutions violated basic elements of procedural justice that underpin Article 1(1) of the Charter. In addition, they violated the core elements of Article 14(1) ICCPR, to which the Security Council is bound as a matter of good faith. It could also be argued that the right to a fair trial has now acquired *ius cogens* status, at least as far as criminal proceedings are concerned. For similar reasons, the Security Council resolutions demanding the freezing of assets of individuals and undertakings listed by the Security Council Sanctions Committee as "associated" with international terrorist organisations would currently suffer from illegality. Unless or until the Security Council provides those affected with a fair hearing where they can disprove the allegations against them, the freezing of their assets for an indefinite period of time effectively amounts to a conviction of involvement with international terrorism without trial.

Other instances of a violation of Article 1(1) of the Charter relate to a violation of states' rights rather than individual rights, as was reflected in the lack of even-handedness and independence of the United Nations Compensation Commission for Iraq. Similar deficits affected the Iraq-Kuwait Boundary Demarcation Commission which, effectively imposed a boundary on Iraq, thereby also violating a core element of state sovereignty.

With respect to authorisations to use force, the measures authorised against North Korea were illegal to the extent that they exceeded the limits of self-defence. The illegality of those measures do not so much relate to any deficiencies in the delegation to use force itself, as to the fact that the Security Council applied the Chapter VII enforcement measures against a state which was not a member of the United Nations at the time. Even if one were to accept that the Security Council could now apply the Chapter VII enforcement mechanism to non-member states by means of customary international law, it is highly unlikely that Chapter VII had already acquired such status by 1950. Consequently, this lack of competence to resort to Articles 42 and 48(1) rendered illegal those military measures that could only be exercised on the basis of these articles. This included, in particular, the authorisation to pursue the North Korean forces beyond the 38 parallel, since these measures could not be justified in terms of the right to self-defence.

As far as the post Cold War peace enforcement operations are concerned, the military mandate against Iraq has proved to be the most controversial due to its open-ended nature. Although the mandate itself had expired with the adoption of Resolution 687 (1991), individual permanent members have (unconvincingly) claimed that the open-ended nature of the mandate placed their subsequent unilateral military action within the ambit of the initial authorisation to use force. Subsequently, a reoccurrence of similar situations elsewhere were prevented by submitting military authorisations to time limits. However, recently the Security Council has once again shown a preference for open-ended mandates when adopting the military and civil mandates for Kosovo and Iraq, after the respective military (air) campaigns of 1999 and 2003. The absence of a time limit to these mandates may ultimately result in their illegality. This will happen where the respective mandate does not enjoy the support of a majority of the permanent members or a general majority within the Security Council anymore.

In Kosovo, East Timor and Iraq the respective mandates for civil administration will also become illegal if they resulted in a persistent and severe violation of the right to self-determination (or other human rights standards) by the United Nations or those acting on its behalf. However, determining the extent to which the respective civil administrations honour their human rights obligations remains a difficult task. The Ombudsperson in Kosovo has no mandatory jurisdiction over the civil actions of KFOR and in Iraq there has not yet been any attempt for providing an independent human rights monitoring system either. This absence of an independent United Nations forum for reviewing the conformity of KFOR's (non-military) actions, as well as those of the Authority in Iraq with international human rights standards, is not in accordance with the notion of accountability inherent to their respective human rights mandates. In order to remain within its human rights obligations, the Security Council or those acting on its behalf would be obliged to remedy this deficit in a fashion that provides for comprehensive and independent human rights monitoring.

2.   RECAPTURING THE ROLE OF THE ICJ IN ENFORCING THE LIMITATIONS TO THE SECURITY COUNCIL'S CHAPTER VII POWERS

The foregoing analysis reflected that the role of the ICJ in reviewing the legality of Security Council resolutions could be developed in the context of the advisory opinions procedure provided for in Article 96(1) of the Charter. An examination of the advisory opinions that resulted in a review of the legality of the political organs of the United Nations reflects that the ICJ gives due consideration to the flexibility and discretion that these organs need to fulfil their duties efficiently. The presumption of legality attached to resolutions of the Security Council implies that only very clear evidence to the contrary would result in a finding of illegality. The advisory opinion procedure would thus usually serve to strengthen the legitimacy of decisions of the political organs, as opposed to delegitimating them. However, if the ICJ were to determine that a particular Security Council resolution is illegal, it would provide member states with a legal basis for refusing to implement the respective resolution *ex nunc*.

An essential prerequisite for this type of (de)legitimisation, is that sufficient use must be made of the advisory procedure as a mode for judicial review. The ICJ can only contribute to the developing of standards for the legality of Security Council action if it is given the opportunity to do so. The General Assembly's under-utilisation of the advisory procedure has played a major role in reinforcing the view that no procedure for reviewing the legality of Security Council resolutions exists within the United Nations system. For example, in none of the above mentioned instances of illegal behaviour by the Security Council was there any attempt by the General Assembly to request an advisory opinion on the matter.

Provided that the context in which the request was submitted was clear and concrete, the General Assembly could have requested advice from the ICJ on the specific (human rights) norms the Security Council has to respect when adopting economic (arms) embargoes; creating quasi-judicial bodies; demanding the extradition of suspected terrorists; authorising the use of force or mandates for civil administration etc. It could also have requested advice on the legality of specific Security Council decisions, as well as the possible consequences in the event that an ICJ opinion concluded that a particular Security Council measure was illegal. This would include, for example, advice as to whether the Security Council should revise the measures in question, whether the United Nations should pay compensation to the individuals or states affected by the illegal measures, and whether third states would be relieved from any obligation to enforce or support such measures. Even though the advisory opinions of the Security Council have no binding force for states or the United Nations, their persuasive force is not to be underestimated. It is therefore possible that an advisory opinion on any of the above issues could persuade the Security Council to review its own measures, or otherwise risk open disobedience by member states who prefer the word of the principle judicial organ of the United Nations to that of the Security Council.

For these reasons it would be important to develop mechanism by means of which the under-utilisation of the advisory opinion procedure could be overcome. Authorising the Secretary-General to request advisory opinions that can guide the United Nations political organs in relation to the legality of their own actions, poses one such possibility. However, as it is unlikely that such an authorisation will be forthcoming, the advisory opinion procedure will probably remain under-utilised in future.

It is also unlikely that judicial review in contentious proceedings against states would be able to compensate for this deficit. First, the situations in which the ICJ will be confronted with the legality of a Security Council decision during contentious proceedings will remain the exception rather than the rule. In addition, the impasse in the debate as to whether the ICJ is entitled to review Security Council resolutions during contentious proceedings is also unlikely to be resolved in the near future. Even though the United Nations represents the core of an embryonic international constitutional order that shows some resemblance to municipal constitutional orders, it would still be premature to recognise judicial review as a general principle of law in terms of Article 38(1)(c) of the ICJ Statute. This means that the deadlock in the debate as to whether the principle of efficiency and the need for cooperation between the principle organs of the United Nations would or would not justify judicial review in contentious proceedings, will not (yet) be resolved by resorting to Article 38(1)(c) of the ICJ Statute.

On the one hand, most countries (at least in theory) now allow for the testing of the legality of decisions of political organs by an independent judicial organ in some form or another. The motivating rationale for this development is the need to legitimate the exercise of political power—an issue which is also of considerable importance in the United Nations system. On the other hand, recognising a general principle of judicial review, based on the existence of some sort of legal testing of the actions of political organs in most countries, would be too general. It would not take account of the fact that the scope of this testing does not necessarily extend to decisions concerning national security. Since this is of direct relevance to the type of judicial review that the ICJ would exercise in contentious proceedings, more information as to the subject-matter of judicial review in municipal jurisdictions is needed, before it could be considered as a general principle of law. As a result, an eventual pragmatic determination by the ICJ that it falls within its "judicial function" to review the legality of Security Council resolutions in contentious proceedings could come across as conceptually unconvincing, as it would not be clear why this "judicial function" necessarily has to imply a power of judicial review.

In essence therefore, the under-utilisation of the advisory opinion procedure combined with the still unresolved controversy surrounding judicial review in contentious proceedings implies that the role of the ICJ in enforcing limitations to the powers of the Security Council will remain limited for some time to come. This raises the question whether member states may determine for themselves that a Security Council resolution is illegal and therefore does not have to be implemented, as this would constitute the only alternative mechanism for enforcing limitations to the powers of the Security Council in a decentralised international order.

3. THE RIGHT OF STATES TO REJECT ILLEGAL SECURITY COUNCIL
   RESOLUTIONS AS A "RIGHT OF LAST RESORT"

In accordance with the rule of the "parallelism of competence",[1] member states generally do not have the power to terminate binding enforcement measures imposed under Chapter VII of the Charter on their own accord. Since the Charter does not explicitly provide for any termination procedure, the competence of termination has to be exercised by the same organ responsible for the competence of initiation, namely the Security Council. Furthermore, if member states had a general right to determine for themselves whether the aim of the enforcement measures had been achieved, they would most likely come to very different conclusions depending on their geo-political interests. This would lead to major legal uncertainty which would undermine the effective functioning of the United Nations collective security system.[2]

However, the previous chapters revealed that extreme situations can arise where the Security Council is unable to terminate or amend enforcement measures which are clearly illegal. This inability mainly results from the fact that the resolution terminating the enforcement measures will also be taken under Chapter VII of the Charter, in accordance with the rule of the "parallelism of forms" which supplements the rule of the "parallelism of competencies".[3] This is problematic to the extent that a Chapter VII resolution can only be adopted if there is consensus amongst the five permanent members to this effect. As a result, the termination of enforcement measures can be blocked by the "reverse veto" of a permanent member. If the exercise of the "reverse veto" resulted in the protraction of illegal enforcement measures, the question arises whether states have the unilateral right to refuse their implementation.[4]

3.1. The Meaning of Article 25 of the Charter

The answer can first and foremost be found in Article 25 of the Charter, according to which members of the United Nations agree to accept and carry out the decisions of the Security Council "in accordance with the present Charter". At first glance Article 25 can be confusing as it is not

---

[1] See ch 6 at s 4.
[2] *Ibid.*
[3] *Ibid.*
[4] Michael Fraas, *Sicherheitsrat der Vereinten Nationen und Internationaler Gerichtshof* 93 (Peter Lang, Frankfurt a/M, 1998); Heike Gading, *Der Schutz grundlegender Menschenrechte durch militärische Massnahmen des Sicherheitsrates—das Ende staatlicher Souveränität?* 65–66 (Berlin, Duncker & Humblot, 1996); Hans-Peter Gasser, "Collective Economic Sanctions and International Humanitarian Law", 56 *Zeitschrift für ausländisches öffentliches Recht und Völkerrecht* 883 (1996).

clear whether the phrase "in accordance with the present Charter" refers only to the member states or the organisation as well. If it referred only to the member states they would be obliged to carry out decisions of the Security Council under all circumstances. If, however, the phrase referred to the organisation as well, the member states would only be obliged to carry out those decisions that were adopted in accordance with the Charter, ie in accordance with its purposes and principles and the norms of *ius cogens*.

If one reads Article 25 together with the first sentence of Article 2(5) of the Charter, it becomes clear that the latter approach is to be preferred.[5] It determines that all members shall give the United Nations every assistance in any action it takes "in accordance with the Charter".[6] From this formulation it clearly follows that the organisation have to act in accordance with the Charter.[7] In addition, a closer look reveals that the "action" that has to be in accordance with the Charter refers to enforcement action under Chapter VII.[8] At first glance Article 2(5) seems to convey a general obligation for member states to give assistance to the organisation.[9] However, since this general obligation is already conveyed by Article 2(2),[10] Article 2(5) must have a narrower scope of application, if it is not to be regarded as merely repetitive and therefore redundant.[11] The reference to "enforcement action" in the last sub-sentence of Article 2(5) indicates that only "action" taken by the Security Council according to Chapter VII could have been envisaged here.[12]

---

[5] Jochen Herbst, *Rechtsbindung des UN-Sicherheitsrates* 295 (Frankfurt a/M, Peter Lang, 1999); See also *Legal Consequences for States of the Continued Presence of South Africa in Namibia (South West Africa) Notwithstanding Security Council Resolution 276 (1970)*, Advisory Opinion, ICJ Rep 1972, at 51–52; Cf Wilhelm A Kewenig, "Die Problematiek der Bindungswirkung von Entscheidungen des Sicherheitsrates", in Horst Emhke *et al* (eds), *Festschrift für Ulrich Scheuner zum 70. Geburtstag* 270 (Berlin, Duncker & Humblot, 1973).

[6] Art 2(5) reads as follows: "All Members shall give the United Nations every assistance in any action it takes in accordance with the present Charter, and shall refrain from giving assistance to any state against which the United Nations is taking preventive or enforcement action."

[7] Herbst, above n 5, at 295.

[8] *Ibid*, at 296.

[9] As is suggested by Jost Delbrück, "Article 25", in Bruno Simma (ed), *The Charter of the United Nations. A Commentary* 414 (Oxford, Oxford University Press, 1994).

[10] Art 2(2) of the Charter reads: All Members, in order to ensure to all of them the rights and benefits resulting from membership, shall fulfil in good faith the obligations assured by them in accordance with the present Charter'.

[11] See Jochen A, Frowein, "Article 2(5)", in Bruno Simma (ed), *The Charter of the United Nations. A Commentary* 129 (Oxford, Oxford University Press, 1994).

[12] Frowein (in Simma), above n 11, at 129–30. As in Art 11(2), the term action refers to collective enforcement measures. The meaning of preventive action in the second part of the sentence is less clear. Even so, it must also be assumed that the main emphasis is on action, which is characteristic of Chapter VII. Therefore, mainly preventive measures under Art 40 must be meant here.

Consequently one can conclude that the obligation to assist the organisation in the first part of the sentence only concerns decisions by the Security Council under Chapter VII *in as far as* they were taken in accordance with the Charter.[13] Thus, since Article 2(5) obliges states to respect Chapter VII resolutions that were adopted in accordance with the Charter, the logical implication is that they are not bound to do so where this is not the case.[14] It then becomes illogical to see how member states can be obliged, in terms of Article 25, to follow binding resolutions which are not in accordance with the Charter.[15] It also implies that the "supremacy rule" articulated in Article 103 of the Charter would only apply to Security Council decisions that remains within the boundaries of the Charter.[16]

The opponents of this view are reluctant to grant member states any discretion in determining whether the Security Council decisions with which they have to comply have been adopted in accordance with the Charter. They fear that this would undermine the efficiency of the Charter system as it would open the door for states to evade their Charter obligations by forwarding pretextual arguments of illegality.[17] As a result, states would be obliged to implement Security Council resolutions, regardless of whether they were taken in accordance with the limits of the Charter.

In the alternative they argue that the wording "in accordance with the present Charter" would only imply a formal discretion.[18] States would only have leeway to decide whether Security Council decisions were taken in accordance with formal requirements, such as the correct voting procedure. In this way the phrase "in accordance with the present Charter" could be interpreted in a way that systematically conforms with

---

[13] Herbst, above n 5, at 296.

[14] *Ibid*, at 295.

[15] *Ibid*, at 295–96. But see José Alvarez, "The Security Council's War on Terrorism: Problems and Policy Options", in Erika de Wet & André Nollkaemper (eds), *Judicial Review of the Security Council by Member States* s 2 (Antwerp, Intersentia, forthcoming). He relies on the drafting history of the Charter to conclude that Art 25 is merely a cross reference to the fact that member states accept Chapter VII decisions as binding and not merely recommendatory.

[16] Art 103 of the Charter reads as follows: "In the event of a conflict between the obligations of the Members of the United Nations under the present Charter and their obligations under any other international agreement, their obligations under the present Charter shall prevail." See also Art 5(g) of the International Law Commission's Draft Articles on Unilateral Acts of States, in its Fifth Report on Unilateral Acts of States, A/CN.4/535/Add/1 11 (2002). It currently determines that a state that formulates a unilateral act "may invoke the absolute invalidity of the act, if at the time of its formulation, the unilateral act conflicts with a decision of the Security Council." However, in light of the above analysis it is submitted that this draft Article should not be read in a way that denies states the right to reject illegal Security Council decisions as a "right of last resort".

[17] Delbrück (Article 25), above n 9, at 414; Alvarez, above n 15, at s 4.2.

[18] *Ibid*.

Articles 2(5) and 25, without jeopardising the efficiency of the Security Council.[19] According to this line of argument, procedural review would allow for an objective assessment, whereas an examination to determine whether a decision conforms to the substantive provisions of the Charter would involve a subjective (ie legally indeterminable) value judgement on the parts of states.[20]

These arguments are flawed in several respects. First, it is incorrect to assume that a refusal to implement illegal Security Council resolutions would necessarily prevent the Security Council from acting effectively. The presumption of legality attached to Security Council resolutions, combined with the requirement that member states execute their obligations in good faith, oblige them to make a very strong case before refusing to implement a Security Council resolution.[21] The opportunity for submitting pre-textual arguments of illegality is thus limited by the fact that states could only reject Security Council resolutions as a "right of last resort".[22]

Second, the efficiency of the Charter system for the maintenance and restoration of international peace and security will ultimately depend on its legitimacy, which will be seriously undermined by enforcement measures that violate the very norms on which the United Nations are based. A refusal to enforce illegal binding Security Council decisions under such circumstances would therefore protect the efficiency of the organisation in the long run, rather than undermine it.

Finally, the assumption that procedural decisions are devoid of value judgements is self-defeating to the extent that the very distinction between procedural and substantive provisions amounts to a value judgement. The previous chapters have also illustrated that the value judgements involved in determining if and to what extent the Security Council has acted in accordance with the substantive provisions of the Charter do not have to be void of objective criteria.

3.2. The Responsibility of Member States Pertaining to their Human Rights Obligations

The second line of argument supporting a "right of last resort" for member states, is based on their obligation under international law to ensure

---

[19] *Ibid.*

[20] *Ibid.*

[21] *Certain Expenses of the United Nations,* Advisory Opinion, ICJ Rep 1962, at 168. Hereinafter referred to as *Certain Expenses* opinion.

[22] Fraas, above n 4 , at 93; Gasser, above n 4, at 883. Cf Georg Nolte, "The limits of the Security Council's Powers and its Functions in the International Legal System: Some Reflections", in Michael Byers (ed), *The Role of Law in International Politics* 365 (Oxford, Oxford University Press, 2000); see also the dissenting opinion of Judge Winiarski in the *Certain Expenses* opinion, above n 21, at 232.

that fundamental human rights are respected.[23] This argument, which focuses on the consequences of state responsibility in relation to human rights obligations, is narrower than that pertaining to Article 25 of the Charter. It is primarily directed at the enforcement of human rights norms to which both the Security Council and member states are bound, as opposed to all legal limitations applicable to the Security Council. It thus concentrates on the enforcement of human rights norms in instances where the "supremacy rule" contained in Article 103 of the Charter would not be applicable, ie when the Security Council itself has violated human rights norms in contravention of the Charter.[24]

Given the fact that most of the limitations to the powers of the Security Council illuminated in previous chapters relate to core human rights norms—notably the right to life, the right to health, the right to self-determination and the right to a fair hearing—this line of argument significantly complements the argument pertaining to Article 25. Under customary international law, as well as the applicable international and regional human rights treaties, states are obliged to ensure the protection of these rights. If states choose to transfer certain powers to international organisations and the exercise of those powers may result in a violation of the human rights that they are obliged to guarantee, they have to secure that proper judicial avenues for addressing these violations are available at the international level. If not, the final responsibility for the human rights violation in question continues to rest with the member states.[25]

This has been underlined by the European Court of Human Rights (hereinafter the European Court) in *Waite and Kennedy v Germany*. This case involved a labour dispute between the applicants and the European Space Agency (ESA). When the German courts granted the ESA immunity from jurisdiction, the applicants argued that Germany thereby violated their right to a fair trial under Article 6(1) of the European Convention for the Protection of Human Rights (hereinafter the European Convention). The European Court held that where states established international organisations in order to pursue or strengthen their cooperation in certain fields of activities, and where they attribute to these organisations certain competencies and accord them immunities, there may be implications as to the protection of fundamental rights. It would be incompatible with the purpose and object of the European Convention if the contracting states were thereby absolved from their responsibility

---

[23] The line of argument relied on here, was extensively articulated by André Nollkaemper in an article co-authored by Erika de Wet & André Nollkaemper, "Review of Security Council Decisions by National Courts", 45 *German Yearbook of International Law* 188 ff (2002).
[24] See above n 16.
[25] See De Wet & Nollkaemper, above n 23, at 188.

under the Convention in relation to the field of activity covered by such attribution.[26]

The responsibility of member states for the protection of human rights by international organisations to which they have transferred powers was also recognised by the European Court in the *Matthews* decision.[27] In this case, the applicant had applied to the Electoral Registration Officer for Gibraltar to be registered as a voter at the elections to the European Parliament. The Electoral Registration Officer declined to do so, because the European Community Act on Direct Elections of 1976 (a treaty instrument entered into by all European Community member states), did not include Gibraltar in the franchise for the European parliamentary elections. According to the applicant, this violated Article 3 of Protocol No 1, which provides that the contracting parties undertake to hold free elections at reasonable intervals by secret ballot.[28]

The European Court held that while the European Convention did not exclude the transfer of competencies to international organisations, states parties must continue to secure the rights under the European Convention. Member states' responsibility therefore continues even after such a transfer.[29] The Court observed that in respect of the obligations of states under the European Convention there is no difference between European and domestic legislation, and no reason why the United Kingdom should not be required to "secure" the rights in Article 3 of Protocol No 1 in respect of European legislation, in the same way as those rights are required to be "secured" in respect of purely domestic legislation. The European Court further determined that, in particular, the suggestion that the United Kingdom may not have effective control over the state of affairs complained of cannot affect the position. For the United Kingdom's responsibility derived from its having entered into treaty commitments subsequent to the applicability of Article 3 of Protocol No 1 to Gibraltar, namely the Maastricht Treaty taken together with its obligations under the Council Decision and the 1976 Act.[30]

From these cases it follows that where states establish international organisations and attribute powers to them in order to pursue or strengthen their cooperation in certain fields of activities, they may remain responsible under international human rights law for the consequences of the exercise of the powers by the international organisations.[31]

---

[26] *Waite and Kennedy v Germany*, App No 26083/94, Judgment of 18 February 1999, at para 67.
[27] Case of *Matthews v the United Kingdom*, App No 24833/94, Judgment of 18 February 1999.
[28] See also De Wet & Nollkaemper, above n 23, at 189 ff.
[29] *Matthews* decision, above n 26, at para 32.
[30] *Ibid*, at para 34.
[31] Cf Karel Wellens, *Remedies against International Organisations* 214–15 (Cambridge, Cambridge University Press, 2002).

This conclusion is based on the fact that the obligation of the European Convention predates the later transfer of competencies to, respectively, the ESA and the European Communities. This conclusion that the European Convention would prevail over later treaty obligations between the same parties would, in turn, be based on two arguments. First, the obligations to respect the human rights laid down in the European Convention are not simply obligations existing between the states parties that can be terminated at any moment in favour of subsequent treaty obligations.[32] The normal conflict rule applying between parties that later treaties prevail over earlier ones[33] would therefore not be automatically applicable. Second, the European Court did not appear to approach the matter in terms of a conflict between treaties, but as a matter of state responsibility which is not affected by any rules of the law of treaties on the relationship between incompatible treaties.[34]

From these cases one could infer that the responsibility for states to secure human rights would only apply in the context of the European Convention and, in particular, to treaty obligations entered into after the entry into force of the European Convention. This would imply that states would not have a similar responsibility under the Charter of the United Nations.[35] However, that would appear to be a too narrow conclusion. The same matter of state responsibility can arise in case of a conflict between international human rights obligations and a subsequent binding decision of an international organisation. Even though decisions of the United Nations (ie the Security Council) are adopted by only 16 members, they are decisions of the organisation as a whole.[36] All members therefore remain responsible, if and to the extent that such decisions violate fundamental human rights to which the member states are bound by customary international law or treaties, such as the ICCPR and the International Covenant on Economic, Social and Cultural Rights (ICESCR). Any other conclusion would create a dangerous loophole by which member states, by exercising powers in the context of an international organisation rather than unilaterally, could evade international responsibility for its obligations to respect human rights.[37]

---

[32] In *Loizidou v Turkey*, Series A 310 (1995), the European Court described the Convention as "a constitutional instrument of European public order ("ordre public").
[33] Arts 30(3) and 30(4) of the Vienna Convention on the Law of Treaties of 1969, reprinted in 8 *International Legal Materials* 679 ff (1969). Hereinafter referred to as the Vienna Convention.
[34] Vienna Convention, above n 33, at Art 73. See also *Case concerning the Gabcikovo-Nagymaros Project (Hungary v Slovakia)*, ICJ Rep 1997, at para 47.
[35] De Wet & Nollkaemper, above 23, at 190.
[36] *Ibid*, at 190–91.
[37] See paras 3 and 17 of the Commentary of the International Law Commission to Art 7 of the draft Articles on State Responsibility as adopted on the first reading (in the second reading renumbered as Art 5), in *Yearbook of the International Law Commission* 277–83 (1974/ II). The ILC applied the same principle to the transfer of competencies for exercising governmental authority to entities separate from the state machinery.

It follows that member states are obliged to take all necessary measures to prevent the infringement. With the exception of the five permanent members, states will most likely not be able to exercise control within the Security Council. However, by refusing to implement Security Council decisions which violate core human rights norms, member states can still provide some protection. Anything less would imply that the organs of member states are participating in an internationally wrongful act committed by the Security Council.[38]

3.3.   Enforcing the Limitations to the Security Council's Chapter VII Powers through the "Right of Last Resort"

In summary, the two lines of argument pertaining to Articles 25 and 2(5) of the Charter and the international human rights obligations of member states, respectively, imply that member states can refuse to implement binding Security Council resolutions, if their illegality is beyond doubt and it is clear that the Security Council has no intention of revoking the illegal resolution. The arguments developed here are a manifestation of the maxim that any restricted delegation of power must have some system of control for ensuring that the institution to whom the power is delegated functions the way it was designed to.[39] Given that neither the Security Council itself nor other organs of the United Nations are likely to exercise the necessary control over Security Council decisions that violate Charter norms, member states constitute the last option for doing so.

Ideally, states should exercise this right within a representative group such as regional organisations. In addition, they should first put the matter before the Security Council itself and allow it the opportunity to take the necessary remedial measures. For example, subsequent to the *Lockerbie* incident the Organisation of African Unity (OAU) threatened to terminate the sanctions against Libya as of December 1998, unless the impasse regarding the extradition of the suspects were negotiated.[40] This decision carried considerable weight, as it was carried by the entire membership of the organisation. It was also only adopted after nine years of fruitless protests against the illegality of the relevant Security Council resolutions and after it became clear that the contentious proceedings before the ICJ had reached an impasse.

---

[38] See a similar argument in the context of breaches of international law by foreign states in FA Mann, "The Consequences of an International Wrong in International and National Law", 48 *British Yearbook of International Law* 30 (1976–1977).

[39] W Michael Reisman, *Systems of Control in International Adjudication & Arbitration. Breakdown and Repair* 1 (Durham, Duke University Press, 1992).

[40] The OAU decision was announced at the conclusion of the OAU Summit in Ouagadougou on 10 June (AHG/Dec XXXIV (1998)). See Tshibangu Kalulu, "La Décision de l'OAU de ne plus Respecter Les Sanctions Décrétées par l'ONU contre la Libye: Désobéissance Civile des États Africains à l'Égard de L'ONU", 32 *Revue belge de droit international* 545 ff (1999).

Another possibility would be to exercise the "right to last resort" through a resolution of the General Assembly. It would significantly strengthen the political legitimacy of the decision and would constitute a step in the creation of an emergency role for the General Assembly, for which it had already set a precedent during the Korean war. Although, the weight of that precedent is weakened by the questionable legality of the Korean military operation as a whole, it does illustrate how the General Assembly could develop a residual role in terminating military or other mandates in future situations where the necessary consensus within the Security Council to do so is lacking.

Although the OAU practice remains the only example of an outright rejection of a binding Security Council decision, it does provide some evidence of an emerging practice of the "right of last resort".[41] Moreover, state practice also reveals that some states are willing to grant limited exceptions to Security Council decisions, in order to ensure that they are implemented in accordance with basic human rights norms. This "human rights friendly" practice is evidenced, in particular, in relation to economic sanctions.[42] Although it constitutes a restricted form of the "right to last resort", it does indicate an assertion by states of a (limited) right to refrain from executing binding Security Council decisions in extreme circumstances.[43] Such a restricted approach effectively amounts to an interpretation of Security

---

[41] See also Marc Bossuyt, "The adverse consequences of economic sanctions on the enjoyment of human rights", Working paper for the Sub-Commission on the Promotion and Protection of Human Rights, E/CN.4/Sub.2/2000/33, at para 109. He stated that sanctions regimes that clearly violate international law, especially human rights and humanitarian law, need not be respected.

[42] See, for example, the Dutch Sanctions Act 1977. Art 9 provides that the minister may grant exemption or dispensation from rules and regulations that implement Security Council resolutions. In a decision of 19 August 1999, the Trade and Industry Appeal Tribunal held that if Art 9 of the 1977 Act is invoked, it will have to be shown in respect of each request what special interests necessitate refusal of the applicant's request. A mere reference to the resolutions is not sufficient for this purpose since the possibility of dispensation is part and parcel of the implementation. This decision was published in 31 *Netherlands Yearbook of International Law* 313 (2000). See also *R (on the application of Othman) v Secretary of State for Work and Pensions*, [2001] EWCH Admin 1022 (QB 2001). According to the English Court, member states were entitled to ensure that individuals affected by economic sanctions—in this case those resulting from SC Res 1333 of 19 December 2000—did not find themselves in a situation where they had no support.

[43] In December 2001 the absence of an independent international review mechanism prompted three Swedish citizens, whose assets had been frozen after they appeared on the sanctions list, to initiate proceedings before the Court of First Instance of the European Court of Justice. The central ground for their plea was that the freezing of their assets occurred in violation of the fundamental right to a fair and public hearing. The choice of the forum was determined by the fact that in the European Union, SC Res 1333 of 19 December 2000 was implemented by means of Council Reg No 467/2001 of 6 March 2001 and Comm Reg No 2199/2001 of 12 November 2001. Due to these regulations, the decisions of the Sanctions Committee became directly applicable throughout the European Union. At the time of writing it was still unclear whether the Court of First Instance would be willing to review the compatibility of the decisions of the Sanctions Committee with fundamental human rights norms. See *Aden and others v Council and Commission*, Case T–306/1, initiated on 10 December 2001.

Council resolutions in a way that gives due consideration to basic human rights (and other) norms to which the Security Council is bound. By interpreting Security Council measures in such a fashion, member states would still honour the presumption of legality attached to Security Council resolutions, whilst also giving effect to the limitations of the latter's powers.

The extent to which member states would be able to reject illegal Security Council measures in this more restricted fashion would depend on the nature and scope of the measures at stake. For example, if states were to reject an illegal Article 39 determination, it would imply that all binding measures exclusively resulting from this illegal determination might be rejected as well. This was arguably the case with the embargo against Libya, as it was exclusively based on Libya's refusal to adhere to the illegal request for the extradition of the *Lockerbie* suspects. States therefore had the right to reject the embargo as a whole, whilst Libya also remained within its rights in refusing to extrade the suspects. However, in the other two instances where the Security Council imposed embargoes in connection with states' refusal to comply with an illegal extradition request (ie Sudan and Afghanistan), these refusals did not constitute the sole basis for the Security Council's Article 39 determination. Instead, the respective determinations were also supported by the threat to peace posed by the Sudanese and Taliban governments' continued training and supporte of international terrorists. Therefore, whilst these states might have been within their rights in refusing to give effect to the illegal extradition requests, the embargoes against them were supported by a legal basis and were therefore to be respected.

However, as indicated, additional difficulties arose with respect to the embargo against the *Taliban*. The controversy related to the scope of the Security Council's direct targeting of suspected terrorists, as it also requested the freezing of assets of individuals and undertakings identified by the Sanctions Committee as being "associated" with *Al-Quaida* and the *Taliban*. Given the impact that these measures had on the right to a fair hearing of those affected, member states would be able to make their continued implementation dependent on whether such a right is granted. As long as the Security Council refrains from granting an independent, impartial and even-handed international procedure by means of which the affected persons can refute the allegations against them, member states would be entitled to provide for a right to a fair hearing on a national level, eg within domestic courts. In states where a fair hearing is provided for in this manner, the continued freezing of assets of those targeted by the Sanctions Committee would then depend on whether their involvement with international terrorism could be proved before an independent judicial organ.[44]

---

[44] See also De Wet & Nollkaemper, above n 23, at 197 ff.

Instances in which the "right to last resort" could only have been exercised in a more outright fashion, include the embargoes against Bosnia-Herzegovina and Iraq, respectively. By the time Bosnia-Herzegovina had requested provisional measures from the ICJ in 1993, it was clear that the arms embargo against the country had undermined Bosnia-Herzegovina's right to self-defence. A refusal to implement this embargo would therefore have been justified until the Security Council took effective measures for the protection of the territorial integrity of Bosnia-Herzegovina. This ultimately occurred with the adoption of the Dayton Accords and their subsequent implementation in Resolution 1031 of 15 December 1995.

Although the Security Council officially terminated the Iraqi embargo in May 2003, states could have rejected the binding character of this embargo (at least) as of 2000. Given the Security Council's unwillingness to amend the embargo in a fashion necessary to remedy its violations of the right to life and the right to health for more than a decade, the exercise of the "right to last resort" would have been justified in this instance. In light of the breadth of the embargo and the difficulty in distinguishing between civilian and so called "dual use" goods, it is clear that any exercise of the "right of last resort" aimed at providing the Iraqi civilians with the infrastructure necessary for sustaining basic human rights, would have implied an outright rejection of the embargo in some form or another.

As far as Iraq is concerned, states could also have refused to turn over Iraqi assets to the United Nations for the purpose of funding the Compensation Commission, until the Security Council had guaranteed the Compensation Commission's independence and even-handedness. However, as it turned out, member states supported the work of the Compensation Commission in spite of the fact that the Security Council's excessive control over this quasi judicial organ constituted a violation of Article 1(1) of the Charter. The Compensation Commission subsequently developed a life of its own and it remains to be seen whether Iraq will acquiesce in its decisions, as it did with respect to the decisions of the Iraq-Kuwait Boundary Demarcation Commission. In this latter instance, Iraq ultimately chose to accept the boundary illegally imposed on it by the Demarcation Commission, and thereby forfeited any right that it might have had to reject it.

Finally, it needs to be emphasised that any residual role for member states in refusing to implement binding Security Council resolutions should remain an *ultima ratio*, even if it were to be exercised through a collective forum such as the General Assembly or a regional organisation. The efficiency and legitimacy of the United Nations would be much better served if the Security Council acted with the self-restraint necessary for ensuring that it remains within the outer limits of its Chapter VII powers. However, in order to do so, the Security Council will first have to come to terms with the fact that its discretion under Chapter VII is not unlimited. The enforcement measures adopted in the early 1990s, in particular with respect to Iraq and Libya, reflected an unwillingness to acknowledge its obligation to act in accordance with the purposes and principles of the Charter and even *ius cogens* norms. The consequences of this behaviour may still haunt the United Nations for several years to come, in particular in terms of a loss of legitimacy of the organisation as a whole.

Although many of the more recent Security Council enforcement measures have shown some self-restraint when authorising the use of force or adopting sanctions regimes (for example by subjecting them to time limits), other measures adopted in the post-11 September 2001 era has indicated that this practice is by no means consistent. The road towards a Security Council practice that consistently remains within the norms of *ius cogens* and the purposes and principles of the Charter is long and arduous. It is, however, the only way by means of which the Security Council can achieve the legitimacy necessary for the efficient restoration and maintenance of international peace and security in the long term and, ultimately, the survival of the international community as represented by the United Nations system.

Bibliography

ABI-SAAB, GEORGES, "Strengthening the Role of the Court as the Principal Judicial Organ of the UN, in Connie Peck and Roy S Lee (eds), *Increasing the Effectiveness of the International Court of Justice* 233–79 (The Hague, Martinus Nijhoff, 1997).

AKANDE, DAPO, "The Role of the International Court of Justice in the Maintenance of International Peace", 8 *African Journal of International and Comparative Law* 592–616 (1996).

AKANDE, DAPO, "The International Court of Justice and the Security Council: Is there Room for Judicial Control of Decisions of Political Organs of the United Nations?", 46 *International & Comparative Law Quarterly* 309–43 (1997).

ALFREDSSON, GUDMUNDUR, "The Right of Self-Determination and Indigenous Peoples", in Christian Tomuschat (ed), *Modern Law of Self-Determination* 41–54 (Dordrecht, Martinus, Nijhoff, 1993).

ALSTON, PHILIP, "The Security Council and Human Rights: Lessons to be Learned from the Iraq-Kuwait Crisis and its Aftermath", 13 *Australian Yearbook of International law* 107–76 (1990/ 1991).

ALVAREZ, JOSÉ, E, "Theoretical Perspectives on Judicial Review by the World Court", 89 *Proceedings of the American Society of International Law* 85–90 (1995).

——, "Judging the Security Council", 90 *American Journal of International Law* 1–39 (1996).

——, "The Security Council's War on Terrorism: Problems and Policy Options", in Erika de Wet & André Nollkaemper (eds), *Judicial Review of the Security Council by Member States* XX (Antwerp, Intersentia, forthcoming).

AMERASINGHE, CHITTHARANJAN F, *Principles of the Institutional Law of International organisations* (Cambridge, Cambridge University Press, 1996).

ANGELET, NICOLAS, "International Law Limits to the Security Council", in Vera Gowlland-Debbas (ed), *United Nations Sanctions and International Law* 71–82 (The Hague, Kluwer, 2001).

ARANGIO-RUIZ, GAETANO, "The 'Federal Analogy' and UN Character Interpretation: A Crucial Issue", 8 *European Journal of International Law* 1–28 (1997).

——, "On the Security Council's 'Law-Making', 83 *Rivista di Diritto Internazionale* 609–725 (2000).

ARNTZ, JOACHIM, *Der Begriff der Friedensbedrohung in Satzung und Praxis der Vereinten Nationen* (Berlin, Duncker & Humblot, 1975).

AZNAR-GÓMEZ, MARIANO J, "A Decade of Human Rights Protection by the UN Security Council: a Sketch of Deregulation?", 13 *European Journal of International Law* 223–41 (2002).

ASTON, JURIJ DANIEL ASTON, "Die Bekämpfung abstrakter Gefahren für den Weltfrieden durch legislative Massnahmen des Sicherheitsrats—Resolution 1373 (200) im Kontext", 62 *Zeitschrift für ausländisches öffentliches Recht und Völkerrecht* 257–91 (2002).

BAADE, HANS W, "Nullity and Avoidance in Public International Law: A Preliminary Survey and a Theoretical Orientation", 39 *Indiana Law Journal* 497–559 (1963–64).

BASSIOUNI, CHERIF, "A Functional Approach to 'General Principles of International Law", 11 *Michigan Journal of International Law* 768–818 (1989).

BATOR, PAUL M et al *Hart and Wechsler's The Federal Courts and the Federal System* (Westbury, Foundation, 1988).

BEDJAOUI, MOHAMMED, *The New World Order and the Security Council* (Dordrecht, Martinus Nijhoff, 1994).

BEKKER, PETER HF, "International Decisions: Questions of Interpretation and Application of the 1971 Montreal Convention Arising from the Aerial Incident at Lockerbie", 92 *American Journal of International Law* 503–08 (1998).

BENVENUTI, PAOLO, "Le Respect du Droit International Humanitaire par les Forces des Nations Unies: La Circulaire du Secretaire General", 105 *Revue Générale de Droit International* 355–72 (2001).

BERNHARDT, RUDOLF, "Normkontrolle", in Hermann Mosler, *Verfassungsrichtsbarkeit in der Gegenwart* 727–37 (Berlin, Springer, 1962).

——, "Eigenheiten und Ziele der Rechtsvergleichung im öffentlichen Recht", 24 *Zeitschrift für ausländisches öffentliches Recht und Völkerrecht* 431–52 (1964).

——, "Interpretation in International Law", 1 *Encyclopedia of Public International Law* 318–27 (1994).

——, "International Organisations, Internal Law and Rules", 2 *Encyclopedia of Public International Law* 1314–18 (1995).

BEVERIDGE, FIONA, "The Lockerbie Affair", 41 *International and Comparative Law Quarterly* 907–20 (1992).

BEYERLIN, U & STRASSER, W, "Völkerrechtliche Praxis der Bundersepublik Deutschland im Jahre 1973", 35 *Zeitschrift für ausländisches öffentliches Recht und Völkerrecht* 71–91 (1975).

BINDSCHEDLER-ROBERT, DENISE, "Korea", 3 *Encyclopedia of Public International Law* 86–93 (1997).

BLOKKER, NIELS M, "Grenzen aan de macht(iging)?", 33 *Nederlands Juristenblad* 1547–53 (1997).

——, "Is the Authorisation Authorised? Powers and Practice of the United Nations Security Council to Authorise the Use of Force by Coalitions of the 'Able and Willing'", 11 *European Journal of International Law* 541–68 (2000).

BLOKKER, NIELS, M & KLEIBOER, MARIEKE, "The Internationalization of Domestic Conflict: The Role of the United Nations Security Council", 9 *Leiden Journal of International Law* 7–35 (1996).

BLOKKER, NIELS, M & MULLER, ALEXANDER S, "NATO as the UN Security Council's Instrument: Question Marks from the Perspective of International Law?", 9 *Leiden Journal of International Law* 417–21 (1996).

BLOOM, EVAN T, "Protection of Peacekeepers: The Convention on the Safety of United Nations and Associated Personnel", 89 *American Journal of International Law* 621–31 (1995).

BOELAERT-SUOMINEN, SONJA, "The Yugoslavia Tribunal and the Common Core of Humanitarian Law Applicable to all Armed Conflicts", 13 *Leiden Journal of International Law* 620–53 (2000).

BÖHMER, FRIEDERIKE, *Die Ermächtigung zu militärischer Gewaltanwendung durch den Sicherheitsrat* (Baden-Baden, Nomos, 1997).

BOJICIC, V & DYKER, D, *Sanctions on Serbia: Sledgehammer or Scalpel?* (Sussex, Sussex European Institute, 1993).

BOTHE, MICHAEL, "Die Erklärung der Generalversammlung der Vereinten Nationen über die Definition der Aggression", 18 *Jahrbuch für Internationales Recht* 127–45 (1975).

——, "Die Bedeutung der Rechtsvergleichung in der Praxis internationaler Gerichte", 36 *Zeitschrift für ausländisches öffentliches Recht und Völkerrecht* 280–99 (1976).

——, "Peace-Keeping", in Bruno Simma (ed), *The Charter of the United Nations. A Commentary* 565–603 (Oxford, Oxford University Press , 1994).

——, "Die NATO nach dem Kosovo-Konflikt und das Völkerrecht", 10 *Schweizerische Zeitschrift für Internationales und Europäisches Recht* 177–95 (2000).

BOTHE, MICHAEL & MARHAUN, THILO, "UN Administration of Kosovo and East Timor: Concept, Legality and Limitations of Security Council Mandated Trusteeship Administration", in Christian Tomuschat (ed), *Kosovo and the International Community* 217–42 (The Hague, Kluwer, 2001).

BOTHE, MICHAEL & RESS, GEORG, "The Comparative Method and Public International Law", in William E Butler, *International Law in a Comparative Perspective* 217–42 (Alphen aan den Rijn, Sijthoff & Noordhoff, 1980).

BOUTROS-GHALI, BOUTROS, "The United Nations and Comprehensive Legal Measures for Combating International Terrorism", in Karel Wellens (ed), *International Law: Theory and Practice. Essays in Honor of Eric Suy*, 287–304 (The Hague, Martinus Nijhoff, 1998).

BOWETT, DEREK, "The Impact of Security Council Decisions on Dispute Settlement Procedures", 5 *European Journal of International Law* 89–101 (1994).

BRAND, MARCUS G, "Institution-Building and Human Rights Protection in Kosovo in the Light of UNMIK Legislation", 70 *Nordic Journal of International Law* 461–88 (2001).

BRAY, CHRISTINE, "Advisory Opinions and the European Court of Justice", 8 *European Law Review* 24–39 (1985).

BRENFORS, MARTHA & PETERSEN, MALENE MAXE, "The Legality of Unilateral Humanitarian Intervention—A Defence", 69 *Nordic Journal of International Law* 449–99 (2000).

BROMS, BENGT, "The Definition of Agression", 154 *Recueil des Cours de l'Académie de Droit International de la Haye* 299–400 (1977 I).

BROWN, CHRISTOPHER, "A Comparative and Critical Assesment of Estoppel in International Law", 50 *University of Miami Law Review* 369–412 (1996).

BROWNLIE, IAN, "The Decision of Political Organs of the United Nations and the Rule of Law", in Ronald St John MacDonald (ed), *Essays in Honor of Wang Tieya* 91–102 (Dordrecht, Martinus Nijhoff, 1994).

——, *Principles of Public International Law* (Oxford, Clarendon, 1998).

BROWNLIE, IAN & APPERLEY, CJ "Kosovo Crisis Inquiry: Memorandum on the International Law Aspects", 49 *International and Comparative Law Quarterly* 878–905 (2000).

BRUHA, THOMAS & KRAJEWSKI, MARKUS, "Funktionswandel des Sicherheitsrats als Verfassungsproblem", 46 *Vereinte Nationen* 13–18 (1998).

BRUNNER, GEORG, "Die neue Verfassungsgerichtsbarkeit in Osteuropa", 53 *Zeitschrift für ausländisches öffentliches Recht und Völkerrecht* 819–70 (1993).

BURCI, GIAN LUCA, "Interpreting the Humanitarian Exceptions through the Sanctions Committees", in Vera Gowlland-Debbas (ed), *United Nations Sanctions and International Law* 143–54 (The Hague, Kluwer, 2001).

BYERS, MICHAEL, "The Shifting Foundations of International Law: A Decade of Forceful Measures against Iraq", 13 *European Journal of International Law* 21–41 (2002).

CAFLISH, LUCIUS, "Is the International Court Entitled to Review Security Council Resolutions Adopted under Chapter VII of the United Nations Charter?", in Najeeb Al-Naumi & Richard Meese, *International Legal Issues Arising under the United Nations Decade of International Law* 633–62 (Martinus Nijhoff, The Hague, 1995).

CARON, DAVID D, "The Legitimacy of the Collective Authority of the Security Council", 87 *American Journal of International Law* 552–58 (1993).

CARON, DAVID D & MORRIS, BRIAN, "The UN Compensation Commission: Practical Justice, not Retribution", 13 *European Journal of International Law* 183–99 (2002).

CARVER, JEREMY, P, "Dispute Resolution or Administrative Tribunal: A Question of Due Process", in Richard B Lillich (ed), *The United Nations Compensation Commission*, 69–76 (Irvington, Transnational, 1996).

CASSESE, ANTONIO, "Ex iniuria ius oritur: Moving towards International Legitimation of Forcible Humanitarian Countermeasures in the World Community?", 10 *European Journal of International Law* 24–30 (1999).

——, *International Law* (Oxford, Oxford University Press, 2001).

CERONE, JOHN, "Minding the Gap: Outlining KFOR Accountability in Post-Conflict Kosovo", 12 *European Journal of International Law* 469–88 (2001).

CHAYES, ABRAM *et al* (eds), *International Legal Process* (Boston, Little & Brown, 1968).

CHARNEY, JONATHAN I, "Anticipatory Humanitarian Intervention in Kosovo", 93 *American Journal of International Law* 834–41 (1999).

CHENG, BIN, *General Principles of Law as applied by International Courts and Tribunals* (London, Stevens, 1953).

CHINKIN, CHRISTINE, "Kosovo, a 'Good' or 'Bad' War?", 93 *American Journal of International Law* 841–47 (1999).

——, "The Legality of NATO's Action in the Former Republic of Yugoslavia (FRY) under International Law", 49 *International and Comparative Law Quarterly* 90–25 (2000).

CHOPRA, JARAT, "The UN's Kingdom in East Timor", 42 *Survival* 27–36 (2000).

CLAPHAM, ANDREW, "Sanctions and Economic, Social and Cultural Rights", in Vera Gowlland-Debbas (ed), *United Nations Sanctions and International Law* 131–41 (The Hague, Kluwer, 2001).

CLARK, ROGER S, "EAST TIMOR, Indonesia, and the International Community", 14 *Temple International and Comparative Law Journal* 75–87 (2000).

CONDORELLI, LUIGI, "La Compatabilité des Sanctions du Conseil de Securité avec le Droit International Humanitaire—Commentaire", in Vera Gowlland-Debbas, *United Nations Sanctions and International Law* 233–40 (The Hague, Kluwer, 2001).

CONFORTI, BENEDETTO, "The Legal Effect of Non-Compliance with Rules of Procedure in the UN General Assembly and the Security Council", 63 *American Journal of International Law* 479–89 (1969).

COTTIER, THOMAS & SCHEFFER, KRISTA N, "Good Faith and the Protection of Legitimate Expectations in the WTO", in Bronckers Marco & Quick, Reinhard (eds), *New Directions in International Economic Law* 47–68 (The Hague, Kluwer, 2000).

CRAIG, PAUL & DE BÚRCA, GRÁINNE, *EU Law: Text, Cases and Materials* (Oxford, Oxford University Press, 1998).

CRAVEN, MATTHEW, "Humanitarianism and the Quest for Smarter Sanctions", 13 *European Journal of International Law* 43–61 (2002).

CRAWFORD, JAMES, "The General Assembly, the International Court and Self-determination", in Vaughan Lowe & Malgosia Fitzmaurice (eds), *Fifty Years of the International Court of Justice. Essays in Honor of Sir Robert Jennings* 585–605 (Cambridge, Cambridge University Press, 1996).

CROOK, JOHN R, "The UNCC and its Critics: Is Iraq Entitled to Judicial Due Process?", in Richard B Lillich (ed), *The United Nations Compensation Commission* 77–101 (Irvington, Transnational, 1996).

CZAPLINSKI, WLADSYLAW, "The Lockerbie Case—some Comments", in 20 *Polish Yearbook of International Law* 37–45 (1993).

DAVID, MANCELLA, "Passport to Justice: Internationalizing the Political Question Doctrine for Application in the World Court", 40 *Harvard International Law Journal* 81–150 (1999).

——, "Rubber Helmets: The Certain Pitfalls of Marshaling Security Council Resources to Combat Aids in Africa", 23 *Human Rights Quarterly* 560–82 (2001).

DAVIDSON, SCOTT, *The Inter-American Court of Human Rights* (Dartmouth, Aldershot, 1992).

DEGAN, VLADIMIR-DJURO DEGAN, "General Principles of Law", 3 *Finnish Yearbook of International Law* 1–100 (1992).

DE HOOGH, ANDRÉ JJ, "The Relationship between Jus Cogens, Obligations Erga Omnes and International Crimes: Peremptory Norms in Perspective", 42 *Österreichische Zeitschrift für öffentliches Recht und Völkerrecht* 183–214 (1991).

——, "Attribution or Delegation of (Legislative) Power by the Security Council? The Case of the United Transnational Administration in East Timor (UNTAET)", 7 *Yearbook of International Peace Operations* 1–41 (2001).

DEKKER, IGE F & MYJER, ERIC PJ, "Air Strikes on Bosnian Positions: Is NATO Also Legally the Proper Instrument of the UN?", 9 *Leiden Journal of International Law* 411–24 (1996).

DELBRÜCK, JOST, "Article 24", in Bruno Simma (ed), *The Charter of the United Nations. A Commentary* 392–407 (Oxford, Oxford University Press, 1994).

——, "Article 25", in Bruno Simma (ed), *The Charter of the United Nations. A Commentary* 407–418 (Oxford, Oxford University Press, 1994).

——, "Proportionality", 3 *Encyclopedia of Public International Law* 1140–344 (1994).

——, "Structural Changes in the International System and its Legal Order: International Law in the Era of Globalization", 11 *Schweizerische Zeitschrift für Internationales und Europäisches Recht* 1–36 (2001).

DEVIN, JULIA & DASHTI-GIBSON, JALEH, "Sanctions in the Former Yugoslavia: Convoluted Goals and Compiled Consequences", in Thomas G Weiss *et al* (eds), *Political Gain and Civil Pain. Humanitarian Impacts of Economic Sanctions* 149–187 (Lanham, Rowman & Littlefield, 1997).

DE WET, ERIKA & NOLLKAEMPER, ANDRÉ, "Review of Security Council Decisions by National Courts", 45 *German Yearbook of International Law*? 166–202 (2002).

DE ZAYAS, ALFRED, "The United Nations and the Guarantees of a Fair Trial in the International Covenant on Civil and Political Rights and the Convention Against Torture and Other Cruel, Inhuman or Degrading Treatment or Punishment", in David Weissbrodt & Rüdiger Wolfrum (eds), *The Right to a Fair Trial* 669–696 (Berlin, Springer, 1997).

DINSTEIN, YORAM, "The right to life, physical integrity and liberty", in Louis Henkin (ed), *The International Bill of Rights* 114–138 (New York, Columbia University Press, 1981).

——, "The Legal Lessons of the Gulf War", 48 *Austrian Journal of Public and International Law* 1–17 (1995).

——, "Humanitarian Intervention from Outside, in the face of Genocide, is Legitimate only when Undertaken by the Security Council", 27 *Justice* 4–6 (2001).

DOEHRING, KAREL, "Self-Determination", in Bruno Simma (ed), *The Charter of the United Nations. A Commentary* 57–72 (Oxford, Oxford University Press, 1994).

——, "Unlawful Resolutions of the Security Council and their Legal Consequences", 1 *Max Planck Yearbook of United Nations Law* 91–109 (1997).

DOSWALD-BECK, L, "The Legal Validity of Military Intervention by Invitation of the Government", 56 *British Yearbook of International Law* 189–252 (1985).

DOXEY, MARGARET, *United Nations Sanctions: Current Policy Issues* (Halifax, Dalhousie, 1999).

DUGARD, JOHN, *International Law: A South African Perspective* (Kenwyn, Juta, 2000).

——, "Judicial Review of Sanctions", in Vera Gowlland-Debbas (ed), "United Nations Sanctions and International Law" 83–91 (The Hague, Kluwer, 2001).

DUPUY, PIERRE-MARIE, "The Constitutional Dimension of the Charter of the United Nations Revisited", 1 *Max Planck Yearbook of International Law* 1–33 (1997).

EITEL, TONO, "The United Nations Security Council and its Future Contribution in the Field of International Law", 4 *Max Planck Yearbook of United Nations Law* 53–71 (2000).

ELIAS, OLUFEMI & LIM, CHIN, "General Principles of Law, 'Soft' Law and the Identification of International Law", 28 *Netherlands Yearbook of International Law* 3–49 (1997).

ERMACORA, FELIX, "Article 2(7)", in Bruno Simma (ed), *The Charter of the United Nations. A Commentary* 139–154 (Oxford, Oxford University Press, 1994).

EVANS, SCOTT S, "The Lockerbie Incident Cases: Libyan-Sponsored Terrorism, Judicial Review and the Political Question Doctrine", 18 *Maryland Journal of International Law and Trade* 22–76 (1994).

FASSBENDER, BARDO, "The United Nations Charter as Constitution of the International Community", 36 *Columbia Journal of Transnational Law* 531–619 (1998).

——, *UN Security Council Reform and the Right of Veto. A Constitutional Perspective* (The Hague, Kluwer, 1998).

——, "Quis Judicabit? The Security Council, Its Powers and Its Legal Control", 11 *European Journal of International Law* 219–232 (2000).

——, "Uncertain Steps into a Post Cold War World: The Role and Functioning of the UN Security Council after a Decade of Measures against Iraq", 13 *European Journal of International Law* 273–303 (2002).

FENRICK, WILLIAM J, "Targeting and Proportionality during the NATO Bombing Campaign against Yugoslavia", 12 *European Journal of International Law* 491–502 (2001).

FIELDING, LOIS E, "Taking a Closer Look at Threats to Peace: The Power of the Security Council to Address Humanitarian Crises", 73 *University of Detroit Mercy Law Review* 552–68 (1996).

FISHMAN, ANDREW K, "Between Iraq and a Hard Place: The Use of Economic Sanctions and Threat to International Peace and Security", 13 *Emory International Law Review* 687–727 (1999).

FITZMAURICE, GERALD G, "The Law and Procedure of the International Court of Justice: Treaty Interpretation and Certain other Treaty Points", 28 *British Year Book of International Law* 1–25 (1951).

FLEURY, JG, "The Plea of Ignorance", *War, Peace and Security WWW Server*, at www.cfcsc.dnd.ca/irc/amsc/amsc1/011.html.

FRAAS, MICHAEL, *Sicherheitsrat der Vereinten Nationen und Internationaler Gerichtshof* (Peter Lang, Frankfurt a/M, 1998).

FRANCK, THOMAS M, "The Emerging Right to Democratic Governance", 86 *American Journal of International Law* 46–91 (1992).

——, "The 'Powers of Appreciation': Who Is the Ultimate Guardian of UN Legality?", 86 *American Journal of International Law* 519–23 (1992).

——, "The Political and the Judicial Empires: Must there be Conflict over Conflict-Resolution?", in Najeeb Al-Naumi & Richard Meese (eds), *International Legal Issues Arising under the United Nations Decade of International Law* 621–32 (The Hague, Martinus Nijhoff, 1995).

FRANKFURTER, FELIX, "A Note on Advisory Opinions", 37 *Harvard Law Review* 1002–09 (1923–24).

FROWEIN, JOCHEN A, "Nullity in International Law", 3 *Encyclopedia of Public International Law* 743–47 (1997).

——, "Die Verpflichtungen erga omnes im Völkerrecht und ihre Durchsetzung", in Rudolf Bernhardt *et al* (eds), *Völkerrecht als Rechtsordnung. Internationale Gerichtsbarkeit. Menschenrechte: Festschrift für Hermann Mosler* 241–62 (Berlin, Springer, 1983).

——, "Collective Enforcement of International Obligations", 47 *Zeitschrift für ausländisches öffentliches Recht und Völkerrecht* 67–79 (1987).

——, "The Internal and External Effects of Resolutions by International Organisations", 49 *Zeitschrift für ausländisches öffentliches Recht und Völkerrecht* 779–90 (1989).

——, "Article 2(5)", in Bruno Simma (ed), *The Charter of the United Nations. A Commentary* 129–31 (Oxford, Oxford University Press, 1994).

——, "Article 39", in Bruno Simma (ed), *The Charter of the United Nations. A Commentary* 605–16 (Oxford, Oxford University Press, 1994).

——, "Article 40", Bruno Simma (ed), *The Charter of the United Nations. A Commentary* 617–21 (Oxford, Oxford University Press, 1994).

——, "Article 42", in Bruno Simma (ed), *The Charter of the United Nations. A Commentary* 628–36 (Oxford, Oxford University Press, 1994).

——, "Obligations *Erga Omnes*", 3 *Encyclopedia of International Law* 757–59 (1997).

——, "Ius Cogens", 3 *Encyclopedia of Public International Law* 65–68 (1997).

GADING, HEIKE, *Der Schutz grundlegender Menschenrechte durch militärische Massnahmen des Sicherheitsrates—das Ende staatlicher Souveränität?* (Berlin, Duncker & Humblot, 1996).

GARDAM, JUDITH G, "Proportionality and Force in International Law", 87 *American Journal of International Law* 391–413 (1993).

GASSER, HANS-PETER, "Collective Economic Sanctions and International Humanitarian Law", 56 *Zeitschrift für ausländisches öffentliches Recht und Völkerrecht* 871–904 (1996).

GATTINI, ANDREA, "The UN Compensation Commission: Old Rules, New Procedures on War Reparations", 13 *European Journal of International Law* 160–75 (2002).

Geiger, RUDOLF, "Article 106", in Bruno Simma (ed) *The Charter of the United Nations. A Commentary* 1149–51 (Oxford, Oxford University Press, 1994).

GIBBONS, ELIZABETH D, *Sanctions in Haiti. Human Rights and Democracy under Assault* (Westport, Praeger, 1999).

Gill, TD, "Legal and Some Political Limitations on the Power of the UN Security Council to Exercise its Enforcement Powers under Chapter VII of the Charter", 26 *Netherlands Yearbook of International Law* 33–138 (1995).

GINTHER, KONRAD, "Die Verfassung der Völkerrechtsgemeinschaft im Lichte der Entscheidung des internationalen Gerichtshofes im sogenannten Südwestafrika-Streit", in René Marcic *et al* (eds), *International Festschrift für Verdross zum 80. Geburtstag* 91–117 (München, Wilhelm Fink, 1971).

GLICK, RICHARD D, "Lip Service to the Law of War: Humanitarian Law and United Nations Armed Forces", in 17 *Michigan Journal of International Law* 53–105 (1995).

GONIDEC, PF *Les Organisations Internationales Africaines* (Paris, L'Harmattan, 1987).

GORDON, RUTH, "United Nations Intervention in Internal Conflicts: Iraq, Somalia, and Beyond", 15 *Michigan Journal of International Law* 520–89 (1993).

GOWLLAND-DEBBAS, VERA, "The Relationship between the International Court of Justice and the Security Council in the Light of the Lockerbie Case", 88 *American Journal of International Law* 643–77 (1994).

——, "Security Council Enforcement Actions and Issues of State Responsibility", 43 *International and Comparative Law Quarterly* 55–98 (1994).

——, "Judicial Insights into Fundamental Values and Interests of the International Community", in Alexander S Muller *et al* (eds). *The International Court of Justice. Its Future Role after Fifty Years* 327–66 (The Hague, Martinus Nijhoff, 1997).

——, "Strengthening the Role of the Court as the Principal Judicial Organ of the UN", in Conny Peck and Roy S Lee (eds), *Increasing the Effectiveness of the International Court of Justice* 233–79 (The Hague, Martinus Nijhoff, 1997).

GRAEFRATH, BERNHARD, "Leave to the Court what Belongs to the Court: The Libyan Case", 4 *European Journal of International Law* 184–205 (1993).

——, "Die Vereinten Nationen im Übergang—Die Gratwanderung des Sicherheitsrates zwischen Rechtsanwendung und Rechtsanmassung", in Klaus Hüfner (ed), *Die Reform der Vereinten Nationen* 43–53 (Opladen, Leske & Budrich, 1994).

——, "Iraqi Reparations and the Security Council", 55 *Zeitschrift für ausländisches öffentliches Recht und Völkerrecht* 1–68 (1995).

GRAY, CHRISTINE, *International Law and the Use of Force* (Oxford, Oxford University Press, 2000).

——, "From Unity to Polarization: International Law and the Use of Force against Iraq", 13 *European Journal of International Law* 1–19 (2002).

GREENWOOD, CHRISTOPHER, "Protection of Peacekeepers: The Legal Regime", 7 *Duke Journal of Comparative & International Law* 185–207 (1996).

——, "International Humanitarian Law and United Nations Military Operations", 1 *Yearbook of Humanitarian Law* 3–34 (1998).

——, "The Impact of Decisions and Resolutions of the Security Council on the International Court of Justice", in Wybo P Heere (ed), *International Law and The Hague's 750th Anniversary* 81–87 (The Hague, TMC Asser, 1999).

——, "International Law and the NATO Intervention in Kosovo", *International and Comparative Law Quarterly* 926–34 (2000).

GREIG, DW, "The Advisory Jurisdiction of the International Court and the Settlement of Disputes between States", *International & Comparative Law Quarterly* 325–68 (1966).

GRIFFITHS, RICHARD L, "International Law, the Crime of Aggression and the Ius ad Bellum", 2 *International Criminal Law Review* 301–73 (2002).

GROSS, LEO, "Treaty Interpretation: the Proper Role of an International Tribunal", 63 *Proceedings of the American Society of International Law* 108–41 (1969).

GUGGENHEIM, PAUL, "Landesrechtliche Begriffe im Völkerrecht, vor allem im Bereich der internationalen Organisationen", in Walter Schaetzel & Hans-Jürgen Schlochauer (eds), *Rechtsfragen der internationalen Organisationen. Festschrift für Hans Wehberg zu seinem 70. Geburtstag* 133–51 (Frankfurt am Main, Vittorio Klostermann, 1956).

GUNN, ANGUS, M, "Council and Court: Prospects in Lockerbie for an International Rule of Law", 52 *University of Toronto Faculty of Law Review* 206–52 (1993).

GUTTERIDGE, HC, "The Meaning of the Scope of Article 38(1)(c) of the Statute of the International Court of Justice", 38 *Transactions of the Grotius Society* 125–50 (1953).

PAUL HAVEN, PAUL, "US-Backed Iraqi Governing Council Meets", *HeraldTribune.com*, 14 July 2003, available at www.heraldtribune.com.

HAILBRONNER, KAY, "Ziele und Methoden völkerrechtlich relevanter Rechtsvergleichung", 36 *Zeitschrift für ausländisches öffentliches Recht und Völkerrecht* 190–26 (1976).

HAILBRONNER, KAY & KLEIN, ECKART, "Article 12", in Bruno Simma (ed), *The Charter of the United Nations. A Commentary* 253–64 (Oxford, Oxford University Press, 1994).

HALDERMAN, "Some Legal Aspects of Sanctions in the Rhodesian Case", 17 *International & Comparative Law Quarterly* 672–05 (1968).

HARPER, KEITH, "Does the United Nations Security Council have the Competence to Act as Court and Legislature?", 27 *New York University Journal of International Law and Politics* 103–55 (1995).

HARVARD Center for Population and Development Studies, *Sanctions in Haiti: Crisis in Humanitarian Action* (Cambridge MA, Harvard School of Public Health, 1993).

HAZELZET, HADEWYCH, "Assessing the Suffering form 'Successful' Sanctions: An Ethical Approach", in Willem JM van Genugten & Gerard A de Groot (eds),

United Nations Sanctions. Effectiveness and Effects, Especially in the Field of Human Rights. A Multi-disciplinary Approach 71–96 (Antwerpen, Intersentia, 1999).

HENKIN, LOUIS, "Kosovo and the law of Humanitarian Intervention", 93 *American Journal of International Law* 824–28 (1999).

HERBST, JOCHEN, *Rechtsbindung des UN-Sicherheitsrates* (Frankfurt a/M, Peter Lang, 1999).

HERDEGEN, MATTHIAS J, "The 'Constitutionalization' of the UN Security System", 27 *Vanderbilt Journal of Transnational Law* 135–59 (1994).

——, "Der Wegfall effektiver Staatsgewalt im Völkerrecht: 'The Failed State'", 34 *Berichte der Deutschen Gesellschaft für Völkerrecht* 49–85 (1995).

——, *Die Befugnisse des UN-Sicherheitsrates: Aufgeklärter Absolitismus im Völkerrecht?* (Heidelberg, Müller, 1998).

HEYNS, CHRISTOF H (ed), *Human Rights in Africa Series 1996* (Kluwer, The Hague, 1996).

HIGGINS, ROSALYN, "Policy Considerations and the International Judicial Process", 17 *International & Comparative Law Quarterly* 58–84 (1968).

——, "The Advisory Opinion on Namibia: Which UN Resolutions are Binding under Article 25 of the Charter?", in 21 *International & Comparative Law Quarterly* 270–86 (1972).

——, "A Comment on the Current Health of Advisory Opinions", in Vaughan Lowe & Malgosia Fitzmaurice (eds), *Fifty Years of the International Court of Justice. Essays in Honor of Sir Robert Jennings* 567–81 (1996).

HOFFMANN, RAINER, "International Law and the Use of Military Force against Iraq", 45 *German Yearbook of International Law* 9–34. (2002).

HOSKINS, ERIC, "The Humanitarian Impacts of Economic Sanctions and War in Iraq", in Thomas G Weiss *et al* (eds), *Political Gain and Civil Pain. Humanitarian Impacts of Economic Sanctions* (Lanham, Rowman & Littlefield, 1997).

——, *The Impact of Sanctions: A Study of UNICEF's Perspectives* (New York, UNICEF, 1998).

HOWSE, ROBERT, "The Road to Baghdad is Paved with Good Intentions", 13 *European Journal of International Law* 89–92 (2002)

HU, YOUNG, "Sechs Jahre Verfassungsgerichtsbarkeit in der Republik Korea", 45 *Jahrbuch des Öffentlichen Rechts* 535–53 (1997).

HUDSON, MANLEY O, "Advisory Opinions of National and International Courts", 37 *Harvard Law Review* 970–01 (1923–24).

HUFFMAN, JAMES L & SAATHOFF, MARDILYN, "Advisory Opinions and Canadian Constitutional Development: The Supreme Court's Reference Jurisdiction", 74 *Minnesota Law Review* 1240–90 (1990).

HULSROIJ, PETER, "The Legal Function of the Security Council", 1 *Chinese Journal of International Law* 59–93 (2002).

HURST, PETER F, "Economic Sanctions: The Lifting of Sanctions against Zimbabwe-Rhodesia by the United States", 21 *Harvard International Law Journal* 253–59 (1980).

JACONELLI, JOSEPH, "Hypothetical Disputes, Moot Points of Law, and Advisory Opinions", 101 *Law Quarterly Review* 587–626 (1985).

JAYAWICKRAMA, NIHAL, "The Right to a Fair Trial under the International Covenant on Civil and Political Rights", in Andrew Byrnes (ed) *The Right to Fair Trial in International & Comparative Perspective* 37–35 (Hong Kong, Centrum for Comparative and Public Law, 1997).

JENNINGS, ROBERT, "Advisory Opinion of July 20, 1962", 11 *International and Comparative Law Quarterly* 1169–83 (1962).

JENNINGS, ROBERT & WATTS, ARTHUR (eds), *Oppenheim's International Law, Vol 1* (London, Harlow, 9th edn, 1992).

JOHARI, ASHOK K, *The Supreme Court's Advisory Function* (Aligarh, Naraina Publishers, 1984).

JOHNSON, DAVID, L, "Sanctions and South Africa", in 19 *Harvard International Law Journal* 887–930 (1978).

JOSEPH, SARAH et al, *The International Covenant on Civil and Political Rights. Cases, Materials, and Commentary* (Oxford, Oxford University Press, 2002).

KAIKOBAD, KAIYAN H, "The Court, the Council and Interim Protection: A Commentary on the Lockerbie Order of 14 April 1992", 17 *Australian Yearbook of International Law* 87–186 (1996).

KALALA, TSHIBANGU, "La Décision de l'OAU de ne plus Respecter les Sanctions Décrétées par l'ONU contre la Libye: Désobéissance Civile des États Africains à l'Égard de l'ONU", 32 *Revue Belge de Droit International* 545–76 (1999).

KÄLIN, WÄLTER, "Humanitäre Intervention: Legitimation durch Verfahren? Zehn Thesen zur Kosovo-Krise", 10 *Schweizerische Zeitschrift für Internationales und Europäisches Recht* 159–91 (2000).

KALKKU, ELINA, "The United Nations Authorisation to Peace Enforcement with the Use of Armed Forces in the Light of the Practice of the UN Security Council", 9 *Finnish Yearbook of International Law* 349–05 (1998).

KAUL, HANS-PETER, "Sanktionsausschüsse des Sicherheitsrates: Ein Einblick in Arbeitsweise und Verfahren", 44 *Vereinte Nationen* 96–103 (1996).

KEITH, KENNETH, "The Advisory Jurisdiction of the International Court of Justice: Some Comparative Reflections", 17 *Australian Yearbook of International Law* 39–58 (1996).

KELSEN, HANS, "Collective Security and Collective Self-Defence under the Charter of the United Nations", in 42 *American Journal of International Law* 783–97 (1948).

——, *The Law of the United Nations* (London, Stevens, 1950).

——, *Principles of International Law* (New York, Holt, Rhinehart & Winston, 1966).

KENNEDY, ROBERT F, "Libya v United States: The International Court of Justice and the Power of Judicial Review", 33 *Virginia Journal of International Law* 899–25 (1993).

KENNEDY, ROBERT, H, "Advisory Opinions: Cautions About Non-Judicial Undertakings", 23 *University of Richmond Law Review* 165–212 (1989).

KERLEY, ERNEST L, "The Powers of Investigation of the United Nations Security Council", in 55 *American Journal of International Law* 892–918 (1961).

KEWENIG, WILHELM A, "Die Problematik der Bindungswirkung von Entscheidungen des Sicherheitsrates", in Horst Emhke et al (eds), *Festschrift für Ulrich Scheuner zum 70. Geburtstag* 260–84 (Berlin, Duncker & Humblot, 1973).

KIRGIS, FREDERIC L, "Claims Settlement and the United Nations Legal Structure", in Richard B Lillich (ed), *The United Nations Compensation Commission* 103–16 (Irvington, Transnational, 1995).

——, "The Security Council's First Fifty Years", 89 *American Journal of International Law* 506–34 (1995).

——, "Book Review", 93 *American Journal of International Law* 970–75 (1999).

——, "Security Council Governance of Postconflict Societies: A Plea for Good Faith and Informed Decision Making", 95 *American Journal of International Law* 579–82 (2001).

——, "Security Council Resolution 1483 on the Rebuilding of Iraq", *ASIL Insight* (2003) available at www.asil.org/insights.htm.

KÖCHLER, HANS, *Etische Aspekte der Sanktionen im Völkerrecht: die Praxis der Sanktionspolitik und die Menschenrechte* (Vienna, International Progress Organisation, 1994).

KÖCK, HERIBERT F, "UN-Satzung und allgemeines Völkerrecht—Zum exemplarischen Charakter von Article 103 SVN", in Konrad Ginther *et al* (eds), *Völkerrecht zwischen normativem Anspruch und politischer Realität. Festschrift für Karl Zemanek zum 65. Geburtstag* 69–93 (Berlin, Duncker & Humblot, 1994).

KOH, HAROLD H, "On American Exceptionalism", 61 *Stanford Law Review* 1479–1520 (2003).

KOLB, ROBERT, "Aperçus sur la bonne foi en droit international public", 54 *Revue Hellénique de Droit International* 1–42 (2001).

KÖRBS, HARTMUT, *Die Friedenssicherung durch die Vereinten Nationen und Regionalorganisationen nach Kapitel VIII der Satzung der Vereinten Nationen* (Bochum, Brockmeyer, 1997).

KRAFFT, MATHIAS-CHARLES *et al*, "Chapter on Switzerland", in Vera Gowlland-Debbas (ed), *National Implementation of Non-Military Security Council Sanctions: A Comparative Study* (Leiden, Martinus Nijhoff, forthcoming).

KRAJEWSKI, MARKUS, "Selbstverteidigung gegen bewaffnete Angriffe nichtstaatlicher Organisationen—Der 11. September 2001 unde seine Folgen", 40 *Archiv des Völkerrechts* 183–214 (2002).

KRECZKO, ALAN J, "The Unilateral Termination of UN Sanctions Against Southern Rhodesia by the United Kingdom", 21 *Virginia Journal of International Law* 97–128 (1981).

KULESSA, MANFRED "Von Märchen und Mechanismen", 43 *Vereinte Nationen* 89–103 (1995).

KUNZ, JOSEF L, "Legality of the Security Council Resolutions of June 25 and 27, 1950", 45 *American Journal of International Law* 137–43 (1951).

LAILACH, MARTIN, *Die Wahrung des Weltfriedens und der internationalen Sicherheit als Aufgabe des Sicherheitsrates der Vereinten Nationen* (Berlin, Duncker & Humblot, 1998).

LAMB, SUSAN, "The Powers of Arrest of the International Criminal Tribunal for the Former Yugoslavia", 75 *British Yearbook of International Law* 167–244 (1999).

LAMMERS, JOHAN G, "General Principles of Law Recognized by Civilized Nations", in Frits Kalshoven *et al* (eds), *Essays on the Development of the International Legal Order in Memory of Haro F Van Panhuys* 53–75 (Alphen aan den Rijn, Sijthoff & Noordhoff, 1980).

LANG, JOHN TEMPLE, "Legal Certainty and Legitimate Expectations as General Principles of Law", in Ulf Bernitz & Joakim Nergelius (eds), *General Principles of European Community Law* 163–84 (The Hague, Kluwer, 2000).

LAPIDOTH, RUTH, "Some Reflections on the Law and Practice Concerning the Imposition of Sanctions by the Security Council", 30 *Archiv des Völkerrechts* 114–25 (1992).

LAUTERPACHT, HERSCH, *Private Law Sources and Analogies of International Law* (Hambden, Conn, Archon, 1971).

LAUTERPACHT, ELIHU "The Legal Effect of Illegal Acts of International Organisations", in *Cambridge Essays in International Law. Essays in Honor of Lord McNair* 88–115 (London, Stevens & Sons, 1965).

LAUTERPACHT, ELIHU *et al* (eds), *The Kuwait Crisis: Basic Documents* (Cambridge, Grotius, 1991).

LEE, ROY S "The Rwanda Tribunal", in 9 *Leiden Journal of International Law* 37–61 (1996).

LENAERTS, KOEN, "Some Reflections on the Separation of Powers in the European Community", 28 *Common Market Law Review* 11–35 (1991).

LISSITZYN, OLIVIER J "International Law and the Advisory opinion on Namibia", 11 *Columbia Journal of International Law* 50–73 (1972).

LOBEL, JULES & RATNER, MICHAEL, "Bypassing the Security Council: Ambiguous Authorisations to use force, Cease-Fires and the Iraqi Inspection Regime", 93 *American Journal of International Law* 124–54 (1999).

LORINSER, BARBARA, *Bindende Resolutionen des Sicherheitsrates* (Baden-Baden, Nomos, 1996).

LUPI, NATALIA, "Report by the Inquiry Commission on the Behavior of Italian Peace-Keeping Troops in Somalia", 1 *Yearbook of International Humanitarian Law* 375–79 (1998).

MACDONALD, RONALD St JOHN, "Changing Relations between the International Court of Justice and the Security Council of the United Nations", 31 *Canadian Yearbook of International Law* 115–49 (1993).

——, "The Charter of the United Nations in Constitutional Perspective", in 20 *Australian Yearbook of International Law* 205–30 (1999).

MALANCZUK, PETER, "International Business and New Rules of State Responsibility?—The Law Applied by the United Nations (Security Council) Compensation Commission for Claims Against Iraq", in Karl-Heinz Böckstiegel (ed), *Perspectives of Air Law, Space Law and International Business Law for the Next Century* 117–28 (Cologne, Carl Heymanns, 1996).

——, *Akehurst's Modern Introduction to International Law* (London, Routledge, 1997).

——, "Reconsidering the Relationship between the ICJ and the Security Council", in Wybo P Heere (ed), *International Law and the Hague's 750th Anniversary* 87–99 (The Hague, TMC Asser, 1999).

MALCOLM, NOEL, *A Short History of Kosovo* (London, Macmillan, 1998).

FA MANN, "The Consequences of an International Wrong in International and National Law", 48 *British Yearbook of International Law* 1–65 (1976–1977).

MANUSAMA, KENNETH, "HIV/AIDS-discussie in de VN-Veiligheidsraad: een kwestie van competentie", *VN-Forum* 23–28 (2000).

MARTENCZUK, BERND, *Rechtsbindung und Rechtskontrolle des Weltsicherheitsrats. Die Überprüfung nichtmilitärischer Zwangsmassnahmen durch den internationalen Gerichtshof* (Duncker & Humblot, Berlin, 1996).

——, "The Security Council, the International Court and Judicial Review: What Lessons from Lockerbie?", 10 *European Journal of International Law* 517–47 (1999).

McDOUGAL, MYRES M & REISMAN, W MICHAEL, "Rhodesia and the United Nations: The Lawfulness of International Concern", 62 *American Journal of International Law* 1–19 (1968).

McGINLEY, GERALD, P, "The ICJ's decision in the Lockerbie cases", 22 *Georgia Journal of International and Comparative Law* 577–607 (1992).

McWHINNEY, EDWARD, "Judicial Wisdom, and the World Court as Special Constitutional Court", in Beyerlein, Ulrich *et al* (eds), *Recht zwischen Umbruch und Bewahrung; Völkerrecht, Europarecht, Staatsrecht: Festshrift für Rudolf Berhnardt* 705–11 (Berlin, Springer, 1995).

MÉGRET, FRÉDÉRIC & FLORIAN HOFFMANN, FLORIAN, "The UN as a Human Rights Violator? Some Reflections on the United Nations Changing Human Rights Responsibilities", 25 *Human Rights Quarterly* 314–42 (2003).

MENDELSON, MH & HULTON, SC, "The Iraq-Kuwait Boundary", 64 *British Yearbook of International Law* 135–95 (1993).

MERISH, BN, "*Travaux Préparatoires* as an Element in the Interpretation of the Treaties", 11 *Indian Journal of International Law* 39–87 (1971).

MERON, THEODOR, "The Humanization of Humanitarian Law", 94 *American Journal of International Law* 240–78 (2000).

——, "The Martens Clause, Principles of Humanity, and Dictates of Public Conscience", 94 *American Journal of International Law* 78–89 (2000).

MOSLER, HERMANN, "Rechtsvergleichung vor völkerrechtlichen Gerichten", in René Marcic *et al* (eds), *Festschrift für Verdross zum 80. Geburtstag* 381–411 (München, Fink, 1971).

——, "General Principles of Law", 2 *Encyclopedia of Public International Law* 511–517 (1995).

MUELLER, JOHN & MUELLER, KARL, "Sanctions of Mass Destruction", *Foreign Affairs* 43–57 (1999).

MÜLLER, JÖRG PAUL, *Vertrauensschutz im Völkerrecht* (Cologne, Heymann, 1971).

——, "Article 2(2)", in Bruno Simma (ed), *The Charter of the United Nations. A Commentary* 89–97 (Oxford, Oxford University Press,1994).

MÜLLER, JÖRG PAUL & COTTIER, THOMAS, "Estoppel", 2 *Encyclopedia of Public International Law* 116–19 (1994).

MÜLLER-SCHIEKE, IRINA, K "Defining the Crime of Aggression under the Statute of the International Criminal Court", 14 *Leiden Journal of International Law* 409–30 (2001).

MURPHY, SEAN, "The Security Council, Legitimacy, and the Concept of Collective Security After the Cold War", 32 *Columbia Journal of Transnational Law* 201–88 (1994).

——, "Democratic Legitimacy and the Recognition of States and Government", 48 *International and Comparative Law Quarterly* 545–81 (1999).

——, "Terrorism and the Concept of 'Armed Attack' in Article 51 of the UN Charter", 43 *Harvard International Law Journal* 43–51 (2002).

NEUHOLD, HANSPETER, "Threat to Peace", 3 *Encyclopedia of Public International Law* 935–38 (1997).

NOLTE, GEORG, "Restoring Peace by Regional Action", 53 *Zeitschrift für ausländisches öffentliches Recht und Völkerrecht* 603–37 (1993).

——, *Eingreifen auf Einladung* (Berlin, Springer, 1999).

——, "The limits of the Security Council's Powers and its Functions in the International Legal System: Some Reflections", in Michael Byers (ed), *The Role of Law in International Politics* 315–26 (Oxford, Oxford University Press, 2000).

NORMAND, ROGER, "A Human Rights Assessment of Sanctions: The Case of Iraq, 1990–1997", in Willem JM van Genugten & Gerard A de Groot (eds), *United Nations Sanctions. Effectiveness and Effects, Especially in the Field of Human Rights. A Multi-disciplinary Approach* 19–34 (Antwerpen, Intersentia, 1999).

NOWAK, MANFRED, *UN Covenant on Civil and Political Rights* (Kehl, Engel, 1993).

NSEREKO, DANIEL D NTANDA, "Aggression under the Rome Statute of the International Criminal Court", 71 *Nordic Journal of International Law* 497–21 (2002).

NYMAN, PRINCETON, L, "Saving the UN Security Council—A Challenge for the United Nations", 4 *Max Planck Yearbook of United Nations Law* 127–46 (2000).

O'CONNELL, MARY ELLEN, "The UN, NATO, and International Law After Kosovo", 22 *Human Rights Quarterly* 57–89 (2000).

——, "Debating the Law of Sanctions", 13 *European Journal of International Law* 63–86(2002).

O'CONNOR, JF, *Good Faith in International Law* (Aldershot, Dartmouth, 1991).

OELLERS-FRAHM, KARIN, "Die 'obligatorische" Gerichtsbarkeit des Internationalen Gerichtshofs, 47 *Zeitschrift für ausländisches öffentliches Recht und Völkerrecht* 243–64 (1987).

——, "Die Entwicklung des Oil for Food-Programs und die gegenwärtige humanitäre Lage in Irak, 59 *Zeitschrift für ausländisches öffentliches Recht und Völkerrecht* 838–62 (1999).

OETTE, LUTZ, "A Decade of Sanctions against Iraq: Never Again! The End of Unlimited Sanctions in the Recent Practice of the UN Security Council", 13 *European Journal of International Law* 93–103 (2002)

OFODILE, ANTHONY C, "The Legality of ECOWAS Intervention in Liberia", 32 *Columbia Journal of Transnational Law* 381–418 (1994).

OOSTHUIZEN, GABRIEL, H, "Playing the Devil's Advocate: The United Nations Security Council is Unbound by Law", 12 *Leiden Journal of International Law* 549–63 (1999).

ÖSTERDAHL, INGER, *Threat to the Peace* (Uppsala, Iustus, 1998).

——, "The Continued Relevance of Collective Security Under the UN: The Security Council, Regional Organisations and the General Assembly", 10 *Finnish Yearbook of International Law* 103–40 (1999).

PARTSCH, KARL JOSEF, "Der Sicherheitsrat als Gerichtsgründer" 42 *Vereinte Nationen* 501–17 (1994).

PASQUALUCCI, Jo M, "Advisory Practice of the Inter-American Court of Human Rights: Contributing to the Evolution of International Human Rights Law", 38 *Stanford Journal of International Law* 241–288 (2002).

PLACHTA, MICHAEL, "The Lockerbie Case: The Role of the Security Council in Enforcing the Principle Aut Dedere Aut Judicare", 12 *European Journal of International Law* 125–40 (2001).

POLLUX, "The Interpretation of the Charter", 23 *British Yearbook of International Law* 54–81 (1946).

POMERANCE, MICHLA, "Advisory Role of the International Court of Justice and its Judicial Character: Past and Future Prisms", in Alexander S Muller, *et al* (eds), *The International Court of Justice—Its Future Role after Fifty Years* 271–323 (The Hague, Martinus Nijhoff, 1997).

——, "The ICJ and South West Africa (Namibia): A Retrospective Legal/ Political Assessment", 12 *Leiden Journal of International Law* 425–36 (1999).

POST, HARRY, "Adjudication as a Mode of Acquisition of Territory? Some observations on the Iraq-Kuwait Boundary Demarcation in the Light of the Jurisprudence of the International Court of Justice", in Vaughan Lowe & Malgosia Fitzmaurice (eds), *Fifty Years of the International Court of Justice. Essays in Honor of Sir Robert Jennings* 237–63 (Cambridge, Cambridge University Press, 1996).

PROVOST, RENÉ, "Starvation as a Weapon: Legal Implications of the United Nations Food Blockade Against Iraq and Kuwait", 30 *Columbia Journal of Transnational Law* 577–639(1992).

PURNAWANTY, J, "Various Perspectives in Understanding the East Timor Crisis", 14 *Temple International and Comparative Law Journal* 61–99 (2000).

QUIGLEY, JOHN, "The United Nations Security Council: Promethean Protector or Helpless Hostage?", 35 *Texas International Law Journal* 129–72 (2000).

RANDELZHOFER, ALBRECHT, "Article 2(4)", in Bruno Simma (ed), *The Charter of the United Nations. A Commentary* 106–28 (Oxford, Oxford University Press, 1994).

REISMAN, W MICHAEL, *Systems of Control in International Adjudication & Arbitration. Breakdown and Repair* (Durham, Duke University Press, 1992).

——, "The Constitutional Crisis in the United Nations", 87 *American Journal of International Law* 83–100 (1993).

REISMAN, W MICHAEL & STEVICK DOUGLAS L, "The applicability of International Law Standards to United Nations Economic Sanctions Programmes", 9 *European Journal of International Law* 86–141 (1998).

RESCHKE, BRIGITTE, "Der aktuelle Fall: Die Aufhebung der Sanktionen gegen Haiti", 3 *Humanitäres Völkerrecht* 134–39 (1994).

RESS, GEORG, "Die Bedeutung der Rechtsvergleichung für das Recht internationaler Organisationen", in 36 *Zeitschrift für ausländisches öffenliches Recht und Völkerrecht* 227–78 (1976).

——, "The Interpretation of the Charter", in Bruno Simma (ed), *The Charter of the United Nations*, (Oxford, Oxford University Press, 1995).

ROBERTS, KEN, "Second-Guessing the Security Council: the International Court of Justice and its Powers of Judicial Review", 7 *Pace International Law Review* 281–319 (1995).

VAN DE ROER, ROBERT, "Resolutie Irak is zege voor VS", *NRC Handelsblad*, 23 May 2003, 5.

ROSENNE, SHABTAI, *Developments in the Law of Treaties 1945–1986* (Cambridge, Cambridge University Press, 1989).

ROSS, JAN, "Daumenschrauben gefällig?", *Die Zeit*, 27.02.2003, at 8.

RUBIN, ALFRED P, "Libya, Lockerbie and the Law", 4 *Diplomacy and Statecraft* 1–19 (1993).

RUFFERT, MATTHIAS, "The Administration of Kosovo and East-Timor by the International Community", 50 *International & Comparative Law Quarterly* 613–31 (2001).

SAROOSHI, DANESH, *The United Nations and the Development of Collective Security* (Oxford, Oxford University Press, 1999).

SARPONG, GA, "The Lockerbie Incident and the International Court of Justice: Reality in the New World Order", *African Society of International and Comparative Law. Proceedings of the Fifth Annual Conference* 64–74 (1993).

SCHARF, MICHAEL P & DOROSIN, JOSHUA L, "Interpreting UN Sanctions: The Rulings and Role of the Yugoslavia Sanctions Committee", 19 *Brooklyn Journal of International Law* 771–826 (1993).

SCHERMERS, HENRY & BLOKKER, NIELS M, *International Institutional Law* (The Hague, Martinus Nijhoff, 1994).

SCHRIJVER, NICO, "Responding to International Terrorism: Moving the Frontiers of International Law for 'Enduring Freedom?', 48 *Netherlands International Law Review* 271–91 (2001).

SCHWARZENBERGER, GEORG, "The Problem of International Constitutional Law in International Judicial Perspective", in Jost Delbrück (ed), *Recht im Dienst des Friedens. Festschrift für Eberhard Menzel zum 65. Geburtstag am 21. January 1976* 241–49 (Berlin, Duncker & Humblot, 1975).

SCHWEBEL, STEPHEN M, *Justice in International Law: Selected Writings* (Cambridge, Grotius, 1994).

SCHWEIGMAN, DAVID, *The Authority of the Security Council under Chapter VII of the United Nations* (The Hague, Kluwer, 2001).

SCHWEISFURTH, THEODOR, "Article 34", in Bruno Simma (ed), *The Charter of the United Nations. A Commentary* 515–26 (Oxford, Oxford University Press, 1994).

SCOTT, CRAIG, *et al* "Memorial for Bosnia: Framework of Legal Arguments Concerning the Lawfulness of the Maintenance of the United Nations Security Council's Arms Embargo on Bosnia and Herzegovina", 16 *Michigan Journal of International Law* 1–140 (1994).

SEGALL, ANNA, "Economic Sanctions: Legal and Policy Constraints", 81 *International Review of the Red Cross* 763–84 (1999).

SEIDERMAN, IAN D, *Hierarchy in International Law: The Human Rights Dimension* (Antwerp, Intersentia, 2001).

SEIDL-HOHENVELDERN, IGNAZ, "Die Rolle der Rechtsvergleichung im Völkerrecht", in FA von der Heydte, *Völkerrecht und rechtliches Weltbild: Festschrift für Alfred Verdross* 253–61 (Vienna, Springer, 1960).

SEYERSTED, FINN, *United Nations Forces in the Law of Peace and War* (Leyden, Sijthoff, 1966).

SHAHABUDDEEN, M, "Municipal Law Reasoning in International Law", in Vaughan Lowe & Malgosia Fitzmaurice, *Fifty Years of the International Court of Justice. Essays in Honor of Sir Robert Jennings* 90–103 (Cambridge, Cambridge University Press, 1996).

SHARPTON, ELEANOR, "European Community Law and the Doctrine of Legitimate Expectations: How Legitimate, and for Whom?", 11 *Northwestern Journal of International Law & Business* 87–103 (1990).

SHAW, MALCOM, *International Law* (Cambridge, Cambridge University Press, 1997).

SHRAGA, DAPHNA, "The United Nations as an Actor Bound by International Humanitarian Law", 5 *International Peacekeeping* 39–59 (1998).

——, "UN Peacekeeping Operations: Applicability of International Humanitarian Law and Responsibility for Operations-Related Damage", 94 *American Journal of International Law* 65–81 (2000).

SHRAGA, DAPHNA, & ZACKLIN, RALPH, "The International Criminal Tribunal for Rwanda", 7 *European Journal of International Law* 501–18 (1996).

SICILIANOS, LINOS-ALEXANDRE, "L'autorisation par le Conseil de Sécurité de Recourir a la Force: Une Tentative d'Évaluation", 106 *Revue Générale de Droit International Public* 5–49 (2002).

SIMMA, BRUNO, "NATO, the UN and the Use of Force: Legal Aspects", 10 *European Journal of International Law* 1–22 (1999).

SIMMA, BRUNO & ALSTON, PHILIP, "The Sources of Human Rights Law: Custom, Ius Cogens, and General Principles", 12 *Australian Yearbook of International Law* 82–108 (1992).

SINCLAIR, IAN, "Estoppel and Acquiescence", in Vaughan Lowe & Malgosia Fitzmaurice (eds), *Fifty Years of the International Court of Justice. Essays in Honour of Sir Robert Jennings* 104–316 (Cambridge, Cambridge University Press, 1996).

SKUBISZEWSKI, KRZYSTOF, "Implied Powers of International Organisations", in Yoram Dinstein (ed), *International Law at a Time of Perplexity. Essays in Honour of Shabtai Rosenne* 855–68 (Dordrecht, Martinus Nijhoff, 1989).

——, "The International Court of Justice and the Security Council", in Vaughan Lowe & Malgosia Fitzmaurice (eds), *Fifty Years of the International Court of Justice* 606–629 (Cambridge, Cambridge University Press, 1996).

SLOAN, BLAINE, "The United Nations Charter as a Constitution", 61 *Pace Yearbook of International Law* 61–126 (1989).

——, *United Nations General Assembly Resolutions in Our Changing World* (Ardsley-on-Hudson NY, Transnational Publications, 1991).

SMITH, ROGER K, "The legality of coercive arms control", 19 *Yale Journal of International Law* 455–507 (1994).

SOHM, STEFAN, "Zur Bekämpfung des internationalen Terrorismus", *Humanitäres Völkerrecht* 163–173 (1994).

SOHN, LOUIS B, "The UN System as Authoritative Interpreter of its Law", in Oscar Schachter & Christopher C Joyner (eds), *United Nations Legal Order Vol I* 169–228 (Cambridge, Cambridge University Press, 1995).

——, "Important Improvements in the Functioning of the Principal Organs of the United Nations that can be Made without Charter Revision", 91 *American Journal of International Law* 652–62 (1997).

SPONECK, HANS C GRAF, "Sanctions and Humanitarian Exemptions: A Practitioner's Commentary", 13 *European Journal of International Law* 81–87 (2002).

STAHN, CARSTEN, "Constitution without a State? Kosovo under the United Nations Constitutional Framework for Self-Government", 14 *Leiden Journal of International Law* 531–561 (2001).

——, "International Territorial Administration in the Former Yugoslavia: Origins, Developments and Challenges ahead", in 61 *Zeitschrift für ausländisches öffentliches Recht und Völkerrecht* 107–72 (2001).

——, "The United Nations Transitional Administrations in Kosovo and East Timor: A First Analysis", 5 *Max Planck Yearbook of United Nations Law* (2001).

STARCK, DOROTHEE, *Die Rechtsmässigkeit von UNO-Wirtschaftssanktionen in Anbetracht ihrer Auswirkungen auf die Zivilbevölkerung* (Berlin, Duncker & Humblot, 2000).

STEIN, ANDREAS, *Der Sicherheitsrat der Vereinten Nationen und die Rule of Law* (Baden-Baden, Nomos, 1999).

STEINBERGER, HELMUT, "Comparative Jurisprudence and Judicial Protection of the Individual against the Executive: A Method for Ascertaining International Law?", in Herman Mosler, *Judicial Protection against the Executive Vol III* 269–79 (Cologne, Carl Heymanns, 1971).

SUGIHARA, TAKANE, "The Judicial Function of the International Court of Justice with Respect to Disputes Involving Highly Political Issues", in Alexander S Muller, *et al* (eds), *The International Court of Justice—Its Future Role after Fifty Years* 117–38 (The Hague, Martinus Nijhoff, 1997).

SUY, ERIC, "Some Legal Questions Concerning the Security Council", in Ingo von Münch (ed), *Festschrift für Hans-Jürgen Schlochauer zum 75. Geburtstag* 676–98 (Walter de Gruyter, Berlin, 1981).

SWINDELLS, FELICIA, "UN Sanctions in Haiti: A Contradiction under Articles 41 and 55 of the UN Charter", 20 *Fordham International Law Journal* 1879–1960 (1997).

SZASZ, PAUL C, "Enhancing the Advisory Competence of the World Court", in Leo Gross, (ed), *The Future of the International Court of Justice Vol II* 499–549 (Dobbs Ferry, Oceana Publications, 1976).

THIRLWAY, HUGH WA, "The Law and Procedure of the International Court of Justice: Part Two", 61 *British Yearbook of International Law* 1–157 (1990).

THÜRER, DANIEL, *Das Selbstbestimmungungsrecht der Völker* (Stämpfli, Bern, 1976).

——, "Self-determination", 4 *Encyclopedia of Public International Law* 364–74 (2000).

——, Der Wefall effektiver Staatsgewalt: "The Failed State", 34 *Berichte der Deutschen Gesellschaft für Völkerrecht* 9–47 (1995).

——, "Internationales 'Rule of Law'—innerstaatliche Demokratie", *Schweizerische Zeitschrift für Internationales and Europäisches Recht* 455–78 (1995).

——, "The 'failed State' and international law", 81 *International Review of the Red Cross* 731–61 (1999).

——, "Der Kosovo-Konflikt im Lichte des Völkerrechts: Von drei—echten und scheinbaren—Dilemmata", 38 *Archiv des Völkerrechts* 1–22 (2000).

——, "Der Krieg gegen Sadam als Testfall. Ist das Völkerrecht wirklich am Ende?", *Neue Zürcher Zeitung Online*, 23 May 2003, available at www.nzz.ch.

TOEBES, BRIGIT CA, *The Right to Health as a Human Right in International Law* (Antwerp, Intersentia, 1999).

TOMUSCHAT, Christian, "Tyrannei der Minderheit?", 19 *German Yearbook of International Law* 278–316 (1976).

——, "Obligations Arising for States without or against their Will", *Recueil des Cours de l'Académie de Droit International de la Haye* 209–309 (1993 IV).

——, "Yugoslavia's Damaged Sovereignty over the Province of Kosovo", in GPH Kreijen *et al* (eds), *State, Sovereignty and International Governance* 323–47 (Oxford, Oxford University Press, 2002).

TUNKIN, G *Theory of International Law*, translation by W Butler (London, Allen Unwin, 1974).

UTTER, ROBERT F & LUNDSGAARD, DAVID C, "Judicial Review in the New Nations of Central and Eastern Europe: Some Thoughts from a Comparative Perspective", 3 *OSCE Bulletin (Office for Democratic Institutions and Human Rights)* 11–24 (1995).

VAN DER GROEBEN, HANS *et al Kommentar zum EU-/EG-Vertrag* (Baden-Baden, Nomos 1997).

VAN HOOF, GJH *Rethinking the Sources of International Law* (The Hague, Kluwer, 1983).

VERDROSS, AFRED "Les Principes Généraux du Droit dans la Jurisprudence International" 52 *Recueil des Cours de l'Académie de Droit International de la Haye* 191–251 (1935 II).

VERDROSS, ALFRED & SIMMA, BRUNO, *Universelles Völkerrecht* (Berlin, Duncker & Humblot, 1984).

VILJOEN, FRANS, "Overview of the African Regional Human Rights System", in Christof Heyns (ed), *Human Rights Law in Africa 1998* 125–205 (The Hague, Kluwer, 2001).

VILLANI, UGO, "The Security Council's Authorisation of Enforcement Action by Regional Organisations", 6 *Max Planck Yearbook of International Law* 535–57 (2002).

VIRALLY, MICHAEL, "The Sources of International Law", in Mark Soerensen (ed), *Manual of Public International Law* 143–48 (London, Macmillan, 1968).

VITANYI, BÉLA, "Les Positions Doctrinales concernant le Sens de la Notion de 'Principe Généraux de Droit Reconnus par les Nations Civilisées", 86 *Revue Générale de Droit International Public* 48–116 (1982).

WALLACE-BRUCE, NII LANTE, "Of Collapsed, Dysfunctional and Disoriented States: Challenges to International Law", 57 *Netherlands International Law Review* 53–73 (2000).

WALLANDER, CELESTE A, "Institutional Assets and Adaptability: NATO After the Cold War", 54 *International Organisation* 705–35 (2000).

WALTER, CHRISTIAN, *Vereinte Nationen und Regionalorganisationen* (Berlin, Springer, 1996).

WATSON, GEOFFREY S, "Constitutionalism, Judicial Review, and the World Court", 34 *Harvard International Law Journal* 1–45 (1993).

WEDGEWOOD, RUTH, "NATO's Campaign in Yugoslavia", 93 *American Journal of International Law* 828–34 (1999).

WELLENS, KAREL, *Remedies against International Organisations* 214–15 (Cambridge, Cambridge University Press, 2002).

WEISSBRODT, DAVID, *The Right to a Fair Trial under the Universal Declaration of Human Rights and the International Covenant on Civil and Political Rights* (New York, United Nations, 2001).

WELLER, MARC, "The Lockerbie Case: A Premature End to the 'New World Order', 4 *African Journal of International and Comparative Law* 302–24 (1992).

——, (ed), *Iraq and Kuwait: The Hostilities and their Aftermath* (Cambridge, Grotius, 1993).

WESTON, BURNS H, "Security Council Resolution 678 and Persian Gulf Decision Making: Precarious Legitimacy", 85 *American Journal of International Law* 516–35 (1991).

WHITE, NIGEL D, "To Review or Not to Review? The Lockerbie Cases Before the World Court", 12 *Leiden Journal of International Law* 378–413 (1999).

——, "The Legality of Bombing in the Name of Humanity", 5 *Journal of Conflict and Security Law* 27–43 (2000).

WHITE, NIGEL D & ÜLGEN, ÖZLEM, "The Security Council and the Decentralized Military Option: Constitutionality and Function", 44 *Netherlands International Law Review* 378–413 (1997).

WILDE, RALPH, "From Danzig to East Timor and Beyond: The Role of International Territorial Administration", 95 *American Journal of International Law* 583–605 (2001).

——, "Accountability and International Actors in Bosnia and Herzegovina, Kosov and East Timor", 7 ILSA *Journal of International and Comparative Law* 455–60 (2001).

WILDHABER, LUZIUS, *Advisory Opinions. Rechtsgutachten höchster Gerichte* (Basel, Helbing & Lichtenhan, 1962).

WOLFRUM, RÜDIGER, "Article 1", in Bruno Simma (ed), *The Charter of the United Nations. A Commentary* 49–56 (Oxford, Oxford University Press, 1994).

WOOD, MICHAEL C, "The interpretation of Security Council Resolutions", in 2 *Max Planck Yearbook of United Nations Law* 73–95 (1998).

WRIGHT SHEIVE, SARAH, "Central and Eastern European Constitutional Courts and the Anti-majoritarian Objection to Judicial Review", 26 *Law and Policy in International Business* 1201–33 (1995).

YOUNG, ROBERT M & MOLINA, MARIA, "IHL and Peace Operations: Sharing Canada's Lessons Learned from Somalia", in 1 *Yearbook of International Humanitarian Law* 262–70 (1998).

ZAIDI, SARAH, "Humanitarian Effects of the Coup and Sanctions in Haiti", in Thomas G Weiss *et al* (eds), *Political Gain and Civilian Pain. Humanitarian Impacts of Economic Sanctions* 189–212 (Lanham, Rowman & Littlefield, 1997).

ZEDALIS, REX, "The Quiet, Continuing Air War Against Iraq: An Interpretive Analysis of the Controlling Security Council Resolutions", 55 *Zeitschrift für Öffentliches Recht* 181–210 (2000).

ZEMANEK, KARL, "Zemanek Was kann die Vergleichung staatlichen öffentlichen Rechts für das Recht der internationalen Organisation leisten?", 24 *Zeitschrift für ausländisches öffentliches Recht und Völkerrecht* 453–71 (1964).

ZIMMERMANN, ANDREAS, "Sovereign Immunity and Violations of International Jus Cogens—Some Critical Remarks", 16 *Michigan Journal of International Law* 433–40 (1995).

——, "Article 5", in O Triffterer, *Commentary on the Rome Statute of the International Criminal Court* 100–03 (Baden-Baden, Nomos, 2000).

——, *Staatennachfolge in völkerrechtliche Verträge* (Berlin, Springer, 2000).

ZIMMERMANN, ANDREAS & STAHN, CARSTEN, "Yugoslav Territory, United Nations Trusteeship or Sovereign State? Reflections on the current and future legal status of Kosovo, 70 *Nordic Journal of International Law* 423–60 (2001).

ZOLLER, ELISABETH, *La bonne foi en droit international public* (Paris, Pédone, 1977).

ZWANENBURG, MARTEN, "Compromise or Commitment: Human Rights and International Humanitarian Law Obligations for UN Peace Forces", 11 *Leiden Journal of International Law* 230–45 (1998).

——, "The Secretary-General's Bulletin on Observance by United Nations Forces of International Humanitarian Law: Some Preliminary Observations", 5 *International Peacekeeping* 133–39 (1999).

Index